MARCUS GRAY is the author of *Last Gang in Town* (1997), the first in-depth critical biography of the Clash, and *It Crawled From the South: an R.E.M. Companion* (1993). He lives in Belfast, Northern Ireland.

Route 19 Revisited

Route 19 Revisited

The Clash and *London Calling*

MARCUS GRAY

Soft Skull Press
New York

First published in the U.K. in 2009 by Jonathan Cape, Random House, 20 Vauxhall Bridge Road, London SWIV 25A

Library of Congress Cataloging-in-Publication Data

Gray, Marcus.
  Route 19 revisited : the Clash and London calling / Marcus Gray.
    p. cm.
  Includes bibliographical references and index.
  ISBN 978-0-224-08564-9 (alk. paper)—ISBN 978-0-224-08565-6 (alk. paper)
  1. Clash (Musical group). London calling. 2. Clash (Musical group)—Criticism and interpretation.
3. Punk rock music—England—History and criticism. 4. Rock music—England—1971–1980—
History and criticism. 5. Punk rock musicians—England—Biography. 6. Punk rock music—
Social aspects. I. Title. II. Title: Clash and London calling.

  ML421.C57G75 2010
  782.42166092'2--dc22

                                        2010026014
ISBN: 978-1-59376-293-3
Cover design by Aaron Artessa
Typeset in Dante MT by Palimpsest Book Production Limited, Grangemouth, Stirlingshire

Printed in the United States of America

Soft Skull Press
New York, NY

www.softskull.com

CONTENTS

CONTENTS

Route 19 Revisited

Introduction

Anyone interested enough to be reading this should need no persuading that the Clash's *London Calling* is an all-time classic. Whether you're a diehard Clash fan, an enthusiastic student or collector (or downloader) of all that's good in rock's back catalogue, someone who happens to have become attached to the album through accident of exposure or association of experience, or you're just plain curious about all the fuss . . . you've probably noticed that *London Calling* has appeared near the top of numerous Greatest Albums Of All Time polls, that several of its songs are firmly lodged in the public consciousness, and that even the front cover has acquired iconic status. ('Iconic' is a word that Pennie Smith, who took the photograph in question, hates. Although much overused and abused, if it's not appropriate here, then it's not appropriate anywhere outside the Eastern Orthodox Church.)

You might not need convincing of its legendary status, but you're presumably interested in how the album came to be. This book considers the Clash's collective and individual circumstances when the album was made. Also, what was going on in the wider world, and what the implications were for the Clash and their fellow earthlings. It discusses which band member wrote which parts of which song, and when, and where (if at all known); what that particular lyric – and even that ad-lib – means (or, in the absence of documentary or anecdotal evidence, is most likely to mean); who played which instruments, and how that downright peculiar sound was created; to whom those album credits refer; where those clothes came from; when and how that photograph was taken, why it was selected, and how that design was conceived; who, and what, inspired almost all of the above; and who, and what, the above in turn inspired.

It's a book about the Clash's *London Calling* . . . so why call it *Route 19 Revisited*?

At the beginning of the album track 'Rudie Can't Fail', Joe Strummer exhorts Mick Jones to 'Sing, Michael, sing . . . on the route of the 19 bus!' This is no random ad-lib: most of *London Calling*'s songs were indeed conceived, polished and recorded at points along the city's Number 19 bus route, south-west to north-east. Some of the lyrics and a couple of the basic tunes were written at the flat where Joe was staying in Whistler Walk, at the World's End in Chelsea. Riffs, tunes and arrangements were worked up and demoed by the band at Vanilla Rehearsal Studios in Pimlico, just down the road from Victoria Station. The songs were completed and recorded for the album at Wessex Studios in Highbury. That's the most straightforward and literal justification for the title.

There are 19 songs on the album: 19 tracks, 19 ways . . . That's the whimsical one.

Even in the early part of the twentieth century, American blues, folk and country made frequent reference to the train. There are countless lyrics where the train is the vehicle for reunion with or abandonment by a loved one, or a symbol of freedom or the lack of it. From Robert Johnson's 'Love in Vain' (1937), as later covered by the Rolling Stones for *Let It Bleed* (1969), to the Depression-era railroad hobo fantasy 'Big Rock Candy Mountain', as revitalised many years later in the film *O Brother, Where Art Thou?* (2000). You could hear a train whistle in the slide guitar or harmonica, but the dominant influence on the music was rhythmic. Huddie 'Lead Belly' Ledbetter's 'The Rock Island Line' – as performed by everyone from America's conscience, Woody Guthrie, to the leading light of the British skiffle boom, Lonnie Donegan – celebrates the train to a primitive backing that sounds like a runaway locomotive. In 'Folsom Prison Blues' (1955), Johnny Cash hears a passing train's 'lonesome whistle blow' while the Tennessee Two echo the clattering rhythm of the wheels down the track . . . a noise so irresistible that 'boom-chick-a-boom' became Cash's trademark sound for many years. Bo Diddley's recreation of the chugging train rhythm was sometimes so relentless that he didn't even let chord changes get in its way. In Chuck Berry's 'Johnny B. Goode' (1958), Johnny sits out by the railroad tracks and learns to play his guitar along to the rhythm that the engines make. Urbanisation, electrification and amplification helped midwife the birth of the music that came to be known as rock'n'roll, the very name of which suggested the cross-rhythms created as the caboose rattles over the points.

Some insist the expression rock'n'roll has its origin in sexual slang – like jazz and funk – and there's no doubt the double entendre was intentional. But even that incorrigibly mischievous purveyor of innuendo Little Richard asserts that 'Lucille' (1957) sounds like it does because he grew up in a house next to the tracks. On the wrong side of the tracks, of course; a phrase which also says much about rock'n'roll's origins and initial audience in the poor, working-class, underprivileged parts of town – both black and white – and its appeal to those in two minds about whether they were privileged to live outside those communities: forbidden thrills, the frisson of danger. Though the music was moving into the future, the lyrics of some early rock'n'roll songs still drew directly upon blues, folk and country source material. Elvis Presley's 'Mystery Train' (1955) is attributed to Sam Phillips, his producer at Sun Records in Memphis, and Junior Parker, the artist who first recorded it for that label, but its minimalist lyric about yet another love lost to the Iron Horse simply lifts and repeats a couple of lines from the folk standard 'Worried Man Blues'. In 1975 Greil Marcus used *Mystery Train* as the title for his seminal book of rock'n'roll criticism. And in 1989 Jim Jarmusch used it again for his equally impressive film, set in Elvis's home town of Memphis, and starring a certain Joe Strummer as an expatriate English rocker called Johnny – Joe's real name – but known as Elvis after the subject of his rock'n'rolling affections.

As is now so well established it's almost embarrassing to repeat, the birth of rock'n'roll followed hard upon the birth of the modern teenager. That's the teenager as state of mind, as personified by fast-driving rebel-without-a-future James Dean. And also the teenager as a significant new player in the marketplace, the young American with enough disposable income to spend not only on records but also on that ultimate status symbol and private luxury transport system, the flash, big-finned Fifties automobile. Pre-fame Elvis earned his living driving trucks; post-fame Elvis spent his money on gold Cadillacs. Arguably the first rock'n'roll record – also recorded for Sun – was a 1951 song called 'Rocket 88', a celebration of the Oldsmobile 88 credited to Jackie Brenston and his Delta Cats, but written by Ike Turner, who allegedly based it on Jimmy Liggins's even earlier 'Cadillac Boogie'. Like many other bluesmen-gone-electric before them, the Delta Cats drove north from the Mississippi Delta to Memphis for the recording session, taking Highway 61, the USA's main north–south route. Another early classic R&B-cum-rock'n'roll song, '(Get Your Kicks On) Route 66' (1946) was written by Bobby Troup after driving the USA's main east-west highway to California. He gave it to Nat King Cole, who had the first big hit with it, turning it into a 'Go West, Young Man' for the new age. That's the New America both symbolically and literally quartered and opened up.

It was the later Chuck Berry version of '(Get Your Kicks On) Route 66' that established it as an R&B and rock standard. Chuck was older than most other rock'n'rollers when the music crossed over in the mid-to-late Fifties, and he was canny enough to realise there was money to be made in pandering to white, middle-class teenage preoccupations. 'Maybellene' (1955), his first single, was about using a car to chase a girl, establishing his two principal – much plagiarised, much parodied – lyrical themes from the get-go. Although, in truth, they weren't exclusively his: Bo Diddley was just as obsessed with fast cars and chasing women. Even as the music and its attendant culture went through changes, the association with the car remained strong. The Beach Boys switched from surf to hot-rodding, from the Chuck Berry rip-off 'Surfin' USA' (1963) to the Berryesque 'Fun, Fun, Fun' (1964). The Rolling Stones got their start with Chuck Berry songs too: their first single was their 1963 version of his 'Come On', about a car that won't start, and their first album opened with their version of his take on '(Get Your Kicks On) Route 66'.

Locomotive and automotive. Rail and road, the train and car, were what you needed to get you there. But only in America or in the imagination. Because in reality, the UK was too cramped for epic journeys, too run-down, too old-fashioned and too poor. Taking years to recover from the Second World War, its rail and road networks were way behind those of other developed countries. The trains never ran on time and their facilities – especially the catering – were a national joke. All but the top-of-the-range cars looked like Matchbox models next to space-age American gas-guzzlers. And unless they were unusually privileged or spoilt – or had been working, saving and thinking of nothing else since they were 14 – the country's 17- to 19-year-olds had no chance of owning their own wheels. (Bicycles and, for a while, scooters excepted.) This was almost as true in the mid-to-late Seventies as it had been in the mid-to-late Fifties. Britain's relationship with the subject of American rock'n'roll was the same as its relationship with American movies about cowboys and gangsters and private eyes: a matter of wishful thinking. Fantasy and projection.

From around 1967 onwards, though, popular music splintered into countless sub-genres, and the word 'rock' was applied to a bewildering range of music, much of which bore absolutely no relation to the original rock'n'roll of just a decade earlier. Although most of these genres still had at least the tip of their roots in the blues and folk and country and R&B, they not only abandoned many of the sounds and rhythms of yore, but also much of the subject matter. They were no longer about pain and loss as a result of – or celebrations in the face of – hard times. They weren't even (not that often, anyway) about rampant consumerism and the latest trends, like so much prime-time rock'n'roll had been. Love still hung on in there as a topic, but in an increasingly stylised way. Lyrics became spiritual or philosophical, and then escapist or solipsistic, or fantastic or futurist, or camp or whimsical. A lot of the music became self-indulgent and complex, or laid-back and bland. There were some keepers of the Old School flame. Bruce Springsteen waxed existential about life on wheels; glam rock rejoiced in . . . well, the glamour of riding in high-end automobiles; and when the UK had a rock'n'roll revival in the early Seventies, it proved encouraging to Woody Mellor, who busked Chuck Berry songs on a ukulele, then formed an R&B band called the 101ers, changed his name to Joe Strummer, performed songs like '(Get Your Kicks On) Route 66' and wrote his own Berry-influenced numbers like 'Motor Boys Motor' and 'Steamgauge 99'. But Bruce sounded melodramatic and wounded by the past, glam was pastiche, and the rock'n'roll revival was faintly grubby nostalgia. Part of what the Class of 1976 UK punk movement set itself up to do was wipe the slate clean, and get back to the original spirit of rock'n'roll; at least, that is, in terms of musical directness and excitement. Subject-wise, though, cars and girls, or – taking it a step further back – lonesome train whistles didn't quite work anymore.

UK punk's determination to be authentic meant that it had to reject fantasy Americana and address the shabbier reality of Britain in the late Seventies. The Clash's debut album opens with 'Janie Jones', whose protagonist owns a Ford Cortina that 'just won't run without fuel'. In 'London's Burning', the cars zoom 'up and down the Westway, in and out the lights' . . . but if they're going some-where, the man who watches them from the concrete sidelines certainly isn't. On the B-side of a single released early in 1978, in a song aptly named 'The Prisoner', the Clash envisage escape from the quotidian in terms of 'bunk[ing] the train to stardom': even that unlikely opportunity will have to be stolen or sneaked. Other travel is restricted to urgent crosstown dashes by the ever-prosaic bus or Tube (the London Underground rail service) in search of short-term highs and cheap thrills. These transport options are closed networks that turn back on themselves at the city's edge, limited travel along predetermined routes within strict confines, impeded and slowed by other traffic or devoid of external stimuli, respectively. The Clash's take on punk delivered a rock that wasn't locomotive or automo-tive, but instead expressed frustration at stasis. Is it any coincidence that the punk dance, the pogo, consisted of jumping up and down on the spot?

Even when the Clash got out on the road for their first trip around the country, the December 1976 Sex Pistols-headlined Anarchy tour, the coach drove from town to town and decanted the bands into their hotels . . . where they remained stuck in their rooms, forbidden to play and besieged by the press and, occasionally, religious zealots. The old Situationist graphic reworked by designer Jamie Reid for the cover of the Sex Pistols' 'Pretty Vacant' single says it all: two coaches with destination boards reading BOREDOM and NOWHERE. During 1977 and 1978, the Clash headlined their own UK tours, and finally did get to play. Punk's preoccupation with offering value for money meant cheap tickets in venues small enough for the audience to see the whites of their eyes, and cover their guitars in gob, but by the fifth circuit of the same charmless run-down ballrooms and cinemas, that too started to feel a bit like being stuck in a maddening loop.

The overdubs for the Clash's second album took place in San Francisco in August 1978. Joe Strummer and Mick Jones had finally made it to America. With mixing sessions scheduled for New York, Joe fulfilled a long-held ambition by jumping in a pickup truck with a buddy and driving cross-country via New Orleans. In late September, Paul Simonon and Topper Headon joined the other members of the Clash in New York for the final couple of days' mixing. A few months later, the Clash were back in the USA for their first tour. It consisted of a mere handful of dates, but offered them their first experience of America by road. They were already thinking in terms of reintro- ducing the USA to a style of rock'n'roll it had invented but forsaken in favour of Aerosmith and Styxx and Journey and Foreigner. There they were – in the company of support act and original rocker Bo Diddley – with their hair slicked back, looking through the coach window at the ever-changing backdrop of the Big Country. With a little imagination, they could see America as it had been for the loco- motive and automotive pioneers in the rock'n'roll and pre-rock'n'roll years.

So it's appropriate that *London Calling* is bracketed by a car song and a train song. After the fanfare of the opening track, it's straight into 'Brand New Cadillac', the Clash's reworked version of Vince Taylor and his Playboys' 1959 original. And, although not credited on the sleeve of the original vinyl double, the album ends with the band's own chugging, syncopated 'Train in Vain', its title intentionally recalling the Robert Johnson-via-the-Stones blues train song 'Love in Vain'. These songs announce that the Clash have opened up to the music's past and to its traditions.

When *London Calling* was released, there was a tendency for a few punk-blinkered reviewers to accuse it of being retrogressive. They looked at the cover and confused black and white with two-dimensional, putting a little too much weight on the Elvis Presley-inspired sleeve design, the band's image and the theme and style of a couple of the songs. Even the more tuned-in, who noticed there was so much more going on – and even appreciated it – charged the Clash with aspiring to be the new Rolling Stones. They were presumably thinking of the gumbo of rock and blues and soul the Stones served up on their (exceptional) run of albums from 1968 to 1972 . . . along with the similar outlaw posturing.

Bob Dylan's the key figure, though. Without Dylan, it is doubtful that either the Stones or the Beatles would have pushed as hard against the lyrically hackneyed as they did. The reference points here are the two albums he released in 1965, *Bringing It All Back Home* and *Highway 61 Revisited*. With this brace of going-electric albums, Bob Dylan didn't just (or even really) say bye to folk and hi to rock: he did something far more complex, and in the process opened up the possibilities and changed the expectations of a certain kind of popular music for ever. Dylan noted 'It Takes a Lot to Laugh, It Takes a Train to Cry'. He saw it all 'From a Buick 6'. Highway 61 – officially Route 61 – not only links the Mississippi Delta to Memphis, thus symbolising folk blues's journey up to the big city and metamorphosis into R&B and rock-'n'roll, but continues on from there all the way to Dylan's home town of Hibbing in the frozen north of the USA. It connected him to what was going on in the south of the country, and enabled him to escape from the boondocks, too.

When, metaphorically speaking, he revisited that road, he brought back home all he'd picked up since he'd been away. Not just imagery from folk and country and blues and the Bible and the church and customs and sayings and traditions – what Greil Marcus, writing about Dylan in the only slightly different, slightly later context of the Basement Tapes, brilliantly summed up as 'the old, weird America' – but also rock'n'roll and art and surrealist poets and the Beats and the left wing and the underground and newspapers and magazines and the movies and, yeah, even the TV, and the stoners and the speed-freaks and the junkies and all their jive, man – and lo: he combined them to create a new country and a new world. Dylan's highway was a symbolic route through a rich popular-cultural hinterland that he more than anyone else opened up as fair game for investigation in song.

And what Dylan did with the old and the new in the mid-Sixties with *Bringing It All Back Home* and *Highway 61 Revisited*, the Clash did at the close of the Seventies with *London Calling*. Yes, they took pointers from Dylan, the Beatles, the Stones, Elvis, the Sex Pistols, and all the others who had gone before, but they went their own way.

On a literal level, Route 19 might have been a bus journey across their hometown; but on a whole other level, it was absolute freedom to go wherever they pleased.

This book sets out to recreate the trip.

1 From the World's End . . .

Eclectic Experience, Punk Purism, Reggae Relaxation and American Aspirations

'I think your sound is a reflection of your personality. It's the culmination of all your experiences to date, so no matter who you are you're going to sound different, you're going to sound like *you* when you play that guitar . . . When I play it, you're hearing my life come out in microcosm.' That's what Mick Jones – touchingly hesitantly – said in Don Letts's *London Calling* documentary, *The Last Testament* (2004). There's a science to musical structure and theory, and certain notes and combinations of notes have been proven to provoke certain responses, but there's no science to overall feel. That's where art and craft and emotion and intuition come in. It's perhaps easier for us to believe that lyrics have a direct relation to experience, because more of us are used to expressing ourselves in words than in music. Listening closely to *London Calling* does not reveal everything about the Clash members' musical and cultural backgrounds – their experience of life – but it does reveal a lot. Conversely, while an investigation of the band members' histories doesn't suddenly spotlight *London Calling* from all angles, it does allow a few previously obscured features to emerge from the shadows.

Joe Strummer embarked upon his first world tour before he was even born. That much is indicated by a pie chart he drew in one of his notebooks – displayed at the *Joe Strummer Past, Present & Future* exhibition at the London Print Studios from 4 to 18 September 2004 – in order to compare his own Heinz 57 pedigree to that of his bandmate Mick Jones. The half of Joe's pie given over to his maternal lineage was Scottish, thanks to his mother, Anna Mackenzie. The other half of the pie reveals that Joe was a quarter English, an eighth Armenian and an eighth German. His father, Ron Mellor, was born and raised in India; and because Ron was serving there with the Foreign Office at the time, John Mellor – later Joe Strummer – was himself born in Ankara, Turkey, on 21 August 1952. Over the next seven years, Ron's job took the family to Cairo, Mexico City and Bonn, Germany.

There had been visits home before, but it was 1959 before the family returned to the UK. Ron bought a bungalow in Warlingham, near Croydon, and Joe and his older brother David attended a local primary school for the next couple of years. Ron's stint in London was always intended to be a relatively brief hiatus in a globetrotting career. In 1962 he was posted to Tehran, Iran, and he and his wife left their sons to board at the City of London Freemen's School (CLFS), a minor public school near Epsom, Surrey. The boys visited their parents during the school holidays, and the arrangement continued when Ron was posted to Blantyre, Malawi, in 1966. As Joe later noted, it wasn't much of a family life, and he felt like he'd been left to fend for himself. He didn't apply himself to his studies at school, but did learn self-reliance and distrust of authority.

His relationship with popular music also began at CFLS. He bought the Beatles' 'I Want to Hold Your Hand' when Beatlemania hit big in 1963, and over the next couple of years also fell for the Rolling Stones, the Beach Boys, Them, the Yardbirds, the Kinks, and the Who. While visiting his parents in Tehran, he bought an EP called *This is Chuck Berry*, with sleeve notes by Guy Stevens. It included 'Bye Bye Johnny' (1960), Chuck's sequel-cum-rewrite of his autobiographical signature tune 'Johnny B. Goode' (1958). Joe was surprised to learn that Berry had written all of the songs, including 'Rock and Roll Music' (1957), which he had previously presumed to be by the Beatles. Inspired to track back, it wasn't long before he also discovered Bo Diddley and the likes of Bukka White.

Record sleeve notes were scoured for information, as was the *Melody Maker*. By 1967 Joe was listening to Jimi Hendrix and Cream, by the following year Fleetwood Mac and Canned Heat, then the year after that Led Zeppelin. When old favourites the Stones entered their dark, spooked and rootsy golden age, he was suitably prepped to appreciate it, and even Captain Beefheart's bizarre *Trout Mask Replica* (1969). He began attending festivals and concerts. Joe was no different from most music enthusiasts in their teens and early twenties, in that his tastes followed the times. He was open to what was new and of the moment. The way he differed from most was that he remained equally intrigued by where it all came from.

Although music was his main passion, it wasn't the only one. He liked all kinds of movies, but especially those that complemented the – in his own words – 'completely dazzling picture' that his love of its various musics had already given him of America: gangster flicks, film noir thrillers, war movies and Westerns. London might have been swinging, but, like John Lennon before him, Joe had been half-American since he first heard a rock'n'roll record, though – not having been there – his America was entirely mythic. An avid reader, as a schoolboy he was a particular fan of the works of T. E. Lawrence – aka Lawrence of Arabia – which, bearing in mind his father's early-Sixties posting, his own place of birth and early experience of globe-trotting, is perhaps not surprising. Later, Beat writers Jack Kerouac and Allen Ginsberg took him off down other roads. His funny bone was touched by Monty Python and cult US cartoonists Robert Crumb and Gilbert Shelton (creator of the Fabulous Furry Freak Brothers).

The cartoonists also appealed to his artistic side: Joe would continue to draw his own cartoons for years. Several featured a recurring character called Gonad, but his most oft-visited subject was Cowboys and Indians. The possibility of pursuing a career as a cartoonist contributed to his decision to apply to the Central School of Art in London. Shortly before he took his place there, his brother David – just 19 years old – committed suicide. It was a devastating event, though the impact was not so much instant as insidious.

Living in student accommodation in Battersea, Joe befriended singer-songwriter Tymon Dogg, who made ends meet by busking. Over the next year, Joe began to live an increasingly hippy lifestyle, dabbling with LSD, listening to singer-songwriters like Leonard Cohen, James Taylor and Carole King, in addition to Bob Dylan's equally laid-back early-Seventies output. Dylan gave Joe another trail to follow, back to Woody Guthrie. John Mellor adopted the pseudonym

Woody at this time, the chrysalis stage for his 1975 transformation into Joe Strummer.

Joe quit his art school course in 1971, but didn't feel any incentive to get a steady job. His retro tendencies began to gain ascendancy the following spring, when Tymon taught Joe some tunes, so that he too could earn a little money busking on the London Underground. Joe's choice of instrument, a ukulele, and ability, barely existent, dictated that these be easy to bash out; his preferred time to play – pub closing time – required that the material be familiar and immediate. His early repertoire consisted of songs like Chuck Berry's 'Sweet Little Sixteen' (1958) and Elvis Presley's 'Heartbreak Hotel' (1956). Bo Diddley had started out as a busker, and had street-tested his beat for years before landing a recording contract. Joe performed Bo's own 'Mona' (1957) and the Stones' Diddleyfied remake of Buddy Holly's 'Not Fade Away' (1964). By summer, he had moved to guitar, on which he could just about manage Chuck's 'Johnny B. Goode'.

After being evicted from a couple of flats in quick succession – the second experience resulting in the destruction of his record collection – a dispirited Joe retreated to his parents' bungalow in Warlingham. In an attempt to put his enforced suburban sabbatical to good use, he had swapped a camera for an old drum kit. As quickly became evident, though, while it's easy to play the drums badly, it's not quite so easy to play them well. Temporarily relocating to Wales, where a couple of his former Central contemporaries were at Newport Art School, Joe took his guitar along with a view to putting in some hard prac-tising. Initially, he stayed with a friend who had a piano, and dabbled on that too, but his musical talents remained rudimentary.

The working-class communities of Wales were still old school in their musical tastes: it's no coincidence that they were producing back-to-basics-style rock'n'roll acts like Shakin' Stevens and the Sunsets and Crazy Cavan and the Rhythm Rockers at this time, both of which acts Joe went to see. The art school had its own version, the Rip-Off Park All Stars. They fell apart shortly after Joe arrived, but he was quick to inveigle his way into the band that grew out of their ashes, the Vultures: he offered them the use of his drum kit, on the condi-tion that he could be the singer. Although themselves technically limited, the other band members refused to let him play anything but very occasional guitar. In addition to a few less retrospectively hip numbers by Jethro Tull and Focus, their repertoire included the Who's 'I Can't Explain' (1965), the Nashville Teens' 'Tobacco Road' (1964) and, latterly, 'Johnny B. Goode'.

The Vultures gradually disintegrated, and in summer 1974 Joe returned to London, settling into the Maida Hill squatting community at 101 Walterton Road. Not for the first time, Joe voiced his interest in becoming a rock star. The band that became the 101ers began rehearsing in the squat's basement shortly after he moved in. The original outfit were a ramshackle seven-plus-piece band, invariably billed as an R&B orchestra. The six-song repertoire for their September 1974 debut included Them's 'Gloria' (1964), Chuck Berry's 'No Particular Place to Go' (1964) and 'Roll Over Beethoven', and Larry Williams's 'Bony Moronie' (1957), all of which would become permanent fixtures in the band's repertoire.

Necessity might have been the mother of invention in those early days, but the 101ers' decision to stick with hard and fast R&B with a strong Fifties and early Sixties feel – in the vein of the Rolling Stones, the Yardbirds, the Animals, Them and even the Kinks and the Who when they first started – is almost certainly attributable to Dr Feelgood, who took the London pub scene by storm in mid-1974. Now tending to monitor the music scene via the *New Musical Express* (*NME*), Joe first saw the Feelgoods at the end of the summer, and watched as they toughened up their act, honed their image, and secured a record deal in relatively quick succession. Over the next few months, the 101ers gradually stripped away the excess baggage, until they too were an edgy four-piece with a Wilko Johnson-style manic guitarist: Joe Strummer. Nor was Joe done borrowing elements of stagecraft: he saw Bruce Springsteen's much-hyped Hammersmith Odeon gig on 24 November 1975, and began to throw a little of Bruce's grandstanding showmanship into his act for good measure.

The 101ers' repertoire increased, but didn't change its basic character. Although eclectic, the cover versions remained retro, drawn from the dark back alleys where the blues first met country with a little rock'n'roll on their minds. The band's repertoire included at least half a dozen more Chuck Berry songs, two or three Bo Diddley tunes, 'Heartbreak Hotel', Gene Vincent's 'Be-Bop-A-Lula' (1956), Little Richard's 'Slippin' and Slidin'' (1956), a few early Stones and Beatles numbers, the Small Faces' 'Sha-La-La-La-Lee' (1966), and 'Junco

Partner' (1952), as learned from a version played by Dr John. Bassist Maurice 'Mole' Chesterton loved reggae, so occasionally, they'd sound-check with a version of Desmond Dekker's 'Israelites' (1969) with Mole on vocals, but the 101ers only really had one direction and they lit out along it full speed ahead. Mole would be sacked en route; and guitarist Clive Timperley and Mole's replacement Dan Kelleher would ultimately also be found wanting because they failed to contribute enough in terms of stage performance to Strummer's declared goal of Maximum Impact.

The other weapon Dr Feelgood had in their arsenal was Johnson's ability to write strong originals in the style of the band's covers. Joe had attempted to write a couple of songs in his last days in Newport, including a skit on his art-school dropout status called 'Crummy Bum Blues'. Tentatively, at first, and then with growing confidence and frequency, Joe now started to write for the 101ers, coming up with lyrics and basic chord progressions to which various of his bandmates would bring changes, melodies and the finer points of arrangement. First came 'Keys to Your Heart', then another dozen or so songs like the automotive 'Motor Boys Motor' and '5 Star Rock'n'Roll Petrol', the locomotive 'Steamgauge 99' and the hedonistic 'Letsagetabitarockin'. While these all betrayed a strong Chuck Berry influence, another of Joe's songs was even more overt in its celebration of influence: 'Bo Diddley's Six Gun Blues'. By early 1976 Joe was inching closer to establishing a voice of his own – again following the lead of Wilko Johnson – and writing lyrics touching on the London lowlife sleaze of 'Rabies (From the Dogs of Love)' and – after a Johnny Cash-style gig at Wandsworth Prison where the 101ers played a themed set of prison-related rockers – 'Lonely Mother's Son', a song that, with some new verses, would be recorded by the Clash in 1978 as 'Jail Guitar Doors'.

Even in Newport, Joe's defensiveness about the material he was limited to by ability had begun hardening into defiance. When with the 101ers in 1975, he told the *Melody Maker* that music had been going up a blind alley since 1967. So he'd already written off the last eight years. In spring 1976 would come his exposure to both the Sex Pistols as a live act and the Ramones' first recorded testament. After that, he'd write off just about everything else as well: not just contemporary prog, dinosaur and West Coast bands, not just solipsistic and fey singer-songwriters, but also all the pre-1967 music he'd been playing with the 101ers and the Vultures and on a ukulele on the London Underground.

Joe knew all about the importance of flash, attitude and verbals in rock'n'roll. He looked around him on stage with his latest band, and then looked in the mirror when he got home, and – always given to the harsh assessment, especially of his own endeavours – saw himself and the rest of the 101ers as a bunch of guys with outmoded musical tastes and values, dirty jumble-sale late-hippy clothes, long, unstyled hair, and no chance in hell of climbing any further up the ladder. The 101ers belonged to an era that was about to end, as did the current incarnation of Joe Strummer. The future – even if it was to be No Future – belonged to the likes of Johnny Rotten. Joe was ready for Year Zero and the Clash.

Mick Jones's early life was also not without its displacements and abandonments. Even if the larger physical distances involved were covered by people other than himself, these shifts would exert as great an influence upon him as the pull of the moon does upon the tides. And even if his entire first-hand experience of the world prior to the Clash did not extend much beyond London, the moves Mick would make within the city's boundaries during his childhood would each require significant readjustment not only to surroundings but also to circumstance. Like Joe Strummer, with his immediate environment and family life subject to frequent disruption, Mick would look else-where for the pillars and touchstones of his existence.

The pie charts Joe Strummer sketched in one of his notebooks comparing his and Mick's genealogical make-up (as displayed at the *Joe Strummer Past, Present & Future* exhibition) show Mick as half English, a quarter Welsh, an eighth Irish and an eighth Russian. This breakdown is at best approximate. Mick's mother, Renee, was of Russo-Jewish stock. Her father, Morris Zegansky, was born in Russia, and although her mother, Stella Class, was born in Whitechapel, her family had also fled the Russian pogroms. The marriage did not last: during the next decade Morris and Stella divorced, and at the start of the Second World War, Stella and Renee moved into the newly built Christchurch House, on Christchurch Road, just south of Brixton in Streatham.

To the young Renee, America – as represented on the airwaves and silver screen, and as embodied by the slick-talking, confident servicemen posted over here from over there – seemed impossibly glamorous in comparison to a Britain enduring the privations first of a lengthy war and then of the following, seemingly interminable, period of austerity. At the age of 19, like her father before her, she tried to stow away on a ship bound for a better future, this time in the States. Unlike him, she was discovered and sent back. Instead, she married Tommy Jones, a taxi driver from Clapham. As his surname hints, his family roots were in Wales. Tommy had spent part of his National Service in Israel, but wanted to stay in London. Their only child, Michael Jones, was born on 26 June 1955.

Elvis Presley and rock'n'roll rekindled Renee's love affair with America and encouraged a sense of dissatisfaction with her lot. The marriage quickly became combative. For the last year or two Tommy and Renee remained together, whenever they wanted to enjoy their periods of truce, or to row without an audience, they would give Mick money to go out and amuse himself. He would go to double-bill movies at the Classic in Brixton on his own, often sitting through both films twice. On other occasions he would explore London with a cheap Red Rover bus pass, visiting all the landmarks and sights. At a very young age, Mick was aware of being a Londoner at a time when London was perceived to be the coolest place on the planet. As there was no musical generation gap in the Jones household, he soaked up the latest sounds, and gave his first concert on the lawn out front of Christchurch House, miming along to the Beatles' 'She Loves You' with a tennis racket as his guitar. By the mid-Sixties, he was a member of the fan clubs of the Animals and the Kinks. Ray Davies's melodies and London-centric lyrics made the latter band especially dear to his heart.

By 1964 Tommy and Renee had split up and divorced. Tommy departed for the southern limits of London. Renee married an American and moved there, eventually settling in unglamorous industrial Michigan. Mick was left in Christchurch House with his Nan – Stella – and a profound feeling of rejection. Renee did keep in regular contact, sending Mick comics and, later, music magazines. That his mother was in America was enough in itself to convey an irresistible appeal of that country for Mick, but the fact that her gifts inevitably celebrated American popular culture made it even more attractive. Renee's fascination with glamour rubbed off on her son. He came to love the idea of fame in all its manifestations: from comic superheroes to movie stars to pop stars.

Although he was three years younger, Mick was moving freely around London on his own when Joe was living a regulated life in the leafy lanes out beyond suburbia . . . but a Red Rover doth not a street urchin make, and there was a cosseted element to Mick's experience: he had a bedroom of his own, and a doting grandmother to attend to his needs. In autumn 1966 he was accepted by Strand School, a selective and strict grammar school with just 500 pupils, conveniently situated just around the corner from Christchurch House.

For years it seemed as though Mick was destined to live vicariously, as a fan. Even his love of football manifested itself as hanging around hotels where the big name players stayed when playing in the capital, and asking them for autographs. By 1967, though, music had taken over. Mick listened to blues and underground music on John Peel's *Perfumed Garden* show on Radio London. Purchased the following year, his first two albums were Cream's *Disraeli Gears* and the Jimi Hendrix Experience's *Smash Hits*. Not long afterwards, Stella took Mick to live with her sister and sister-in-law in Park West, another flat block towards the Marble Arch end of Edgware Road. This new central location meant it was now even easier for him to visit Swinging Sixties London hotspots like the Kings Road and Carnaby Street, and he and his friends regularly spent Saturdays staking out the homes of Rolling Stones Mick Jagger and Keith Richards in Cheyne Walk, Chelsea.

Park West was also just around the corner from Hyde Park, and the first live gigs Mick attended were free shows there. Both the nature of the events and the type of bands they showcased furthered Mick's immersion in the culture of what was then not yet even known as 'rock music'. The Hyde Park gigs were organised as an extension of the late Sixties underground clubs UFO and Middle Earth. They were the brainchild of Peter Jenner and Andrew King of Blackhill Enterprises, the Notting Hill-based bookers for underground scene bands like Tyrannosaurus Rex and Pink Floyd. The first show Mick saw took place on 27 July 1968 and featured Traffic, the Nice and the Pretty Things. Later that summer came two more shows featuring the likes of Fleetwood Mac, Fairport Convention, the Move and the Strawbs. The following year's Hyde Park events kicked off on 7 June with Blind Faith headlining, a concert that attracted 120,000 people.

Nine days after his fourteenth birthday, Mick was present at the most famous of the shows: held on 5 July, it was headlined by the Rolling Stones and dedicated to founder member Brian Jones, who had drowned in his swimming pool just two days earlier.

Back at school in the autumn, Mick turned up for a maths lesson to find himself sitting next to Robin Crocker. Robin was a year older, but being forced to resit a year because of his incessant trouble making. Mick and Robin fought, and then bonded over their subsequent punishment. Mick could now count on the bolder and more streetwise Robin as a concert-going buddy. Another London underground venture had started in autumn 1969. The underground's first musical event, Barry Miles's launch party for underground newspaper the *International Times* (*IT*) had taken place at the Roundhouse in Camden Town back in 1966, and both the UFO and Middle Earth clubs had later spent their dying days there. Now the venue became home to the scene's latest – and last – regular club event, Implosion. Among Implosion's co-founders was Caroline Coon, an *IT* contributor and mainstay of Release, an organisation dedicated to providing legal advice to drug-busted hippies. Implosion lasted all day every Sunday, cost just a few pence to get in, and offered several bands plus a DJ playing records in the breaks. At Robin Crocker's instigation, he and Mick would usually bunk in anyway, setting something of a precedent – whenever possible – for future gig-going activities. Some big names did appear at the Roundhouse during this time – the Who and Stones among them – but it was more common to see Ladbroke Grove outfits like the Pink Fairies, the Edgar Broughton Band and Hawkwind, whose ubiquity and willingness to play for peanuts or nothing for any cause or no reason had earned them the status of 'people's bands'. In summer 1970 Mick also attended the Phun City festival near Worthing to see the MC5, Detroit's high-energy rebel rock band, on their first visit to the UK.

As Seventies cynicism set in, the underground scene dissipated, and the British music scene became, like the American one, more success and status oriented – the music *business* – Implosion became a showcase for new groups hoping they were on the way up, but more often than not finding out they were going nowhere. This distinction meant little to Mick. He was young, and it was all bright lights and loud noise to him. Implosion would finally live up to its name in 1973 – though the Roundhouse's tradition of multi-band showcase gigs would continue well into the punk era – but long before then Mick and his friends had started going to more conventional rock shows on a regular basis, seeing just about anyone anywhere. He read the music press, especially the *NME*, and bought all the records he could afford.

The Stones' early-Seventies Tax Exile on Main Street made them appear increasingly remote from their audience. This was great news for two spin-off bands from the Small Faces: Steve Marriott's ever-so-earthy Humble Pie and, especially, the Faces, whose boozy, bawdy and bovversome image, presentation and songs made them not so much the perfect people's band as the perfect lads' band. Mick and Robin loved them. Robin had introduced Mick to some older boys, including Kelvin Blacklock and John Brown, who also attended Strand Grammar, and who shared their enthusiasm for rock'n'roll music. Free were highly popular in their circle, but the schoolfriends' allegiance increasingly shifted towards another new British band, Mott the Hoople. A hard-rockin', no-nonsense combo put together and managed by Guy Stevens – by then an A&R man for Island Records – and fronted by Ian Hunter, their accessibility and exhilarating live shows ensured they built up a loyal following of young rock'n'roll fans. Their road manager, Stan Tippins, would let regulars in through the back doors for free, and the Strand boys further cut down on expenses by bunking trains to Mott gigs around the country. By early 1972 Mick had caught the glam bug, getting into Slade, T.Rex, David Bowie and Alice Cooper in quick succession. Thanks to Bowie's gift of 'All the Young Dudes', Mott soon went glam, too.

Kelvin Blacklock, John Brown and a couple of others had started fooling around in a rehearsal band together playing R&B, because it was all they could manage. When, in May 1972, encouraged by Ian Hunter, Schoolgirl began playing low-key gigs in and around London, Mick Jones acted as roadie, but whenever he got the chance, he would slip behind the drum kit and teach himself the basics. The hapless Schoolgirl fell apart that October.

Mick's mother Renee used to send two of the leading American music publications of the day, *Rock Scene* and the highly irreverent *Creem*, which featured the standard-setting rock journalism of Lester Bangs, among others. Being based in Detroit, *Creem* reflected that city's penchant for no-bullshit, street-smart, high-energy rock'n'roll. Mick's interest in the Motor City's home-grown talents the MC5 was rekindled. He also discovered Iggy Pop and the Stooges, being part of the audience who saw the band's legendary show at the King's Cross Cinema in London on 15 July 1972. He saw the New York Dolls on *The Old Grey Whistle Test* on TV and also live, supporting the Faces at Wembley Pool on 29 October 1972. Bangs's pro-proto-punk outpourings also inspired Mick to investigate the 1972 *Nuggets* compilation of Sixties-vintage garage rock. London's independent record stalls, especially Rock On!, enabled Mick to track down other genre gems, from the Flamin' Groovies to the Standells.

Around the same time, Mick and Stella found themselves moving home again, to flat number 111 on the eighteenth floor of Wilmcote House, a 20-storey high-rise council tower block just off the Harrow Road, to the north of Notting Hill. It was in the tiny second bedroom here that Mick spent hours learning to play guitar, after Robin taught him a few chords. Mick admits that his main motivation in electing to go to Hammersmith Art School was to meet someone with whom he could form a band. It didn't work out. He asked Schoolgirl's former bassist John Brown to teach him bass in order to increase his opportunities. Instead, the two hit it off so well that, in May 1974, they decided to stick with their current instruments and form a band together. The lessons weren't wasted, though: Mick's familiarity with the other instruments used in the standard rock band line-up would stand him in good stead later on.

When the Delinquents launched themselves in September 1974 – at almost exactly the same time as Joe Strummer's 101ers – although heavily influenced by Mott the Hoople and Free spin-off band the Sharks, they were already advertising themselves as 'loud and punky', and including covers of songs by the MC5 and the Flamin' Groovies in their set alongside originals, most of them Mick's. He taught himself to write as he taught himself to play, using a reel-to-reel tape recorder to make home demos. The Delinquents lasted for just nine gigs at various art schools and a couple of minor London pub venues before half their number revealed themselves to be anything but untamed youth, and left to go straight.

Late in 1974, Mott frontman Ian Hunter published *Diary of a Rock'n'Roll Star*, which an undeterred Mick adopted as his own guidebook to rock stardom. By this stage, though, his passion for the New York Dolls was at its height. In January 1975, he and John Brown started putting together another band, this time with the ambition to play similarly decadent and debauched rock'n'roll. By the spring, they had a flash guitarist and good-looking drummer, and a repertoire including the Rolling Stones' 1970 live version of Chuck Berry's 'Little Queenie' (1959), the Yardbirds' 1965 version of Mose Allison's 'I'm Not Talking' (1964), the Standells' 'Sometimes Good Guys Don't Wear White' (1966), and a number of originals by Mick.

They brought in former Schoolgirl vocalist and Strand old boy Kelvin Blacklock, which ultimately led to a power struggle. Kelvin wanted the band to perform his songs, and also wanted to link the band up with former Mott the Hoople producer Guy Stevens. Guy assumed control, changed the band's name from Little Queenie to Violent Luck, and – as if to illustrate that concept – ousted Mick from his own group.

Mick dusted himself down and within days formed a new partnership with a bassist called Tony James. In mid-July 1975 they placed a *Melody Maker* ad for additional musicians. Lead guitarist Brian James played them a tape of his band Bastard, based in Belgium, which impressed them, but said he wouldn't be available until October. In the interim period, Mick and Tony met Bernie Rhodes at a Deaf School gig. Bernie had been involved in printing and designing some of the T-shirts Malcolm McLaren and Vivienne Westwood sold in their Kings Road shop, Sex. From late 1974, while Malcolm had been away in the USA trying and failing to hold the New York Dolls together as their makeshift manager, Bernie had done some preparatory work with a young London band that liked to hang around the Sex shop. Upon Malcolm's return from the States in mid-1975, he and Bernie had resumed plotting to instigate a street-level music movement. In New York Malcolm had witnessed the scene centred on CBGBs club. Back in 1974 poet Patti Smith had formed a punk-style band with *Nuggets* compiler Lenny Kaye, and not long afterwards the original version of Television – formed by childhood friends Tom Verlaine and Richard Hell – had started playing the club. The Ramones and a slew of other bands had followed their lead. It was Bernie who nominated Johnny Rotten as frontman for the Sex Pistols, but when he asked for an equal partnership in managing the band, Malcolm refused and pushed him out. In conversation with Mick and Tony, though, Bernie claimed he was still Malcolm's close associate. As they knew about Malcolm's involvement with the Dolls, they were impressed no end.

Bernie became their unofficial manager, despite being unhappy with the band name Mick and Tony wanted to use: London SS. He found them a basement rehearsal room in the red-light district of Praed Street, underneath a café where they could hang out and quiz prospective new bandmates when Brian James returned from Belgium. As well as covers of the Flamin' Groovies' 'Slow Death' (1972), the Strangeloves' 'Night Time' (1966), the MC5's 'Ramblin' Rose' (1969), the Modern Lovers' 'Roadrunner' (1972) and the Standells' 'Barracuda' (1967), the band's repertoire consisted of a mixture of Brian's songs and Mick's songs. Tony did write, but concentrated more on lyrics. For the next three months, they strove to complete the line-up by running ads in the *Melody Maker*. Among the drummers auditioned: Nick Headon was offered the position but went off with a soul band instead; Terry Chimes was told to wait for a call; Rat Scabies sat in for a while, before Mick and Tony decided his face didn't fit; and Roland Hot lasted longer than most. Roland was accompanied to his audition by his friend Paul Simonon, whose looks impressed the others enough to ask him to try out on vocals. His voice put paid to that possibility.

Brian James had little interest in how the candidates looked. Mick and Tony were aware of the whole gamut of proto-punk possibilities, but cleaved to the high-concept glam style of the New York Dolls. Although Patti Smith's *Horses* was released in the UK in December 1975, precious little other music had emerged from the contemporary New York scene. It had received enthusiastic coverage in *Rock Scene* and a couple of write-ups in UK music papers *Melody Maker* and *NME*, but was still a relatively well-kept secret. Bernie trusted Malcolm's conviction that the ragged urchin look of the New York punks was the way forward, and endeavoured to wake up his protégés to the fact that the long-haired pouting and preening of the New York Dolls was passé, and it was time for a new thing. Finally, he brought Malcolm along to a London SS rehearsal, and Malcolm obliged with a thumbs down. Sick of all the talking, Brian James left to form the Damned with his favourite London SS reject, Rat Scabies.

Bernie took a good look at what he had left. Much as he had previously done with the Pistols, he had been encouraging Mick and Tony to think about goals other than rock stardom and subject matter other than romance or fantasy. As a duo, Mick and Tony continued to re-inforce each other's dreams and aspirations, and were still pig-headed enough to fight for doing things their way. Following the divide-and-conquer principle, Bernie first berated Tony for being too middle-class and predictable, both lyrically and personally, and then fired him – Mick's best friend – in January 1976. Belatedly fully embracing the Rhodes Principle, Tony went on to write the punk-pop anthem lyrics for Generation X.

Although, at the time the band formed, he would be the only member of the Clash who had seen the MC5, the Stooges, the Dolls and Lou Reed, and could genuinely call himself a fan of garage and proto-punk rock, Mick's own songs were more typical of the *Nuggets* end of the spectrum. They were upbeat melodic guitar pop songs exploring teen romance themes, albeit with a cheeky twist or sharp edge, like 'Ooh, Baby, Ooh (It's Not Over)' '1–2 (Crush on You)', 'I'm So Bored with You', 'Deny' and 'Protex Blue'. Bernie didn't think much of Mick's lyrics, and didn't respect the craft of the tunesmith enough for it to be a major factor in his decision to persevere with him. More important to Bernie was the fact that Mick worked hard, consistently produced raw material, and was both passionate and deter-mined. On his own, now, and depressed by the failure of London SS – his third band in two years – Mick was also more malleable than before. Not that Bernie had to work too hard to beat him into shape: as soon as Mick saw the Sex Pistols at Andrew Logan's party on 14 February 1976 the light went on and his commitment to Bernie's vision was total. There would be a couple more false starts, including a part-nership with Chrissie Hynde: she helped Mick polish a couple of his lyrics and also cut his waist-length hair, but she refused to take direc-tion from Bernie, instead going on to form the Pretenders.

At a Roxy Music concert, Mick met Alan Drake and Viv Albertine, who were squatting a flat at 22 Davis Road in Shepherd's Bush. It wasn't long before Mick started hanging around there as well. As a result, the first-floor squat became the latest hub of Bernie's efforts to build a band around him. A friend of Alan's called Keith Levene turned out to be a precociously talented guitarist, with an aggressive, questioning attitude that impressed Bernie. Remembering Paul Simonon's audition for the London SS, Bernie persuaded Mick to invite him to join, too.

Paul Gustave Simonon was born on 15 December 1955 in Thornton Heath, three miles south of Brixton in south London. His mother, Elaine, was just 19, and a librarian. His father, Gustave Antoine Simonon, known as Antony, was 20, just coming to the end of his National Service with East Kent regiment the Buffs. The couple had married in a Catholic church in Streatham a few months before. Elaine was English and Paul's father was of French origin.

Like Mick Jones's father, Tommy, Antony spent part of his National Service abroad and it had proved a life-changing experience. The Buffs were posted to Kenya between April 1953 and December 1954 to assist with the suppression of the so-called Mau Mau rebellion. At the time, Antony had been considerably younger than his son would be when he joined the Clash, and it would have been impossible for him to avoid witnessing some gruesome sights. The biographical notes accompanying an exhibition of Antony's paintings at the Raw Arts Festival in August 2004 described him as 'one of many traumatised by his army experiences in Kenya'. In those days, such trauma went largely undiagnosed, untreated and undiscussed. Antony's desire to study art after leaving school had been thwarted by his obligatory spell in the armed forces. Immediately afterwards it was thwarted by the demands of family life. At the same time, the aftermath of his recent experiences made it difficult for him to settle to any job or stay in any location for long, and the family moved often.

Although in interviews Paul prefers to dwell on the time he lived in south London, specifically Brixton, his parents' nomadic lifestyle initially took the family on a whistlestop tour of largely well-to-do south-east English towns. Paul's brother Nick was born in Ramsgate in 1959. By autumn 1961, though, the Simonons were living just off Ladbroke Grove in Notting Hill, an area with cheap housing, a large West Indian community, and considerable racial tension. Paul was therefore the first member of the Clash to live in the area that would become so closely associated with the band. By 1964 the family had moved to Shakespeare Road in Brixton, an area with a similar demographic, culture and underlying unease. Although it was hardly a new experience after Notting Hill, Paul was now of an age when he was spending more time hanging around on the street, playing with friends from families of Jamaican origin, and hearing Jamaican music. Antony also began a tradition of taking Paul along to see action films on Saturday mornings.

Paul's parents split up when he was roughly the same age Mick was when his parents went their separate ways. Shortly after Antony moved out, Elaine's new partner Michael Short, a pianist and composer, moved in. This presaged another upheaval. In early 1966 Michael accepted a scholarship to study music in Italy for a year, and Elaine and her sons went too. Ultimately, his time abroad meant that Paul missed a year of schooling. When his new family unit returned to London, again settling close to Brixton in Herne Hill, he soon began attending William Penn School on Red Post Hill. Before long, he became part of the skinhead youth cult, devoting his time to posing, causing trouble and dancing to early reggae instrumentals at Streatham Locarno (see 'The Guns of Brixton' in Part 4). By autumn 1970 Paul had been playing truant for most of the year, warring with his 'stepfather'.

His mother's solution was to send him to live with his father at 27 Faraday Road, off Ladbroke Grove, a tiny flat where his bed was set up in the kitchen. Antony gave Paul chores, including housework, and made him deliver Communist Party leaflets door-to-door. Antony had a job manning a stall on Portobello Market; Paul was persuaded to get one, too. Although the idea of the move was to keep him away from bad influences, Paul was living in a similar inner-city area, and his new school – Isaac Newton in Wornington Road – was no better than his last. He still ran wild whenever he could, a tendency which only calmed down when he became aware of the opposite sex, and vice versa. He was still more interested in street style than music. By 1972 he had adopted the then-popular Budgie look, the feathered blonde haircut and dandy threads sported by Adam Faith on the TV series about the perennial London loser of the same name, and by early 1976 he was affecting David Bowie's plastic soulboy look. He was briefly infatuated with the Sensational Alex Harvey Band after seeing them play at the Hammersmith Odeon in 1975, but that was about the extent of his interest in contemporary rock music.

Father and son resumed movie-going together in Notting Hill. Most of the heroes of Paul's mid-teens derived from the silver screen, from films involving war, gangsters, cowboys, guns and hard men. Circumstances had prevented Antony from going to art school, but he had continued to pursue his interest in art throughout Paul's youth. The Faraday Road flat was crammed with Antony's work. Having copied his father's pictures as a child, Paul now began to paint alongside him: it was another pastime he and Antony could share, and his enthusiasm grew as his own talent became evident. In 1973 his father retrained as an art teacher and moved to 61 Western Avenue, the western continuation of the Westway in East Acton. Despite his school's poor standards, Paul was encouraged by one of his teachers, and by his parents, to apply for art school, and after spending a year working on a portfolio he was accepted on a foundation course at the Byam Shaw School of Art in Notting Hill. During this period, he continued to live with Antony, though home life had again become complicated: Antony was by now involved with fellow teacher Marion Clarke, and they married towards the end of 1975, as did Paul's mother Elaine and Michael Short.

Paul enjoyed the social life at the Byam Shaw, but couldn't get to grips with the teaching style. In autumn 1975 he was asked to resit his foundation year. A couple of months later, he failed his 'audition' as vocalist for the London SS, but Bernie Rhodes couldn't help noticing that Paul had the right kind of style and look for the kind of band he had in mind: he was tall, thin and strikingly good-looking and had always favoured short hair. It was, eventually, decided that he would play bass: never having played before was not seen as an obstacle. Bernie certainly didn't worry about such minor considerations. He had seen Steve Jones of the Sex Pistols learn guitar in a matter of a few months, and knew that Richard Hell had only picked up a bass when he and Tom Verlaine formed Television. He had proposed Johnny Rotten for the Pistols without ever hearing him sing. For his part, Mick Jones was comforted by the fact that Stu Sutcliffe had been a cool-looking art-school student who couldn't play bass when his friend John Lennon recruited him for the Beatles. Paul was won over to the idea after seeing the Sex Pistols at the Nashville in April 1976. He was already spending a lot of time at the Davis Road squat, which was not far from Western Avenue. It wasn't long before he dropped out of art school, and moved in. Shortly afterwards, Bernie instigated the recruitment of Joe Strummer.

Although Terry Chimes, the Clash's original drummer, would attempt to hand his notice in within six months of joining the band in June 1976, he wouldn't quite get away until March 1977, when the Clash finally managed to find an acceptable replacement.

Philip Headon and Margaret Williams were born, grew up, met and got married in Wales. They both trained as teachers, and afterwards moved where job opportunities dictated. First stop was Bromley in Kent, where Nick 'Topper' Headon was born on 30 May 1955 and spent his early childhood first attending the primary school where his father taught, then going on to secondary school in Dartford. He grew up with music in the house. Margaret liked the Beatles, and Topper's own tastes moved on to the Who and the Blues Boom bands of the late Sixties, including Canned Heat. He learned to play basic acoustic guitar. When he was 13, his father was offered a headship in Dover on the south coast of the county, so the family moved there. Topper began to attend Dover Grammar School. Finding it hard to adjust, he overcompensated by misbehaving and clowning around for attention. Never academically inclined, he eventually stopped trying altogether, reserving his interest for music and football.

At 14 he broke his leg so badly playing football that he had to spend several months in a cast, followed by several more convalescing at home. This ultimately required him to resit a year at school, adding to his sense of dislocation. Even in the short term, the enforced confinement was purgatory for the normally highly active teenager, and Topper began to show symptoms of depression. When the cast came off, in order to help him build up strength in his damaged leg, and allow him to blow off a little steam, his parents gave in to his pleas for a drum kit. Already showing signs of the addictive personality that would manifest itself in other less positive ways in years to come, Topper practised for up to eight hours a day. His early hero was Keith Moon, and that kind of exuberant showmanship became an important part of his drumming style . . . and his personality.

Topper's first band, formed with schoolfriend Steve Barnacle – brother of saxophonist Gary – was called Crystal Carcass, and performed 12-bar boogie instrumentals. Steve's father Bill played trumpet in a jazz band at Dover's jazz venue, the Louis Armstrong pub. Topper guested on one occasion and – having demonstrated his precocious versatility – was invited to sit in from time to time thereafter with the in-house trad jazz band led by landlord Bod Bowles. His desire to play, and the fact that even such a young drummer could earn decent money around town, led to him sitting in with a variety of other local groups, too. After playing with a local blues band called Back to Sanity, he joined a more serious prog-rock outfit called Mirkwood, which specialised in long songs with complicated rhythms. Next came a more straightforwardly hard-rock band called Expedition, which also operated the strictly for fun spin-off band Dead Dogs Don't Lie. By the early Seventies, Topper's drumming heroes were Man's Terry Williams (who later joined Rockpile and Dire Straits), and the showier jazz players Buddy Rich, Gene Krupa, Elvin Jones, and Billy Cobham, but he would listen to everyone and try to learn as much as he could. A musical natural, he continued to play guitar at home, and also taught himself piano.

Inevitably, his schoolwork suffered. Topper wasn't interested in a conventional career. The year after he left school, 1974, he moved up to the capital with the intention of joining a band with prospects. He took a room in Tooting, south London, and auditioned for Sparks, but lost out after reaching the final two. With money running out, he returned to his parents' house in Dover, and he briefly worked on building the Channel Tunnel. In May 1975, at just 19, he married his girlfriend Wendy Wood, a typist, and the couple returned to London, this time basing themselves in Finsbury Park, north London, while Topper tried out for other bands via the *Melody Maker* classifieds. A brief stint with Canadian guitarist Pat Travers came to nothing, and Topper went straight back to auditioning. One of the ads he responded to was placed by the London SS. Another was placed by a soul band called the IGs (most of the band were ex-GIs). This time, Topper was successful in both auditions. He opted for the IGs, because they had work and – unlike the London SS – they paid: £50 a week.

Next, Pat Travers put him in touch with a couple of fellow ex-patriate Canadians looking for a rhythm section to complete their bluesy hard-rock band, Fury. Topper persuaded his Dover friend Steve Barnacle to join him, and they began rehearsing material and playing gigs on the London pub-rock circuit. In early 1977 they were auditioned for CBS records, and given the impression it was just a formality and a deal was already in the bag. This was around the same time CBS signed the Clash, though, and when the record company turned down Fury, Steve Barnacle, for one, felt it was probably because the UK branch of the company had committed their new-signings budget to punk. The excuse CBS gave Fury was that the small and slight Topper didn't hit the drums with enough power for a band with a name like theirs.

On 24 March 1977 Mick Jones bumped into Topper at a Kinks gig at the Rainbow in Finsbury Park and invited him to audition for the Clash. Still stung by the recent criticism of his drumming style, Topper made sure he hit the drums as hard as he could. Combined with his skill, it ensured that – after a haircut and dye and a quick change of clothes – he was installed as the Clash drummer in time for the band's White Riot tour.

Most bands that get together in any sort of organic way – at school, at college or as neighbourhood friends; meeting at gigs or in record shops; via advertisements on notice boards or in the music press – do so because they share musical and other cultural tastes, or because they're simpatico individuals prepared to pool more diverse influences. Looking through the Clash members' potted pre-Clash biographies, it's immediately obvious that they came from very different backgrounds. It's possible to join enough dots together to come up with a musical sketch for an album like *London Calling*: retro rock'n'roll and R&B from Joe; more forward-looking Sixties guitar pop from Mick; reggae from Paul; soul, funk and jazz from Topper. There is also enough crossover of the four individuals' experience to provide pointers for the album's lyrical concerns: high-rise and inner-city ghetto living; a fascination with London, America and Jamaica and their mythologies; an understanding of folk, blues and rock'n'roll archetypes; a familiarity with a wide variety of movie genres; a keen interest in popular culture and the popular arts generally. Assessing the situation in this superficial way, it would be tempting to say that, if four musically creative people with such histories went into a rehearsal room together, determined to be open-minded and co-operative, they would almost inevitably come out with something that sounded at least a little like *London Calling*.

So why didn't the Clash produce something more like it in spring 1977, instead of *The Clash*? An obvious point to make is that Topper wasn't part of the line-up at that time. This wasn't the only issue with regard to the band's musicality, though. At the time, it pretty much began and ended with Mick Jones. Topper's predecessor, Terry Chimes, was only a real member of the Clash for a few months from June 1976, and thereafter fulfilled the role of temp, because the Clash had so much trouble finding a replacement. Terry could play, but he was a straight-forward rock'n'roll drummer anyway, and because he was just acting as a session player on *The Clash*, Mick told and showed him what he wanted. By the time of recording that album, Paul could still only find his way around his instrument with the aid of notes painted onto the fretboard. All his bass lines were devised by Mick and learned by rote. Joe Strummer was a very basic rhythm guitarist whose barely tuned guitars made such a horrible noise that his rhythm parts were mixed very low, and then overdubbed by Mick. And Mick himself had been playing rhythm guitar for just two years when he joined the Clash. For the first few months of the band's existence, fifth member Keith Levene was the lead guitarist. It was only when Keith was sacked in September 1976 that Mick had to cover his role, too, learning to play a mixture of rhythm and lead during live performances. And it was just six months later that *The Clash* was recorded. In other words, the band's musical director was pretty much a novice in his role, too. That the Clash's debut turned out to be such a towering album speaks volumes for Mick Jones's raw talent ... but it's also clear that the Clash simply would not have been capable of making *London Calling* in 1977, even if they had wanted to, or set out to.

And, of course, they didn't. The Clash didn't assemble in an organic way in order to express themselves and explore shared interests. Instead, they were put together by a man with a plan, Bernie Rhodes, who, responding to the Sex Pistols and what he'd heard about New York's New Wave, was intent on coming up with something similarly new and challenging. This high-concept project intrigued and excited the various band members, but they didn't originate it. The details were thrashed out collectively in meetings, but the overall scheme was shaped and guided by Bernie. Initially, at least, it required their individual identities and interests to be subsumed to serve the needs of the Big Idea.

*

The earliest indication of what was going on inside the Malcolm McLaren–Bernie Rhodes think tank was provided by their November 1974 T-shirt design collaboration, *You're gonna wake up one morning and* _know_ what side of the bed you've been lying on! It was a clumsy attempt at a Situationist slogan, but the underlying design concept was inspired: dividing the whole of experience – or, at least, Malcolm and Bernie's experience – into a list of Loves and a list of Hates. Highly subjective, arrogant and provocatively absolutist (and in places, an opportunity to settle petty personal scores), its purpose was to deny the option of fence-sitting, insisting – as late-Sixties revolutionary jargon put it – 'If you're not part of the solution, you're part of the problem.'

The lists are wide-ranging, covering music, film, television, theatre, art, comedy, fashion, advertising, publishing, the press, philosophy, and both political ideology and the tawdry reality of central and local politics. The Hates are boring, stale, Establishment, conventional, safe, repressive, glossy, superficial, passive, obligatory, money-oriented, exploitative and ultimately soulless. The Loves are raw, wild, exciting, daring, challenging, passionate, amoral, sexy, violent, anti-Establishment, anarchic, subversive, transgressive and highly imaginative. Together, they outline subject matter that would subsequently be tackled in early songs by both the Sex Pistols and the Clash, which very much supports Malcolm and Bernie's claims to have provided the core ideas for that material. The T-shirt manifesto might have been a rough blueprint for punk in terms of its very black-and-white position taking, but the battle lines would shift considerably before the concrete foundations were laid for the walls and sentry towers.

There has been a tendency to identify the musical malaise of the mid-Seventies as being the fault of tax exile superstar bands and pompous, noodling prog rockers. But there were also tasteful, technically proficient West Coast rock bands, self-obsessed singer-songwriters, cliché-ridden heavy metal bands, banal mainstream pop groups, and far too many so-called 'supergroups': that is, various permutations of well-known musicians being offered album deals simply because they were various permutations of well-known musicians, regardless of the fact they had been creatively bankrupt for years. Even soul music seemed to have become a chicken-in-the-basket nightmare of polyester jumpsuits and slick choreography, with very little actual soul in evidence.

The _what side of the bed_ T-shirt's list of Hates includes prog-rock bands Yes and ELP – it's easy to see why Bernie Rhodes was impressed when he first saw Johnny Rotten walking down the Kings Road in his customised *I Hate Pink Floyd* T-shirt – jet-set rock aristos Mick Jagger, Brian Ferry and Elton John, the presenter of BBC2's *The Old Grey Whistle Test*, Whispering Bob Harris, toothsome pop crooner David Essex, and 'clockwork soul routines'. On the Loves side appears *Raw Power* by proto-punks Iggy Pop and the Stooges, with a positive nod also given to early New York New Wave scenesters Television. Ian Dury's pub-rock band Kilburn and the High Roads are praised – Malcolm had designed stagewear for them – as are the then still largely imaginary Sex Pistols. Bernie was a reggae enthusiast, and was running a reggae stall at the time, explaining the nods to Bob Marley, King Tubby's sound system, dreadlocks, the Four Aces club in Dalston and Sixties Jamaican rude boys.

As if to underline how unsatisfactory they found the current music scene, almost everything else on the musical Loves list belongs to the past, like the rude boys: original American rock'n'rollers Eddie Cochran and Gene Vincent, early British rocker Screaming Lord Sutch (Malcolm's shop was, after all, originally called Let It Rock, catering to Teddy Boys and rock'n'roll revivalists), 'Guy Stevens records' (early Sixties soul and R&B as played at mod hangout the Scene club where Guy was the DJ, and leased by him from the USA for release on the Sue label), original soul artist Sam Cooke, original funk artist James Brown, plus the genre-bestriding Jimi Hendrix, and (again reflecting Bernie's personal tastes) 'New Thing' jazzmen Archie Shepp and John Coltrane.

Also on the Hates list, though, is 'old clothes, old ideas'. With another couple of years to refine the punk manifesto before the scene took off in the fanzines and music press and then the national news media came along and fixed its ideas for good, Malcolm and Bernie – jointly and separately – came to the conclusion that punk couldn't be about the past; or not openly, at least. Malcolm wanted to be free of his former customer base's inherent conservatism, so first-generation rock'n'roll was swiftly removed from the Loves list. Malcolm and Bernie were both ex-mods raised on a highly charged early Sixties culture of cafés and all-nighters, dandy threads and catchy, no-nonsense dance singles, and although both had in mind the early-mid-Sixties London live music scene – with bands like the Rolling Stones, the Kinks and the Who – as the archetype for the new London scene they hoped to instigate, they didn't want to be seen to be recycling any of the above.

The situation was further complicated by the fact that a section of the contemporary pub-rock scene was already engaged in doing exactly that. Bands like Dr Feelgood, the Count Bishops, the 101ers and Eddie and the Hot Rods played mid-Sixties R&B and guitar pop music (and their own material in that vein), but – in Malcolm and Bernie's opinion – in the wrong type of venues and with a complete lack of flair. To distance themselves from the smell of stale beer and patchouli oil and version 1,000,001 of 'Johnny B. Goode', the schemers deleted mod, Sixties guitar pop and the first half of the Sixties from the Loves list, too.

By the late Sixties, Malcolm – an art student at the time – had involved himself in student protest and was on nodding terms with the London branch of the Situationist International. Both he and Bernie were excited by the street-level revolt of *les Enragés* in Paris in 1968, and fascinated by the actions of the Yippies, the Black Panthers and the Weathermen in the USA. They knew that the MC5 were managed by John Sinclair, founder of the White Panthers. They were aware that, by the end of the decade, the White Panthers' representative in the UK was London underground scenester Mick Farren. After sacking him, Farren's former band the Deviants renamed themselves the Pink Fairies, and set themselves up as Ladbroke Grove's answer to the MC5. Together with the other 'people's bands', they followed a policy of playing benefits for deserving causes and local community action groups. The punk-plotting duo also took note when, in 1971, a high-concept, revolutionary rock band named Third World War was launched by Sixties music business maverick John Fenton. While Malcolm and Bernie were happy to continue claiming personal involvement with the underground – though it was minimal: Malcolm was a trouble-making dilettante, and Bernie's direct involvement doesn't appear to have gone much further than making use of free arts lab facilities – they were quick to belittle the achievements of the supposedly revolutionary bands and artists of the period. Wariness of being caught walking in their Jesus-sandalled footsteps was the root of punk's antipathy towards hippies and their baggage: long hair, flared jeans, smoking dope. So that was the second half of the Sixties dismissed, too.

Malcolm lifted a lot of his ideas for London punk from the contemporary New York CBGBs scene, which itself owed much to the Dolls, the Stooges and the *Nuggets* bands. Lester Bangs would write convincingly about this type of garage or proto-punk rock as a wild mutation: music birthed from the blues via R&B and rock'n'roll, but three or four generations away from its roots in the Mississippi Delta and the black experience, adapted by mostly white urban working-class and suburban middle-class bands, distorted by incompetence and amplification, pinged backwards and forwards from the USA to the UK to the USA, until it was a Xerox of a Xerox of a Xerox, something so degraded it was almost unrecognisable. Black music with all the black blanched out; white noise in more than one sense of the phrase. Soul and funk and swing and jazz were also dropped from the Loves list, quietly, because no one wanted to come over like an overt racist . . . but this was to be a white riot. There's a distinct lack of R&B or soul-style syncopation in the early Clash material. Frenetic it is; funky it most certainly ain't.

When the nascent Clash heard the first Ramones album in April 1976 it helped them devise a sound of their own that was different to that of the Pistols. The Ramones wrote short, repetitive songs with instant hooks, garbled lyrics and no solos, and recorded them cheaply and close to live with limited overdubs. They claimed they played how they played and what they played because it was all they could play. Although the Ramones were barely credited as the source, their approach became part of the punk manifesto for the Clash and many other UK punk bands that formed in their wake: songs had to be played fast, kept concise and simple, with no technical expertise on show. This was the antithesis of prog, and of successful Californian bands spending a year in the studio making an album.

Malcolm and Bernie were determined for punk to be considered a London movement, and Bernie, in particular, stressed that the Clash should write about their personal experience. Joe Strummer's insistence that he 'sang in English' was a handy device to distance the Clash and UK punk from other UK rock bands whose vocalists affected American accents to sing about imaginary American experiences, like that well-known Mississippi Delta bluesman, Mick Jagger. But the statement – and the intent behind it – also dismissed genuine American bands of all types: not only the despised West Coast AOR, but also quality material from the Fifties, Sixties and Seventies. In 'I'm So Bored with the USA', Joe has the decency to salute the New York New Wave, but then appears to express the hope that it will wipe out all other American music. In 'New York', Johnny Rotten pretends to have no time at all for the Manhattan scene, heaping cheap insults upon the New York Dolls, without whom his manager would have still been selling drape jackets and rubber gimp suits, and he himself wouldn't have been allowed anywhere near a microphone. The McLaren–Rhodes party line was that all music from America – that is, all the truly *popular* popular music of the twentieth century – was worthless. Again, the baby went out with the bathwater. This was the origin of UK punk's Year Zero philosophy.

Terry Chimes was taken on as the Clash's original drummer precisely because he played in a straightforward, no-frills style, and the *Melody Maker* ads Bernie and the band ran for his replacement in January 1977 stressed 'No funk, no jazz, no laid-back'. What Topper Headon brought to the mix a couple of months later was not only unavailable to the Clash in 1976 and early 1977, it was very pointedly not required. Having had a previous visible – if not exactly high-profile – life in the 101ers, Joe Strummer could hardly pretend that he had never had any interest in rock'n'roll and R&B. What he did instead – after an appropriately biblical rending of his garments (and the slightly less biblical safety-pinning of them back together again) – was betray it two times before the cock crowed. He customised a shirt to read *Chuck Berry is Dead* and came up with the line 'No Elvis, Beatles or the Rolling Stones' for the Clash's Year Zero celebration, '1977'.

Mick Jones was the last of the band to get his shoulder-length hair cut, lose the Kensington Market peacock finery, and start wearing the ripped and torn punk uniform. In another early interview for premiere punk fanzine *Sniffin' Glue*, he made a valid case for the socio-political awareness of Ray Davies of the Kinks and Ian Hunter of Mott the Hoople, but after that his love of what had gone before was rarely allowed to speak its name. The Clash's first appearance in the *Melody Maker* had already provided him with an opportunity to denounce one of his great heroes, Rod Stewart, and elsewhere he joined in with the general band razzing of the long-haired and be-flared, despite being just a couple of months out of both himself.

Paul Simonon, meanwhile, could breathe easy: he didn't have a highly visible musical history. Despite being black music, laid-back music, long-haired music, with a strong Sixties as well as Seventies tradition, reggae was considered OK because it was made in ghetto conditions, and also had a tradition of tackling social and political issues. The cool tough-guy poise that was a legacy of Paul's period as a skinhead also helped define the Clash's no-nonsense look.

All of the shunning and fie-ing that was going on was taken at face value by large sections of the UK music press and by the new punk audience. By the time Elvis Presley succumbed to both his own weight and the weight of Joe Strummer's prediction in August 1977, the audience at London's leading punk club of the time, the Vortex, had been so conditioned by the movement's rhetoric that they cheered the news of his death. They seemed oblivious to the many contradictions. Here are just some of them . . .

However he cut his hair and overhauled his wardrobe, Joe Strummer still performed like a hot-wired Eddie Cochran. Even by early 1977 he had started slicking his hair back on his nights off and regularly attending rock'n'roll revival shows . . . out of town. Johnny Rotten's microphone technique was pure Gene Vincent (via Ian Dury). And when Johnny left the Pistols, Malcolm McLaren would keep the rump of the band in the charts by having Sid Vicious gurn his way through a couple of Eddie Cochran songs.

The Pistols' early set included several of the sort of mid-Sixties standards that were also gracing the sets of pub-rock bands like Eddie and the Hot Rods, including the Who's 'Substitute' (1966) and the Small Faces' 'Whatcha Gonna Do About It' (1965), while a pre-Strummer version of the Clash played the Troggs' 'I Can't Control Myself' (1966) and the Kinks' 'Dead End Street' (1966). Both the Pistols and the Clash's early originals were very much influenced by this period of music, something which is perhaps most obvious in the case of the latter band: Mick Jones's tune for '1977' lifts the riff from the Kinks' 'All Day and All of the Night' (1964), and 'Clash City Rockers' is a close relative of the Who's 'I Can't Explain' (1965). (In fairness, Mick was usually a more talented and subtle 'thief': he took a little from everywhere, which made it not plagiarism, but research.)

Despite Malcolm and Bernie's professed revulsion for 'old clothes', the early Sex Pistols look was pretty much mod-meets-Pop Art with a few pervy designer touches, while the early Clash look was Oxfam mod-meets-Pop Art put through the shredder. Punk's drug of choice was the mod drug of choice: speed. Even Bernie wasn't above living the lie: it was he who hired Sixties mover-and-shaker Guy Stevens to produce the Clash's November 1976 demos for Polydor Records.

One of Malcolm and Bernie's more impressive bits of flimflammery was rubbishing the late Sixties underground while making free with its subject matter, values, presentation and infrastructure. *Passion is a fashion*, as stencilled on Joe's boiler suit in late 1976, is a Situationist slogan of the type used on posters and as graffiti during the Paris riots. Jamie Reid's sleeve and poster design for the Pistols appropriated elements from Situationist flyers. The title 'White Riot' was previously used for a version of 'White Christmas' in the 1969 Weathermen songbook. It was intended to be to the 'black riot' of late Seventies Notting Hill what the White Panthers had been to the Black Panthers in the late Sixties: a gesture of support, while acknowledging a difference in experience.

Mick Farren believes that Class of 1976 punk owes a debt to London's 'people's bands' of the late Sixties and early Seventies. Many of the punk scene's leading lights were certainly exposed to them at an impressionable age, including Mick Jones, Johnny Rotten, Rat Scabies, Brian James, Captain Sensible and Tony James. The Pink Fairies' 'Do It' (1971) may well be the first recorded articulation of what would become UK punk's trademark DIY philosophy, and like the Kinks and Mott the Hoople, the Fairies also wrote songs acknowledging the inner-city condition, like 'Street Urchin' and 'City Kids' (both 1973). Malcolm was still checking out the band for pointers at a reunion show in January 1976. In 1971 Third World War released their eponymous debut album with songs declining to kiss the monarchy's arse and threatening to take Molotovs and automatic rifles onto the streets of west London. It's hardly wild theorising to imply that there might have been some seepage, via Malcolm and Bernie, into songs written by the Pistols and the Clash. Also, punk in general and the Clash in particular followed the precedent these bands set for playing benefits for deserving causes. Even the Clash's conscious self-association with the Westway and Notting Hill takes its lead from the previous generation of Ladbroke Groovers.

Most tellingly of all, the individuals that Bernie, in particular, selected to help him sell the 'new' musical revolution had been key players in the underground scene. Without the support of Barry Miles and, especially, Caroline Coon – the first music journalist to describe the music made by the new British bands as 'punk rock' – it's doubtful the Clash's rise to prominence would have been quite so vertiginous. Bernie 'borrowed' – they were never returned – photographer Joe Stevens's collection of Sixties underground publications to aid Joe Strummer's political education. Another photographer more closely associated with the Clash, Pennie Smith, also started out working for underground press magazine *Friends*, and was also credited with the album sleeve for the Pink Fairies' *Never Never Land* (1971).

Try as they might, the Pistols and the Clash couldn't really deny the influence of New York New Wave. Steve Jones learned guitar playing along to a Dolls album on a guitar Malcolm 'borrowed' – he never gave it back – from the Dolls' Syl Sylvain. Live, Steve's stage poses were modelled on those of the other Dolls guitarist, Johnny Thunders. Mick Jones bought the guitar he used in the early days of the Clash, a Gibson Les Paul Junior, because Thunders had one, and he too threw some of his hero's moves into his live routine. The punk spiketop haircut as worn by Johnny Rotten, Sid Vicious and Paul Simonon – UK punk's definitive style, pre-Mohawk – was originated by Television's Richard Hell. Television also wore narrow-lapelled jackets held together by safety pins.

Some genuinely new, awkward and challengingly avant-garde music did come out of the London punk scene, but not too much of it was to be found on the first few releases by the Sex Pistols or the Clash. This was not so obvious in 1977 as it is now that time and familiarity have taken away much of the shock and awe of punk's initial impact. Steve Jones's wall of guitars and Johnny Rotten's mannered non-singing diverted attention from the fact that the Pistols repertoire evolved from playing those songs by the Small Faces, the Who and the Monkees, and that main tunesmith Glen Matlock wasn't averse to throwing in a little Abba. And the frenetic pace, harsh treble and Joe Strummer's mush-mouthed bellow temporarily obscured his and Mick Jones's shared love affair with almost the entire back catalogue of popular music.

Class of 1976 UK punk's selling of itself as a wholly new and original musical form beholden to no one and nothing – either from across the waves or from the recent or distant past – was a con. A brilliant con. It was put over with such charismatic certainty that the majority swallowed it. As has been noted many times before: very George Orwell, very Joseph Stalin. Also very Emperor's New Clothes.

*

The *what side of the bed?* T-shirt finds Malcolm and Bernie beginning to stake out common ground among cults celebrating their apartness from mainstream society: youth cults like mods and skinheads; lifestyle cults like rubber and S&M fetishists; street urchins, amoral through force of circumstance, getting by as thieves, hustlers and prostitutes; and Left Bank intellectuals, dissident for the sake of ideology or mischief. While Malcolm was in New York, and Bernie was left in charge of the Sex Pistols, he gave the Pistols' Glen Matlock a reading list-cum-cultural primer. A few months later, he did much the same for Mick Jones and Tony James of the London SS. Considering punk's character prided itself on being so very English, this new list was decidedly European (and particularly French): Dada, Jean-Luc Godard and Nouvelle Vague film, Jean-Paul Sartre and – zoning in on the punk archetype – Jean Genet's *The Thief's Journal* (1949).

As has been remarked before on more than one occasion, there was a distinct sense of Charles Dickens and *Oliver Twist* about Malcolm and Bernie and their respective gangs of lost boys. When the two managers went their separate ways, it quickly became clear that Malcolm was more interested in sexual provocation: hardly surprising for a man who had renamed his clothes shop Sex, started selling rubber fetish wear and pornographic T-shirts, and called 'his' band the Sex Pistols. The first *Sex Pistols* T-shirt features a photograph of a naked, underage boy lifted from a paedophile magazine. The Pistols themselves posed for some early photographs as teenage victims. Jordan, who worked in Sex, and Siouxsie Sioux of the group of Pistols fans known as the Bromley Contingent both adopted a fetishwear dominatrix look. Other hangers-on experimented with prostitution. Sid Vicious flirted with rent-boy life. Mischievous Malcolm lived vicariously through the Sex Pistols and their followers. Although his home background was anything but conventional, he was a spoiled, indulged and cosseted child, and had flitted from art school to art school as a young man before teaming up with Vivienne Westwood to sell clothes.

Bernie Rhodes's background was more authentically grim. The Dickensian aspects of punk and of the archetypal punk character, as determined in discussions between Malcolm and Bernie, were not entirely literary, artistic or cinematic. They owed much to Bernie's true-life experience.

His mother, Millie Rotman, was of Russo-Jewish stock. Her parents, David and Liebe, had fled the pogroms, ending up in south Wales, where Millie was born and her father David worked in a steel mill. What happened next is sketchy, but it appears that sometime after the Russian Revolution of 1917, Liebe returned to Russia, taking Millie with her. They got caught up in the civil war that followed. It lasted until 1922, and resulted in the death of nine million people, most of them civilians, including Liebe. Millie, apparently, was placed in an orphanage. In the meantime, David moved to London, entered the tailoring trade, found a new partner, and started another family.

David was finally able to bring Millie to London when she was approximately 15. Understandably traumatised by her experience, and finding it hard to come to terms with her father's new family situation, she left home as soon as she could to make her own way in tailoring, despite speaking hardly any English. In 1942 she married divorcee August 'Cecil' Rhodes, and in 1944 Bernie was born in Stepney. Bernie claims he never knew his father. As it was Cecil who remained at the family home for many years afterwards, it can only be assumed that it was Millie who chose or was asked to leave. Until the early Fifties she and Bernie lived in one of the Nissen huts the Government erected as temporary housing on East End bombsites, with Bernie having to fend for himself while his mother did piecework as a tailor's finisher. By the time Bernie was eight, Millie (or the authorities) had decided the position was untenable. Millie's father David had died before Bernie was born, she didn't feel close enough to her sister or half-brother to turn to them for help, and she was receiving no assistance from her ex-husband. Bernie was placed in the Jewish Orphanage in Norwood, south London.

Bernie has claimed in more than one interview that he ran away from the orphanage and was on the streets by the age of eight, but although it was common for residents to abscond, they rarely got far or stayed away long. Bernie remained at Norwood until he was 15, and from 11 onwards attended Aristotle Secondary School in Brixton.

Like Paul Simonon a decade later, Bernie would soak up the West Indian immigrant culture in Brixton market. He continued at school until he took O levels in 1960, but by his last year he was living back with Millie in a small flat in Kilburn. As his mother was now doing finishing work for Hawes & Curtis in Dover Street, off Piccadilly, Bernie began to spend his spare time hanging around near Soho. Even 15 years after the war, it was still full of spivs and prostitutes, and – unlike Malcolm – Bernie became a participant in the life, a self-proclaimed 'West End hustler' on friendly terms with the working girls. He relied on ducking and diving to make his money, and not exclusively in the schmutter trade. Via Millie, Bernie met John Pearse, a tailor's apprentice at Hawes & Curtis. When Bernie was 16, they began sharing a flat together, and launched themselves on the mod scene. Within a couple of years, they were joined on the town and in their Maida Vale flat by Richard Cole.

Bernie liked some R&B and soul music, and spent time at the all-nighters at the Lyceum on the Strand, the Scene club in Ham Yard listening to Guy Stevens, and at the Flamingo club in Wardour Street, where he could keep up with the development of ska, but his own tastes were more Old School Modernist: he liked jazz. Richard Cole began to roadie for bands like Unit 4 Plus 2 and the Who, though, and John Pearse co-founded Granny Takes a Trip on the Kings Road, a shop frequented by the new psychedelic pop aristocracy. When Mickey Finn – the soon-to-be bongo-playing partner to Bernie's mod-era acquaintance Marc Bolan in underground scene duo Tyrannosaurus Rex – also moved into the communal Maida Vale flat, Bernie could boast an across-the-board knowledge of contemporary UK pop culture. Always possessed of an enquiring mind, he kept up to date with current affairs, read widely, assimilating the information and questioning everything.

One of the reasons that Bernie wasn't more directly involved with the underground is that his girlfriend Sheila gave birth to a son in 1967. Bernie moved out of the bachelor pad in Maida Vale and into a family flat in Camden Town. By the early Seventies he had become jaded with the mainstream music scene, and was unimpressed by the now electric T.Rex's teenybop pop, or by Richard Cole's latest gig as road manager of the increasingly self-indulgent Led Zeppelin. Bernie continued to hustle, dealing second-hand clothes and running a reggae stall in Antiquarius in the Kings Road. Noticing the popularity of slogan and image T-shirts, he also acquired a printing machine. It was in late 1973 or early 1974, while hawking his wares around the funky part of the Kings Road where Antiquarius, Granny Takes a Trip, the Don Letts-run Acme Attractions and Let It Rock (the future Sex) were all located – the World's End – that he and Malcolm first fell into conversation. Their shared dissatisfaction with the way that youth culture seemed to have been appropriated by safe, mainstream popular entertainment was what got them interested in stirring up a new street-level scene. Even by 1976, though, Bernie still maintained a more prosaic sideline, running ads in *Time Out* offering to fix up Renault cars, work that he then sub-contracted to Harry's Garage in Camden Town's British Rail Yards. It would be no coincidence that his own Clash-era car (the one with the CLA5H number plate) and the Clash's first van were both Renaults.

Bernie's take on street culture differed from Malcolm's because it was so much more real to him. As he had moved and lived among working girls, his interest in prostitution was more socio-economic: to Bernie, in the pre-feminist era, it was what girls of a certain social class and limited education who had been led to believe they have no other marketable skills did if they didn't want to work in a factory and couldn't make the grade as a showgirl. It was at his urging that Mick Jones wrote 'Janie Jones', named after an infamous early Seventies madam. Otherwise, Bernie was less interested in titillation than in political provocation. Bernie saw the contemporary economic down-turn and the resulting rise in youth unemployment as presaging an upsurge of violence on the streets and a draconian authoritarian response.

The Clash members were not politically minded before they took up with Bernie. London's underground scene had influenced Mick's thinking, but he had always considered himself to be 'of the left' without getting actively involved or even thinking about it too much. Paul's father had embraced Communism by the early Seventies, and made his son deliver leaflets, but it didn't rub off. Paul was more hedo-nistically inclined, and remained so for much of the Clash's existence. Joe would later claim that he himself had been politicised by his forceful evictions in the early Seventies. He did drop out of society at that time, but it was because he didn't want to work (and possibly because he was clinically depressed following the death of his brother). He did sell the Communist newspaper the *Morning Star* at pitheads in South Wales for a while, but that was to impress a girl. And he did squat upon his return to London, but that was so he could live cheaply while putting a band together. It was Bernie who took and shaped this rough clay into the intensely political and pro-active Clash.

His success in communicating his theories to the songwriting members of the band, most importantly chief lyricist Joe Strummer, goes some way to explaining such first-album songs as 'Remote Control' and 'Hate & War'. The sense of living not only a life with no values, but also a life not valued by society – and with no prospect of change for the better – informs the disappointed hedonism of '48 Hours', 'Deny' and 'Protex Blue', and the howls of frustration and despair that are 'London's Burning', 'What's My Name' and 'Garageland'.

Bernie had been a mod – a member of a youth cult produced by an economic upswing and disposable income – when the 48 hours of the weekend had been more promise than curse, but he'd witnessed worsening times since beget skinheads and bovver boys – football hooligans – and he also knew the history of the rude boy in Jamaica. When the youth of Kingston got out of control in 1966 it prompted the declaration of the country's first state of emergency: curfews and harsh jail sentences. Ten years later, Jamaica was going through it all again, only worse. Of all the music from other times and places it had been considered acceptable to Love in 1974, only reggae was still on the list two years later, and the reason was that reggae was a versatile, constantly evolving, powerful music made (for the most part) by people who knew all about real ghetto life. Its lyrics celebrated good times and good things when appropriate, but by 1976 they dealt mostly with hardship, oppression and conflict. The Notting Hill Riot of August that year brought the Kingston vibe to London, and provided rich lyrical pickings for Joe Strummer.

Bernie was interested in throwing down a few cultural challenges to late Seventies Britain, using the Clash as his gauntlet. One was about passivity: audiences at gigs sitting down to watch musicians noodle; and audiences at home spending hours in front of the television. He wanted to protest at the death of 'free' radio: that is, radio willing to take a risk and get behind new sounds rather than radio giving its target market exactly what market research indicates that target market wants.

He also wanted to query the tyranny of work: people continuing to do jobs they hate because they lack the gumption or courage to leave. (A timely topic for debate, given rising unemployment.) All of these subjects appear on the *what side of the bed* T-shirt, and all became burning issues for the Clash. During early gigs, Joe would rail at audiences to get up and give something back; and even when former Sex and Acme Attractions accountant Andrew Czezowski beat both Malcolm and Bernie to establishing a punk venue and hangout with the Roxy, the Clash continued to express their interest in opening a club of their own to showcase exciting music for excitable people. TV as soporific provokes the Clash's ire in 'London's Burning' (Mick Jones came up with that line). The band berate their local radio station for its failures in 'Capital Radio', and Joe Strummer also repeatedly expressed interest in establishing a Clash radio station. And what Bernie perceived to be the central issue of employment struck such a chord with the band – none of whom had attempted to hold down a proper job for any length of time – that they came at it from different angles in 'Janie Jones', '1977', 'Career Opportunities' and 'Clash City Rockers'.

It was entirely coincidental that Paul's father had left home, and Mick's parents had split up and left him with his Nan, and Joe's parents had deposited him at boarding school, at almost exactly the same age that Bernie had been placed in the orphanage, but it was useful common ground, and good material for Bernie to work with when it came to adding some authentic flavour of childhood disadvantage. The gang element of punk was important. As kids from broken, or at least less than solid and secure homes, the future members of the Clash had also sought other collective structures to give them a sense of belonging. Paul had been a skinhead and a football hooligan. Mick had hung around with Robin Crocker's gang, and on the edges of the underground scene, and with the bunch of kids that followed Mott the Hoople. At the time of the first album's release, he told Tony Parsons of the *NME* that the Clash was now his family. Joe was more of a loner by inclination, but was used to living communally, first at school and then in the squats. He had briefly been a member of the Divine Light Mission during his art-school foundation year, providing some context for the utter conviction of his conversion to punk a few years later: like Malcolm, Bernie had more than a little of the Fagin about him; but he also did a mean cult leader.

Class was and is a contentious subject when discussing punk. People from outside the UK don't always understand it, and many people born there like to pretend it has never been an issue. While it is true that money and success have blurred the dividing lines, and changes in the structure of society have fogged the definitions, class does still impact upon British life today, and certainly did between the early Fifties and the late Seventies. Bernie wanted the Clash to represent the dead-end kids, the scrap-heap dwellers, the underclass. That none of them came from anything like this background was obscured by rhetoric. The Clash members were dole bums by inclination rather than circumstance. Joe and Mick were both intelligent and educated. The songwriting duo were widely read enough to be able to work through Bernie's educational primers and relate them to other cultural input, like Stanley Kubrick's film *A Clockwork Orange* (1971), and J. G. Ballard's *Concrete Island* (1974) and *High Rise* (1975), and accustomed enough to academic debate to thrash issues through with Bernie in band meetings. Paul wasn't educated, but was smart enough when he chose to be. He was responsible for naming the band after noticing the word 'clash' recurring in the *Evening Standard*'s headlines. Mostly, though, he and (when he joined) Topper read comics. Paul was also responsible for nicknaming the drummer, after noticing his resemblance to the character Mickey the Monkey on the cover of that week's *Topper*. Fittingly for a band formed by three art students at the behest of a self-styled street philosopher, the Clash of *The Clash* was an exercise in conceptual performance art.

Bernie found a rehearsal space for the band not far from his flat in Camden Town, in the British Rail Yards which also housed Harry's, the garage where he had his Renaults done up. He named it Rehearsals Rehearsals (whether in an unusually literal-minded moment or as a Jewish in-joke, no one seems to know). Despite being based at Rehearsals – with Joe and Paul also living there or close by for the next few months – the Clash were encouraged to make much of their association with Notting Hill and Brixton, areas with transitory, strongly immigrant populations, in order to enhance their street credibility. It was Mick Jones's time in high-rise council housing that was usually stressed in early band interviews, because – if painted with broad enough brush strokes – it provided the required picture of underbelly life. It was forgotten that Mick was almost an adult when he and

Stella first moved into Wilmcote House, and that for the preceding five or six years they'd lived just off Hyde Park in a private Art Deco flat block with a porter on the door.

Because Bernie had spent his entire life in the capital, and because the Clash's voice was to be the authentic voice of inner-city London – in 'Hate & War' the band declare their intention of staying there even when their house falls down, an encapsulation of the East End spirit during the Blitz – focus was diverted away from certain band members' time spent outside the capital. It would be many years before Paul's early years in towns around the Home Counties and year out in Italy would be admitted to. There were too many people on the punk scene who knew Joe's history to prevent him being as selective with it as Paul was with his, but as many details as possible were omitted, and his accent moved several notches further towards Cockney prole than his background warranted.

*

Looking at the Clash's career from the punk perspective, then, as everyone was instructed to do by the Clash themselves in 1976 – and many continued to do so until approximately 1996 – aside from Joe's grittier 101ers material, and Mick's love of the Dolls, the MC5 and garage rock, and Paul's skinhead-inspired street style, much of what the Clash members did and liked in the years pre-Clash was kept quiet or even denied, like an embarrassment best forgotten. Consequently, much of what they produced in the years post-1978 was perceived by the punk faithful to be a sell-out, a letdown or at best a failed effort to deliver on the promise. In truth, though, for this particular punk band it was the punk period that was the anomaly, the aberration.

Keith Levene lost interest in the Clash with 'White Riot'. It was at this point he realised the band's output was going to consist of what he thought of as Mick Jones's facile pop tunes married to Joe Strummer's Agit-Prop for Beginners lyrics. Left to his own devices when writing for the 101ers, Joe had developed a verbose style with lots of Chuck Berryesque internal rhymes and cartoon, late hippy argot: transatlantic Beatnik. Following Bernie Rhodes's instruction, Joe not only started writing songs about Key Topical Subjects, but jettisoned about 70 per cent of his vocabulary, and dispensed with any grammatical structure longer than the most basic of clauses in an attempt to put across urgency and anger, yes, but also to pretend that he was an impassioned but barely articulate man of the people. His new faux-impoverished style was memorably described by one critic as 'telegrammatic'.

Which is not to agree with Keith Levene that the likes of 'White Riot' signalled the corruption of the Original Great Idea. Joe's intelligence was not dumbed down, and his wit was not suppressed; they were just delivered in a new way. Mick's skills were not compromised, just challenged and stimulated. The compositional brief he was given, combined with the loss of Keith – and Mick's resultant need to take on lead as well as rhythm guitar for the 50 per cent of the gig and 95 per cent of the record Joe wouldn't be playing – forced Mick to learn how to make a number glue together and grab and hold the listener's attention with the minimum of elements: how to arrange, use dynamics, use space. Some of the best art results from the friction between ambition and limitation, whether that limitation be technical shortcomings or self- or externally-imposed rules. *The Clash* was a landmark album, and is still worthy of a placing much higher in the Greatest Albums Of All Time polls than it has.

What the album, the rhetoric and the revised band member biographies threatened to do, though, was catch the Clash in a trap of their own making. Not allowing themselves to develop – or to use an unacceptable word, progress – would doom them to delivering more of the same only less so, or, at best, refining their schtick until it became unschtuck. The Ramones quickly ceased to be good role models: second album, same as the first; third album, same as the second. The Damned and pub-rock/punk-rock crossover bands the Jam and Stranglers delivered weak follow-up albums six months after their debuts. Scene leaders the Sex Pistols sacked their main tunesmith Glen Matlock in early 1977, and – not entirely coincidentally – split up in early 1978. None of the first bands to emerge from the UK punk scene rode this period of transition well, with the arguable exception of the Buzzcocks. In 1980 Mick looked back on this time for *Rolling Stone*, telling James Henke, 'We had just been reaching the same people over and over, and the music – just *bang! bang! bang!* – was getting to be like a nagging wife.' For the Clash, the option of continuing to just be themselves was made even less palatable by the number of bands who emerged during the course of 1977 with Clash-influenced songs and lyrics and clothes, only – for the most part – lacking much of the prototype's invention, humour and style: the remodelled Jam, Chelsea, Generation X, 999, Sham 69, the UK Subs, the Tom Robinson Band and Stiff Little Fingers, to name but several. It was important for the Clash to find a way out without having to recant and embarrass themselves too much.

They had three things going for them.

The first was reggae. Paul Simonon might have learned the (very) basics of bass by playing along to *The Ramones*, but when he started to work on his playing, he did so by playing along to the reggae songs on the jukebox at Rehearsals Rehearsals. As reggae was bass-dominated, the bass lines stood out and were easier for him to grasp. His bass playing naturally developed a reggae flavour, becoming one of the elements that made *The Clash* more than standard-issue punk ramalalama. Also, during rehearsals, he would fill downtime by running through a few bars of a favourite reggae tune. After a while, one of the other musicians would start to play along. The first song the Clash worked up as a light relief jam was the Wailers' 'Dancing Shoes' (1966).

By early 1977 the band were taking a stab at Junior Murvin's 'Police & Thieves' (1976). And when they realised they were short of material for their first album – recorded just eight months after they formed, by which time they had played no more than 30 gigs – someone suggested they include it. The decision to proceed wasn't taken lightly. The song had been blaring out of the speakers at the 1976 Notting Hill Carnival before, during and after the riot that had inspired 'White Riot'. It was the perfect complement to the Clash's own composition, addressing the same subject from the West Indian immigrant point of view. But although reggae was seen by the punk scene-setters as thematically and ideologically aligned with punk, there were those – including the highly vocal and influential Johnny Rotten – who saw it as cultural imperialism for people who were not suffering the Jamaican's burden to play the Jamaican's music. Like, say, Eric Clapton's 1974 reading of the previous year's Bob Marley and the Wailers release 'I Shot the Sheriff'. The archetypal punk song was rigidly structured, angular, trebly, and over and done in three minutes or less, but 1976-era reggae – notably that produced (and co-written) by Lee 'Scratch'

Perry, as was 'Police & Thieves' – was by comparison a slow-motion groove running twice as long. Mick Jones arranged the Clash's version as a punk treatment of a reggae song, but it still lasted for six minutes, and sounded like it came from a third genre somewhere in the middle. It broke all of punk's rules and helped set the Clash free.

In fairness, this didn't happen entirely in isolation. Mick might have learned to bite his lip when discussing matters musical in front of the music press, but his tastes remained catholic. When the band joined CBS in January 1977, he took the entire Bob Dylan back catalogue as his signing present, and when he went on tour, he brought and bought cassettes of a wide variety of current music. On the summer 1977 Out on Parole tour, *NME* journalist Chris Salewicz made a note of just one day's purchases: *Legalise It* by Peter Tosh, *On the Beach* by Neil Young, *Little Criminals* by Randy Newman, and *Let's Stay Together* by Al Green. Mick would listen to all of it for pleasure, but also to take from it whatever he needed to make himself a better songwriter, arranger, guitar player and – ultimately – producer. He was always inquisitive, always looking for new ways to combine chords and notes and sounds.

The great myth is that Mick's early Clash tunes were ultra-basic, with no more than three chords apiece. Of the 14 Clash-composed tracks on the debut album and single, though, only two qualify as three-chord tricks, with – including relative minors and occasional chromatic forays – 10 of the others having five or more, and two boasting as many as eight. Even at this stage, Mick was pushing and pulling at rigid structure, adding coda sections to more than half of the songs. In the wake of the album, a combination of his urge to test the limits of the punk form and the complete otherness of form represented by reggae allowed him to write a couple of singles that many believe to be the Clash's two finest individual moments: 'Complete Control', with its rule-flouting guitar solo – 'You're my guitar hero!' – and extended coda, which was produced in east London by none other than Lee 'Scratch' Perry; and '(White Man) In Hammersmith Palais', the Clash's first self-penned song in a true reggae style. (In 2003, *Uncut* magazine polled 63 music business figures to determine the best ever Clash songs, and placed these two at numbers 2 and 1, respectively.) In between came the reggae- and self-glorifying 'Clash City Rockers', with another extended coda. Invoking the spirit of Brian Wilson's *Pet Sounds* and *Smile*-era pocket symphonies, and Pete Townshend's rock operas from 'A Quick One While He's Away' onwards, Paul Simonon described Mick's songs from this period as 'mini-operas'.

The last piece of the jigsaw – musically speaking – was Topper Headon. By the time the Clash finished the May 1977 White Riot tour, they had notched up more gigs with Topper than they had previously played without him. As 1977 wore on, the other three members of the band improved as musicians and gained confidence onstage, in the studio and in the rehearsal room. The fact that Topper could, would and did play anything gave the Clash the freedom to widen their scope in rehearsals, and encouraged Mick to write accordingly. It took a while for Topper to earn the right to assume full control of his instrument from the band's musical director, but his versatility added considerably to the sound of the 1977–8 inter-album singles, and by the time recording began for the Clash's second album, *Give 'Em Enough Rope*, he was making suggestions and having them heeded.

Which is not to say it was all easy going for the Clash from then on. When it came time to write the second album – in late November 1977 – Mick and Joe were dispatched to Kingston, Jamaica, for ten days, presumably with the expectation that they would further hone the promising punk/contemporary reggae hybrid that 'Police & Thieves' had kick-started. Unfortunately, Mick and Joe immediately found themselves completely out of their depth: if their punk threads were considered provocative in London, they were unearthly in downtown Kingston, where they were asking for trouble merely by being white. This, remember, was a country in crisis, with robbery and knife and gun violence a daily event, and murder not far behind. It was like dropping a couple of canaries into a cattery. Petrified, they hid in their hotel, the Pegasus, with a big bag of ganja. The positive result was that they did nothing but write, and came back with enough material for an album. The downside was that they had an attack of guilt and shame, feeling like frauds for co-opting a musical genre reflecting a truly desperate situation as a vehicle for Clash songs. The true implications of all those conversations about cultural tourism hit home, and hard: the Third World reality of ghetto life in the city reggae came from was so much harder and scarier than anything they had encountered back in their relatively cosy First World environment.

The last punk/contemporary reggae hybrid song they attempted was their admirably frank confession, 'Safe European Home'.

It was, by a long way, the best thing they wrote on the trip, and would be the best song on their second album. Consequently, it's hard not to feel some selfish regret that the Clash did not record an entire album mining the rich claim staked out by 'Police & Thieves', 'Complete Control', 'Clash City Rockers' and '(White Man) In Hammersmith Palais'. That said, there was another reason for the Clash's – as it subsequently turned out, temporary – decision to abandon contemporary reggae in early 1978: as had happened with their 'White Riot' punk prototype, a Hamelin's worth of groups had danced along in their punk and reggae crossover footsteps, whether it be with one-offs, like Elvis Costello's 'Watching the Detectives', Generation X's 'Wild Dub', ATV's 'Life After Life' and Stiff Little Fingers' Bob Marley cover 'Johnny Was', or extensive explorations of this new genre by the likes of the Police, the Ruts and the Members . . . with, as it turned out, more to follow.

*

This section of the book does not aspire to provide a complete biography of the various band members pre-Clash, or of the Clash pre-*London Calling*. Its function is to set the scene and provide the context for how *London Calling* came to be. Other essential background details are as follows . . .

By January 1977 Bernie Rhodes had lined up a deal with Polydor Records, but at the last minute managed to finagle a contract with CBS for four times as much, an advance of £100,000. (Using the retail price index as the point of comparison, that would have been roughly the equivalent of £448,000 in 2007; using average earnings, it would have been £755,000.)

It was an enormous amount, but it was a contract not without its Faustian elements. Bernie almost certainly had the precedent set by Malcolm McLaren in mind: signing for as much money as possible upfront, and walking away with the entire haul of swag when first EMI and then A&M found the Sex Pistols too hot to handle. However, the UK Head of CBS was expatriate American Maurice Oberstein, a canny operator who had every intention of getting his money's worth.

Unlike the Polydor contract, the CBS contract did not offer tour support or to cover recording costs. An advance is not a gift; it has to be paid back from earnings. Declaring that it was far too raw for American tastes, the two American CBS labels – Epic and Columbia – both refused to release *The Clash*. Without an outlet in the world's single biggest market, the Clash's long-term future did not look promising.

A much-trumpeted clause in the CBS contract gave the Clash total artistic freedom: the band could decide what they recorded, with whom they recorded it, what the record company released, and how it was presented. Or rather, that was the Clash's reading of the small print. After the Clash released their debut single 'White Riot' in mid-March 1977 and album *The Clash* in early April (in Clash-approved sleeves), they set out on the White Riot tour at the beginning of May. Two weeks in, CBS released the single 'Remote Control' in a sleeve of their own design and against the band's wishes. Upon his return, a furious Mick Jones wrote 'Complete Control' to protest at this humiliation, and the Clash insisted CBS release it as the band's third single that September, pointedly named the supporting tour Out of Control. So far, so much tit for tat.

But if the Clash were to survive, Bernie knew they had to keep their bargaining position strong. So when pressure came to choose a producer who would be more likely to ensure an American release for the second album, Bernie was prepared to play along. In November 1978 Mick Jones admitted to *Sounds'* Garry Bushell that the Clash had agreed to the big production in order to be able to take on American groups like Aerosmith. From the short list of possibilities they were offered, the best candidate was Sandy Pearlman, producer of Blue Oyster Cult, but also, more recently, of American cartoon gonzo 'New Wave' band the Dictators. The long drawn-out process of recording began.

Initial sessions had to be postponed when Joe Strummer contracted hepatitis and was hospitalised in February 1978, so it was not until May that the sessions proper began in Basing Street Studios in Notting Hill. And then they were interrupted by the Clash's touring obligations. It wasn't until August that Joe and Mick were able to record vocal and guitar overdubs in San Francisco, and late September until the album was mixed at the Record Plant in New York, on the corner of 44th Street and 8th Avenue. The Clash celebrated the last address in the rewritten lyric to an old song of Mick's, henceforth known by what would turn out to be the highly significant title 'Gates of the West'.

In April 1978 Bernie committed the Clash to taking part in a quasi-documentary film to be made by David Mingay and Jack Hazan, trading as Buzzy Enterprises Ltd. The duo collaborated, but Jack handled the camera and David the people. They were not regular music film-makers, and their previous documentary, *A Bigger Splash*, had been about the artist David Hockney. Their initial contact with the band was limited to filming a few live performances and a couple of vocals recorded during the Basing Street studio sessions. Their relationship with the Clash would become more significant during 1979.

Chief among the problems facing the Clash from early 1977 through to late 1978 was the gradual breakdown of their relationship with their manager. The imperious nature of Bernie's decision-making had already begun to grate. In January 1977 Bernie held a meeting at which he had insisted that the only way he could make the Clash work was if he were allowed 'complete control'. The band responded with outright mockery – Mick used the phrase for the title of his song attacking CBS – but Bernie did plot with Malcolm McLaren to swap Paul Simonon with Glen Matlock at that time, and did plot to replace Mick Jones with Steve Jones in mid-1978. He denied Paul – the band's true Jamaican music fan, but at that time a non-writer – the opportunity to accompany Mick and Joe to Jamaica in November 1977. He neglected to visit Joe when he was in hospital with hepatitis in February 1978. He made no effort to come to the aid of Paul and Topper when they were arrested – on suspicion of terrorist activity – for shooting pigeons with an air rifle on the roof of Rehearsals Rehearsals in March 1978, and instead left it to Mick and Caroline Coon to post bail. Paul responded by painting a large mural on the wall of Rehearsals showing a naked Bernie being defecated upon by circling pigeons. Failing to see the funny side, Bernie refused to come to Rehearsals when the band was present. In truth, though, he'd long since ceded the day-to-day personal management of the Clash to roadie Johnny Green. Bernie was interested in new ideas and opportunities, not in keeping existing situations chugging along. His energies were being directed into developing other bands, like the Subway Sect and the Black Arabs, and establishing his peripatetic London club night, Club Left. When he did hear the Clash's new material, he wasn't particularly complimentary, reacting – as Joe Strummer later noted – with scorn. The Clash felt abandoned.

Lacking Bernie's input, Joe struggled with subject matter for *Give 'Em Enough Rope*. He didn't want to repeat himself, but didn't really know where to go next. With the reggae route closed down, a growing cocaine habit affecting his judgement, and Sandy Pearlman encouraging his guitar hero inclinations, Mick Jones was similarly adrift. The album was self-indulgent and largely misguided. Lyrically, Joe seemed far too interested in terrorism, gunrunning, drugs and mythologising the Clash, drawing his material from newspaper headlines and late-night squat conversations. Mick chipped in with a tribute to his school friend, Robin Crocker. Musically, Mick had tried to stretch into several new – for the Clash – areas, but the production disguised much of this: a hard-rock adaptation of punk, which is another way of saying not particularly slick hard rock. It isn't fair to blame Pearlman entirely for this. He clearly tried to meet Mick halfway, which perhaps explains why the album sounds like the Dictators play Mott the Hoople, or vice versa. Even mentally stripped back to their bare bones, though, only about half the songs are engaging on any level, and all of them bar the opening track are below the standard and expectations established by the band's canon so far.

The second half of 1978 was unsettled, and something of a grind. It was brightened for Mick and Joe by the American trip to complete the second album, but this caused further upset at home. This time, both Paul and Topper were annoyed at having been left behind. For his part, Bernie was unhappy that Mick and Joe had been removed from his sphere of influence, suspecting that Epic were plotting to drive a wedge between himself and the band, with the collusion of Sandy Pearlman. It also bothered him that the second album was running up far greater studio costs than the first, because he knew the Clash would ultimately have to pay them. He pushed he matter by arranging a London gig for the Clash to try to force Mick and Joe's return. With work still to be done on mixing the album in New York, they were in no position to honour the engagement, and it had to be cancelled. This embarrassment proved to be the last straw. In late September, when Paul and Topper flew over to New York to be present for the mixing of the album, the band made the decision to sack Bernie immediately upon their return to London.

Having been closely if unofficially involved in promoting the Clash's career since they formed, Caroline Coon was asked to step in as manager (see Part 2). The band set out on the mid-October–end–December 1978 Sort it Out tour of the UK, a tour almost exactly like every tour they'd played since the White Riot tour of May the previous year, only much longer, reinforcing the feeling of stagnation. Buzzy Enterprises again filmed a few performances. *Give 'Em Enough Rope* was released in early November, and although reviews were generally good, there were caveats – indications that the reviewers had wanted to like it more than they did – and although it climbed higher in the UK charts than the band's debut, it faded away far more quickly.

Some of the rumblings of discontent had to do with the album's perceived Americanness, that the band who had protested about their annoyance at American culture swamping the UK in 'I'm So Bored with the USA' had spent so much time there recording an album with a sound (it was presumed) geared to the American market. While the approach to recording *Give 'Em Enough Rope* was indeed a concession to CBS and the American market – and it worked, because this time Epic agreed to release it – the Clash hardly pandered to the moral majority and the patriotic hordes. One of the songs has the word 'cunts' in its chorus, and the cover features a representation of a dead cowboy being eaten by vultures while the Chinese Red Army march victoriously past on horseback. A significant proportion of Americans don't find that kind of thing amusing.

By the time 1979 – the year of *London Calling* – began, the Clash were already a couple of months into a period of transition. With Bernie gone, and most of the rest of the original punk bands split up or in disarray, and their own recent album not entirely an unqualified success – Joe would later admit it was a 'lash up', and none of the other members of the band has ever challenged that summation or expressed a high regard for it – they knew they would have to find their own way. To do so, ultimately, they would sideline much of the 1976–7 Year Zero rhetoric and start to access their own experience and acknowledge their own true musical taste. Which is not to say that it was to be as if punk had never happened: the Clash's two and a

half years as a punk band was now a significant part of that experience and taste, and the band members were neither willing nor able
to deny it.

Punk had kicked open a locked door for them (and many other
bands), but that door had led into something that seemed worryingly
like a broom cupboard: short on space, vista and ventilation. What
the Clash needed to do in 1979 was find the hidden exit on the other
side. It was a matter of pushing past a few old paint-spattered overalls, and some even older *what side of the bed* T-shirts, and locating
Route 19 to Vanilla, Wessex and beyond.

2 Passport to Pimlico

The Three Rs (i): Riting and Rehearsing

The Clash's Sort it Out tour of the UK began on 13 October 1978 in Belfast, and ended with three London shows at the Lyceum on the Strand on 28 and 29 December and 3 January 1979. As early as the White Riot tour of May 1977 the Clash had established a tradition of introducing a new self-composed song or cover version to their set. For the Sort it Out tour that song was 'I Fought the Law'. It was written by Sonny Curtis of the Crickets in 1959, but the version first heard by Mick Jones and Joe Strummer in August 1978 – on the jukebox in the café at the Automatt studio, San Francisco, where they were recording overdubs for *Give 'Em Enough Rope* – was the 1965 Bobby Fuller Four recording. Joe, who was trying to improve his skills on the instrument, initially learned it on the piano. Back in London, he and Mick taught it to the rest of the band. A rocked-up version of an outlaw or badman ballad, like Johnny Cash's 'Folsom Prison Blues' (1956) and Jimi Hendrix's cover of 'Hey Joe' (1966), it fitted in neatly with the Clash's own songs of incarceration, 'The Prisoner' and 'Jail Guitar Doors', and provided a wry comment on the band's first-hand brushes with the law over the last couple of years. It went over well live, and the Clash enjoyed playing it.

For what would become *Rude Boy*, the Buzzy Enterprises team of David Mingay and Jack Hazan had filmed snatches of earlier shows on Sort it Out to add to those already in the can of other dates, going all the way back to the band's appearance at Rock Against Racism and the Anti-Nazi League's Carnival Against the Nazis in Victoria Park, Hackney on 30 April 1978. Much of the earlier footage was shot with just one camera, albeit expertly handled by Jack Hazan. In the hope of capturing something a little more polished for their Big Finish, Buzzy arranged with the Clash and CBS to record one of the Lyceum shows on the Rolling Stones' mobile studio, while they positioned five cameras in different parts of the venue. (The night the recording and filming took place is uncertain: Bill Price, who later mixed the sound recordings, insists that the tape box he accessed is dated 28 December, whereas the 2003 DVD version of *Rude Boy* lists the filming date as 3 January.)

The song Buzzy particularly wanted to capture was 'I Fought the Law': not only powerful, but also thematically appropriate. In November 1978 Mick Jones even told *Sounds'* Garry Bushell that the film was going to be called *I Fought the Law*. The sequence shows the Clash performing the song dressed mostly in black with little touches of white, and this, too has become a subject of debate because of what it symbolised or can be seen to symbolise. In an interview extra included with the DVD release of *Rude Boy*, Jack Hazan said that he and David Mingay had watched the Clash start to become organised during autumn 1978, as the day-to-day running of the band was taken out of their control. After adopting individual styles for most of 1978, they had begun to dress alike again, as they had done in the punk period of 1976 and 1977. Only now the clothes and hair were, like their new cover version, more rock'n'roll than punk. Both David Mingay and the Clash's chief roadie, Johnny Green, attribute this newfound restyling and the organisation that went with it to new manager Caroline Coon. 'She was acting like a boss figure, telling them what to do,' says David. 'They liked the way she looked after their image,' says Johnny. Jack Hazan claims it was his idea for the band to all wear black for the filming of the 'I Fought the Law' sequence. Johnny thinks it was Caroline's. David says the Clash were already favouring black around the time – at Caroline's behest – and that he and Jack just asked them to make sure they were wearing it on the night. 'We wore what we wanted, nobody told us,' Mick Jones told *Uncut's* Simon Goddard in 2003. 'Bloody cheek!' 'What the Clash wore was always and absolutely the Clash's idea,' confirms Caroline Coon. 'Any notion that David Mingay or Jack Hazan could be credited with any Clash "look" is simply daft.' It might seem like a trivial issue, but this monochrome style would go on to play a large part in how the band presented themselves and *London Calling* during 1979 and 1980.

Jack and David wanted the 'men in black' look for the *Rude Boy* Lyceum sequence, not only because it was visually strong, but also in order that they could exploit what they perceived to be the subtext of the Clash wearing a uniform, like the early Beatles. As if his antennae picked up the filmmakers' intent, or maybe simply because the funereal nature of the band's clothing sent his mind spinning off on a tangent, Joe subverted the performance of the song, and consequently the scene in the film. On 12 October 1978 the Clash's friend Sid Vicious – with whom Mick Jones had played a pick-up show in New York a month earlier – had been arrested and remanded on suspicion of stabbing to death his girlfriend Nancy Spungen. At the Lyceum, Joe altered the lyric of 'I Fought the Law' from 'I left my baby . . .' to 'I *killed* my baby . . .' Johnny Green recalls David being furious – 'very unlike him' – in the dressing room afterwards, shouting 'You've fucked the plot!' at Joe, who simply laughed. David has no recollection of this exchange and, looking back, enjoys Joe's substitution immensely, believing that it adds a whole new twist not only to the band's performance but also to the film: as David sees it, the Lyceum sequence now has the Clash saying a metaphorical graveside farewell not only to Sid, but also to their own amateur-hour punk-rock incarnation, and to the fragmenting UK punk-rock movement and market, as they prepare to take on rock'n'roll, careerism and America. 'There had been a kind of passing,' says David. 'It signified the death of *something*, the black.'

The Clash's primary concern at the time was escaping the punk pigeonhole, but David's conceit works well enough in retrospect. So well that the live version of 'I Fought the Law' recorded for posterity at Buzzy's behest would be used to close the first, punk period, CD of the Clash's 1991 career retrospective box set *Clash On Broadway*.

In mid-January, the band decided to record a studio version of 'I Fought the Law', with the intention of releasing it as the lead track on an EP. Hoping for a quicker, more straightforward and less enervating experience than working with Sandy Pearlman on *Give 'Em Enough Rope* had turned out to be, they were looking around for a new recording studio collaborator. It isn't difficult to come up with a number of reasons why the Clash might have decided to record with Bill Price at Wessex Studios, but it isn't quite so easy to pinpoint the exact one. Wessex was where the Sex Pistols had recorded their singles and *Never Mind the Bollocks* with Chris Thomas and Bill Price in 1977, and where Chris had subsequently produced material with Bill acting as chief engineer for one of Mick's favourite artists, Philip Rambow. Bill had also worked as an engineer with Guy Stevens, Mott the Hoople and – quite recently – former Mott songwriter Ian Hunter, who as well as being Mick's great hero was now occasionally moving in his social circle. Muff Winwood, who had been appointed the new Head of A&R at CBS UK the previous year, claims it was his idea. 'I'd worked with Bill when I was a producer, and knew how good he was,' he says. Bill is prepared to believe that any of the above might have led the band to his door. 'I was doing an audition,' is how he recalls the session. 'For me!'

The production on the EP was jointly credited to Bill and the Clash – which in reality meant Bill and Mick Jones – with Bill also functioning as chief engineer. Although credited as a humble tape operator, Jerry Green (unlike Johnny Green, it was his real surname) had been working closely with Bill at Wessex for a couple of years by this stage, and was already functioning as second engineer, a role he would officially assume later in 1979. During their three-day Wessex stint, in addition to 'I Fought the Law', the band recorded a new version of 'Capital Radio'. The explanation for the re-recording was that copies of the original *Capital Radio* EP – given away free with *NME* coupons at the time of *The Clash*'s release – were exchanging hands for £40 on the collectors' market or as bootlegs. Bill recalls that the band were well-rehearsed, and the songs needed no further arrangement in the studio. To record the backing tracks, he set them up almost as if they were about to play live (see Part 3 for detail of his methods). Having learned a thing or two about overdubbing with Sandy Pearlman, the Clash were relaxed enough to add extra instruments like acoustic guitar and Mick's harmonica on 'Groovy Times', handclaps, and even some sound effects: a guitar explosion on 'Capital Radio Two', metal percussion on 'I Fought the Law', and a reprise of that song faked up to sound live, with a reggae DJ-style toast from Joe. Although the other two songs included on the EP would receive the same production credits, both the backing tracks and many of the overdubs for

'Groovy Times' and 'Gates of the West' dated back to the sessions for *Give 'Em Enough Rope*. They had been tinkered with periodically during 1978 before being left off that album. 'We did any overdubs and fixes they required, and then mixed them,' says Bill.

The band believed their collaboration with Bill promised great things for the future, and after the grim slog of the sessions for their second album, the EP sessions had proved to be a quick and painless process for the Clash. The pain came immediately afterwards.

The band presented the songs to CBS, requesting that they be released in late February 1979, upon their return from a planned tour of America. The label responded by announcing that 'English Civil War', a second track pulled from *Give 'Em Enough Rope*, backed with the band's year-old recording of Toots and the Maytals' 'Pressure Drop', was already scheduled to be released as the next Clash single on 23 February. As a sop to the band, it was agreed that the EP could be released next, in May. For a band keen to turn the page and move on, four months seemed like an age away.

On 30 January the Clash flew out to Vancouver, Canada, from where they were to launch their debut tour of America, due to end in Toronto on 20 February. It was a short but eventful visit. Although *Give 'Em Enough Rope* had been released by CBS label Epic in the USA, the American branch of the company tried hard to dissuade the Clash from coming over at this early stage. When the Clash insisted, further problems arose: they refused to support another band, or take some other Epic act on the road as their support. Instead, they insisted on touring with Bo Diddley, who Epic clearly thought of as an inappropriate has-been novelty act. The Clash's purpose was to challenge both preconceptions, and present America with a package featuring both one of the originators and the new torchbearers of rock as it should be rolled. It cost them dear. Caroline Coon had to beg $30,000 from Epic to allow the tour to go ahead, which was only reluctantly handed over after she had invested £3,000 of her own savings in setting up the dates. Shortly afterwards, she tracked Bo Diddley down on tour in Australia, and had to guarantee him $20,000 to join the bill.

Having heard Johnny Rotten's horror stories about the cultural divide between the Sex Pistols and the American crew they used on their ill-fated US tour a year earlier, the Clash paid to take their own crew of Johnny Green and drum roadie Baker along. They also took

Barry 'Scratchy' Myers, the regular DJ at Dingwalls, Camden Town, who had provided play-on music at their four late July 1978 Out on Parole tour Music Machine gigs. 'We used to hang around at Dingwalls when we were based at Rehearsals, used to go and pull there,' says Johnny Green. 'Mick and Joe thought back to the old Roundhouse concerts that they'd been to in the early Seventies, where they'd had a DJ. And they thought, that's a good idea. Rather than pre-recorded tapes, which is what they'd had before, let's have someone create an ambience. They had him play their favourite tracks. The idea of taking an English DJ to the States was seen as quite esoteric. The idea was to create a whole package show. It worked.'

The tour got off to a bad start when the Clash were informed of Sid Vicious's death from a heroin overdose on 2 February 1979. Shortly afterwards, Mick Jones learned his London flat had been burgled in his absence. Before they left, the band had made the decision to honour the kamikaze nature of the venture by christening it the Pearl Harbour tour. Epic failed to see the joke, and boringly promoted it as the Give 'Em Enough Rope tour. About as far as they were prepared to go to acknowledge that the Clash might in any way present a challenge to the status quo was to illustrate ads and posters with a representation of the Statue of Liberty trussed up in rope. And, as the band discovered when they arrived at the venues, promotion was at best half-hearted – a few record covers stuck to a wall at one venue – and at worst non-existent.

On 9 February several Epic representatives gathered backstage at the Santa Monica Civic Auditorium for the traditional record company reps and band group photograph. The Clash walked away in disgust before the shutter clicked. 'The feeling was, we weren't just another rock'n'roll band, but we were being treated like one,' says Johnny Green. Caroline Coon was dismayed: she knew how damaging such insults could be for the band's future. Still unaware – or uncaring – that edgy and provocative British humour does not always travel well, the band also habitually opened the shows with 'I'm So Bored with the USA'. The mood in the Clash camp remained buoyant. 'There was a real feeling of, "It's a long way from Camden Town, boys!"' says Johnny. Upon his return to the UK, Joe Strummer filed an exhilarated UPPER CASE tour diary with the *NME*, but his enthusiasm was not necessarily realistic. The Clash had loved America, and the audiences at the shows had loved the Clash; but the jury was still out on the band's long-term commercial prospects there.

A couple of days after the band arrived back in London, CBS released 'English Civil War'. On 8 March 1979 the Clash travelled up to Newcastle-upon-Tyne to appear on ITV's new kids' music show *Alright Now*, playing live and being interviewed in front of an invited audience by 'zany' presenter Den Hegerty, bass vocalist for doo-wop revival band Darts. The Clash performed 'English Civil War', but followed it up with a seething 'Hate & War', a track from their first album. Instead of single B-side 'Pressure Drop', the Clash played a different reggae cover, their sometime soundcheck version of Desmond Dekker's 'The Israelites'. It was followed by a few crowd pleasers the cameras neglected to record for posterity. As the show was not broadcast until 18 April, its impact on the single's fate was negligible. That was the full extent of the Clash's promotional effort.

From CBS's point of view, the last album was still a long way from recouping the outlay on recording costs. The idea behind releasing a second single from *Give 'Em Enough Rope* in the UK was to prolong the album's shelf life, and give sales another boost. It made sound financial sense, but the Clash's financial sense had always been limited; so far, at least, the 'artistic freedom' clause in the contract had been the only one that interested them. The band had already lived too long with the material on their last album, almost all of which was now over a year old. They had wanted to leave it behind them in the New Year of 1979, and take bold strides into the future through the 'Gates of the West', spurs jangling. Instead, it seemed – very much like the Statue of Liberty on the Epic promotional posters – they were expected to spend another few months tied up with old *Rope*.

By the spring of 1979, on the surface at least, the band's relationship with both CBS in the UK and Epic in the USA seemed strained. In the *NME* news pages, Bernie Rhodes's sacking had been characterised as a coup on behalf of a CBS intent upon making the band more malleable. It didn't appear to have worked: the argument over the EP release was the latest skirmish in a guerrilla war now entering its third year . . . or that was how it was portrayed by the Clash. While there's no doubt that both sides felt genuine irritation at times, Muff Winwood insists the relationship was by no means poisonous. CBS understood that the punk ethos required them to be cast as the bad guys. Like the Clash, they had observed the Sex Pistols do their dance with EMI and A&M, and seen the resultant media coverage and sales spike. The Clash–CBS show-downs had more than an element of theatre about them.

'The whole ethos around the band was such that it shunned normal record label life, and didn't really want to be involved with day to day record company business,' says Muff Winwood. 'So, in the beginning, it was all down to our relationship with the manager, Bernie Rhodes. Bernie was a lovely, lovely guy, actually. He was an odd character, a bizarre character. I *think* I got on with him really well. More im-portantly, Maurice Oberstein was a classic eccentric who loved other eccentrics. Therefore he loved Bernie, and he loved the Clash. Absolutely loved them.' The leading figures in the major record compa-nies of the day liked to be considered characters, and enjoyed playing head games. The 50-year-old transplanted American Head of CBS UK, Maurice Oberstein, aka Obie, was no different. His schtick involved wearing a fedora, taking his dog to work, and affecting to consult it on business decisions. He enjoyed his own sense of humour immensely, and kept his staff on their toes by vacillating between displays of kind-ness and consideration and of outrageous personal abuse. A uniformed female chauffeur would drive Obie around town in a Rolls-Royce, but when Muff asked him for a new company car, Obie chased him through the CBS building with a baseball bat.

He died in 2001, but in a 1993 interview for the *Guardian* with Adam Sweeting, he described the Clash as his pride and joy. Like many outsiders who had regular dealings with the Clash, the loquacious Muff Winwood quickly acquired a less-than-flattering nickname – Duff Windbag – but the same fate did not befall Maurice Oberstein. And this was more to do with respect than fear and awe. 'They all loved him,' says the Clash's regular photographer, Pennie Smith. 'They thought he was a really, really nice bloke. It might have been total war with the contract-signing department, but Maurice was a real, real sweetie. They loved him to bits.'

'The Clash were very intelligent guys, and the fact of the matter is they were presenting an image,' continues Muff. 'They enjoyed presenting that image, and they felt that image, but when you've got to present it, you've got to present it properly. You've got to go the whole hog. And they did. Mainly because Maurice was up for this, we as a record company played along. We gave them a far longer lead than we would have done with a lot of other artists. We accepted the jibes, we accepted all the so-called bad press we got, and we went along with the whole game that the Clash had nothing to do with their record company, but in fact we had a reasonably good line of communication through Bernie, and most of the things both of us wanted to do got done. It's only an entertainment. Bernie Rhodes played the game well, and I don't think he was disliked by us at all. I certainly can't ever remember discussions between us in the CBS hierarchy that Bernie needed to be moved on. It was disquiet within the band about Bernie that led to that . . . possibly because they thought he was taking *too much* notice of the record company. At the end of the day, managers are always stuck in the middle. Sometimes they come to the record company with difficult information, and sometimes they go back to the band with difficult information. They're the messengers.'

Epic were not so easygoing about either Bernie or the Clash. There was no punk culture point of reference for CBS's senior staff in America, and even if there had been, their egos would not have made allowances for it: it was the record company's way or no way. Bernie's unsettlingly unfamiliar approach to management simply did not translate, and there can be little doubt that Epic were glad to see him go. They were probably labouring under the illusion that he was the sole architect of the band's 'awkward' stance. By mid-February 1979 they knew otherwise. As Bernie's successor Caroline Coon feared, the band's snubbing of several of Epic's influential personnel on the Pearl Harbour tour ensured that the little that had been done to promote *Give 'Em Enough Rope* before the band arrived in America remained the album's lot. To their American label, the Clash appeared ungrateful, rude, uncooperative, demanding, disorganised, costly and unrealistic. If – in the band's opinion – too many singles had been released from the album in the UK, then – in anyone's opinion – too few were released from the album in the USA. None.

When it came to taking sides, Maurice Oberstein aligned himself firmly with his troublesome British signings rather than the record company's American HQ. 'It became my great joy to attend a CBS convention in America, and have the presidents of Epic and Columbia asking for my acts for their labels,' he told Adam Sweeting in 1993. 'I got my satisfaction, having absorbed the pain of those sons of bitches ignoring my artists and ignoring my people. They weren't nice, but then they were Americans.'

★

The contract with CBS entitled Bernie Rhodes to 20 per cent of the band's earnings before deductions . . . which meant that the band's income was paid to him in the first instance. While he was still their manager, the Clash and their crew had experienced trouble extracting payments from Bernie for everything from rent to guitar strings. Being sacked had not made him any more co-operative. Despite having only the sketchiest of accounts to back up his claims, Bernie maintained that the band owed *him* £25,000, and used his hustler's legal nous to freeze the bulk of the Clash's monies until such a time as the matter could be resolved. Estimates about the extent of the Clash's debt to CBS at this time have varied wildly. In 1981 Paul Simonon told *Rolling Stone*'s David Fricke that it was £98,000; in 1985 Topper told *Sounds'* Jane Simon that it had reached £250,000. Weighing up the prevailing circumstances at the time of both interviews, Paul's version is likely to be more accurate.

When considering Bernie's replacement, the band had eschewed traditional management companies in favour of approaching several trusted Clash champions and supporters they thought might be capable of doing something creative with the position. They asked *NME* journalist Chris Salewicz and, separately, *NME* photographer Pennie Smith; and then Sixties underground mover and shaker and more recently *NME* journalist Barry Miles to team up with CBS press officer Ellie Smith (which in itself indicates that the Clash's relationship with their record company was not wholly adversarial). All four passed on the opportunity, considering the situation too complicated to take on: a band involved in litigation with their former manager, with little in the way of paperwork to show what had happened to their income to date, and with a determinedly naïve and impractical approach to the music business. Furthermore, Joe Strummer was still highly protective towards Bernie and would not allow any aggressive action against him.

When Caroline Coon, another underground mover and shaker and, more recently, *Melody Maker* journalist, was offered the position, however, she accepted. Her experience with Release, the legal advice service she had co-founded in the late Sixties to assist those busted for drugs offences, meant that legal and contractual red tape and loopholes did not intimidate her. The Clash appreciated the way she had got Paul and Topper out on bail in the wake of the Pigeon Shooting Incident, and – subsequently – delayed Johnny Green's court appearance on a drunk-driving charge, thus prolonging the period he could continue to drive the band's van. Caroline insists she had her own career, and that neither she nor the band saw her appointment as a long-term one: rather more of a caretaker role to see them through a difficult period. Like a favour for a friend . . .

Discussing Caroline's managerial relationship with the band is not a straightforward matter. Johnny Green, David Mingay and Chris Salewicz, among others, were – and still are – under the impression that Caroline and Paul Simonon entered into a personal relationship sometime during late 1976 or early 1977, and refer to Caroline as Paul's girlfriend. Paul and Caroline went on holiday to Russia together in January 1978. They appear in poses that imply they are 'an item' in a 1978 Pennie Smith photograph and a taxicab scene filmed around the same time for Rude Boy. Also, Johnny, David and Chris, among others, are under the impression that Paul shared Caroline's accommodation from mid-1977 onwards, firstly in Tregunter Road, Chelsea (given as Paul's official address when he appeared in court in respect of the Pigeon Shooting Incident in June 1978) and, from the autumn of that year, at 35 St Andrews Square, Notting Hill. The NME news item announcing Caroline's appointment as Clash manager was as follows: 'At the moment, their affairs are being handled by rock journalist Caroline Coon, who lives with Clash bassist Paul Simonon.'

Caroline refutes this, saying that the information is 'factually inaccurate' and has been 'garnered from notoriously sexist and misogynist second-hand sources'. She goes on to state: 'Unlike some of those who preach leftist World Revolution whose personal lives are steadfastly dishonest, reactionary, right-wing and sexist, I have, since I was a teenager, successfully lived my personal life according to the independent feminism I preached. I have never lived with a man or a woman. I never lived with Paul. Paul never lived with me.' Caroline allows that Paul did pay her visits, but insists that his home base throughout 1977 and 1978 was Rehearsals Rehearsals. He had indeed lived rough in the band's Camden Town rehearsal space from late 1976 until early 1977, but there were no heating, washing or cooking facilities, and it is hard to imagine Paul – alone of the Clash members – continuing to put up with such conditions once the band had signed their recording contract. Johnny Green did endure them for several months from January 1978, and doesn't recall having to share floor space with Paul.

Subtract the personal element, and Caroline's motive for involving herself professionally with the Clash is not immediately obvious. She had been intrigued by their political stance in 1976, but their material, presentation and day to day behaviour did not stand up to hard-line feminist scrutiny. Despite occasional flashes of sensitivity to the female condition, they were a pretty typical band of late-Seventies rock'n'rollers when it came to macho posturing, *Boy's Own* fantasies and enthusiastic philandering. Because of her gender, she was discouraged by the band from even using the term 'manager', which made things difficult when she was trying to negotiate on their behalf. 'In the Seventies, a woman manager could cause sexist consternation,' she says. 'Joe worried that having a woman manager might be considered cissy, so to make a joke of it, I sometimes called myself the not-the-manager of the Clash.'

Around the time the Clash signed to CBS, Bernie Rhodes had bought a series of off-the-shelf limited companies, including Nineden, originally set up as a painting and decorating concern, subsequently devoted to handling the band's music publishing. Caroline Coon officially replaced Bernie as secretary of Nineden on 24 October 1978. She appointed Peter Quinnell as the Clash's new accountant, and his office, at 100 Baker Street, became the new official address of Nineden and the other Clash-related companies. 'I arranged with Peter Quinnell for them to receive a reasonable weekly wage and to have their expenses paid,' says Caroline. With Bernie's legal constraints in place, though, other expenditure had to be approved first by Peter, which caused the notoriously casual band and crew to bridle, and the restraints became all the more obvious once the Clash returned from the American tour. At first, the band used to call their accountant Quister the Twister. Which is not to imply that there was anything bent about him. 'I'd never met a straighter figure in my life,' says Johnny Green, the go-between. 'It got to the stage where he became the paymaster, because we had nowhere else to go for the day to day cash flow you need to run a band. This bloke in a three-piece suit, and he's bailing us out. It's like he's your bank manager: your nightmare when you're broke.'

After the Pearl Harbour tour, the Clash's confidence hit an all-time low. 'There was a strong feeling of paranoia at the time,' says Johnny. 'A feeling that they were about to be booted off the label, basically. I don't know if there was any substance to that, but that was the talk. They realised the contractual position Bernie had consigned them to, and were very worried about it.' To the band, it felt like they had reached a stalemate with CBS, and were still stuck on a very basic income with no chance of changing their circumstances for the better. After nearly three years in the band, having made two albums, the first hailed as life-changing, the second – largely – well-received, both of which had sold well, they appeared to be in a worse position than when they started.

Upon splitting with Bernie, the Clash had lost the use of his Renault van. Transport for the band and their gear was essential. Peter Quinnell promptly handed over the money for a second-hand Ford Transit: no more Renaults for the Clash. Used to having a secure – if hardly salubrious – home base at Rehearsals Rehearsals, from late October 1978 onwards the Clash had to get used to renting a series of rehearsal facilities by the hour. Invariably located in railway arches in south London, they were – as such highly evocative names as Base, the Vault and Black Hole imply – cramped, airless, dark, smelly and damp. They hardly symbolised a bright new future.

The band members' personal circumstances were similarly unpromising. Whatever his current romantic situation and wherever he might unofficially be laying his head, Paul did not officially have a home of his own. Mick's relationship with Slits guitarist Viv Albertine was strained. The top-floor flat in Pembridge Villas, Notting Hill, he had shared for the previous year with Tony James had been looted of its musical and electrical equipment within a couple of days of his departure to America. Its location was obviously too well known for Mick to remain there – his periodic absences on tour were invariably advertised in the music press – so upon returning, he had retreated to his old room in his Nan's council high-rise flat to lick his wounds.

Topper had shared a flat in Finsbury Park, north-east London, with his wife Wendy until his new lifestyle put paid to their marriage in autumn 1978. As it was now vacant, Topper moved in to Sid Vicious's former flat at number 3 Pindock Mews, Notting Hill. When Topper inherited it, blood sprays from Sid's sloppy shooting up habits were still in evidence on the bathroom walls. Sid's subsequent progression from murder suspect to overdose victim-cum-suspected suicide didn't do anything to cheer the place up. At least Topper was in a new relationship, with a 17-year-old called Dee.

After flitting from rented room to rented studio for much of 1978, Joe was back squatting at 34 Daventry Street with former 101ers roadie John 'Boogie' Tiberi. Like Topper, he had a new romantic interest in his life, a school friend of Dee's named Gaby Salter. Joe had first met Gaby at a Christmas party in 1977, but their relationship began towards the end of 1978. At first, Gaby moved in with Joe at Daventry Street. Faced with the prospect of her 17-year-old daughter squatting with a 26-year-old punk musician, Gaby's recently divorced mother Frances proved to be remarkably progressive in her thinking. She invited Joe to live with Gaby, plus Frances and Gaby's two brothers, in the family's three-bedroom council flat at 31 Whistler Walk, on the massive World's End Estate, Chelsea.

None of the Clash were living high on the hog, then. And conditions were generally harsh, which impacted further upon their mood. Setting a pattern for the rest of the year, the winter had been stormy. It snowed and then it froze. As ever, the country's transport and communications network collapsed under the strain; but because conditions were much worse than usual, the upset was greater and lasted longer. There is nothing like a spell of bad weather to highlight other deficiencies in the quality of life.

When punk first emerged in 1976 the movement's anger and desperation had been – in part at least – a response to Britain's already advanced decline: by late summer 1976 the economy had become so weak that the Labour government had been forced to apply to the International Monetary Fund for a loan. By the end of 1978 conditions had deteriorated even further. Fewer new council homes had been built that year than in any year since the Second World War. Since 1974, 25,000 hospital beds had been lost in ward and hospital closures. Over the same period, unemployment had risen from half a million to 1.6 million. Inflation had caused prices to double between

February 1974 and December 1978, yet the Government had imposed a 5 per cent limit on pay rises. In November 1978 a brief bakers' strike led to the panic buying of bread. At the end of that month, that bastion of British Establishment values, *The Times*, was forced to suspend publication due to industrial action. On 5 January 1979 a lorry-drivers' strike led to shortages of heating oil and fresh food. Ten days later, there was a 24-hour rail strike. A week after that, 1.5 million public sector workers staged a walkout. Garbage was left to pile up in the streets, hospitals had to turn patients away, and – with no one to bury them – bodies were left to pile up in morgues. (The last of these was exaggerated by the tabloids for ghoulish effect; but given the prevailing circumstances, it hardly stretched credulity.) With the greater part of the population just scraping by joylessly, civil unrest gained momentum. There were mass demonstrations with people demanding wages reflecting the true 'cost of living'.

The Labour Party, supposedly socialist in ideology, the 'party of the people', was perceived to be letting the people down. Prime Minister James Callaghan exacerbated the problem on 10 January 1979 by denying there was a crisis. On 14 February he was forced to make a deal with the trade unions to bring the strikes to an end. But the damage was already done: following a no-confidence motion brought by the opposition, the Labour government fell on 28 March and a general election was called for 3 May. Overall, then, life in the last few months of 1978 and first few months of 1979 was cold, pinched and grim, and by the time the Clash returned from America, it had already been dubbed the Winter of Discontent.

Whenever a country's economy is in distress it is always the poor that suffer the most. And immigrants are all too often made the scapegoat. In August 1976 the Notting Hill Carnival had attracted a provocatively large and aggressive police presence, which provoked a full-scale riot. British fascist party the National Front (NF) raised its profile; over the next year, first Rock Against Racism and then the Anti-Nazi League were formed in direct response to the perceived threat from the extreme right. In August 1977 the NF was given permission to march through the multi-racial south-east London borough of Lewisham. This time, the massed ranks of the police were there to protect the fascists from protesters. Another riot erupted. On 23 April 1979 the NF would hold another rally in Southall, and once again the massed

Metropolitan Police presence seemed more interested in targeting protesters. After an encounter with the force's Special Patrol Group, Clarence Baker, the manager of local reggae band Misty in Roots, was hospitalised with a fractured skull. Teacher Blair Peach received similar treatment, and subsequently died of the injuries he sustained.

It was easy to believe that everything was on the point of falling apart, an atmosphere that understandably encouraged all manner of doom-mongering. The extreme weather was interpreted as Mother Nature not waving, but drowning. On 31 March 1979 the threat of imminent natural disaster was followed by the threat of an imminent man-made one, when the news broke that nuclear catastrophe had only just been averted at the Three Mile Island nuclear power plant at Harrisburg, Pennsylvania. The End of the World had always been nigh, but in the first half of 1979 it seemed just that bit more nigh than usual.

The only regular activity on offer to the Clash was related to the ongoing *Rude Boy* film project. The Clash co-operated with some last-minute filming requests, dressing in togs of an approximately appropriate vintage to play the early 1977 song 'Garageland' live in Black Hole rehearsal studios. And Joe performed a couple of numbers on piano in Base rehearsal studios, one of them written especially for that purpose. From 9 March 1979 until early April, though, the band spent most of their time in first the Wessex recording studio, and then a film-editing suite at AIR on Oxford Circus (Bill's former home studio), working on the film soundtrack.

Most of the live filming by Buzzy Enterprises had been done on a limited budget, with one 35 mm camera, operated by Jack Hazan, and one soundman, and just enough film stock to record one or two songs per gig. Which meant there weren't a lot of performances to choose from. Although the film footage was impressive, the same could not be said of the sound. David Mingay had tried to upgrade the equipment used to record it periodically throughout the latter half of 1978 – from mono to stereo to 8-track – but there were too many glitches and gremlins, and the standard of the band's performances was also widely variable. Even when Buzzy brought in the Rolling Stones' 24-track mobile studio to record the last show filmed – at the Lyceum – it produced just one song for the film. Bill Price was asked if anything could be done to salvage the other 13 live performances. The answer was no. 'They sounded like they'd been recorded on a cassette machine zipped up in a girl's handbag,' he says. 'Eventually my suggestion that the only answer was to fake it up in the studio was agreed.'

Faking it wasn't simply a case of setting up live in the studio and bashing through the songs for an hour. The venues were all different sizes with different acoustics, and the instruments and voices had to be in sync with the film. A couple of significant ironies were involved. The first was that the Clash had always refused, and would continue to refuse, to appear on BBC1's hugely popular music show *Top of the Pops* – audience figures in the Seventies regularly reached 16 million, making it the single most powerful promotional opportunity in the UK – because it involved singing along to pre-recorded backing tracks, and the band maintained faking it in this manner was selling the audience short. It was a principled stand that had and would continue to cost them dear in terms of single sales and chart placings, and consequently of album sales and placings. The second was that, even for normal studio recording, the Clash usually set up as if for a live show to record the master take, but in order to recreate their live performances for *Rude Boy*, each member of the band had to play their part separately.

The original live recordings were transferred to one track of Wessex's available 24 as a rough guide. The drums were then miked differently for each song to replicate the venue acoustics. 'It was only possible because of Topper's uncanny ability to dub over himself in perfect time,' says Bill. 'We would then separately dub on the bass, guitars and vocals, in that order.' Each band member took his turn to play along to a video of the sequence 'in a bit of a rough lock with the 24-track', as Bill puts it, in order to stay in sync. Both he and Jerry Green estimate that each band member took three or four passes at his part to get an acceptable composite. 'Then all the ambient noise from the crowd at the actual gig was synched back onto the stuff we'd recorded,' says Jerry. They could occasionally salvage some of Joe's live vocal, too. Because David Mingay wanted the sound to be mixed to 35 mm film stock for editing purposes, the last few guitar and vocal overdubs – mostly those relating to close-ups – and the mixing took place at AIR. 'When I was mixing, Mingay was constantly asking me, "Is any of the live sound in there?"' says Bill. 'I would reply, "Yes, there is a bit, Dave."'

The re-recording proved to be a hugely expensive process – Jack Hazan has estimated that it doubled the entire budget for the film – and it was also time-consuming, which made for a fraught atmosphere. Both Jack and David grumble that Mick would habitually show up late in the day for studio sessions. Bill counters that the Clash members came in as and when he required them to record their parts. David does allow that Mick was meticulous in his determination to get it right: he took recording seriously, and enjoyed the opportunity to learn about a different kind of studio work. More so even than the brief January sessions for the EP, the *Rude Boy* sessions allowed him to develop a close working relationship with Bill Price, whose technical knowledge and resourcefulness impressed him greatly.

The other members of the band didn't feel the same way about the project. 'They were not happy about it at all,' says Johnny Green. 'It was a source of great contention.' But with cash flow being a problem, the money they were paid for the work was incentive enough. 'The amount wasn't huge, but it was worth their while, and they needed it,' says David. 'It was regularised and it was fair.' There were also unregularised 'bungs', too, mostly to Topper and Johnny Green. David points out that the band were working for their own benefit. They were being paid to soundtrack the film, but had the rights to release the results as a soundtrack album, if they so wished. Buzzy had no option on such a release.

As if to symbolise the general vaguely dissatisfying feeling of obligation, frustration and stagnation of life in the Clash at this time, the one opportunity that came up for the band to play live fell through. In late March, the Beaufort Market on the Kings Road, just around the corner from Joe's new home in Whistler Walk, was threatened with closure. Like the nearby Antiquarius, originally a collection of antique outlets, since the early Seventies it had been a glorified flea-cum-rag market. Various punk and post-punk second-hand stalls were now based there. The nature of its wares and its proximity to Malcolm McLaren and Vivienne Westwood's shop Seditionaries – the latest name for Sex – ensured that Beaufort Market was a popular haunt for the punks hanging around the Kings Road. The Clash responded to stall holder Jock McDonald's entreaties by agreeing to provide the climax to a planned demonstration on 31 March 1979 with a benefit gig on site. The police heard about the plans and refused permission. When the

Clash turned up to apologise to and show support for the 2,000 protesting punks, the abrasive police protest ensured that things turned nasty, and 70 arrests were made.

All gloom then, in spring 1979. Or so it seemed. Contrary to how the Clash characterised their situation at the time to friends, crew and music-press journalists, Caroline Coon believes the band were far from being in dire straits, financially or otherwise, though does admit that morale was low. 'Part of a manager's job is to help musicians over the raging emotions and deep depression that can crash into them at the end of tours,' she says.

When discussing Bernie Rhodes's 1977–8 business dealings on behalf of the Clash, the tendency is to characterise them as inept or even corrupt. While the terms he agreed to with CBS look, in retrospect, to have put short-term gain above the long-term best interests of the band, he no doubt had Malcolm McLaren's experience with the Sex Pistols in mind: take a large advance, so that if and when the record company 'lets you go', at least you've got the money. But Bernie was also smart enough to know what music-business lawyer Don Engel told Frederic Dannen for his 1990 book *Hit Men: Power Brokers and Fast Money Inside the Music Business*: that the standard record company deal in the Seventies was 'the most onerous, impossible, unfair contract'. The contract Bernie negotiated with CBS required all the costs incurred by the Clash – living expenses, equipment, support staff, rehearsal space, hiring a producer, promotion, touring, and almost everything else – to be met by the band. This would not only quickly dispose of the advance, no matter how large, but would mean it was a long time, if ever, before the band started earning royalties from record sales. Major record companies liked to keep their artists in the red – and therefore needing to beg for further advances in order to keep functioning, thus putting them further in the red – in order to maintain 'complete control'. It was standard operational procedure.

Had the Clash been prepared to play *Top of the Pops*, they would have increased their sales, and perhaps been in a royalty-earning position much sooner in their career. Had they kept recording costs to a minimum, their debt would not have increased so quickly. Another possible way for artists to earn money was via live performances. Properly costed, tours could make serious money, which went directly to the artists, not via the record company. Wearing their punk principles in much the same way Mick Jones wore his 'Red Guard' armband, the Clash insisted on offering value for money to their followers, which meant tours featuring a three-band bill, small venues with limited capacity, and low ticket prices . . . The Clash always made a loss on tour, and invariably had to ask for loans from CBS or Epic, which further increased their debt. Yet another option for earning money was merchandising, but again, hard selling promotional material to their audience was not something the Clash were comfortable with.

Bernie was not to blame for any of these decisions to throw money away. The remaining area where he did have control was over music publishing, which – since the early Sixties – had been recognised by music business insiders to be the most important area of all. A recording contract could provide initial working capital, but all too frequently ceased to be a source of further income. Conversely, providing an artist made popular records that continued to sell over a period of time, a good music publishing deal guaranteed a regular and steadily increasing income. When Bernie set up Nineden as a publishing company to handle the Clash's songs, shares were issued equally, 33 per cent each, among named directors Joe Strummer, Mick Jones and Paul Simonon, the three official members of the Clash at the time the band signed to CBS. This meant that while the music publishing revenue would go to songwriters Mick and Joe, all three would receive company profit as directors. Bernie merely acted as secretary, and made no attempt to divert a substantial or even token part of the band's publishing revenue into his own pocket. In the past, other managers – of such artists as Elvis, the Beatles and the Rolling Stones, for instance – had not been so kind.

Furthermore, instead of making an immediate administration – that is, songwriting royalties collection – deal with CBS's in-house music publishing arm, or another established publishing company that would have taken a sizeable proportion of that revenue in return for an advance, Bernie left it until *The Clash* had been selling for nearly six months before he went looking for such a deal. By which time he had something of proven value, and could dictate advantageous terms. In October 1977 he signed an administration contract with Riva Music Ltd, based at 3 New Kings Road in Chelsea.

Rod Stewart's manager Billy Gaff had originally founded Riva in 1975 as a record label for Rod's UK releases. By the autumn of 1977

Gaff had decided to branch out into publishing and had brought in Dennis Collopy from RCA to look after that side of things. The Clash were one of their first signings. Mick Jones had been a huge Faces fan in the early Seventies, but had ended up feeling betrayed when Stewart instead opted for life in the international jet set as part of a celebrity couple with actress Britt Ekland. Rod was a soft target during the early punk years, and Mick took a potshot at him in the Clash's first ever interview, conducted by Caroline Coon for *Melody Maker* in July 1976: 'We want to get rid of rock'n'rollers like Rod Stewart who kiss royalty after gigs.' Had any of the Clash's critics paid attention to the small print on record labels from the 'Clash City Rockers' single onwards, then the Rod Stewart connection might have proved as big a stick with which to beat the Clash as 'selling out' to CBS or going to America.

'Bernie was a bit of trailblazer,' says Dennis Collopy. 'He had a real political view of what he wanted from a business deal. I think he saw us as a way of controlling CBS, because if CBS had the music publishing, too, the band would have lost all control of their repertoire. We offered them a deal that no one else would. It was a five-figure advance, which by the standards of the day was quite a lot, but by the standards of today seems quite small. [The Nineden accounts indicate the deal was for £10,000.] But if you think about what we paid for: we didn't own the songs, the band owned the songs. We administered them for a short period of time, just three years, and we couldn't really do anything much with them. This is what got us the deal. We gave the band compete control, and specifically we agreed that no audio-visual use of their songs would be permitted by us without their prior consent, which again is normal today, but at the time was very unusual.' The terms were generous towards the songwriters. 'They had good legal representation and we were starting a new publishing company from scratch, and were in a position to just tailor the deal to what they wanted. It was what I would call a New Generation publishing agreement. We accounted to the band at source. It meant they had a percentage of all the gross income everywhere, they weren't paid on net. We all made money from the very beginning. It was quite a successful deal.' Initially, it covered the UK, Ireland, Europe and Australasia. Cannily, Bernie elected to sit on American administration rights until such a time as the Clash took off in the States.

Soon after the October 1977 signing, Riva did a subsidiary deal with Wise Publications to put together the *Clash Songbook,* a project that creatively involved Mick and Paul from the Clash, and Caroline Coon and Barry Miles, among others. 'The idea we had was that anybody who had a very basic knowledge of guitars could pick up that book and play the songs,' says Dennis. 'We wanted the basic chords, plus – most importantly – the lyrics, putting them together with sympathetic graphics.' Because it offered photos, illustrations, imaginatively Clash-appropriate design, and the otherwise unavailable early Clash lyrics, the songbook proved highly desirable for even non-guitar-playing Clash fans. 'It sold incredibly well,' says Dennis. 'We got a royalty from Wise Publications, which we paid on to the band.'

By spring 1979 it had sold well enough for Dennis to think about doing a second songbook, covering subsequent record releases, only this time with Riva editing, designing and publishing the book themselves, thus keeping more of the income in-house. Around April 1979 he contacted Caroline Coon to discuss the project. 'The first book had been really successful, but I felt it still looked quite corporate,' says Dennis. 'With the second one, we wanted something that was a bit more representative of the band's image. We wanted something that really captured the Day-Glo politics of the band, very striking, right down to the cover. At that stage I mainly communicated with Caroline, who I think got the idea pretty quickly. They had complete creative freedom. That was the nature of our relationship with them. The suggestion of Derek really came from Caroline.'

Derek Boshier had been Caroline's fine art tutor at the Central School of Art. She believed his Pop Art graphic style, typically combining photographic images and rough, hand-drawn images with handwritten lettering, would be a perfect fit with the Clash. Coincidentally, Derek had also taught Joe Strummer at Central, but Caroline didn't know that, and Joe didn't tell her. 'I showed the Clash illustrations of Derek's graphic work, and suggested he would be a good designer for the project, because I thought his style was in sync with the by then well-established Clash aesthetic,' says Caroline. The creative freedom demanded by the Clash from Riva was passed on. Derek asked for some photographs of the band, intending to use the work of several different photographers, but he was so impressed by Pennie Smith's work that he decided to use that exclusively. The other collage materials used were all his choices, too, which demonstrates how closely attuned he was to the Clash style: he used the same kind of gun catalogues that Topper and Paul liked to pore over to illustrate 'Guns on the Roof', and the overall feel he achieved for the book was not dissimilar to the sleeve designs for the 'Tommy Gun' and 'English Civil War' singles. The *Clash 2nd Songbook* was published in autumn 1979. 'The rights to that vested primarily in the band,' says Dennis Collopy.

Dennis was aware of the size of the band's debt to CBS, which meant that anything the Clash earned by way of royalties from record sales would go towards repaying this debt for quite some time. 'It was a big black hole,' he says, maintaining that publishing royalties collected by Riva went a long way to keeping the Clash going during this period. Riva's office was just around the corner from Joe's new home in Whistler Walk, and Joe got into the habit of calling in from time to time to see if there was any money 'in the kitty'. Caroline Coon says it was seeing the music publishing royalties start to come through at this time for Mick and Joe that got Paul Simonon interested in the idea of writing songs. As Paul dryly noted some years later, his own contributions in the area of clothes, style and presentation didn't have the same kind of return; or, indeed, any. While the income from Riva was useful, though, it had little to do with getting the Clash moving forward again.

'The Clash's relations with CBS were conflicted,' concedes Caroline. 'But anyone who maintains that by 1979 it looked like any debt the Clash had was a non-recoupable "black hole" does not understand finance. The debt was normal and, given the creative potential of the band, easily manageable. The Clash's earnings were in the pipeline. By 1979, on paper, they were very wealthy indeed, if not millionaires.' This assessment is so at odds with those of the other people involved that at first it seems like a deliberately contrary, eccentrically misguided or naïvely optimistic point of view. On closer inspection though, it's justifiably sanguine. The one point that issue could be taken with is Caroline's claim that the Clash themselves were wealthy, even on paper. Better, perhaps, to say that they were generating wealth.

As Frederic Dannen pointed out in *Hit Men*, just because an artist is in debt to the record company that does not mean that the record company is not making a profit from the artist. For CBS, the Clash was a proven cash cow, and it was clear there was plenty more milk left in the udder. In the UK *The Clash* had reached number 12 on the album charts within a couple of weeks, and stayed on the charts for 16 weeks. In December 1977, just eight months after the album's release, the British Phonographic Industry (BPI) determined that it had sold enough copies in the UK – 60,000 – to be awarded a Silver disc. By April 1979 it was well on its way to turning Gold, with sales of more than 100,000, which status it would achieve in December 1979. *Give 'Em Enough Rope* went quickly to number 2, and although it stayed on the UK charts for just 14 weeks, still went Silver within a month of release, in December 1978. By April 1979 it was also well on its way to turning Gold, which it did in December 1979.

Top Of The Pops might not have been an option, and mainstream radio plays might have been rare, but the Clash were seldom out of the UK music press. The leading inky, the *NME*, boasted a quarter of a million readers per issue. It adored the Clash, with very few dissenting voices at this time. The band were also usually positively and generously covered in the other two main papers, *Melody Maker* and *Sounds*. Even the uncomfortable second album had been given a relatively easy ride. *Sounds* awarded it the full five stars. While the *NME*'s Nick Kent took issue with the subject matter of some of Joe's lyrics, he was kindly disposed overall. Only at *Melody Maker* did Jon Savage strike a truly disappointed note, accusing the band of squandering their greatness. The Clash still had a rabidly passionate following among their UK fans, as had been proved on the Sort it Out tour, and was again proved in the inkies' end of year readers' polls: in the *NME* the Clash were voted the Best Group, '(White Man) In Hammersmith Palais' the Best Single, and *Rope* runner-up in the Best Album category.

Thanks to a chicken-and-egg combination of the Clash's reluctance to turn on the charm for their American record label and Epic's non-existent application, *Give 'Em Enough Rope* had failed to chart in the USA, but it sold steadily, notching up 200,000 sales by the end of May 1979. It had also received good reviews, including one by *Rolling Stone*'s highly influential Greil Marcus: 'Imagine the Who's "I Can't Explain" as a statement about a world in flames, not a lover's daze, and you've got the idea.' The clincher for the band's future in America came when Epic became aware of another statistic that spring: the band's first album, *The Clash* – which Epic had refused to release in April 1977, citing unacceptable production values – had sold what was at that time a record 100,000 copies in the USA on import. Epic now decided to give the album a belated official American release, with some changes to the tracklisting, supposedly to improve its commerciality (but at least partly to save the label's blushes for what was now quite clearly an egregious error of judgement). Some horse-trading ensued. The Clash agreed to a few tracks being dropped from the UK track listing in order to make way for the 1977–8 non-album UK singles, also as yet unreleased in the US, and Epic agreed to include with the album a freebie 7-inch single, pairing 'Groovy Times' and 'Gates of the West'. *The Clash* would be released in late July 1979, trailered by the band's debut American single, 'I Fought the Law' backed with '(White Man) In Hammersmith Palais'.

CBS would have been foolhardy indeed to drop the band at this point, and it was never even discussed. 'Absolutely not!' says an incredulous Muff Winwood. 'There was no way we wouldn't want a third album!' He admits that relations with the band had become more strained since Bernie Rhodes's departure, but firmly puts that back on the Clash. 'We had an uneasy relationship with Caroline Coon,' he says. 'Much more so than we ever had with Bernie. When she became their manager, the band probably told her the strict dos and don'ts . . . and one of the dos would have been to keep the record company at arm's length. It was difficult. They absolutely wanted to run their own lives their own way, and I suppose that's fair enough. They were making money for the record company, so it made good sense to run along with them.' Again, the inkys were being manipulated to cover a showdown that didn't really exist . . . with CBS UK, at least.

'I'm absolutely convinced that a lot of their problems with the record company were to do with how it was dealing with them in America,' says Muff. 'In Britain, they could use the media, and do the bizarre things that British bands have always done with the media, because the country's small enough to be able to do it, but in America it's much more difficult. You can't just replicate how you do things in England. You have to do it a different way. You need big business to flow things through. The media is a whole different thing, and you have to deal with it differently.' What complicated and confused matters was that, as CBS UK was the band's home label, a lot of Epic's communications with the Clash camp came via CBS UK. 'So we almost took the managerial role there, passing on the bad messages from one side to the other,' says Muff.

Muff finds it hard to comprehend the Clash's financial concerns at this point. 'The record company would loan them money to get them through, and then recoup it as the record sold,' he says. The loans did have to be explained and justified, however. 'In order for there to be a steady flow of funds, I had to have regular discussions with CBS about the Clash's plans,' says Caroline Coon. Making and sticking to plans was not really the band's forte, so in the absence of direction from her charges, she assessed the situation herself: 'I sketched a future plan for the Clash to CBS. It was obvious that the band needed (a) a rest, (b) time to write new songs, (c) to record their next album, and (d) a return tour of the USA. Rest and time to write were first and fundamental.' Money released by CBS, and deemed essential expenditure by Peter Quinnell, was passed on to the band.

Since she took over, Caroline had been trying to impress upon the Clash members how important it was for them to have their own secure places to live. 'I explained to the band that they were in a financial position to all buy small properties of their own,' she says. 'I said that I would, with their accountant, arrange their mortgages. I suggested that paying a mortgage was a better use of their earnings than paying rent. Paul Simonon took me up on this offer and he was enabled to buy a small flat on Oxford Gardens.' In spring 1979 Paul moved into a tiny basement flat in Notting Hill, number 42b Oxford Gardens, and went from being officially homeless to being the first home-owning member of the Clash.

After a few weeks back at his Nan's, Mick decided it was also time for him to move into a new place of his own, but wanted to resume sharing with Tony James, and something slightly larger and more salubrious than Paul's basement. To have this relative luxury, he would have to continue paying rent. Caroline found a selection of suitable properties, and in April Mick and Tony moved into a small mews house at 5 Simon Close, off the south end of Portobello Road. It was just around the corner from their former flat, but this time they were a little more circumspect about giving out the address. Ex-Pistol Glen Matlock remained a regular visitor, and remembers the design and décor being 'like something out of *Jason King*', the 1971–2 ATV series starring Peter Wyngarde as a dandy dilettante spy (and the inspiration for the 1997 spoof film *Austin Powers: International Man of Mystery*). 'It had a little spiral staircase, and everything,' says Glen. 'Funniest sight I ever saw, going around there in the morning, and Mick would be lying in bed, while Tony would be doing the washing up and making a cup of tea in his rock'n'roll gear and a little pair of rubber gloves.'

As Topper was still not officially a full equal member of the Clash, he had no choice but to continue renting, moving into a flat in Pimlico with Dee. That left Joe. 'I remember Joe being worried that buying property and relinquishing squatting would damage his street credibility,' says Caroline of their initial conversation in late 1978. Joe was the one who had been held to account at the beginning of that year for living in a 'White Mansion' – he'd taken a small room in Sebastian Conran's large Camden Town terrace house at 31 Albany Street – and was understandably wary of giving the snipers any more ammunition. In addition, as Caroline – thinking only in terms of improving his circumstances – possibly didn't quite grasp, he drew strength and inspiration from his bohemian lifestyle, and quite possibly even depended upon it for his sense of self. That still held true in spring 1979. For the rest of the year, into early 1980, Joe would remain based at the Salters' council flat at 31 Whistler Walk. It might have been a family home, but it hardly qualified as a settled arrangement. When *London Calling* sleeve designer Ray Lowry visited in November 1979, he noted that Joe and Gaby still 'lived out of suitcases, like Bonnie and Clyde'.

In order to write new songs, the Clash also needed a place to work. Hiring Black Hole, Base or the Vault by the hour was expensive and inconvenient. Having to spend half the allotted time setting up and taking down the equipment was irritating. The Clash wanted a new version of Rehearsals Rehearsals: somewhere exclusively theirs, homely, where they could leave the gear set up and ready to go the next day, and where they could negotiate a reasonable weekly or monthly rent rather than a punitive hourly rate. 'With the roadies, I looked for studio workspace for the Clash,' says Caroline. 'This was to be a rehearsal and songwriting base, a safe place for the Clash to be as the emotional dust settled and the band came to terms with the shocking and dramatic changes that had occurred in their lives.' Johnny Green's memory is that it was he and Baker who were tasked with finding the space, scouring the classified ads in *Melody Maker* for likely candidates, before – Johnny having by now lost his licence for drinking and driving – Baker drove them around to check out the few possibilities. Among the places they looked at were the Who's rehearsal studio and Nomis in Earl's Court.

Meanwhile, with typical brisk efficiency, Caroline turned her attention to the remaining item on her list: getting the Clash back to the USA for a second tour. Contacting the New York agent she had used to book the Palladium show on the Pearl Harbour tour, she provisionally arranged two further shows at the Palladium for June. She then, once again, approached Epic for a contribution to the cost of bringing the band over. On the surface at least, her timing looked good, but Epic refused, arguing that the planned shows did not coincide with the proposed release dates for 'I Fought the Law' or *The Clash*. This required a postponement, nothing worse, so Caroline shrugged it off. 'Cancellation and rescheduling is normal,' she says. Bernie had certainly had to do quite a lot of both while he was in charge.

Proof that the Clash had not been forgotten by their UK fans came when the *NME* ran an alternative Prime Minister election to coincide with the bona fide general election that brought Margaret Thatcher and the right-wing Conservative Party to power on 4 May 1979. Joe Strummer and his fictional Riot Wing Party received the lion's share of the votes, and Joe entered into the spirit of the occasion by posing for a photograph with a Winston Churchill-style cigar, and providing the music paper with his 'manifesto'. In addition to cracking a few jokes, he addressed some of the topical issues that had been influencing his new lyrics: he demanded affordable and suitable public housing and transport, the banning of police from demonstrations, the cancellation of the nuclear programme in favour of solar power, and more inspirational television and radio programmes.

On 11 May 1979 the EP comprising the four tracks the Clash had recorded or completed back in mid-January was finally released in the UK. The title *The Cost of Living* was a reference to both the hard times the Clash themselves were experiencing and also one of the key issues – almost a catchphrase – of the Winter of Discontent. The elaborate gatefold sleeve with inner bag, designed by Rockin' Russian, illustrated the theme: the front cover was a mock-up of a washing-powder packet, Joe's idea. The toast in the reprise of 'I Fought the Law' advertises the very EP that contains it. This extended conceptual joke – with its implied 'art as commodity' dig at their record company – rebounded on the Clash before the record even hit the shops. Concerned, as ever, with giving their fans value for money, the band had tried to persuade CBS to release the EP for the price of a standard single, £1, but the record company had insisted that two extra tracks and the expensive-to-produce packaging warranted a price tag of £1.49. Forty-nine pence might not seem worth haggling over at this remove, but it was worth more then: both literally, and – with the evidence of a depressed economy all around – symbolically. The Clash were unhappy about the 50 per cent mark-up. For all the hard-sell humour of the packaging, no significant attempt was made to promote the new record.

In spite of Caroline's unruffled response to the Clash's situation, by early May 1979 the Clash were still on edgy terms with both the UK and American branches of their record company, and their hopes of getting back to the USA on tour had been temporarily thwarted. Perhaps predictably, it was Caroline who carried the can. Her manner with the band verged on the authoritarian, which rubbed Joe up the wrong way, and her (perceived) relationship with Paul added a Yoko Ono frisson to her role. 'It was Mick and Joe, really: I don't think they thought she was up to the level they needed,' says Johnny Green. 'To put it bluntly, I think they thought she was on the make. And by that point, people were missing Bernie in a funny sort of way.' This assessment of Caroline's capabilities and motives – whoever's it might be – is unfair and unfounded. Closer to the mark is Jack Hazan's observation that she was the first manager of a rock group to be fired for being *too* efficient. Johnny's comment about the band – or, at least, certain members of the band – missing Bernie is more pertinent. Bernie might have been told to go away, but he hadn't actually gone: Bill Price remembers him paying a visit during the January sessions for *The Cost of Living*. In retrospect, it seems evident that Joe acted as something of a double agent throughout Bernie's period of supposed estrangement from the band, keeping him in the loop and always looking for an opportunity to press his case with the other members of the Clash. He liked Bernie's anarchic, maverick approach to management. Mick didn't, but he also had an alternative to Caroline in mind (see Part 3).

As for the charge that Caroline was 'on the make': her position as manager was only ever supposed to be temporary. 'I wanted to hand over to another proficient manager,' she says. 'I was waiting.' Consequently, she was also looking around for opportunities for herself, so she would not be left high and dry when that handover occurred. Discussions had taken place about the possibility of her becoming creative consultant for a proposed American punk-themed film, at that time going under the working title *All Washed Up*, but eventually released as *Ladies and Gentleman, the Fabulous Stains*. It could be argued that her association with the Clash helped make this happen for her; but it could also be argued that Caroline made it happen for herself by being among the first two or three music journalists to cover the UK punk scene (and give the nascent Clash a future in the process).

Either her imminent departure to America to firm up her appointment was the trigger for her dismissal, or – altogether more likely a reason – it enabled Joe to play the assassin without having to face up to any immediate consequences. 'The day I was flying to the USA to take a meeting with Paramount, Joe suddenly called me to a meeting,' says Caroline. 'I walked in and sat down next to him. "You're sacked!" he said. "Right!" I said. And I laughed and walked out. I thought it was really very funny. I went straight to the airport. I stopped off in New York to say thank you to the Clash's American agent and to the Clash people at CBS and explain to them that the band were looking for a new manager. The Clash have since said that they liked chaos, but chaos tends to block the money pipeline.'

This abrupt and ungrateful ending to her tenure aside, she was content enough. 'My mission was accomplished,' she says. 'I had enabled the Clash to stay together. They were working on their third album. I believed their future was assured and, whatever happened to them next, they would have a modicum of financial security for the rest of their lives.' She did go on to work on the movie, and offers as proof that she harboured no grudge against the Clash in general or Paul Simonon in particular the fact that she later arranged for Paul to audition for a role in the movie. He got the part and filming took place in April 1980 in LA and Vancouver. 'Paul resented the way that Coon had gone, and the way he was treated in that situation,' says Johnny Green. 'After that, he started to get a lot more assertive about his position within the group dynamic.'

Joe made it clear that he wanted Bernie back. Mick made the opposite equally clear. As the next couple of months would be low-key, devoted to preparing material for the new album, there was no need to force the issue. The Clash announced they would be managing themselves for the time being, 'taking it in turns to carry the briefcase'. Joe went first. On 14 May 1979 Caroline Coon resigned as secretary of Nineden and Joe assumed the role. Not quite ready to embrace total chaos, the band decided to keep Peter Quinnell on as their accountant. He seemed to be enjoying the job, and was no longer thought of as The Enemy, or even Quister: band and crew were now on first-name terms with Peter. 'Within a few months, he's got his feet up on the desk, his tie's loose, and he's a rock'n'roll accountant,' laughs Johnny Green. 'Marvellous geezer. Very sweet man. Very understanding. He held us together. *He* should have managed them.'

★

Meanwhile, Johnny Green and Baker had found Vanilla Rehearsal Studios at 36 Causton Street, a side street towards the southern end of Vauxhall Bridge Road. The premises had originally housed Haley's Industrial Motors, then the Midland Rubber Company. Immediately following the Second World War it was home to Vauxhall Motors, a taxi firm. By the mid-Seventies, number 36 had again caught up with the times, and was occupied by Stereo Thirty Six Ltd, Hi-Fi Sound Equipment Suppliers. Thereafter – perhaps appropriately – cars and music shared the premises. By 1978 they housed Motor Doctor Auto Electrical Repairs Ltd and New Sounds Rehearsal Studios.

Although both Johnny Green and Joe Strummer have said that the Clash used the studio as their base for around five and a half months, it was just under three. New Sounds was relaunched as Vanilla Rehearsal Studios in 1979, and was first listed in the classified section of *Melody Maker* under that name on 5 May that year, which is where Johnny saw the ad. On their initial recce, Johnny and Baker discovered that the two-storey building fronting Causton Street was just the first (roughly speaking) third of a deep and sprawling site that was completely roofed over and filled with a variety of jerry-built constructions. Double garage doors opened from the street onto a ramped drive leading into the interior, and – if followed to its end – an underground carpark at the back of the site. A left turn halfway along, though, led into the covered courtyard occupying the middle third. The courtyard gave access to the two old but massive hangars – incorporating various smaller buildings – taking up the back third (over the carpark). This was the garage.

The omens looked good for a self-professed garageband whose previous long-term base, Rehearsals Rehearsals, had been adjacent to such an establishment. Rather than fixing up old Renaults like Harry's in Camden Town, though, the motor doctoring in the Causton Street courtyard appeared to consist largely of re-spraying top-of-the-range sports cars and Rolls-Royces. Johnny thought it looked dodgy, but when he discovered the tough-looking car-coated gentlemen who ran the garage also let the studios, he decided not to enquire any further. (Mick Jones was later wont to compare Vanilla to a typical gang hideout in a black-and-white British heist movie.) Johnny and Baker were shown the two studios: an unsuitably small one on the ground floor of the garage, and then, up a flight of stairs, a larger – 30 feet by 10 feet – low-ceilinged room with no windows. A six-inch-high platform ran down one side. Baker was not impressed by this studio, either, but the built-in 'stage' helped sell it to Johnny: the Clash had always set up to rehearse as though they were playing live.

Twelve years later, Joe Strummer would describe Vanilla to *Rolling Stone* as 'a dirty room in Pimlico with one light and filthy carpet on the walls for soundproofing', but he was always inclined to exaggerate the Clash's privations for dramatic effect. The lack of light – both natural and artificial – might have given Vanilla a seedy aspect, but it was relatively clean, had cream paint rather than carpet on most of the wall space, had a carpet where it should have been, on the floor. As with their former home, the reason for Vanilla's name was and remains a mystery, with the best-guess suggestion being that it was inspired by the (lack of) colour scheme: unremarkable though it was, it was still the most remarkable thing about the place. 'We didn't want somewhere flash,' says Johnny. 'We wanted somewhere we could make a base, that offered virtually nothing except somewhere to plug in a kettle.' And, of course, some amps.

Causton Street is both oddly shaped and positioned: a short

circumflex linking Vauxhall Bridge Road with one of its larger eastern tributaries, Regency Street. On the opposite side of the road to Vanilla was and is a residential terrace and a playground. Next door to the rehearsal room in 1979 was the back of publisher Random House, still there, and on the other side the London Diocesan House. Exploration of the immediate surrounding area revealed a pub, the White Swan, at the south end of the street, and a serviceable café just around the corner on Vauxhall Bridge Road. Johnny enquired about a rate for sole occupation and use, and was given a quote by one of the car coats. He then secured the necessary funds from Peter Quinnell. Baker fetched the band's gear in its hot pink flight-cases, and he and Johnny set up the amps, speakers, drums and guitars ready for the band. Johnny made the room homely by bringing in a few chairs and a table, and invested in the makings of a cup of tea. The band members were faced with a fait accompli: Vanilla was their new base.

What made the location perfect was all the things, and people, that weren't close by. Causton Street was neither a chic hangout nor close to one. Very much off the beaten track, the room promised seclusion and respite. 'I can remember the band saying, "We don't want anybody knowing where we are,"' says Johnny. 'For the first time since I'd known the Clash, hangers on – even close friends like Robin Banks [Crocker] and Kris Needs – were not allowed to hang around in the rehearsal room.' CBS were also kept at arm's length. Muff Winwood took this in his stride. 'It's a syndrome that every band goes through,' he says. 'When you're creating something, you don't really want anybody to criticise or critique it until all the parts are together. Somebody coming in and saying you should do a bit more of this and you should do a bit less of that, and this doesn't sound very good, but that does . . . it's not an easy thing to live with when you're still trying to create. They were guarded because they didn't feel confident about what they'd got at the time.'

That's almost correct. 'I can remember the first day they went into Vanilla,' says Johnny. 'They didn't have a single tune. They had nothing. I can remember being very surprised, and Baker was as well. We'd spent a long time setting the equipment up and getting the ambience in the room.' This, then, was the underlying reason for Mick and Joe's discomfort at Caroline Coon's attempts to make firm plans and commitments on their behalf with CBS, and for their decision to reject outside representation and retreat into one anonymous room with no one but their two closest and most trusted crew members. 'There was very much a beleaguered atmosphere in the early days at Vanilla,' says Johnny.

What had gone unremarked about *The Cost of Living* was that, of its four tracks, one was a cover version, one was a remake of a Clash release from spring 1977, one song dated from the early 1978 writing sessions for *Give 'Em Enough Rope*, and one – 'Gates of the West' – was Mick Jones's 1976 pre-Clash song 'Ooh, Baby, Ooh (It's Not Over)' with a new lyric by Joe. By May 1979 Mick and Joe had not produced anything from scratch for a whole year: a third of the Clash's entire existence.

In November 1978 Mick had boasted to Garry Bushell of *Sounds* of having 15 unreleased songs in various stages of completion, dating back to before spring 1978. Two of these had since appeared on the EP. One song mentioned by name in the interview with Bushell, 'Heart and Mind', would be revived at Vanilla. Unless the other dozen were made over in some so-far unacknowledged way, they were either forgotten or abandoned as substandard or old hat. Whether it was due to the Clash's hectic touring schedule, his struggle with cocaine in 1977, the tussles with Bernie Rhodes, his tempestuous relationship with Viv Albertine, the recent burglary at his flat, or depression brought about by permutations of any of the above, Mick's writer's block was now celebrating its first anniversary. 'Mick had been very unproductive, coinciding with the period of our filming,' says David Mingay, meaning from April 1978 to March 1979. 'He just wouldn't turn up some days, and he said he couldn't write. It was a difficult time for him.' Joe had filled in by writing the piano song he performs in *Rude Boy* on his own, but that he didn't take it very seriously can be deduced from the fact that he didn't even give it a title. It was certainly never considered as a contender for the next Clash album.

This period in the doldrums was naturally a cause of great consternation for both Mick and Joe. They had struggled to find a satisfactory combination of words, music and approach for the second album, but at least they had produced that album. Now deadlines were in place and the pressure was on: could they deliver again, and from a standing start?

They had hoped that *The Cost of Living* might at least allow them to find a new style and sound, but following a critical mauling in the *NME*, of all places, were no longer even fully confident about that. Recent *NME* recruit Ian Penman had already signalled his refusal to join the inkies' chorus of adoration for the Clash in October 1978, when he reviewed a show at the Harlesden Roxy thus: 'A joyless, emotionless, directionless, self-important music, something like a shambolic HM quartet converted to Mao minutes before a show, but still retaining the original ego-pushy set, swaggers and all . . . The Clash don't know what to do with themselves, don't know what to do with rock music, but I and you know what it's doing to them.' If it had been spiteful and wide of the mark, it wouldn't have hurt so much. But Penman's assessment of the Clash's music and stance circa *Rope* and his intuition that the band were flailing around in their search for a new direction were both spot on. That didn't stop him going on the band's hate list, though. Penman also happened to be in the singles-reviewing chair six months later when *The Cost of Living* was released. 'If they've re-thought, then this EP doesn't betray the fact. The Clash "sound" is mellower and more cluttered than it's possibly ever been, the structures more obvious, the solos longer . . . The Clash are prancing as would-be "traditional" rock'n'roll heroes while still projecting some totally unfounded sense of the "brave" and the "new".' Again, the review was scarily perceptive about the band's underlying malaise, but this time it was far too hard. Yes, *The Cost of Living* is cluttered, at times sounding like it's trying too hard to make a point about the Clash's versatility and musicianship. In retrospect, however, it can be seen as a trial run, if not quite a blueprint, for what was to come next. It was the sound of the Clash members putting a line through Year Zero and opening themselves up further than ever before to all the musics they had encountered in their lives.

There had been hints on *Give 'Em Enough Rope*, too – there's the rockabilly rhythm and lyrical references to Cajun and zydeco in 'Last Gang in Town'; the fact that 'English Civil War' is a new lyric married to the trad. arr. folk anthem 'Johnny Comes Marching Home'; the horn-led R&B swing of 'Julie's Been Working for the Drug Squad'; as well as all that slightly overripe Mott the Hoople – but most of them had been buried by the hard-rock avalanche, were lying trapped under too many strata of guitars. By including a wider range of textures, the EP is more able to wear rock's rich tapestry on its sleeve.

There's the late Fifties rocker 'I Fought the Law'. Then the early Sixties folky Dylanesque harmonica (credited to 'Bob' Jones) and acoustic guitar-flavoured intro to 'Groovy Times' is followed by its big pop-soul chorus and slick mid-Seventies folky Al Stewart 'Year of the Cat'-style middle eight. The tune of 'Gates of the West' is a straight lift from Booker T. and the MGs' 1969 soul groover 'Time is Tight'. The song's lyric makes reference to original rock'n'roller Little Richard in the kitchen, rattling utensils (like Bill Haley and the Comets in 'Rock Around the Clock'). What would become known as 'Capital Radio Two' in order to distinguish it from the 1977 original has a 'sophisti-cated', noodling acoustic guitar intro. It was Topper who conceived the disco-funk coda to the song, which explains Joe Strummer's ad-lib about the drummer being in the box office counting all the money. And there's the reggae DJ toasting on the reprise of the lead track. Including a reprise is a very late-Sixties rock thing to do: see *Sgt. Pepper's Lonely Hearts Club Band* (1967), *Electric Ladyland* (1968) and *Mott the Hoople* (1969).

For a year, Mick and Joe had been paralysed by indecision, depression, lack of conviction and lack of self-belief . . . and by sneering so viciously at the EP via which the band were hoping to get themselves back on track, Ian Penman had not exactly cheered them on their way.

Those first days in Vanilla, in the absence of new original material, the Clash did what they always did in rehearsals or at soundchecks: loosened up and tried to get themselves in the mood by playing their own older material and some cover versions. By this stage in their career, the Clash had been together long enough to be able to play together for fun. Or – as pre-punk bands would have put it – jam. They didn't choose material with recording in mind; they just played music that popped into their heads.

As 'Heart and Mind' is far more of a piece with *Give 'Em Enough Rope* than the two songs that ended up on *The Cost of Living*, it's doubtful that it was ever really worked up as a genuine contender for inclusion on the new album. The same applies to 'Remote Control', already included on *The Clash*, and the song that originated – and was therefore symbolic of – their tussle with CBS.

Joe had always liked rock'n'roll and R&B-style music from the late Fifties and early Sixties that nodded back to even earlier blues, country, folk and New Orleans boogie. 'Joe would be into Clifton Chenier or whoever, a new person every week,' says Johnny Green. 'Often the most obscure people you'd ever heard of, but always retro or genre stuff.' Mick was fond of the sort of mid-to-late Sixties R&B, soul, pop and garage music that looked more to the future. Paul had continued to work on his bass technique by playing along to reggae records, and his teenage affection for mid-to-late Sixties Jamaican music of the rock steady to early reggae period – the skinhead era – had been rekindled in early 1977 by the re-release of the five-year-old cult Jamaican film *The Harder They Come*. At heart, Topper preferred rhythmically challenging music from improvisational power rock to prog to funk to jazz to fusion.

As a rough guide to how the Clash chose other artists' songs to cover, that breakdown of inclinations is useful, but ultimately simplistic. To attribute the band's selections strictly along those lines would certainly be misleading. As well as playing together for two-to-three years, the band members had been living in each other's pockets and exposing themselves to each other's tastes. The Clash evolved out of playing some of Mick's Sixties favourites, but Joe and Topper had grown up listening to most of them, too, and Mick put others on the jukebox at Rehearsals Rehearsals, so they were practically wired into the entire band's DNA. He himself could find something to like and respond to in all kinds of music, including Paul's vintage reggae and Joe's pre-rock'n'roll Americana. 'Mick was just into music,' says Johnny Green. 'He listened to it all the time, and wanted to know all about new stuff.'

When Paul first starting sharing a squat with the newly recruited Joe Strummer in mid-1976, he was intrigued by the R&B and rock'n'roll record sleeves littered around – Paul later complained the records themselves were usually either so badly scratched they couldn't be played or else were missing altogether – and as soon as he had the money started buying that kind of music himself. The rawness of rockabilly reminded him of punk. 'It's interesting because a lot of that period is like today, there's similarities,' he told John McKenna of *Hot Press* in late 1979. 'That's why I enjoy it: there's a desperate feel to it.' As well as becoming an enthusiastic collector – unlike Joe, keeping his discs pristine in plastic sleeves – he also spent time lovingly compiling tapes to take on the road. For the Pearl Harbour tour, his carrying case of custom-illustrated tapes – as photographed by Bob Gruen – included one side of reggae tapes, four labelled *Dreadnought*, four labelled *Dread Control*, one *Natty*, one *Dub*, one *Big Youth*, one *Ska-Reggae*, and one labelled *One Badd Gun*, plus a side of rock'n'roll tapes, three labelled *Rockabilly*, one *Elvis Presley*, one split between *Screaming Jay Hawkins* and *Eddie Cochran*, a *Bo Diddley*, a *Chuck Berry*, two *Little Richards*, a *Lee Dorsey* . . . plus a *Blues*, and, covering the soul department, a *Motown* and a *Temptations*.

Joe's interest in reggae was piqued by Bernie's additions to the jukebox at Rehearsals, by Paul's enthusiasm for the music, by the Notting Hill Carnival sound systems, and by Don Letts's DJ sessions at the Roxy in Covent Garden. He followed in Paul's footsteps back to *The Harder They Come*, and by 1978 was also a champion of Sixties Jamaican music. And Topper? Topper could play anything, and took great pleasure in demonstrating the fact. 'He would bring in Weather Report, and say, "I can do that,"' says Johnny Green. 'And it was, "Yeah, Topper . . ." But when the others found out he could, his musical impact started to come through. It wasn't just a stylistic or technical thing. It meant their musical register could open.'

The Clash had covered Toots and the Maytals' 'Pressure Drop' (1969) on their White Riot tour, recorded it in March 1978, and released it a year later. Desmond Dekker's 'The Israelites' (1969) – as previously covered by the 101ers – was in their soundcheck repertoire by mid-1978. For all Joe's comments about leaving contemporary reggae behind as an influence, the Clash didn't turn their backs on it entirely, largely because Paul still liked to play along to reggae old and new on his ghetto blaster, and the others couldn't resist the cue. Althea and Donna's 'Up Town Top Ranking' got a few run-throughs in rehearsals before it became a Number 1 hit in the UK in February 1978, and Joe would even quote snippets from the lyric onstage. 'Fire in Soweto' (1977) by Nigerian afrofunk-highlife-reggae musician Sonny Okosun (aka Sunny Okosuns), made it as far as a set list on that July's Out on Parole tour, and Topper estimates Danny Ray's 'Revolution Rock' (1976) had made it to the rehearsal room by late autumn 1978.

The Clash might not have gone public with their reversal of policy vis-à-vis Old School rock'n'roll until they recorded 'I Fought the Law', but rock'n'roll had been let in through the back door a little earlier than is generally acknowledged. In early 1978 Joe had been approached by American filmmaker Diego Cortez to provide a recording of Elvis Presley's 'Heartbreak Hotel' for his never-released film *Grutzi Elvis* (*Hello, Elvis*), which took its inspiration from the approximate synchronicity of the emergence of punk, Presley's death on 16 August 1977, and the death in custody of Andreas Baader, co-founder of the German terrorist Baader-Meinhof Gang (aka the Red Army Faction or RAF) on 18 October 1977. All three topics were high on Joe's list of personal interests at the time. He did two versions, one that he described as a 'Cajun' version with some German musicians, and another as a 'terrorist' version. The most significant thing about Joe's reworking of the song is that he makes up his own lyric, darkly witty musings on buying pills in Germany, blowing up his friends, and turning yellow . . . which had happened to Joe at the time, thanks to his bout of hepatitis. It was an irreverent and free approach to the lyrics of cover versions that he would continue to favour, allowing the Clash to personalise other people's songs.

By the spring of 1978, or so Joe told Pete Silverton of *Sounds* at that time, the Clash were covering the Johnny Burnette Trio's 1956 rockabilly classic 'Train Kept A Rollin'', and a song Joe named as 'Your Rockin' Mama' and attributed to Sun Records veteran Carl Mann, having recently seen him perform it live at a London gig. He possibly meant the Hi-Tombs' 1958 rockabilly number 'Sweet Rockin' Mama'. Leiber and Stoller's 'Riot in Cell Block #9', first recorded in 1954 by black R&B vocal group the Robins – and again previously covered by the 101ers – made it into the Clash's set for their 7 February 1979 Berkeley Community Theater show on the Pearl Harbour tour. In March, Joe took a stab at a solo piano rendition of the Shirley and Lee song 'Let the Good Times Roll' (1956) for *Rude Boy*, which he subsequently admitted he had probably learned from the Animals' 1965 version. The more forward-looking Sixties side of things was represented by Booker T. and the MGs' 'Time is Tight' (1969), which crept on to the band's set list in October 1977, and which they recorded in the studio the following March. During the sessions for *Give 'Em Enough Rope* that May, obviously recognising a lyrical if not a musical connection, Sandy Pearlman persuaded the band to record a version of Thunderclap Newman's 'Something in the Air' (1969).

As early as May 1978 Joe had told Pete Silverton that the Clash knew their way around an album's worth of covers, and might well be releasing their own take on David Bowie's *Pin Ups* (1973) some time in the near future. It was most likely meant in jest, but the band did have enough favourites to warrant it, and it's quite possible in their darker moments during the early days at Vanilla that the Clash thought this was the way they might have to go. (Twenty-seven years later, Paul Simonon would help compile Trojan Records' *Revolution Rock: A Clash Jukebox*, featuring 21 original versions of songs covered by the Clash.) Any and all of the above songs may have been attempted at Vanilla, but only 'Revolution Rock' was played for certain. The band had a bunch of new old favourites . . .

At first, a cover of Matumbi's 1976 lovers-rock-style cover version of Bob Dylan's 'The Man in Me', from the often overlooked 1970 album *New Morning*, seems a doubly strange choice: even when Clashified, it remained a laid-back reggae take on a laid-back country-style love song. Having just toured with him, it was more predictable that the Clash would attempt a few of Bo Diddley's classic recordings. During a 4 August 1979 interview with Mikko Montonen for Finnish music magazine *Soundi*, Joe said the band had also played Elvis Presley's 'Crawfish' at Vanilla. It hails from the soundtrack of the 1958 film *King Creole*, a video of which had been on the Pearl Harbour tour bus. Much later, Joe would name it as his favourite Presley song. An odd choice: it's either a literal salute to a freshwater lobster, or a way-overextended sexual metaphor. DJ Barry Myers had played Vince Taylor and the Playboys' 1959 rocker 'Brand New Cadillac' on Pearl Harbour too, and it was also worked up in Vanilla. 'I Fought the Law' and 'Riot in Cell Block #9' having already explored crime and punishment R&B-style, it was natural enough for the Clash to have a go at Sam Cooke's 1960 hit 'Chain Gang', another song Joe mentioned in the *Soundi* interview. And entirely suited to a band settling into a daily routine.

Soon enough, they started to come up with their own ideas for songs . . . tentatively at first, then more and more confidently and consistently. 'There was a great relief,' says David Mingay, who visited the Clash in the rehearsal room in June. 'At Vanilla, Mick suddenly got his old facility back, and that was marvellous.' The answer the band stumbled upon was to play what they wanted to play, to write about what interested them . . . and to worry about other people's reaction to it later. Unsurprisingly, the covers set the template for the type of material they began to write. Which in turn explains why an unprecedented three covers eventually made it to *London Calling*, and why those three covers – and the fourth that joined the title track on the album's UK single – fitted in so well with the band's own material.

The feeling of being up against it brought out the more determined side of the Clash: they had always had a strong work ethic, and while they reacted badly to structure imposed from outside, and believed a little chaos spiced things up, they were not averse to self-imposed rules and regulations. One thing that was never going to change was Mick Jones's inability to get out of bed and to rehearsals under his own steam, but the others worked around this. As always, Johnny would arrive first by Tube, turn on the equipment, tune the guitars, tidy up the previous day's detritus and vacuum the carpet. Based nearby, Topper Headon would usually be the first band member to turn up, and start messing around on the drums to warm up. Either Paul Simonon or Joe Strummer would arrive next – Paul usually toting his ghetto blaster – and join in. They would swap instruments and goof around. Finally, Baker would head off in the van to fetch Mick. By this stage, late morning had usually crept into early afternoon. After lunch at the café, the brewing of more tea, and the rolling of the first of many joints, rehearsals would begin in earnest.

The Clash might not have clocked on at the crack of dawn, but they would continue to play right through until the late evening. 'It was an extremely disciplined programme of work at Vanilla,' says Johnny Green. 'Yeah, the spliffs were flying and, yeah, we did adjourn to the café for egg and chips, but I was always asked to time 'em. "How long have we been here, Johnny?" "Thirty minutes." "OK, let's go." And we'd all go back. And then at seven o'clock, it'd be, "Let's go and have a drink." Round the pub, we'd all have a couple, then back we'd go. Very structured approach. Impressively so.'

Another recreational break began as an accident, developed into a ritual, and ultimately made an important contribution to the mood of the sessions. Early one evening, Baker got a football out of the band's van and started kicking it against the wall in the courtyard area. Johnny joined in, and then Paul, whose enthusiasm was greater than his control. With a yard full of expensive cars to dent, one of the car coats quickly put the mockers on that. Instead he directed them to the Causton Street Children's Playground, diagonally opposite. It had an unforgiving asphalt surface, high fence to stop balls escaping and smashing windows, and an unlocked gate. Over the next few days, the football match became a regular occurrence, with all the other members of the band joining in and, as word got around, band friends like Robin Crocker, *Rude Boy* actor Terry McQuade, DJ Barry Myers and *ZigZag* editor Kris Needs began turning up from time to time. These were not gentle kick abouts, with care taken not to sprain wrists and fingers that would shortly be shaping chords, plucking strings or wielding drumsticks. They were fast, furious and highly physical. Even Topper, whose teenage football injury had left him bedridden for half a year, and who needed all four limbs to be fully functioning in order to play his instrument, was a wholehearted participant.

Johnny Green recalls that Robin and Topper were the real talents upfront, Robin being a natural goalscorer, while Topper excelled at controlling and passing the ball. Mick was a little more full of himself than he had reason to be, running down the wing with his arm in the air shouting, 'To me! To me!' while the others largely ignored him. Joe and Paul certainly didn't believing in passing: they were out and out cloggers, gravitating towards defence, where they could concentrate on going in hard. As did Johnny himself. And as they were playing in boots on an asphalt surface, hard meant hard. When and if he got the ball, Paul hoofed it up the yard; Joe preferred to take time to size up the options, and then ran straight for goal until he was dispossessed. 'Meanwhile, Mick would be running about trying to beat 27 people, shouting at everyone and being very demanding,' says Johnny, who likes to see a parallel between how the Clash members were on the pitch and their roles within the band. 'Those football sessions were lovely,' he says. 'They made that album. It sounds a silly thing to say, but they actually built up team spirit.'

It sounds anything but silly: all kinds of businesses use similar team-building exercises with great success. Though, perhaps, discouraging quite so much swearing and casual violence. Following the match was the early evening pub visit; but after the agreed couple of drinks, no matter how enjoyable the banter or how severe their aches, scrapes, bumps and bruises, the band would leave the other players in the pub and go back to Vanilla for another couple of hours.

It might not have been the Beautiful Game the way the Clash played it, but it was fun, and a much-needed release. And all four members of the band later agreed with Johnny that these games of football were symbolic of a growing sense of self-belief, and mutual appreciation and support; all the stronger for being forged in adversity. 'There was a lot of communication and ideas in the air,' says Johnny. 'There was a real buzz. The first week, it had been all this, "Oh we've got another album to do, we're still with *that* record company, and we haven't got a manager!" but within a very short space of time there was an immense feeling of, "Oh, we are *very* special!" There was very much a feeling of, "Hey, there's something happening, here!" because the music was gelling in a very interesting way. Ideas were flowing.' The Clash might have been in seclusion – in self-imposed exile – awaiting a verdict on their future from CBS, the critics, and the public, but after the stresses and divisions of the previous 18 months, they were a band again; and arguably more of a band than they had ever been before, or would ever be again.

*

Reviewing their songwriting partnership after the band split, both Mick Jones and Joe Strummer liked to make it sound almost effortlessly natural. 'Joe used to sit there with a typewriter, and I used to sit in front of him. Once he had something, he'd hand me the sheet of paper and I'd bang out a tune,' is the typical Mick Jones version, on this occasion offered to *Guitar World*'s Matthew Caws in 1995. 'By the time I was done, he'd have another one.' In the *Clash On Broadway* booklet, Joe Strummer said that if a song took more than a day to come together while he and Mick were writing the first album, they would abandon it.

It could be argued that they were staying true to the punk ethos by demystifying the creative process: making songwriting seem straightforward and spontaneous, and refusing to conform to rock's tortured artist stereotype. But by claiming it was so casual and effortless for them, Joe and Mick were buying into another rock myth instead. As lifelong music fans, both knew the stories about John Lennon and Paul McCartney sitting down at a piano, or with a couple of guitars, and writing a classic 'eyeball to eyeball' within a few minutes;

and stories about Stones manager Andrew Loog Oldham deciding that non-writers Mick Jagger and Keith Richards had to become the Rolling Stones' Lennon and McCartney, and locking them in the kitchen of their shared flat until they came out with a song. Bernie Rhodes had made a similar decision about Joe Strummer and Mick Jones: as soon as Joe signed up to join the band, he was told he would be writing with Mick. Compatibility was not a consideration. And ego certainly wasn't. Joe had written some intriguing lyrics for the 101ers, but to Bernie his tunes were stale old pub-rock R&B. Before Joe's recruitment, Mick Jones had been the embryonic Clash's tunesmith *and* lyricist. But Bernie knew that Mick's lyrics were not strong or unusual enough to go up against Johnny Rotten's. It was logical that Joe should write the words – following Bernie's guidelines – and Mick supply the music. And that, mostly, was how it did work. Only not immediately, not always, and not always as straightforwardly as Joe and Mick would later claim.

Of the songs Mick had written in their entirety before Joe joined, a handful survived for the first album and early single B-sides, some intact, like 'Protex Blue' and '1-2 Crush On You', some after minor lyrical tweaking by Joe, like 'Deny', and others after being substantially lyrically reworked, like 'I'm So Bored with the USA'. Whether for diplomatic reasons or lack of inspiration, what rewrites there were rarely happened quickly and, in the case of the last of these songs, it took Joe the entire seven months up until the band recorded *The Clash* to arrive at something he – and Mick, and Bernie – was happy with. Mick briefly, and unusually, turned the tables in 1977: he took a 101ers song called 'Lonely Mother's Son', which the Clash had played in early rehearsals, and rewrote Joe's original verses to come up with 'Jail Guitar Doors'.

Not someone willing to be demoted or dictated to, even after Joe joined, Mick continued to write songs entirely on his own, words and music both. If such a song was personal to Mick, and Mick wanted to sing it – or, as was sometimes the case, Joe didn't want to sing it *because* it was personal to Mick – Joe would usually leave the lyric well alone . . . though on other occasions he wouldn't be able to resist an edit. 'Janie Jones', 'Complete Control' and 'Stay Free' received a couple of minor tweaks, but were recorded largely as Mick intended. Sometimes Mick – and in the case of 'What's My Name', Mick and

Keith Levene – would come up with a tune and maybe a few words of a chorus, and give it to Joe to fill in the rest.

When Joe started to feel comfortable in the role of chief mouthpiece for Project Clash, he began originating songs by writing the lyrics first, as he had done for the 101ers, usually alone in his squat and late at night. Although he often did type up finished lyrics (and by the time he was working on *Sandinista!* and *Combat Rock*, would work on a typewriter from scratch, at one point with four machines lined up with four different lyrics on the go), for his first few years with the band Joe did rough drafts by hand, in pen or pencil, usually on whatever scraps of paper were available. (Even in the year or two before his death, he could still sometimes be found in the vocal booth using a napkin or pizza box as a prompt.)

Sometimes his draft lyrics would also have rough ideas for chords, but more often not. In the early days of the Clash, Joe would take these drafts round to Mick's place, or to Rehearsals Rehearsals, and hand them over. Mick would then either sit and work up a tune on the spot, with Joe offering comments, as with 'London's Burning' and 'White Riot', or Mick would work on the song overnight, or during a longer break from rehearsals, as with 'Hate & War', 'Remote Control' and 'Garageland'. Joe's words had internal rhythms which, Mick found, naturally dictated how the accompanying tune should go. From time to time he would make a suggestion to improve a line of the lyric, or fill in a blank. '1977' was again unusual: a lyric Joe already had the bulk of in his notebook married to a tune Mick already had . . . borrowed from Ray Davies.

Less than a third of the first album's songs were genuinely written eyeball to eyeball at Rehearsals, usually after a decision had been made to come up with something about a particular topic, or simply because a number was needed to replace one about to be dropped from the set. Joe would write the words, sometimes with input from Mick, while Mick would fashion the tune, sometimes with input from Joe. The result could be inspired, as with 'Career Opportunities', or fairly obvious hackwork – if still enjoyable – as in the case of '48 Hours' and 'Cheat'. The late 1977 Strummer-Jones Jamaican writing trip in respect of the second album produced the largest batch of songs written in this way, as Joe and Mick were stuck in a hotel room together. And even then, the process was anything but bish, bash, bosh. 'Safe European Home' was originally more of an epic poem, or a Dylanesque marathon to rival even 'Sad-Eyed Lady of the Lowlands', before Joe cut it down from its original 52 lines to the final 16.

Unlike the Beatles, the Clash didn't telegraph the identity of the chief writer by making him the lead vocalist on the song. That Joe sings 'Janie Jones' and 'Complete Control' cannot be taken to indicate that he wrote the words, anymore than the fact that Mick sings 'Hate & War' and 'Remote Control' can be taken to indicate that he wrote the words.

Largely by luck, Bernie had put two creative people together who could collaborate in a number of ways. It might not have made for such a slick soundbite, but the versatility both of them demonstrated in reality was far more impressive than the official fiction allows. While it is true that if they didn't nail a song in a day they might abandon it, those are the forgotten songs that no one else will ever hear. Some of the keepers did come relatively quickly, and it's clearly those collaborations that Mick and Joe chose to look back on fondly in retrospective interviews. A significant number of what came to be considered the major Clash songs gave them problems for one reason or another, but had enough potential to make the duo return to them time and time again over weeks until they could make them work. And however they wrote a first draft, and however long it took, Mick would continue to hone the arrangement, and Joe the words, until such a time as the song was recorded . . . Even when he was in front of the microphone in the studio, if Joe got carried away, he was liable to extemporise additional lyrics, and Mick would be thinking of refinements up to – and sometimes after – the mixing stage.

While their ultimate commitment was to ensuring the Clash produced the best music they could, there's no doubt that there was a competitive rivalry between the two songwriters. Lennon and McCartney, and Jagger and Richards, began writing together, then drifted apart. Strummer and Jones began writing separately, and were then pushed together. Joe had lost much of his outlet for tunes, and Mick had lost much of his outlet for lyrics, and they both felt disgruntled about this from time to time. It's no coincidence that Joe began to work on his piano playing a few months into Mick's writer's block: he knew that *someone* would have to come up with songs. Even when

Mick started producing again, it meant Joe now had more options: his technique on the piano remained as limited as his guitar playing, but it suggested different chord progressions, and could give him more control over the way the songs he originated turned out. (Unfortunately, there was no piano at Vanilla.)

Something happened back in spring 1978 that indicated another possible way to fill the gap left by Mick's dry spell. During the course of a rehearsal session, the entire band jammed up a tune together, to which Joe put a lyric loosely inspired by Paul and Topper's recent run-in with the police over the Pigeon Shooting Incident. 'Guns on the Roof' became the first Clash song to receive a four-way writing credit. It's unremarkable in itself, being for the most part – like 'Clash City Rockers' before it – a variant on the Who's 'I Can't Explain' riff, but it indicated that Paul and Topper would be ready to take part in the writing process in future. Like Mick, Topper had long been able to play guitar and piano as well as drums, and could take an overview of the way a song's musical elements might fit together. Paul, always the least musical person in the band, had come on considerably over the last year. Having worked hard on his bass playing, he had begun to hear music rather than play patterns by rote to order, and was now able to devise most, if not all, of his own bass lines. He also showed some interest in bashing out a few basic rockabilly chord progressions on Joe's guitar. In Chris Salewicz's Joe Strummer biography, *Redemption Song* (2006), Gaby Salter recalled Joe tabling the motion to introduce a collective group credit for new songs around this time. When it became clear Mick would once again be writing most of the new tunes for the album, and that Joe would be coming up with most of the lyrics, though, they thought better of the more democratic credit, and decided to stick with Strummer-Jones.

By spring 1979, Joe was writing in notebooks, drafting and redrafting over successive pages. He still found his best ideas came to him in contemplative moments, often late at night. 'I write from line to line,' he told *Melody Maker* in 1988. 'If I get to line four and find I've gone on to another subject completely, I have to go back, otherwise it would just be completely indecipherable. It really annoys me because I write in a flood. I write the sort of thing that comes to you when you're lying in bed thinking.' In 1980 he told *Musician*'s Vic Garbarini, 'I find that when I write a really good song, it's a blur in my mind when

I actually wrote it. I know the song exists, because I can play it for my friends, but I just can't remember what happened between thinking of the idea for the song and finally playing it for my friends. Something happened that I don't remember.' Late-night lateral thinking and subconscious connections would be a particular feature of his lyrics for *London Calling*, with many of the dramatic jump cuts from subject to subject surviving through to the final draft.

As quoted in Pennie Smith's Clash photo book *Before and After* (1980), Strummer's Law is: 'To get output, you must have input.' The musical input was all the music the Clash members had listened to and played, not just recently, but all their lives to date. The lyrical input was what had happened to the band and in the world around them during the year so far, in the period roughly spanning the beginning of the Winter of Discontent and the advent of the Nuclear Winter of Thatcherism. It included the books and films, and sex and drugs, the American tour, *Rude Boy*, Sid's death, losing homes and girlfriends, gaining homes and girlfriends, the tussles with CBS, depression, defiance, hard times, consumerism, the rise of the Right, the response of the Left, and the End of the World. Topical though this raw information was, it also allowed Joe to disappear down wormholes to explore connections in different times and places.

'I personally like a pokey lyric, because unless there's something really good about it, it bores me to hear about jealousy and hetero-sexual complaining songs,' Joe, who could have been channelling Bernie Rhodes, told *Melody Maker*'s Chris Bohn in December 1979. 'I prefer a lyric covered in barbed wire.' He also said he hated lyrics that just stated the obvious. Since the disappointment of *Give 'Em Enough Rope*, Joe had been doing a lot of thinking about his craft, and the processes involved. His lyrics for *London Calling* represented a significant development. While retaining the punk-era poke, Joe relaxed his internal self-censor enough to let his pre-Clash Beat lyrical flow and more of his offbeat sense of humour through. In so doing, he found something that sounded more than ever like his authentic voice. While not in any superficial way derivative of the work of Bob Dylan in the mid-Sixties, his new lyrics did have a similar quality, in both senses of that word.

'I just listened to a lot of music fanatically from a young age,' is how Mick Jones explained how he came up with tunes to the team behind the *Q Classic* Clash special in 2005. 'I do it naturally, but I must have worked out what those people did. When you're writing music, you start with nothing, then you do something, then that tells you where to go.' 'I would sing my parts first,' he told *Guitar World*'s Matthew Caws in 1995. 'That's how I made sure they were melodic. I'd listen for a while, hum a tune and then have a go at it . . . A lot of the music I was into was from the Sixties, and Pop Art was the visual side of that period. I think if you relate to music in a visual sense, it's easier to cross boundaries.' From May to July 1979, this happened both home alone at Simon Close and at Vanilla.

'This is when we worked best together: two heads better than one,' Joe told *Uncut*'s Gavin Martin in 1999. 'Unless you're superhuman like Bob Dylan – people like that are on another level as far as I'm concerned – then you need a team. One guy's expertise comes in when the other's falls short. You up the ante, challenge each other.' This was such a dynamic process that Mick had to admit to *Q Classic* that he didn't 'remember the particulars' of who wrote what.

The memories of the surviving band members, and of Johnny Green, are also fuzzy about the order in which the new songs came. Mick thinks 'Rudie Can't Fail' was first. Though it's probably too neat, it's tempting to presume that all the early songs were those most obviously derived from playing the cover versions: 'Rudie Can't Fail' clearly betrays the influence of late Sixties reggae, Bo Diddley and 'I Fought the Law'; 'Hateful' is also set to a Bo Diddley beat; 'I'm Not Down' sounds like an answer song to the Beatles' 'I'm Down'; 'Lover's Rock' does just what it says on the tape-box label; and, likewise, 'Jimmy Jazz' came about because Topper wanted to play something jazzy.

The two new songs that were most blatantly derivative of cover versions would not make it to the album at all. Mick's solo composition 'Lonesome Me' has a different tune to Don Gibson's 'Oh, Lonesome Me' (1968) – as covered by long-time Jones favourite Neil Young on *After the Gold Rush* (1970) – but it does share a genre (late-Fifties-style country), a mood (maudlin), a lyrical subject (his baby done left him), and a title and chorus refrain . . . the last two being perhaps a tip of the Stetson too many. Similarly, the Clash came up with their own musical backing for the reggae number they named 'Where You Gonna Go (Soweto)?', but Joe's lyric-in-progress draws heavily upon 'Fire in Soweto' by Sonny Okosun . . . and, again, the title kind of gives the game away.

If it were still possible to dispute that the band wrote the songs collectively, then it was no longer possible to deny that the rehearsal room arrangements were a genuine group effort. And that, in itself, was a new way of working. Mick – formerly the sole musical director – would later describe it as an 'organic' process. The band members wouldn't just determine their own parts, but would also propose styles and refinements to the others. There was now three guys' expertise coming in when the other guys fell short, upping the ante and challenging each other. 'On some numbers, we'd say, "Let's do it reggae-style," or "Let's do it rockabilly," or in whatever style,' Paul Simonon told Adam Sweeting in 2004. 'I suppose that was probably the beginning of our opening up as musicians and working as a group, because everybody had their own idea, as a group does, and things went one way in the verse and maybe another way in the chorus.' All four musicians' influences could sometimes come out in the same song.

The Clash seldom concentrated on one composition exclusively all the way to completion. They would only persevere so long as ideas were coming. As soon as they got stuck or bored, they would take a break, play another cover or oldie, or start in on something else. Which is not to insinuate that they lacked focus or stamina: but after working with Sandy Pearlman, they knew it was healthier to keep it fresh rather than keep on banging it into the ground. Whether brought in nearly whole, or derived from jams, some tunes didn't get further then instrumentals at this stage, including the never-completed 'Walking the Slidewalk' – musically very similar to 'Where You Gonna Go (Soweto)?' – and 'Working and Waiting', 'Up-Toon' (aka 'Canalside Walk'), and 'Paul's Tune', the last three of which would receive their lyrics later. (When they became, respectively, 'Clampdown', 'The Right Profile', and 'The Guns of Brixton'.)

Within a month of the Clash moving into Vanilla, the band began discussions with Rock Against Racism (RAR) about doing something to benefit the Southall Defence Fund, relating to the riot following the National Front march there in April 1979. RAR set up two benefit shows on consecutive nights at the Rainbow Theatre in Finsbury Park. The first – on 13 July 1979 – was to be headlined by Pete Townshend, who also volunteered the loan of the Who's PA. The Clash were to headline the second night.

The Who connection was to prove significant for other reasons. Although the Clash had been playing together on a daily basis since early May, they had not played live since the *Alright Now* TV show in early March. As well as being performance-rusty, they were conscious that their UK fans were starting to feel neglected. And they were also keen to try out some of their new material in front of an audience. It was decided to schedule a couple of low-key London shows as warm-ups for the Rainbow gig. The Who's long-serving soundman Bob Pridden, in charge of the Who-funded equipment rental company ML Executives, agreed to supply the PA at a knock-down price.

The Clash wanted an audience to hear their new material, but they also wanted to hear it themselves, and to be able to present it to CBS. Mick had recorded rough demos for *Give 'Em Enough Rope* at Rehearsal Rehearsals in January 1978 on his own reel-to-reel recorder; a likely victim of the February 1979 burglary at his flat. Bob Pridden was asked to advise on the best method of recording the Vanilla rehearsals. He proposed a TEAC 4-track. Baker took the responsibility for reading the manual and operating the controls, so that Mick would be able to concentrate on playing and arranging. As soon as the band got a song – or, in the absence of a lyric, a tune – into some kind of shape, they would record it live, and then add a couple of overdubs where necessary. 'Having tapes, you could listen to them back away from the environment of the rehearsal studio and ponder over how it was going, then come back with a new adjustment or improvement,' Paul told Adam Sweeting. Which describes what had previously been Mick's – and was now apparently the whole band's – working method with demos. 'It was all being made up there in the room,' says Johnny Green. 'It wasn't a case of Joe or Mick walking in and saying, "Here's a song. I'll tell you what I want." They were very laboured sessions in terms of actually building the song up.'

The Clash's time in Vanilla is usually characterised as highly prolific. The fact that the Clash would end up making a double album perhaps gives the wrong impression about the quantity of new music they produced there. The Clash came up with 16 songs during rehearsals, 13 of which were ultimately considered strong enough for *London Calling*. Over the three months the band spent in Vanilla, then, they wrote roughly five songs per month, and kept roughly four per month: slightly less than one per week. It's hardly a flood.

In the three years of their existence prior to the Vanilla sessions, the Clash had written just 32 songs they considered worthy of release: a strike rate of considerably less than one per month. But that's misleading. Six of those songs were written before the band formed in June 1976; 12 in the first flurry of activity between then and February 1977, before the Clash had any recording commitments or much in the way of live commitments. After that, when demands on their time increased, Joe and Mick wrote just four songs between tours over the summer of 1977; maybe as many as eight during their 10-day holiday in Jamaica in November 1977; and the remaining couple (one of them the communal effort) between then and late spring 1978; since when, as already stated, nothing. Statistics can be soulless, but these facts and figures give the lie to the notion that Joe and Mick were a writing machine, regularly bashing out a song to order in half an hour, or even during the course of a day.

Far more important than quantity is quality. At Vanilla, the Clash did escape the broom closet, did manage to slip free from the limited and limiting time-and-place-bound angry-young-man stylings of UK punk, and into the timeless, universal sounds and spirit of musics like reggae, rock'n'roll, rockabilly, R&B, blues, country and folk, without completely losing sight of their original incarnation. In the process, they invented post-punk roots music.

While the Clash were weighing up potential venues for the Clash's pre-Rainbow benefit warm-up gigs, Paul Simonon remembered the Notre Dame Hall at 6 Leicester Place, just off the north side of Leicester Square. Scene of the Sex Pistols' warm-up gig for the Anarchy tour in November 1976, it was also – something that perhaps had more sentimental resonance – the scene of Sid Vicious's first gig with that band on 21 March 1977. Nothing like as grand as its Parisian namesake, Notre Dame was a church hall connected to the Notre Dame French Catholic Church, but only dated from 1953, when it was erected on the site of an earlier building destroyed during the Blitz. It had the benefit of being centrally located, and – even more importantly, as it was hired out by priests rather than hard-headed rock venue managers – it was cheap. The Clash booked it for two nights, 5 and 6 July 1979.

Everything about the Clash's Notre Dame gigs was arranged on a low budget and in a rush by the still self-managed band . . . and was appropriately attributed to Panic Promotions. Support acts for the shows were drummed up from among the Clash's acquaintance. The Mo-dettes had been formed by Kate Korus, formerly of the Slits, the girlfriend of former 101ers roadie Boogie, and still a resident at Joe's most recently vacated squat at 34 Daventry Street. The Low Numbers were managed by Terry McQuade. As well as supplying the gear, Bob Pridden offered to do the front-of-house sound. In punk tradition, Joe himself designed the photocopied collage flyer the band used to advertise the gigs.

It was left to a small number of these flyers, which the band, Baker and Johnny themselves distributed around the Camden Town and Notting Hill areas, and the word of mouth they generated, to publicise the shows. The 600 who turned up for the first night were treated to a mixture of established Clash rabble-rousers and new numbers, and the larger second-night audience got much the same. In total, eight new songs received their live debuts over the two nights: 'London Calling', 'Hateful' (its lyrics pinned to a microphone during soundchecks), 'Rudie Can't Fail', 'Death or Glory', 'I'm Not Down', 'Lover's Rock', 'Jimmy Jazz', and the cover of 'Revolution Rock'. A recording of the first night has emerged on bootlegs.

Journalists Chris Bohn of *Melody Maker* and Dave McCullough and Garry Bushell of *Sounds* were among those who turned up for that first night. Although Chris Bohn was more open to the 'broadening of the Clash's horizons', he did add that others might see the change as a 'dilution of their initial commitment'. And in assessing the new songs, he thought 'Hateful' 'strident and excitable', 'I'm Not Down' and 'Death or Glory' to be not particularly inspiring 'traditional Clash rockers', despite the electric performance of the latter and, although he felt 'Lover's Rock' and 'Revolution Rock' were 'appealing eulogies to reggae song styling' found both 'appallingly trite, lyrically speaking'.

The other pair preferred their punk rock edgy, and Bushell liked it ultra-basic. They were concerned about the extent of the Clash's move away from their original template, and pushed hard for an interview. It took place with Dave McCullough following the soundcheck on the second day – Bushell had to leave early – and resulted in a three-page *Sounds* cover feature. In an edgy discussion, during which tempers occasionally flared, the Clash made the point that they couldn't just keep on rewriting 'White Riot' – too many other bands were already doing that – and stressed that punk was about change rather than conformity. McCullough allowed himself to be swayed to some extent by Joe's impassioned defence, but the interview was tacked on to the end of the joint gig review he and Bushell had already filed, and the overall tone of the piece was dubious, even alarmist, about the latest Clash developments.

The *Sounds* journalists didn't know the names of the new songs on the first night, but as they responded to them in the order in which they were played – and helpfully referenced the other Clash songs they recognised in between – their verdicts were that 'I'm Not Down' was 'not too earth-shattering', while 'Death or Glory' was better, being a 'bit harder'. 'London Calling' was good, being 'punchy', but the chorus of 'Rudie Can't Fail' was a 'direct retread of '(White Man) In Hammersmith Palais'. (They appear to have assumed that 'Lover's Rock' was part of the same song, because it isn't mentioned at all.) 'Jimmy Jazz' was better, being 'slower, but catchy', but the 'nice fast start' to 'Hateful' was let down because 'it don't seem like they mean it', while 'Revolution Rock' was just more 'dull reggae'. Eight new songs is a lot for anyone to take in at once in a live situation, and their response was knee-jerk stuff. Hearing the songs again at the sound-check the following day, the duo admitted they sounded tighter and fiercer, and, finally picking up the titles, McCullough described 'London Calling' as 'best of the lot . . . ominous, pounding', but the *Sounds* writers felt duty-bound to be true to the general feeling in the room the night before: 'The new songs are naff. The Clash have run out of ideas.'

Coming so soon after Ian Penman's trashing of *The Cost of Living* in the *NME* – which record McCullough admitted he hadn't liked, either – this amounted to a grand slam vote of no confidence in the new material from the UK inkys, which could not help but worry the band. It was most painful to Joe Strummer and Mick Jones, who had read the music press religiously since their early teens, and saw it not only as a potential shaper of wider public attitudes, but also an indicator of those attitudes. 'They paid a great deal of attention to what the music press said about them,' says Johnny Green. 'It came to a head with that very long, very serious discussion at the back of the hall with Bushell and his mate. They were basically saying, "This is all shit, and you've had it!" The band were very upset by that. Not that they cared about Bushell, but it was the fact that a writer with a reputation would say that about them. That conversation carried on among the band for a good few days afterwards.'

At the following week's performance at the Southall Defence Fund gig at the much larger Rainbow, the Clash still played five of their new compositions, and also gave their version of 'Brand New Cadillac' its live debut. On this occasion, Paul Morley filed a review for the *NME*. He praised the Clash for rejecting established music business practices, observing that 'they operate with a strange value on the perimeters'. The lack of detail about the performance and the new songs – described as 'masterpieces, but then you've probably learned not to trust me by now' – came over as a little detached, but at least it was positive. It was enough to convince the Clash to keep moving forward.

The recording of demos continued through the first weeks of July 1979, in amongst rehearsals for the live shows. While their prime function was to let the band hear their own work, they were not the only interested parties. A delegation from CBS went down to Vanilla to hear them. 'That was the Americans,' says Muff Winwood. 'It was a big jolly for them, to come over on bloody Concorde. They often did that. There would probably be four or five of them, and they'd go and see four or five different artists in a four- or five-day stint. We would have set it up for them and then let them get on with it.'

Once the tapes had been played, the Epic representatives were invited over the road for a game of football. After a few puzzled glances were exchanged, they accepted the challenge. 'The band treated them like dirt,' says Johnny Green. 'Oh, they were really beaten at football. Clobbered severely! I mean, Crocker was told to go in hard. It was pathetic. In retrospect, they should have said "Bollocks! We're record company executives. Why are we trying to prove we're one of the lads?" It was such a bizarre thing!' 'Often those visits were completely useless,' says Muff. 'But I suppose in a way they then went back to the people who had got to work the new album in America, and talked it up to them.' In different circumstances, this mass roughing-up disguised as a sporting event could well have been another Clash own goal with Epic, but the band knew their American career had been firmly back on track as soon as Epic had decided to release the amended version of *The Clash*, due out that very month.

In late July, the Clash left Vanilla – their home for one of the most creative periods in their career – to record *London Calling* in Wessex, back in charge of their own destiny.

3 Highway to Highbury

The Three Rs (ii): Recording

The recording of *Give 'Em Enough Rope* by producer Sandy Pearlman and his regular chief engineer Corky Stasiak had taken around two and a half months, spread out over the best part of a year, involved four different 24-track studios, each of them more expensive than the last, and had ended up accounting for a significant proportion of the band's total paper debt to CBS as of the end of 1978. *The Clash*, by way of extreme contrast, had been recorded over three consecutive long weekends in CBS's own 16-track Studio 3 in Whitfield Street by original Clash soundman Micky Foote and junior in-house engineer Simon Humphrey at a total cost of just £4,000.

Listening to the playbacks of the Vanilla demos of the band's new material, and believing them to be raw but full of energy, Joe Strummer came up with a plan to simultaneously sidestep huge studio bills, minimise the Clash's dependency on CBS front-money, and give the band's fans even more value for money than usual. 'We've got some crazy ideas like, some LPs – like a Bee Gees LP – will cost hundreds of thousands of pounds to make, so it's gonna cost six quid an album soon,' he told the *NME*'s Charles Shaar Murray in June 1979. 'Suppose a group came along and decided to make a 16 track LP on two TEACs, which dramatically reduces studio costs? Suppose you presented that tape to the record company and told 'em that it cost just these few quid to make. So, even when they've added their fucking mark-ups, you can still get a fucking LP for two or three quid. Why can't that be cost-related?' The Clash could produce their own album, and record it at Vanilla on twinned 4-track TEAC machines for no more than the expense of hiring the rehearsal room and the recording equipment and buying the actual tape.

Mick Jones has since laughed off the possibility that this was ever seriously considered. But even following *London Calling*'s release in December 1979, Joe was still talking about it as a missed opportunity to *Melody Maker*'s Chris Bohn. His favourite records – as he would later admit – tended to date from pre-1965, and were mostly live or near-live takes recorded on between one and four tracks, when what really mattered was whether or not you could capture an expressive performance. Which is not to say it had to be ultra-primitive. Even in 1967 the Beatles had recorded *Sgt. Pepper's Lonely Hearts Club Band*, an album that at the time had been considered the pinnacle of pop-musical sophistication and invention – and over a decade later, was still rated one of the best ever made – on a pair of twinned 4-tracks. Admittedly, these were studio machines, but portastudio development was coming on in leaps and bounds. The TEAC portastudio the Clash used in Vanilla was brought in on the advice of the technologically savvy Bob Pridden. That – and Baker needing to read the manual before operating it – indicates new technology that, paradoxically, was right up even the most Luddite member of the Clash's cobbled street: 1979 was the year that Tascam introduced the TEAC 144, which offered high-quality recording using standard cassette tape.

It could be done. But perhaps not by Baker and the Clash, at least on the evidence of the demos recorded at Vanilla, and included on a separate disc as part of the *London Calling* 25th Anniversary Edition package as *The Vanilla Tapes*. Although the CD booklet notes described them as 'clean, bright recordings', it would have been a little closer to the truth to characterise them as rough and ready, patchy, occasionally muffled and generally of little better than bootleg standard. 'You can't even say, "Oh, look how this turned into that, isn't that fascinating?"' long-time Clash supporter Greil Marcus told Oliver Hall of *Perfect Sound Forever* in 2005. 'Or even, "God, this doesn't sound like it ever could become anything, but it did!" No, you just can't listen to that crap, it sounds so bad.' As Marcus had spent lengthy periods listening intently to Bob Dylan and the Band's 1967 home demos – the famous Basement Tapes (not the album released in 1975 as *The Basement Tapes*) – before writing his appreciative study *Invisible Republic* (1998), his tolerance of lo-fi is fairly high. Contrary to what he says about their value as documents of the songs' evolution, though, several of the Vanilla demos do provide a fascinating insight into how the Clash got from initial inspiration to final article.

Even Joe recognised that his alternative recording option was doomed. 'To do that, we knew that we'd have to pay the recording costs ourselves,' he admitted to Chris Bohn. 'Otherwise CBS would have told us to fuck off, and sent us another list of debts when we asked them to put it out cheap.' The twinned TEAC plan was never even put forward to the record company, but the Clash did make it clear that they wanted to choose their own producer, someone who was sympathetic to their music and their production values. Last time, Epic had been in the driving seat, making it a condition of an American release for *Rope* that the Clash use a producer with whom they were familiar and in whose track record they had confidence, and the American label had even provided a shortlist. In 1979, had anyone drawn up a similar list of candidates based on such criteria as consistency, reliability, responsibility and bankability, not only would Guy Stevens have been nowhere near the top, he wouldn't have been on it at all. Unless it was overleaf, underscored and circled with red biro, under the separate heading 'Avoid at all costs'. And it's not as though the Clash were innocent of his reputation.

Guy Stevens liked to say he was never the same again after hearing Jerry Lee Lewis's 'Whole Lotta Shakin' Goin' On' (1957) when he was 14. He was expelled from school just a short while later, and devoted much of his time thereafter to gig-going and record collecting. By 1963 Guy had become the raving DJ at premiere mod hangout the Scene Club in Soho's Ham Yard. He sent off to America for the latest sounds and had the best R&B record collection in the country. In those days, R&B was a catch-all term that could be extended to cover rock'n'roll, soul, proto-funk, some jazz and ska and even folk blues. A man of eclectic tastes, Guy revered Chuck Berry and Bob Dylan in particular. Between 1963 and 1965 he made recommendations, played records and compiled tapes that provided significant parts – and in some cases, all – of the early live repertoires of the Rolling Stones, the Yardbirds, the Animals, the Small Faces, the Who, the Spencer Davis Group, the Paramounts and the VIPs. Among others.

In 1964, as head of the UK branch of the Chuck Berry Fan Club, Guy put pressure on Chuck's record label bosses to help get him out of jail – where he had languished since 1959 – and was heavily involved in promoting his music in the UK. He proselytised the music he loved via the pages of the *NME* and *Record Mirror*, and wrote many record sleeve notes; including those for the Pye *This is Chuck Berry* EP purchased by a 13-year-old Joe Strummer while on holiday in Tehran. In 1965, Guy was asked to head the UK branch of Sue Records as an offshoot of Chris Blackwell's independent distribution company, Island – itself set up to sell ska in the UK – with the intention of licensing the best of American music. 'I wanted everything to be on Sue,' Guy told the *NME*'s Charles Shaar Murray in 1979. 'I wanted Bob Dylan to be on Sue.' So enthusiastic was Guy's spending spree that it nearly bankrupted Island.

Sue was shelved in early 1967, but as Guy had already shaped British pop music once, his good taste couldn't be denied. He became an A&R man for Island, which was about to follow the trend of the times away from genre dance singles into rock band albums, a direction that Chris Blackwell's management of the Spencer Davis Band, and Guy's own production of Island's 1966 signing the VIPs had helped signpost. Guy continued to write sleeve notes for Island albums like *Club Ska '67* and the following year's *Guy Stevens' Testament of Rock and Roll*, which he also compiled, a truly barnstorming collection of not-too-obvious Fifties and early Sixties classics. In those days it was rare for a club DJ-cum-music writer-cum-record licenser-cum-A&R man-cum-novice producer to have his name in front of a record's title, and it gives some indication of Guy's status.

In summer 1966 Keith Reid had shown Chris Blackwell a screed of Dylanesque lyrics. Blackwell palmed him off on the Dylanophile Guy, who teamed him up with Gary Brooker, former pianist for the recently disbanded Paramounts, urging them to collaborate on songs and, ultimately, form a band. 'So the three of us – me, Keith and Guy – used to sit around and say, "Well, what do we need, what do we want?"' says Gary. In late 1966 they were listening to a lot of Stax soul round at Guy's flat at 23c Gloucester Avenue, Camden Town – a popular party venue with Guy spinning the records and enthusing loudly over the top of them – and noticed the common ground between that sound and Bob Dylan's recent hook-up with the Band. 'Generally speaking, the two keyboards – the piano with the Hammond organ – was an important part of the concept behind the band,' says Gary. 'The reason was that it had always been a good sound, from Booker T. and the MGs via the Young Rascals to Dylan and the Band, and it also gave you a lot of power.'

Guy called the new band Procol Harum after the pedigree name of a friend's cat, and even (admittedly inadvertently) came up with the title for 'A Whiter Shade of Pale'. Sometime before the end of March 1967, Guy Stevens produced a full band demo of the song at Marquee studios, and offered it to Chris Blackwell . . . but as he was preoccupied helping Steve Winwood assemble a new band to record for Island as Traffic, and nothing happened. Shortly afterwards, Procol Harum left Guy and took their single to Decca's Deram label. Over the summer of 1967 'A Whiter Shade of Pale' became a worldwide monster hit, the defining single of the Summer of Love. Guy was devastated that the band he had put together and directed – very much the way Bernie Rhodes would put together and direct the Clash a decade later – had gone on to such glory without him. He would later blame Chris Blackwell for the missed opportunity, but the fault really lay closer to home. Although he'd discovered speed comparatively recently, he'd quickly become an enthusiastic drug-taker, which he advertised by hanging around with the Stones' notoriously dissolute Brian Jones. It had brought Guy to the attention of the police. 'Guy went away around that period,' says Gary Brooker. 'I think it was a bust. He had been going off the rails, and he was getting a little bit unpredictable.'

Guy had produced and Brian played on a project built around acid-imagery poster and record cover design team Hapshash and the Coloured Coat, which resulted in the jamming'n'chanting jug band trippy concept album *Hapshash and the Coloured Coat Featuring the Human Host and the Heavy Metal Kids*. Bernie Rhodes's friends and former flat-mates John Pearse and Mickey Finn were also involved. It was not a hit. The second half of 1967 was overshadowed by Procol Harum's success, and Guy succumbed more and more often to Lost Weekend binges. Following his professional disappointment came two personal ones in fairly rapid succession: his beloved massive, rare and irreplaceable record collection was stolen, and he had a nervous breakdown. He left Island for a while.

In April 1968 Chris Blackwell threw Guy a lifeline, inviting him to produce the debut album by a bluesy young guitar band named Free. They were strong-willed enough to resist Guy's attempt to rename them the Heavy Metal Kids – recycling a name from the previous year – but did let him call the album *Tons of Sobs*. He recorded them live in the studio, without separation, and nailed the album in just a week. That summer, though, Guy was again arrested on drugs charges. Because it was the second time in little over a year, he was sentenced to a year in Wormwood Scrubs, of which he served eight months. Free went their own way to glory without him.

Guy's release in spring 1969 found him back at Island. In prison, he had obsessed about replicating the success of the Band That Got Away with a Stevens-named and produced band featuring two keyboards – organ and piano – playing R&B-influenced music with, preferably, Dylanesque words. The R&B element would now be more in a contemporary Rolling Stones vein: music that referenced all Guy's favourites, from Stax to Jerry Lee Lewis to Chuck Berry. His determination was reinforced by the death of Brian Jones on 3 July. He signed a Hereford band named Silence, largely – he later admitted – because he was impressed by the commitment they demonstrated in hauling Verden Allen's heavy Hammond C-3 organ up the stairs to the rehearsal room. His need to meddle with line-ups now bordered on a compulsion, a trait Bernie Rhodes would later exhibit. He demoted vocalist Stan Tippins to road manager, and held auditions for a Dylanesque writer-singer-pianist, hiring the seasoned Ian Hunter – a bass player faking it – to fill that role. Guy renamed the band Mott the Hoople – after a novel he had read in prison, and set out to manage and produce them to stardom.

Initially, Guy required the band to play endless cover versions by or in the vein of Dylan and the Stones. It succeeded in getting the band, especially Ian Hunter, writing along those lines. After just a week and a half of rehearsals, before they had even played a gig, Guy took them into the studio to record *Mott the Hoople* in five days of sessions spread over three months. 'I used to stack up chairs during Mott sessions and then keep knocking 'em over to get 'em at it,' he told the *NME*'s Roy Carr in 1979. The album was released in November 1969, with Guy re-titling some songs and even designing the cover, as he would continue to do for the band.

The second Mott album, *Mad Shadows*, was released in September 1970. Guy had given away its original title, *Sticky Fingers*, to the Rolling Stones. According to Campbell Devine's 1998 Mott the Hoople biography *All the Young Dudes*, although sessions took ten days over five months, four songs – of the album's total of seven – were culled from the final day's marathon studio session. Guy cajoled Ian into extemporising a lyric for one song on the spot. The previous year, Guy had been an effusive and confidence-building cheerleader, but his mood was no longer upbeat and encouraging: he was using lots of speed, going through another dark period, and seemingly intent on taking the band with him. He mixed the record on speed, too, which distorted his perception of the sound balance.

Thanks to their live schedule, Mott had evolved into a powerful rock'n'roll band. Shortly after the second album's release, Guy recorded a concert for a proposed live album, but the band had tired of his mercurial behaviour. He had recently tried on separate occasions to fire both Ian Hunter and Verden Allen, and Mott turned the tables and told him his services were no longer required. Their third album, *Wildlife*, was largely self-produced, and largely unremarkable. In August 1971 they began work on a fourth, at Island's new Basing Street studio, but gradually lost confidence in what they were doing. With recording almost complete, they invited Guy to take over. Less than fresh from his latest binge, he demanded payment upfront, insisted the band dump everything they'd laboured over so far, and booked a few days in the studio in late September. He and his favourite engineer turned up for work a day late with Zorro masks, water pistols and a crate of booze, setting the tone for proceedings. Deciding the whole album would be recorded live in one take, Guy decided to further liven matters up by leading the band in trashing the studio, piling up the furniture and fittings in the centre and setting them on fire. The result was called *Brain Capers*.

Although Mott were supposed to be Guy's masterpiece, the four albums they recorded for Island were of decidedly mixed quality, and were all commercial flops. His charges lost patience with him again, before disbanding early in 1972. Whereupon David Bowie persuaded them to have another go, made them a gift of 'All the Young Dudes' and more than a little of his glam image, and in turn took much of the credit for their chart breakthrough with CBS during 1972-4.

Guy's own career stalled at this point. Following the end of his association with Island, his consumption of booze and speed increased as his ability to cope with them decreased. In a reversal of the usual pattern, in late 1974 he was brought in to 'save' the debut album by a new band called the Winkies, formed by expatriate Canadian Philip Rambow and an early fixture on the London pub rock scene with an atypical glam-flash look that had also brought them to the attention of Mick Jones. Signed to Chrysalis, they had already begun and abandoned at least one set of sessions. *The Winkies*, released in spring 1975, includes a Bob Dylan cover, sounds a little like glorified demos, and a little like the Rolling Stones and Mott the Hoople. In a 2004 *Observer Music Magazine* poll, Mick Jones listed it as his third favourite British album of all time.

Formerly seen as a madcap eccentric with a musical sixth sense, Guy was well on the way to being considered a liability. Nonetheless, in 1975 Warner Brothers' Mo Ostin put him on a retainer. Fans of both Free and Mott, Mick Jones's musically-minded contemporaries from Brixton's Strand School remained largely blind to the change in his status, continuing to think of him as one of the main architects of the music they loved. They would periodically attempt to woo Guy with their own latest bands. In mid-1975, when two of them, Kelvin Blacklock and John Brown, found themselves back together in a group called Little Queenie with Mick Jones, Kelvin again appealed to Guy. He took the band on, but could not resist meddling. First came a name change, to Violent Luck. Next came a transparent attempt to remake the band in the image of Mott the Hoople, which involved replacing one of the guitarists with a keyboard player. That guitarist was Mick Jones. Guy recorded three songs with the rest of the band as demos for Warners, one of them being a Mott the Hoople cover . . . and he brought in Mott's Verden Allen to play keyboards. When no record deal materialised, Violent Luck and Guy went their separate ways, and the band were subsequently swept away in the punk deluge.

In late 1976 Bernie Rhodes approached Guy and asked him to produce the Clash's demos. He listened to the band playing 'White Riot' at Rehearsals, and approved. The band subsequently visited him at his mother's flat in Swiss Cottage, his marriage having broken up some time before. Guy started pouring invective upon Led Zeppelin's monstrous ego-fest of a movie *The Song Remains the Same*, getting so excited in the process that he picked up the album and flung it across the room . . . hitting Joe Strummer in the eye.

In November 1976 the Clash went into Polydor Studios in Stratford Place to record five songs with Guy. Demos they might have been, but Guy didn't deal in half-measures. He started off by living up to all the stories the band had heard about him, encouraging and urging, raving and yelling, driving the band to give it their all. 'It was fantastic when we were doing it: he was really inciting us,' Mick told Kris Needs of *ZigZag* the following April. 'But when it came down to the mixing, it was a bit untogether.' Wary of the studio environment, and self-conscious about his voice, Joe didn't enjoy recording the vocals quite so much: the non-musical Guy's only criteria for the music was that it be exciting; but being a fan of Chuck Berry and Bob Dylan, he believed the words were of vital importance, and should be enunciated clearly. 'So I did and it sounded like Matt Monroe,' Joe told the *NME*'s Tony Parsons in 1977. 'I thought, "I'm never doing that again!" To me, our music is like Jamaican stuff: if they can't hear it, they're not supposed to hear it.'

Polydor A&R man Chris Parry and engineer Vic Coppersmith-Heaven – who would subsequently team up to produce the Jam – found the producer hard to fathom. 'Guy was a bit all over the place,' says Chris Parry. 'It was difficult to tell if he was pissed or not, really. I think the band were a bit disappointed. I got Vic in to oversee the session.' Before long, it became all too easy to tell how inebriated Guy was, and Coppersmith-Heaven had to complete the recordings on his own. Polydor prevaricated over the admittedly not very impressive results for a fatal two months, and in late January 1977 the Clash signed to CBS instead. At that time, Bernie told *Melody Maker*, 'We picked Guy Stevens because we wanted a nutcase to produce the band. But there are different kinds of nutcase, and it didn't work out with him.' When the band began recording *The Clash* shortly afterwards, Guy was not offered a second chance. Upon the album's release that April, Joe explained how Clash soundman Micky Foote had come to be producer. 'We tried the famous ones,' he told Tony Parsons. 'They were all too pissed to work.' At that time, Guy was the only other producer they had worked with.

So why, with another two and a half years of hard living on the clock – he had not stayed sober, had rarely worked, and certainly not on anything high profile – should Guy Stevens suddenly be considered the prime candidate to get the best out of the Clash in the studio for their make-or-break third album? In the 1991 *Clash On Broadway* booklet notes, Mick Jones claimed that Guy might have been his idea, but by the time of *The Last Testament* documentary filmed by Don Letts to accompany the release of the 25th Anniversary Edition of *London Calling*, he had revised that statement. Paul Simonon has since also admitted that the person who proposed Guy as producer was none other than ousted Clash manager Bernie Rhodes. The financial dispute had been all but resolved – basically, the band agreed to pay him the £25,000 he said they owed him – and Bernie still had the Clash's ear via Joe.

Bernie had been genuinely disgusted by the lengthy, meticulous and expensive over-production afforded *Give 'Em Enough Rope*. Whatever his faults, no one could accuse Guy of hanging about. His philosophy had always been to slam an energetic live take down as quickly as possible, gussy it up if absolutely necessary, throw on a vocal, and get it out. That recording approach was very much in the spirit of *The Vanilla Tapes*. Joe might not have been able to bring Bernie back, but the next best thing was to follow Bernie's advice, and bring Guy back. 'I think something dies in the music when everything is so strait-laced, with accountants monitoring every move,' Joe told *Rolling Stone* in 1989. Asked separately, both Bill Price and Wessex's assistant engineer Jerry Green say they got the distinct impression that – of all the band members – it was Joe who had most wanted Guy.

When they thought about it, though, both Joe *and* Mick – the band's decision makers in such matters – could find all kinds of links between their own personal tastes, the nature of the band's recent material, punk's championing of feel and immediacy over technique and perfection, and Guy's contribution to the history of British music. Guy was legendary, and Joe wanted the Clash to be legendary, too. Mick could be tardy, moody and self-centred, but he was also fiercely loyal. Despite having been sacked from Little Queenie/Violent Luck by Guy, he still thought of him as one of the all-time great inspirational music business figures. Mick's hero worship of Ian Hunter had led to him inviting the former Mott frontman to both of the Clash's previous album sessions, eager to receive what he called 'the blessing'. Similarly, he believed Guy's presence at the third could confer something magical upon the Clash. In the end, nobody in the band was against the choice. 'It was a united decision,' says Johnny Green. '"Let's go for the maverick."'

Joe volunteered to find Guy, and later recounted the tale of his search often enough to make it mythical. He knew the producer frequented the pubs off Oxford Street, and worked his way through them systematically until he found him propping up a bar. 'I went up to him and tapped him on the shoulder, he looked around, and it was like son-finding-father in one of those corny films,' Joe told Charles Shaar Murray in 1979. 'He looked up at me and said, "Have a drink."'

Understandably, Muff Winwood was aghast. He had known Guy since his days as bassist for the Spencer Davis Group, and both had joined the A&R team at Island at much the same time. Muff knew how much of a wild card Guy was even back then, and – like all music business insiders – was aware of how badly things had gone for him since. Staring almost certain disaster in the face, Muff racked his brains to come up with a damage limitation plan. And as there was no current Clash manager for him to use as a go-between, he turned to the only person that had ever been able to get through to the band.

'I'm convinced that Bernie Rhodes helped me do this,' says Muff. 'I can remember making this argument to Bernie, probably desperate, saying, "You've got to help! If they must go this mad way, then the least we can do is make it as non-dangerous as possible." I said, "If you're going to use Guy, you have to have someone in the studio that has total and utter control, because Guy will fall off the wall many, many times during the sessions."' That someone was Bill Price: Muff had worked with Bill successfully, knew the Clash had recently worked with Bill successfully, and – most importantly – knew that Bill had worked with Guy, and would not be overwhelmed by him. 'Bill agreed to do it if the album was recorded at Wessex,' says Muff. 'That was fine as far as I was concerned. I still knew there were going to be problems, but I knew if Bill was behind the controls we would get something.' 'The only people I had official discussions with on setting up the *London Calling* sessions were CBS,' says Bill. 'They were booked a little in advance. Guy's involvement came as a complete surprise to me: I only heard of it at the last minute before the sessions started.' When the arrangement was finally explained to him, it was presented as a fait accompli. 'Guy, me and Wessex were a job lot,' he says. 'CBS thought I could keep Guy under control.' CBS made Bill rather than Guy their first point of contact: it would be his responsibility to make sure the job was completed to schedule. That Bill would be as important to the process as Guy was signalled by both of them receiving a royalty – rather than just a flat fee – for working on the album. There was one more CBS pre-condition, more in hope than expectation: 'Guy agreed to stop drinking in order to get the *London Calling* gig,' says Bill.

From their own experience on the 1976 Polydor demo sessions, as well as from Ian Hunter's stories, the Clash knew that Guy was enthusiastic and committed at the start of projects but bad at finishing them, and that he was a 'vibe merchant' producer who relied upon feel and his own taste rather than in-depth musical or technical knowledge. In his own words: 'I deal in emotion.' Guy would be a motivator. He would get the Clash going on the right path . . . and Bill and Mick were capable of completing the album if and when Guy lost it. It was an acceptable compromise.

'Guy was brought down to Vanilla,' says Johnny Green. 'They made him a cassette of the songs on the portastudio, but he didn't have a tape recorder, so he said "How am I going to play that?"' Johnny had to visit 100 Baker Street and ask Peter Quinnell for £50 to buy one on Tottenham Court Road. The purchase was duly made, and Baker gave Johnny the cassette, marked *Val Doonican*, to deliver to Guy. After a few refreshing beverages, Johnny set out on the Tube, taking the Victoria Line north from Pimlico . . . and woke with a start in Seven Sisters, having missed the stop where he was supposed to change trains. He scrambled off, only to realise he'd left the cassette player, complete with cassette, on the Tube. The next day a shamefaced Johnny made up some cover story to explain the loss to the band. They were relaxed about it. Which would have been surprising if – as would be reported on more than one occasion afterwards – the *Val Doonican* tape had been the only existing copy of the Vanilla demos. Luckily, this was not the case: even the Clash weren't quite *that* lackadaisical. Johnny made another visit to Peter Quinnell, who raised an eyebrow before handing over another £50 for another tape recorder, and this time Johnny successfully delivered that and a second tape to Guy.

The Vanilla demo recordings did not emerge even on bootleg for the next 25 years, which reinforced the popular belief that the only copy of the tape had been lost on the Tube. Clash representative Kosmo Vinyl even said as much in an interview with *Vox* in 1994. Then, in February 2004 – some might say conveniently close to the 25th anniversary of *London Calling*'s release – Mick Jones cleared out the lock-up in which he had stored some of his more treasured possessions since the Eighties. Among his finds were the Vanilla demos. It was decided to include one take of each of the songs preserved on a special edition of the album to be released in time to celebrate the anniversary. There were 37 demos, including several variations of the same songs, which were whittled down to 21 tracks for *The Vanilla Tapes*. Interest at the time of release was largely directed towards the previously unreleased and – to the general public – unknown songs, *Give 'Em Enough Rope* holdover 'Heart and Mind', the instrumental 'Walking the Slidewalk', 'Lonesome Me' and 'Where You Gonna Go (Soweto)' – all four of which were attributed to 'the Clash' – and the cover of Matumbi's cover of Bob Dylan's 'The Man in Me'.

★

With the album given the go-ahead, and the recording team and studio arranged, one remaining detail needed to be sorted out before the band started work: it was clear the Clash needed proper management. Again, it seems highly likely that CBS pushed hard for this, but it's unlikely they met much resistance. The Clash had enjoyed opting out of the music business machine for the summer, but after two and a half months taking it in turns to carry the briefcase, they had also come to the realisation that it was more cumbersome than they had anticipated, and was beginning to restrict their forward movement. 'Those were heady days, when we actually sat down and talked a lot,' says Johnny Green. 'Very free-flowing conversations about money, record contracts, American tours, publicity, anything to do with the band. But I think we were all aware that we couldn't hack it on our own. There was just too much to do. The band had really wanted to manage themselves, but decisions were being put off and knocked back.'

Perhaps the best illustration of the Clash's limitations as organisers was the gig schedule, or lack of it. It was one thing arranging a couple of low-key London shows from a payphone, but neither the band nor Johnny Green had the experience and resources to sort out anything more substantial. For one reason or another, discussions about one-off shows in Europe and Cuba came to nothing, as did an invitation from the Undertones to headline a festival near Derry in Northern Ireland. The two shows the Clash did commit to shortly before commencing recording also came about through invitation rather than action on the Clash's behalf. Enthused by the band's attempt at self-sufficiency, a San Francisco acquaintance named Mo Armstrong fixed them up with a slot at the Tribal Stomp Festival, to be held on 8 September 1979 in Monterey, California, scene of one of the most feted late Sixties counter-cultural festivals. The Clash were keen to accept any opportunity to go back to America, and as the new album was due to be completed by the end of August, the timing was perfect.

Then Ian Flukes, who had booked the Sort it Out tour at the end of 1978, called and offered the Clash a last-minute support slot at the Ruisrock Festival in Turku, Finland, on 4 August 1979, as a late stand-in for Johnny Winters. The Clash were accustomed to topping the bill, and on this occasion the timing was not so good: the show was scheduled a week into the newly arranged recording sessions for the new album. Not only would appearing at the festival disrupt their flow, it would – or so it at first appeared – involve removing all the band's carefully miked-up gear and transporting it to Finland at considerable expense. On the other hand, the Clash and their trusty crew were in their usual impecunious state. The fee was negotiated up to £7,500, which meant that the Clash would be paid more than the actual headliner, Graham Parker. After a little more hustling on the phone, Johnny managed to hire some gear for the Clash in Scandinavia – from Abba, no less – which meant the Clash's own equipment could remain undisturbed in the recording studio. It would be a case of flying out over the weekend, playing, getting paid, and flying back, without losing any recording time and leaving nobody in authority any the wiser. Later that year, Joe told Chris Bohn the band agreed to play because the 'dough would pay for' the recording of London Calling at Wessex, but this was a bit fancifully Robin Hood. As usual, CBS would be picking up the tab for the Wessex sessions (which would cost far more than £7,500), the money to be deducted, like – or so it seemed – the rest of the national debt, from future Clash royalties. The fee from

Ruisrock just gave the band and crew some ready cash to live on while recording.

Epic had finally come around to the idea of an autumn tour in support of the American release of *The Clash*, and the obvious thing to do was schedule it after the Monterey show. For that, the band needed to call in the professionals. Bernie Rhodes had already thrown his hat in the ring, but he was by no means the only one pressing his suit.

Kosmo Vinyl was a London wide-boy with a mouth big enough and suit loud enough to establish that much before he was halfway through the door. He had put in time working for Keith Altham, who handled publicity for the Who, among others; acted as MC on the first Stiff records tour, featuring Elvis Costello and the Attractions and Ian Dury and the Blockheads; and gone on to work in a PR role for Dury's management team, Peter Jenner and Andrew King of Blackhill Enterprises. In summer 1979, after two years of promotion and touring, an exhausted Dury had decided to take some time off to recuperate.

Sometime around the start of July 1979 Kosmo began popping down to visit Mick Jones at Vanilla. He was no more encouraged to hang around in the studio than any of the band's other acquaintances, but he and his friend Jock Scott attended the Notre Dame shows, and Kosmo ingratiated himself into the Clash camp remarkably quickly. 'Baker and I were very wary of him early on,' says Johnny Green. 'Kosmo appeared to be a court jester because it suited his purposes, but he wasn't there for a laugh on a Tuesday afternoon. He was there for a reason, and that reason – and we all knew it – was that we needed management. He was a forerunner for Jenner and King coming in, the pitch man. He was the one with the streetwise talk, the Johnson's suits, the one the band could relate to. And they fell in love with him pretty quickly, I have to say that. He was sharp, amusing, stylish, and he opened them up to all kinds of new influences. Kosmo coming in was not an accident. The idea had to have come from somewhere, and I think it came from Mick.'

According to Chris Salewicz's Joe Strummer biography, it did come from Mick, and had been coming for some time. Over Christmas 1977 Mick and Joe had attended a party at Philip Rambow's house (the same party where Joe first met Gaby Salter). The ex-Winkie was in the process of launching a solo career, and Blackhill were his new managers. Mick got into conversation with them at the time, and kept in touch. A lot of paths seemed to be crossing in meaningful ways at this time: Blackhill booked Philip into Wessex to record some tracks with Chris Thomas and Bill Price. When the Clash played a benefit for the Sid Vicious Defence Fund at the Music Machine on 19 December 1978, Philip was support, and Mick joined him onstage. In the late spring of 1979 Mick was invited to play guitar on a track on Philip's solo album, *Shooting Gallery*, and talked to his managers again.

By the time Blackhill's PR started showing up at Vanilla, Mick had already decided who he wanted to be the Clash's new managers, and could offer compelling arguments in their favour on a number of fronts. They might have been a professional music business operation, but they had left-field origins, coming from the same Notting Hill-centred counter-cultural milieu that had produced those other Bernie-approved Clash champions, and subsequent Clash management candidates, Barry Miles and Caroline Coon. More recently, Blackhill had shown enough faith in Joe Strummer's pub-rock contemporary Ian Dury to represent him, and enough imagination to recognise that the tiny independent label Stiff could offer more than a hiding to nothing as an outlet for his 1977 album *New Boots and Panties*. That Blackhill and Stiff initially had offices in the same building, at 32 Alexander Street, Notting Hill, helped, of course. Stiff had since moved a couple of doors down the road, and the booker Ian Flukes had taken over their old office . . . His offering the Clash the lucrative Ruisrock Festival date might well have been part of Blackhill's charm offensive.

Blackhill had no problem demonstrating that they could get things done. They might have come from the left field, but that hadn't stopped them from helping to make Ian Dury a success; and by the summer of 1979, *the* success du jour. *New Boots and Panties* had made Number 5, spending 90 weeks on the UK charts, and turning Platinum with sales of 300,000 by June 1979; 'Hit Me with Your Rhythm Stick' had made Number 1 in the UK in November 1978; the follow-up album *Do It Yourself* had reached Number 2 in June 1979; and the single 'Reasons to Be Cheerful (Part 3)' had reached Number 3 that July. And with Ian Dury now taking a sabbatical, nobody could accuse them of being too wrapped up in promoting the career of their current star to have time for anyone else.

Joe was still carrying a torch for Bernie, but Mick got his way. Blackhill offered to work for a trial period without a contract, on a handshake, and be judged on their achievements. With the need for someone to set up the new American tour growing ever more pressing, Joe finally, reluctantly, accepted those conditions. Peter Quinnell was kept on as accountant. As of this time, according to Andrew King, the Clash were just £50,000 in debt to CBS. Blackhill immediately contacted the William Morris Agency to reschedule the Clash's post-poned American tour to commence in mid-September. Blackhill's appointment would also impact upon the sessions themselves.

With Guy on board, the Clash block-booked Wessex Studio One for a month from the beginning of August 1979. Bill Price cannot be more specific about the date, unfortunately, or any of the dates to do with the *London Calling* recording sessions. 'Some rude boy stole my bag from Wessex shortly after, with four years of diaries and note-books,' he says. But as the sessions were initially Monday to Friday, it's likely that the first day was Monday 30 July.

It is one of the injustices of recording that the credit for the sound of an album so often goes to either the band or to the producer – or some combination of the two – when, oftentimes, the only person in the room with the ability to select the appropriate equipment, arrange the mikes, set levels, and operate the console is the engineer. Bill Price is too modest to make such a claim for himself. 'The sound I get comes from the music and people the other side of the control-room glass,' he says. But at Wessex, it was up to Bill to get the best sound possible and capture it on tape.

At the start of the Sixties, Bill Price became bored with working on guided-missile control systems for Plessey, and decided to take his electronics expertise into the recording studio. In 1962 he joined Decca and was based in their West Hampstead studio. There he worked with a variety of artists and learned his craft recording not only some of the best singers around, including Tom Jones and Englebert Humperdink, but also some of the best session men and full orches-tras. In 1970, when EMI's George Martin and three other leading producers decided to go independent and set up their own studio, AIR, in Oxford Circus, Bill's versatility ensured that he was headhunted for the new venture. At AIR, Bill worked on soundtrack scores, including the James Bond movie *Live and Let Die* (1973), as well as rock albums, including Mott the Hoople's *Mott* (1973) and *The Hoople* (1974), and Ian Hunter's eponymous debut solo album (1975). By 1975 he was AIR's Chief Engineer.

That same year, Chrysalis Records decided to invest in recording studios, and purchased both AIR and Wessex, at 106 Highbury New Park, Highbury, north London. Highbury New Park is a long, diagonal residential street running from Canonbury at the south end to Green Lanes and Clissold Park at the north. Wide and tree-lined, it offers an unusual mixture of housing types: sections featuring very grand semi-detached, four-storey Victorian villas interspersed with more recent low-rise council estates dating from the Thirties to the Fifties. Wessex was housed in the former Victorian Church Hall hidden from the street by St Augustine's Church, which it was originally built to serve. It had been converted into a studio during the Sixties by a family who originally hailed from Bournemouth, Wessex, explaining the name. A 4-track facility, it was largely used for live recordings and boasted a room large enough to accommodate extra session players and even full orchestras.

In the mid-Seventies, when 24-track facilities were commonplace, and even the most basic studios boasted 16 tracks, it was hopelessly outdated. Pioneering experiments with layering sounds carried out by the likes of the Beatles and the Beach Boys had established new norms for constructing songs in the studio: recordings tended to be pieced together track by track, with musicians screened off by baffles, or in separate booths, to record their individual instruments and avoid any extraneous sound leaking into their microphones. As fewer musicians were recorded at any one time, studios could be smaller, with the acoustics in a room tweaked to give a fuller, richer sound. By contrast – and, to a layperson, perplexingly – Wessex's large live room sounded dead. On top of its other deficiencies, the soundproofing was primitive, which, given that the area was primarily residential, meant that recording had to stop at 10.30 p.m., the time that many typically night-owl rock'n'rollers hit their stride. Chrysalis offered Bill Price the opportunity to overhaul and update it, and then take over as studio manager as well as resident engineer.

Roughly the shape of an L tipped on its side, the leg parallel to Highbury New Park, and the foot pointing towards the street, the building was reconfigured to house two studios. The shin housed Studio

One, the main studio, and the foot the smaller Studio Two, used mainly for overdubs. The control room was situated between them, at the ankle. An office was positioned at the knee, with the tech room behind it, a kitchen ran in a thin strip down the calf behind Studio One, and the toilets were in the heel. A recreation room with a pool table, TV and – by 1979 – a Space Invaders machine (as featured on the Pretenders' album track of that title) was situated on the top floor.

Ken Shearer, the 'acoustic architect' who had designed AIR, was consulted with regard to the sound-proofing issue. A heavy concrete ceiling was duly fitted underneath the building's Victorian roof. An unfortunate side-effect, though, was that it reduced the volume of Studio One by 30 per cent. Keith Slaughter, who was studio manager at AIR and had also worked on the acoustics there, was brought in to redress the balance. Meanwhile, Bill updated the studio equipment, investing in a range of microphones and installing a 3M M79 24-track recorder and a Cadac console for each studio. Interviewed by another former AIR engineer, Chris Michie, for *Mix* magazine in 2000, Bill told him 'the Cadac, to my ear, is still probably the best audio chain I've ever heard'. The desks had an unusual configuration, and boasted hundreds of small toggles, the functions of most of which were a mystery to all but regular users. This became a problem when Wessex tried to entice freelance engineers to use the facilities in the Eighties, and Bill would have to replace the desks in 1984 for something a little more user-friendly. In the late Seventies, though, they were still in place, Bill and Jerry Green both knew their way around them, and Wessex was very much up to industry standard as a 24-track facility.

Even with all these changes, Wessex Studio One remained quite a dead room, more acoustically suited to old-fashioned live recording than the layered approach introduced during the late Sixties and early Seventies. This became a blessing when punk ripped up the contemporary recording rule book, placing the emphasis on the credo – courtesy of original Stiff house producer Nick Lowe – 'bash it down now and tart it up later'. Chris Thomas, an engineer-turned-producer who was also ex-AIR, and who had worked with Bill there, was the first to fully exploit Wessex's church hall ambience. The two former colleagues renewed their professional relationship in 1977 during sessions for the Sex Pistols' *Never Mind the Bollocks*. By this time there was no band to speak of, with – a couple of tracks aside – only Paul Cook and Steve Jones present and able to record the music. Nevertheless, Chris decided to put them at ease by setting them up at one end of the hall, so they could run through the band's set live, as if at a Sex Pistols gig. Or, perhaps more accurately, the right-hand half of a Sex Pistols gig. Steve overdubbed bass and many more guitars later. Chris came back to work at Wessex with the Tom Robinson Band and the Pretenders, and with full bands was even more keen to achieve a live sound. Because the room was dead, he could do this without having to use too many screens to separate the different instruments: the sound from the different instruments did not bleed or leak or spill into each other too much, allowing individual tracks of guitar, bass or drums to be isolated and then patched up, replaced or reinforced with overdubs later. Chris also encouraged Bill to be creative with his positioning of the microphones, working to get the best possible combination.

Bill and Jerry Green miked the instruments for *London Calling* using a refinement of these techniques. For *Give 'Em Enough Rope* it had taken three days just to get an acceptable drum sound in what was – to the visiting American production team – an unfamiliar room. Bill and Jerry could set up the mikes for all the instruments almost immediately because they worked at Wessex nearly every day. 'Recording almost always started with the Clash playing as if on stage, with Joe singing a guide, if he had the lyric,' says Bill. 'We used minimal screening, so wearing headphones was optional.' Looking out into the rectangular Studio One through the control-room window – Bill's-eye view – the drums were positioned towards the back and left, surrounded by low-level screens, with stacks of plastic orchestra chairs behind them. At the back on the right were the band's flight cases, which Joe would arrange to form a hidey-hole – the first of his many spliffbunkers – where he could continue to work on his lyrics in downtime. Halfway back on the right was the studio's Bösendorfer grand piano, the body of which was surrounded by high-level screens with only the keyboard showing. Joe's guitar amp was also set up on the right, just in front of the piano keyboard, Mick's on the left, in front of the drum screens, and Paul's in the middle – with an optional bar stool – so they could all face Topper in a semi-circle as they were accustomed to doing in the rehearsal room. None of the guitar positions was screened. Immediately up against the control-room window, to the right, was the vocal overdub booth, with high-level screens to either side.

Topper had a low-key sponsorship deal with Pearl – he didn't have to plug their wares, but they could cite him as a Pearl user – and played a slightly customised silver Pearl drum kit: 24 x 17-inch bass drum, 14 x 10 top tom-tom, and 16 x 10 and 18 x 10 floor tom-toms. He'd found that the Pearl snare didn't stand up to the beating he gave it when tuned as tight as he liked it to be, so used a Ludwig Black Beauty instead. His drum heads (skins) were Evans Hydraulic. All his cymbals were Zildjian: two 15-inch Heavy Rock hi-hats, plus a 16 and an 18 crash. His stands were Premier Lokfast Trilok, and he got Baker to bulk order the military-style Premier sticks he liked, which were long and fat, but light, and produced a really powerful sound when whipped.

'Chris Thomas and I had earlier developed a drum recording set-up that relied on the particular acoustics of Wessex Studio One,' says Bill. 'By the Clash sessions it had evolved, but still relied on capturing the best ambience of each part of the kit in the right place in the room, with the right microphone, and then gating this with a trigger from the relevant close mike.' In 2000 Bill described the set-up for the track 'London Calling' to *Mix*, providing a precise snapshot of his approach to recording the drums for the album in general. For the close mikes, Bill used a Shure SM57 and a Neumann KM86 on the snare drum, Sennheiser 421s on the tom-toms, and AKG 451s on the cymbals. Each of the hi-hats was miked with Neumann KM84s. For the bass drum, Bill used a dynamic AKG D-12 placed inside the shell and a Neumann U47 tube condenser just outside. Bill also put two Neumann U87s about 15 feet up and 10 feet in front of the drum kit as general ambience mikes, and a pair of STC (the equivalent of today's Coles) 4038 ribbon mikes were placed on the floor 8 feet behind the kit, 6 inches off the floor for bass-drum ambience, keyed by the close bass-drum mikes.

Bill recorded onto Ampex 406 2-inch tape, and usually applied Dolby A noise reduction to minimise tape hiss on anything he might be required to move, composite or mix down onto another track, but did not use Dolby on the drums. 'Two-inch 24-track running at 15 ips [inches-per-second] is quite a noisy medium, particularly if you make composites of vocals, or layered guitars,' he explains. 'The drum tracks, however, would remain as recorded on the same tracks, and as they would be highly modulated, they didn't contribute a lot of noise. Hence there was no need for Dolby on these tracks.' The drums were allotted a generous proportion of the 24 available tracks from the beginning – six for the close mikes, and another four for the ambience mikes. Not using Dolby on the master made the most of the high frequencies, especially the cymbals.

At the time of recording, Paul owned two white Fender Precision basses which he used for live work: one acquired in 1978 with *Paul* scratched onto the body; and the second better quality model at the start of 1979, customised with a sticker reading *Positive* (among other touches), which became his main bass. He liked the Fenders because they were solid-bodied and could take a lot of punishment . . . though not quite as much he would give his main bass on the tour immediately following the Wessex sessions. In the less demanding conditions of the studio, he also used a semi-acoustic sunburst Epiphone Rivoli. He can be seen playing both the main Fender and the Epiphone in the *Wessex Studios Footage* included with the 25th Anniversary Edition of *London Calling*. (The former bass would also star on the *London Calling* album cover, and he would use the latter in the 'London Calling' video.) Paul used an Ampeg amp and an Ampeg speaker cabinet. Bill recorded the bass for the initial live take via a Neumann U87 mike against the cabinet plus via direct injection into the console. These were recorded separately onto a track apiece – kept as backup – and also mixed together onto a third track.

Joe was a Fender man, too. He had at least two Telecasters he used regularly at the time of recording: his original 1966 three-colour sunburst, bought in 1975, sprayed black in 1976 and bearing an *Ignore Alien Orders* sticker; and a 1964 butterscotch one with a strip of adhesive tape reading *240 volts*. He also had a white 1962 Fender Esquire (identical in look to a Telecaster, and the name under which Telecasters were originally marketed), which he referred to as his 'Number One' guitar. He took them all into the studio with him – Jerry Green was appalled by the state of them, saying the strings and pick-ups were covered in rust – and both he and Topper can be seen playing the butterscotch model in the *Wessex Studios Footage*. Joe used a Music Man combo amp and cabinet.

Mick was partial to Gibsons. His main guitar from the formation of the Clash onwards was a Gibson Les Paul Junior, but after it was damaged a couple of times in 1977 he stopped using it for live work and graduated to adult Les Pauls. At the time of recording he had three: a 1958 Sunburst Standard, and two Customs, one black, one white. Around the time of recording, he acquired a white 1952 Gibson ES hollow body (a semi-acoustic with the depth of a real acoustic), which he also used on the sessions. In the *Wessex Studios Footage*, he is seen playing a new-looking black Fender Stratocaster. For *London Calling*, he put his guitar through a Roland Space Echo, and used a Mesa Boogie amp (with disconnected speaker) and Marshall cabinets.

For the live tracking takes, Mick and Joe's guitars were both miked with an Electro-Voice RE20 and a Neumann U87 and mixed to one track apiece. Mick initially played a combination of rhythm and lead, as he would have done onstage, and would subsequently replace his track with tracks of individual rhythm and lead. Joe played straight-forward rhythm. As he wasn't interested in overdubbing – and Mick took care of the detailed guitar work – Joe's rhythm guitar track, like the drums, was seldom replaced. Joe would also usually sing a guide vocal while playing, recorded onto another track, and this would be replaced later.

'They had trouble tuning the guitars, the Clash,' says Jerry Green, something of a muso's muso at the time, with a Brian May perm to prove it. 'In the studio, Bill's great at knowing when something's not in tune, but he can't tell if it's sharp or flat. He doesn't have that fine ability. So it became my job to say, "Well, the G is slightly sharp or slightly flat."' After Johnny Green had tested his mettle by setting fire to his perm, and Jerry had taken the hint to get a more up-to-date haircut in reasonably good spirit, the Clash were prepared to listen.

Everything was set up and ready to go in time for Guy Stevens's first day. Which was all to the good because, when he arrived, all further technical considerations were brushed aside, along with his sobriety pledge. 'I can remember Guy walking into the control room, and he had an old lady's shopping bag with a bottle of tequila and a bottle of something else in there,' says Johnny Green. 'It was early afternoon. And I said, "Oh, great, the booze has arrived!" and picked it up, and he nearly knocked me over.'

'Are we ready?' Guy demanded, as was his wont. 'Let's *gooooooooo!*' There's no doubt that the Vanilla demos played an important part in

developing the songs during rehearsals, but in terms of their importance in the actual making of the album, it wouldn't have mattered
that much if they had been lost on the Tube. 'Do you know, I don't
think the band wanted me to hear the demos,' says Bill. '*They* may
have referred to them, but we never dissected them in the control
room.' He also doubts that Guy had spent much time – if any –
listening to the tapes. 'He seemed to have no knowledge of the
well-rehearsed songs when we started recording them,' says Bill. 'In
fact, Guy got the band to play and quickly record all the songs they
had ready on the first day of sessions for his benefit.' As it is usual
for bands intending to record basic tracks live – or tracking, as it is
usually known – the Clash expected to warm up with a couple of
numbers to play themselves in, while Bill did some final checks on
levels. As ever, Guy had his own agenda.

The band took their places in the studio and, as Guy instructed Bill
to roll the tape, launched into Vince Taylor's 'Brand New Cadillac'.
When the band finished, Guy shouted 'It's a take!' Topper, who relished
the nickname Sandy Pearlman had given him – the 'Human Drum
Machine' – pointed out that it sped up. 'Great!' retorted Guy. 'All
rock'n'roll speeds up. Take!' According to Topper, 'After that, those
sessions just cooked.' Grandstanding though it might have been, it
was a smart move, because it immediately put the band at ease. 'We'd
built up this whole spirit at Vanilla,' says Johnny Green. 'We had all
this stuff down, demoed and logged in a fairly rough fashion, which
was what the band wanted, and then suddenly to be faced by a big,
expensive studio . . . there was a buzz, but also a certain trepidation
about how it was going to go.'

Having decided that the first song recorded was of high enough
standard for the album, Guy saw no reason not to continue at the
same pace. 'We cut 12 tracks in just three days flat,' he told the *NME*'s
Roy Carr at the end of the first week. 'It was just a question of cutting
out all the bullshit.' That was just two fewer tracks than had been
recorded for *The Clash*, and two more than had been released on *Give
'Em Enough Rope*. Of the 12, Guy named only two, 'Brand New Cadillac'
and . . . the inevitable Bob Dylan cover version, a 'personalised' version
of 'Billy' from the 1973 soundtrack album *Pat Garret and Billy the Kid*
with Joe on piano. In between takes on the guitar, Joe would gravi-
tate towards the Bösendorfer, and run through some of his rock'n'roll

party pieces. The Roy Carr interview appears to be the only record of 'Billy' being attempted, the actual recording having apparently been lost or wiped, and not just from the tape, but also from the memory of everyone else involved. It seems unlikely that Guy would have made it up though, or misremembered just a day or two after the event: he might have been erratic, but his power of recall was extraordinary. He encouraged the Clash to dip further into their repertoire of cover versions, especially of early rock'n'roll songs. Two of these covers have survived, unofficially on bootlegs (the quality indicating they were taken from cassette reference tapes): Bo Diddley's 'Mona (I Need You Baby)' (1957) and Bo's version of Willie Dixon's 'You Can't Judge a Book (By Looking at Its Cover)' (1962), the latter's lyric wittily reworked by Joe as 'You Can't Judge a Woman (By Making Love to Her Mother)', arguably a bit near the knuckle given his domestic arrangements at the time.

In his chat with Roy Carr, Guy implied the album was all done bar the mixing. The band were certainly in high spirits by the time they flew out to play the Ruisrock Festival over the weekend of 4–5 August, taking assistant Jerry Green – who'd already proved his ability to tune a guitar under pressure – with them as extra crew, but they were just pleased by the spirit of the recordings thus far, and optimistic about how things would turn out. Whatever impression the Vanilla demos, and the talk of recording the album on a portastudio might have given, nobody else – not even Joe – was interested in going so far back to basics that they intended to release an album of rough live takes, at least a third of them cover versions. 'I think it was Guy's direction, really,' says Jerry. Although 'Brand New Cadillac' was kept, and kept rough'n'ready, even that would be overdubbed. Of the other 11, Bill Price says, 'I don't think any of them were masters.' What happened to them – other than the bootlegged Bo Diddley songs – is a mystery. They may still be still in the Sony BMG (formerly CBS) tape vaults, but Bill doesn't seem to think so, and none of them were discovered while remastering London Calling in 1999, or five years later when preparing the 25th Anniversary special edition of the album.

Upon their return from Finland, with the band confident and thoroughly relaxed, Wessex became an open house in a way that Vanilla had not been. 'It's very rare that you have the free-for-all party atmosphere which happened on that album,' says Jerry. 'People would come and go.

It never got rowdy, but there were always people hanging around.' Members of the Clash's usual circle would drop in, including Robin Crocker and Kris Needs. Topper's girlfriend Dee and Joe's girlfriend Gaby were regulars. 'Kosmo hung out lots, and so did many others,' says Bill. 'Andrew King and Peter Jenner occasionally came by.' Even former producer Sandy Pearlman turned up.

The Clash's old rivals the Damned had reformed in the spring without original guitarist Brian James, and with original bassist Captain Sensible having switched to guitar. They were now signed to the independent label Chiswick. Roger Armstrong, the label's co-owner and in-house producer, with whom the 101ers had recorded their one and only single before splitting three years earlier, brought the band to spend several days between 3 and 28 August completing their third album, *Machine Gun Etiquette*. After a couple of sessions tracking in Studio One – fitting in around the Clash's shifts – they moved into the smaller Studio Two for overdubs. Both bands and producers knew each other, and they not only crossed paths in the kitchen and the recreation room, but also visited each other's studios.

In 2004 Kosmo unearthed a couple of video cassettes containing 84 minutes of black-and-white home-movie footage of the Clash at work and play in the studio, shot by Johnny Green, Baker and – when he wasn't needed elsewhere – Paul Simonon. With all the 'experimental' work edited out, it provided enough raw material for a short feature included on the DVD accompanying the 25th Anniversary Edition of *London Calling* as the *Wessex Studios Footage*. As well as a mock-up of TV game show *The Golden Shot*, it includes a lengthy meandering R&B jam of the kind punk had supposedly buried, with an understandably bored-looking (and unusually serious) Captain Sensible on drums, Joe on piano, Paul on bass, Topper on Joe's rhythm guitar, Mick on interminable lead, and Guy periodically bellowing into a microphone, which – thankfully – does not appear to be switched on. In another sequence from the tapes, the Captain and Ray play the Damned's debut single 'New Rose' on banjo and spoons, respectively, before Joe bursts into the frame in time to sing the chorus, then turns around to bash along on the piano. The trio then attempt a version of the Clash's debut single, with the Captain and Rat changing the chorus to 'White Christmas' (unwittingly taking the song back to its Weathermen origins). The Damned didn't contribute to *London Calling* for real, but Joe and Topper would be drafted in to contribute to the hooligan backing vocals on the Damned's 'Noise, Noise, Noise'.

The approach to recording the live basic tracks that would be used on the Clash's album continued to be much the same as for the initial run-throughs, though the number of takes required to get a master Bill and the band thought they could work with varied considerably from song to song. 'One to fifty,' is Bill's half-joking guesstimate. Most of the first original songs to be tracked required just a handful of takes, because the better-rehearsed songs were attempted first, and the more experimental or more recently written ones left until later in proceedings.

As Bill Price notes, the recording term 'direct injection' meant something entirely different to Guy Stevens. The producer and technicians were supposed to stay in the control room and leave the musicians to it in the soundproofed and carefully miked studio, but Guy would charge out onto the studio floor mid-take and run around shouting, getting right up into the band members' faces, and pulling and pushing at them. 'He was getting all this aggression going,' says Jerry Green. The first time it happened, Paul Simonon – the band's resident hard man – came close to downing his bass and punching Guy out, but the anarchic side of his personality recognised a kindred spirit, and he instead just grinned and kept playing. Used to being told off for fluffs and dropped notes, Paul appreciated that Guy had other priorities. For a while, it worked. Apparently.

The Stevens Direct Injection technique is preserved on the *Wessex Studios Footage* during a Clash performance of garage-band classic 'Louie, Louie', written by Richard Berry in 1955, but made famous in 1963 (although initially only in the vicinity of their own garage) by the Kingsmen: Guy kangaroo hops around the studio, plays air guitar, and invades the musicians' personal space. All of which appears to be making it difficult for them to hold the three-chord riff together. At one point Guy castigates Mick Jones for stopping playing. When he starts repeatedly slamming a plastic orchestra chair down onto the studio floor, the ramshackle take finally peters out. Guy yells, 'We've got it!' Everyone else just looks embarrassed, as well they might. This is another cover that – had it not been for the camera's presence – would never have been heard (or heard of) again.

Second engineer Jerry Green found all this bemusing. Being the assistant, he was responsible for the studio's equipment, fixtures and fittings, and was unhappy about Guy's casual vandalism. On the *Wessex Studios Footage* he can be seen trying to restrain Guy from throwing a heavy pole the length of the studio, while Guy insists he can do what he likes and, ultimately, does. 'Bill's going, "Don't worry about it. Just let him break what he wants,"' says Jerry. 'Though he did get me to sort out the chairs, so the older ones were the ones nearer the front and most likely to get smashed up.' Bill knew that CBS – and therefore, ultimately, the Clash – would be picking up the tab for breakages. Even his patience could be found wanting, though. After he had spent hours arranging the faders to get the exact levels he wanted on the tricky Cadac, it was not unknown for Guy to throw himself on the console and try to push everything into the red, where-upon Bill would have to fend him off with one hand while doing his job with the other. On one occasion, this resulted in the two of them rolling around the control-room floor like a pair of all-in wrestlers. 'The late Guy Stevens was one of my oldest and most loved friends, and I always had time for him,' is Bill's admirably loyal – if slightly frosty – response when asked if he found Guy's contribution counter-productive at times. Like all four members of the Clash themselves, he has gone on record to say that the band responded well to Guy's approach; the implication being that the end justified the means.

The more upbeat anecdotes about Guy's eccentric behaviour during the recording of *London Calling* have eclipsed even those from the prime of his career. Wired to the point he was almost frothing at the mouth, Guy would habitually shower anyone he talked to in spittle, requiring Joe to invent a cardboard screen he dubbed the 'splatterboard'. Guy would be required to hold it in front of the lower half of his face during close-quarters conversation. He didn't walk down stairs, he fell down them. The Clash had agreed to pay his taxi fares to work each day, so Guy brought in every taxi receipt he could find, no matter how old. An Arsenal fan, Guy made the most of recording just around the corner from the team's home ground by wearing his Liam Brady scarf and getting the cab driver to stop at Highbury en route to Wessex so he could walk onto the pitch and pay homage. (A member of staff at Highbury phoned Wessex to check Guy's credentials.) One day, Guy turned up with a heavy-set guy and installed him at the back of the control room for an entire session, and then casually demanded the money required to pay him. He was that day's cab driver, and had left his meter running the whole time.

It was not long before the band's honeymoon period with Guy came to an end. 'He piled the chairs up and knocked them over,' says Johnny Green. 'And we all watched that and laughed. And then he did it again. And then, suddenly, the quiet talk was – and I don't wish to be rude about Guy, who I loved – that he was trying to recreate something he'd already done.' Not for the first time. As recording continued, and the immediacy of live takes of well-rehearsed songs gave way to the more laborious and detailed work of overdubbing and writing and arranging new songs, he became more and more of a problem. As well as being creatively and philosophically opposed to the kind of detailed work the band were now embarking upon, he didn't have the patience or – it must be said – the understanding or skills for it. It was also difficult for the Clash to explain that he had already provided everything they needed from him: the record's spirit.

Whether he was aware of this or not, as his alcohol intake increased, so did Guy's unhappiness. When he was feeling feisty, he would push the issue, moaning loud and long at Mick about the time overdubbing was taking. As the illusion of control slipped away from him, Guy began to flounder. On several occasions he made lengthy calls to Ian Hunter in America from the Wessex payphone – also on the Clash's tab – seeking reassurance. More often, though, he would drink himself into a stupor, and either be left flaked out under the console in the control room, moved into the tech room to sleep it off, or taken home. 'I remember going down there one night when the roadies were carrying Guy out,' says Muff Winwood. 'Completely poleaxed.'

Guy was also given to petulant and destructive acts that had nothing to do with inspiring great performances. In a bid to force Mick to get a move on with one guitar overdub, Guy grabbed a ladder – the same one he can be seen using to climb up onto the piano stool, and then throwing across the studio in the *Wessex Studios Footage* – and swung it around, requiring Mick to duck to avoid being decapitated. 'Frightened the shit out of Mick, basically,' says Jerry Green. 'Came a bit too close.' While the Clash had anticipated Guy not going the full distance, that didn't make his behaviour any less stressful at times. Roger Armstrong remembers overhearing Mick yelling to Joe on one occasion that he couldn't take much more of it. 'Mick got annoyed sometimes,' concedes Bill.

On another occasion, according to Joe – interviewed by Charles Shaar Murray for a December 1979 *NME* feature on Guy – he poured beer into the piano 'to make it sound better'. In the 2004 *The Last Testament* documentary, Bill offered his version: Joe was sitting at the piano, concentrating on working out a part for a song, when Guy approached him and told him to play like Jerry Lee Lewis. Joe ignored him and carried on, whereupon Guy picked up a bottle of red wine and poured it all over Joe's fingers and the keyboard to gain his attention. 'A quick wipe with a J-cloth and the piano was fine for the rest of the sessions,' says Bill now, saving the sting in the tail for later.

Jerry Green is a little less breezy. He maintains the taxi driver-minder incident and the piano-christening incident happened on the same night, and were part of the same twisted tale. He says Bill and the Clash members had all left for the night, and only learned what happened when he told them the following day. He was about to close up the studio when Guy lurched up to him and demanded £55. 'I went, "I don't have it, Guy." I had about £3, or something. He said, "I need it to get home and pay the cabbie." This was when I learned that this guy who had been there all day was a taxi driver. I asked him to take Guy home and come back the following day for his money. Guy went, "No, you've got to pay him now!" And he picked up this huge two-litre bottle of red wine, walked over to the piano and said, "If you don't give me £55, I'm going to throw this in the piano." We'd bought the Bösendorfer Grand for the studio about eight months previously. A glorious instrument. It cost an absolute fortune. I went, 'Look, Guy, *please* don't do that. It's not necessary," but he emptied the wine into the piano. At which point I rushed up to Guy and grabbed him to get him away from there . . . but he was quite a light man, and I'm six foot six, so I ended up throwing him about 10 feet across the studio, which I felt awful about. He was just off his head. I didn't mean to hurt him. He then buggered off with the cabbie, and I spent the next three hours cleaning out the piano, trying to get the red wine off the soundboard. It was a fucking disaster.' More than a quick wipe with a J-cloth, then.

When he confessed all the next day, Jerry expected to be reprimanded for assaulting the producer, but for once everyone was appalled at Guy. Joe could be pretty rough on the piano himself – leaving aside his style of playing, the *Wessex Studios Footage* shows him with his brothel creepers up on the keyboard – but neither he nor the rest of the band were happy with the possibility of it being put out of action. 'It was one of the best recording pianos in London, because its sound was so hard,' says Jerry. 'The band were up in arms about it, because they used it all the time.' Even in the sanitised version they gave Charles Shaar Murray, they admitted that this particular act of sabotage had been a step too far. 'I nearly killed him,' said Mick. The Clash were able to use the Bösendorfer for the rest of the sessions, but the next time the piano tuner visited, he had some bad news for Bill and for Wessex. 'The wine's effect was slow, but unstoppable,' says Bill. 'Many months later, we had to hire a new piano, and send the action back to Bösendorfer to be rebuilt. Most of the bass strings had to be replaced. It cost about £6,000, and it was way too late to bill the Clash.'

The basic live tracks for the material previously rehearsed in Vanilla were recorded in the first couple of weeks, but Guy was not necessarily there when all of them were recorded. Topper broke ranks during *The Last Testament* documentary to remark that Guy was only 'occasionally' in the studio. 'Guy was there for about two weeks in spirit, and he was in and out throughout that period,' agrees Jerry Green. For the first part of the overdub stage – which crossed over with the tracking stage – Mick managed to work around Guy, taking particular advantage of those lengthy periods when he came in late, skipped a day, or was passed out in the tech room. Other times, he signalled to Johnny Green to take Guy for a walk, or to the pub, or both. As the sessions progressed, and time became more pressing, he and the rest of the band at first resorted to lying to Guy from time to time, telling him they were having a rest day and not to bother coming in. After the piano incident, Guy was rarely seen at all.

'The band basically took over and the rest of the stuff was pretty much produced by them and Bill,' says Jerry. 'As I remember it, as soon as Guy was out of the way, we got on with the serious work. Before that, it was pretty much playtime and trying it Guy's way.' Johnny confirms this. 'I was aware, within a few days, really, that Mick had taken over,' he says. 'Of course, Bill Price was there, and Jerry Green: a pretty solid team. A lot of help. But Mick suddenly knew what he was doing. I could see a difference in him in the control room from how he'd been previously. He was very much on top of the whole thing.'

'We would record a backing track, fix any mistakes and do any overdubs anybody could think of, before moving on,' says Bill Price. 'We would then come back to it later to add any new ideas.' The process went like this: 'Record some good takes of the backing track. Edit together to get the best drum track. Fix any bass mistakes, or redo if needed. Record the guitar ideas that Mick already had in mind. Do the lead vocal. Do Topper's percussion ideas and Mick's backing vocals. Job done: easy. Come back to it next week, wipe this, redo that and struggle all night with the other . . .'

All Topper's drum tracks were live takes, but Bill would edit the tape to 'get the best bits', and then dub in 'the odd missed cymbal or tom-tom idea'. Repairs were minimal, but extra toms appear in key places on many of the tracks, including on 'London Calling' itself, where they can be heard at the beginning and towards the end.

Unlike Topper, Paul rarely produced a live bass take that could not be improved upon later. For 'London Calling', in addition to the original live take, Bill Price recorded two further passes onto four further tracks. He then mixed the best sections from all the bass takes onto a composite single track, with which he replaced the original track. This approach was standard operational procedure for the rest of the album.

The extent to which Paul's bass playing appears on Clash recordings has been a matter for conjecture for many years. He did play on *The Clash*, but Mick devised his parts and Paul learned them parrot-fashion. With such a rough and ready album, the deficiencies did not really matter. Johnny Green recalls Paul – late back from his Russian holiday with Caroline Coon – having to sit upstairs and learn his parts for the second album from demos on which the bass lines had been similarly devised and played by Mick. Being a more demanding taskmaster, Sandy Pearlman made Paul redo his bass again and again for *Give 'Em Enough Rope*. Johnny Green maintains that, even then, Sandy was rarely satisfied. 'Paul Simonon had a concentration span of about four minutes then,' says Johnny Green. 'One of mine or the Baker's jobs was to take him home when he'd done his take, and then Mick did the bass again. Paul was a lot better on bass by the time *London Calling* was recorded, but he still went home early! He played a lot of pool . . .' Damned producer Roger Armstrong remembers walking into Studio One and seeing Mick Jones recording bass overdubs. 'I can't remember which tracks,' he says. 'But it was in the same context that the Captain over-dubbed bass on *Machine Gun Etiquette* tracks.'

'Quite a lot of time was spent teaching Paul bass lines,' says Jerry Green. 'Mick might have picked up the bass to show him the riff, but it was generally Paul who recorded it, even if we came back and spent a lot of time dropping in on his tracks to patch them up. I mean, Paul wasn't the world's greatest bass player. He knows that, so I'm not nervous about saying it. But he would work at something if shown what was required. I can't specifically remember any occasion where Mick replaced any bass line of Paul's. For someone who doesn't under-stand the recording process, or someone who is in and out of the studio, if they see Mick with the bass in his hand when Paul's gone home, they make a natural assumption. But Mick might have been recording a guide bass line for Paul to re-record so that we could get on and do something else.' Bill Price's track sheet for 'London Calling' includes a track marked 'Mick DT bass', which was Mick augmenting – not replacing – Paul's existing bass part. 'Paul practised very hard,' says Bill Price. 'Mick helped him come up with some of the bass parts, but Paul's bass is on every track. Mick's "double-track" bass is more often than not a counterpoint or added accent, rather than the same part.'

So this was the context in which Mick recorded bass parts that made it to the final mix: on a few of the songs worked up in the studio, rather than those much rehearsed at Vanilla, or when – working longer hours and more intensively than the others – he came up with a new detail, or decided on a late change in a particular area, and wanted to sort it out there and then and get on with the overall sound picture.

'Joe's live rhythm guitar was normally perfect, and he didn't tend to add new parts,' says Bill, who is consistently kind about Joe Strummer's guitar playing, which was as unpolished as his guitars. Talking to *Mix*'s Chris Michie in 2000 he described it as 'intuitive', noting that Joe would 'bash the living daylights out of his guitar' and had a 'sort of unconscious way of damping the chord with his right hand, which used to produce this incredibly urgent, clanging and clashing sound, which I've never heard any other guitarist ever produce'. Joe's thrashing style was at least partly attributable to his being a left-handed guitarist playing a right-handed instrument: acknowledgement of his limitations had prompted his choice of stage name. He was barré chords only and – in his own words – 'fuck the fiddly bits!' While the driving, percussive noise he produced was fine for a live performance, it had been deemed too harsh and unmusical to appear on the Clash's previous albums other than as a ghost in the mix: the audible rhythm guitar had been almost entirely Mick's. While this is also true of some of the more delicate tracks on *London Calling*, Bill did keep Joe's live rhythm guitar upfront for most of the others.

'Mick is an amazingly accomplished guitar player,' Bill told Chris Michie. 'Whenever I worked with him, he was always coming up with melodic lines and neat rhythmic accents. And he's always been very into discovering what he could get out of his guitar.' By August 1979 Mick's influences and touches recognised no barriers of taste and had no truck with inverted punk snobbery. The guitar stylings of Seventies hard rock, country rock, and West Coast funk rock are as evident on the album as of Sixties garage, R&B, pop and soul. There are even nods to Thirties jazz. His playing and ideas were truly eclectic. He was also fond of effects, his latest purchase being the Roland Space Echo. 'He used it all the time, on every song!' says Bill. 'Quite often I would rig it so I had it in the control room and could do subtle tweaks.'

Mick's live tracking take was typically a combination of rhythm and lead, held as a guide, but subsequently replaced. Using 'London Calling' as an example: he overdubbed two tracks of rhythm, two passes of feedback-drenched lead, which Bill then composited to one track, and then two tracks of backwards lead. Although the amount and type of guitars Mick recorded would vary from song to song, the five tracks finally devoted to his guitar contribution to 'London Calling', as compared to Joe's one track, is not proportionately unrepresentative. According to Bill, over half the time afforded to overdubs in Wessex was devoted to Mick's guitars. While Guy was still there, as Bill wryly notes, it was the tracks where Mick was intent on 'assembling double-tracked guitars in three-part harmony' which were most likely to promote conflict.

With *The Clash*, Joe had wanted to record his vocals live with the band, while simultaneously playing guitar. Even when persuaded to replace the vocal later, as was customary, he showed little interest in doing what most vocalists did: recording take after take so the engineer could edit together the best bits. In 1977, for Joe, it was one or two takes all the way through, cough and walk off. He also insisted on bashing away on an unplugged guitar while singing, meaning that the final mix had not one but two barely audible Strummer guitars on it. When it came to *Give 'Em Enough Rope*, Sandy Pearlman had made Joe record far more vocal takes, and really push himself as a singer. By the time the Clash were ready to record *London Calling*, Joe had come around to studio craft, and would make several overdub passes at a lead vocal in order to help Bill make a composite to replace the live guide. As Joe didn't have a finished lyric for 'London Calling' when the band first recorded it, it was one of relatively few songs tracked without a guide vocal. When Joe came to dub on the lead later, he made three passes at it, initially recorded on three separate tracks, which were then composited down to one track. Again, this was roughly standard for his lead vocal work.

Joe's approach to the actual recording of vocal overdubs had not changed much. He still preferred to play an unplugged guitar while doing so, claiming it helped him with his timing and phrasing. When he could be persuaded to sing without the prop, he would often keep time by beating his right fist against his chest. That was not the only challenge to Bill Price's recording talents. He usually favoured a tube Neumann U47 microphone when recording vocals, but it quickly became apparent that this would not work with Joe, who had a baritone voice to begin with, something unusual about the formation of his palate that added a slightly roofless, consonant-damping quality, and teeth in an advanced state of decay, which threw in random sibilance. The U47 required so much EQ to combat the last of these problems that Joe ended up sounding like one of the more speech-impeded Looney Tunes cartoon characters, somewhere between Daffy and Sylvester. Bill opted instead for an SM58 mike for necessary 'punch and clarity'.

More punch, if not necessarily more clarity, came from Guy, who – while still present – respected the privacy of the vocal booth no more than the studio as a whole. 'He believed that the record producer's job was to maximise the emotion and feeling that an artist revealed on mike in the studio when doing the song,' Bill told Chris Michie.

'He would challenge the artist verbally and physically to get more emotion out of him when he performed. Funnily enough, this worked better on some people than others. It worked very well with Joe, actually.' The *Wessex Studios Footage* opens with a guitarless Joe clinging as if for dear life to the frame of Studio One's vocal booth, swinging his brothel-creepered feet and almost lifting himself off the ground with the amount of energy he's expending recording a lead vocal overdub for 'Four Horsemen'. 'Nearly there, Joe,' remarks a hovering Guy, as though encouraging a mother-to-be through a difficult birth. Guy makes some remark to Bill – who can be seen through the control-room glass – about being OK with an earlier, 'relaxed', vocal for 'Death or Glory', but when Joe starts to sing 'Koka Kola', Guy starts to give him some stern instruction about clarity of diction. (This is doubly rich: not only is Guy himself slurring badly, but when Guy gave him the same order when recording the Polydor demos three years earlier, Joe had insisted it would never happen again.) 'I'm producing now,' explains Guy. 'Guy LOVED that camera,' deadpans Bill. These three songs, and 'The Right Profile', which the entire band can be seen running through on the *Wessex Studios Footage*, were among the first Clash originals recorded at Wessex.

Guy was no longer around by the time most of the backing vocals were recorded, and when interventions would have been less productive. Overall, the album was to remain the crowning achievement of the vocal interplay between Mick and Joe. As singers, neither was blessed with great range. Mick's voice was high-pitched and wispy, lacking power and projection. Nonetheless, thanks to some inspired arrangements by Mick and Jerry Green – who says he helped work out root notes for harmonies – the two main singers managed to blend and weave their contrasting voices like they were born to complement each other. Mick reinforces choruses, and adds oohs and ahhs, but also plays slick call-and-response, swapping and overlapping lines with Joe. 'Backing vocals are a particular speciality of Mick's,' says Bill. 'All I needed was enough tracks, and enough patience, to get what Mick wanted onto tape.' The usual roles are reversed on the songs for which Joe adds emphasis and shading, while Mick takes the lead. What Mick lacked in natural ability as a lead singer he was more than prepared to make up for in hard work. With Bill's assistance, he was experienced enough in the studio to know how to play to his strengths and mask his weaknesses. And double-tracking helped.

Topper did not have much to do on the drum kit after the initial live takes, but he continued to hang around at Wessex. Making a stand against both increasingly popular synthesised percussion effects and – perhaps – Mick Jones's dominance of the overdub process, Topper insisted on renting a box of percussion instruments and tapping, shaking, clattering, scraping, stroking and ting-a-linging just about everything therein wherever he could find the space. 'I even use finger cymbals on one track,' he claimed, proudly, at the end of the year. 'Topper was always open to the suggestion to overdub some percussion,' says Bill Price. 'He's a genius. He'll continue until everything in the box is broken or all the tracks are full, whichever happens sooner. The hire company charged us for a new box every week.' Roger Armstrong admits the Damned may have contributed to the wear and tear on one occasion: he snuck them into Studio One late one night and borrowed Topper's box of tricks for the *Machine Gun Etiquette* track 'Anti-Pope'.

That takes care of the full complement of punk-approved, keep-it-basic recording elements: drums, bass, guitars and vocals. But the band – mainly Mick – had been ignoring such restrictions for some time. The Clash had already experimented with occasional overdubs of other instruments on *Give 'Em Enough Rope* and *The Cost of Living*, including pianos, horns and harmonicas. The variety of song genres and textures on *London Calling* called out for both more of the same and more that was different. The Clash had added the piano to their own performing arsenal. Joe was particularly keen to make his presence felt on the instrument with which he had recently reacquainted himself. His approach to it was almost exactly like his approach to guitar: frantic staccato pounding in the rough and raw style which has long served to generate excitement in English pubs and music halls, in addition to the barrel houses and honkey-tonks of the American south. 'I can stay in rhythm, but I can only handle three-prong chords,' Joe admitted to *Musician*'s Bill Flanagan in 1986. Having named himself Strummer in recognition of his deficiencies on the Telecaster, Joe would credit himself with 'pianner' on the sleeve of *London Calling* in acknowledgement of his brutality to the Bösendorfer. According to Bill Price, in a major new departure for the Clash, and indicating the extent of Joe's love affair with his new instrument, he occasionally played the instrument during the basic live take of songs. He is playing piano on the *Wessex Studios Footage* warm-up for 'The Right Profile'. Mick's more considered (and musical) piano parts were all overdubs.

The piano had another important role. The band wrote and arranged two entirely new songs, 'Spanish Bombs' and 'The Card Cheat' during the Wessex sessions, and also worked up their version of 'Wrong 'Em Boyo', another Sixties reggae song they all knew from the jukebox at Rehearsals Rehearsals back in 1976. The arrangements of the last two of these songs were developed on the Bösendorfer, as well as additions to some of the older material. 'A lot of things, Joe would sit at the piano and work out,' says Jerry Green. 'There were certain elements of some songs they were still getting together in the studio. The album wasn't completely formed.' On *The Last Testament*, Mick agreed that the band liked to have some parts that weren't worked out in advance. He described the process of arriving at the finished article as 'instinctual', with the fine detail added as the band went along. That detail would also include a melodica, a jew's harp and apparently random sound effects.

Input was encouraged from all sides. 'It was a great time to work with them,' says Jerry. 'They would take on board anybody's idea, unlike other bands that I worked with at the time, and have worked with since. There was none of that, "Shut up! You're just the tea boy!" sort of thing. I was Bill's assistant by then, and would take over some of the overdubs, so maybe that helped. Plus me being a musician. All ideas were given a fair airing, and they either took them on board or they didn't. A lot of the punk-era bands would just show up and play, but the Clash were technically quite on the case: they knew what they wanted, and how we could achieve it. They were interested in investigating the possibilities of the studio.'

Although overdubs would normally proceed in roughly the above order on individual songs, not all of the songs were at the same stage of development at any given time. Several different types of overdubs might be happening on different songs at different times on the same day. It might have become chaotic, had Bill not kept his track sheets up to date, and Mick not maintained a personal cassette tape library of each song, so he could stay abreast of what still needed to be done.

He would study these further at home. 'On every project I've done with Mick, he keeps his tapes in running order as soon as each track is recorded, long before the mix,' says Bill. Joe, meanwhile, would still be working on lyrics. 'If we were doing guitar overdubs with Mick, rather than hanging around in the control room, Joe would be in his bunker with his anglepoise lamp, writing the lyrics,' says Jerry. Roger Armstrong remembers seeing Joe in his bunker late at night, still refining ideas.

When it came to overdubs involving external musicians, the band had to be a little more prepared, with all the songs requiring contributions needing to be ready at much the same time. Sometime in the latter half of August, the Clash agreed the retro rock'n'roll-reggae-soul-funk-blues-folk flavour of much of the material recorded for *London Calling* was begging for a judicious touch of organ, and both Joe and Mick knew it was beyond them. 'While they liked to have a little dabble, no one in the Clash could really play keyboards,' says Johnny Green. 'I mean, Joe couldn't play them *efficiently!*' If the piano arrived in rock'n'roll from houses of ill-repute, via boogie-woogie, then the organ came from the House of God, via gospel and soul. Its thick, full sound and ability to sustain notes and chords was perfect for expressing both joy and mourning, and when it moved over into the secular tradition it carried with it overtones of uplift and sorrow, depending on context and emphasis. A Hammond electric organ is able to offer lead lines as fluid as any guitar or saxophone, but is also able to produce an atmospheric wash. In the recording studio, the organ has something else going for it: when buried deeper in the mix, it can provide the perfect pad, a sort of aural cement or glue holding together the other instruments and elements.

The Clash were still wary of bringing in a bona fide session musician. It was the first opportunity for Kosmo Vinyl and Blackhill to offer practical assistance. They nominated Ian Dury and the Blockheads' keyboard player Mickey Gallagher. The Clash – and Mick in particular – would have been aware of Mickey's pedigree: as far back as 1965 he had briefly replaced Alan Price in Mick's beloved Animals, before forming Skip Bifferty, a band that, in 1969, had even more briefly moonlighted as Heavy Jelly for a Guy Stevens-produced single.

'Blackhill got me involved,' says Mickey Gallagher (he prefers Mick these days, but sticking with Mickey here will avoid confusion with

Mr Jones). 'When they asked me to go up, they gave me the *Give 'Em Enough Rope* album to listen to. I thought, "What the *hell* is this?" It was just a mess to me. Horrible! I really couldn't get it, and I thought, "What will I be doing on this?" I just went up there the first time thinking, "Oh, I'll just do one session. The Office want me to do it. Because Kosmo was working there.' He wasn't paid a standard session fee. 'It was Mates' Rates, which I regretted later. My whole relationship with the Clash was like that, because they were with Blackhill, and I was with Blackhill through Ian. So anything that was done through the Office was always cheaper than what you'd do it for outside. You'd think, we're all in this together, we'll get paid later, or get paid in kind, or be considered for something at some point . . . *Were we bollocks!*'

Mickey walked right into another alcohol-ownership tussle, which did nothing to ease his misgivings. 'One of the first things I did was nick Topper's beer without realising it. I just picked one up, and it was, "Hey, that's *my* beer!" Really confrontational.' It was quickly smoothed over, and Mickey was taken into the control room, introduced to Bill Price and the rest of the Clash, none of whom would actually be recording. 'They'd hang out at the studio,' says Mickey. 'It was a nice place to be, Wessex. It was very sociable whenever I went up there. The girlfriends would be there, too.' Guy, though, was not present on any of the occasions he visited.

'When I heard the first track, I was very surprised to hear what they'd been doing,' says Mickey. 'It was chalk and cheese to what they'd done before. All the publicity had been that everything before the Clash was crap, and how the Clash were breaking new ground, and all that, and I think what people like Guy Stevens did for them was make them realise that some of the stuff that went before them was fucking good, man! They were avid learners. They were unschooled musos, but they picked up really fast from that point on. Doing all that work in the studio, they started listening, and it made a hell of a difference.'

He was directed to the Hammond that had been hired in for him – 'a C-3, I think' – but that was the extent of the direction. 'The Clash didn't speak in musical terms at all,' he says. 'It was more they played me the track to listen to, and then I'd go and play along to it, mess around on it, and we'd just put it together like that, really. It was at the overdubbing stage, just building up. If they had any specific idea what else was still to go on there, like horns, they'd tell me. And we would cut the parts how they wanted. I was new to the relationship then. It was all very polite.' He thinks he went up for two or three sessions in total, during which he dubbed four songs. Mickey provides glue and fattens the sound on 'Clampdown' and 'Spanish Bombs', and is more obviously to the fore on the reggae covers 'Wrong 'Em Boyo' and 'Revolution Rock'. He doesn't remember any specifics. 'I liked it – it was my sort of thing – but I haven't listened to it for 20 or 30 years,' he says.

The tradition of augmenting a basic four- or five-piece strings, skins and keys combo with horns had always been a staple of Fifties and Sixties rock'n'roll, R&B, soul and funk live shows. It was synonymous with the mid-Sixties Stax sound, and even before that had hopped across the Caribbean to Jamaica, where ska had been carried along as much by the strident brass section as by the rhythm section. Horn sections had experienced something of a renaissance in the early-to-mid-Seventies too, when, in a bid to revisit the rootsy origins of their music, numerous established rock outfits including the Rolling Stones and Van Morrison's band had started to tour with brass. Pub rockers like Ian Dury's first band Kilburn and the High Roads and the original incarnation of the 101ers followed suit. As soon as he had the budget to extend his backing band the Rumour in 1976, Graham Parker had joined the club by adding the Rumour Brass. As their new music referenced most of the above, it seemed appropriate for the Clash to hire a brass section for several cuts on *London Calling*. So they also added the Rumour Brass; or at least three-quarters of them.

Baritone and tenor sax player John 'Irish' Earle, tenor sax player Ray Beavis, trumpet player Dick Hanson and trombonist Chris Gower were already seasoned players when they teamed up and joined Parker. Their live work with him is preserved on the 1978 album *The Parkerilla*, but they had been dropped for Parker's subsequent studio album, *Squeezing Out Sparks*, released in March 1979. The horn section had not been with him in Finland, where his path had last crossed the Clash's. Even before splitting with Parker, though, as Stiff Records had been co-founded by his manager, Dave Robinson, they had become the label's in-house brass section, and knew the Blackhill team well.

'We were the staff horns for Stiff,' says Dick Hanson. 'But, basically, any left-of-centre sessions in England that needed horns, we were doing. I think Kosmo Vinyl booked us for the Clash. He started off as a Graham Parker fan, turning up everywhere and coming back with us on the bus after concerts.' The quartet would continue to work together as the Rumour Brass until 1992, but those of their number who played on *London Calling* would be credited as 'the Irish Horns', after their leader and the only Irishman among them.

'They specifically wanted two saxes and a trumpet,' says Dick. Chris Gower's services on trombone were not required. 'Trumpet and two tenors is the classic Stax brass line-up,' explains Bill Price. John Earle is no longer with us, and neither Dick nor Ray Beavis can remember the date of the session. Dick recently binned his work diaries, but he does remember that Bill Price ran the session – no Guy – and that only Mick and Joe of the Clash were present. 'It was one session, and very quick,' says Dick. 'About three hours. Not bad for an afternoon's work!' Ray Beavis remembers it as an evening session lasting five to six hours. 'All first takes,' continues Dick. 'It was a two-way thing, that: you had to be quick to get re-employed, but you also wanted to stretch it out to get paid more. It would have been Union Rate.' 'The arrangements went as they always do with rock horn sections,' says Bill. 'Everybody sung them lines, and told them records they liked, the horns listened to the chords and the rhythm of the guitars and vocal . . . and then promptly went out and played whatever they wanted, to fine effect. They would sometimes be open to "Don't play here," or "Put a bit in there."' 'They were head arrangements,' says Ray. 'We devised them ourselves,' agrees Dick. 'That's pretty much how we worked. We said, "How about this?" and the guys said if they liked it or not. Working like we did, you had to be creative all the time. Irish would come up with some great ideas, and Ray was really good at harmony. It always came pretty much together, but Irish was particularly good at originating things.'

The horns recorded as a group, lined up as if for a show. 'We always did,' says Dick. 'We were a specialist rock horn section. You had to play like you were onstage, at full tilt. We used to have our cans so loud that the engineer would sometimes ask us to turn them down, because the sound was spilling over. It was about getting the same energy as in a rock concert.' 'I can't remember if all the vocals were in place, but there would almost certainly have been at least guide vocals for working purposes,' says Ray. 'Almost certainly, the microphones used for that session were Neumann U87s, large diaphragm condenser mikes. That's what we used on pretty much all our recordings. I liked the songs immediately, and thought we played appropriately on them.' Dick thinks they dubbed 'Wrong 'Em Boyo' first, but doesn't remember any more details. Like Mickey Gallagher, he isn't over-sentimental about his contribution. 'Ray bought a copy of the album when it came out. I borrowed it, listened to it, and gave it back. I was never really a Clash fan. And you have to remember, a three-hour creative session is pretty exhausting, and when you do another one, you have to completely wipe your memory and start all over again or else you'll lose your concentration.'

The album sessions had been booked for the five weeks of August 1979, Monday to Friday, with the band arriving late morning or early afternoon and leaving ten hours later. For the last couple of weeks of that period, various permutations of band members – mostly Joe and Mick – and engineers Bill and Jerry were working at the studio up to 16 hours a day, spelling each other in a frantic attempt to finish the job. 'We worked till we dropped every day,' says Bill, simply. As pressure started to build from within, so did it start to build from without. CBS did not exactly leave the Clash to their own devices. Bill Price was contacted regularly for updates and check-ups on Guy Stevens. Paul Simonon remembers trying to record his first ever Clash lead vocal for 'The Guns of Brixton' with a visiting Epic representative staring at him through the control-room glass. Muff Winwood also dropped in 'two or three times', and – apart from the time he passed Guy being carried the other way – efforts were made for the official producer to be there to meet him. Politeness stopped there. 'You got this really daft thing that, when I turned up the band refused to play anything!' laughs Muff. '"It's not finished!" and all that stuff. Guy was OK with me, and Bill was OK with me, so when the guys left the room Bill would play me a quick bit of something. Often this whole thing was like a game, you know. What I heard sounded fantastic. Now on record you got the real fire of the band. Before, their records had always been a little muddy, but this sounded like the one that would cross over.'

On a less positive note, the album was behind schedule, and the

Clash asked for extra money to continue working over the few days before they were due to depart for America. There was usually a six-week production turnaround for albums. CBS would have liked *London Calling* to be delivered at the end of August in time to make the ideal mid-October release date: when there would still be plenty of lead-up time for Christmas sales. Even though this clearly wasn't going to come to pass, Muff wasn't overly concerned. 'This happened with every act that was popular,' he shrugs. 'They were always late on delivering their albums, and they were always running over schedule into the time they were due to start a tour. You just had to fiddle your way around it, put the tours back, or put the releases back.'

'The thing with the Clash was, you could go in to record a certain number of songs, but it never ever happened that way,' says Jerry Green. 'There was always anywhere between 30 per cent and 100 per cent more stuff recorded than needed.' It was not unusual for bands to record more tracks than required during sessions, enabling them to choose the strongest material for an album, and leaving some potential singles B-sides and other extras in the can. On this occasion, though, the Clash felt strongly that the 15 tracks (all but two of them originals) they had re-recorded from *The Vanilla Tapes*, plus the three tracks they had worked up while in the studio (two of them originals), belonged together, and were all strong enough to make the cut. Mick, as was his wont, already had his reference cassettes for all 18 in what he had already decided should be the final running order. Rather than apologise for running over schedule, the Clash were proud they had done (nearly) twice the work expected of them, and wanted to release the results as a double album.

Muff explained the economics of the situation. Doubles used twice the vinyl, and – with a gatefold sleeve – twice the packaging, therefore incurred twice the manufacturing costs. Furthermore, when the weight was doubled, so were the distribution costs. Just a couple of months earlier – when he was still talking to the music press about recording the album on a portastudio and passing on the savings to the customer – Joe Strummer had bellowed at *Sounds'* Dave McCullough: 'THERE WILL BE NO SIX-QUID CLASH LP EVER!' The record company line was that increased costs meant a double album would have to be sold for more than that. The higher price would result in some sales being lost, as would the amount of material:

existing fans would probably buy it, but more casual buyers would find it too great a commitment of both money and time. This was the market the Clash needed to attract if they were going to have a long-term future. Most successful double albums were by well-established acts, or were greatest hits or live albums compiling already proven material. There was also a new factor to consider, peculiar to bands of the Clash's ilk: doubles were against the punk ethos, which was all about pogoing on the grave of the album as lavishly presented magnum opus, being instead concerned with keeping both the music and packaging fast, clean and cheap.

These arguments washed over the Clash, who, despite having recorded it in an expensive 24-track studio, still wanted to sell the album at a twinned TEAC 4-track rate: a double album for £5, at the time the lowest UK price category for a single album. Their mantra throughout negotiations was 'two for the price of one'. *London Calling* would be the embodiment of punk's Value For Money ethos.

It was at this stage, close to the end of August, that Maurice Oberstein himself decided to pay a visit to Wessex to listen to the Clash's material. Hasty arrangements were made to put a rough mix together, and ensure the entire band, Bill and Guy were all present at the appointed time. But Obie's visit wasn't intended to intimidate. It was unusual for him to visit a recording session in person, but he was eager to hear what one of his favourite signings were up to. 'He gave up unnecessarily large amounts of time to visit the studio just because he was having fun,' says *NME* photographer Pennie Smith. She was also present on the day of the meeting, entirely by coincidence. Pennie was asked to take a photo of Obie posing with the Clash, Bill and Guy in Guy's frequent haunt, the tech cupboard. (It's hard to believe Joe would have worn that Elvis Presley *Return to Sender* shirt had he known it was going to be preserved for posterity . . . though it did presage the album cover design.) The group is all smiles, and the picture gives no sense of the drama about to unfold when Obie was taken into the control room to hear the rough mixes.

Although the atmosphere was not unduly tense, Guy was in a frazzled state, and having the album evaluated by the Big Boss proved too much for him. When Roger Armstrong arrived to start work with the Damned shortly afterwards, he walked past Obie's chauffeured Rolls and into Wessex to find Guy repeatedly smashing one of the orchestra chairs into the floor while shouting 'Fuck CBS!', among other things. After the playback, Obie made appreciative noises, but refused to get into a serious discussion about a double. 'I never worked out exactly why Maurice made that visit,' says Bill. 'The shock and horror of it, as it dreadfully unfolded, instantly wiped my memory of everything that was said.' When Obie moved out back through the studio en route to his car, Guy grabbed hold of the back of his jacket and refused to let go until the Head of CBS UK admitted that the Clash's music was 'magnificent'. Embarrassed, Bill faded away and 'played with Maurice's dog and some ping-pong balls'. There followed a loud, long and excruciatingly embarrassing harangue, before Obie finally managed to free himself and dive into the Rolls. He urged his chauffeuse to make a speedy getaway, only to be informed that the way was blocked by the balding and extremely agitated gentleman lying on the ground in front of the vehicle. Guy was yelling that the only way Obie was going to get away without agreeing to increase the budget was over his dead body, and with reversing not an option, he wasn't exaggerating. Eventually, Bill and Jerry Green came out, picked Guy up and carried him back inside.

This might have proved to be an episode too far for Guy, but it turned out to be the makings of an anecdote in which, for once, he could genuinely be cast in a vaguely heroic role: Don Quixote tilting at the giant windmill of CBS. Either tickled by Guy's bizarre protest or convinced by his passion, Obie OK'd the money for the Clash to do the last-minute tweaking over the next few days, and for Bill Price to mix the album, while the band went off to tour America. If work was completed and approved by late September, it would still allow CBS UK to go ahead with an early November release, like the previous year's *Give 'Em Enough Rope*.

At what point consent was given for the double is difficult to pin down, but, realistically, it must have happened before the Clash's departure. The band headed off the packaging costs objection by stating that a gatefold sleeve was not necessary. Although admittedly not associated with double albums, the band argued, punk had been associated with gimmicks from day one: limited editions, picture sleeves for singles (previously a rarity in the UK, other than for EPs), coloured vinyl, and even 12-inch singles. Originally introduced for DJ-only mixes in the early disco era, the 12-inch single (aka Disco 45) had allowed an extended, bass-heavy mix of a dance tune to be cut and played loud without the needle jumping out of the groove. Demand then grew for the general release of records in this format, usually in limited editions. The 12-inch single crossed over to reggae, and later hip hop, for the same reasons: it was perfect for groove-based music with a running time too long and a bottom end too big to squeeze into the tight-packed grooves of the traditional 7-inch disc. But the format was used for punk singles purely because it was 'different'. Extra tracks were thrown on to fill up the space, and it became another standard record company gimmick, as was giving away a free 45 rpm 7-inch single or EP with an album, which in what the Sex Pistols had done with the original pressing of *Never Mind the Bollocks*, Elvis Costello had done with *This Year's Model* and *Armed Forces*, the Stranglers had done with *Black and White* . . . and Epic had just agreed to do with the American edition of *The Clash*.

This, according to the Clash, is how the negotiations went: CBS agreed to the Clash's £5 selling price, but for a single album; CBS agreed to include a free two-track 7-inch disc with the single album; CBS agreed to make the free single a four-track EP; CBS agreed to make the free 7-inch disc a 12-inch disc; CBS had to accept that a 33 rpm 12-inch disc with eight tracks on it cost no more to produce than a 45 rpm 12-inch disc with four tracks on it . . . by which time the record company found they had been manoeuvred into agreeing to *London Calling* being an 18-track double album sold for the price of one, exactly what the Clash had wanted from the beginning. 'It was our first real victory over CBS,' Joe told *Melody Maker*'s Chris Bohn that December . . . words that he would come to rue within a few short months.

Muff Winwood concedes that the band got their own way in the UK, but maintains CBS's capitulation was quicker and more good-natured than the Clash version implies: it wasn't a case of the wily band getting one over on the record company; more a case of the band exploiting the strong position they happened to be in. 'At the end of the day, an album is only successful if the record company puts it out, and if the band go to the media and tell them how much they love it, and then they go out onstage and play it to people,' he says. 'The album won't be successful unless those three things happen. We can't put it out in a way the band don't want, because they'll just go to the media and say, "We hate this!" and nobody will buy it. All you can do is try to convince a band that the best and most commercial way to put out an album is this way, and if they bluntly refuse, you have no choice. No album is successful without the artist fronting it up.

'If the alternative is nothing, then it's best to do the double for a price of a single,' he continues. 'In Britain you could do that, because you could speak to the distributors and the retailers very quickly and almost personally, and you could make them understand the situation. There were only a couple of distributors that were powerful, and anyway the record company itself did most of its own distribution, and there were only a certain amount of shops in the UK. We had representatives who got to virtually every shop in the country once a week, so we could tell each record shop what was happening and why . . . You've got to remember that every retailer in the country wanted a Clash album out. Soon as that happens, the retailer's making money. So you have to present to the retailers the fact that if they didn't accept the album this way, they won't get the album for Christmas, which would be a big disappointment for them. They had to accept it like we had to accept it. It wasn't the best, but it was the best that we could get.' So deals could be and were cut at all levels – production, distribution, retail – to ensure no one party took too heavy a hit from the reduced profit margin on the album.

The real resistance came from Epic, with CBS UK once again forced into the mediator role. 'In America, the way records were distributed and the power and control that the American distributors had was very different,' says Muff. 'The band was not well known yet at all. It had a very good underground following among cool people, but in mass audience terms was an unknown act. There was no way you could get American distributors to put an album like that in the shops. You just couldn't do it.' There were lots of separate – and different – regional markets, numerous powerful distributors unwilling to take a cut in profits, too many retailers to talk to, and Clash material wasn't as yet as in demand as it was in the UK. 'It wasn't a problem for us in England, but it was a massive problem for America,' says Muff. 'Massive!' The rumblings of discontent would continue for the next four months.

*

The Clash continued working at Wessex until two hours before they were due at the airport to fly to the USA on 4 September 1979, in order to rehearse a set in time to play the Tribal Stomp in Monterey on 8 September, followed four days later by the first date on the Take the 5th tour that had been set up for them by Blackhill. Being a typical last-minute job, little about the organisation of this trip was slick. In addition to Johnny Green, Baker, lighting man Warren Steadman, DJ Barry Myers and Kosmo Vinyl, the band decided to take their girlfriends. Joe took Gaby, Topper took Dee, and Paul took New York-based model Debbie Kronick. Since his split with Viv Albertine, Mick had been single, but he did take a travelling companion along: old friend Rory Johnson, now based in LA. Epic supplied a tour manager, Mark Wissing. *NME* photographer Pennie Smith would be along for a large part of the tour, along with *NME* cartoonist Ray Lowry. Journalists from that paper, *Sounds* and *Melody Maker* would also be flown out for selected periods by CBS as part of a campaign to win back the hearts and minds of the inkys themselves, and by extension of the band's UK following.

Just before the band was due to leave, Mickey Gallagher received a phone call. 'Ian Dury was still on holiday, and Joe got wind that I wasn't doing anything,' he says. 'So he rang out of the blue, just as I was talking to my wife about what we should do with all this time off. He said, "Hey we're going to America, man, why don't you join us?" It was always like that with Joe. Something would pop up, and you'd have to make a decision on the spur of the moment. I said, "I was thinking of going on holiday with the family." So he said, "Bring 'em." So I was able to take my missus and a couple of kids out halfway through the tour to travel on the bus.' The tour was called Take the 5th after the Fifth Amendment to the US Constitution – part of the Bill of Rights – but it was also the first time since Keith Levene left the band in 1976 that the Clash had taken a fifth musician on the road.

It was an excessive entourage for a group of the Clash's still relatively lowly stature to take to America on a 22-date tour of medium-sized venues, but it was not motivated by delusions of grandeur. The Clash had been in each other's pockets for three years non-stop without a significant break, and had been working together at close quarters for long hours under considerable pressure in studios or rehearsal rooms for the last six months. They were about to spend another five weeks together in a tour bus, which – despite its attractive name, Arpeggio – they knew from their previous visit would soon start to feel very much like a submarine. The reason the womenfolk were there – and Scratchy and Rory and Uncle Ray Lowry and all – was to provide some variety, and keep the band members apart long enough during the day so that they could do what they needed to do together at soundchecks and during the shows without losing it. On the very first night, in St Paul, they nearly did lose it, with Mick and Joe openly squabbling on stage and Joe at one point biting Paul's arm. Mickey Gallagher arrived a week later. 'They sat in separate corners with their girlfriends as often as possible,' he says. 'They weren't really talking to one another, and I was supposed to be a catalyst. I didn't realise at the time that that was a large part of the job.' It was an environment in which an upbeat, inquisitive, talkative character like Kosmo Vinyl could excel. Johnny and Baker resented him as an interloper, and Ray Lowry considered him a buffoon, but it was Kosmo more than anyone else who kept the band amused and enthused and away from each other's throats. The tour guaranteed his future as the Clash's PR, a role which in this case involved dealing with publicity and press, supplying sartorial direction and entertainment, and doing a lot of cheerleading.

Adding to the expense of the tour, as ever, was the Clash's generous array of support artists: Derry band the Undertones played the first leg, and there were other one-off appearances by American punk outfits: the Cramps and the Dead Kennedys, both on 13 October at the Kezar Pavilion in San Francisco; and Godfathers of Punk like former New York Doll David Johansen, who supported at the Civic Center in Saint Paul, Minnesota, on 12 September, and Gang War, featuring former MC5 member Wayne Kramer and another ex-Doll Johnny Thunders, who supported in Worcester, Massachusetts, on 28 September. Contemporary country rocker Joe Ely joined the Clash onstage at the Tribal Stomp in Monterey, California, on 8 September to play his Jerry Lee Lewis-flavoured song 'Fingernails', and repeated the guest spot when his band supported the Clash on the southern leg of the tour. The appreciation of the greats of yesteryear tone set by the Pearl Harbour tour was revisited when Bo Diddley returned to play support at the Aragon Ballroom in Chicago on 14 September. Sixties Stax soul men Sam and Dave took over as support for the northeastern dates in late September, and hoodoo bluesman Screamin' Jay Hawkins also made a couple of appearances.

In addition to the reggae and rockabilly tapes Paul had made to liven up the long journeys on the tour bus, the Clash had Scratchy to warm up the audiences at gigs with more material in the same vein, including regular outings for Sam Cooke's 'Chain Gang'. Ray Lowry was a rocker from way back, and – to his great delight – the band's walk-on music on 20 September at the New York Palladium was his old favourite 'The Shape I'm In' by Johnny Restivo (1959). Nor were the Clash above playing their entrances for laughs: on 21 September at the New York Palladium, it was Frank Sinatra's 'High Hopes' (1961); on 11 October at the Hollywood Palladium, it was 'Gee Officer Krupke' from *West Side Story* (1961) which Ray had been sent out to buy especially; and on 26 September at the O'Keefe Center in Ontario, it was the Temptations' soul-funk classic 'Papa Was a Rolling Stone' (1972). On 22 September – the night after Paul Simonon smashed his bass in New York – the Clash took the stage at the Walnut Street Theater, Philadelphia, to the sound of Little Richard's 'Rip It Up' (1956). It was at the O'Keefe Center, however, that the audience really did rip it up, or rather smash up – depending on the source – between 16 and 30 seats.

Willi Williamson's 'Armagideon Time' became the band's latest contemporary reggae cover. The band learned it the day of their Tribal Stomp appearance, and kept it in their set as the first encore, and another highly visual set piece, for the duration of the tour. Most of the other covers reflected the bias of Scratchy's play-on music: old style R&B and rock'n'roll. At the New York Palladium soundcheck on 21 September, the Clash played Bo Diddley's 'Road Runner' (1959) and Big Joe Williams's 'Baby Please Don't Go', first recorded in 1935, but revved up by Them 29 years later (it was the A-side to the B-side of 'Gloria', a song Joe knew inside out, and – evidently – flipside up). At the Kezar Pavilion, San Francisco on 13 October the Clash encored with Gene Vincent's 'Be-Bop-A-Lula' (1956), another veteran of the 101ers songbook. On 7 October Ely took the Clash to visit the grave of Buddy Holly in Lubbock, Texas. On 12 September, at the Civic Center, St Paul, Minnesota, Bob Dylan came to watch the band, bringing his family backstage to say hello. On 14 September, in Chicago, they visited the site of bankrobber John Dillinger's fatal 1934 shooting at the Biograph Theater, and Joe put his fingers in the bullet holes in the walls. In early September, near Monterey, they met Clint Eastwood; on 20 September, in New York, Robert De Niro came to the show.

It was all soaked up and reflected. There was nothing pre-meditated about the way the Clash dressed on the tour. It just grew from their fascination with Americana. 'Some days the Clash would all walk out of their hotel rooms, and they all happened to look like cowboys that day, or gangsters, all independently,' says Pennie Smith, who got it all down in appropriate black and white. 'It was chemistry, absolutely.' Mostly, though, they looked increasingly like Fifties rockers. Inspired by the music they were playing and the music they were listening to, the Clash had bought Johnson's suits and brothel creepers in London, and further accessorised as they went along in America, adding vintage Fifties shirts from New York's East Village thrift shops and pointy shoes in Atlanta. Joe was even given a Casey Jones hat in St Paul. They greased their hair back. (Hair pomade became a cult item, a sickly sweet unguent named Tres Flores becoming Ray Lowry's personal favourite.) The already bequiffed and besuited Kosmo is given some credit for helping this transformation along. Not so Mickey Gallagher, who had been affecting a rocker style, complete with quiff, for some time with the Blockheads, but clearly wasn't considered cool enough to copy. The notion of re-introducing America to proper roots-style rock'n'roll with a punk atti-tude, and in the process banishing from the radio what the band called 'flared rock' – in a reference to Joe's infamous 1976 *Sniffin' Glue* quote, 'Like trousers, like brain' – as epitomised by current airwaves favourites the Eagles, Steely Dan, Boston, Kansas, Foreigner, Styxx and Journey, became a campaign, which the band took every oppor-tunity to sound off about during interviews on local radio stations, and which the ever-gung-ho Kosmo dubbed the Quest.

Live, the Clash would play tracks from *The Clash*, the album they were nominally there to promote, but they were now a different band. They gradually introduced material from the new album during the course of the tour to the point where it typically accounted for around a third of the set. From 19 September's show at the Orpheum Theater in Boston onwards, Mickey Gallagher was there to help them play it, which could not help but draw attention to a change in emphasis. Mickey – who had never even seen the Clash live before – joined the band onstage for the second half of the set to prod hopefully at a locally rented organ that, as often as not, didn't work properly. He got neither the degree of rehearsal nor the signals and cues he was used to. 'Topper turned out to be the one I got closest to, musically,' he says. 'We'd actually play off each other. Mick would come over and stand in front of you, but just do that glazed look, just concentrating on playing his part. Good, but no real eye contact, no playing together, like there was with Topper.' While Bill Price had managed – for the most part – to keep Mick's love affair with the Roland Space Echo under control during the album sessions, it came close to getting out of control on the tour. Mick always played INCREDIBLY LOUD onstage, and on the nights he got carried away, or the front of house levels got out of whack, he could sound like an asthmatic having a panic attack into an over-amped set of bagpipes.

'I'm Not Down', 'Hateful', 'Death or Glory', 'Rudie Can't Fail', 'Lover's Rock' and 'Revolution Rock' had all been played at the Notre Dame shows on 5 and 6 July, and the first three had also received an outing at the Kampuchea Benefit at the Rainbow a week later, but none of them was attempted again on Take the 5th. 'Four Horsemen', played at the Ruisrock Festival in Finland on 4 August, was not revisited either. What these seven songs have in common is that they were among the first the Clash worked up at Vanilla. Familiarity had evidently led to boredom: the Clash were more interested in playing more recent compositions.

Of the other songs from the new album, the Notre Dame veteran 'London Calling' – its lyric still in a state of flux – and the previously untried 'Koka Kola' were in the set from the beginning to the end of the tour proper, and 'Clampdown' and 'The Guns of Brixton' were also regulars from the second night onwards. The last two became big production numbers, visual as well as musical cornerstones of the show. Requiring organ, 'Wrong 'Em Boyo' made its debut with Mickey on 19 September, and also stayed in the set thereafter. These five songs were the core *London Calling* tracks for the Take the 5th tour.

In addition, 'Jimmy Jazz', having made its debut at Notre Dame on 5 July, was the expectation-confusing opening number on the second night of the tour, and was heard a couple more times over the next week before being dropped; 'Brand New Cadillac', having previously been played at the Rainbow on 14 July, got an outing in Toronto on 26 September, and reappeared for the last couple of dates in October; and 'Spanish Bombs' was played for the first and possibly only time at the Aragon, Atlanta, on 2 October. By the time the tour ended, the only three songs so far recorded for the album that had never been played live were: 'The Card Cheat', a piano song with a studio production that could not be reproduced on stage; the disco ballad 'Lost in the Supermarket'; and 'The Right Profile', which simply wouldn't have sounded the same without the horns. (Joe did, however, ad-lib the New York-referencing part of the lyric to the last of these songs during 'What's My Name' at the New York Palladium on 21 September.) On the whole, then, *London Calling* was more than adequately represented. Whatever Epic wanted from the tour, the Clash were looking to their future.

It proved to be a successful and uplifting visit, but no one could claim it ran smoothly. The tone was set the day before departure, when Johnny Green had to visit the CBS offices in Soho Square to beg an advance to buy guitar strings.

Moving an entourage this size around America did not come cheap, and Epic baulked at contributing $20,000 to the costs, while – according to the band – CBS in London tried to make a further advance of cash from home, conditional upon the band agreeing to release the amended US version of *The Clash* in the UK, which they refused to do. Funding was a saga that would last the duration of the tour. As early as Chicago on 14 September, the touring party of 30 had to book into a hotel for three nights on the credit card of *Sounds* writer Peter Silverton. By this time, original road manager Mark Wissing had departed, to be replaced by Bruce Wayne. By 2 October, in Atlanta, there was no money to pay the American road crew, and they mutinied, staying at the hotel and running up an enormous drinks tab on room service until a briefcase of cash arrived. The Blackhill management team joined the tour for its last two weeks. In San Francisco on 13 October Andrew and Peter finally at first refused to pay the increasingly drunk and out-of-control Johnny Green until he threatened them with violence. Three days later, the American road crew, their wages again overdue, refused to operate the equipment for the final night's show in Vancouver until Johnny and Baker tied up the crew boss and threatened him with more of the same. At this point, Bruce Wayne wrapped his cape around himself and melted into the night.

Plans for the tour to continue to Mexico, Cuba and Jamaica had already fizzled out, due largely to the lack of cash. The morning after the Vancouver show, a frayed Johnny Green claims he tried to wake the exhausted band members in time to catch the plane to London, was told to fuck off, and so headed for the airport with Ray Lowry. The band's version is that everyone else involved with the tour did a flit and left them stranded without even enough money to get home.

*

As soon as the band left for America on 4 September 1979 Bill Price started mixing the album. 'Jerry Green was my sounding board,' he says. 'Guy was too far gone by now. Mixing is always hard. It seems to take forever, but at the same time, the hours and days seem to fly by.' He made a couple of transatlantic phone calls to the band to OK some last-minute ideas, but for the most part was left to his own devices, and trusted his own ears and talent. 'It doesn't take 24 tracks to record a band,' says Jerry Green, but for 'London Calling' and a good few of the other songs, the Clash had used every single one of them, so blends and balances were not straightforward. Different songs had different requirements, or suggested little tricks or fine touches. There were some straightforward elements, though. 'Joe's rhythm left, Mick's rhythm right, Mick's lead half-right is Clash Standard guitar stereo layout,' says Bill.

Nothing that had been worked on in Wessex – that is, that was taken further than the live tracking stage – was left out. 'If it was on tape, Mick would have had it on the album!' says Bill. 'I mixed everything we had.' Which confirms that the songs included on *The Vanilla Tapes* that do not appear on *London Calling* were discarded before the Wessex sessions, not during. And that the Guy Stevens warm-up songs like Bob Dylan's 'Billy' and the Bo Diddley covers were never considered as anything more than that, and were forgotten as soon as the real work started.

On 21 September Bill flew out to New York with a cassette of his mix. 'I played it to the band in New York after a gig,' he says. 'The Palladium was the first playback to the band. They loved absolutely everything. They were all totally smashed at the time.' Bill came home, and the band continued to Philadelphia in high spirits, listening to the tape on the bus. 'I think Mick phoned me with a couple of "What happened to the double of that guitar?" and "Don't use that harmony till the last chorus!" type issues. I probably sent him a cassette of the changes.' The Clash received this upon their return to California, around 12 October. After some more hard listening, Mick decided he still wanted to make a couple of alterations, and the last stage of the process was put off until the band's return to the UK, which meant a further delay to the release date.

The Clash arrived back in London on 18 October. After just a two-week break to recuperate, they went back into Wessex studios with Bill Price and Jerry Green to allow Mick to do his last-minute tweaking of certain album tracks and to record 'Armagideon Time'. The band's latest regular cover version was always intended to be paired with 'London Calling' as the UK single, rather than included on the album, and the Clash had habitually looked after their own singles production . . . but sadly, Guy Stevens would have been incapable of contributing, even if he had been invited.

'Armagideon Time' was tracked on Monday 5 November 1979, and overdubbed and versioned over the next day or two. Then the Clash got to work on wrapping up the album. 'Mick did a little recording on a few of the songs, mostly backing vocals and guitar,' says Bill. Part of the lyric, and therefore lead vocal, for 'I'm Not Down' was also changed at this late stage. 'So after that, a remix was needed on those songs.' This took the band through until the end of the week. Once again, the pressure was on. The album had to be at the pressing plant by the end of Tuesday 13 November if *London Calling* was to be released on 14 December in the UK, the last possible pre-Christmas slot. Bill had already booked the mastering lathe at CBS studios in Whitfield Street for Tuesday morning.

At some point during this last, already tense, week of work – according to legend – Mick was motivated to work up another song, 'Train in Vain'. It was finished on Sunday 11 November, and the decision to tack it on to the end of the album was made on Monday 12 November. (See Part 4.) The band, crew, friends like Robin Crocker and Kris Needs, and Guy were all in attendance from the early afternoon onwards on this last day in Wessex, when the already agreed running order became a reality, and the details of the segues between tracks was finalised. A party atmosphere prevailed in the rec room where, according to the *ZigZag* report Kris Needs wrote the following day, the usual suspects indulged in pool tournaments, Space Invaders marathons, food fights, water fights and trussing Kris up in gaffer tape until, finally, at 5 a.m. on the morning of Tuesday 13 November, they were called downstairs to Studio One to hear a playback of the finished mix of the now 19-track album for the first time. Pride, joy and relief were uncontained. Afterwards, the band members headed home for some much-needed rest.

No such luck for Bill Price and Jerry Green, who had just enough time to get themselves and the tapes to Whitfield Street to make their 10 a.m. appointment with mastering engineer Tim Young. Of all the individuals involved with the recording of *London Calling*, Tim is the only one who kept a work diary and still has it. 'I distinctly remember they both looked completely fucked,' he says. 'I think they'd been up all night and come straight to CBS Studios in Whitfield Street – as it then was – from Wessex. The thing was, when you were cutting lacquers in those days, there was a train used to go up to the pressing plant in Aylesbury at 11 o'clock at night, so the idea was, it had to go up to Aylesbury that night at the latest to get the pressings done in time to meet the release date.' If they failed to make it, not only would they miss their release slot, but they would also be in breach of their contract with CBS. That contract called for at least one album a year. There had been 18 months between the release of the first and second albums, but those release dates had fallen in 1977 and 1978. The Clash could not afford *London Calling* to become a 1980 album in the UK. (Urgency wasn't so much of an issue in America: Epic had already released *The Clash* in 1979.) With this in mind, the brinkmanship involved in the last-minute inclusion of 'Train in Vain' seems even more daring . . . or foolhardy.

Not being in-house CBS staff, Bill had no particular obligation to use a CBS facility for mastering, and Tim did wonder why he had been chosen. 'I hadn't been cutting records so very long,' he says. 'I'd only really been doing it full time for about a year by then, so I was very inexperienced. I think that was the very first time I worked with Bill. The master was quarter-inch tape, 15 ips [inches per second], and what happened in those days – before digital audio, which swept all before it in the Eighties – you played it back on a specialist machine that was just used for cutting vinyl. It went through a console – bass, treble, middle, EQ – and then onto a cutting lathe. We'd only had the lathe since that summer. It was brand new. We were the first studio in the UK to have that model of lathe, and I was just finding my feet around using it. You can imagine, you've got really, really short sides, this fantastic new cutting lathe, so the thing is: "Right, how loud's this gonna make it, son?" And that was basically the brief.'

It also answers the question why Bill chose Whitfield Street and Tim. 'Tim's lathe was reputed to be able to cut at the high levels that were achieved at Decca Classical by the old half-speed cutting,' he says. 'I wanted high level. That also explains the side lengths.' Even with the extra track, *London Calling* is a short double. The typical single rock LP was around 35–45 minutes long, but the Clash album is just over 65 – the four sides running for approximately 15.35, 18.00, 12.45 and 18.45, in that order – allowing enough room for the sound to be maximised. 'I was able to cut it very, very loud,' says Tim.

A lot can be done to influence the sound at the cutting stage in ways other than volume-related, which made Tim nervous. 'If I'm to be 100 per cent honest, I didn't really know what I was doing in those days,' he says. 'Whereas Bill is one of the great engineers of his gener-ation, and his skills were as good then as they are today. I seem to remember him taking a very close interest in what I was actually doing to it. He didn't interfere, but he was keeping a close eye on me! I added some high treble and a bit of light mid-range presence to it.' 'You pay a mastering engineer to bring in a new pair of ears,' says Bill. 'You don't buy a dog to bark yourself, as they say. Tim did a fine job. I trust his ears.' Tim's ears told him that what made the album special was the band's songwriting hitting a peak, plus Topper's drum-ming, plus Bill's engineering and mixing. 'One thing I can say without fear of contradiction, that when it came to mixing that record, Bill was pretty much on his own,' he says. 'I know Bill's work well enough now to know that *London Calling*'s got all his characteristics. In the use of stereo, the fact that it's very, very wide, the stereo picture. The way the echo's used on it as well, in a very creative way, a way you don't get with young engineers today. All of the guys of Bill's gener-ation were absolute masters at producing echo. When you think of the tools that they had for manipulating sound in the Sixties – when he learned his craft at Decca – they were so restricted compared to today, and they ended up being creative with what was available, what they had, developing skills to an extent that you don't get these days.' Paul Simonon would later describe it as a 'Cinemascope sound'.

Mick Jones turned up at Whitfield Street in the afternoon to see how things were going. Work continued through into the evening. Normally, a test pressing would have been cut and played through to make sure everything had worked, but there was no time for that if *London Calling* were going to make the 11 p.m. train to Aylesbury. 'What I did then, which I would *never* do today, was just cut the master lacquers and send them off to the factory,' says Tim. 'It just went straight to manufacturing. Risky, I know. Fortunately, it all worked out OK.'

Another indication of the tightness of deadlines was that the single of 'London Calling' was cut after the album, not before: as singles traditionally trailer albums, and the turnaround time is usually about the same, it's usual for them to be cut first. 'I cut the album two days before I cut the single,' says Tim. 'In my diary, I've got "Mick Jones, single" pencilled in for Thursday 15 November at 3 o'clock in the afternoon. And I'm cutting both the 7- and 12-inch singles.' As well as being issued as a standard 7-inch single, it had also been agreed to issue 'London Calling' as the Clash's first ever 12-inch single. Because two lengthy dub reggae versions of 'Armagideon Time' were to be included, for once a punk band could justify the format. Both formats were scheduled for release the week before the album, on 7 December. Time was very, very tight.

Even after both the album and single were cut onto disc and delivered to the factory, Tim's work was not finished. In late December – about a week after the album had been released in the UK – he received an unusual request from CBS. 'They rang up and said, "Can you cut the whole thing on one album?" I think it worked out at about 34 to 35 minutes a side as a single album. [It would have been approximately 33.35 for side one and 31.30 for side two.] And I managed to get it on, but it was like on the level of a K-Tel album. Not to blind you with science, it was about 6 dB quieter. I think the idea wasn't so much for the UK, I think it was that if other overseas bits of CBS had baulked at the idea of releasing a double album, they could have released it as a single. It might have come from Muff, actually. I just test-cut it.'

'It probably was me that went down with him to do it,' says Muff Winwood. Epic were still giving CBS UK hell. 'The American company was saying, "No way! You tell these fucks that they're gonna have one album. They've gotta cut it down!" and all this. We would have just been testing it to see if it was physically possible: does it affect the loudness of the album? Obviously, you couldn't let the sound drop, particularly on an album like this. From something that really punched through the speakers to something that ended up softer and quieter than every other album you had in your collection . . . no. That was just us trying it out to find out what we could do.' The 6 dB drop was unacceptable, so the possibility of an American single album version was, finally, dropped instead.

Taking his business hat off, Muff was highly impressed by *London Calling*. 'When you heard this album, the band are in front of the speakers playing: right there, crisp and hard and tight,' he says. 'It really punches above its weight. That's a lot to do with how the studio is set, how the whole thing is recorded, and I give Bill Price a majority of the credit for that.'

★

Guy Stevens died just two years after the recording of *London Calling*, and the Clash and Bill Price would clearly prefer him to be remembered as a loveable, gifted eccentric and the album as his Last Great Work. Guy certainly did more than enough in the Sixties and early Seventies to be honoured as one of the founding fathers of British popular music, but by the late Seventies he was an out-of-control alcoholic, and – typically for the music business of the day – this was not something that anyone was prepared to – or knew how to – address. 'We didn't realise at first that Guy really couldn't handle it,' says Johnny Green. 'He got drunk extremely quickly.' The inclusion of the *Wessex Studios Footage* on the 25th Anniversary Edition of *London Calling* did Guy's myth few favours. The stories enhance the legend; the reality, as seen in grainy black and white, is a man about to spin out of a 20-year feedback loop of obsession and addiction: dishevelled, destructive, childish, egotistical, deluded . . . and being humoured, when that clearly wasn't helping.

The Clash did do something hugely important for Guy Stevens, though. On what turned out to be his last significant recording session, they delivered to Guy what he had been chasing with obsessive determination for over a decade: an album featuring soulful Hammond organ and attacking Jerry Lee Lewis piano, made by a band with a nearly Rolling Stonesian quality of rootsiness, charisma and stature (if not a strictly Stonesian sound), fronted by a lyricist demonstrating an almost Dylanesque facility and range of reference (if not in a strictly Dylanesque style).

All four members of the Clash have always told Guy Stevens anecdotes with affection, being careful to feed the legend rather than undermine the reputation. They have also been careful to balance accounts of wayward behaviour with glowing testimonials to the producer's more positive contributions. Mick, the band member who suffered most from his wiles, was most gracious when he defined Guy's role to Charles Shaar Murray: 'His presence in the studio definitely makes all the difference. It's like all the mess goes into him, like Dorian Gray's portrait, or whatever. All the messy sound goes and it becomes *him*, and what's left on the tape is . . . clarity.' As Mick did so much of the production work on the album himself, it was a modest remark, and it stands as a touching eulogy. Asked by *Mojo* to name his all-time hero in 2002, Mick picked Guy.

It could be argued that the way the album turned out was a long way from the Vanilla demos, the idea of recording the album on a couple of TEACs, and the whole point of hiring Guy as producer. There's no doubt that there was a discrepancy between what Joe had envisaged in the beginning and what Mick went for at the end, and no doubt that a certain amount of largely unspoken tension developed from that (which would cause more serious problems for the Clash further down the line). But it's not being glib, or putting a spin on it, to claim that, somehow, the Clash managed to get the best of both worlds on *London Calling*.

They chose relatively early basic takes to work with, when there was still some spontaneity and spirit in the performance, and more than a little of the Guy Stevens wild-card factor. They kept the driving elements of the music live – the drums and rhythm guitar – and many of the overdubs stayed true to that feel, with finger squeaks on fretboards, demented piano, blurts of feedback, vocal ad-libs, and found sounds all flaunted as badges of authenticity. With this as a sometimes eccentric but always sturdy foundation, Mick – with the help of the session players, Topper's exuberant percussion and Joe's ever-intriguing lyrics – was able to add a wide variety of fine detail, hooks both blatant and subtle, counter-melodies and layers of backing vocals. And Bill Price recorded and mixed it all to perfection. The result manages the neat trick of sounding at once rude and sophisticated, rough and polished, organic and structured. A fine line is stretched between the album's twin towers, and over potential pitfalls of considerable depth and size, is walked with consummate grace and style . . . by a punk band wearing brothel creepers and biker boots (spurs optional).

4 Across the Tracks

London Calling Song by Song

Recordings that feature regularly in the Greatest Albums Of All Time polls (see Part 6) are seldom just collections of 10 to 20 consistently memorable songs, well performed. More than a few actually feature material of decidedly variable quality. Somehow, this doesn't matter so long as the songs inform and illuminate each other, and are sequenced to make the most of this interaction. Although upon first hearing certain tracks may make a greater initial impact than others, what elevates an album to the pantheon is the impression it gives of being a coherent body of work.

In other words, Great Albums are at least loosely thematic or conceptual. That is not to say they all tell the story of the search for a lost chord or the deification of a deaf, dumb and blind boy, but they do create and sustain their own moods, feels, outlooks and backgrounds. They go where only the Germans, it seems, have a vocabulary bold enough to follow: they capture the *Zeitgeist*; they express a *Weltanschauung*; they open up an extensive *Hinterland* for further exploration. Or, in more approximate English: a Great Album will speak meaningfully of the human condition, and of the word, and of its own time, in a timeless way. It may not use words to do so, or the words might be secondary to the music in achieving this communication. There will be much going on in the background that escapes notice on first hearing, and that only moves into focus with repeated plays. There are some connections and truths that might not become apparent for many years, perhaps until the listener's own experience has caught up. No matter how extensively it is explored, a Great Album will always tease the listener with the promise of further discoveries yet to be made. (With the possible exception of *Never Mind the Bollocks*, a Great Album that comes with its own warning notice to anyone tempted to indulge in flowery analysis.)

Some will argue that a Great Album *is* simply a collection of a dozen or so great songs, nothing more and nothing less. The polls beg to differ. Others might more credibly claim that this kind of discussion is a pastime belonging to a past time . . . an age that began to change tense with the advent of the CD, which, as well as offering greater capacity and therefore stretching the form, introduced the shuffle facility to undermine pre-planned sequencing, and the skip facility to make it easier to omit less immediate tracks as well as disliked ones. Since then, file sharing, downloading and the iPod have turned all the music ever made in the world into a giant random-play personal jukebox. Even as form seems to be readying itself to follow function into the ether, though, artists have begun to hold high-profile live concert events in which they perform their classic albums of yesteryear in their original sequence. A money-grubbing exercise in nostalgia aimed at an ageing section of the populace unwilling or unable to keep up with changing times? The death throes of an obsolete means of musical consumption? Or an indication that the album – like the print novel – is intent upon rallying, digging in and holding on in some vaguely recognisable form whatever the future might bring?

There is no one true reading of an album, just like there is no one true meaning of a song. When it comes to popular music, tunesmiths and arrangers often work instinctively. By his own admission, this was very much true of the Clash's main tunesmith and arranger, Mick Jones. Wordsmiths aiming for more than banal sentiment or straight narrative tend to work allusively, associatively. By his own admission this was very much true of the Clash's main lyricist, Joe Strummer. In both cases, there is considerable room for happy accidents, lateral connections and subliminal blips. Mick has talked of tunes dictating their own development, especially when being written to fit Joe's lyrics. Joe has talked of experiencing a gap in consciousness between starting to write and ending up with the finished article: a sense of . . . where did *that* come from? Looking back, Mick has also admitted that he simply can't remember the details about how certain songs were constructed, or even in many cases, who wrote what. Joe, of course, is no longer available for consultation. Fortunately, Mick wore his musical predilections on his composer's sleeve, and although Joe tended not to write in a directly autobiographical manner, he did draw upon his personal experience to an unprecedented degree for *London Calling*, as well as upon contemporary events, and such other 'input' as records, books and films. Demos and live recordings reveal how some songs developed prior to recording. Joe kept notebooks of his draft lyrics. From 4 to 18 September 2004, these notebook drafts were put on display at the London Print Studio's *Joe Strummer Past, Present & Future* exhibition. Several were also displayed from 21 October 2006 to 15 April 2007 at the *Revolution Rock: The Story of the Clash* exhibition at the Rock and Roll Hall of Fame in Cleveland, Ohio, and again from 24 November 2008 at the Hall's new Annex in New York.

Lyrics are not reproduced in full here, but are part of the packaging for all officially released versions of *London Calling*. And no pirate of the cyber seas or information superhighwayman is more than a couple of clicks away from an online trove.

'London Calling'

Mick Jones tends to describe his songwriting collaboration with Joe Strummer as being swift and straightforward, with one or other of them knocking out their contribution in a matter of minutes and handing it over the table for the other party to do likewise (see Part 2). The tortuous process of writing 'London Calling' gives the lie to that. From an early stage, Joe and Mick knew they had a song with the potential to be truly great, but Joe really had to struggle to arrive at the finished article. What is far truer to their compositional work ethic is Joe's 'note to self' preserved on the sleeve of *Streetcore*, the third, posthumously released, Mescaleros album: 'Nothing in the world can take the place of persistence.' Or, even closer to home, as another track on *London Calling* would have it: sometimes it's necessary to march a long way for glory . . .

'London Calling' was among the batch of new songs worked up in the Vanilla rehearsal studio sometime in May or June 1979, but it was among the last to be completed to the band's satisfaction at Wessex in late August. The original version of the lyric came first, but the final version of the lyric came last.

After working late at Vanilla, Joe would splash out on a taxi home. Especially if his girlfriend Gaby Salter had turned up to meet him. One night, as the cab took them along the bank of the River Thames from the rehearsal room in Pimlico to their council flat in Chelsea, the couple had one of their frequent conversations about the State of the World. Joe had read what he described to *Melody Maker* in 1988 as 'about 10 newspaper reports in one day calling down a variety of plagues upon us, like the Ice Age is coming and the sun's getting closer to the Earth, and London's gonna drown next time there's a heavy rain'. In June 1979, talking to the *NME*'s Charles Shaar Murray, Joe referred to another of the predictions of doom he'd read about: 'There's 10,000 days of oil left. It's finite.' Another concern was the possibility of crop failure and mass starvation. It was Gaby who urged Joe to write something about this. Back in the flat at 31 Whistler Walk, sitting at the window looking down over Edith Grove, he set to work on the lyric.

In 1988 Joe described what he said was the first draft to *Melody Maker* as a song simply about London in 1979: 'I was annoyed by a lot of people who came down to London and seemed to roam through the streets of Soho. They didn't want to come into the bars and drink with us or see our movies or dig the capital.' Three years later, interviewed by Kosmo Vinyl for the *Clash On Broadway* box set booklet, he specified that it was about mobs of people flooding Soho whenever big football matches were scheduled. Joe credited Mick Jones with slipping into what had once been Bernie Rhodes's role, and urging him to rewrite those early verses and come up with something more worthy of the chorus: 'That's not important. Write about something that's important.'

The process was a little more drawn out than that, and the version Joe describes as his first draft in these interviews was at least his fourth. After his death in December 2002, a notebook found among piles of archive material stored in an outbuilding of his home near Bridgwater, Somerset, revealed that the lyric of 'London Calling' had gone through several substantially different incarnations before the Clash even demoed the song at Vanilla; and it changed at least once more before the final version was recorded at Wessex. Bill Price still has Joe's working copy of the finished lyric, the one he consulted while singing in the studio, which Bill annotated with notes about which vocal passes to use. From beginning to end, getting a version everyone was satisfied with took Joe three to four months . . . though he would continue to tinker with it live for another two.

The notebook drafts for 'London Calling' were put on display at *Joe Strummer Past, Present & Future* in September 2004, with one of the later drafts reproduced to illustrate an August preview of the exhibition in the *Independent*'s Arts & Books Review supplement. What they reveal is that Joe started out with something thematically similar to what he ended up with, but took a couple of detours along the way. Not that these detours were a complete waste of time and effort: the final lyric developed by a process of accretion, with the best and most memorable lines and phrases from the numerous versions tending to stick – or even to be reinstated after being dropped – even if the shifting contexts made for unusual juxtapositions and an impressionistic overall effect.

Right from the start, the chorus betrayed the original inspiration: the planetary scale of the devastation threatened by (and recounted in the style of) tabloid newspaper banner headlines of the day; and the more local and personal sense of vulnerability experienced during the course of a nocturnal cab ride along the apparently soon-to-be-flooded river to a Thames-side flat in an area apparently all too fittingly named the World's End. Not unlike Bob Dylan with 'A Hard Rain's a-Gonna Fall' (1962), Joe had so many Prophesies of Nostradamus to consider, it was hard for him to decide on his final selection for a four-line chorus. Throughout his drafts, phrases are shuffled and refined, dropped and added to, but the prospect of oil and wheat running out, the threats (two of them related, two apparently paradoxical) of the sun getting closer, the city drowning and an imminent Ice Age are all present and correct in some form or other from the beginning. The last line of the chorus would stay the same throughout. It clearly presented Joe with one of the lyric's major obstacles: finding a rhyme for 'river' in the penultimate line. (Wisely, he eventually stopped trying to force the issue, and went for the – at best – half-rhyme 'no fear'.)

The debate about whether the world would perish in fire or in ice was not new, but it was heating up . . . so to speak. *Newsweek* published an influential article entitled 'The Cooling World' in 1975, the same year Harold Wilcox published his book *Hothouse Earth*, and the year before Lowell Ponte published *The Cooling: Has the Next Ice Age Already Begun?* The issue was the same as today's concern about global warming; only scientists were not sure whether the effects of pollution were going to take us up or down the thermometer. By 1977, weather was the stuff of conspiracy theory, as signalled by the publication that year of *The Weather Conspiracy: The Coming of the New Ice Age* by the self-styled Impact Team. The following year, a specialist telescope was launched into orbit to monitor solar-flare activity, which prompted media musings about the degree to which that activity, and solar radiation, might be increasing. The First World Climate Conference was held in Geneva between 12 and 23 February 1979, ensuring that a hotchpotch of weather-related theories made the newspapers that spring.

The oil scare dated back to 1956 and the Hubbert Peak Theory of American oil production, which predicted it would hit its maximum in the late Sixties and decline thereafter. Subsequent revised models for global production, factoring in discoveries of new reserves and improved extraction methods, have indicated that oil demand will start to exceed supply sometime before 2020, making Joe's 10,000 days comment not far off the mark. But oil was a specific cause for worry in the Seventies for other reasons. Tensions in the Middle East resulted in an OPEC boycott of oil supply, and prices continuing to rise steadily. The consequences of the revolution in Iran hit the UK hard, with a price hike in June 1979 making oil 50 per cent more expensive than at the start of the year. There was more at stake than engines running down. Increasing fuel costs also meant increasing food prices: these were the economics of the Winter of Discontent. More generally speaking, the fear of population outstripping available supplies of food was a hardy perennial dating all the way back to Thomas Malthus in the early years of the nineteenth century.

The River Thames had always been vulnerable to high spring tides, which could be dangerous when combined with a North Sea storm surge. And, with global warming, the sea level was rising. Fourteen people had died in a 1928 flood that had collapsed part of Chelsea Embankment, not far from where Whistler Walk would be built 50 years later. That was the last time there was significant flooding in central London, but a massive storm surge in 1953 had killed a total of 307 people along the eastern coast of Britain, more than a third of them in towns around the Thames Estuary. Work had begun on a Thames Flood Barrier at Woolwich Reach in 1974, but would not be completed until 1984. Bad weather in early 1979 brought high tides and storms that breached sea defences along the south coast of England. London was spared, but Joe was clearly given pause to wonder for how long.

Also from his earliest draft, the newspaper headline and strapline feel of the chorus encouraged Joe to think in terms of radio and TV news announcements for the rest of the lyric. 'London calling . . .' which gave him the opening phrase for each verse and, of course, the song's title, was the call sign associated with BBC Overseas Service Radio, used to ID the station just before the regular news bulletin. In a couple of the early draft versions of his lyric, Joe immediately followed it with the expression 'News of Clock Nine', another lift from the BBC, this time from their nightly BBC1 TV bulletin *The Nine O'Clock News*, its title clumsily inverted presumably for the sake of a stronger rhyme. This phrase appears to have been considered for the song's title for a while.

The rest of the original first verse is straight reportage from the Winter of Discontent, covering chaos and strikes in central London. After that, well . . . the second verse heads out of the city and off on a couple of wild tangents in quick succession. A couplet about crows roosting in deserted reactor towers evokes a post-nuclear disaster wasteland. On their February 1979 Pearl Harbour tour of America, the Clash had been amused when Bo Diddley boasted about having his own fallout shelter. When news of the only-just-averted disaster at Three Mile Island broke on 31 March, it no longer seemed so eccentric. It is followed immediately by a couplet describing blood dripping on the flowers in the Puerto Rican Embassy: references to Federico Garcia Lorca's 1932 play *Blood Wedding* and to contemporary 'Nuyorican' poet Pedro Pietri's Seventies performance piece, *El Puerto Rican Embassy*, squeezed into the same too-tight phrase.

The next verse takes the action back to London, down in the Tube station with mice on the line, and bowler-hatted gents prodding people with brollies. Mention of rationing reinforces the impression that Londoners are taking shelter in the Underground, as they did from the Blitz during the Second World War. It's relatively easy to follow Joe's thought processes here: the BBC's Overseas Service was at its most influential and authoritative during wartime. The next verse again switches focus to more exotic locations, referring to the Far East's Golden Triangle of opium production, and planes 'flying oceans high' to deliver narcotic balm to soothe northern itches and southern jangles. All of this scattershot material was destined for the chop . . . though the nuclear threat, war and junkie imagery would reappear in the final version in different guises, and Lorca would get his own song elsewhere on the album, 'Spanish Bombs'.

Joe's notebook also contains the second draft of the song, which finds him arriving at something close to the finished version's first verse. There are still some real clunkers, like 'we've had a little murder and bombings of late' – a reference to IRA activities again addressed with more finesse in 'Spanish Bombs' – but the line about the faraway towns and the use of 'phoney' are now in place . . . as is 'ain't got no swing'. While Roger Armstrong was taking a break from recording the Damned's *Machine Gun Etiquette* in Wessex Studio Two one day, Guy Stevens slumped down on a sofa next to him and said, 'Your guys swing. How can I get my guys to swing?' If Guy repeated his criticism or something like it to the Clash – and he was hardly discreet or diplomatic even when sober – it's possible that Joe incorporated it into the lyric. The inspiration for 'Cheapskates' had come from similar casual criticisms made by Bernie Rhodes; as would the opening line of 'Rock the Casbah'. The phrase 'ain't got no swing' also alludes to London's erstwhile role as the epicentre of the Swinging Sixties. In 1965 Roger Miller's country crossover song 'King of the Road' went to Number 4 in the USA mainstream charts, and then Number 1 in the UK. The following year he celebrated with 'England Swings' ('. . . like a pendulum do'), which reached Numbers 8 and 13, respectively. Joe knew the song well: two years later, he would quote a line from it in his lyric for 'Red Angel Dragnet'.

The main function of the line is to remind the listener that Swinging London is a thing of the past . . . other than swinging like a police truncheon do during a riot, demonstration or peaceful protest, in which case it's *bang, bang, bang* up to date. As Misty in Roots manager Clarence Baker could well attest, having had his skull fractured during the 23 April 1979 Southall Anti-Nazi League protest.

The third draft of the song is recorded in the notebook pages reproduced by the *Independent* in August 2004, and is also – more or less – the one preserved on *The Vanilla Tapes* demo version of the track, as included on 2004's 25th Anniversary Edition of *London Calling*. Joe now adds a nuclear meltdown to the list of apocalyptic possibilities in the chorus. While the chorus draws ever closer to its final shape, however, the verses have been almost completely rewritten to reflect a new Strummer obsession . . . Or rather, a re-heated Strummer obsession, which Joe outlined to Charles Shaar Murray in his late June 1979 *NME* interview: 'The Sixties are really in, aren't they? We've got *Juke Box Jury* and everything.' The BBC's pop music panel show had originally run from 1959–67, but was briefly revived in 1979. 'I'm so sick of delving into the past,' continued Joe. 'It's on short-cycle now, as well. It's stupid. Everyone's looking for yesterday because tomorrow's so shitty.'

By mid-1979 the UK's latest musical and sub-cultural craze was the mod revival. Kick-started by the Jam when they released *All Mod Cons* in November 1978, it had continued to build ever since, and would be rein-forced by the summer 1979 release of *Quadrophenia*, the film inspired by the Who's then six-year-old mod concept album of the same title. In his third draft lyric for 'London Calling' – evidently inspired by the surviving 'ain't got no swing' couplet – Joe gives short shrift to the Swinging Sixties wannalives coming on pilgrimages to former Soho mod tailoring centre Carnaby Street, which, by the late Seventies was wholly given over to tourist tat, and finding it wanting because it hadn't been sealed in a time bubble back in 1964. Joe's knee-jerk loathing for these retread mods causes him to mutter all kinds of snide remarks about 'the right kind of parka', 'the Sixties in gear', '*Juke Box Jury* retir[ing] inside', and – bearing in mind the chorus's prediction of imminent extreme weather conditions – to rub his hands in glee at the prospect of 'mods on the run' during their next bank holiday seaside outing. He comes over a little like Travis Bickle, the central character in the 1976 cult film *Taxi Driver*, as again later quoted in 'Red Angel Dragnet', wishing for a real rain to come and wash all the scum off the sidewalk.

The bile is completely out of proportion to the supposed crime. Why was it less acceptable for the youth of 1979 to play the music and dress in the style of the early to mid-Sixties than it was for Joe Strummer and the rest of the Clash to play the music and dress in the style of the late Fifties? At times, Joe's self-awareness could appear to be lacking to the extent that he couldn't see the accusations he was so liberally spraying around at everyone else could be – and would be, and already had been – directed right back at him.

The Jam not only took over the Clash's role as the darlings of the UK music press and its readers during 1979 (glowing reviews, regularly topping readers' polls) they were destined to back it up in the UK marketplace in a way that – thanks largely to their refusal to play *Top Of The Pops* – the Clash would never manage. In November 1979 the Jam would hit the Number 3 spot with 'The Eton Rifles', on their way to even greater glories. Joe's highly developed competitive streak was in danger of turning his eyes green (rather than yellow), and in this version of 'London Calling' it shows.

Even in 1979 there was something intrinsically Swinging Sixties about *any* song written about London, as had been semi-acknowledged in earlier Clash songs like 'London's Burning', '48 Hours' and 'Capital Radio', and which would be noted and exploited by Blur some 15 years later. From the Kinks' reference to a 'Carnabetian army' in 'A Dedicated Follower of Fashion' (1966) to the Rolling Stones singing about the Grosvenor Square anti-Vietnam War demonstration in 'Street Fighting Man' (1968), the mid-to-late Sixties British music scene had been built on songs promoting London, and its red telephone boxes, red buses, black cabs and Big Ben as the Centre of the Happening Universe. And 'London Calling' was not only a London song, but also a River Thames song, and so would have to go up against the Kinks' near-perfect pop moment 'Waterloo Sunset' (1967).

By the time 'London Calling' made its live debut at the Clash's 5 July Notre Dame show, the lyric had moved towards something that sounded a little more like the version described by Joe in the retrospective 1988 *Melody Maker* and 1991 *Clash On Broadway* interviews, with the crowd now being outsiders from the faraway towns roaming Soho. This just involved a slight tweak from the previous version, with the 'fools' and 'clowns' who 'jeer their way around' simply changing from mobs of mods to mobs of provincial yobs. Joe had evidently finally realised his anti-mod proselytising did not reflect well upon him. The Sixties revivalists would leave their mark on the final version, though, surviving as echoes in the references to Beatlemania and the 'imitation zone'. As Joe had recently visited 24-hour cities like New York, and was a keen imbiber and night owl, he also took the opportunity offered by mention of Soho to object to Central London's 'midnight shutdown': an unofficial curfew which did nothing to improve the good cheer of the city's indigenous population.

The Soho mob version of the lyric was still current when the Clash went into Wessex to start recording *London Calling*. It was at this juncture that Mick Jones made his objections about the lyric not being up to standard, so the song was initially recorded as an instrumental. '"London Calling" was one of the few tracks we recorded without Joe singing,' confirms Bill Price. Evidence that Joe's initial response to Mick's criticism – after all the work he had already put in – was not quite as easygoing and accepting as he would later suggest was offered by the sarcastic introduction to the song he made during the Clash's appearance at the Ruisrock Festival in Turku, Finland, after the first week of recording in Wessex. 'I hope you've all got your pens and notebooks ready to make sure you get all these wonderful lyrics,' said Joe. 'This song's now going to be called "London's Burning".'

Bill is certain that all the songs intended for the album at that stage had vocals in place by the time he mixed the album, prior to taking a tape out to play to the band in New York on 21 September. While one or two other songs received overdubs upon the band's return to Wessex in early November 1979, there are no marks on either the Wessex track sheet or the final draft of the lyric in Bill's possession to indicate that any late changes were made to the master of 'London Calling'. Which means the song as it was released was recorded in its entirety, and the lyric as it is widely known both complete and recorded, before the end of August. What makes this peculiar is that Joe continued to sing a mixture of older and alternative lyrics to the song for the entire duration of the Take the 5th tour: both before 21 September and afterwards, when he had every opportunity to refer to the cassette of the studio recording. Either he wasn't yet entirely happy with what he'd recorded for the album's lead track and UK single . . . or he simply couldn't remember it.

*

What helped everything fall into place for Joe was going back to first principles: the phrase 'London calling . . .' itself. 'News of Clock Nine' still appears at the top of 'Bill's' final draft lyric, as part of a couplet Joe considered singing over the introduction . . . but he abandoned the idea during the vocal dubbing session. Dropping the reference to television's evening news in favour of focussing solely on the more venerable medium of radio worked in the song's favour in several ways.

Joe and Mick Jones had grown up listening to radio stations that delivered urgent packages of pop-cultural information straight to their eager teenage ears. It was an exciting time for youth, with the counter-culture coming into its own and influencing the wider culture in unprecedented ways. The music scene not only reflected the Zeitgeist, but also helped move it along. Joe recalled hearing the Rolling Stones' 'Street Fighting Man' in 1968 and believing it to be accurate reportage of what was going on in the capital. Keith Richards has talked about the pressure to deliver a new killer single every couple of months in the Sixties, and the immediacy of the process. 'Every eight weeks you had to come up with a red-hot song that said it all in about two minutes 30 seconds.' Those hot new songs could be composed, recorded, released, played on the radio and sitting pretty in the charts within six weeks: just a month and a half from first chord to *Billboard*. Popular music was able to be topically relevant because it was so fast moving. Most artists recorded at least one album and three singles a year, and that tradition continued from the mid-Fifties to the late Seventies.

In 1972 David Bowie proved he was both on the same wavelength and very much tuned in to the moment when he wrote his State of the Nation in Decay song 'All the Young Dudes' for Mott the Hoople, in which his titular heroes 'carry the news'. Bowie's apocalyptic futurist vision goes full circle to the days of the wandering minstrel, part of whose function was to pick up news and pass it on in song. This was at the root of the Broadside ballad tradition, Woody Guthrie's Depression-era protest songs, and their ultimate arrival in rock'n'roll via the folk revival, Greenwich Village and the likes of Phil Ochs and Bob Dylan.

In early and mid-Sixties Britain, contemporary music radio was hard to come by. At first it meant scrabbling around the dial for Radio Luxembourg, which came and went on a wave of phase, until pirate stations like Radio Caroline and (the original) Radio London set up to operate from outside British territorial waters on rusting trawlers and docking platforms in 1964. Even when the BBC's popular music station Radio One was launched to supersede them in 1967 it wasn't exactly up to the minute and on the money 24 hours a day, seven days a week, and many still pined for the more anarchic and inspired alternative. In the mid-Seventies, the 101ers had appeared on, played a benefit for, and – on one occasion – offered broadcast space in their squat to itinerant west London pirate station Radio Concorde. Bernie Rhodes and Malcolm McLaren's *what side of the bed* T-shirt praised Free Radio: as in, politically and artistically free.

In his earliest interviews as a member of the Clash, Joe in particular had expressed his ambition for the band to set up their own radio station. In August 1976, when Keith Levene broke a string on his only guitar halfway through one of the band's first gigs, Joe had filled what could have otherwise been an awkward gap by holding up his transistor to the microphone, sound engineer Dave Goodman improvising heavy echo to send a news report of an IRA bombing echoing around the 100 Club. It didn't escape Joe's notice that this dubbed-up news broadcast was very much in the Clash spirit. Paul Simonon had auditioned for the London SS on a version of Jonathan Richman and the Modern Lovers' 'Roadrunner' (1972), and in March 1977 the Clash began playing around with a version in rehearsals, modifying the refrain from 'radio on' to 'Radio One' in order to berate the BBC's designated youth outlet for ignoring punk and short-changing its target audience. The band soon dropped the idea in favour of writing their own 'Capital Radio', which takes London's independent station to task for the same failings. Instead of being, as its station ID boasted, 'in tune with London', Joe's chorus sneers that Capital is 'in tune with nothing'. In addition to their Guthriesque and Dylanesque songs of protest, the Clash continued to use songs like 'Remote Control', 'Garageland', 'Complete Control', 'Clash City Rockers', '(White Man) in Hammersmith Palais', 'Safe European Home', 'Cheapskates' and – note the Bowie–Mott reference – 'All the Young Punks' to file first-hand reports from the frontlines of punk as the movement grew, mutated and splintered.

Re-recording 'Capital Radio' as 'Capital Radio Two' in January 1979 for *The Cost of Living* EP clearly brought both the medium and the message back to the forefront of the Strummer brain. The original 'Capital Radio' ends with the heavily echoed warning 'don't touch that dial!'; and in another sort of echo, 'London Calling' closes with Joe adapting that traditional piece of hourly radio news bulletin jargon 'at the top of the hour' to 'at the top of the dial' . . . 'London Calling' can be seen as evidence of the Clash's commitment to keeping the notion of the pop song as three-minute news bulletin alive. When released as a single, it would communicate suppressed information, disseminate notes from the underground, and carry the news to all the young dudes, both via the medium of radio and direct from disc.

The initial licence given to BBC Radio when it formed in 1922 was 2LO. 2LO began broadcasting on 14 November that year, from Marconi House in London to anyone in London who could receive the signal. Broadcasts began, 'This is 2LO London calling . . .' Four years later, the original company was dissolved, and the BBC began to operate with a Crown Charter as Britain's national radio station. Even by this time its call sign had caught the public imagination. As early as September 1923 the Duke of York's Theatre staged a revue called *London Calling* featuring a number of skits and musical numbers written by Noël Coward and choreographed by Fred Astaire. It ran for 367 performances. In 1930 a Geoffrey Kerr play called *London Calling* opened on Broadway in New York, telling the story of two brothers who were separated at birth and brought up on separate sides of the Atlantic.

Meanwhile, the BBC was spreading its radio waves far and wide, at home and abroad. The Empire Service was founded in 1932, with various foreign language services added from 1938 onwards, including German. The station ID was now simply 'This is London calling . . .' In August 1939 the BBC began to publish its own overseas journal, also, inevitably, entitled *London Calling*. That year the Empire Service changed its name to the less chest-beating Overseas Service. Shortly afterwards, Europe was thrown into the turmoil of the Second World War, when the Overseas Service really came into its own, fighting the propaganda war against Nazi Germany and relaying information in all the major European languages to occupied nations and their resistance movements. It's almost impossible to overstate the importance during those years of the calming and authoritative declaration, 'This is London calling . . .' The words were the audio equivalent of a beacon, bringing comfort and offering hope to millions. Just a decade or so after the end of the war, during his nomadic Foreign Office childhood, Joe would get first-hand experience of the Overseas

Service's ability to reach out and connect, not only functioning as an umbilical cord between British expatriates and their motherland, but communicating across frontiers and cultural, racial, religious and political divides. (Although often retrospectively referred to as the World Service, the Overseas Service didn't change its name again until 1988.)

In choosing 'London calling' as his verse-opening hook, then, Joe was consciously co-opting the gravitas associated with the phrase. This was to be an important broadcast for the public good, positive propaganda in direct contrast to that produced by Joseph Goebbels for the Nazis, as previously invoked by Joe in the condemnatory 'Capital Radio'. Earlier in the writing process for 'London Calling', the war association had taken Joe back to the Second World War, but his final draft of the lyric quickly establishes a scenario – by the second line, no less – where the world is looking down the barrel of a Third. War has been declared, we learn. The phrase 'battle come down' is highly evocative, simultaneously hinting at the sudden violence of a descending axe blade, the relentless pressure drop of modern day engines of destruction, and a biblical judgement from on high.

This, too, continues an established Clash tradition: in '1977' Joe envisaged 'sten guns in Knightsbridge', and by 1978 he was predicting an 'English Civil War' and 'Guns on the Roof' of the world. Jack Hazan and David Mingay of Buzzy Enterprises, the team responsible for making *Rude Boy* – still going through the editing process while *London Calling* was being demoed and recorded – had picked up on this tendency in Joe's lyrics, and were intent on highlighting it in their movie. The film ends with Margaret Thatcher's triumphant May 1979 arrival in Downing Street, heralding the long reign of the UK's most radical and socially divisive right-wing government in living memory. Existing problems would be exacerbated and exploited for political ends.

All this was in the air during the writing of 'London Calling', and Joe's antennae were tuned in and receiving. Right from the beginning of the song, now, we know this is a radio broadcast with some very bad news to impart.

Although uncomfortable and bombastic, the militaristic flavour of *Give 'Em Enough Rope* had been typically influential (or, arguably, slightly ahead of the pack): in 1979 alone there would be similarly themed albums from Elvis Costello (*Armed Forces*) and the Jam (*Setting Sons*), while the less serious Damned at least released an album with a title that sounded ready to go to war: *Machine Gun Etiquette*.

Joe's fascination with terrorism was evident in 'Tommy Gun' and on his custom-designed T-shirts referencing everyone from the IRA to the Baader-Meinhof Gang to the Brigate Rosse. During 1979 Talking Heads recorded 'Life During Wartime', a driving, inexorable funk-punk song inspired by the Baader-Meinhof Gang, and painting a breathless, on-the-run scenario that is not so much post-revolution or post-terrorist atrocity as post-apocalypse. It recalls David Bowie's pounding Bo Diddley-goes-Salsa number 'Panic in Detroit' (1973), which compares the last of the White Panthers to Che Guevara, and places him in a city plunged into chaos. The sci-fi line of enquiry that led Bowie from 'All the Young Dudes' to 'Panic in Detroit' to 'Diamond Dogs' (1974) is not much different from the one that brought Joe Strummer to 'London Calling' . . .

The cab journey which provided the initial inspiration for 'London Calling' and the towering council estate where the lyric was first drafted maintain a subliminal presence throughout the lyric's many stages of development, and in the final draft they combine with the radio and catastrophe themes to present Joe with the conceit that ties everything together. The sense of having made a late-night run across town to a place of questionable safety in a world spinning out of control recalls disaster scenario sci-fi movies like *The Day of the Triffids* (1962) and TV series like *Survivors* (1975–7) wherein a few arguably fortunate survivors of some event or disease or predatory force that has laid waste to almost everyone else dig in and attempt to repel anything from their fellow man gone to the bad to aliens to the undead to overgrown weeds.

The most inspirational text in – and arguably the originator of – this sub-genre is Richard Matheson's 1954 novel *I Am Legend*. Set in future Los Angeles – between 1976 and 1979, appropriately enough – it features the character Robert Neville as the sole survivor of a pandemic virus . . . apart from the hordes of vampires created by the virus roaming the city at night. In placing vampires in a futurist setting, and multiplying them so they become a terrifying swarm, the book introduced the modern-day version of the zombie to popular culture. It spawned the film *The Last Man On Earth* (1964). Made and set in Rome and starring the familiar ghoulish face and voice of Vincent

Price, it became a cult American hit, and one that – by his own admission – directly inspired George A. Romero to make his zombie movie *Night of the Living Dead* (1968). In 1971 *I Am Legend* was itself remade in LA as *The Omega Man*, starring Charlton Heston (as was obligatory for all sci-fi films at that time). In this version, now set in 1977, biological warfare appears to have wiped out the rest of mankind, but Neville has self-vaccinated. He scavenges through a devastated city during the day, and at night retreats to a fortified LA high-rise to battle waves of attacks from killer vampire-zombies known as the Family (in a then-contemporary reference to Charles Manson's real-life troupe of predators). Three years later, this film inspired David Bowie's New York-set 'Diamond Dogs', and five years after that it seeped into Joe Strummer's 'London Calling', with its high-rise viewpoint, myriad impending disasters and 'zombies of death'.

More importantly, a convention of this futurist-alarmist-survivalist sci-fi horror sub-genre is the attempt to make contact with other possible tattered remnants of humanity, usually via radio. In keeping with genre tradition, and in the context of the lyric's references to nuclear meltdown, there's an implication that the war in 'London Calling' is an end-of-civilisation-as-we-know-it war. London is attempting to communicate with the faraway towns, perhaps even to give them its last testament. So what should this valediction be? As Mick Jones had so rightly pointed out at the start of August, what the Clash shouldn't waste time doing was grumbling about the capital's licensing laws, belittling retro youth cults or dismissing listeners as provincial tossers.

On a literal level, the first verse now has Joe beseeching the wannabe survivors to emerge from their hiding places in cellars and cupboards. The hicksvilles addressed are no longer just British, but international, and the tone has changed from patronising and dismissive to solicitous and inclusive. On a metaphorical level, Joe appeals to youth and counter-culture figures (the underworld/underground) and the marginal, oppressed and scared (in the cupboard/closet) to step out and step up, take centre stage and take responsibility. This is not – to paraphrase Bob Dylan – a time to be following leaders. Or worshipping rock bands, even the Clash. And it isn't a time to be looking back to the Sixties, either (Joe couldn't resist leaving that in). The second verse starts with a summation: don't imitate, whether the object of your affections be the Clash as a band or, ahem, mod as a movement: be original and think for yourself. And then Joe makes one of his freely associative jump cuts, reviving the heroin reference from the early notebook version of the lyric. Having warned against apathy, he identifies its ultimate manifestation: zombies. Although they nod their heads to the sci-fi bogeymen, his zombies are a different kind of walking corpse. 'The "zombies of death" were shooters [as in, junkies shooting up]. "Draw another breath": start living again. "Saw you nodding out": a lot of people were getting down on heroin at the time,' Joe explained to Musician's Bill Flanagan in 1988. It was another plague or tribulation of the times.

As Joe knew only too well, heroin use in inner-city America in the late Sixties and early Seventies had helped defuse and dissipate the revolutionary spirit of the counter-culture, particularly that of the Black Panthers (so much so that it was widely suspected in radical circles that its supply was encouraged by The Man). To nod out was to opt out. Heroin was death to activism, death to creativity, and – all too often – real death. By 1979 heroin use was spreading through the London music scene and had already reached many of the faraway towns. Clash hero Johnny Thunders's first band the New York Dolls had fallen apart as a direct consequence of his addiction; his second band the Heartbreakers had gone down the tubes, and his solo career had stalled before it really started for the same reason. Clash buddy Sid Vicious had died of a heroin overdose in February 1979. Former Sex Pistols guitarist Steve Jones was hooked. Former Clash member Keith Levene had graduated from injecting speed to injecting smack. Closer to home – 'I saw you' – Clash road manager Johnny Green was dabbling with the odd snort. So was drummer Topper Headon. Following the Clash's Take the 5th show at the Rox club in Lubbock, Texas, on 7 October 1979, Topper overdosed and had to be revived. 'I walked him up and down the road for about an hour trying to keep him conscious, because we couldn't risk taking him to hospital,' says Johnny Green.

Interestingly, in his choice of words, Joe chooses to point the finger of suspicion at himself. He is, or was, the 'one with the yellowy eyes': yellow eyes were the most visible symptom of the hepatitis Joe had contracted back in February 1978. This was Joe's second reference to his condition in song, the first being in his rewrite of Elvis Presley's

'Heartbreak Hotel' for 1978's *Grutzi Elvis* film. Sid Vicious's hospital stay with the disease in 1977 – which prevented him from playing on much of *Never Mind the Bollocks* – had been as a result of sharing dirty needles, and hepatitis did have this particular association in rock culture. In interviews he gave both at the time and much later, a defensive Joe blamed his own stay in hospital – which caused a two-month delay in the recording of *Give 'Em Enough Rope* – on inadvertently swallowing a gob of spittle from an infected member of the audience. It would seem that the lyric-writing part of his brain was prepared to be a little more honest. In Chris Salewicz's 2006 Strummer biography *Redemption Song*, Joe's girlfriend of early 1978, future PiL member Jeannette Lee, went on record with the information that Joe *had* caught the disease from a dirty needle when shooting up for his first and only time with Keith Levene and some others in a spirit of 'what the hell' experimentation. In corroboration, Salewicz further revealed that Mick Jones had told him a version of the story at the time of Joe's illness. Joe's somewhat unlikely alternative explanation of how he contracted the disease was more a matter of embarrassment and regret than complete denial. Jeannette was not sure if the drug injected had been speed or heroin, which Keith had moved on to by the time he joined PiL. Mick gave Salewicz the strong impression it had been heroin.

Despite the serious nature of his subject matter, Joe teases, puns and quips throughout the song, and the third verse continues to play with the listeners' heads: both the fictitious listeners to this broadcast, that is, the survivors in the distant towns; and the real listeners, that is, the purchasers of the song and those who might hear it on the radio. It opens with a first-person testimony as to the veracity of, uh, *some* of the information contained in the song 'London Calling' – and, by extension, the album *London Calling* – Joe having already disputed the wisdom of following leaders or taking anything at face value. Then the mood goes through three more rapid switches, guaranteed to disconcert. Joe has London calling 'at the top of the dial', that is 12 o'clock . . . The witching hour. The zombie hour. The end of the day. Or, metaphorically, another kind of Midnight Shutdown: the End of Days. He then asks for a smile. Is it a sign of hope? Does he need a gesture of comfort, the expressional equivalent of a last cigarette? Or has the whole song been a joke at our expense: gallows humour? Maybe all of the above.

Gates of the West: the Clash at the border. Standing (l–r): Manager Caroline Coon in Pearl Harbor tour T-shirt, Topper Headon, Paul Simonon, Joe Strummer and Mick Jones; crouching (l–r): Crew members Baker and Johnny Green in Stetsons, February 1979.

The Clash in standard rehearsal formation, July 1979.

Melody Maker
classifieds, May 5, 1979.

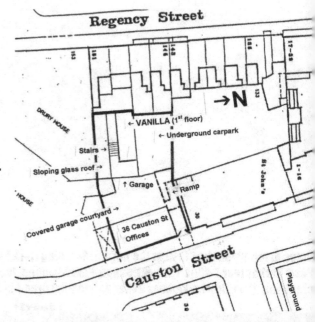

Plan of 36 Causton Street, Pimlico, as it was in 1979, showing the position of the larger Vanilla Rehearsal Studio – as used by the Clash – in relation to the rest of the site.

Composite photograph of the 36 Causton Street site taken at different times during demolition for redevelopment, circa 1993. 1 is the courtyard, 2 the entrance to the garage, and 3 the floor of the room where the Clash wrote and rehearsed *London Calling*.

The Clash in the tape cupboard at Wessex with (l–r): Engineer Bill Price, producer Guy Stevens and head of CBS UK Maurice Oberstein, August 1979.

Wessex Recording Studios, 106 Highbury New Park, before conversion into luxury apartments. Studio One to the right, Studio Two to the left, Rec Room up the fire escape.

The Clash behind Wessex, August 1979.

Truncheons about to swing: Joe Strummer and Gaby Salter at the World's End, King's Road, Chelsea, March 31, 1979.

Living by the river: the World's End Estate, Chelsea, from the south bank of the Thames.

Wessex Studios tracksheet for *London Calling*, August 1979.

The Clash meet Bo Diddley, the Pearl Harbor tour bus, February 1979.

Mick Jones soundchecks "Hateful," Notre Dame Hall, July 6, 1979.

MICHAEL WHITE presents

THE CLASH

RUDE BOY

Produced and Directed by
JACK HAZAN
DAVID MINGAY

Ray Gange drinks Brew for breakfast, *Rude Boy* film poster, 1980.

The Slits, 1978. Spanish bombshell Paloma "Palmolive" Romero far right, atypical girl Viv Albertine far left.

"Ten newspaper reports in one day": the Clash uptown.

Montgomery Clift blows his own bugle: Flyer for the Notre Dame shows, July 5 & 6, 1979.

The Right Profile: *Montgomery Clift* by Patricia Bosworth, as presented to Joe Strummer by Guy Stevens, July 28, 1979.

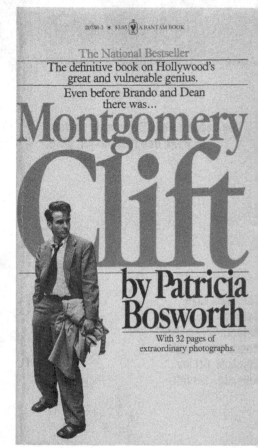

20788-3 ★ $3.95 A BANTAM BOOK

The National Bestseller

The definitive book on Hollywood's great and vulnerable genius.

Even before Brando and Dean there was...

Montgomery Clift

by Patricia Bosworth

With 32 pages of extraordinary photographs.

The verse is abandoned halfway through in favour of a snatch of another song. 'I never felt so much a-like . . .' begins Joe, before he is dramatically cut off, leaving the last word to echo into the void. This is a slight misquotation of the first half of the opening line – the second half being the song's title – of the country-goes-mainstream song 'Singing the Blues', written by Melvin Endsley. (Joe would sometimes sing the whole line when performing 'London Calling' live.) In 1955 the song was taken to Number 1 in the US country charts by Marty Robbins, and Number 1 in the US pop charts by Guy Mitchell. Mitchell repeated his feat in the UK early the following year, and was closely followed by Tommy Steele with his homegrown copycat version. Singing the blues is nothing if not an appropriate response for someone at the point of oblivion . . .

So, after all this talking around the subject, in a nutshell: the world might be on its way out. There's going to be a period of violent upheaval, which will impact upon our sense of security, our values and beliefs. The broadcast is about to be cut off. You can't rely upon the messenger anymore. But then, you never could. Rely upon yourself instead, and those you know and trust. Stand up and be counted. Be resourceful, be creative. Things can't ever be what they were, so don't try to go back. Don't numb yourself to life. Try to enjoy yourself. It's later than you think . . . Joe might have had a prolonged struggle with the lyric, but he got there in the end. There are some 'typical Clash' elements here, but they are put together in an altogether new and impressive way.

Greil Marcus picked up on the sci-fi radio theme in his review of the album, later included in his book *Ranters and Crowd Pleasers* (1994). He compared Joe's vocal to the chilling voice of Orson Welles in his infamous October 1938 radio play update of H. G. Wells's *The War of the Worlds*: so convincing was that supposed 'live as it happens' performance that the general public took it as a genuine news broadcast about an alien invasion, and mass panic ensued.

★

Appropriately for such a heavyweight lyric, the tune is one of the most arresting and unusual on the album. It has inspired some apparently conflicting descriptions over the years. Writing in *Discoveries* in

1994, Ralph Heibutzki heard a 'furious jazz-like swing', and various other reviewers have commented on the martial beat, the dirge-like vocal, and the slightly incongruous reggae-like bass line. It appears to have the capacity to be all things to all men and women. What it isn't is bog-standard fizzing 90 mph punk rock.

By his own admission, Joe was a limited guitar player and most of his original compositions on the instrument in the 101ers days revolved around standard R&B/rock'n'roll chord progressions. For that reason, and because Mick Jones had previously originated most of the music for the Clash – it's tempting to attribute the tune exclusively to Mick. But chord options accompany Joe's very first notebook draft of the lyric, and Joe claimed it for himself in an interview with Judy McGuire of *Punk* magazine, first published shortly after his death: 'I can knock a tune out, which I do occasionally, like "London Calling," or whatever.' Joe was aware of his melodic limitations, and true to form, 'London Calling' doesn't have much in the way of a melody.

To balance that, though, Pat Gilbert's liner notes for the 2004 25th Anniversary Edition of *London Calling* recounted Topper's vivid memory of Mick turning up at Vanilla and excitedly demonstrating an idea for the main two-chord riff, so he at least contributed to Joe's vision. The identity of those two chords has long been a matter of debate, with tab websites opting for Em and C or Em and Am7, while the official *The Clash: The Complete Chord Songbook* (2004) states Em and F and, in his liner notes, Pat Gilbert goes with Em and Fmaj9. He is closest. While the main staccato guitar thrashes four Em chords and then four F chords, a second guitar, lower in the mix, thrashes Em all the way through. When the F and secondary Em coincide, they produce a dissonant effect, and a chord that, technically – according to music theorist Patrick Clark – would have to be described as Fmaj9#11. This, then, was Mick's tweak.

In the introduction, the staccato riff is reinforced by Topper's drum beats, which not only set up the imminent warning of battle, but also keep the listener in suspense about the metric structure of the song until just before the vocal comes in. In keeping with both the combat and announcement themes, the intro's bass figure is written more like a brass figure, sounding a fanfare. Played almost entirely on the A string, it involves a slide followed by a fluttery little triplet. It's more than faintly reminiscent of the 'Main Theme' from John Williams's soundtrack to *Star Wars*, a movie released in 1977 . . . and one of just four videos that the movie-loving Clash had watched repeatedly on the tour bus during their February 1979 Pearl Harbour tour of America, providing plenty of opportunity for either a direct lift or subliminal influence. The guitar riff's altered F is supported by C on the bass: not the chord's root, but its fifth. A trick beloved by Brian Wilson – as evident in the opening line of 'God Only Knows' (1966) – it weakens the structure slightly, and creates further suspense by leaving the impression that the chord is striving to resolve. Although Joe was a huge Beach Boys fan, it's easier to imagine Mick, with his superior pop nous, being the one to take musical inspiration from Wilson. It wasn't Paul's area of expertise.

When Topper does announce Joe's address, it's with a snare drum fill involving 12 rather than eight or 16 hits, the first clue that the song is in 12/8 time. A first for the Clash, it's a simplified shuffle beat that could conceivably be called swing; though as it swings more like a truncheon do than a pendulum do, the effect would perhaps better be described as 'a swing feel'. (It may well have been the lilting way Joe delivers the vocal that first made 'Singing the Blues' pop into his head: it's just about possible to fit that song's lyric to the Clash's tune, and vice versa.)

The guitar riff continues throughout the verses – although it now ascends to G at the end of each couplet – also maintaining the tension and drama. Because the F chord doesn't belong to the scale harmonically, the tune isn't in any specific key, and would have to be described as modal: that mode being Phrygian. The significant changes in the verse are that Topper is now playing the beat and Paul has dropped the fanfare in favour of a more conventional bass pattern. Although not quite the out-and-out reggae bass line it is sometimes described as, Paul's contribution is bouncy enough to feel slightly alien to its context. In the chorus, the guitars now swing from Em to G, ending on D in time to restore harmony for the 'I live by the river' section.

This first track on the album moves some distance away from the Guy Stevens model of spontaneous live recording. With Bill Price's assistance, the live tracking take of 'London Calling' was rebuilt from the ground up, making everything bigger. Topper's live drums and Joe's rhythm guitar were kept. All the other tracks were re-recorded, composited and overdubbed. Paul's original bass take was replaced with a composite put together from three subsequent passes. Mick also overdubbed a second bass in parts. The introductory bass fanfare is present but not overt on the Vanilla demo version, but in Wessex it is really punched up. 'The bass intro blends so well it could almost be single-tracked,' says Bill Price. 'It's probably Paul louder than Mick.' Mick's original live mix of rhythm and lead was replaced with two further tracks of rhythm guitar, the riff proper and the dissonant secondary riff. Not content with the lead guitar break on the Vanilla version, in Wessex Mick recorded two tracks of feedback lead for the 'solo', and then had Bill turn the tape over, so he could record two tracks of backwards lead: more dissonance.

Topper overdubbed tom-toms with heavy reverb, which come to the fore just before the guitar solo. When Joe finally had his lyric ready to go, he recorded three vocals on three separate tracks, which were then composited to another track. He, Mick and Paul each recorded separate backing vocals, all of which were double tracked. Mick also followed the abrupt cut-off of Joe's snatch of 'Singing the Blues' with a burst of controlled feedback – created, as Bill confirms, 'with the pick-up switch on the guitar' – emulating Morse code: as though the desperate survivor has had to move further back down the evolutionary chain of communications from failing radio to the telegraph in order to get his last message through. Morse was used for interval signals by the BBC Overseas Service from 1941 onwards, but not for this purpose: what Mick is spelling out is the emergency distress signal S-O-S: Save Our Souls.

During the middle eight of the Vanilla demo version, Joe had let loose with an unearthly sounding howl, heavily echoed by Baker. He reproduced these cries again when recording the final version of the lyric in Wessex. For years, most listeners presumed these were supposed to be wolf noises (or even werewolf noises – that undead theme just won't lie down), but Joe was trying to emulate the seagulls that swooped around the river near the World's End Estate when the weather was rough out at sea. His final draft of the lyric has 'gulls' written in the relevant place, and he told Bill he wanted the final mix to conjure up an image of mist swirling along the Thames with the seabirds circling overhead. Bill used a series of reverb, varispeed and delay tricks, with the echo effects in the instrumental break intended to evoke the mist, and the slow multiple repeat on Joe's mouth noises the harsh, keening gull cries: Cinemascope mixing.

The result is a colossus of a track, which could not be placed anywhere other than at the start of the album. There was a possible downside to this. Reviewing the double LP following its initial US release, *Creem*'s Billy Altman wrote, 'The unavoidable fact of *London Calling* is that the very first track almost makes the rest of the other two records immaterial. So explosive is it in its depiction of apocalypse now, so strong is its message . . . that the rest of the album's lyrics just seem to be a weak addendum to a case already stated as well as it can be.' A hard act to follow though 'London Calling' undoubtedly is, Altman overstates the case. Twenty-three years later, Mick Jones told Simon Goddard of *Uncut*, 'It was the pivotal track on that album. It's like 'London Calling' is at the top and it encompasses all the rest, like an umbrella, like the world in microcosm.' Its themes of social struggle, personal accountability and responsibility, and an underlying threat of apocalypse recur throughout the subsequent songs.

In 2004, when *Rolling Stone* placed 'London Calling' at number 15 in its list of 'The 500 Greatest Songs Of All Time', a mischievous Mick Jones pointed out that Joe had been unlikely to drown in the case of a flood, because he was living in a high-rise at the time. The entrances for the Whistler Walk flats lead off from the first floor, and the flats – which vary in size – are reached via stairs going either up or down from there. The three-bedroom Number 31 is on the second floor. Not quite a Thames-side eyrie, then, but, as Mick said, high enough off the ground to make sure that, even if the worst came to the worst, Joe was in little genuine danger of getting his feet wet.

'Brand New Cadillac'

The live tracking take of 'Brand New Cadillac' was the first take of the first song the band recorded at Wessex. 'We started with it because it looked like an easy one,' says Bill Price. It could not come first on *London Calling*, but it had to come as near to the beginning as possible, because one of its key functions is to demonstrate the Clash warming up, having fun, reflecting the Vanilla vibe and Guy

Stevens's methodology. The quote from 'Singing the Blues' at the end of 'London Calling' also offers a neat, understated link: back to the Fifties. So successfully had the band adapted 'I Fought the Law' that many people had been unaware of its past history, and believed it to be a Clash original. But this is cards on the table time. After three years of 'we sing in English' and 'I'm So Bored with the USA', 'Brand New Cadillac' finds the Clash unapologetically playing rock'n'roll with American subject matter.

Whether or not it is American rock'n'roll, though, is something they were quick to dispute. 'Brand New Cadillac' was originally recorded by Vince Taylor and his Playboys in 1959. Taylor might have been raised in the States, might have been inspired by Elvis Presley, and might have begun singing in LA nightclubs . . . but he was born Brian Holden in Isleworth, Middlesex, England, where he was raised until the age of seven, and he moved back to England in 1958 at the age of 19 in order to make his bid for rock'n'roll stardom in London. In the first edition of *The Armagideon Times*, prepared in December 1979 to be sold on the January 1980 16 Tons tour of the UK, Topper described 'Brand New Cadillac' as 'the first British rock'n'roll song'. Twenty years later, Joe told *Mojo*'s Kieron Tyler, 'Vince Taylor was the beginning of British rock'n'roll. Before him there was nothing. He was a miracle.'

Neither was strictly correct. 'Brand New Cadillac' wasn't even Vince Taylor's first British rock'n'roll song. His debut release in November 1958 – on Parlophone, accompanied by the Playboys – was 'Right Behind You, Baby', backed with 'I Like Love', both covers. The self-penned 'Brand New Cadillac' was the B-side of his April 1959-released follow-up. Vince came to London because the domestic scene, hothoused at the 2i's Club, a tiny basement at 59 Old Compton Street, Soho, was already thriving. Tommy Steele had enjoyed the UK's first major rock'n'roll hit with 'Rock with the Caveman', a Number 1 in 1956. And Cliff Richard had reached number 2 with 'Move It' in 1958. There was even a hugely popular UK rock'n'roll TV show, Jack Good's *Oh Boy!*.

Although it was Guy Mitchell who first reached Number 1 in the UK in January 1957 with 'Singing the Blues' – he had been a chart regular in Britain since 1952 – Tommy Steele was quick to cover this sure-fire but non-rock'n'roll hit, and had ousted Mitchell from the top spot with the same song later that month. This is what both Topper and Joe were getting at when they insisted upon Vince Taylor's primacy: most UK rockers seemed a little too clean-cut to be entirely convincing, and as soon as they missed the charts with a rock'n'roll flavoured song, they would turn their voices to anything in order to earn half a sixpence: jaunty singalongs, cheesy ballads, musicals, pantomimes. The ever-opportunistic Steele had opted for the Mitchell cover after he flopped with his second single, 'Doomsday Rock' – now *there's* an alternative title for 'London Calling', if ever one were needed – and three years later he would be up to his cheeky Cockney chappy grin in 'Little White Bull'. Even Vince Taylor was required to play the game on record – Parlophone insisted that the A-side of 'Brand New Cadillac' should be a bland cover of Johnny Ace's 'Pledging My Love' – but his live performances always had a feral, unpredictable quality. Although he never did have any chart success, he didn't lose his edge. He might not have been the first British rocker, but he was the wildest.

The four- to five-piece Playboys had a fast-changing line-up, usually drawn from members of the 2i's house band and their friends. By the time of the first recording session the band included Tony Sheridan on lead guitar, Tony Harvey on rhythm, Brian Locking on bass, and Brian Bennett on drums. The band dressed all in black with white ties and two-tone black and white shoes and caps. For the 'Brand New Cadillac' session, pianist Brian Pugh (aka Perry Ford) was brought in, and Tony Sheridan was replaced by another 2i's regular, Joe Moretti.

In his 2000 *Mojo* feature on Vince Taylor – revised for the sleeve notes of the 2009 Taylor career retrospective album, *Jet Black Leather Machine* – Kieron Tyler indicated that Moretti was merely hired to play the session. Moretti's own 2002 account (to be found on his eponymous website) claimed that he was approached in the 2i's to be Sheridan's full-time replacement after Tony quit in January 1959. At that point, he and his family moved in to the flat Vince and the Playboys were sharing in Knightsbridge. Joe recalled wearing the black and white gear onstage and off, and taking part in about a week's worth of gigs. Vince nicknamed him Scotty Moretti, because Elvis Presley's guitarist was Scotty Moore, and it allowed the singer to emulate his hero by urging 'Scotty' to take it away in the middle eight. Joe was present when Vince started work on the lyric to 'Brand New Cadillac' in the Star Restaurant at 5 Old Compton Street (now the West End

Tandoori). He brought the finished lyric in the following day. The band worked up the tune and their respective parts just before they went into EMI's Abbey Road studio – the same room where, three years later, the Beatles would make their first record for the same label – and recorded the song in a couple of takes with Norrie Paramor producing.

'Scotty' Moretti plays the kinetic main riff fast, using the classic Fifties string damping technique. A point of reference would be Duane Eddy's guitar-led version of Henry Mancini's 'Peter Gunn' . . . but that was released a few months after Taylor's song, going on to reach Number 6 in the UK charts. In contrast, Moretti's lead guitar intro and solo have a stinging urgency. Despite the limitations of the British studio equipment of the day, the rest of the band also deliver. Brian P. reinforces the rhythm guitar with his piano, throwing in the occasional showy Jerry Lee Lewis glissando to push the excitement button. Brian L.'s bass is loud and propulsive, not something to take for granted given the standard of British recording equipment at the time. If Brian B. relies a little too much on agitating his metalware, he's quick to taking an energising roll around the toms at the end of the verses. And Vince's vocal . . . is OK. The sad truth is, he had the moves and the attitude, but he never had much of a voice. (Brian B told Kieron Tyler that he had problems with both pitch and timing when performing live.)

Compared to Chuck Berry's earlier 'Maybellene' (1955) and 'You Can't Catch Me' (1956), Vince's lyric is a less eloquent and witty take on the eternal quest for girls and cars, or girls in cars . . . but it has rebellious attitude to spare. Baby takes off in the flash ride after announcing her departure. Whether she's made her own money, come into an inheritance, stolen the vehicle, or met a guy with more in the bank than poor ol' Vince is left unsaid, but the fact she addresses her erstwhile lover as 'Daddy' – from Sugar Daddy – makes the last of these options the favourite. He gives chase in his own wheels, and even manages to keep up with her for a while, pleading with her to 'turn that big boy around'. Despite having been ditched by the suddenly rich lady, Vince hasn't learned his lesson yet. He's still all swagger and holler. She just gives him That Look: she ain't ever coming back.

The song was relegated to the B-side of the single partly because it was considered too wild and unpolished, but partly – according to

Joe Moretti – because it was deemed to be 'advertising' the Ford Cadillac. It became an instant jukebox favourite, but the A-side received little airplay, and Parlophone let Taylor go. Even by May 1959 he could no longer afford to keep the version of the Playboys responsible for the single on the payroll. Joe Moretti had already guested as lead guitarist on that other 1959 British rock'n'roll classic, Johnny Kid and the Pirates' 'Shakin' All Over', and went on to become a rock'n'roll session guitarist for hire. His predecessor Tony Sheridan ended up in Hamburg, where he would record with the pre-fame Beatles as his backing band. The bass and drum Brians went on to join first Marty Wilde's Wildcats and then the Shadows. Vince marked time by opening his own club, the Top 10 on Berwick Street, but it was more of a hangout than a moneymaker. He persevered with further Playboys line-ups, but had trouble holding them together and became increasingly unreliable, argumentative and aggressive.

By 1961 he was dressing in black leather outfits like Gene Vincent (though some maintain that the true originator of this look was another London rocker, Joe Brown). His wild act went down so well in Paris – where he was known to inspire audience riots that would have made the Clash proud – that he was offered a contract by Barclay Records, and relocated there. Drugs like Preludin, as taken by the Beatles in Hamburg, and similar to amphetamine, were washed down with booze. By the end of 1962 it was evident that he had serious problems. His behaviour became ever more erratic as the decade progressed. He discovered LSD in May 1965 at a London party thrown by Bob Dylan, renamed himself Mateus after the bottle of wine he happened to be drinking at the time, and told his sister, visiting from America, that he was the Son of God. After a show in Paris he walked out of the venue and started preaching to his fans. Two years of psychiatric treatment followed, with Vince reduced to a near-catatonic state. In 1967 a comeback attempt failed, and the Mateus character resurfaced. He spent the next four years hanging around London, sometimes affecting long white robes. It was during this period that David Bowie made his acquaintance, eventually going on to use him as the principal model for the messianic character of Ziggy Stardust.

In 1970, drummerless good-time jug band Mungo Jerry had a surprise international Number 1 with 'In the Summertime'. Their live set included a semi-improvised approximation of 'Brand New Cadillac', introduced by frontman Ray Dorset as 'Cadillac'. After racking his brains for a way to follow up the monster for nine months, he wrote new verses for this live favourite, in which the love interest acquires a micro-mini dress and a see-through sweater, and altered the chorus so that instead of leaving him behind in her car, she succumbs to the inevitable and jumps into his dream. (In Ray Dorset songs, Ray Dorset always gets some.) Re-titling the result 'Baby Jump', he took the full writing credit, despite the fact that the chorus still contains the give-away 'Baby, baby, baby, what you doing to me?' The single reached Number 1 in the UK in March 1971 and stayed in the charts for 13 weeks. Two years later, Dutch band Golden Earring paid a more upfront homage by recording the leather-clad fantasy romance saga 'Just Like Vince Taylor' for their breakthrough international hit album *Moontan*.

Meanwhile, Vince Taylor and his Playboys' original 'Brand New Cadillac' continued to enjoy cult status among London's Teddy Boy faithful. It was on the Fifties-vintage Ami jukebox at Malcolm McLaren and Vivienne Westwood's Kings Road Ted clothing emporium Let It Rock, and stayed there when the shop became Sex in 1974. (In 2003, Marco Pirroni – former shop regular and member of Adam and the Ants – compiled *Sex*, a 20-track album of his Ami favourites, including 'Brand New Cadillac'.) Like many a rocker, Malcolm sourced his records from the Rock On! stall on Golborne Road, Notting Hill, and the original Taylor single remained a coveted item throughout the early Seventies, fetching up to £20 a go, a fortune at the time. This prompted stall owners Ted Carroll and Roger Armstrong to license 'Brand New Cadillac' from EMI, and make it the second release on their newly formed independent Chiswick label on 3 March 1976. At almost exactly the same time, another independent label, Charly, released another cult rock'n'roll song, Hank Mizell's 'Jungle Rock', with a similarly 'Peter Gunn'-flavoured riff. Originally released 20 years before, 'Jungle Rock' went on to become a freak Number 3 UK hit. Roger Armstrong credits it with helping sales of 'Brand New Cadillac' along. Although the Chiswick record didn't make the charts, it did go on to shift an impressive 10,000 copies before it was deleted in 1978.

Shortly after its release, Chiswick approached Joe Strummer's 101ers to record 'Keys to Your Heart' as the label's third release. 'I'm sure Joe had a copy of "Brand New Cadillac",' says Roger Armstrong.

'Maybe I even gave him one when we signed the 101ers.' Joe was not the only member of the band who knew about it. Ian Hunter mentions covering the song with Mott the Hoople in *Diary of a Rock'n'Roll Star* in 1974, all the recommendation Mick Jones needed. According to Paul Simonon, though, neither Mick nor Joe consciously introduced the song to the Clash repertoire. A copy of the Chiswick release just happened to be lying around in the upstairs flat at 22 Davis Road, Shepherd's Bush, when the prototype Clash were using the squat for a base in April and May 1976. Paul recalls band members trying to work out how the song went even before Joe Strummer joined, and the Clash would return to it from time to time thereafter. 'Most of the copies we sold will have ended up in London,' says Roger. 'It's certainly a record that young guitar bands could aspire to, as it isn't that complicated.' Structurally, it's about as straightforward a 12-bar blues as you could find. By the start of 1979 Paul had his own copy of the Chiswick release, and Barry Myers used the song as the Clash's play-off music on 20 February 1979, the last night of the Pearl Harbour tour, at the Rex Danforth Theatre, Toronto.

'Brand New Cadillac' shares its fascination with '59 Fords and getting the girl with Eddie Cochran's 'Somethin' Else', which was released in the autumn of 1959, so not an influence on Taylor. (Twenty years later, though, Sid Vicious would enjoy a posthumous Number 3 UK hit fronting the rump of the Sex Pistols on his version of 'Somethin' Else' . . . just a couple of months before the Clash chose to work up the Taylor song in Vanilla.) As with 'I Fought the Law', the first of the Clash's rock'n'roll covers to make it to disc, 'Brand New Cadillac' had strong cult standing, but wasn't overly familiar to either the band's core audience or the mainstream audience, which enabled the Clash to put their own stamp on it, if not quite – on this occasion – claim it as their own

For all the oft-repeated tale of Guy Stevens overruling Topper's request for a second take because the Clash's version of the song speeds up, the Clash take it slightly slower than the Playboys. And the famous pick-up in pace (about a minute in) is so slight that only a precision-tuned instrument like Topper would notice. The Clash rely more on restrained power – the implication of plenty more to spare under the hood – than speed for their recounting of this tale of automotive heartbreak. Because the Clash and Guy Stevens were so excited about nailing the master take first take, the other assumption often made is that the unadorned live recording is what appears on the record. Again, that's not the case. 'Joe's guitar on the left is almost certainly live,' says Bill Price. 'Mick's on the right and half-right with three guitar parts: the "Peter Gunn" riff; the choppy rhythm; and the lead bits and solo. He would have done a combination of these live, then overdubbed them separately. There could still be some of his live guitar in there. I can't tell.' Mick's main rhythm guitar riff is close to being a straight lift of the original Fifties style, but for his other parts, Mick takes a tip from the MC5, who based their sound on the noise from the Detroit drag strips: the choppy, snarling rhythm that cuts across the main riff sounds like an engine revving and ready to go, and instead of the original's stinging lead, he lets loose like the sound of squealing tyres. You can almost smell the burning rubber.

Partly because Joe had trouble remembering even his own lyrics on occasion, and partly because he preferred to customise covers by taking key phrases and improvising something a little more personal around them, he goes for an even more minimalist approach than the laconic Taylor. He doesn't cut to the chase; he cuts *out* the chase, and instead cuts straight to the confrontation. For Joe's Baby, just giving him That Look isn't enough. You can hear his incredulity when she pulls away with the line, '*Balls* to you, Big Daddy!' *Big* Daddy was the domineering father in Tennessee Williams's *Cat on a Hot Tin Roof*, played by the heavyweight Burl Ives in both the 1955 play and 1958 film. This subtly increases the taint of power and corruption in the relationship, making the kiss-off even stronger. It also makes the song very punk in attitude – no one would have got away with 'balls to you' in 1959, even on a rock'n'roll B-side – and even transforms it into a quasi-feminist anthem. Who cares how Baby got the car? She's her own woman now, leaving Big Daddy a broken man, jaw on the kerb, choking on her exhaust fumes.

Joe Strummer and Paul Simonon finally got to meet Vince Taylor at the Pigfoot restaurant in Paris in late May 1980, during the European leg of the 16 Tons tour. He told Paul he had just appeared on a TV show with the Muppets and the Sex Pistols, and told Joe that the Duke and Duchess of Windsor were planning to kill him with poisoned chocolate cake. He continued to be plagued by mental illness and alcoholism, but married in 1983 and moved to Geneva in Switzerland, where he underwent treatment for his drink problem, played the odd small club gig, and died of cancer in 1991. In 1999 Van Morrison recorded a song called 'Goin' Down Geneva', which announces that Vince Taylor used to live there, before, somewhat poignantly, adding that nobody had ever heard of him.

Which, as indicated above, is not strictly true. Taylor remained a huge star in France. He had a sort of second-hand UK chart-topper with Mungo Jerry's 'Baby Jump', and gained a sort of second-hand international immortality via *The Rise and Fall of Ziggy Stardust and the Spiders from Mars*. More than any other single contributory factor, though, it is the Clash's souped-up version of 'Brand New Cadillac' that has ensured the real Vince Taylor will never be forgotten. Roger Armstrong has also remained true to the cause: in 2009 it was Chiswick's successor, Ace, that released the definitive Taylor compilation *Jet Black Leather Machine*. It proves that, although he might not have been a songwriter or even a technically gifted singer, there was considerably more to him than his most famous song.

To return to the question left hanging by the anti-mod version of 'London Calling': what's the difference between reviving the Sixties and reviving the Fifties? The Clash's argument was that the late Seventies mod revivalists were merely offering a fading Xerox of what had gone before; that in wanting to bring back the past by copying it, they were merely serving to diminish it. Conversely, in their own minds – or at least, in their own talk – the Clash were taking a step backwards in order to move forwards. They wanted to admit and celebrate the connection that they and their Class of 1976 contemporaries had previously denied between punk and its original rock'n'roll antecedents. They intended to remind their American audience that rock'n'roll had once been and could again be something a lot more vital than the 'flared rock' clogging up that country's airwaves in 1979. This thinking would in turn produce *London Calling*'s working title *The Last Testament*, and contribute to Ray Lowry's Elvis Presley-referencing album cover design for the album and its associated promotional campaign.

The Clash's version of 'Brand New Cadillac' does move forward with considerable determination, but their argument has a whiff of sophistry about it. Maybe success is its own justification. How many mod revival recordings have since reached the Top 5 in polls of the

Greatest British Albums Of All Time, or the very top spot in polls of the Greatest Albums of both the Seventies and the Eighties?

'Jimmy Jazz'

Self- and punk-imposed restrictions lifted, the Clash had felt increasingly free to go in any direction they chose at Vanilla, playing covers and working up their own tunes in an unprecedentedly wide variety of styles, from rockabilly to ska to R&B to country to soul. Sometimes all in the same song. They tried things out to educate and amuse each other. Arguably the most radical result of this was 'Jimmy Jazz'. It had caused consternation among *Sounds* reviewers when performed at the Notre Dame shows in London on 5 and 6 July 1979, but the Clash were evidently not going to be cowed. They played the still unreleased and therefore unfamiliar song as their opening number on the second night of the Take the 5th tour, 14 September 1979, at the Aragon Ballroom in Chicago, after Mick Jones had introduced it with a teasing, 'This is the Home of the Blues, right?' A week later, the Clash played it as one of their encores at the Orpheum Theater in Boston. It is placed third on the album with the same intent: throwing down the gauntlet to those who didn't expect or want to hear the Clash play anything other than prole punk.

If 'Brand New Cadillac' takes the listener back to the Fifties, then – musically, at least – 'Jimmy Jazz' goes back two decades further. It was written at Vanilla, officially by Joe and Mick working together, but the style of music and unpolished lyric point to it having its origins in a band jam, and one in which Topper was significantly involved. It's peculiar that the Vanilla demo was recorded without a lyric. The song title at that time was the eventual lyric's entire first line, 'The Police Walked in for Jimmy Jazz', which would indicate that Joe did have at least some of the words at the time the demo was recorded. The lyric was certainly in place by the time the Clash performed the song at the early July Notre Dame shows.

Its musical influences are not hard to discern, but 'Jimmy Jazz' evades a neat genre encapsulation, usually causing it to be described as bluesy jazz or jazzy blues. It's an 8-bar riff with a swing feel (like, yet so unlike, 'London Calling'). While technically not a blues, it features a common or garden R&B turnaround, and a jazzy impression is created by the A to F# chord trajectory and some of the instrumental and vocal touches. It's a Thirties hybrid, really, the sort of thing a US nightclub band might have played in those days, with touches of Tin Pan Alley show-tune harmony: as if the nightclub combo had stolen a few tricks from something sophisticated they'd heard on the radiogram; something owing more than a little to the popular Rhythm Changes progression (named after George Gershwin's 1930 tune 'I Got Rhythm').

The playing has a lazy feel, that unobtrusive, early-hours sound usually described as cocktail jazz or lounge. Mick's introductory guitar work alludes to that of Django Reinhardt in terms of style, if not finesse. The first D in the chord sequence is a D9, a variant of the D7, and a typical Django chord. Mick must also be responsible for the jazzy little piano run around three minutes in. Paul provides a relaxed walking bass. Joe goes so far as to scat in the middle eight. The Irish Horns make their first appearance on the album. 'I liked that one,' says trumpet player Dick Hanson. 'They wanted us to give it a Count Basie feel. They specified that.' Ray Beavis's sax solo at 'what a relief' obligingly does just what the words suggest, and Mick's electric guitar solo also tries to sound like a horn. Having played in pub jazz bands since the age of 14, Topper was confident in his ability to man the traps for such music, and is admirably nimble here. Towards the end, he also gets to make his first raid on the percussion cupboard for over-dubs, contributing flexatone, vibraslap and bird whistle.

As if the introductory guitar noodling didn't already sound casual enough, crewmember Baker whistles the song in. After the Clash had left Wessex for the Take the 5th tour on 4 September, Bill Price phoned Joe in America to propose mixing the track to sound like it had been recorded live in a smoky, after-hours dive. Given the go-ahead, Bill dubbed on the sound of clinking glasses and bottles from a sound effects record. It's all very *Nighthawks at the Diner*-era Tom Waits. Joe was something of a Waits fan, having caught at least two nights of his early June 1976 Ronnie Scott's residency, taking a number of his new punk pals along with him on the second occasion.

Such Cinemascope touches are appropriate, because the starting point for Joe's lyric was the late-night, sleazy, low-life, underground ambience of the music. In the comments he contributed to the first issue of *The Armagideon Times*, the picture Joe painted was in the bleak, melodramatic, cynical, morally compromised, ominous, stylised, heavily shadowed, black-and-white B-movie style known as film noir: 'All crosstown – elevator broken down – no lights at the edge of the building sight [sic] – suspicious entry and retreats – wind blows too hard – the band corner turned four figures in a car – maroon colour – no answer . . . again!'

It's fitting, because Joe also claimed the opening line of the first verse came to him like the opening scene in a movie. It's possible he neglected to record his vocal at Vanilla because he planned to work on the lyric further before committing it to tape, but in he end, he chose to stay with what he already had. The lyric for 'Jimmy Jazz' is not quite improvised, but it's evidently not as worked over – as *written* – as, say, 'London Calling' or 'Spanish Bombs'. 'It's not only the message, it's the way it's said,' said Joe, when discussing 'Jimmy Jazz' with *Melody Maker*'s Chris Bohn in 1979. 'So a piece of nonsense can have a powerful meaning to me.' Laughing, he went on to cite the Cadillacs' novelty 1955 doo-wop hit 'Speedo' and Gene Vincent's 'Be-Bop-A-Lula' from the following year as examples of ostensibly inane lyrics in which 'the meaning of life is revealed immediately'.

'Jimmy Jazz' is as oblique-verging-on-cryptic as Joe's notes about it in *The Armagideon Times*: all gossip, rumour, Chinese whispers, drunken mumbles . . . In other words, impressionistic, with the 'story' being as hard to grasp as the smoke hanging in the air of the nightclub. Are Jimmy Jazz and Jimmy Dread in cahoots or deadly enemies? Or are they the same person? Is there a contract out on Jimmy Dread, or is he already dead? Is the message for Jimmy Jazz a warning? If so, are the police warning Jimmy, or is Jimmy to be warned that the police are looking for him?

There are a couple of movie references in the song: not to bona fide noir films from the genre's Forties and Fifties heyday, but more recent pictures with an appropriately bleak noir mood. In addition to recalling the denouement of the 'Oranges and Lemons' nursery rhyme (as previously employed in 'Clash City Rockers'), the second verse's threat to 'cut off his ears and chop off his head' recalls the 1974 movie *Bring Me the Head of Alfredo Garcia*, where impotent US barroom pianist Warren Oates goes to Mexico in an attempt to regain his manhood by taking the titular trophy. And the 'suck that!' preceding the final verse is a little too close for coincidence to the 'suck on that!' Robert

De Niro's mentally disturbed vigilante-assassin Travis Bickle delivers to Harvey Keitel's pimp in 1976's *Taxi Driver*, immediately before shooting him in the stomach. Both films, like the song, have a highly ritualistic quality.

The character(s) Jimmy Jazz/Jimmy Dread come from a different source, though. One of the challenges set by discussing an album's songs in the sequence they appear on an album is that they were not necessarily written in that order. Joe's lyric for 'Rudie Can't Fail' predates that for 'Jimmy Jazz', and the Clash had been immersing themselves in rebel rock songs like the Bobby Fuller Four's 'I Fought the Law' and rude boy anthems like Desmond Dekker's '007 (Shanty Town)' (1966) for many months before that. Joe was knowledgeable enough about musical history to know that both genres share the same point of origin: the outlaw ballad.

The earliest known examples are the British Robin Hood ballads, which provided the foundation stone of noble-spirited outlaw mythology. ('He robbed from the rich, and gave to the poor / As you do, as you do.') Balladeers went on to sing the praises and number the fates of infamous highwaymen and cut-throats before folk music travelled to the States, and subsequent generations of folk, country and blues singers sang songs of gunfighters, bankrobbers and homicidal barroom brawlers. The most famous of these last figures was Staggerlee, who crops up later on the album. Less and less effort was put into justifying the outlaw's actions: they were increasingly celebrated as anti-heroes, bad men. And that type of outlaw ballad became known as a badman ballad. As the musics that propagated these legends intermingled, cross-pollinated and produced rock'n'roll, they brought the outlaw image with them. Johnny Cash borrowed a line from the traditional ballad 'Duncan and Brady' for his own 'Folsom Prison Blues' (1955), where he shoots a man in Reno 'just to watch him die'. Jerry Lee Lewis was known as the Killer. Sonny Curtis of the Crickets wrote 'I Fought the Law' (1959). Chuck Berry customised gunslinger mythology to fit his talented guitar slinger 'Johnny B. Goode' (1958).

Ska developed in Jamaica in the early Sixties as a locally flavoured take on imported American R&B; and some of the lyrical content and the attendant mythology travelled, too. The music's development into rock steady roughly coincided with a wave of local gangster or rude-boy violence, which inspired a slew of songs either lauding or berating the rudie. (See 'Rudie Can't Fail' below.) Outlaw legends were strong narratives, and inspired as many films as they did songs. The Clash's beloved *The Harder They Come* was based on a true story of Jamaican outlaw, Ivanhoe 'Rhygin' Martin, who was involved in a series of shoot-outs with the police in 1948. (His given first name was either a blessing or a curse: the modern day image of Robin Hood derives from Walter Scott's 1819 novel *Ivanhoe*, where Hood appears as a supporting character.) The soundtrack of *The Harder They Come* includes a song in which the Slickers take Chuck Berry's character 'Johnny B. Goode' and turn him back into a gun- and knife-toting rude boy named 'Johnny Too Bad'. The Clash's own movie, *Rude Boy*, would include 'I Fought the Law' and their own rude-boy anthem 'Rudie Can't Fail'. Back in 1978 Joe had already pulled the reggae rude boy and rock rebel strands of the badman ballad tradition back together in his lyric for 'The Prisoner', where 'Johnny Too Bad meets Johnny B. Goode in the Charing Cross Road'.

Thin Lizzy weren't really Joe Strummer's bag, but there was some contact between the Clash and Lizzy camps in 1978. Bernie Rhodes (albeit inadvertently) titled Lizzy's 1978 double album *Live and Dangerous*. When it was released towards the end of the year to considerable sales and media attention, Caroline Coon hired Lizzy's publicist Tony Brainsby to do the same job for the Clash. Phil Lynott was accepted by most of the punk crowd. Like Berry and Hendrix, as a black man in rock'n'roll, when assembling his own lyrics and persona he had found the image of the Staggerlee dandy badass a little too hard to resist. It's not beyond the realms of possibility that Joe was familiar with the muted, late-night, low-life, shady double-dealing of Lizzy's late 1976 song 'Johnny the Fox Meets Jimmy the Weed', a version of which appears on *Live and Dangerous*.

When Jimmy Jazz meets Jimmy Dread the location is shifted to somewhere in B-movie Hollywood, but the precedent and scene are both set for *London Calling*'s other badman ballad/film noir characters, about to introduce themselves not only in 'Rudie Can't Fail', but also 'The Guns of Brixton', 'Wrong 'Em Boyo', 'The Card Cheat' and 'Revolution Rock'.

'Satta massa gana' is Amharic, the language spoken by Ethiopians and quoted by devout Rastafarians, like the Abyssinians, whose 'Satta Massa Gana' (recorded 1969, and first released in 1971) Joe is referencing here. It means, very roughly, and just a little incongruously, 'give thanks'.

'Jimmy Jazz' is a song with a lot of menace and violence, both threatened and implied, but that's not the impression the listener is left with. This is in part due to the Irish Horns' boisterousness, and in part to Topper's percussive pay-offs: most of the noises he makes with his box of tricks are associated with slapstick cartoon comedy. The flexatone is traditionally employed to augment the vision of an eternal sucker like Wile E. Coyote dazedly wobbling back and forth on his heels after his latest purchase from ACME has misfired, toppled or rebounded.

'Hateful'

When Joe Strummer was asked to pick his all-time hero by *Mojo* in 2002 it was Bo Diddley, real name Ellas McDaniel, who received his vote, because the musical style he developed and all but trademarked was so well-suited to its purpose: primitive and raw, compelling and uplifting. Joe told the magazine's Jon Bennett, 'He was playing on the street corner, and he knew that he needed something else. He wasn't the greatest fretsman in the world. Everybody else was playing 12-bar blues at the time . . . So he came up with something even more African than the blues is. People can get caught thinking it's all about technique, when it's not really about technique at all. It's about something more exciting and indefinable.' This was the essence of Joe's revised punk philosophy of 1979, one that he and the rest of the Clash were now willing to admit not only linked punk to original rock'n'roll but also to blues and to busking; which – hardly coincidentally – was the view back along the route that Joe's personal musical journey had brought him. Forget Year Zero: the band now chose to view itself as part of a tradition of primal, energetic, passionate, inventive music that went back to Year Diddley, and earlier.

The first record to really grab Joe's attention in his youth had been the Rolling Stones' 1964 version of Buddy Holly's 'Not Fade Away' (1957), which the Stones had personalised by grafting Holly's lyric and tune onto Bo Diddley's trademark 'shave-and-a-haircut-two-bits' hoodoo rhythm. Like his favourite mid-Sixties band before him, Joe built the 101ers on a foundation laid by Bo Diddley and Chuck Berry in the late Fifties and early Sixties. The 101ers' repertoire included Diddley's 'Who Do You Love?' (1956) and 'Don't Let It Go' (1959). Joe even wrote a song in the same style for the band. Entitled 'Bo Diddley's Six Gun Blues', it features the line, 'So I sit by the light bulb / Just Bo Diddley and me.' But the decision to employ Bo Diddley as support for the February 1979 Pearl Harbour tour was by no means unilateral. Mick Jones had also been a Stones fan from childhood, and like any music buff interested in investigating the inspiration for his favourite music, he had also backtracked to discover both Chuck Berry and Bo Diddley. When Mick met Robin Crocker aka Robin Banks at school, their very first conversation ended in a fight about which of those two colossi was the most colossal. Mick said Bo. Mick's favourite mid-Seventies band, the New York Dolls, included a cover of Bo's 'Pills' (1961) in their recorded repertoire. By the beginning of 1979, Paul Simonon was also a convert.

All four members of the band found Bo immensely entertaining company on the Pearl Harbour tour bus, with his advice about taking the money upfront – which the Clash implemented on their trip to play the Ruisrock Festival that August – his insistence on sleeping sitting upright and giving up his bunk to his guitar, his constant slugging from a lethal alcoholic drink named rock'n'rye, and his bottomless fund of homespun wisdom and anecdotes about life on the road. Paul started calling him Uncle Skiddley Daddley, but probably not to his face. At the time, Vince Taylor was just a name to the Clash, but Bo Diddley was flesh and blood, if larger than life, and became the embodiment of the Clash's 'Quest'. And who was better suited to fulfil that role than a man whose alias derived from the African one-stringed instrument, the diddley bow? How much closer to the point of origin could you get?

Back in the UK it was perhaps predictable that the Clash would jam on a few of his songs. At Vanilla, warming up at Wessex, and at soundchecks later in the year, they would play 'Mona' (1957), 'You Can't Judge a Book (By Looking at Its Cover)' (1962) and 'Road Runner' (1959). It was also inevitable that the Clash would try their hand at an 'original' song in the Diddley style. Like 'Jimmy Jazz', 'Hateful' was demoed as an instrumental at Vanilla, but again, Joe had the lyric in time for the band to perform the complete song at the Notre Dame gigs on 5 and 6 July 1979. During soundcheck on the second day, Mick still had the words on a piece of paper stuck to his microphone stand.

It's not worth spending time debating who 'wrote' the verse sections of the music, but the Clash do an excellent job of doing the Diddley in the version recorded at Wessex, with Topper's two bars on, two bars off maracas recalling the sterling work of Bo's original onstage foil, Jerome Green. The double-tracked handclaps with slight delay in the chorus pay homage to the Stones' version of 'Not Fade Away'. This is the first of several songs on the album to use call-and-response vocals, a feature of black R&B music drawing inspiration from church services and work songs, and – before that – African folk traditions.

That's it for authentic tribute, though: Mick the Arranger couldn't leave it so raw and rootsy. The chorus ('Anything I want . . .') finds – according to Bill Price – no less than three strummed electric rhythm guitars lending a really satisfying depth and resonance to Mick's powerful payoff flourish. Both the harmony and arrangement in this section are strongly reminiscent of 'A Well Respected Man' (1965) by Mick's faves, the Kinks. At the end of the chorus ('it's paid for'), there are a few bars of held chords over descending (vaguely disco-style) bass. This half-tempo change of feel inverts but still recalls another popular Sixties songwriting trick: the double-tempo change of feel that can be heard in the Beatles' 'A Day in the Life' (1967) and – perhaps more pertinently in this instance – Thunderclap Newman's 'Something in the Air' (1969), which the Clash had covered during the sessions for *Give 'Em Enough Rope*. While Thunderclap Newman accelerate to exhilarate, though, the Clash do the opposite, and unexpectedly drop the listener into the doldrums: a manipulation of mood that coincides perfectly with the drug-related relaxation occurring in the lyric. Straight after this sophisticated touch, the band round off the chorus with an almost comical straight up the scale turnaround.

The intro sounds as though it's played on some combination of organ and bagpipes. 'It's Mick on his melodica,' says Bill Price. 'Everybody else left the room when he got it out.' The melodica is also responsible for the high-pitched tweeting noise that can be heard periodically throughout the song. Given that reggae artist and producer Augustus Pablo did so much to legitimise the instrument, notably on

King Tubby's Meets Rockers Uptown (1976), it would have been more obvious for Mick to use it on one of the album's several reggae tracks. Instead, he chooses to set a precedent here for confounding expectations and juggling contexts: on *London Calling* the Clash have no truck with laws of genre or instrumentation. Which also explains the Ronnotone (that is, Mick Ronsonesque) guitar solo.

This wilfulness extends to the relationship between lyric and music: with a perversity that is by now already typical of *London Calling*, save for the short-lived chorus mood swing mentioned above, the hugely enjoyable romp of a tune is completely out of emotional sync with the subject of the lyric

If making Uncle Skiddley Daddley's acquaintance was one of the best things about the Pearl Harbour tour for the Clash, then one of the worst things was hearing about the death by heroin overdose of Sid Vicious, who had been part of the band's entourage from the day they formed until he landed his own gig as Glen Matlock's replacement in the Sex Pistols. The 'friend who's a man' introduced in the first verse is the same guy Lou Reed is killing time for in the Velvet Underground's 'I'm Waiting for the Man' (1967): a mainman, a dealer. The apparent generosity he shows in the first line of the chorus is quickly undermined by the second line – 'not for free' – and the conclusion, 'it's hateful'. The 'grateful to be nowhere' conclusion is not so much a contradiction as an acknowledgement of the ebb and flow of the junkie's living-death cycle; what William Burroughs once described as the 'algebra of need'. Joe's lyric is about becoming trapped in a relationship with someone growing rich from feeding your habit.

The line in the second verse about losing friends could be taken one of two ways: the protagonist has lost friends, because they can no longer condone his drug use or forgive his behaviour; or some of his drug buddies have died. Either way, he's oblivious. His dependency and intake increase. Last verse, and his memory and mind are going. He's driving but he's not steady and he can't see too well . . . and is shaping up for the fate met a few songs later by Montgomery Clift, or worse. This is a stern morality tale. 'All this junkie "he's so out of it" rock'n'roll stuff doesn't appeal to me at all,' Joe told *Melody Maker*'s Chris Bohn in December 1979. 'That's the easy way out, you know?' Just as they fetishise the ritual of copping and shooting up, there is a tendency for junkies to get off on the not-so-cryptic code attached to their badly kept secret. Heroin is variously known as Harry, as Horse, or H . . . which is how the song came by its title. On Joe's original notebook lyric draft, as displayed at the *Joe Strummer: Past Present & Future* exhibition, the song is even titled 'H for Hateful'.

Other than the synchronicity of their respective arrival in and departure from the Clash's story, and their respective influence on the music and lyric of this song, links between Bo and Sid are not immediately obvious: the chunky, black, middle-aged, bespectacled originator, and the skinny, white, young, spike-topped chancer. But Bo Diddley was not some cuddly showbiz character. He came up the hard way, and carried a whiff of menace in his early years. In amongst the proto-rap macho bragging of 'Who Do You Love?' he declares, 'A tombstone hand and a graveyard mind / Just 22 and I don't mind dying.' By the end, that was pretty much Sid's philosophy, too; though his death was pathetic rather than defiant or brave, and he was just 21 when he or heroin decided it was time for him to go.

The Clash played 'Hateful' live three times in July 1979, at the Notre Dame and Rainbow shows. After recording it in August, they never played it again. It was perhaps a little too musically derivative for comfort.

'Rudie Can't Fail'

More detail about the original early-to-mid-Sixties Kingston rude boys seems called for. An economic squeeze at that time led to a larger than usual number of young men from rural parts of Jamaica going to the capital in search of work . . . where there wasn't any, as the local youth knew all too well. With mobs of impoverished young men hanging around all day with nothing to do but brood and complain, the inevitable result was a wave of robbery and violence. As they were country boys, 'rude' originally meant 'unsophisticated', but the definition was soon expanded to cover 'antisocial' and 'offensive'. Some amused themselves by breaking up sound-system dances; others got paid to do the same by rival operations, hence Alton Ellis's 'Dance Crasher' (1965). Some rudies teamed up in gangs for their hoodlum antics. There was considerable overlap between the music business, the police force and the political parties of Kingston. Much blame about the cause of the current economic climate was flung around, and some rude boys became hired (or, at least, bribed) thugs for one or other of the two main political parties, the Jamaica Labour Party (JLP) and the People's National Party (PNP).

This wasn't schoolboy fisticuffs they were indulging in, either. Rude boys habitually carried ratchet knives. Although folding knives with relatively short blades – around four inches long – they were more like cut-throat razors than penknives, and the experienced user could have one open and ready for action with a lightning-quick flick of the wrist. A number of the really heavy-duty toughs also carried guns. The violence escalated over the period 1965–7, and was not contained among their own kind: whether affiliated to gangs or not, many rude boys simply ran wild, mugging, robbing, looting, fighting and assaulting anyone who remonstrated with them, and – if some of the more sensationalist anecdotes are to believed – raping at will. A heavy-handed and somewhat arbitrary clampdown from the forces of law and order further escalated tensions and increased the workload of the courts to the point that Jamaica's first state of emergency was declared by the ruling JLP on 2 October 1966. Police and the military cordoned off the western part of the Kingston area and imposed a curfew from 10 p.m. to 6 a.m., thus hitting those involved in the music and entertainment business harder than the gangs. The state of emergency lasted until 4 November 1966, but the problems continued.

Kingston is a perfect example of a community using songs – in this case, disseminated more via sound systems than radio – as an alternative local newspaper, and for a couple of years, the rude boy was rarely off page one. The emergence of the rude boy problem was followed in 1966 by a period of unusually hot weather. This is given as one of the reasons that the style of the local music started to change during the course of that year – this being Jamaica, there are several other explanations to choose from, including the wider availability of the electric bass and improved studio technology – with the frenetic ska giving way to the slower, more stately rock-steady. While the bass and drums gained prominence – the bass playing a strong, repetitive pattern emphasising certain notes – and the vocals were also highlighted, the horns receded further into the background. The early rude-boy songs were transitional, but by mid-1966, form and content had made their match, with the brooding new rock-steady sound complementing the cocksure strutting and posing of the young toughs.

Rude-boy songs varied considerably in message and integrity: some artists voiced deeply held beliefs and offered what they believed to be sage advice; some saw an opportunity to sell records and make money by stirring up the 'debate' or pandering to the vanity of the rudies. The Wailers' very first single, 'Simmer Down' – a hit in early 1964 – is a prototypical rude-boy song, a warning to the youth to 'control your temper'. By the following year, this concern for the well-being of their Kingston contemporaries had hardened into unquestioning support. Bunny Wailer's composition 'Rude Boy' (aka 'Rude Boy Ska' or 'Rude Boy Skank') advises his 'friends' to 'walk the proud land'. In 1966 the Wailers followed up with Bob Marley's downright militant 'Jailhouse' (aka 'Rudie' or 'Good Good Rudie'), an overtly pro-rudie song, which warns that jails can't hold rudies, and that the police's baton sticks will diminish in size as the rudies grow taller (a strong but slightly surreal *Alice in Wonderland* image which appears in several other rude-boy songs of the period).

A comparatively obscure vocal group named the Rulers took the opposite stance: their debut release, from mid-1966, was 'Don't Be a Rude Boy' (aka 'Don't Be Rude'), which advises rudies to mend their ways, get wise, avoid jail and gain the respect of their fellow citizens. In a nutshell, 'It's not good to be a rude boy / But it's good to be a good boy.' In case the point hadn't been made clearly enough by now, the flipside was 'Be Good'. Not that the Rulers were wholly unsympathetic to the plight of the downtrodden: their October 1966 follow-up, 'Copasetic', denounces the state of emergency as a draconian response. The main drift of the Rulers' rather pious and earnest argument was that everyone should be striving to be a better person, rather than giving in to their baser natures. 'Wrong Emboyo' (sic), another similarly intentioned song from their oeuvre, is covered later on *London Calling*.

Polar opposites were the Pioneers with 'Rudies Are the Greatest' and Justin Hinds and the Dominoes with 'No Good Rudie'. (Jamaican release dates are not well documented, but the bulk of these rude-boy songs date from late 1965 to early 1967.) Many just wanted it all to end. Echoing the sentiments of the Wailers' 'Simmer Down' came

Derrick Morgan with 'Cool Off Rudies', Lloyd Robinson with 'No More Trouble' and the Valentines with 'Stop the Violence', while Stranger Cole and the Conquerors advised 'Drop the Ratchet'. But there was an undeniable fascination with the violence, from Baba Brooks and his Band's 'Guns Fever' to the Heptones' 'Gunmen Coming to Town' to Clancy Eccles's 'Guns Town'. Even the title of the Maytals' 1966 Jamaican Song Festival Competition winner, 'Bam Bam', evidenced guns fever. In Winston & George's 'Denham Town', the rudies start off with hatchets and ratchets, but then run for their guns. In 'Rudies All Around' Joe White observes that if the police shoot rude boys, rude boys will shoot the police. Such tit-for-tat escalation was inevitable, not least because of all the attention the problem and the perpetrators were being given in song.

Desmond Baker and the Clarendonians' 'Rude Boy Gone a Jail' – like the Wailers' 'Jailhouse' – takes as its subject another recurring theme in rude-boy lore: the court appearances and prison time that were an inevitable part of the miscreants' story arc. Their rude boy insists that he won't go to jail, because he's so rude that he cannot fail. Count Lasher (with Lyn Taitt and the Baba Brooks Band) disagrees: his 'Hooligan' *will* fail . . . and go to jail. In the Clarendonians' follow-up, 'Rudie Bam Bam', a rude boy is released from jail . . . having just got bail – truly, this is the rhyme that just keeps on giving – but gets involved in a knife fight and is sent straight back for life. In early 1967 Prince Buster recorded the legendary 'Judge Dread', bestowing multiple life sentences upon the rudies in his dock. Derrick Morgan voiced the rudies' defiance in the courtroom drama 'Tougher than Tough' and a brace of sequels. Lee 'Scratch' Perry – recording with the Defenders – also came down on the rudies' side with the double-header 'Set Them Free'/ 'Don't Blame the Children', but he at least offers a reasoned socio-historical argument for clemency: rudies are poor, uneducated, unemployed and desperate, and consequently forced to steal to survive (conveniently, perhaps, Scratch omits the random violence and other atrocities). His pithy observation that a 'hungry man is an angry man' would later do service in the chorus of Bob Marley's 'Them Belly Full (But We Hungry)' (1974).

What all of this added up to was a powerful mythology. As already stated (see 'Jimmy Jazz', above), there's always been a tendency for the balladeers of the day to romanticise robbery and violence during hard times, especially if there's a perception that those hard times are due to or exacerbated by the policies of an oppressive or unheeding Establishment. And other media fed the flames. Cinema-going was an important part of Jamaican social life. Rudies on the street picked up poses and attitudes and wisecracks from their silver-screen action heroes, the cooler and tougher the better. And just as rude boys took tips from the latest heroes of spaghetti westerns, spy films, action films and buddy-buddy films of the day, so did the Jamaican musical community. The two mythologies quickly became intertwined. The Slickers' 'Johnny Too Bad' ostensibly warns the rudie that he is bound for hell, but for all his robbing and stabbing and looting and shooting, and his spaghetti western or mobster movie name, and his habit of swaggering down the road with a pistol and a ratchet in his belt, the subject of the song comes over as more cult hero than vicious thug.

It was left to Desmond Dekker to take the romance to the next level with his 1966 single '007 (Shanty Town)', a title that says it all about the gap between fantasy and reality. His lyric consists largely of magpie borrowings from other rude boy songs of the era (common practice rather than heinous crime). He begins by evoking both James Bond and the Rat Pack (007 and *Ocean's 11*) as rude-boy role models, and then has his rude boys loot and a shoot like 'Johnny Too Bad'. Dekker enjoys this insistent rhyme scheme so much – and it really does capture something of the compulsive frenzy of the rudies' antics – that he just keeps on running with it. Like countless others before them, his rudies get bail, get out of jail, and cannot fail . . . but they also wail.

In the early Sixties, Jamaican records released in the UK were primarily targeted at the West Indian immigrant population in London. There was a West Indian club on Carnaby Street called the Roaring Twenties which played a lot of ska, where many of the regulars dressed in a Jamaican rude-boy style, with loafers, and trousers cut slightly too short to show off white socks, set off with that relic of the be bop jazz era, the pork-pie hat. By 1964 a sizeable West Indian contingent was regularly showing up for the all-nighters at the Flamingo club, just around the corner in Wardour Street. Thanks largely to Georgie Fame and the Blue Flames' highly danceable jazz-influenced soul, the Flamingo also attracted mods in their Italian-cut three-button suits, and (mostly black) American GIs. Considerable sartorial and musical crossover ensued. Meanwhile, Millie Small's 1964 Number 2 hit 'My Boy Lollipop' declared the mainstream UK charts were fair game for Jamaican music.

In summer 1967 it was the turn of '007 (Shanty Town)' to catch the public imagination. Released in the UK on the Pyramid label, it climbed to Number 14 in the charts that June, helped by a hastily arranged concert tour by Dekker and his backing singers, the Aces. These shows also attracted a crossover audience. In addition to UK-based Jamaicans, there were some late-period mods. But the original mods were getting long in the tooth by this stage, and many of the next generation had moved on to what would be the dominant style over the next few years for the UK's rock-steady and reggae enthusiasts: skinhead, a look – not coincidentally – initially based on that of the Jamaican rude boy.

In the latter half of the Sixties, the bright new future promised in the first half of the decade was already beginning to seem like a bad joke to many young Britons, not least those from the working class who toiled long hours on factory assembly lines – the country still had a manufacturing base at that time – and lived on council estates or in high-rise blocks, or in the country's vast stock of decaying Victorian terraces. The hippies, with their long hair, mysticism, peace and love and bohemian pretensions seemed like so many spoiled, fey, privileged middle-class students. And even if that wasn't quite the truth, then they undeniably inhabited a different world. Skinhead supporters will argue until they are red, white and blue in the face that it was not a cult devoted to mindless violence; that, like mod, it was more about posing and preening and dancing and looking cool. But mindless violence did play a large part not only in its reputation, but also in its mythology and its appeal to its followers. Even if skins didn't have access to guns, their identification with the rude boy went further than the clothes. In his early teens, between roughly late 1967 and 1970, Paul Simonon was one of their number.

London-based reggae artists had been keeping one eye on developments at home and the other on opportunities in the UK ever since Millie Small hit the big time. Dandy Livingstone recorded 'Rudy, a Message to You', the message being, simmer down . . . or else you'll go to jail. Desmond Dekker had already followed up his Jamaican hit with the celebratory cash-in 'Rudy Got Soul', and in response to the

UK success of '007 (Shanty Town)', he recorded 'Rude Boy Train', which even recycled part of its lyric. It was not to be another rude-boy anthem, though, but rather 'The Israelites', a song about a family man's struggle to make ends meet, recorded in London in 1969, that was to provide Dekker's next UK hit, taking him to Number 1. By which stage the rude-boy song cycle had ground to a halt, and the story of reggae had moved on. Well, almost. In 1971, a little late for the rude-boy train, London-based Jackie Edwards – who, like the Rulers, will make another appearance in the *London Calling* story – recorded 'Johnny Gunman' for Trojan in belated response to 'Johnny Too Bad': it starts with gunshots and police sirens, and warns Johnny that he will fail . . . and go to jail.

In 1972 Jamaican director Perry Henzell fulfilled his ambition to make a film set in Jamaica about Jamaica. *The Harder They Come* is based on the story of Ivanhoe 'Rhygin' Martin, Jamaica's Public Enemy Number 1, who became a folk hero in the late 1940s after shooting a policeman and going on the run. The story is updated to the (early Seventies) present day, and set within the Jamaican music business, with Ivan portrayed by contemporary reggae singer Jimmy Cliff in *Superfly* threads and shades. But as the nickname Rhygin translates, roughly, as 'Badman', the material's connection with the rude-boy era was too strong to ignore. Cliff recorded some new songs for the sound-track, including the title number about fighting for what's yours on earth and refusing to bow down to the police. Toots and the Maytals' 'Pressure Drop', a suitably dread warning about the retribution conse-quent upon bad behaviour, is an early reggae song from 1969. Also included on the soundtrack, and the soundtrack album, are two of the struttingest vintage rude-boy songs, the Slickers' 'Johnny Too Bad' and Desmond Dekker's '007 (Shanty Town)'.

Upon its initial release, *The Harder They Come* was mismarketed as just another blaxploitation movie with funny accents. In early 1977 Perry Henzell decided to try again, and the film was re-released in conjunction with the soundtrack album. It made an instant connection with members of the punk scene. Paul Simonon prac-tised bass by playing along to the LP at Rehearsals Rehearsals, and took a tape of the soundtrack on tour with him for at least the next couple of years. The frequent tour-bus airings of its songs and rehearsal run-throughs of its bass lines firmly established both movie and soundtrack in the collective Clash consciousness. It was from this source that they took their May 1977 cover of 'Pressure Drop', and Joe went on to make numerous allusions to the film and its songs in the lyrics he wrote for the band's own material during 1977. 'The Prisoner' refers to 'Johnny Too Bad' and rude boys getting rude. The title of *Give 'Em Enough Rope* (. . . 'and they'll hang themselves') is consciously similar to *The Harder They Come* (. . . 'the harder they fall'). 'Safe European Home' not only namechecks *The Harder They Come* but also borrows the phrase 'Rudie can't fail' from '007 (Shanty Town)'.

Don Letts, the dreadlocked DJ at the Roxy club during its time of serious influence (late December 1976–April 1977), was largely responsible for establishing the wider punk community's interest in the heavier sounds of contemporary roots reggae. Joe became friendly with him, and in late 1977, Don – at the time more interested in contemporary reggae – made Joe a present of an unwanted Trojan compilation album of classics from the ska, rock-steady and early reggae period. From Joe's description, it sounds like the 1972 triple album *The Trojan Story*. (Joe responded to Don's generosity by poaching his girlfriend, Jeanette Lee.) Already in thrall to *The Harder They Come*, and prone to musical crazes, Joe listened to little else but this vintage Sixties Jamaican music for the next few months. In May 1978 Joe told Pete Silverton of *Sounds* he'd written a 'couple of Blue Beat numbers' (Blue Beat being the name of an early UK record label specialising in ska that became a generic UK term for the music).

'Rudie Can't Fail' could be taken as an attempt by the Clash to mimic the popular music of a bygone era. The title phrase, recycled from the 18-month-old 'Safe European Home', is generic to the Jamaican rude-boy song cycle. As are the lyrical references to problems finding a job, feeling the pressure drop, and the need to simmer down or 'cool your temper'. At the end of the Vanilla demo version of the song, Paul Simonon gleefully shouts out, 'Don't be a naughty boy!' a reference to the Rulers' 'Don't Be a Rude Boy'. The Clash's Rudie even swaggers around in a pork-pie hat and suit thinking he's hot stuff. Jail is not mentioned, but the threat of it hangs in the air like the ghost of a rhyme.

The instrumentation of the album version also draws heavily upon Jamaican styles of yore. Aficionado Paul Simonon is naturally in his element on bass, sliding from note to note in the verses, leaving the all important spaces, but keeping it lighter and tighter and staying more on top of the beat than would be required for a more up-to-date Seventies reggae sound. The Irish Horns help the tune sashay along in an appropriately rousing style. Trumpet player Dick Hanson had some useful previous experience. 'I was a staff musician for Trojan Records for several years,' he says. 'God knows how many tracks I played on or who they were by. Don't ask! I did about eight a day, and I never even knew who I was playing for half the time. I did play for Desmond Dekker. And I was on the road with the Pioneers for a while.'

★

The Specials, the Selecter, Madness and the Two Tone-led ska revival hit big in the UK over summer and autumn 1979, in the wake of the success of the Specials' debut single, 'Gangsters', which was released that May and charted in August. When the band covered Dandy Livingstone's 'Rudy, a Message to You' (as 'A Message to You, Rudy') for their follow-up single and the opening track of their debut album, *The Specials*, both released in October, it helped re-establish the rude boy phenomenon in the UK. Cue songs with the character in the title – usually addressed as Rudy, Rudi or Rudie for short – and the rude-boy-inspired suits'n'hats styling of the Two-Tone bands, quickly adopted by many of their fans. Because the Clash's 'Rudie Can't Fail' was not released until December 1979, and the Clash-starring movie *Rude Boy* was not released until spring 1980, it was easy for the casual onlooker to get the impression the Clash were jumping on a band-wagon.

In late 1977 and early 1978 punk seemed to trigger revived, mutated and hybrid cults at a bewildering rate, letting them loose to roam the post-punk landscape like armies of custom-designed zombies. The rock'n'roll revival predated punk by many years (it hardly qualified as a revival, as it never went away), giving the nascent punk movement a tribe to do battle with in the shape of the Teds. But AP (After Punk) came power pop and the mod revival, the skinhead revival, the Two Tone ska revival and Mowhawk punk. Like most gangs, they didn't warm to members of other gangs. As Joe Strummer noted in 'Last

Gang in Town', his witty early 1978 commentary on these bewildering developments, 'kids fight like different nations'. However purist its rhetoric, no revival movement is ever wholly pure, because it's impossible to erase or ignore every musical or sartorial development that has occurred since it happened first time around. The second-generation mods and skins and Two Tone rude boys all had some punk in the blood, and were therefore even more closely related to each other than the first generations of their movements had been.

Even while Joe was playing the part-amused, part-appalled observer in 'Last Gang in Town', the Clash themselves were reverting to subcultural type. As 1978 progressed, and manager Bernie Rhodes's interest, influence and control relaxed, the band gave up on the short, spiked punk hairdo, doffed the zippered and stencilled Rock'n'Roll Army Fatigues item by item (though they didn't dispense with them completely for several months to come), and when offstage, began to wear clothes that reflected their musical interests pre-Clash. This was least true of Topper Headon, who had never been a punk: upon signing up he had been given a punk haircut and a set of punk duds to wear when he was on duty, and he doggedly continued to do that. Mick Jones, though, grew his hair out long and curly, wore high-heeled boots, waistcoats and scarves, and floppy sleeved shirts open at the neck: the Kensington Market glam-meets-lads-rock look from the mid-Seventies (with a little touch of punk). Joe Strummer combed his hair into a quiff, affected a turn-up on his drainpipes, and wore brothel creepers and flecked jackets of near drape-length: a rock'n'roll revival look based on late Fifties styles (with a little touch of punk). And Paul Simonon cropped his hair close, bought a blue Johnson's suit in the three-button mod style, and wore it with Fred Perry shirts and DMs, and from time to time, red braces and a pork-pie hat: somewhere between the rude boy and the skinhead looks of the mid-to-late Sixties (with a little touch of punk).

Soon after the Specials got together in Coventry, they talked their way into a support slot on the Clash's June–July 1978 Out on Parole tour of the UK. At the time, the band were still dressing in a strange assortment of clothes, with various members favouring punk or rockabilly-type gear, and one or two still sporting wide-lapelled jackets and flat caps. They played a set that reflected the variety of influences, ages and cultural origins of the band members, with a not always comfortable mix of punk songs and early reggae songs. It was band-leader Jerry Dammers's idea that the band should play skinhead-era rather than contemporary reggae. 'At the time I wasn't keen, as I had grown up being picked on by original skinheads in the late Sixties and early Seventies,' says the band's rockabilly-loving lead guitarist Rod Byers (aka Roddy Radiation).

Shortly after the tour, Bernie Rhodes began to manage the Specials, during which period they rehearsed and lived semi-rough in Rehearsals Rehearsals in Camden Town. This was a period of great hardship for the band, which culminated in the unpleasant experiences documented in 'Gangsters' and brought their relationship with Bernie to an end. But it was also at this time that everything started to come together for the band. The Specials' social commentary lyrics already owed a lot to the Clash, and Bernie stressed the need for a more coordinated sound and image.

It was Jerry who realised that the rhythms of ska would combine better with punk than did those of reggae's later, more laid-back incar-nations, and the band's material was reworked in a ska-punk hybrid style. It was evident to the Specials from their time on the Clash tour that punk as a unified movement was over. For the section of the former punk audience who had bought into the tabloid view of punk as a licence to behave like cretinous yobs – and thought the mod revival was too effete – the skinhead revival offered an opportunity to keep on misbehaving in a different drag. As the original skins had been the audience for late Sixties reggae first time around, post-punk revival skins represented the most likely audience for a band playing post-punk Sixties reggae. The Specials had already encountered enough skin revival aggression while supporting Sham 69 – a band dogged by a notoriously problematic following – and at a couple of venues on the Clash tour to feel ambivalent about this audience. Naïvely, perhaps, they opted to try to change it. 'Jerry has said since he was trying to get the new skinheads away from racist organisations like the National Front,' says Rod. In the Specials' first significant music press interview, in April 1979 with *Sounds*' Dave McCullough, in an effort to distance the band from the negative associations of skinheads and establish an identity of their own, Jerry pointedly referred to Two Tone as a rude-boy movement. At the time, the Specials were thinking of rude boy as a sort of Jamaican mod thing, rather than as a hoodlum mob thing.

What they hadn't considered, as Specials bassist Horace Panter notes in his memoir *Ska'd for Life* (2007), was that neither the mainstream press nor the general public made such subtle distinctions between mods, rude boys and skins. And why should they? All three subcultures, in both their original and revival strains, came from the same source.

The Specials got the disruptive skinhead audience they didn't want anyway. But they did succeed in making the ska revival a rude-boy revival. Distinctions between original ska, original rock steady, and original early reggae/skinhead music collapse at this point: the Specials threw it all into the liquidiser – or should that be 'The Liquidator'? – with a stiff shot of punk energy. 'Gangsters' is based on Prince Buster's 'Al Capone' (1965). The Specials not only covered 'Rudy, a Message to You', they brought in the trombonist on the original song, Rico Rodriguez, to guest on their debut album and subsequent tours. Over the next year they recorded a medley of skinhead-era instrumental classics as the 'Skinhead Symphony' and their own take on 'Judge Dread' in the guise of 'Rude Boys Outa Jail'.

It might or might not be entirely coincidental that the Clash began rehearsing 'Rudie Can't Fail' the month after the Specials' *Sounds* feature and the same month 'Gangsters' was first released. Although the Specials beat the Clash to releasing a ska/punk hybrid recording, though, they did so a year after the Clash first covered 'Pressure Drop' and 'The Israelites' – Rod Byers remembers watching the band sound-checking with the latter on the Out on Parole tour – and Joe first sang about rude boys and rudies, made reference to 'ska punk' in the lyric of 'Last Gang in Town' and talked to the music press about having written his 'couple of Blue Beat numbers'.

It's well known that it was an early Sixties photograph of the Wailers' Peter Tosh in a black suit, white socks and sunglasses that inspired the Two Tone emblem, Walt Jabsco. However, Rod maintains it was Paul Simonon's mid-1978 style that was the chief inspiration for what would become widely recognised as the Two Tone look. 'Paul looked cool in his rude boy gear, and I reckon that's where Jerry Dammers got our image from,' he says.

It would be taking too much away from an inspired and innovative band to claim that the Clash provided the Specials with the complete template for their image and music, but it would be equally unfair to claim that the Clash ripped off their former support band's ideas when it came to exploring Jamaican music of the rude-boy era. 'I think we both influenced each other, but we had our different ways of playing it,' says Rod, diplomatically. 'Having two Jamaicans in the band who had grown up with the music, plus Rico, gave us a more coffee-coloured sound than the Clash's white-rock style. But there were bands up and down the country experimenting with that mix of ska and punk, the Beat and Madness to name just two. It seemed an obvious direction to all of us at the time.'

The Specials' first recordings marry punk speed to ska rhythms, to the soul and funk touches Jerry Dammers and Horace Panter had picked up in their earlier bands, to the Chuck Berry-cum-Johnny Thunders guitar stylings of Rod Byers. 'I wasn't trying to be different,' he says. 'It was all I could play at the time.' The Clash also refused to be hamstrung by slavish attention to period detail, either lyrically or musically. While the pork-pie hat aside in Joe's lyric for 'Rudie Can't Fail' could be a reference to first-generation rude-boy fashions, it's far more likely – in the wake of his pointed jibes at the 1979 mod revival in an early draft of 'London Calling' – to be a sideswipe at the Specials-orchestrated 1979 ska revival. 'I guess we were the new fashion, and the Two Tone thing was all getting a bit teenybop by then, so Joe had a slight dig,' laughs Rod.

The Clash weren't fixated on the revival, though. Joe also mentions a doctor 'born for a purpose' and the suit he describes is not tonic or mohair but 'chicken skin', references to contemporary reggae DJ Dr Alimantado's single 'Born for a Purpose' (1977) and his best-selling Greensleeves compilation album *Best Dressed Chicken in Town* (1978), respectively. 'Sky juice' is the poetic – more literally, it means water – Jamaican name for cones filled with shaved ice flavoured with fruit syrup, and in autumn 1979 it was also the title of a popular reggae single by Nigger Kojak and Liza. Meanwhile, Mick's lead guitar line around 2:17 has more to do with the way he used to dress in 1978 than the way Paul Simonon used to dress in 1978. There's also more evidence of Mick's studies at the feet of the master Sixties pop song-writers under the title refrain, where he doubles the bass line with a guitar line played an octave higher to fatten the sound.

The most obvious musical incongruity has more to do with the way Joe Strummer used to dress in 1978: the incorporation of the

Bo Diddley beat, present even in the Vanilla demo version. This is no accident: Joe's notes about the song's structure identify these parts as the 'Bo Diddley Sections'. In addition, the structure of the vocal line owes much to that for 'I Fought the Law': there's the same syncopated pause towards the end of the line, accompanied by what music theorist Patrick Clark describes as the 'upper neighbour' tone: the vocal goes up a step before returning to the note it started on. The three key musical elements of the song might be retro by themselves, but the band's fusion of them makes the song something else entirely.

The first rule of sequencing: don't put similar-sounding songs together. It can diminish both by drawing attention to how alike they are. Over the course of a double album, had they so wished, the Clash could easily have hidden or at least played down the Bo Diddley connection between 'Hateful' and 'Rudie Can't Fail'. That Mick Jones, who was in total control of sequencing, placed one after the other was both typically contrary, and typically witty. In this context, the intro to the latter song becomes a wicked tease: Topper's drum punctuations give the song the same feel as 'Hateful', but are deliberately impossible to anticipate – one on the first beat, then two on the first beat, then one *off* the first beat – adding up to a stumbling, lurching effect . . . just like one too many Brews for breakfast. When he brings the backbeat in, though, Topper switches into highly proficient bona fide Sixties reggae playing, with plenty of genre-appropriate work on the rim of the snare . . . but he also keeps the maracas going through the verses, emphasising the half-beat – as Jerome Green did for Bo Diddley – and uses the hi-hats for the same purpose in the chorus, thus providing the tune with much of its energy and groove.

*

In 1978 David Mingay and Jack Hazan of Buzzy Enterprises began filming the Clash for a movie they were making, with no clear idea what final shape that movie would take. Some months before starting, they had come to the conclusion that they wanted to include footage of a punk band, and while taking in a few gigs for research, David got talking to 20-year-old Ray Gange at the Marquee club in Wardour Street. 'I asked him what group he would recommend as being the best punk group, and he was undyingly loyal to the Clash,' says David. Ray, who also liked Fifties rock'n'roll, was an occasional drinking acquaintance of Joe Strummer. After the inevitably complicated negotiations with Bernie Rhodes, Jack Hazan was able to shoot his first footage of the band for what would become *Rude Boy* on 30 April 1978, at Rock Against Racism and the Anti-Nazi League's joint Carnival Against the Nazis in Victoria Park, Hackney.

A reluctant Ray had been talked into taking a role in the film, and was pushed in front of the camera on the day, initially with the idea that he might act as a roadie. Genuine roadies Johnny Green and Baker would appear in the movie as themselves, but Ray was supposed to be an everypunk Clash fan-made-good, a foil providing Buzzy with an opportunity to examine some of the band's actions and beliefs. His interaction with the band became ever more important as David and Jack came to realise the live performances they filmed at several different UK venues through the remainder of 1978 were true gold dust: impassioned deliveries of strong and highly topical songs caught by Jack's quite inspired (given the limitations of manpower and equipment) camerawork. 'I thought Joe's lyrics were a hundred times better than the norm,' says David. 'I thought, like Dylan, he was an authentic voice, not just an imitator of other people.' He set up semi-improvised dialogues between Ray and members of the band – part-scripted or at least cue-carded, but usually either recreated from or inspired by real conversations – in order to give Ray the opportunity to debate points raised in songs the film was recording, in particular those relating to the left/right and black/white tensions of the time.

Ray's main function was to play devil's advocate, which at times put him close to expressing right-wing or racist views. Whether or not those were his real views remains a matter of some argument. 'Ray has been wrongly interpreted as some kind of fascist, when he was merely pointing out contradictions in those kinds of issues,' says David Mingay. In the 'extras' interview Ray gave to accompany the 2003 DVD re-release of *Rude Boy*, he claimed he was instructed what to say by David, and that the co-writing credit he receives for the film 'stitched him up'. He wished he'd insisted upon a fictional name for his character, or a disclaimer making it clear that the views expressed by the screen Ray Gange were not necessarily those of the real Ray Gange.

The semi-improvised exchanges are awkward and often unsatisfactory. The band members usually fail to take the bait Ray is giving them, which makes them appear to lack as much in the way of conviction as they do in acting ability. And Ray doesn't come over any better. As filming progressed, it became clear his main talents were for ligging and drinking copious amounts of Special Brew. Ever adaptable, David worked this into the 'script': Ray freeloads, loafs and louses up, and then is (at long last) warned for voicing dubious opinions by Mick Jones, is beaten up by bouncers, has the mickey taken out of him by Johnny and Baker, is dumped in a bath by the roadies plus Paul and Topper, and is eventually abandoned by the Clash.

As filming progressed, the band had begun to think of the film as theirs and, furthermore, their own British punk version of *The Harder They Come*. The Clash mentally cast themselves in one highly romanticised aspect of the outlaw persona – the dangerous rock'n'roll band riding into town to hit, split and quit the way bankrobbers in cowboy or gangster movies might – while Ray Gange personified another, less glamorous side of being young and rebellious in late Seventies Britain: lacking money, the ability to find a steady, interesting job, having no direction or obvious skills, he seems doomed to drink and drift. Similarly, his on-screen friend, played by the diminutive Terry McQuade – who, had a swearbox been anywhere nearby, would have been skint within two minutes of stepping into frame – doesn't appear to have much other than a convincing skinhead look going for him.

Off-screen, Mick Jones's schoolfriend Robin Crocker, the self-styled Robin Banks, who had roadied for the Clash in the past – just as drunkenly as Ray Gange, and more violently – illustrated another option which the Clash, again romantically, liked to see as a possible fate for themselves had rock'n'roll not saved their souls: after being expelled from school, Robin had embraced a life of petty crime and hoodlum behaviour, but had quickly progressed to involvement in armed robbery and to jail time, as previously celebrated by Mick in the 1978 Clash song 'Stay Free'. Hanging around with the Clash, Robin tended to dress down in jeans and Doc Martens, and liked to wear a trilby. By the middle of that year – some time before the idea took root in the Specials' camp – extrapolating from Robin and the other 'street' people around them, the Clash had come to see their UK fan base as a predominately white equivalent of latter-day black Jamaican rude boys. 'I was really impressed by this,' says David Mingay. 'They were making it so there wasn't any difference between a black rudie and a white rudie. And they didn't regard that as fake. It was coming from the reggae culture. And Joe had tackled this crossover successfully, and nobody else had [at that time]. This was not what the other groups were particularly interested in, but ever since "Police & Thieves", the Clash had been involved in that: "They must live as rebels and outcasts!"' According to Bill Price – their engineer for four recording sessions spread out at intervals throughout 1979 – the band frequently used the term 'rude boy' as a term of address during casual conversation within their immediate circle.

The Buzzy team did not take the Clash's mythic view of the Clash or their friends and followers at face value, but being aware of the band's many rude-boy reference points, they were politically astute enough to recognise their resonance in and for contemporary Britain. They filmed a sequence for the film showing Paul lying on a hotel bed listening to the Slickers' 'Johnny Too Bad' from *The Harder They Come* soundtrack, and also used the Wailers' 'Jailhouse' (credited as 'Rudi') as incidental music. David and Jack also conceived and shot a sub-plot showing some black pickpockets in London being monitored by police, then arrested and finally locked up. Live footage of the Clash at the Lyceum on 28 December 1978 (or 3 January 1979) performing 'I Fought the Law' was included partly to highlight the contrast between the fate of the band and the fate of the pickpockets . . . and, by extension, of the real rudies back in Jamaica. 'The Clash get away with it, and the black guys get put in prison,' says David.

For his part, having risked far more money on the venture than he had intended, David was keen to ensure that the film be as marketable as possible. He began to press the Clash for a new, previously unreleased song that would have specific relevance to the movie. With Mick suffering from writer's block, it was left to Joe Strummer to oblige. 'I had seen Joe play a piano in some bar or somewhere,' says David. 'With him just hammering away.' David floated the idea of a pivotal late scene in which Joe and Ray Gange would discuss Ray's situation, and Joe would perform a song relating to it. 'The film is intended to be more like a musical than a rock concert film, where one song just carries on after another,' says David. 'In a Hollywood musical, often the main characters get down to intimate discussion over a piano. It's almost a convention.' In what would be one of the last scenes shot for the film to feature a member of the Clash, Joe sits at a piano among the band's trademark hot-pink flight cases in Base rehearsal studios, Tooley Street – hired by Buzzy specifically for the shoot – and sings the solo R&B number 'No Reason', while Ray mooches about swigging from his ever-present can of highly potent Special Brew. 'Joe wrote that song specifically for the film, as a song about Ray,' says David. 'In fact, the song is an address to Ray in the form of a song. So we got there, and to wind us up, Joe at first said he hadn't got anything, and then that he might be able to play a bit, and then – typical for him – he brought out his notebook and it was all there, all the words written out and ready. It wasn't properly titled. I think we called it "No Reason" in the film because it was in the first line of the song, but he didn't commercialise it like that. It was just an aid to his performance in the scene.' Joe knew that, musically, it was a generic-sounding bit of sub-New Orleans boogie. 'That scene was intended to be a transition in the film where you suddenly see things from a different point, or there's a development in the character's mentality, where he has to admit something', continues David.

The lyric is mostly in the first person, and does seem to describe the lifestyle and express the viewpoint of Ray Gange the character: the protagonist is jobless, penniless, resentful, convinced that the country is going to the dogs, and highly race-conscious, believing himself to have no more chance in life than the disadvantaged black youth in his home area of Brixton. When Joe finishes 'No Reason', Ray offers him a swig from his can of Special Brew, and Joe pointedly replies that he's off it now, because 'it was fucking me up'. He then asks Ray what he's going to do with himself. Echoing 'No Reason', Ray blurts out that he might as well be black because people treat him 'like a nigger'. True to form, Joe avoids confrontation by choosing to mishear the word as 'ligger'. Ray then tells Joe that the Clash ought to leave politics out of music, because the two don't belong together. Joe responds – appropriately enough – by playing Shirley and Lee's 'Let the Good Times Roll'. Ray does a little jig.

It might enhance a key scene in the film, but the not-very-original original 'No Reason' is hardly premier-league Clash, and Johnny Green remembers David Mingay being disappointed. He continued to push for a theme song performed by the entire band. Johnny believes that what Buzzy really wanted was a song that would be exclusive to the film, something that would increase box office and ensure a soundtrack album, and help make back some of the money spent on the studio re-recording of the live shows (see Part 2). David dismisses this theory. 'No, because we never stood to make money out of the music,' he says. 'We couldn't exploit the soundtrack in any way without their approval. That was the agreement we had.'

As with 'No Reason', the Clash delayed and hedged, but in June 1979 Joe invited David down to Pimlico to hear the demo of the band's new offering. The Clash – or at least, Joe – had taken the commission seriously, and again, any show of reluctance was largely a cover for the difficulties the band had been experiencing writing anything at all. As well as the lyric, Joe is the most likely candidate to have come up with the chords for the main body of the tune, and brought both in to Vanilla together.

'"Rudie Can't Fail" was originally written and recorded specifically for the end credits of the film,' says David. 'The line about drinking Brew for breakfast: that was Ray.' The list of adjectives in the remainder of the opening verse also fit: rude, reckless, crude, feckless. In the second verse, the protagonist acknowledges that his lack of direction is a matter of concern to others, but says he can't cope with the indignity of labour at another's command. (There is no bridge section in the Vanilla version: it was added later.) In the third verse, he's advised to control himself, and consult the situations vacant advertisements. But by the fade out, ever irrepressible, he's already insulting his new boss. That's not all there is to the lyric, but it is most of it and, like 'No Reason', it sums up Ray as we see him in the film and also tallies with the autobiographical material he provided for the film's promotional pack. (That said, although the real Ray Gange did hail from Brixton, his life wasn't quite as dead-end as that of his screen character. Like Mick Jones, he was grammar-school-educated and didn't live in the hellish Brixton tower block he is shown leaving in the film's opening scenes, Jack Hazan's camera taking time to linger on the Ku Klux Klan and National Front graffiti.) 'It was Joe's rather generous adios to Ray,' says David of 'Rudie Can't Fail'. Adios to both Ray the character and Ray the real person, who – having been paid for his role – promptly emigrated to Hollywood to enjoy the good life . . .

working in construction. The song is undeniably generous: it conveniently ignores the fact that, by most people's standards, Ray the character does fail.

During his visit to Vanilla, David also heard some of the other demos, including 'Death or Glory', and expressed interest, but was told that 'Rudie Can't Fail' had been written for the film and that's what he was getting. During an interview with Joe in late June – conducted shortly after David's visit to Vanilla – NME journalist Charles Shaar Murray started enthusing about the new Quadrophenia movie. 'Wait till you see our film,' shot back Joe. 'It's called Rudie Can't Fail. Ray Gange is the boy from nowhere.' (He phoned Murray the following day and said, 'Make that the slob from nowhere.') Which demonstrates two key things: how closely Joe associated the song with the film and with Ray; and how quickly Buzzy had embraced the song as being ideal for their purposes, a musical theme so closely suited to their creative theme, and so readily identifiable with their principal character that they had already adopted its title as the film's working title. Even the title the film was eventually released under, Rude Boy, doesn't stray too far away . . . and the poster and ads used to promote it feature a still of Ray drinking Special Brew for breakfast.

It all seems straightforward enough. But both Ray Gange and Joe Strummer went on to deny David Mingay's interpretation. 'I never thought "Rudie Can't Fail" was anything to do with me,' says Ray. 'As far as I know, the film was named after the song at the last moment.' He insists a can of Special Brew was pretty much a standard punk accessory – 'Shame I didn't know about product placement at the time!' – and he was hardly the only person around the Clash who drank it. While his refusal to play the gloryhound is admirable, Ray was never party to David and Jack's planning and sub-plotting, and had left the country before the song was offered for the film, never mind delivered and attached to it, and so was not aware that Rudie Can't Fail, in Johnny Green's words, 'was the working title for a long time'.

Joe Strummer proved even more determined to distance the song from Ray and the film. He insisted that 'Rudie Can't Fail' was drawn from first-hand experience and observation, and that any relevance to the movie was coincidental. In the first issue of The Armagideon Times, produced in December 1979, he reminisced about waking up one morning at 11 o'clock in a flat empty save for some left-over Special Brew 'so we had some Brew for breakfast'. In his roughly contemporaneous interview with Chris Bohn, he stated, 'I wrote "Rudie Can't Fail" about some mates who were drinking Brew for breakfast. They think nothing of it. Me, I'm past the stage where I can. I can drink Brew for breakfast, but not every day, and that's what made me notice them. I thought it was a hell of a way to start a day.' Twelve years later, he again cast himself as one of the morning boozers in the *Clash On Broadway* booklet, but showed some confusion about the date, stating that the song wasn't written for *Rude Boy*, but 'a long time after', following a summer spent going to reggae blues parties.

As the lack of consistency might reveal, these scenarios were attempts to rewrite history. There are a number of reasons for that. The Clash saw a rough cut of the film in August 1979, while they were working on *London Calling* in Wessex. This was after they acquired the new Blackhill management team of Peter Jenner and Andrew King, who also attended the screening. Shortly afterwards, Andrew phoned David Mingay to demand that Buzzy remove all the political content from the film and release it as a 50-minute presentation of the Clash performing 'live'. He explained that Mick Jones in particular objected to the fact that all the white people in the film were portrayed as fascists, and all the black people as thieves.

This accusation is both an exaggeration and a distortion of David Mingay's and Jack Hazan's creative intent and political stance. It's also somewhat hypocritical. The Clash were chosen for the film because their lyrics and stance reflected the times, and the dialogue in the film was either reworked from real conversations overheard by David Mingay or introduced in order to explore themes raised by Joe Strummer's lyrics. The preoccupation with the issue of fascism is understandable in a context where the first footage of the Clash was shot at the Carnival Against the Nazis, shortly before the band recorded 'English Civil War' – a song envisaging a Nazi-like takeover of the UK – and the last scenes of the film show a right-wing government coming to power. It's hard to see how including footage of black pickpockets in the film is inherently racist. The Notting Hill Riot of 31 August 1976 started when police tried to arrest a black pickpocket, and while Joe and Paul were taking part in the resulting mayhem, a gang of black fellow rioters tried to mug them. It was this that prompted Joe to write 'White Riot'. '(White Man) In Hammersmith Palais' was partly inspired by Joe witnessing black 'sticksmen' – his word – trying to steal girls' handbags during a reggae show at that venue. In 'Safe European Home' being white in Kingston invites robbery by blacks. The knife-wielding pickpockets in 'Last Gang in Town' are also identified as black. In all four songs, Joe is clearly making a point about a lack of unity between rude boys of different hues, cultures and musical tastes rather than identifying all black men as petty criminals. The first three songs are performed in *Rude Boy*, and all of them are relevant to the film's plot. 'Joe was always involved in examining black people and white people,' says David. '*He* was sometimes misunderstood. There was absolutely no reason for the misunderstanding, except for the stupidity of some people. Because he didn't spell it out to them as such, but it was quite clear what he was saying.' By extension, the same applies to the examination of the issue in *Rude Boy*.

The Clash had other, perhaps more genuine, concerns about *Rude Boy*, some of which were, and some of which were not, expressed to David Mingay at the time. The live footage and one or two golden moments of behind-the-scenes footage aside, the film can be a little earnest and boring. The improvised dialogue lacks sparkle. The actors, including the band members, are not very accomplished. And gallingly, given the amount of time, money and effort put into getting them right, the visuals and the sound do slip out of sync too often during the live segments. (Bill Price blames this on additional editing after he delivered the soundtrack, which was in sync with the cut he and the band worked with.) 'Mick also said that he didn't like the film because he'd changed his hairstyle since it was filmed,' laughs David. 'He really meant that. He was obsessed with his hair. And I think he thought that Joe was too charismatic in the film. I came to realise later that by making the kind of film where we tried to reveal things about people by being close to them, that something would offend those people slightly. Probably the truth, actually. Or else other people watch the film, and then say things about it to them. Instead of seeing themselves in the way that I saw them, they wanted to see themselves in another way. And sometimes there's a sense of humour failure, or a lack of . . . not humility, but self-deprecation.'

The largest unvoiced objection of all, though, came from the Blackhill management team. More so than the band: they were appalled that the Clash had made and would make so little money from the film. David did sense this when he spoke to Andrew King. He thought he was hearing the opening gambit in a forced renegotiation of terms, and – having long ago exhausted the budget – he decided he was not going to play along. Relations deteriorated rapidly from then on.

Even so, after the album was mixed in early November 1979, the Clash gave David the studio version of 'Rudie Can't Fail' as promised, but with very bad grace. Today, David plays this down, but three weeks after his visit to Wessex to collect the song, he spoke to *Melody Maker's* Michael Watts about the project, and claimed a threat had been made to cut him at the studio, and upon returning home he had to take the phone off the hook after receiving numerous further threats. The song was added to the closing credits, and described as the Main Theme . . . but the title of the film was now changed from *Rudie Can't Fail* to *Rude Boy*. David recalls Mick being very much against the film being named after the song, but doesn't think this was the main reason it was changed. 'I think it was a copyright issue, that it wouldn't have been viable for CBS,' he says. 'Plus, the Clash hadn't written the film. You don't want two different pieces of work in different media by different people with the same title.'

Squabbling and talk of injunctions preceded and followed a limited press preview at the end of November 1979. Formerly so proud of the venture that he had boasted about it to the *NME* as 'our film', Joe now began disowning *Rude Boy* in interviews . . . and it was from this time on that he began claiming that 'Rudie Can't Fail' was neither commissioned nor composed for the film, a position which he never publicly revised. More threats of legal action preceded the film's consequently belated official release in April 1980. Without the band's support, UK screenings were limited. There was no soundtrack album. (The film went on to do well in Europe, and had several releases on video, and was released on DVD, with extras, in 2003.)

Joe was being disingenuous when he strove so hard to play down the song's association with *Rude Boy* and Ray Gange, but not when he claimed the song had a wider application. It is also about the Clash, and 'some mates' of the Clash, and the Clash's followers in general. *Those* rude boys; the ones that Ray Gange's character was supposed to represent in the film. (In this respect, the song is a more upbeat close cousin of Mick's earlier 'Stay Free'.)

Joe's MC-style introduction for Mick at the beginning of the song establishes ownership and feeds the Clash's inclusive personal mythology. Mick's vocal is clearly double-tracked, and painstakingly pieced together. It's given even more emphasis when Joe joins in halfway through the last line of each verse, and then hangs around for the title refrain and a bassy 'oh no' or two. The two singers – panned to the left and right channels – overlap each other to insistent, hypnotic effect, and then reverse their call-and-response roles for the chorus. In a marginal note on his draft lyric for what he refers to as the 'Market Bit' – the new bridge section added after the Vanilla demo recording – Joe offers further wry illumination of the limited choices on offer to his protagonist in terms that reflect the day to day life of the perennially cash-strapped Clash members and their friends from mid-1976 to early 1979: 'So where you wanna go today? / Shall we look round the market? / Or shall we look round the market?' Although the first three verses and the bridge section are either in the first- or the second-person singular, the inter-verse links are plural – 'hear them sayin' and 'so we reply' – presaging a change to the first-person plural for the final verse. At this point, suddenly, the positive is accentuated: 'we' are still none too keen to get a job, but are now no longer feckless but 'cool and speckless'. This shift in perspective makes the title-chorus a little more believable, gives the song a more universal feel, and encourages the listener to identify. Even if that listener gets to work or college on time every morning after drinking nothing stronger for breakfast than milky tea with two sugars.

'Joe was trying to include the audience as well,' says David Mingay. 'He was whipping them up to be rebels, and he had that thing of solidarity. "Rudie Can't Fail": what he meant was the Clash were on the side of Rudie. Rudie is the thing of the future. He's not the boring one. What they were expressing in the song was partly what they had picked up from working on the film, because they knew the film by the time they wrote it. They saw it in reels on several occasions, as a work in progress.'

The period of the Clash's direct contribution to *Rude Boy* began in April 1978 and lasted for more than a year, and it was inevitable that their creative efforts during this period influenced the project, and vice versa. When filming, the band dressed in black to play 'I Fought the Law' at the Lyceum on 28 December 1978 (or 3 January 1979), David Mingay and Jack Hazan not only helping to open the doors for the Clash's rebel rock'n'roll period, but also to set the precedent for the monochrome retro rocker look that would accompany it. Overall, *Rude Boy* captures the period during which the rebel rock and rude boy strains started to come together in the Clash's work, providing an insight into the mindset that would produce 'Jimmy Jazz' and 'The Card Cheat', as well as the more obvious 'The Guns of Brixton', and the band's takes on 'Wrong 'Em Boyo' and 'Revolution Rock'. Joe also began to think about the likely fates of the band's 'rude boy' friends and followers as they aged and were compromised even further by life, providing him with the central lyrical concepts for 'Death or Glory' and 'Clampdown'.

There are several other ways in which 'Rudie Can't Fail' – the last track of side one of the original double LP, and therefore the end of the album's first chapter – speaks to the rest of *London Calling*. There are some filigree-delicate little high-pitched touches of Roland Chorus-treated guitar at the end of each line of the chorus – subtle, but hard to block out once they've been noticed, sorry – which recall the melodica tweets on 'Hateful', and anticipate the full-immersion Chorus-bath of 'Lost in the Supermarket'. Musically, the Market Bit provides a reflective, even mournful, pause, before the resumption of the hectic ska-Diddley. Lyrically, it enables Joe to reference two other songs on the album. The first two lines – not getting what you need at the market for what ails you – pre-echo 'Lost in the Supermarket', while the third line – about being put under pressure so great it causes physical pain – pre-echoes the crushing and bruising of 'The Guns of Brixton'. The use of the syncopated pause and 'upper neighbour' vocal technique borrowed from 'I Fought the Law' reappears in both 'Clampdown' and 'The Card Cheat'. In the closing breakdown section, along with some 'hep, hep, hep' ska toasting, there are some calypso 'wayos' mimicking the horn lines, and some strictly-for-fun Strummer ad-libbing, all of which presage the even longer party section in 'Revolution Rock'. And, recalling the seagulls in 'London Calling', Joe gets so carried away at the end, he howls like a dog. Or maybe this time it really is a werewolf . . .

Though there's a distinct possibility it's supposed to be a wilde-beest. On 20 March 1979 – partly as a favour to another member of the Clash's rude-boy posse, *ZigZag* editor Kris Needs, and partly because he was keen to get into the studio control room at Olympic studios in Barnes – Mick had produced the 'Danger Love' single for Kris's hobby band the Vice Creems, with Topper also helping out on drums. The B-side was a cover of Fabian's 'Like a Tiger', which featured Kris, Robin Crocker et al howling like wildebeest. Topper had been so taken with this sound that it had become a running joke in the Clash camp, with Paul happy to join in. Kris would like to believe that Joe's sudden interest in random animal noises on *London Calling* owed much to the precedent established by the Vice Creems' 'Like a Tiger' . . . and he might very well be right.

'Spanish Bombs'

Although a late addition to the album, the song opening side two of the album was almost as demanding to write as 'London Calling'. Also like the title song, it has its origins in a cab ride . . . or, at least, it did in the accounts Joe Strummer gave to *Melody Maker* in 1988 and the *Clash On Broadway* booklet three years later. In the first week of the Wessex recording sessions for *London Calling*, Joe and Gaby Salter took a taxi from the studio in Highbury to Whistler Walk in the early hours of the morning. There was a newsflash on the driver's radio about a bombing by Basque separatist group Euskadi Ta Askatasuna ('Basque Homeland and Freedom': ETA for short). Joe turned to Gaby and said, 'There should be a song called "Spanish Bombs".' Two other accounts would seem to contradict this version, though. In the first issue of *The Armagideon Times*, Joe claimed the song was written in seat 18b of a Braniff Airlines DC-10 aeroplane. Twenty-five years later, Mick Jones appeared to back this up when he told *Uncut* that Joe wrote the song after having recently visited Spain.

The water was further muddied by another of Joe's remarks, alluding directly or indirectly to the start of the Spanish Civil War: 'I'd also been thinking about Granada in 1936, when the repression was extremely heavy,' he told *Melody Maker* in 1988; 'I got [the song] from reading Orwell and people like that,' he told that same music paper in 1979; 'Spanish Bombs' the song was 'drenched in Federico García Lorca' he told the *NME*'s Sean O'Hagan in 1988. To really confuse matters, in the latter interview, he also said, 'I was going out with Palmolive of the Slits at the time and she came from Andalusia. It's a kind of love song.'

So what part of the above is true? The answer is: all of it, almost . . . but not exactly. 'That's another complex lyric . . . It moves back and forth through time from Spanish history to package holidays,' Joe told Sean O'Hagan. He was right: it's one of his more ambitious – and successful – exercises in associative writing, involving matters historical, topical, political, geographical, poetical, folk musical and personal.

The genesis of the idea did come in the cab. Although Joe recalled the bombs being placed in tourist hotels on the Costa Brava – which actions ETA had threatened, and would carry out – the incident that made the news on 29 July 1979 was the simultaneous bombing of Madrid's airport and two railway stations, killing six and causing 130 injuries. Contrary to Mick's claim, Joe didn't visit Spain at all in 1979, and hadn't for some years. But Joe's 'seat 18b' and 'Braniff Airlines' details were not invented: at least part of the lyric was written on a plane. Braniff Airlines was a bargain-rate American-based company that expanded rapidly during 1978. This later proved to be the company's undoing – it overstretched itself, and folded in 1982 – but during their brief growth spurt, they did establish some London-to-Europe routes. One of these was to Stockholm in Sweden, where the Clash changed planes on the hit-and-run trip they made to Turku, Finland, in order to appear at the Ruisrock Festival. This has Joe working on his lyric the week after the Madrid bombing incident.

The reference to the DC-10, both in the lyric and in Joe's account of the song's writing, is poetic licence. Though Braniff did have some ageing McDonnell Douglas DC-8s, most of its fleet was composed of Boeing 727s, and they had no DC-10s. The reason Joe chose to refer to that particular make of plane was to accentuate the song's portents of doom. First flown in 1970, DC-10s had been involved in five high-profile incidents between 1973 and 1978, and on 25 May 1979 an engine ripped off the wing of a DC-10 while it was taking off from Chicago, resulting in 273 fatalities. Four days later, all DC-10 airliners in the US and UK were grounded for emergency checks. Overall, the DC-10's safety record was no worse than that of other planes of its age and size, but that was not how it was perceived, at least by Joe Strummer. 'DC-10s were crashing all over the place,' was his explanation for the plane's appearance in 'Spanish Bombs'.

In 1931 Spain abolished its monarchy and became a republic. In February 1936 the left-wing People's Front won the general election. Thereafter, violence between right- and left-wing factions escalated. In July that year, General Francisco Franco of the right-wing Nationalist movement led a coup d'état, and took over as head of state. Civil war broke out. Poet and dramatist Federico García Lorca was a vocal supporter of the Left, and evidently not secretive enough about his homosexuality. At dawn on 19 August 1936 soldiers belonging to one of the right-wing militias dragged him into a field in Viznar, near Granada, Andalusia, shot him, and threw his body into a mass unmarked grave. Lorca's subject matter had always been highly romantic, dark and brooding, marrying the earthy rituals of Andalusian gypsy life and death to a private mythology revolving around recurring images like blood and the moon. His violent early death made him one of the first and most significant martyrs of the left-wing cause, now even easier to characterise as a fight for freedom. While the Nationalists were backed by the Fascist powers in Germany and Italy, the People's Front were backed, and assisted in the trenches, by a cosmopolitan brotherhood of left-wing sympathisers known as the International Brigades.

Training and access to arms were limited for those who first rallied to the left-wing militias, and many of the local soldiers were little more than ill-disciplined schoolboys. There was also much squabbling between the various factions: parts of the Popular Front were not so popular with other parts. One of the British volunteers was Eric Blair. Better known by his pen name George Orwell, he wrote *Homage to Catalonia*, first published in 1938, about his experiences fighting on the Aragon front in the hills around Zaragoza in the first half of 1937, before being shot in the throat and invalided out. Orwell had joined the Communist group POUM, which was declared illegal while he was recuperating from his injuries in Barcelona. Key members were arrested, and in some cases, shot, requiring Orwell to flee the country. With internecine squabbling rife among the opposing forces, it was small wonder the Nationalists prevailed in 1939, allowing General Franco to establish a dictatorship that lasted until his death in 1975. For much of that time, Lorca's works were banned in his home country.

The monarchy was nominally restored in 1947, but Franco remained in charge. In 1959, as his dictatorship entered its twentieth year, the most determined opposition came from the Basque population. Indigenous to the north of Spain, the Basques spoke a different language, considered themselves a different people, and were pushing to be recognised as a separate nation. The more militant among them formed ETA. In 1968 they began a programme of assassinations. Five years later, they blew up a car carrying Admiral Luis Carrero Blanco, the Spanish Prime Minister and Franco's intended successor. When Franco died in 1975, the country instead became a constitutional monarchy under King Juan Carlos. A process of democratisation and decentralisation followed, with the Basque region being granted a degree of autonomy in 1978. A degree was not considered enough: ETA promptly escalated its activities, and a total of 76 people died as a result in 1979 alone. The intention was to threaten the communication, transport and power infrastructures, and undermine what had become the foundation of Spain's economy: tourism.

Others who craved freedom during the Franco years simply left the country. When Joe Strummer moved in to the squat at 101 Walterton Road in summer 1974, he became friendly with Richard Nother, destined to be one of the longest-serving members of the 101ers. Joe called him Snakehips Dudanski, and the second name, at least, stuck. Richard was living with Esperanza Romero, a young Spanish woman who had come to London to pursue her interest in ceramics, and live in a climate where books and films were not subject to censorship. In early 1975 her 20-year-old sister Paloma moved into 101 Walterton Road, and quickly entered into a relationship with Joe. The very first song Joe wrote as a member of the 101ers was for Paloma: 'Keys to Your Heart'. Even then, Joe talked a lot about the Spanish Civil War. Paloma described it to Joe's biographer Chris Salewicz as 'part of our courting'. The two sisters – whose names translate as Hope and Dove – and the two bandmates became a tight-knit foursome. Over summer that year, they hitchhiked down through Spain to Morocco, stopping along the route to stay with the girls' parents in Malaga, Andalusia.

When Joe left the 101ers to join the Clash in late May 1976, his new band- and housemate Paul Simonon pretended to mishear Paloma's name, and instead called her Palmolive, after the soap. It was a time of upheaval for Joe: in order to convince as a member of the Clash, he felt a lot of pressure to sever ties with his 'hippy' past, and coupledom was considered too cute and cosy for the early punk scene. Paloma was already finding the torn and conflicted Joe difficult to live with. She left for a while, then returned. Soon afterwards, Joe proposed a more casual arrangement . . . which was the beginning of the end. Before their relationship ground to a halt, though, encouraged by the emerging movement's have-a-go spirit, Paloma embraced her new identity of Palmolive, and decided to play drums in a punk band. She got together with some of the new friends Joe had made via the Davis Road squat where he first rehearsed with the Clash: Sid Vicious, Viv Albertine, whose relationship with Mick Jones was also due to suffer considerable punk-imposed stress, and – after he left the Clash in September 1976 – Viv's friend and sometime guitar-tutor Keith Levene. The Flowers of Romance never got past the rehearsal stage, though, and at the end of 1976, Palmolive decamped to form the Slits. The all-female band were offered a support slot for the Clash's 11 March 1977 gig at the Harlesden Roxy, and then, with Viv Albertine now on guitar, they were taken along on the Clash's May 1977 White Riot tour of the UK. By this time, Joe and Palmolive had not been an item for some months. Joe was not one for voicing his feelings, and the punk-era Clash didn't have any room for songs about broken hearts, but the end of the relationship coincided with a period of heavy drinking and unhappiness for him.

When the restless Palmolive left the Slits in November 1978 she was invited to join another all-female band, the Raincoats. After recording a single and album, she left them, too, in late spring 1979. Always interested in New Age spirituality, she decided to give up drumming and go in search of answers with her new partner Dave McLardy, who had formerly helped out as a driver for the 101ers. They left to study with a guru in India, but lost faith in him after a couple of months and came back. They married, had a daughter, and briefly moved to Spain.

Joe's break-up with Palmolive occurred nearly three years before he wrote 'Spanish Bombs', so she was definitely not his girlfriend 'at the time', but both parties had continued to move in much the same social circles. Her departure for India, however, was a physical parting of the ways, and although that did not turn out to be permanent, marriage and motherhood drew a firm line under the Joe Strummer phase of her life at this time.

When he began writing the song, Joe had been involved with Gaby for around eight months. Chris Salewicz's *Redemption Song* reveals that he wasn't remotely monogamous, either then or later, but he did have strong feelings for Gaby, as Johnny Green attests, and the fact their relationship went on to last 14 years and produce two daughters confirms. In choosing to write even obliquely about Palmolive, Joe wasn't being disloyal to his current partner, just acknowledging that a new romantic beginning is also the true end of whatever went before. Also, the Bernie Rhodes diktat about love as a subject had only recently lost its authority. This was the first opportunity since 'Keys to Your Heart' for Joe to explore these sorts of feelings in song. It might seem strange on the surface, but although Gaby was the sounding-board when the initial inspiration for 'Spanish Bombs' came to Joe, it is – at heart – the valedictory love song to Palmolive that he had not been able (or allowed) to write any sooner. As he was still uncomfortable with the outpouring of personal feelings that came perhaps too easily to Mick Jones, it's semi-fictionalised, and hidden behind the screens of war, politics, Lorca, and the chorus's mangling of Palmolive's native tongue, but – in Joe's own words from *The Armagideon Times* – 'The Spanish is Clash Spannish and it means – "I love you and goodbye! I want you but – oh my aching heart!"'

The lyrical structure requires the listener to have a feel for cinematic flashbacks and jump-cuts. The first verse allows Spanish songs to convey us straight back to 1939. The line 'Oh, please leave the vendanna open' is a bastardisation of the opening and closing refrain from Lorca's short poem 'Farewell'. Lorca's lines are 'If I die / Leave the balcony open!', meaning the balcony window; in Joe's version, 'vendanna' is a Clash Spannish approximation of *'ventana'*, meaning window. (Another Lorca poem exploring much the same theme is entitled 'Nocturnes of the Window' [*'Nocturnos de la Ventana'*].) Shortly after meeting Palmolive, Joe announced that the knack to speaking Spanish was sticking an 'o' on the end of every word. Over four years later, despite their close relationship for a good half of that time (and the fact that he'd attended a Spanish-speaking school in Mexico for a year as a child) Joe clearly hadn't progressed much further with the language than his own peculiar version of O level.

Supposedly in transit on the DC-10, Joe recalls seeing bullet-hole evidence of the battles of 40 years before in the walls of the cemeteries, and mentions the Guardia Civil's black cars to evoke ongoing Nationalist oppression. The Guardia Civil are a threatening, brutish presence throughout Lorca's work, and his 'The Ballad of the Spanish Civil Guard' contains the couplet 'Black are their horses / Black the horse's shoes . . .'

The last line of Joe's first verse brings us back up to date with bombs planted in tourist hotels along Spain's Mediterranean coast . . . or does it? Joe sings (and the inner-sleeve lyric sheet reads) 'Costa Rica' . . . the former Spanish colony in Central America, which declared itself independent from Spain in the early nineteenth century. Although Costa Rica had two bloody internal upheavals at roughly the same time Europe was hosting its world wars, it had been relatively peaceful since 1949. So it's unlikely that Joe seriously intended to switch his lyrical focus to somewhere half a world away . . . a slip of the Clash Spannish tongue into the Spannish cheek, then. Next time around, Joe sings 'Costa Brava' instead: far more relevant.

The second verse cuts from the imaginary package holiday – discos and casinos being among ETA's targets – back to 1939 and the Spanish Civil War, this time to take a look at the Popular Front's lines. The different factions flew their own flags: the red flag was Communist, the black flag was Anarchist (and just to confuse matters, the Anarcho-Syndicalists fought under a red-*and*-black flag). In Joe's lyric, the red flag is sung rather than flown, because 'The Red Flag' is also the anthem of the international Socialist movement. It was written in 1889 by London-based Irishman Jim Connell, inspired by that year's London Dock Strike. It's a song about standing firm together, and fighting to the death for what you believe in. Which underlines the secondary purpose of Joe's invocation of red and black: as quasi-Lorcan images of, respectively, blood, fire and freedom, and death, sorrow and darkness. After the left-wing forces die, Joe throws in an apparently incongruous reference to 'Mockingbird Hill'. Written by Vaughn Horton in 1949, and recorded by Les Paul and Mary Ford among others, it's a paean to the joys of home sweet home and a life of bucolic contentment. This is presumably intended to evoke the calm and silence after all the gunfire and screaming.

Following this briefest of brief pauses in the bloodshed, the action resumes in the present day, 'back home' with the bombs of another paramilitary organisation. The aims and methods of ETA and the Irish Republican Army (IRA) were not dissimilar. London landmarks, stations, hotels and clubs had been subjected to bombing campaigns by the IRA and breakaway groups throughout the Seventies. On 30 March 1979 a car bomb planted by the breakaway Irish National Liberation Army (INLA) killed Conservative MP Airey Neave as his car pulled out of the House of Commons car park. (Too late for Joe's lyric, but adding weight to it, nonetheless: on 27 August a bomb planted on his fishing boat by the IRA caused the death of Earl Mountbatten and three others; and on that same day a landmine explosion and ambush at Warrenpoint resulted in the death of 18 soldiers.)

Joe then cuts back to the ETA bombs in Spanish hotels, and to the dramatic tie-in-cum-creative-sleight-of-hand that lets him get away with his un-Clash-like chorus: in the song, he's heartbroken and saying farewell because the object of his affections has been killed in one such explosion. When he bemoans the fact that his 'senorita's rose was nipped in the bud', he's taking extreme risks with the listener's tolerance for corny romantic imagery.

The threads of the narrative come together in the third verse. Joe's imagination finds him wandering hills no longer silent after battle, but crowded with the ghosts of memory and resounding with the cries and music of the past: the Civil War and the poets in the trenches preparing for battle in the Thirties are as real and present as the terrorist bombings of the Seventies because they share the same historical root. As Joe's ill-fated DC-10 prepares to land, the last Clash Spanish chorus circles in on the region of Andalusia, where Palmolive was born and raised, and its inland capital Granada, where Lorca was born and raised. The close positioning of the words 'mandolina' and 'corazon' recall the line *'turbio de corazon y mandolina'* from Lorca's 'Nocturne of the Void', which (if the association was intended) is the equivalent of dollying back to let us see Joe, the singer-narrator, with a frog in his throat and with 'clouded heart and mandolin'.

Mick acknowledged that this song was 'one of Joe's' to Adam Sweeting of *Uncut* in 2004, but although Joe may have brought the first draft of the lyric into Wessex with chords attached, it was Mick who added the fine detail, while Joe polished this and other lyrics in his spliffbunker. The Wessex studio clock was ticking as the band worked up and recorded the song, but Mick did not allow this to impinge on the time he put into either the arrangement or the recording. In his 1980 *Rolling Stone* album review, Tom Carson refers to the song's 'jangling flamenco guitar work', and other commentators have apparently heard echoes of Spanish folk music and even a touch of Django Reinhardt's Thirties acoustic Belgian Gypsy jazz. This would have been appropriate to the mood of Lorca's *Gypsy Ballads*, to the period of the Spanish Civil War, and to Joe's lyrical allusions to Spanish songs, mandolins and 'music from another time'. It would also have been perhaps too literal a musical interpretation of the words. And it really isn't there, unless – at a real stretch – some of Mick's acoustic rhythm guitar flourishes could be described as mimicking the passion of flamenco, while the repeated notes in his lead lines could be likened to mandolin tremolo. The illusion of anything more overtly period- or place- or genre-appropriate taking place is testament to the evocative power of the lyric, helped by a touch of the loving tongue (albeit slightly tongue-tied) in the chorus.

The musical tangent that Mick does pursue complements the lyric in a more subtle way. The harmony of the main riff goes from A to F#m to Bm to Dm. It would have been more predictable to end with a D major, but the closing minor – foreign to the key – gives it a regretful feel, in keeping with the lyric's sense of nostalgia and loss. Overall, the clutch of minor chords makes it sound like the Beatles at their most McCartneyesque. After Topper's introductory tattoo, the rhythm appears to be hijacked by strummed acoustic guitars. Bill Price disputes this – he says he always did his best to bury Mick's acoustics in the mix because he only ever had 'crap' ones – and maintains the dominant sound here is 'long spread chords on electric guitar'. But what sound very much like two acoustics are clearly audible – albeit with the percussive grating noise produced by striking the strings with the plectrum admittedly louder than the actual chords – panned hard left and right in the mix, which makes them stand out rather than buries them. Then, at the start of the chorus, at least one acoustic guitar appears to be attempting to play a lead countermelody, only without any power to sustain. So, if – as

Bill claims – these guitars aren't acoustics pretending to be electrics, then they're electrics pretending to be acoustics pretending to be electrics.

Guitar that sounds more obviously electric reinforces the strumming, and Mick also scatters wiggy bursts of lead throughout the climactic third verse. Mickey Gallagher's Hammond organ becomes more audible towards the end, still fairly low in the mix, but with the Leslie on full. Meanwhile, Topper's drums drive this 'folksy' song along at a cracking rock'n'roll pace. Overall, the anachronistic use of modern electric instruments and technology to create an old-time ambience perfectly reflects the rapid and disorienting time shifts in Joe's lyric.

Even more so than the preceding 'Rudie Can't Fail', the vocal work is a mesmerising weave. Joe's baritone dominates the verses, singing almost all the lines, with Mick's tenor coming in to double up an octave higher on every other phrase . . . and just when that starts to be predictable, Mick gets an occasional phrase to himself, before Joe butts back in. The chorus reverses the leads, with Mick singing 'Spanish bombs' alone, then being joined by Joe for the Clash Spannish. Again, there's a hint of the call-and-response of the field holler, folk blues, gospel and soul traditions, but the abiding impression given by all this overlapping and unison singing is of camaraderie amidst confusion and chaos. Which is also the abiding impression of Orwell's *Homage to Catalonia*.

A remarkable coincidence: Orwell's book was by no means the only autobiographical account of the Spanish Civil War. Spanish broadcaster Arturo Barea fled into exile following the conflict, and ended up in England working for the Spanish-language division of the BBC's Overseas Service. (London calling . . .) In 1946, Faber and Faber published his memoir of his own role in the conflict under the title *The Clash*.

'The Right Profile'

Accounts by both Joe Strummer and road manager Johnny Green have attributed this song to Joe, and dated it to the August 1979 Wessex sessions. Like the preceding 'Spanish Bombs', they said, it was one of the late additions to *London Calling*. Consequently, one of the biggest surprises thrown up by the rediscovery of the Vanilla demos in 2004 was that the tune, at least, had an earlier life. Or rather, more than one earlier life: two instrumental versions were among the 37 Vanilla demos that Mick Jones found in his lock-up.

One of them, entitled 'Up-Toon', is included on *The Vanilla Tapes*. Working titles for demos are throwaway, but as they are intended as a guide to recognition, they usually give some clue as to the nature of the song, the instrumentation used, or the source, place or time of inspiration. Here, the title is a layered pun. It's an *up tune*, in both tempo and mood. It might even be described as *cartoonishly buoyant . . .* or is that reaching a little too far? Looking at it from a less charitable angle, the reason it has such a generic working title could be that there isn't much else to say about it. The other, slightly different, demo take, not included on *The Vanilla Tapes*, was labelled 'Canalside Walk', which could be yet another attempt to evoke the tune's carefree breeziness, or possibly even provide a record of the circumstances of its conception. (The Vanilla demo 'Walking the Slidewalk' is another punfest on the same theme, but is an entirely different tune.)

It wasn't Joe's intention to mislead about how the song came to be. Like a lot of songwriters whose main contribution is writing lyrics, that part of the process tended to dominate his thinking. At times, when he talked about composing a song, he did mean the whole song (or at least, the words and the beginnings of a tune); at other times, when he talked about writing a song, he meant writing his part of it: the lyric. Even though this particular tune did not come with words attached, it's not beyond the realm of possibility that Joe instigated it, because it's a simple, obvious sequence played round and round and round, and then – when that's in danger of getting boring – shifted up a fifth and played there instead. Again, like 'London Calling', it's a 12/8 shuffle with a 'swing feel', and the overall sound is staccato. (Having said that, one of the working titles points to Mick: Joe might have been living reasonably close to the river at the time, but Mick had only just stopped living even closer to the canal: Wilmcote House, where his Nan had her flat, is next to the towpath promenade of the Paddington Branch of the Grand Union Canal.)

Joe can be seen playing the piano during the recording studio warm-up run-through of the song preserved for posterity on the *Wessex Studios Footage*. Bill Price maintains that he did not play the instrument live on the recorded take, though, because Joe's rhythm guitar – which he always recorded live – can be heard in the final mix. The piano is overdubbed, then, but there are still strong indications that Joe was the perpetrator: the style is rollicking, reckless, Jerry Lee Lewis-dahn-at-the-Old Bull and Bush-of-a-Sat'day-night stuff, with lots of glassy tinkling at the top end and metallic rumbling at the bottom . . . degenerating into an even more damaged-sounding crashing and bashing, like someone attempting to play the instrument while it's being pushed down a flight of stairs. (Or perhaps being filled with wine by Guy Stevens.) 'There is a certain madness to the piano part,' acknowledges the ever-dry Bill.

More than anything, 'The Right Profile' as it appears on the album is another advertisement for the feel-is-all approach to recording: the song structure might be run of the mill, but the players are clearly having a great time, and the fun is highly contagious. The Irish Horns have to take most of the credit for delivering the *London Calling* version from ordinariness. They *blast* through it on full Stax soul strut. This is a sound that Dexys Midnight Runners – who at the time of recording were still Bernie Rhodes protégés, having followed in the footsteps of the Clash and the Specials to Rehearsals Rehearsals – would not bring back to the UK charts until the following year. The horns are mixed higher even than the vocal, and they only let up the barrage to make way for the stratospheric tenor sax solo. 'I think I was inspired at that point by Dick Parry's solo on Pink Floyd's "Money",' says Ray Beavis. (What's the betting he didn't mention that to the Clash?) Topper joins in with similarly gung-ho percussion. There's also what sounds like an intermittent doorbell or distant fire alarm, which, after close listening, Bill thinks is 'the piano and one of Mick's guitars, both playing 16ths in some spots': frenetic stuff.

Joe finally got his subject matter for the lyric when Guy Stevens was taken on as producer for the album. Johnny Green recalls Guy pulling Patricia Bosworth's *Montgomery Clift* from his bag and singing its praises. First published in 1978, it was only recently out in paper-back. Guy made a present of the book to Joe, signing and dating it 28 July 1979 – it was found among Joe's effects after his death – which, as it was a Saturday, ties in with Johnny's claim that Joe 'took it home for the weekend, and came back Monday and there it was: "The Right Profile".' The chronology might not be so straightforward, though:

Johnny also says he was the first to borrow the book from Guy. 'I went home and read it in two days, and I said, "Joe this is fantastic! An amazing life!"' Whatever the sequence, the book did the rounds. 'Everybody read it during that period,' confirms Wessex second engineer Jerry Green. When Mikko Montonen interviewed Joe on Saturday 4 August in Turku for Finnish music magazine *Soundi*, he noted that Joe was still reading the book. And in December 1979 Joe told Chris Salewicz that he followed it up by reading a second biography to get a better overall perspective. At the time, the other widely available account was *Monty: A Biography of Montgomery Clift* by Robert Laguardia, first published in 1977. Work continued on this particular lyric in the spliffbunker for some days.

Intriguingly, the collage flyer Joe had designed to promote the Clash's Notre Dame shows on 5 and 6 July 1979 features a photograph of Monty Clift playing the bugle as his *From Here to Eternity* character Robert E. Lee Prewitt. Either this is a remarkable coincidence, or it was seeing the flyer that prompted Guy to bring in the book.

At the time, Monty was not so well-remembered as his approximate contemporaries Marlon Brando and James Dean, something that Joe establishes in his half-spoken introduction – while simultaneously indicating that he ought to be – by wondering where he might have seen him before, and then running through a list of some of his films: the Howard Hawk western *Red River* (1948), in which Monty starred opposite John Wayne; the George Stevens movie *A Place in the Sun* (1951), with Elizabeth Taylor; the John Huston modern-day western *The Misfits* (1961), the last film for both Clift's co-stars Clark Gable and Marilyn Monroe; and, his most famous role, the Fred Zinnemann war movie *From Here to Eternity* (1953), with Burt Lancaster, Deborah Kerr and Frank Sinatra. Like Brando and Dean, Monty was a gifted and meticulous method actor who would go to great lengths to give an authentic performance. He nearly broke his back learning to break in a horse for one of his cowboy roles, and – even though he wasn't required to supply the music – he learned to play the bugle for *From Here to Eternity* so that his breath control and facial expressions would look convincing.

That he had disappeared from the radar by the early Sixties was hardly surprising. Monty's is a grotesque and alarming story. He was raised by an overbearing, hysterical mother who was herself adopted, but who was obsessed by social status and breeding. Unable to come to terms with his homosexuality, Monty hid his true nature as best as he could. At war with himself, he found it difficult to sleep, and began to rely on increasing quantities of booze and pills, mostly – but not exclusively – barbiturates to try to get some inner peace. He began an asexual relationship with an older woman, former torch and jazz singer Libby Holman, whose own tragic history included the shooting of her first husband and the early death of her only son. She was a more libertarian, maternal figure than Mrs Clift, but she had her own reasons for taking refuge in drink and drugs, which in turn exacerbated Monty's problems. Another of Monty's maternally inclined pals was the young but similarly troubled Elizabeth Taylor.

His self-administered medication and questionable support network ensured that, even by the early Fifties, Monty was hopelessly addicted. He had a 14-feet-long medicine cabinet in his bathroom packed with Tuinal, Seconal, Nembutal and a dizzying assortment of other pills. Joe's reference to a 'roll' in the last verse comes from the term used by dealers for 1,000 pills, an unofficial prescription that Monty had refilled every couple of months. Even by the time he played the role of Prewitt, he was regularly having to be put to bed at night after losing control of his bladder, and he was losing friends like brain cells. Joe addresses this period of his life in the second verse, where a bedraggled Monty is 'recognised at dawn' in the then highly insalubrious Times Square area.

In May 1956, while filming *Raintree County*, Monty went for dinner at Liz Taylor's place. While driving home, he blacked out and crashed the car. As Joe describes it in the third verse, his face was broken against the steering wheel: his jaw and nose were smashed, he suffered heavy lacerations to the left side of his face, and, when she arrived on the scene, Liz had to save his life by preventing him from choking on his own staved-in teeth. Months later, Monty was able to complete the film, but director Edward Dmytryk had to shoot him from the right in order to hide the damage on his left: hence Joe's title, 'The Right Profile'. With his looks gone and suffering from constant pain in his neck, Monty's addiction to pills and booze only worsened over subsequent years. He stopped getting good parts, and then any parts at all. For a while, he continued to stumble around New York disgracing himself, but then became a recluse until his heart finally gave out on

22 July 1966, all as described (complete with somewhat insensitive sound effects) at the close of the last verse.

It's a knowing lyric. The stage directions – 'dim the lights' – and terse descriptive passages make much of it sound like the shooting script for a film, while the gossipy speculation in the chorus recreates the salacious voyeurism of the media and public. Overall, it conveys the sense of Monty always being watched, of his life being out of his control and treated like cheap entertainment by others (including, by extension, listeners to this song). As he admitted in a rare open moment to a friend – which the friend subsequently recounted to Patricia Bosworth – Monty's greatest concern was how others perceived him. And, like the drugs, fame was addictive. An early notebook draft of Joe's lyric contains the subsequently abandoned pay-off line: 'Waking up in darkness / I need the sound of applause.'

Again, the downbeat subject matter runs very much against the grain of the upbeat music. This discrepancy sets up one of the album's more extreme tensions, but Joe's delivery – almost gleefully unfeeling in places – works the contradiction brilliantly. In his 1980 *Rolling Stone* review, the ever-perceptive Tom Carson noted: 'Over braying and sarcastic horns, Joe Strummer gags, mugs, mocks and snickers his way through a comic-horrible account of the actor's collapse on booze and pills, only to close with a grudging admiration that becomes unexpectedly and astonishingly moving.' The Irish Horns do yakety yak it up to almost vaudeville comic effect. The bursts of 'fire alarm' hint at drug-fuelled mania, and the pianner does a good job of recreating both the car crash and the nervous breakdown. John Earle's baritone saxophone part is double-tracked, producing a slightly phased, woozy effect. Similarly, the 'everybody says' backing vocals are doubled, and panned hard left and right, with a delay between them that gives them the effect of pinging from speaker to speaker, and of sounding, in Bill Price's words, 'big but distant'. Both tricks mimic Monty's whacked-out state, with the latter suggesting the paranoia-feeding whispering and snickering of the gossips.

The sheer volume of the horns – 'tracked to make it sound like we could afford a bigger horn section,' according to Bill Price – and the unfettered nature of the tenor solo recalls a passage in the biography that details what attracted Monty to the character of Robert E. Lee Prewitt in the first place. A closed book, Prewitt can only truly express himself when playing his bugle 'richly and fully, honking, smearing, trilling out the notes in a spray of jazz and blues'. Monty could relate to that. So could the Clash.

So could Guy Stevens. And, given Guy's own prodigious intake of pills and booze, and his own episodes of public embarrassment, that was not the only thing in the book with which he identified. In his memoir *A Riot of Our Own*, Johnny Green offered the opinion that Joe was very much aware of this, and that, as well as paying tribute to Monty by writing 'The Right Profile' he was also paying tribute at one remove to the man who lent him the Bosworth biography. It's a theory encouraged by his opening line for the song: 'Say, where did I see this *guy*?' Joe's spluttering at the end could almost be a parody of an overexcited Stevens soaking the splatterboard. Or a reference to Guy's vocal instruction. In the *Wessex Studios Footage*, Guy can be seen standing next to (almost inside) the vocal overdub booth coaching Joe in his vocal for 'Koka Kola'. Objecting to the singer throwing the lyric away by slurring the words, he insists that Joe 'come up on the vocal properly'. 'I don't want to hear you going: *waargh, wargh, buh, wargh, waarghhhhhhh*,' Guy tells him, sternly. 'We need to write that down,' murmurs Joe. It sounds like a throwaway sarcastic retort . . . but write it down, or at least remember it, is exactly what he did for the last line of this song, recorded soon afterwards.

'Lost in the Supermarket'

Because 'Lost in the Supermarket' appears to be, in part, about living in a high-rise flat, and Mick Jones was the member of the band most closely associated with such accommodation; because Mick had been responsible for 'Stay Free', the closest thing to a sensitive ballad in the Clash's repertoire prior to the release of *London Calling*; because he also sings the other three sensitive songs on *London Calling*, 'I'm Not Down', 'The Card Cheat' and 'Train in Vain'; and because Joe, unlike Mick, had always been loath to talk directly about his own feelings in song . . . for all these reasons, 'Lost in the Supermarket' was assumed for many years to be a Mick Jones solo composition.

In 1988 Joe set the record (almost) straight to *Melody Maker*: 'Everybody blames Mick for this, but I came up with the chorus and the verses and he wrote the tune. A lot of people go *that wimpy bull-shit!*' Mick has since stated, on numerous occasions, that he believes Joe wrote the lyric from his perspective – imagining what life must have been like for him growing up on the 18th floor of Wilmcote House with his Nan, his only contact with his mother being via post and long-distance calls – and gave it to him to sing as a sort of present. Other people close to the Clash – including Johnny Green, Kosmo Vinyl and Chris Salewicz – have gone on record to say that Joe told them he had written the song for Mick.

When it came to public utterance, Joe was almost pathologically averse to naval-gazing or self-pity. Some of this is attributable to upbringing. Spending his early years in the stiff upper lip world of overseas Foreign Office enclosures, and the ages of 9 to 18 in the stiff upper lip world of a public boarding school had inculcated in him the belief that it was 'a sin to bore people' with his own problems and fears. Behind this front, Joe was a highly sensitive soul with a tendency to bouts of depression. He'd moved around from country to country as a small child, been sent the City of London Freemen's School (CLFS) by his parents while still very young, lost his brother to suicide when he was 18, and experienced the inevitable anger and guilt that came with that. He'd dropped out of conventional society at 20 and spent (at least) five years living on the breadline while drifting from squat to squat. He'd abandoned his friends and girl-friend of the previous few years in order to join the Clash at 23, whereupon he had undergone Bernie Rhodes's cult-style brainwashing (with rapid rinse and plenty of spin). He'd drunk heavily for the next two years, and sometimes drugged unwisely, and had suffered a debili-tating bout of hepatitis at the age of 25, meaning he wasn't able to drink at all for the next six months. On the other side of the scale, of course, there had been a lot of fun, creativity, achievement and adulation along the way. But Joe Strummer's life had not been without its trials, and even if he didn't like to dwell on them in conversation, they had left their scars.

He had always tapped into them for his work. In 1981, asked by *Musician*'s Vic Garbarini if it was necessary to suffer to create some-thing worthwhile, Joe paraphrased philosopher Søren Kierkegaard's musing that: 'A poet is an unhappy being whose heart is torn by secret sufferings, but whose lips are so strangely formed that when the sighs and the cries escape them, they sound like beautiful music . . . and then people crowd about the poet and say to him: "Sing for us soon again," that is as much as to say, "May new sufferings torment your soul."' To which Joe added, slightly less poetically, 'Happy people don't create anything. I find creativity hinges on being well fucked up.'

Nearly three years before 'Lost in the Supermarket', the Clash wrote 'London's Burning', the lyric of which song has also been construed to be an example of Joe putting himself in the mind of those who, like Mick Jones, lived in the grim watchtowers standing sentry along multi-lane, inner-city freeways. For many years, Joe encouraged people to believe that he and Mick wrote the song together at Wilmcote House. (Pennie Smith's 1980 photobook *The Clash: Before & After* even includes a photo of Mick on the balcony there, accompanied by the Strummer caption, 'Incidentally, "London's Burning" was written on this ledge.') As a result, Mick's high-rise home was established as one of the concrete pillars of Clash (and punk) mythology, rooting the band firmly in the Notting Hill area, and giving rise to such oft-recycled music press headlines as 'Tower Block Rock' and 'The Sound of the Westway'. Much later, Joe admitted he had written the song alone in the top bedroom of his then squat at 42 Orsett Terrace – which was also right next to the Westway – while Palmolive slept nearby, after he had spent a cold and miserable day wandering around the local streets with Paul Simonon. He did go over to Mick's flat the following day so Mick could add some of his magic to the tune, but the lyric was about *Joe's* headstate: by the time the wind starts howling through the empty stone, it's as vivid a depiction as you're likely to get of a waif hungover and coming down to find a bad case of the urban alienation blues waiting to mug him for his Tube fare.

In the case of 'London's Burning', the sensitivity is masked somewhat by volume, velocity and aggression. With such trademarks-turned-clichés of punk now largely out of favour, Joe was in danger of being left exposed, just as his writing for *London Calling* found him exploring ever more personal terrain. So he relied upon humour, allusion and narrative twists as distancing devices, and – when all else failed – he gave songs like 'Lost in the Supermarket', 'The Card Cheat' and 'I'm Not Down' to Mick Jones to sing, ostensibly because they were better suited to Mick's plaintive warble, but really to ensure that they became associated with Mick instead. To help this sleight of voice along, Mick was deputised to write the notes about them in the first issue of *The Armagideon Times*. Anticipating the inevitable criticism from the pierced and tattooed hordes, Mick described 'Lost in the Supermarket' as a 'whimpering ballad'.

Unusually, the song opens with its chorus, which – less unusually – also provides its title. The listener is immediately plunged deep into consumer alienation: that sense of being surrounded by specials and deals, bright packaging promising everything necessary to make life complete, but not being able to believe it or even care anymore while reeling under the tired, flyblown strip lighting at the fag end of another long, hard day. 'It was me sitting in the World's End flats,' Joe confessed, eventually, to *Melody Maker* in 1988. 'There's a big supermarket next to the car park. You know when your mind goes blank and you find yourself wandering through all this bright, garishly lit stuff and you don't really know what you want or why you're in there? I always lose my shopping list . . .' Located at numbers 471–473 Kings Road, on the corner with Edith Grove, and backing on to Edith Way, for the duration of Joe's time in Whistler Walk, the supermarket in question was the International. Having changed hands several times since, it is currently a branch of Somerfield.

The Winter of Discontent, with its shortages of goods, failures in supply and devaluation of wages, had recently highlighted the pointlessness of looking to the material world to provide spiritual answers, or to consumerism to establish identity: 'I buy, therefore I am' having become 'I can't buy, therefore . . . *what am I?*' In May 1979, not long before Joe wrote the lyric, the Clash released *The Cost of Living* EP, with Joe's idea for a soap packet cover design, and its other visual and lyrical puns on the theme of selling out and shifting units. As already discussed, in one of *London Calling*'s many examples of lyrical cross-pollination, similar shopping-place-related existential angst can be found in the Market Bit of 'Rudie Can't Fail', while the Big Sell as Big Lie also informs 'Koka Kola'.

May 1979 also saw the Raincoats release their debut single on Rough Trade. Their new drummer, Palmolive, didn't write the A-side, but Joe would naturally have paid attention to his ex's latest: 'Fairytale in the Supermarket'. The lyric is far more oblique than Joe's for 'Lost in the Supermarket', but in addition to the similar title – which also features strongly in the chorus – the Raincoats' song does share a sense of blankness and disorientation. The difference between night and day is difficult to discern, the passing hours are measured out in cups of tea – T.S. Eliot, take a bow – Polaroids and mirrors offer opportunities for musings about identity, there's a search for comfort in familiar books, a strong sense of loss, and the observation 'nobody tells you how to live'.

Joe didn't have to borrow the high-rise experiences recounted in verses from Mick. They were his own. The World's End Estate is a massive council development situated where the Kings Road squeezes closest to the River Thames. Built by the Borough of Kensington and Chelsea in the Seventies to replace war-damaged slum terraces, it was completed in 1977, the year punk broke. Architects Eric Lyons & Associates were nothing if not bold: the development resembles an enormous, futuristic, orange-brick castle: the Castle at the End of the World, no less. The seven Towers are between 16 and 19 storeys high, and are connected by an outer wall of five-storey terraces, each of which contains two Walks on separate levels: for instance, as well as Whistler Walk, which offers access to its flats from the first floor, there is also Upper Whistler Walk, which offers access to its flats from the fourth. To give some idea of the scale: there is a total of 744 properties on the Estate, split roughly half and half between the Towers and the Walks, housing an approximate total of 3,000 residents. Number 31 Whistler Walk – at that time the Salter family flat – is in the section of five-storey terrace 'wall' joining Greaves Tower to Whistler Tower, running north-south along the east side of Edith Grove. The entrance door is situated on the inner side, leading out onto the enclosed 'castle courtyard', a raised communal garden on the first-storey level, only accessible to residents. Underneath the garden is the estate's car park, the entrance to which is via Edith Way, off Edith Grove, just behind the supermarket.

The first verse opens in the suburbs (where inner-city kid Mick never lived). After travelling the world for years with the Foreign Office, Joe's parents bought a small bungalow at 15 Court Farm Road in suburban Warlingham, near Croydon, to the south of London. Although it would remain the family home until his parents died in the mid-Eighties – and it would be another 10 years before he finally sold it – Joe only lived there full time from the ages of six to nine. There is some home-movie footage of a young Joe, his brother David and their parents larking about in the garden at the beginning of Julien Temple's 2006 Joe Strummer film biography, *The Future Is Unwritten*. Joe was small for his age, and although there was no hedge as such, there was a rickety wooden fence and a fair few bushes and shrubs . . . though, admittedly, the sizeable gaps between them meant that their height wasn't really an issue: if he couldn't see over, he could see through. Joe was then sent to the CLFS in Ashtead Park, Surrey – plenty of hedges and trees there – while his parents set off on their travels again. Because of the distances involved, for the next eight years – until they finally returned to settle at Court Farm Road in 1969 – he usually only spent time with them during school vacations. Hence the feeling he expresses of being abandoned, neglected and unwanted as a child.

So how did we get from the supermarket next to the World's End Estate in 1979 to a bungalow in Warlingham 20 years earlier? By the quickest route of all: association. Getting lost in a supermarket for real is a fate most likely to befall children. Joe was sharing his new home with Gaby, her mother, and her two younger brothers. The Salter boys may have reminded him of himself and his brother David when they were young. If not, then the trigger was the 'kids in the hall' Joe mentions in the last verse. The residential Royal Borough of Kensington and Chelsea Children's Home was and is based just three doors away from Number 31 Whistler Walk, at Number 28, with a playground situated in the courtyard directly outside: more children learning to live without their parents.

The second verse brings the protagonist right back to the Estate, and drops him off at the flat, listening to the folks above his head in Upper Whistler Walk arguing and shouting. 'The flats have reasonable soundproofing – for example, they have suspended floors – but it's certainly possible to hear your neighbours if they're loud enough,' says World's End Estate Residents' Association Secretary Jules Montero. The part of the song that isn't *exactly* true to life is when Joe claims it's always been like this for him. There are two ways of looking at this. One is that Joe is using his imagination in order to empathise with those destined to spend their whole lives racked and stacked in a council-estate development with 3,000 other people. That the environment is new to him is what provides the awe that helps him paint such an evocative picture. (The experience was also new to the Salters, who spoke Home Counties posh, and – prior to family financial woes and Frances's recent divorce from Gaby's father, Tom – had owned a large house in a more fashionable part of Chelsea.)

The other way of looking at it is to be less nit-pickingly literal. Joe might not have spent years on a council estate, but he knew more than a little about loud and crowded. At the CLFS he had boarded at Philp House for nine years with 50 or so other boys, sleeping in dorms with very little in the way of privacy. When he first moved to London in 1970 to attend the Central School of Art, he stayed in the Ralph West Hall of Residence, a high-rise packed with fellow students just over the Thames from Whistler Walk at 45 Worfield Street, Battersea. And since then, he had spent years living in a series of three- to four-storey Victorian town-house squats around the Notting Hill area, with anything up to 20 fellow occupants, and assorted rowdy anarchists, refugees, Hell's Angels, musicians, drug addicts, alcoholics, psychopaths, and, latterly, punks for neighbours.

The third verse takes its cue from the chorus, and finds Joe expanding on the spiritual emptiness of modern life: television as a soporific (as in 'London's Burning'); the 'be part of the Zeitgeist' hard-selling of disco music compilation records to people who don't go to discos or even (usually) buy music; the saving of special-offer, money-off coupons as a hobby; the reliance upon alcohol for any fleeting sense of escape. The disco compilations were another true-life detail. In 'Capital Radio Two', Joe satirised the dominance of the ultra-successful *Saturday Night Fever* and *Grease* soundtracks, the second of which had topped the UK album charts for 13 weeks from 7 October 1978. Depressingly for those who had fought the punk wars, nothing had changed for the better by the first few months of 1979. As well as compilations by middle-of-the-road artists like the Carpenters, Neil Diamond, Wings, Barry Manilow, Cliff Richard, Leo Sayer, and Barbra Streisand, the album charts were dominated by TV-advertised, pseudo-disco compilations like EMI's *Don't Walk, Boogie* and K-Tel's *Midnight Hustle* and *Action Replay*, the last of which reached Number 1 on 10 February 1979.

After pausing to appreciate the true soundtrack to the Winter of Discontent, it's back to the din of the estate for the fourth verse. In addition to the children in the walkways, the plumbing's playing up. The heating and hot water for the entire World's End Estate was and is provided by four enormous gas boilers in a central communal boiler house: the pipes that radiate out from there run throughout the flats, with the result that the inevitable gurgles and clanks sound louder and travel further than would those in a property with its own individual heating system. In context, the 'long-distance callers' are more likely to be bellowing passing drunks in Edith Grove and the Kings Road than neighbours talking down their home phones to Delhi, Dallas, Dubai or Darwin. And after the questionable comfort of these stray background noises comes the silence of solitude and long hours of insomnia as that elusive identity slips away . . .

God, it's miserable. But so is 'Eleanor Rigby'. And there's a convenient link: the Strummer-Jones partnership had some parallels to the Lennon-McCartney partnership. John Lennon was an endlessly inventive and often startlingly perceptive and witty wordsmith, but was a limited tunesmith. Paul McCartney could be banal and soppy as a lyricist, and – while he could and did write all-stops-out screaming rockers – he excelled at delicate, inventive melodies, and found it difficult to resist adding a little too much sweetener to the mix. Much the same could be said, respectively, of Joe Strummer and Mick Jones. 'Lost in the Supermarket' finds Joe going against type with his lyric; so what about Mick's music and arrangement?

Mick might not have written the words, but he took them home to 5 Simon Close and responded to them so quickly that he brought the tune in to Vanilla complete. The demo version on *The Vanilla Tapes* is a light and elegant sponge cake, but lacking much in the way of decoration. Mick more than made up for that at Wessex. The Roland Space Echo has a Roland Chorus circuit built into it that can be used without the Echo. On the album version of 'Lost in the Supermarket', the guitars are heavily swathed in Chorus, producing an almost sickly-sweet effect. Bill Price sometimes succeeded in persuading Mick to let him regulate Roland's effects . . . but not always. 'Obviously Mick had it out in the studio in this case, away from my grasp,' he says. Mick also plays harmonics. Instead of holding the strings hard against the fretboard, harmonics are produced by touching them lightly, then pulling the fretting hand away, resulting in ethereal high notes . . . a sprinkling of caster sugar.

He seems determined to ensure the musical action doesn't wander too far away from the supermarket's confectionery aisle. Could it be that the treatment afforded the album version is intentionally evoking the saccharine muzak supermarkets played in those days, something they had in common with airport lounges and the lifts of department stores, office buildings and major corporations? Bill is having none of this. 'Mick's relative leaning towards the pop side of the music spectrum helped the Clash to be more than just another punk band,' he admonishes.

There are other indications that the Clash arranged and played the album version of the song with smirks on their faces; had their cake and ate it, so to speak. In *The Armagideon Times*, Mick declared 'there are no disco instruments on this cut'. This echoes Queen's habitual album sleeve note about not using synthesisers. Until they gave in and went disco for 1980's *The Game*. There might not be any synths on 'Lost in the Supermarket', but there's plenty of treated guitar and – as if to illustrate Joe's reference to the discotheque compilation album – Mick plays funky little lead licks and Paul a muted disco bass line throughout, as he had done on 'Capital Radio Two'. Topper went to see Taj Mahal play in London the night before the band recorded 'Lost in the Supermarket'. Although known as a blues artist, Taj Mahal always refused to recognise boundaries. His International Rhythm Band included musicians from Jamaica and Africa as well as the USA, and their sound incorporated elements of jazz, reggae, funk and other musics from around the world. Topper noticed that drummer Kester Smith played a lot of what would usually be snare drum beats on his floor tom instead. So Topper does the same in the first half of each verse of 'Lost in the Supermarket'. Determinedly going for groove in the final breakdown section, he overdubs a guiro: a piece of bamboo with parallel notches cut into so that when a flat piece of wood is rubbed along, it produces a grater effect. Latin percussion evokes Samba and Latin jazz, but is also prevalent in disco, which is pretty much uptight processed funk with sophisticated Latin touches, usually horns, strings and percussion. Just to make sure none of this passes unnoticed, Paul performs a deeply corny rising octave funk-flourish during the breakdown section.

As the infamous T-shirt of the period attests, in the late Seventies there were a lot of established rock musicians who believed that *Disco Sucks*, just like there were a lot of established rock musicians who believed that punk was junk. But Queen wouldn't be the only band to try it on for size towards the end of the decade. The Clash's Riva bedfellow, Rod Stewart, asked 'Do Ya Think I'm Sexy?' at the end of 1978. The answer might not have been an unqualified yes for Rod, but that same year the Rolling Stones released *Some Girls*, which proved their best album for four or five years – arguably, their last ever good album – and the band owed their rejuvenation not to punk, as some have claimed, but to Mick Jagger's time down the disco in New York. The disco touch is also there in late Seventies records by artists as diverse as Abba and Blondie. Even ska revivalists found it hard to resist the lure: Horace Panter gets his disco on in the chorus of the Specials' May 1979 debut single 'Gangsters'. As Taj Mahal had just illustrated to Topper, music benefits from musicians being open to everything, from demanding avant-garde to disposable pop. When the Clash were in New York on the Pearl Harbour tour, all four members of the band visited Studio 54 to see how the beautiful people lived. (Joe went two nights running, the first night with Andy Warhol's in-crowd.) They might have started out adding disco inflections for entirely humorous reasons, but they clearly found they enjoyed playing that type of music. As with *Some Girls*, there is more than one cut on *London Calling* in thrall to the mirror ball.

Bill is right to insist that concentrating for too long on the kitsch aspects of 'Lost in the Supermarket' is to do both the song and the band a disservice. On one level, yes, it's like everyone involved is following Joe in trying to distance themselves from their own sensitivity. And yet, whatever its treatment, 'Lost in the Supermarket' remains endearing, even moving. There are some glorious details. Mick's vocals are double-tracked (as usual), which makes them sound breathy and upset, so that when Joe comes in on the choruses it's like he's bringing comfort. When he takes over to sing lead on the chorus around 2.30, his solo voice no longer sounds reassuring, but bruised, beaten and utterly desolate. Just short of the three-minute mark, Mick and Joe's vocals are split apart and panned hard left and right in the mix. 'Mick's lost and can't find his mum: Joe, in this case, on the right,' explains Bill. 'The solo guitar does something similar just before that.' It does indeed: it wanders forlornly around the entire store, aisle by aisle.

'Clampdown'

Another tune that Mick Jones brought into Vanilla ready to go, but this time it came first. As if to demonstrate that he had more than intricate melodies in his bag of tricks, it's the album's most aggressive, loud, four-on-the-floor rocker. The Vanilla demo version is listed as 'Working and Waiting', but in the notes in the *Clash On Broadway* compilation booklet Joe recalls it as 'Working and *Awaiting*'. And this is what the Clash were doing in Vanilla: working on new material, while awaiting the green light from CBS to make an album. It was also the working title of a tune by Mick awaiting a lyric from Joe, which, by the latter's own admission, he took 'a few weeks' to get around to. Which explains why the Vanilla demo is still an instrumental . . . and might also explain why the track was later briefly known as 'For Fuck's Sake' before finally acquiring that lyric.

'Working and Awaiting' rolls off the tongue more easily than 'Working and Waiting', and it scans better with the chorus line Joe eventually did supply for Mick's tune. And, tellingly, it also scans with and echoes a line from one of the cover versions the Clash played at Vanilla.

Sam Cooke was one of the founders of what came to be known as soul music. It is a genre that can trace its roots back, via gospel, to the black church – where Sam got his start – and also, via the blues and field hollers, to the hard-working and hard-playing life of poor blacks in the Southern states of America. Both church and work songs were often built on a call-and-response format. While the former were concerned with spiritual affirmation, field hollers were born of communal endeavour, the antiphonal chants interspersed with grunts of effort over the steady rhythm made by picks, shovels and axes striking in unison. It was back-breaking work for tough men (and women), with plenty of opportunity for fights to break out, especially with some recreational liquor thrown into the equation, and it could lead all too easily to a spell on a prison farm. Here the prisoners sang songs similar to the field hollers, but to a more insistent beat as they swung hammers against railroad ties or picks against rocks on the chain gang. More hard labour. Cooke's voice might have been gospel-sweet, and the bulk of his secular output might have been geared towards the sophisticated supper-club market, but in 1960 he wrote and recorded a song called 'Chain Gang' with a chorus featuring rhythmic grunts and clangs over the refrain, 'That's the sound of the men / Working on the chain gang.' It reached Number 2 in the American mainstream charts, and Number 9 in the UK. The Clash had already sung about 'breaking rocks in the hot sun' in their cover of 'I Fought the Law', and had added appropriate sound effects to the January 1979 Wessex recording of that song: the 'clang, clang' noises at the end are made by the band banging on the pipes in the Wessex toilets. Covering 'Chain Gang' at Vanilla four months later was a logical progression.

For the Clash's own song, Topper smashes down what band buddy Kris Needs described in his *ZigZag* preview of the album – written after listening to a Wessex playback, with the Clash passing comments the while – as a 'metallic piledriver beat emphasising the monotony of factory work'. Following the introduction, he doesn't indulge himself in anything that resembles a fill, and he avoids the tom-toms at all costs: he's a straight-four machine, his only release in the main section of the song being his lunges at the crash cymbals to mark significant chord changes: the machine changing gear. It's another modal tune (this time Mixolydian), and Mick's guitar is liberally dosed with distortion and feedback. Mickey Gallagher's solid Hammond C-3 playing acts like glue to make the sound even denser, a truly claustrophobic industrial assault. Sonically, then, the original unpleasant working environment of the chain gang has been updated to evoke something even more unpleasant. The lyric Joe finally produced follows the call-and-response structure of a chain gang work song. Vocally, Joe supplies the call and Mick supplies the repetitive response: the men are no longer 'working on the chain gang' or even 'working and awaiting', but 'working for the Clampdown'.

The allusion to jail time with hard labour also leaps the fence between the songs, with the judge threatening a sentence of five to 10 years at the start of Joe's second verse: very 'Judge Dread'. This is so much metaphorical grandstanding, though: a lifetime of factory work is its own hard time. Joe had been urging against giving in to dead-end jobs like factory work since the Clash formed: 'Career Opportunities', 'Clash City Rockers' and 'All the Young Punks' are just three earlier songs advising listeners to just say no. And no one could accuse the band of failing to put their dole cheques where their mouths were: with the exception of the year Mick spent as a Civil Service clerk between school and art school, none of the Clash had ever held down a 'proper' job for longer than a few months.

To an extent, 'Clampdown' picks up from the verse in 'Rudie Can't Fail' where Rudie's free spirit is threatened by the need to control himself and toe the employment line: here characterised as growing up and calming down. But 'Clampdown' isn't solely an anti-work diatribe. Only in the bridge section does Joe's lyric directly address the daily factory grind, urging boys (rude or otherwise) to get running. Most of the lyric is concerned with making connections between the day to day behaviour of individuals – whether in the workplace or in the street – and groups of people on the larger stage.

The first line of the first verse is borderline surreal, enough of a head-twister to make the listener sit up and pay close attention: 'Taking off his turban, they said is this man a Jew?' There's a hint of Middle-Eastern conflict here – the Clash would later juxtapose caricatures of Arabs and Hasidim in the video and on the single sleeve for 'Rock the Casbah' – but turbans are more closely associated with Sikhs than Sheiks. The line is either intended as an illustration of the ignorant taunting of immigrants – the forcible public removal a Sikh's turban being a serious religious affront – or ignorance of cultural difference. The next line, in which 'they' brag about their fatter pay packets, adds one-upmanship. Such wrong-headedness is passed on from generation to generation, keeping bigotry and envy alive. And it's a deliberate tactic of divide and rule by the 'Old Men': the powers that be, the bosses, the already compromised generation.

The allusion to racial difference is echoed at the end of the first verse, where 'blue-eyed men' are trained to become 'young believers'. This begs to be interpreted as a reference to prized Aryan physical characteristics and to the Hitler Youth. In the third verse, the young get older and start wearing 'the blue and brown', which could be (and has been) similarly interpreted as an allusion to the uniforms of the Nazi Party's pre-war paramilitary arm, the Brownshirts, and of the Nazi armed forces during wartime, mostly brown or grey-blue in colour. When the men in Joe's lyric attain a position of authority, their power corrupts, and then corrupts absolutely: rather than question right and wrong, they go along with it all until they brutalise and even kill. As his invocation of Joseph Goebbels in 'Capital Radio' might indicate, back in 1977 Joe had read William Shirer's *The Rise and Fall of the Third Reich* (1960) in early 1977, as part of his Bernie Rhodes-inspired self-education programme, and the book was discussed among the Clash. Not long after the band played the 30 April 1978 Carnival Against the Nazis in Victoria Park, Mick disputed the opinion that the National Front didn't represent a serious threat by reminding an anonymous *Record Mirror* interviewer: 'In 1928, Adolf Hitler got 2.8 per cent of the vote. By 1939 there was no one voting for anyone else.' This was a trick Hitler and his fellow Nazis managed by playing on prejudice, ignorance, envy, resentment, greed and – increasingly – fear of being singled out for reprisals by offering any opposition. And propaganda, like the twisted speeches aimed at the country's impressionable youth. Plus, of course, clampdowns: displays of the iron fist.

There are other ways of interpreting the significance of blue and brown. In the UK of 1979, the uniform of the police force (and the navy and RAF) was blue, while that of the army was brown. As already explored in 'London Calling', the police – especially in London – were proving themselves willing to whack first and not bother asking questions at all, and there was a distinct whiff of impending militarism in the air. In the context of a worksong becoming a song about the oppressiveness of work, the colours could even be construed as relating to the blue of rep suits, the blue and brown of trades and factory overalls. Discussing the song in the *Melody Maker* in 1988, Paul Simonon offered the opinion that is was about 'shopfloor fascism'.

'Clampdown' is not literally (or solely) a song about capital-letter Nazism or Fascism, then, more a song about how easy it is for normal everyday people to find themselves condoning despicable things by failing to object. And how easy it is for those despicable things to escalate from teasing to bullying to harming, and even to murder. Once the uniform – any uniform – has been donned, the mindset follows close behind. (Which knowledge didn't prevent Paul Simonon modelling a Waffen SS uniform for a *Sounds* photoshoot in May 1978.) Harry Champion's 1910 music hall ditty urging dress code conformity, 'Ginger, You're Barmy' ('. . . you'll never join the army'), might explain the yelp with which Joe concludes the song. In 1965, when Bob Dylan declared he wasn't going to work on 'Maggie's Farm' no more, he wasn't objecting to digging potatoes or cleaning out the cowshed; he was refusing to co-operate with a system he didn't believe in, because if he neglected to voice his opposition, his silence might be construed as approval. Since 4 May 1979 everyone in the UK had been faced with the option of working on Maggie's farm, or not working at all.

In *A Riot of Our Own*, Johnny Green recalled Joe telling him that 'Clampdown' was inspired by the introduction of wheel-clamping in London . . . Johnny has a mischievous sense of humour, as did Joe, so it's tempting to dismiss this story as one or other of them working for a cheap laugh. But wheel-clamping was symbolic of the kind of petty restrictions on personal freedom beloved of both central and local government, and it helped make 'clampdown' something of a media buzzword at the time. Joe had a track record of responding to the phrase of the moment.

As his notebook draft for 'Clampdown' reveals, before that inspiration struck, the song's title and chorus was briefly 'Working for the Breakdown'. That would have been too passive. 'Clampdown' is far more forceful: it's the equivalent of the Jamaican concept 'under heavy manners', a slogan Joe had stencilled on his boiler suit back in late 1976, during Jamaica's last state of emergency, implying the powers-that-be are bringing extreme pressure to bear in order to make the people, unruly and otherwise, bend to their will. When it was his turn to explain 'Clampdown' to the *Melody Maker* in 1988, Joe – who, after all, wrote the lyric – said, 'Mainly, it's a song about freedom, or the lack thereof.'

Repression and control were the subjects of another song the Clash covered – and demoed – at Vanilla: their own 'Remote Control'. In the first *Clash Songbook*, edited in 1977 by Mick Jones and Paul Simonon, 'Remote Control' is illustrated with a still of a 'Big Brother is Watching You' poster from the 1954 BBC television play of George Orwell's *Nineteen Eighty-Four*. (Julien Temple repeatedly dropped scenes from the same play into his 2007 Joe Strummer documentary *The Future Is Unwritten*.) There's more than a hint of *Nineteen Eighty-Four* about 'Clampdown'. Joe changed a line in his notebook draft of the lyric, 'Like no film, this time it's for real,' to the even less hopeful version as recorded, 'Only a fool would think someone could save you.' That bleak fatalism is reminiscent of Orwell's famous line, 'If you want a picture of the future, imagine a boot stamping on a human face – for ever.' Which brings us back to Mick Jones's inexorable, piledriving riff: stamp, stamp, stamp.

(The Clash evidently found Orwell irresistible: in addition to the *Nineteen Eighty-Four* references mentioned above, and *Homage to Catalonia*'s inspirational contribution to 'Spanish Bombs', a still from the 1954 animated film version of *Animal Farm* graces the cover of the 'English Civil War' single. In 1979 Mick Jones's preferred nom de hotel – which he also used for his production work on the Vice Creems single that March – was Michael Blair, inspired by Orwell's real name, Eric Blair.)

Joe's lyric wasn't finished there. 'And then for some reason it goes into an anti-nuclear rant,' he told the *Melody Maker*. 'I think Three Mile Island must have happened just before.' It did. The second part of the last verse – omitted from the lyric sheet transcribed by Ray Lowry – refers to the Harrisburg incident, and contemplates waiting to be melted down. Joe's use of the expression 'for some reason' to explain this shift makes the nuclear threat sound tangential, which to some degree it was. But only to some degree. On 31 March 1979 the existence of a potentially explosive bubble of hydrogen gas inside a crippled reactor at Three Mile Island was discovered. It was explained that this could possibly lead to the reactor overheating, and then melting down to disastrous effect. Thus, a new apocalyptic scenario was added to mankind's already extensive portfolio. This was headline-grabbing news throughout the world, and the media's vocabulary immediately gained another new buzzword: meltdown. The crisis lasted a very tense week, but the emotional fallout lasted much longer. Clampdown, meltdown: for Joe, the connection was begging to be made. But wordplay aside, the possibility of nuclear obliteration by accident or design is also the most extreme limitation of all on the freedom to enjoy life.

Just as personal, national and international politics and local and global ecological threats combine to make up the lyric of 'London Calling', so too do they combine to make up the lyric of 'Clampdown'. Join the forces, and look what will become of you. Stay at the factory, and look what will become of you. Surrender meekly to your peer group or government's demands, and look what will become of you. Fail to consider the consequences of messing with the mighty atom, and look what will become of us all.

If that were all there were to the song, it would be both earnest and depressing. But in the verse before the bridge, Joe spits, 'anger can be power' and incites his listeners to take on the Establishment: the Clash are still pressing their audience to assume responsibility for their lives and make a stand for their beliefs. The contrasting bridge section itself provides welcome relief from the barrage of noise and doom (though it does sound like it was welded on with less than Mick's usual care and attention). Even as Mick's backing 'aahs' approximate the wailing of souls in torment, his lead vocal urges escape, whereupon Topper whacks his congas and sounds the vibraslap and flexatone alarms, while Mick detonates a guitar explosion: an aural jailbreak; or if you prefer, a *Cool Hand Luke*-style getaway from the chain gang.

In the verse following the bridge, age and circumstance again appear to be blunting the will to be free. This reversal of the sense of liberation sets us up for a *Nineteen Eighty-Four*-style unhappy ending, with Big Brother triumphing after all. But in the first part of the final verse – added to Joe's draft notebook lyric in a different ink, presumably at a later date – he crows about some 'evil *presidentés*' having recently suffered their comeuppance. Things *can* change for the better . . .

There had indeed been an outbreak of hard karma in 1979. Joe's reversion to Clash Spannish points to the 17 July 1979 ousting of Nicaraguan dictator General Anastasio Somoza Debayle by the Sandinistas. (Who would inspire the title of the Clash's next album.) Even before Somoza's flight to Paraguay via Miami, though, despots were beginning to look like an endangered species worldwide. On 8 January 1979 Vietnam invaded Cambodia, ending the reign of Pol Pot and the Khmer Rouge, and leading, a few months later, to the outside world's discovery of the horrors of the killing fields. (The Clash would play a benefit for the country, newly and briefly renamed Kampuchea, on 27 December.) On 16 January 1979 Shah Mohammed Reza Pahlavi of Iran, whose control over the huge oil wealth of his country meant that few benefits had reached the average citizen, was forced into exile in Egypt. On 29 March Idi Amin ran from Uganda, leaving his regime to collapse, and the full extent of *his* depravity to emerge. (That the Shah and Somoza had been previously backed by the USA also demonstrates that the Clash were not prepared to soft-soap Americans in order to improve their chances of success in America.)

It was good riddance to bad rubbish, as Joe gleefully – if slightly bizarrely – celebrates in fine singing cowboy style. His 'ha, gitalong, gitalong!' ad-lib comes from the traditional cattle-herding song 'Git Along, Little Dogies' (aka 'Whoopie Ti Yi Yo'), as made famous by recording and movie star Gene Autrey in the 1937 film of the same name, and also recorded by Roy Rogers and Woody Guthrie, among countless others. The full refrain is 'Git along, little doggies, git along / It's your misfortune and none of my own.'

Over the closing funk breakdown – that giant hits discotheque album was evidently getting some serious needle time – Mick tries to put the damper back on proceedings by dolefully and insistently intoning 'work, more work', but he lets loose with all kinds of showy little chops and trills on guitar, while Mickey Gallagher makes another break for the border with some cheery organ. Joe then insists he's given away no secrets . . . which is true . . . and that nothing he's said could be dismissed as the ravings of a madman . . . which might depend upon the listener's political leanings.

Immediately following the August sessions for *London Calling*, the Clash rented a rehearsal room in Cannery Row, Carmel-by-the-Sea, California, to prepare for their 8 September 1979 afternoon appearance at the 2nd Annual Tribal Stomp Potluck Picnic and Dance in nearby Monterey, and the subsequent Take the 5th tour of America. Cannery Row life during the Great Depression was examined by John Steinbeck in his novel of that title. A rail spur ran behind the rehearsal room, and the connection proved too much for the Clash to resist. They stripped off their shirts, grabbed some nearby sledgehammers, and posed for a photograph taken by DJ Barry Myers as though they were part of a chain gang working on the railroad. For the first few dates of the tour, their play-on music again included Sam Cooke's 'Chain Gang': the Clash were back at work, more work.

Rewind to the beginning. 'Clampdown' is introduced by a hushed and slurred, spoken-word monologue, Joe's voice double-tracked and positioned to sit low in the mix, while Mick and the others warm up the machinery of doom. It is not included on the lyric sheet, so what Joe says is difficult to decipher, which, over the years, has been enough in itself to make it the subject of much speculation.

Mick Jones admitted he didn't know all of it in a 1999 online interview on the *Spin* website, but confirmed the first three lines. For a
long time, an Internet consensus version nearly made sense . . . but
not quite. Then Ade Marks worked out, if not the definitive, then
at least the best-guess, most likely version, which was subsequently
printed in a 2005 issue of *Q Classic* magazine devoted to the Clash.
To paraphrase: the kingdom is ransacked, the jewels are recovered,
and the chopper descends. The passengers hide in the back,
enveloped by the smoke, while a recorded message revolves on a
tape spool, saying 'I'm back in this place and I could cry.' It could
be a self-aggrandising account of a rock'n'roll band facing an unwelcome gig – Joe and Paul would remain fond of combat metaphors
for many years – or it could be an imaginary scenario depicting
genuine soldiers involved in a coup, counter-coup or covert op
against one or other of the evil *presidentés*.

What it most closely recalls, though, is a hallucinatory action
sequence from Francis Ford Coppola's Vietnam war film *Apocalypse
Now!*, released in the USA in summer 1979. The Clash saw it for the
first time in early September, in California, at the beginning of the
Take the 5th tour, and a few members of the touring party caught it
again in Philadelphia towards the end of the month. 'That's an incred-
ible film,' Joe told *Sounds*' Robbi Millar in January 1980, not long after
London Calling's release. 'You know, it doesn't leave you, it's like a
dream.' If the movie were the inspiration for Joe's hushed monologue
– and his pseudo-American drawl, the descending choppers, the smoke
and the slightly surreal feel add up to a pretty good case – then the
voiceover must have been added after the band's return to the UK,
during the 5–13 November 1979 mixing stage of the album. (Bill Price
is unable to confirm or deny this.) When the band performed the
song live, Joe omitted the monologue, instead usually introducing
the song by saying it was time to bring on the tanks and planes, whereupon Mick Jones would throw off a salute and count in the first verse
military style, 'Hup, two, three, four . . .'

Immediately following the spoken-word monologue on the album
version comes Joe's shout of, 'What are we going to do now?' It makes
a logical enough conclusion to his mutterings. But considered in its
own right, it could also be taken as a knowing wink at the difficulty
he had thinking up a lyric for the song: another way of saying 'For

Fuck's Sake', and so acknowledging that stage of the song's evolution. It's the kind of remark all the members of the Clash made to each other on a daily basis while rehearsing at Vanilla – the demo version of 'Up-Toon' on *The Vanilla Tapes* is preceded by Paul asking 'What we doin' now?' – so it preserves that part of the process of making the album for posterity.

It's also a catchphrase Spike Milligan used throughout his *Q* comedy series, from *Q5* to *Q9*. *Q8* was broadcast between 4 April and 9 May 1979, and Joe was a keen comedy fan. In his 1999 autobiography *The Family Album* Milligan recalled that the cast members would end any sketches that didn't have an obvious punchline or natural resolution – and as he was aspiring to free-form comedy, this was more than a few – by pacing towards the camera lens as one, chanting in unison 'What are we going to do now?' That this was the source of the phrase used by the Clash is supported by the band's typical live performance of 'Clampdown': the three frontmen would retreat to the drum riser for the introduction, pumping out the riff with their backs to the audience, and then wheel around and rush their microphones as one just in time to deliver this line. Not so much Going Over the Top as doing a Milligan.

'The Guns of Brixton'

The freewheeling Vanilla rehearsals encouraged the creative side of all four members of the Clash. One day, instead of warming up by playing a bass line of a favourite reggae tune, Paul Simonon played one of his own.

Bernie Rhodes liked the band to have clear and defined roles: the contract he signed with Riva in the autumn of 1977 made it clear that only Strummer-Jones songs were covered by the agreement, and when the writing trip to Jamaica was planned that November, nobody seriously considered taking Paul along. Paul has himself admitted that his early efforts to originate songs came to nothing. 'I just sort of wrote things and they weren't no good,' he told *Hot Press*'s John McKenna in December 1979. Like Topper, he received a co-credit for 'Guns on the Roof', written in spring 1978, but it wasn't that which spurred him on so much as the music publishing royalties Mick and

Joe started to receive for Clash songs later that year. 'Paul began writing the song "The Guns of Brixton" in 1978, before he moved into Oxford Gardens,' says Caroline Coon. 'I had suggested that instead of feeling resentful of the Clash songwriters he should perhaps write songs himself. He worked at it on visits to my place. The determination to write his first song gave Paul a deep appreciation of Joe and Mick's songwriting genius.' When he played the bass line at Vanilla, and admitted originating it, the other members of the band were admirably quick to encourage him, filling in an arrangement which was then demoed as the instrumental 'Paul's Tune'. 'The music just happened at rehearsal, the rhythm and all that stuff,' Paul told John McKenna.

The Vanilla Tapes treatment is noticeably different from the finished song, the bass line fluid rather than strident, and the whole a little more restrained and typical of contemporary reggae productions than the album version. Catchy as it is, it's questionable whether 'Paul's Tune' would have been a serious contender for inclusion on the album proper, had not Paul pulled a sheet of paper out of his pocket at Wessex and asked Joe what he thought of the words he'd written to go with it.

Paul was insistent that the Clash were as capable of – and justified in – playing the music as any black Jamaican outfit. 'People say white blokes can't do reggae, but that's a lot of shit. We [that is, Paul and Mick Jones] grew up in Brixton,' he told *Musician*'s Clint Roswell in 1981. 'All the people I knew were black. We shared the same common experience. I didn't discover reggae in a book, I grew up with it. It's part of me.'

Paul often talks of having been raised in 'the slums of Brixton'. Although this overstates the case slightly, he did spend a significant portion of his youth in south London. He was born at 1 Beulah Crescent, Thornton Heath, three miles south of Brixton. The road is not so much a crescent as a complete circle: a target on the *A-Z* page. The family didn't stay there long, though, and continued to move at frequent intervals for the next seven or eight years, leaving London altogether for much of that time to live in small towns of varying degrees of quaintness throughout southern England, including Ramsgate, Canterbury and Bury St Edmunds. But life wasn't all cockles and conkers. In 1961, when Paul was five, the Simonons spent a year in a flat at 81b Oxford Gardens, off Ladbroke Grove.

Already Notting Hill was host to significant numbers of the West Indian immigrant community that would provide so much of the area's character and identity over the next few decades. Notorious slum landlord Peter Rachman was active in the area, ruthlessly exploiting the immigrant population, and race riots had erupted for the first time in summer 1958.

It was early 1964, by which time Paul was eight years old, before the Simonons took up residence at 271 Shakespeare Road in Brixton proper. Belated though his arrival there was, Paul's description of his new home as a slum was not much of an exaggeration. At that time, Shakespeare Road was a long street of decaying terraces, running parallel to a rail line, and the basement of Number 271 was strewn with old newspapers, providing the ideal nesting material for rats. Like Notting Hill, many of the area's human residents were of West Indian origin, though others hailed from Ireland. It was here that Paul was really exposed to Jamaican culture for the first time, in and out of the homes of his neighbourhood friends, encountering different food and a different lifestyle, hearing patois talked, watching the men peacocking around in tonic suits and pork-pie hats.

He also first started going to see Saturday matinee film shows with his father at the Brixton Astoria (which would later become the Brixton Academy music venue), where the audience responded in the traditional Jamaican participatory style, best suited to films that were action rather than plot- or dialogue-driven, and loud with it. At that time, the staple fare was made up of westerns, war films and thrillers: anything with chases and fights and guns. Soon after Paul's parents split up, his mother's new boyfriend Michael Short moved in to Shakespeare Road. And soon after that Michael was awarded a year-long scholarship to study music abroad and took his new family with him. Paul spent most of 1966 in Italy, missing a year of school but getting to see one spaghetti western, Sergio Corbucci's *Django*.

When the Short-Simonons returned to the UK, they moved into a new flat just around the corner from Shakespeare Road at 54 Herne Hill, in the area also known as Herne Hill, but still close enough to Brixton to qualify. While many of the first wave West Indian immigrants had been prepared to do the dirty jobs and take the abuse, this veneer of subservience had been wearing thinner each year since the first Notting Hill race riots of the late Fifties. By the mid-Sixties, parts of Brixton were rumbling with discontent; by the end of the decade, with the Black Panthers making Black Power noises in the US, and Enoch Powell stirring up anti-immigrant feeling in the UK, that rumbling had risen in both pitch and urgency. The Short-Simonons' new home, like their old one, was just around the corner from Railton Road, a notorious trouble spot soon to become known as the Front Line (from whence Virgin Records would take the name of their mid-Seventies reggae offshoot label).

Paul began attending the local William Penn School, an over-crowded inner-city comprehensive with an ill-served student body that was 90 per cent black and a troubled reputation. Pictures of Paul taken in the mid-Sixties show a somewhat fey-looking, pale-skinned pretty-boy. He hadn't lived a pampered life, but in his new environment he might as well have been a boy named Sue. The quality of his official education was poor, but he proved quick on the uptake when it came to survival. He had little choice about learning to fight, but was also savvy enough to befriend the toughest kids in school. His social life became gang life. Intent on proving himself and fitting in, he was regularly involved in petty mischief, playing truant, vandalism, football violence and shoplifting. He became a skinhead.

For as long as Paul had lived in the area, he'd been hearing Jamaican music booming out from blues parties in neighbours' houses, from ska to rock-steady and then early reggae. He didn't own a record player so didn't buy records, but even without his financial support, the skinhead market in Britain was large enough to push favourite moonstompers high into the singles charts. Catchy instrumentals based on or named after action and war movies and spaghetti westerns were as popular in the UK as they were in Jamaica: in 1967 the Skatellites reached Number 36 in the UK charts with 'Guns of Navarone', and in 1969 madcap reggae producer Lee 'Scratch' Perry's Upsetters took 'Return of Django' to Number 5.

Paul and his friends hung around outside Desmond's Hip City record store on Brixton Road, and attended the Saturday morning dances at the Streatham Locarno in their Doc Marten boots, Ben Sherman shirts and red braces. In an account he gave to *Another Magazine* in 2005 Paul described a rowdy scene: dressing flash, dancing to Lee Perry, fighting on the dancefloor. Skinheads did not constitute reggae's sole market, but they were its core, as was acknowledged in 1970 by the London-based Symarip's 'Skinhead Moonstomp'. It was Lee Perry's response to spaghetti westerns – incorporating certain musical elements associated with the genre – rather than Paul's own fleeting, first-hand Italian experience of *Django* that can take the credit for kick-starting his enthusiasm for spaghetti western soundtrack material.

By the end of 1970, when he was coming up to 15, Paul was so out of control that his mother sent him to live with his father Antony. It brought to an end his time in Brixton, but only took him as far as Notting Hill. Here, he attended an equally problematic comprehensive school. For the next year or so, Antony kept Paul on a short leash in and around the tiny flat they shared at 27 Faraday Road, but over time, he was able to meet old friends and make new ones, many of them from the local West Indian community. He spoke patois without thinking about it. His hooligan behaviour diminished as his interest in girls increased, and he also rekindled his interest in art. Antony moved to 61 Western Avenue in East Acton in 1973, and Paul was still living there when he began to attend art school in west London. After joining the Clash Paul spent 1976 to 1979 moving between Camden Town, Notting Hill and Chelsea. By the spring of 1979 he was in his new home, 42b Oxford Gardens, on the very same street he had lived on when his family first tried life in Notting Hill 18 years earlier.

Although he was now a property owner, at the time his purchase hardly represented a significant move up the socio-economic ladder. Oxford Gardens is a tree-lined street of grand Victorian town houses, and the last couple of decades have seen it gentrified and renovated to something like its original glory, but in 1961 it was run-down and had been sub-divided into small, overcrowded flats catering for a transient population. In 1979 it hadn't improved much. On the north side of the road, between Ladbroke Grove and St Lawrence Terrace, 42b was a basement flat of a modest 590 square feet, the original layout consisting of a lounge and a compact bedroom either side of an internal bathroom, with a tiny kitchenette at the back looking out onto a small yard. As is the case with all mid-terrace dwellings, light could only enter from the front and back, and as the flat was small and not only subterranean but at the foot of a five-storey cliff of a building, had security bars over the windows, and rooms linked by a long, narrow corridor running front to back, it felt like a dingy and claustrophobic tunnel.

On the positive side, Paul got it very cheap and all he needed was a bed, a table, a couple of chairs and some shelves and it was furnished. His art school painting of a car dump went up on one wall, and over the next few months, he began to accumulate the rest of the décor, including shooting gallery targets and replica guns. He and Topper Headon had always played around with air pistols and air rifles at Rehearsals Rehearsals. On 30 March 1978 they'd been arrested for shooting pigeons on the roof, leading to a night in the cells and, subsequently, 'Guns on the Roof'. They also liked to pore over gun and ammunition catalogues, which Derek Boshier picked up on when he used cuttings from one such catalogue to illustrate that song in the *Clash 2nd Songbook*. Paul was also responsible for devising the gun and target illustration for the label of the '(White Man) In Hammersmith Palais' single, released in June 1978 to tie in with the Out on Parole UK tour that followed their court appearance. In 1978 he told *Negative Reaction* fanzine, 'I'd like to act in films like Clint Eastwood,' and his fantasies were clearly still very much movie-led. Within a year of moving into Number 42b, to his soundtrack album of Jamaican gunslinger movie *The Harder They Come*, he would add a copy of the novel and a videocassette of the film itself.

The title Paul gave his new song is a nod to the Skatellites' 'Guns of Navarone', though its style came from somewhere further along on reggae's evolutionary chain. 'When people hear what I man do, them hear a different beat, a slower beat, a waxy beat, like you stepping in glue,' Lee 'Scratch' Perry told *Black Music's* Chris May in autumn 1977, around the same time he was in London producing the Clash's 'Complete Control'. 'Them hear a different bass, a rebel bass, coming at you like sticking a gun.' Paul could have almost had this very quote in mind when honing the bass line for 'The Guns of Brixton', but it was his fondness for *The Harder They Come* that got him started on the lyric. 'That was the initial inspiration,' he told the *Melody Maker* in 1988. Which should hardly come as a surprise: both the film's title and main character Ivan are namechecked in Paul's song – the latter inviting a rhyme of considerable chutzpah, "survivan" – and both protagonists face a climactic confrontation with the law. The true-life gangster the film character was based upon and named after (Ray Gange-style confusion between fiction and reality is a very real possibility here) died on 9 September 1948 from injuries sustained in a gun battle with police in Lime Cay, Jamaica. In the film, Ivan's rebel stance is hardened by watching a spaghetti western: *Django* (1966), the very movie Paul had seen in Italy the year of its release.

Bringing all this home, and making a credible connection between the life of Ivan and the life of a white former art student member of a rock'n'roll band didn't give Paul too much pause for thought. It was, he claimed, a time of heavy manners in areas of inner-city London with a significant black population, something that affected all residents of those areas. The antiquated Sus Law allowed the police to stop and search anyone they considered to be a 'suspected person', which usually translated as either 'not white' or 'not rich or wise enough to live somewhere else'. The crepuscular ambience of Paul's new flat did little to set his mind at ease, and nor did the replica guns and targets on the walls. 'I was kind of scared the police would come bursting in through the front door,' he told *Melody Maker* in 1988. Talking to Adam Sweeting of *Uncut* in 2004, Paul allowed that it was 'possibly a paranoid situation. I was living in a basement flat at the time and, I dunno, lack of sunlight can sort of turn your mind a bit.'

The lyric's jumps in tense are disorienting. The 'you' in the first three verses could be addressed to a third party in the song; it could be self-addressed, an internal monologue; or it could be addressed to the listener. Together, these parties make up the 'us' on the receiving end of the pressure in the chorus. Meanwhile, the 'you' in the chorus is the same as the faceless 'they' in the final verse: namely, the police, the Man, the people applying the pressure. Somehow, from both a dramatic and psychologically manipulative perspective, this works: it's not immediately obvious where the threat is coming from, or how real it is, which establishes and feeds the sense of paranoia.

Given that Paul first visualised the showdown happening at the front door of Number 42b Oxford Gardens, it's not immediately obvious why the song isn't 'The Guns of Notting Hill' rather than 'The Guns of Brixton'. Even if Herne Hill is counted, Paul had only lived in the latter area for five or six years in total, while by 1979 he had chalked up eight years in and around Notting Hill. His late teenage and adult life was not only spent in the west London area, it was – thanks to Clash mythology – strongly associated with it: the Westway had been celebrated in 'London's Burning', and the Notting Hill Riot of 1976 in 'White Riot'. Part of the answer is that, although Notting Hill might have been where Paul had become a punk, Brixton was where he felt he was 'from'. It was close to where he was born, and was where he had reached teenage, discovered street life and Jamaican music. It was where he had become a skinhead, or – if you like – a rude boy, and sub-cults are nothing if not tribal and territorial. It was where he had first learned to handle himself, and started to get an idea of himself. It was also where he'd first seen the sort of movies that helped inspire the song. It is 'The Guns of Brixton' partly in honour of home, and partly as tribute to his friends from the area and their shared past.

There are three other points to consider, though . . .

Firstly, as already established, *Rude Boy* was greatly inspired by *The Harder They Come*. Joe's song 'No Reason', exclusive to *Rude Boy*, mentions Brixton, home base for the song's subject, Ray Gange. Joe's 'Rudie Can't Fail' is closely tied to 'No Reason' via a shared – albeit, in the former case, disputed – association with the Gange character, and by the inclusion of both songs on the film's soundtrack. '"The Guns Of Brixton" isn't about me, either,' is Ray Gange's unsolicited comment. Absolutely not, Ray. But 'The Guns of Brixton' *is* linked to 'Rudie Can't Fail' by their common use of pressure imagery, and both convey the sense of victimisation, shame, anger, restriction and limitation faced by young men from inner-city, immigrant communities. The crushing and bruising – the heavy manners, the pressure drop – was also something the Clash could relate to as a band. It expresses the sense of creative suffocation they were trying to throw off with *London Calling*, drawing upon reggae and other roots musics in their bid for universal freedom of expression. In this reading, the oppressors can be seen as CBS, the punk purist element of the band's audience, and certain sections of the formerly – but no longer – universally pro-Clash UK music press.

Secondly, after cutting his teeth as a filmmaker with *Punk Rock Movie*, a mix of performance and offstage antics shot in 1977 on Super 8 at the Roxy and elsewhere, Don Letts had applied the same guerrilla-documentary approach to reggae artists for *Rankin' Movie*, which was released in London in August 1979. At this time Chris Salewicz interviewed him for the *NME*, and Don spoke about a new film script he had written called *Dread at the Controls*. Its title came from a Jamaican radio show hosted by Mikey Dread – who would shortly be touring and recording with the Clash – but the script was inspired by Brixton poet Linton Kwesi Johnson's 'Five Nights of Bleeding'. First published in 1975, it was recorded by LKJ with production and dub backing by Matumbi's Dennis Bovell for the 1978 Poet and the Roots album *Dread Beat An' Blood*. The patois poem details five nights of violence at sound systems, in blues dances and pubs, and outside concert halls, four of these confrontations taking place in the Brixton area (including Railton Road), and one of them involving police-on-black violence leading to retaliation by ratchet.

As Don elaborated in his 2007 memoir *Culture Clash: Dread Meets Punk Rockers*, his planned film was to be a modern-day 'reggae Western' set in the office of a Brixton taxi company, with taxis as horses, Rasta drivers as cowboys, and the action leading up to a full-scale Brixton race riot. On the back of the positive press for *Rankin' Movie*, Don took his script to Michael White, who had helped finance *Rude Boy*. White took an option on the project, and it got as far as casting before it got stuck in development hell and was abandoned. Don Letts has never made anything of the crossover between LKJ's poem, his own script and Paul's lyric, but given that he was a longtime Clash associate, the soon-to-be director of the 'London Calling' video, and was first interviewed about his *Dread at the Controls* project by another Friend Of The Clash, Chris Salewicz, for a feature run on the same page as Roy Carr's interview with Guy Stevens about the first three days of recording for *London Calling* . . . well, it's quite some coincidence.

Thirdly, Graham Greene's *Brighton Rock* (1938) – named after the seaside town's traditional and ubiquitous souvenir – had been one of the texts on Paul's O level English syllabus. The central character is a 17-year-old Catholic gangster and killer named Pinkie Brown, whose apparent fearlessness and icy stare allow him control over much older villains. At the end of the book, he makes a desperate last stand against the police. The attraction to a 15-year-old lapsed Catholic former skinhead is self-evident.

When the Clash started working with the Buzzy team of David

Mingay and Jack Hazan in spring 1978 Paul discovered they had access to old black-and-white British films, and took advantage of their eagerness to please in order to make requests for loans. In addition to the war films from the Imperial War Museum that he showed on the studio wall during breaks in recording *Give 'Em Enough Rope*, he got hold of a print of the Boulting Brothers' 1947 film of *Brighton Rock*. In no hurry to return it, he started taking it home for private showings. Shot in an almost American noir style, it's still a very English movie, with a cast of character actors led by Richard Attenborough as Pinkie. Pinkie's gang live in a damp and peeling Victorian slum building, but, like mods and rude boys and skins in their respective times and places, dress meticulously in the spiv fashions of the day: brilliantined hair, trilby hats and sharp suits in thick chalk stripe or loud check. Also like rude boys, they carry folding cut-throat razors, and – in the final scene where the police come for him, ultimately leading to his death – Pinkie carries a gun.

Pinkie could never have been mistaken for a Robin Hood – as portrayed by Attenborough, he's a creepy psychopath – but the pre-echo of the denouement of *The Harder They Come*, and therefore of 'The Guns of Brixton', is clear. Although not part of London, Brighton is so close to the capital in distance and mood that it is known as London-on-Sea, and the Cockney accents of Pinkie's gang and most of the other characters in the film betray them as transplanted Londoners. Brighton and Brixton: they even sound similar. Paul became increasingly fascinated by the look of the film, and after the first flurry of interest in Fifties American rocker styles that dominated the autumn 1979 Take the 5th tour, started incorporating elements of *Brighton Rock*'s spiv look into his personal style upon his return to the UK. The rest of the band quickly followed suit. And hat. As is evidenced by the 'London Calling' video (see Part 5).

★

Part of the reason the bass line on the Wessex version of 'The Guns of Brixton' sounds different to the Vanilla demo version is the amount of work Paul devoted to it in between. 'He wore his bass everywhere in the studio, all day for nearly a week, constantly practising it,' says Bill Price.

Paul wanted Joe to sing the song, but Joe and the others insisted Paul do it himself. An encouraging gesture though it was, it made for an uncomfortable hour or so in the studio and, for some, makes for an uncomfortable few minutes listening to the end result. In the *Clash On Broadway* booklet, Paul noted that he didn't consider himself a singer, and the experience was made even harder for him by having an 'American CBS bloke' sitting just two feet away from him on the other side of the control-room glass while he was in the vocal booth. Nerves and irritation might have contributed to the iffy pitching and awkward phrasing, but even at the best of times, Paul's singing voice was hardly mellifluous. Reggae is all about groove, and the best singers float over it. There's no flow to Paul's delivery: for the most part he sticks doggedly to the beat, and when he dares to leave it for a couple of notes, it sounds like he's made a mistake rather than taken flight. Mick would later describe this peculiarly stilted effect as 'Jamaican Marlene Dietrich'.

In a strange way, though, the limitations of the lead vocal are the making of the song. Firstly, the tense delivery lends the lyric a not inappropriate pugnacious edge. Secondly, the band and Bill Price resort to various tricks to divert attention from the voice, thus creating a highly individual sound. The bass line – one of the most distinctive and memorable ever recorded – is mixed right up front. Not far behind are the drums, with Topper's playing as full of flair as ever. He contributes to the mood of sweaty exotica with overdubbed clattering tom-toms. At around 1.30 he introduces a similarly elongated snare motif, which he then revisits with increasing frequency until it all but elbows everything else out of the way. Giving the mix even more of an inverted feeling, the backing vocal 'aahs' are allowed to overwhelm Paul's lead, and the rhythm guitar skanks in the left channel are also distractingly loud.

The 'last stand' lyric inspires Mick to add a bunch of sound effects which would have been at home in one of Lee Perry's spaghetti western instrumental dubs. In the intro, Mick sets the scene by scraping his plectrum along a string a couple of times to get a lovely descending scrunch: instant dynamic tension. At the end of the chorus, he does some string bending: not just single notes, but entire chords, to give a tremulous, vaguely south-of-the-border feel. Composer Ennio Morricone helped Sergio Leone establish movie characters with individually themed signature flourishes, which Mick acknowledges by playing a Jew's harp in the instrumental break. But even that's not the strangest overdub on this Cinemascope epic. While listening to the playback in the control room, the Clash sat fiddling with the Velcro fasteners on Bill Price's control-room chair cushions. 'People were always doing that to my chair,' says Bill. Deciding they liked the noise this made, the Clash pulled the chair into the studio, and recorded it. That sound under the opening bars, like the surface noise on a bad Jamaican pressing of a dub plate: all cheap shellac full of airholes and grit? That's the Velcro. Collectively, all these tricks and effects don't quite succeed in masking Paul's shortcomings as a singer but – despite their novelty value – they do work with it to create a deadly serious Lee Van Cleef, snake-eyed mood. Bits might be ugly, bits might even be bad, but the overall impression is . . . pretty good.

Not everyone agreed. 'The Guns of Brixton' proved to be one of the more instantly contentious songs on the album. In his *Sounds* review of *London Calling* Garry Bushell found it 'truly embarrassing . . . Simonon's limp vocals gracing a feeble reggae setting for more of the Clash's degenerating "guns and gangs" outlaw vision – lumpen lyrical fantasy world populated by druggies, crooks, gambling dens, dingy basements and gun-toting niggers.'

In two songs' time, when Joe Strummer seems to be offering 'Death or Glory', what he'll really be offering is neither. His lyric for that song addresses the grey area in between that most folk end up falling into instead: a fairly long, disappointingly inglorious life. In 'The Guns of Brixton' Paul's contrasting couplets in the first two verses set up the quiz as though he, too, is offering a choice between death or glory. But in the way he phrases it – you gonna do this (like a wimp); or you gonna do that (like a man)? – what he's really promoting is a combination of both: a supposedly glorious death. What Americans now term 'suicide by cop': that is, going out in a hail of bullets.

So maybe Garry Bushell had a point, if not a winning way of making it. Paul's teenage life had been tougher than those of the other members of the Clash: he grew up on rough streets in edgy areas and went to genuinely poor schools. In truth, though, Paul still had a few more things going for him than desperados like Ivan, or even most of his contemporaries in Brixton and Notting Hill. Excuse the social worker report, but: his parents and their subsequent partners

were engaged, creative, pro-arts and pro-education. His family background was questioning bohemian rather than uncaring underclass.
When Paul's skinhead activities and truancy peaked at the end of
the Sixties, strenuous efforts were made to help him turn his life
around. He was ultimately encouraged to follow his interests and
talents and attend art school. In short, there was a safety net there
for him that made it unlikely that the scenario depicted in 'The Guns
of Brixton' could ever have happened to him . . . unless he had been
absolutely determined to make it happen. Of course, it's a fantasy,
but its autobiographical touches blur the dividing lines. It would be
easy for someone a little closer to the edge to mistake it for an
Outlaw Code to be followed to the letter.

At the end of 1979 Hot Press's John McKenna denounced the song
as irresponsible in the wake of the Brenda Spencer incident. On 29
January 1979, 16-year-old schoolgirl Spencer had barricaded herself in
her house opposite the Cleveland Elementary School in San Diego,
California, and used a rifle she'd been given for Christmas by her father
to take potshots at figures on the playground, hitting eight children
and three adults, two of them – the headmaster and janitor – fatally.
It would have been impossible for Paul and the rest of the Clash not
to be aware of this incident when recording 'The Guns of Brixton'.
When asked to explain her actions during telephone negotiations with
the police, Spencer had replied, 'I don't like Mondays.' Recognising an
unforgettable phrase when he heard one, Bob Geldof of the Boomtown
Rats wrote a song inspired by the incident. In July 1979 it topped the
UK singles charts.

Nine years after London Calling's release, Joe claimed that, by
persuading Paul to sing his own song, he had deliberately distanced
himself from what he knew would be a problematic issue. Apparently,
he hadn't really approved of the sentiments of the song either, but
had not felt it was his place to censor other band members' lyrics:
'"The Guns of Brixton" was Paul's song. I had a go at him about that,'
he told the NME's Sean O'Hagan in 1988. 'I said, "Here, how would
you like to get shot, eh?" And he said, "I don' care." So I said, "Fair
enough." Can't argue with that, really.' This not only smacks of a
position assumed with the benefit of hindsight, it's also a bit sly. There
are more than a few casually brandished weapons in the Strummer
lyrical oeuvre. London Calling alone has Jimmy Dread threatened with

a beheading in 'Jimmy Jazz'; Staggerlee threatened with a knife in the back, to which he responds by shooting Billy dead, in 'Wrong 'Em Boyo'; the gambler forced to his knees and shot dead in 'The Card Cheat'; and the cheerful protagonist of 'Revolution Rock' boasting about having the biggest knife and knowing how to use it. Joe himself was sometimes blinded to the reality of violence by movie and song mythology.

Some might find it strange – or even suspicious – that Paul's first recorded 'solo' Clash composition proved to be so musically arresting and lyrically coherent, bearing in mind he never again wrote anything else remotely as strong musically, and immediately gave up on writing lyrics altogether. Perhaps, though, it's not quite so odd, after all: 'The Guns of Brixton' is such a thorough exploration of the mythopoetics of Paul Simonon that, by the time he had completed it, he had not only written a song about his fantasy life, but also the song of a lifetime. Shortly after its release, he proved how much it meant to him by having a pistol tattooed close to his Brixton heart; or, at least, a couple of inches above his left nipple.

Whatever the moral issues the song raises, Mick ensured it was sequenced perfectly on the album. After getting in touch with their inner child on 'Lost in the Supermarket', the Clash have fully reasserted their machismo with first the hard-rock rampage of 'Clampdown', and now the heavy reggae menace of 'The Guns of Brixton'. Plus, the end of the five-track side two balances the end of the five-track side one: echoes of the upbeat 'Rudie Can't Fail' are to be found in the contrastingly brooding, but thematically linked, second original Clash reggae composition on the album.

'Wrong 'Em Boyo'

For years, the character of Staggerlee – or, as he is variously known, Stagger Lee, Stagolee, Stag O'Lee, Stackerlee or Stack-a-Lee – seemed to have emerged fully formed from the folk consciousness like, inevitably, a latter-day Robin Hood. In the Thirties, American folk music archivists John and Alan Lomax collected two very different variants of the song which bears his name (or names) for their *American*

Ballads and Folk Songs, both of them dating back to the last years of the nineteenth century. Of their A version and B version, the latter would prevail, being the variant from which countless blues, jazz and R&B piano versions – the last of these something of a New Orleans speciality – were derived. One such piano version was recorded in 1950 by Archibald Cox. Eight years later, Lloyd Price reworked it for the rock'n'roll audience as 'Stagger Lee', reaching Number 1 in the US mainstream charts and selling over a million copies, and even making Number 7 in the UK.

Different genres and different times have different requirements. Folk ballads, field hollers and barrelhouse numbers helped dreary hours fly by in the days before TV and even radio, so tended to be lengthy, taking their own sweet time to set the scene, develop the story, bring in the bit-part players, explore a few subplots, and eventually, all things being equal, put the shaggy dog to bed. The Lomaxes' A version – only partially recollected by the contributor – runs to 10 verses; the B version runs to 40 couplets. The pithier forms required by the early recording age, where a song had to be between two and four minutes long to fit on the disc, tended to shed the scene-setting, subplots and asides and cut right to the heart of the matter: crime and retribution. In the countless versions of the Staggerlee saga recorded since, most of these core details remain much the same: Stag and Billy have an argument in a bar, usually over a gambling matter, often around Christmas time. Billy further provokes Stag by taking liberties with his hat. In some cases, he also pulls a knife. Stag responds by drawing a gun and killing Billy. The law comes after Stag. He doesn't go quietly, but is eventually caught. In the Lomaxes' A version, Stag's woman gets him out on bail. In other versions, he is either shot while resisting, or jailed and then executed. The Lomaxes' original B version even follows him down to hell to watch him giving the Devil a hard time.

Why, when there were so many badman ballads to choose from, should Staggerlee's story have hit such a resounding chord? The fact that Stag recurs and features so prominently in so many black musical forms testifies to the fact that the black population claimed him as their own. Unlike Robin Hood, he didn't give to the poor. He quite clearly didn't give a good goddamn. But he did unintentionally give something else of value to a black community in a racist society where every day brought a hundred and one humiliations from the mouths and at the hands of the ruling white classes: pride.

This might be hard for some to understand. In almost every variant of the song, Stag is depicted as an evil son of a bitch, who, for the most trivial of reasons, shoots (and sometimes keeps on shooting) Billy, a man with a wife and children, who pleads for his life, *on Christmas Day*, of all the days for clemency and forgiveness . . . But those were tough times with a tough code. Whether he has cheated in a gambling game, accused Stag of cheating, or even if he has just touched Stag's hat, Billy has clearly dissed Stag in the most public of public places, a bar, and he has to pay, and be seen to pay, in order for Stag to retain his reputation and public status. Even more importantly, in the song, Stag is not only unafraid of Billy, he is also unafraid of the police: he doesn't run and he doesn't hide. If anything, the police are usually depicted as being more than a little scared of Stag. The details – the bar, the gambling, the Stetson, the weapons – make this as close as black America was going to get at the time to their own western outlaw legend. Fast forward to the early Seventies, and the same principle underwrites the appeal of the Superfly characters in Blaxploitation movies – and *The Harder They Come*, a film made in another former slave colony – fast forward again to the end of the twentieth century, and it's there again in the psychotic world of gangsta rap. Stag was arguably the first black anti-hero, which meant a lot to a section of the population long denied access to conventional heroes.

Details about Staggerlee's antecedents remained vague until comparatively recently, when authors Greil Marcus and Cecil Brown started digging around in the historical records. They discovered that, although very different in their focus, both the Lomax versions turned out to be surprisingly accurate, and vestiges of the true story are retained in almost all the B-version derivatives. The action did take place late on Christmas Day in 1895 in St Louis, Missouri, not far from the River Mississippi docks. The Bill Curtis Saloon was situated in the black part of town at 1101 Morgan Street, on the corner with 11th Street. (Now long gone, the site is at the corner of Convention Plaza and 11th.) It was a joint with a fearsome reputation for bloodshed, where even the police were reluctant to go. Twenty-five-year-old levee hand Billy Lyons lived a few blocks down Morgan at Number 1410. When he arrived that night, he asked his friend Henry Crump to lend him a knife for protection. Shortly afterwards, Lee Shelton turned up in his outrageous multicoloured finery, set off with a gold-topped cane and milk-white Stetson. Also local, living at 911 North 12th Street (the house is still there, but the street is now known as North Tucker Boulevard) he was supposedly a 'carriage driver', but as his style might indicate he was really a pimp, one of a group known locally as the Macks.

Witnesses later reported that Lyons bought Shelton a drink, and they talked and laughed awhile, until they got drunk enough to start discussing local politics: not wise, as they were affiliated to different parties. At this juncture, Shelton grabbed and crushed Lyons's ordinary brown derby hat, quite possibly in an ill-judged jest. Lyons responded by grabbing Shelton's Stetson, whereupon Shelton suddenly lost his sense of humour. He pulled his gun, a Smith & Wesson .44 (sometimes described in song as a .41, but only to serve a rhyme) and pistol-whipped Lyons with it, demanding he return the hat on pain of death. Lyons refused to give it up, pulled his knife, and challenged Shelton to do his worst. In true Wild West style, most of the bar's 25 or so customers promptly made for the exits. Shelton shot Lyons in the abdomen. Then he calmly picked up his hat, walked home, gave his landlady his gun for safe-keeping, and went to bed. Lyons was taken to the hospital, where he died at 4 a.m. on Boxing Day.

Shelton was still in bed at 911 North 12th Street when the police came for him, and when they knocked at his front door, he put up no resistance at all. Probably because he was wealthy and well-connected enough to afford a good lawyer and two separate bail bonds; the first, in January 1896 for $4,000 (about $100,000 in 2007), the second that June for $3,000. This was around the time the Lomaxes' A version of his story was composed. The trial began on 15 July 1896. The St Louis Globe-Democrat preceded it with a sloppy and erroneous report that Shelton and Lyons had been playing the dice game craps immediately prior to the incident. The jury could not decide whether it was murder in the first degree, in the second degree, or – as Shelton's lawyer argued – self-defence. A retrial was ordered. No record of this survives, but Shelton must have been found guilty, and of murder in the second rather than first, because instead of being set free or sentenced to death, he was sent to the Missouri State Penitentiary on

7 October 1896 to begin a 25-year sentence. His connections ensured he was paroled in 1909, a relatively lenient (both for the times and for his colour) 13 years later. Just two years after that, though, he was back in prison following another pistol-whipping incident. He died there of TB on 11 March 1911. The Lomaxes' B version could have originated at any time after publication of the *St Louis Globe-Democrat* article, because – although it throws in the apocryphal gambling detail – it chooses to rewrite the arrest and punishment part of the story in typical outlaw ballad fashion, with execution and damnation as the punchline. Well before his death, then, Staggerlee was not so much a man as an archetype.

The original Jamaican blues dances, the forerunners of the sound systems, relied upon R&B discs imported from the USA, mostly from New Orleans, until local musicians started cutting their own records and customising the style into what became ska. The precedent was set for cover versions or adaptations of American material. Bob Marley's 'One Love', first recorded by the Wailers in 1965, interpolates Curtis Mayfield's 'People Get Ready' from that same year. The Rulers did much the same with Lloyd Price's 'Stagger Lee' for their 1967 single 'Wrong Emboyo' (*sic*). In the first issue of *The Armagideon Times*, Joe Strummer describes it as 'a genuine example of three-dimensional Jamaican feeling and thinking . . . Dig the imported blues from Florida! Music buffs!'

The Rulers' backing band start attempting to play Price's 'Stagger Lee' as a sparse barrelhouse New Orleans R&B piano number with trebly guitar skanks grafted on. The vocal also starts off faithful to the original lyric, including the line about Staggerlee throwing seven and Billy claiming eight, the gambling detail that dates all the way back to the original Lomax B Version. Then, 45 seconds in, there's a shout of 'Breaks! Wrong emboyo! Start all over again, huh?' and the Rulers and musicians obey, commencing their own substantial reworking of the song. So what *was* wrong? The metre of the original is 12/8 – more swing feel – which means it has three sub-divisions, not two. Ska puts the chord on the second half of every beat. It doesn't fit.

The rolling piano makes way for a slower, rock-steady rhythm and the backing band stretch out the form to suit. When consulted, music theorist Patrick Clark says the Rulers' song is still a blues, but with a form so loose and meandering it qualifies as neither a 12-bar nor a 16, but instead something 'a little strange'. Heavier bass and fatter-sounding guitar skanks now underpin the doleful vocals. What Joe described as the 'three-dimensional feeling and thinking' is a conceptual joke: the musical mistake and need to start afresh become both the lyrical theme and the chorus of the new song. There are no details about Stetsons or violence by gun or knife in the Rulers' version; after the intro, theirs is purely and simply a song about how wrong it is to cheat or bully a 'trying man'. In short, whenever you do something wrong or bad; stop: start again; and this time Do the Right Thing. Don't be a rude boy, be a good boy.

The Clash didn't – as has been claimed on more than one occasion – originate the song's false start, then, but they did make other significant changes. Tightening and simplifying the structure, they follow their 16-bar intro with a bona fide 12-bar reading of the song proper; halving the repeats of 'Don't you know it is wrong' from four to two; and dropping the Rulers' chorus of 'Why do you lie, steal, cheat and deceit', instead incorporating that line of the lyric into their repeating verse structure. Joe's rewrite also drops the sanctimonious line 'Someday you're gonna fail', and elsewhere adds two couplets of his own, both of them highly significant in that they restore to the narrative the violence excised by the Rulers. In the intro, before the break, Joe has Billy threatening to use his knife; and at the start of the third verse, he announces that Billy has been shot and that 'Stagger Lee's come out on top'. Overall, though, the message is still the opposite of 'The Guns of Brixton': another point underlined by Mick's clever sequencing.

This is a piano song, which explains why it wasn't demoed at Vanilla. The Clash worked it up in Wessex. Bill Price is hazy about details, but thinks the initial live take might have been 'possibly with not the whole band', and describes it as 'one of the more experimental tracks'. The intro has Strummer-style staccato piano, but it doesn't get to dominate, having to fight for space with Mickey Gallagher's organ wash, the rasping Irish Horns and what Bill terms Mick's 'tremulando guitars', all of which combine to build a wall of sound almost as large of the Wall of Sound in 'The Card Cheat'.

When the Clash start all over again for the song proper, they do so at a jaunty ska pace, which serves to change the mood: rather than

shaking their heads in sorrow at man's shortcomings, they're celebrating his ability to reform his character. It's as though the band
really believe the Staggerlee tale is going to have a happy ending this
time around, despite all the evidence to the contrary. The mix is
dynamic. The R&B piano continues throughout, placed centrally, while
Paul reinforces the R&B/ska crossover feel by playing a reggaefied
version of a boogie-woogie bass line, arc-shaped, going up and down
every two bars. Very much out of keeping with the Rulers' original –
and, for that matter, any other song previously recorded by the Clash
– Mick's guitar is barely to be heard after the time change. It's there,
playing the skank, but is mixed down low to blend in with the piano
and brass.

Even more unusually for a Sixties reggae cover, Topper's drums
also drop out for the entire duration of the second and last verses,
leaving his overdubbed tom-toms to carry the momentum until he
rejoins on his main kit. 'Break it down, man, so you can bring it right
up,' says Bill. 'Topper must have played throughout, or it would
have fallen apart. I can't remember if he played full kit, or just kept
time on the hat. Either way, he's been taken out.' Topper also uses
the vibraslap for occasional releases of tension. Making the most of
all this extra space, Mickey Gallagher (mixed to the left) gets to really
show off on the Hammond for the first time on the album. The Irish
Horns (mixed to the right) balance him perfectly. They are in Stax
mode once more, their countermelodies, also arc-shaped, rising up to
the seventh – the blue note – then descending again, while the baritone sax brings some of the ska by slipping in a cheeky *ba-doom* on
the upbeat of nearly every bar.

'I remember doing that one,' says trumpet player Dick Hanson. 'I
think it was the first one we did. We said, "Tell you what, let's just
try it. Just play the track and we'll come up in the control room and
play along and see if you like it." We'd played together for so long
that we slipped straight into a three-part harmony, just picked up a
riff and played along. They said, "That's it!" Then we went down into
the studio and did it in one take. It was all over within half an hour.'
In his December 1979 *Sounds* review of *London Calling*, Garry Bushell
was the first but not the last to observe that their horn part sounds
almost exactly like that on Frankie Ford's 1959 New Orleans R&B hit
'Sea Cruise'.

'Sea Cruise' was written by Huey 'Piano' Smith, and recorded with his backing band the Clowns, and his regular vocalist, the black female impersonator Bobby Marchan. The record company wiped Marchan's vocal and replaced it with Frankie Ford's because he was considered a 'more commercial' prospect, being youthful, white, and not a female impersonator. But the horn part remains how Smith wrote it and the Clowns played it. A genuinely surprised Dick Hanson denies the brass on 'Wrong 'Em Boyo' was a conscious lift, and as Bill Price points out, 'It's a pretty classic horn riff for that type of song.'

So, to recap: this is the Clash's unconventional R&B-ska hybrid tightening up of a rock-steady loosening up of a rock'n'roll reworking of a barrelhouse reworking of a folk blues song . . . with a fairly standard R&B horn part grafted on from elsewhere. Both the stylistic crossover and the subject matter tie in with 'Jimmy Jazz' and 'Rudie Can't Fail', and as the Rulers' original was a song addressing the role of the Staggerlee archetype in creating the musical legend of the rude boy, it's tempting to identify it as one of the starting points for the Clash's extensive exploration of this theme on *London Calling*. Even though they hadn't demoed the song at Vanilla, the entire band had been familiar with the Rulers' 'Wrong Emboyo' for at least three years before recording it.

*

The Rulers recorded a handful of songs for a Kingston jukebox distributor turned record salesman turned record producer named Carl Johnson, who styled himself Sir JJ, and initially released his material on the JJ label in Jamaica. London-based label Rio made a deal for the UK rights, and released the singles until late in 1967. After 'Don't Be a Rude Boy' and 'Copasetic', both released in 1966, 'Wrong Emboyo' was their third Rio single, released in early 1967. The exclusivity of such licensing agreements was questionable – or at least, questioned – and 'Copasetic' is also included on a compilation album called *Club Ska '67*, released that year on Island, with sleeve notes by Guy Stevens.

When the Clash were interviewed in September 1976 for the fourth edition of *Sniffin' Glue*, Paul Simonon claimed the Rulers and the Ethiopians as his influences. 'I've never heard of 'em!' admitted Joe

Strummer. In his 2006 liner notes to *Revolution Rock: A Clash Jukebox*, Paul said he knew 'Wrong Emboyo' from the late Sixties, but credits Bernie Rhodes for being the one who put it on the Rehearsals Rehearsals jukebox when the Clash first started rehearsing there in summer 1976. According to Paul, Bernie had 'a whole stack' of this particular Rio single, which he used to sell from the reggae stall he ran at Antiquarius in the Kings Road. Even 30 years later, Paul had to admit that he still didn't know who the Rulers were. This is no reflection on him: no one else does, either. What is known is that the Rulers were a vocal group, probably – but not necessarily – a trio in the style of the Wailers. They apparently recorded on and off for little over a year, from mid-1966, and exclusively for the self-styled Sir JJ.

Carl Johnson's aristocratic pretensions were relatively modest for the day, when it was common for sound-system owners and label bosses to style themselves Dukes and Princes and Lords. The Rulers might have been following this convention when they – or Sir JJ – chose their name. Alternatively, they could have been referencing the revolutionary sentiments of the Wailers' 'Jailhouse' – 'we're gonna rule this land' – and aligning themselves with disaffected youth even as they advised rude boys to take it easy. The third possibility is that their name was intended as a tribute to Emperor Haile Selassie, 'King of Kings, Elect of God, and Conquering Lion of the Tribe of Judea', who visited Jamaica on 21 April 1966, an event which helped legitimise the Rastafarian faith and spread it more widely. Although the first few Rulers A-sides are aimed at rude boys, they evidence a proto-Rasta moral code which is even more to the fore in the group's even less widely known but more overtly spiritual songs 'Exodus 9' (aka 'Let My People Go') and 'Got to Be Free'.

No photograph of the Rulers seems to have been taken for promotional purposes, and – worse – no one still living appears to remember their names. Carl Dawkins, who recorded for Sir JJ at the same time, and who appeared on the B-side of a couple of the Rulers' Rio singles, remembers them only as teenagers up from the country. Unlike the rude boys they sang about, they did make it in the big city without recourse to bad behaviour. Or, at least, they got to make records there, most of them intriguing, but some distinctly amateurish, preserving fluffed vocal cues. That they didn't like much of what they saw is partly evidenced by their songs' sorrowful sermonising about the Hell's Kitchen of mid-Sixties Kingston, but they made their point even more strongly by heading back off to the country between sessions, and ultimately – evidently – staying there for good. No new Rulers recordings appeared on Sir JJ's label or any other label in Jamaica after the end of 1967, and although one single, 'Got to Be Free', was released on Trojan in the UK as late as 1969, it was doubtless a late licensing arrangement for an old recording.

Most likely, the only reason the Rulers got the opportunity to record at all was that Sir JJ was a small operator interested at the time in breaking into the recording business. He ran his jukebox distribution business from 133 Orange Street – Kingston's Tin Pan Alley – and by the mid-Sixties his shop was also home to JJ Record Sales. After supplying machines to play records on, and then supplying the records, the next logical step was making the records to supply. A daily motivator was right next door at Number 135 Orange Street, on the corner with North Street: Beverley's record label, owned by Leslie Kong and his brothers, used to be an ice-cream parlour until a hopeful Jimmy Cliff sang the song 'Dearest Beverley' to Kong in 1961. Since then Beverley's had gone on to record some of the most successful artists of the Sixties, including Desmond Dekker.

Carl 'Sir JJ' Johnson came from money and was well-connected via his family, and doubtless felt a certain pressure to diversify and succeed. His father was Bromley Johnson, who had built up the successful nationwide Magnet Bus Company from scratch. One of his older brothers was Millard Johnson, a barrister and leader of the radical People's Political Party, who advocated redistribution of wealth and forging economic ties with Africa. Another brother, Copley, ran one of Kingston's leading restaurants and nightspots, Johnson's Drive-In on Maxfield Avenue.

In the mid-Sixties Sir JJ started buying time at Jamaica Studios, 13 Brentford Road, the official name for what was more widely known as Studio One, owned by Clement 'Coxsone' Dodd. Sir JJ employed as his studio band the established and highly regarded Carib-beats, featuring Bobby Aitken – brother of the original king of ska, Laurel – on guitar, Winston Grennan on drums, Vincent White on bass and Bobby Kalphat on piano. Occasional members included Ansell Collins on organ, Mark Lewis on trumpet, Alphanso Henry on sax, Dave Parks on trombone and Iron Spratt on percussion. The core band, at least, played on all the Rulers material, as well as that recorded by Sir JJ's other acts Carl Dawkins and the Kingstonians, either under their own name – they are so credited on the early Rulers JJ singles labels – or, later, as the Sir JJ All Stars. Grennan died in 2000, but shortly before then made a bid to ensure his immortality by listing the many artists he had played with on his website, and claiming to have originated several different reggae drumming styles along the way, including the 'flying cymbals' (aka 'flyers') beat. As an early example of this style he offered 'Copasetic' . . . but, typically, he couldn't remember the name of the artist.

That the Rulers apparently made next to no impression on most of the people whose paths they crossed would be more depressing if they had been responsible for writing their own material, but that was not the case. 'Staggerlee' is a traditional song, in the public domain, but the Clash felt the Rulers' version was different enough to count as an original composition. They followed the advice of the lyric to do the right thing, and ensured efforts were made to establish the identity of the author before *London Calling* was released. The information is not provided on either the JJ or Rio record sleeves, but behind-the-scenes publishing enquiries came up with the name C. Alphanso in time for it to be included on *London Calling*'s label credit. In *The Armagideon Times*, Joe misspelled this as C. Alfonso, before adding that the individual in question had unfortunately since died in a car crash, but 'his next of kin will cop some royalty'. Subsequent releases of the Clash album have added a forename: Clive Alphanso. The individual presently 'copping some royalty' is his son, Michael Campbell. Still a young boy when his father died, he has learned everything he knows about Clive from his mother, his paternal grandmother and his aunt. 'He just wrote songs for the Rulers,' he says. 'He didn't sing with the Rulers. I don't really know who the Rulers were, but I know he wrote for them.'

Carl Alphanso Campbell was born on 6 May 1944 in Jubilee, the Kingston Public Hospital. His mother was from the country, Point Hill, St Catherine, just to the west of Spanish Town, but the family settled in Kingston's Trench Town in what Bob Marley would later immortalise as one of the 'government yards'. 'My aunt tell me that my father used to sing while taking showers, and by the time he was finished there'd be a whole group of people gathered around the shower listening to him,' says Michael. Around 1961, when he was 17, Clive joined a four-piece vocal group called the Sylastians. They split soon afterwards, but all went on to more memorable things: Keble Drummond formed the Cables, Barry Llewellyn and Earl Morgan formed the Heptones, and around 1962 Clive Campbell became one of the Four Aces. This group recorded two or three singles for Leslie Kong at Beverley's, one of which, 'Hoochy Koochy Kai Po' (1964) was a Jamaican hit.

Despite their success, it was felt that the Four Aces lacked a strong lead singer. Meanwhile, another Beverley's act, Desmond Dekker, had taken note of the fact that vocal groups were starting to dominate the local music scene. Dekker always claimed the idea that the Four Aces should become his backing band came from their side, but subsequent events demonstrate that certain members, at least, were not happy with the arrangement. It's easy to see why: the individual Aces would be getting even less of the limelight than before, and from now on they would be recording only Dekker's songs. 'Get Up Edina', one of their first recordings together, was a hit in 1965, but Patrick Johnson left the group soon afterwards, precipitating a name change to Desmond Dekker and the Aces. Clive Campbell was the next to go. The Aces carried on until early 1969, when the remaining two members, Easton Barrington Howard and Winston James Samuels, also dropped out, returning Desmond Dekker to solo status.

Accounts vary as to the exact date of Clive's departure from the Aces, but it was most likely sometime in 1965. 'My father decide he wanted a solo career, so he started doing little songs in clubs,' says Michael. In July 1965, at the age of 21, Clive Campbell made the finals of the Jamaica Festival Popular Solo Singing contest under the name Clive Alphonso (sic). All of the Aces enjoyed playing around with various permutations of their first names, middle names, surnames and nicknames, with the last two members to leave racking up as many as half a dozen noms de stage each before the bitter end. Clive had also started to write songs under his new name, but had no outlet for them via Desmond Dekker and the Aces. That was to change in mid-1966, when he began to provide material for the Rulers. Instead of singing on the rude-boy-glorifying '007 (Shanty Town)', he wrote the condemnatory 'Don't Be a Rude Boy'.

A first-hand account of how he came to supply the Rulers with songs is missing, but an interview conducted by reggae writer and historian David Katz – for his 2003 book, *Solid Foundation: An Oral History of Reggae* – with Leonard Dillon of the Ethiopians, the other band Paul cited as an influence in that 1976 *Sniffin' Glue* interview, raises the strong possibility that the crucial discussion took place not between Clive and the group, but between Clive and the power behind the Rulers' throne, Carl 'Sir JJ' Johnson. Leonard was doing the customary rounds of the Orange Street record stores one day in 1968, charming the mostly female sales staff to persuade them to push his latest recording, when his own association with Sir JJ began. He was walking past Sir JJ Record Sales, when the owner called out to him. 'At that time, all essential services, them in Jamaica, was on strike,' said Leonard. 'He just say, "Make a song named 'Everything Crash'!" and I wrote it.'

As Clive Alphanso was an artist affiliated to Beverley's, located next door to Sir JJ's, it's easy to see how he might have ended up having a similar conversation with Sir JJ two years earlier. And given that Sir JJ and several of his family members were businessmen who frequently suffered from acts of rude-boy robbery and vandalism, it's just as easy to see how Sir JJ might have said, 'Make a song named "Don't Be A Rude Boy" for this new group of mine!' And how, shortly afterwards, when the state of emergency was declared – which would affect the income of a jukebox distributor and his brother the restaurant and night-club owner, as well as offend his other brother, the anti-authoritarian politician – how Sir JJ might have gone back to Clive and said, 'Make a song about how the state of emergency is not "Copasetic"!'

As for 'Wrong Emboyo': its insistence on fair play and doing right reflected the Rulers' beliefs, but was also those of writer Clive Alphanso and producer-mentor Carl Johnson. 'He was a very quiet guy, a very spiritual man,' is what Michael Campbell has – perhaps predictably – been told about his father by his relatives. 'And very kind. They say he would give the shirt off his back. Very polite. He would help the old people in the neighbourhood, do stuff like carrying their groceries in.'

Of Sir JJ, Leonard Dillon had this to say to David Katz: 'He was a conscious black man, sensible manner, irie man, cool. My best producer. He look up on me and say, "You no have to sign a contract, you know. Me live up to my word, you just have to live up to yours." That's what happened, so that's why I stick with him so long.' Sir JJ was friendly with Alvin Ranglin, who might have been his twin by another mother: known as GG, he was another jukebox distributor, turned GG sound-system operator, turned record-store owner, turned record producer who also set up his own label, called GG. 'I know he was a good guy, a good person to do business with, very calm, never been hostile,' GG told David Katz. 'He's been successful, but somebody who always take a little time out to talk to you, even if it is not for long. He's a good person.' There was a feeling abroad, though, that, while Sir JJ's moneyed background enabled him to buy radio time – the Jamaican music scene was very upfront about its payola – he was something of a dilettante, and destined to remain small time. 'He wasn't really in the business too tough,' said Leonard Dillon. Roy Shirley, another JJ artist, told David Katz, 'He was always a little guy in the production field, like say Beverley's was big, you couldn't put them man against Beverley's and Federal and all them guys and Coxsone. The thing about JJ, he had a lot of money and his father had some bus company before that, but the guy look so simple, he always dress like them way-out cowboy and walk that way.'

Clive Alphanso's arrangement with Sir JJ appears to have come to an end by the end of 1967. Possibly because the Rulers stopped coming to Kingston to record, or possibly because their records stopped selling. A few Alphanso-penned Rulers tracks were only available as pre-release white labels, which indicates that demand wasn't sufficient for them to be given a full release. The most likely reason for the end of his association with Sir JJ, however, is that Clive had made a deal with another producer to write and sing his own material. In 1968 he recorded some of his songs for Clement 'Coxsone' Dodd's Studio One label. Had this worked out, it would have been a significant step up in the world. However, that year saw just one track emerging, 'Moving Together', and that only on the compilation album *Reggae in the Grass*, credited to Clive Alphonso. The following year came a single 'Good Enough', even less correctly attributed to Clyde Alphonso. And that appears to have been the end of Clive Alphanso Campbell's recording career. 'Exodus 9' (aka 'Let

My People Go') – previously only available as an obscure Rulers white-label pre-release – was covered by yet another mystery figure named Keith Wilson in 1971, again for Studio One, under the new title 'God I God I Say'. And that appears to have been the end of Clive's career as a supplier of songs . . . until the Clash covered 'Wrong Emboyo' in 1979.

By which time Clive had been dead for six years. According to Michael, the story Joe Strummer heard about a fatal car accident was untrue. 'My father, he died on 22 December 1973. He was performing at a nightclub at Lane Plaza, uptown in Half Way Tree. My grandmother told me, he had just eaten a bowl of chicken soup, and he was on his way to work. He left the house some minutes after 11 o'clock, and from where we lived to where he was going was a good five minute, 10 minute ride, so he probably got there around 11.30. Usually the entertainers enter from the back of the building, and when he tried to enter he was fatally shot by the security guard. During that time the club used to get robbed a lot, and they rob it from the back entrance. They thought he was coming to rob the place, so when he went to see if he could get in, they just shot him. *Three times*, as a matter of fact! Just before Christmas. It was devastating. I was just six years old.'

The irony of a man who wrote songs advising rude boys against violence and robbery, and against a heavy-handed and indiscriminate official response to such behaviour, being mistaken for a robber and gunned down by security guards is not lost on his son. 'It just so happened he lost his life in a way he used to preach against,' he says. As a conclusion to Clive's musical career and life, it directs a new and harsh spotlight onto the attitude struck by 'The Guns of Brixton'.

The date of Clive's death is confirmed by records held by song publishing body MCPS. As befitting a man whose life has so successfully escaped documentation, however, almost all the issues of Jamaica's newspaper of record, *The Gleaner* covering the period 23 December 1973 to 2 January 1974 are missing from the archive. No retrospective references to the shooting incident could be found in the available issues for the remainder of 1974. During the time this book was being written, due no doubt to Jamaica's current period of unrest, the facility for ordering copies of death certificates from Jamaica's Registrar General was unavailable. (Before that, according to complaints on the Internet, it was just highly unreliable.)

In 1968 the Ethiopians' 'Everything Crash' was a sizeable hit for Sir JJ and gave the group's career a much-needed boost. They would go on to enjoy more success over the next year or two, but Leonard Dillon noticed that the producer's heart wasn't really in it any more: 'He could not take the fight.' And there was plenty of fight. Aside from the day-to-day wheeling and dealing to get records played, it was widely known around town that Carl Johnson came from wealthy stock, which made him and his business regular robbery targets. He stopped recording new material some time in late 1971, and the last Sir JJ productions emerged during 1972. Leonard Dillon says Sir JJ abandoned the recording business to concentrate on his jukebox operation for the rest of the Seventies. Several others describe a more sudden and dramatic end to his career as a producer and label boss. All accounts agree that he was ultimately killed, in even more violent circumstances than Clive Alphanso Campbell, though the time, place and means of his dispatch vary from version to version, which goes to illustrate the adage, 'In Jamaica, there's no such thing as a fact.'

Roy Shirley moved to the UK in the early Seventies, and when he returned to Jamaica a year or two later he was told that Sir JJ had been targeted by some hoodlums new to the island who had learned he liked to bank his business earnings personally. They broke into his home one night, 'stick him up, and stuff him throat with some cloth and kill him and take away his things'. As part of his generous efforts to assist with this book, David Katz discussed the matter anew with veteran Jamaican producer Niney the Observer. Niney heard that robbers followed Sir JJ home, or were lying in wait for him there, and shot him to steal either his money or the gun that he carried for protection. Leonard Dillon's version has Sir JJ living slightly longer, but having a few close calls along the way: 'It's just something intending, because it's three times them shot him, and he was living with shot in him. The fourth time they shot him, and then they cut him throat.' Australian-born Graeme Goodall, who worked as a recording engineer in Jamaica in the ska and rock-steady era, before setting up the Doctor Bird label in the UK, heard something similar. 'His premature and completely unnecessary death was clearly a case of being in the wrong place at the wrong time,' he says.

Despite all the entries in The Gleaner about other members of the influential Johnson family – both prior to and following the period of

Sir JJ's supposed demise – there appears to be no record of his death as a result of robbery, random violence or targeted hit. Even when the family patriarch Bromley Johnson died in 1979 at the age of 92, and a list of mourners was published that included Millard and Copley and the other Johnson sons, no reference was made to a living Carl Johnson or the fairly recent violent death of a Carl Johnson.

For a band called the Rulers, this story couldn't be any less straight. And there's one more kink to come . . . Eagle-eyed readers will have noticed two different spellings of the title in the above song history. On the original JJ and Rio single labels, the Rulers' version is listed as 'Wrong Emboyo'. As the precise meaning of this expression – a peculiar turn of phrase even by Jamaican patois's traditionally free-spirited take on the English language – is not immediately apparent, the tendency has been to presume a misspelling on behalf of either the song's author or the individual who logged the original label information in his absence. When Trojan included the song on a Nineties box set compilation, they altered the title to 'Wrong Embryo'. This makes absolutely no sense in the context of the song: the foetal state is a little too early for even Staggerlee to have gone to the bad. Plus, the Rulers clearly sing 'embaya', not 'embraya'.

In his own bid to impose order on the title, Joe Strummer elected to list the Clash's version on *London Calling* as 'Wrong 'Em Boyo'. In Dylan Thomas's radio play *Under Milk Wood* (1953), there is a character named Nogood Boyo, which roughly translates as Rude Boy. Sadly, the chances of this being directly relevant to a single recorded over a decade later on the other side of the world are slight. It does, however, highlight that 'boyo' is Welsh slang, not Jamaican. 'In Jamaican patois, we take out letters and we add in letters,' muses Michael Campbell. 'These days we would say "wrang" for "wrong", and "dem" for "'em", and "bwai" not "boyo", but it changes over the years. So maybe at that time, the slang was "'em". Even today, some people here say "Watch 'em!" I don't know why my father used the word "boyo". But as a whole, it's slang for "Don't wrong them, boy."'

But is it? 'Wrong 'em' might just have made sense if the chorus line was 'you will' or 'it will . . . wrong 'em, boyo', but it runs, 'It *is* the wrong emboyo' . . . and, at the end of the song, the miscreant is told if he changes his ways he will find 'It is the right emboyo.' Investigations and queries made on reggae and Jamaican community websites have failed to throw up an obscure patois word or phrase that fits the bill, but whatever Clive Alphanso meant by 'emboyo', it needs to translate as something like 'thing to do' or 'approach'. Perhaps it should be 'It is the wrong *end*, boyo', as in, the wrong end of the stick? Which is probably a good place to stop.

'Death or Glory'

It was inevitable that an expedition into the hinterland of *London Calling* would, eventually, stumble into the arms of the Knights Templar. Alternatively known as the Poor Fellow-Soldiers of Christ and of the Temple of Solomon – no surprises that it was the shorter version that caught on – the military order was formed at the end of the eleventh century, in the wake of the First Crusade, initially to protect Christians making the pilgrimage to Jerusalem. Over the next 200 years, the Templars became wealthy and powerful – they were both the first international bankers and the first multinational corporation – but their influence faded at the end of the thirteenth century, when the Ninth Crusade failed and Christians lost their footing in the Holy Land. King Philip IV of France was severely in debt to the Templars, having borrowed heavily to fund his war against the English. He pressured his puppet pope Pope Clement V to disband the order. Much torture, execution and confiscation of property followed, the last of these being Philip's primary motive.

Legend has it that the Templars were the first to adopt the skull and crossbones as one of their symbols: the crossed bones representing the cross upon which Jesus died, and the skull representing Golgotha – 'Place of the Skull' in Aramaic ('Calvary' is a rough Latin translation) – where he was crucified. There are two possible explanations for how the image of the skull and crossbones passed into the world of piracy. One is that Mediterranean pirates began hoisting a skull and crossbones flag in order to deceive pilgrims and traders into believing that they were Templars offering protection rather than scurvy sea dogs intent on plunder. The other is that, lacking any other means of support following the unjust persecution of their order, some surviving Templars turned to piracy themselves. Either way, it didn't take long for the skull and crossbones flag, white on a black background, to lose its association with good deeds on the high seas. Traditionally, it would be shown as a warning to stand and deliver; if the target vessel failed to pay heed, a second flag would be hoisted, this one plain blood red, indicating that no quarter would be given, and known – with piratically grim humour – as the Jolie Rouge. Again, over time, or so one theory has it, the name of the second flag transferred to the first, slightly corrupted: the Jolly Roger. Having acquired this association with mortal danger, the skull and crossbones symbol also eventually came to be used as a hazard warning symbol to denote poison.

Christianity initially celebrated victory over death, with positive emphasis placed on the afterlife in the Kingdom of Heaven. The Black Death of 1348 put a different spin on things. Estimates are that it wiped out between a third and two thirds of the total population of Europe. Having lost so many of their kith and kin, the survivors had plenty of cause to fixate on mortality, and on the urgent necessity of repenting sins while there was still time. As lesser plagues continued to lay waste to Europe periodically over the next 400 years, and the death toll was increased further by famine and war – including the Anglo-French Hundred Years War (1337–1453) over the right to the throne of France – this tendency to the morbid became entrenched in the Middle Ages. Men of religion and power were keen to ensure no one forgot death was a constant lurking threat. It kept order, if nothing else. In some countries, cemetery gates were topped with a real skull and crossbones, and it was not uncommon for tombstones to be marked with the image. Some chapels were even built of skulls and bones.

In series of illustrations intended to remind people from all walks of life of their mortality – *memento mori* – Death began to be personified as first a skeletal man, and then a walking skeleton, taking the lives of the godly and wordly, warlike and peaceful, rich and poor alike in what became known as the *Danse Macabre* (Dance of Death). The first examples from the early fifteenth century usually show the dead being led away all together in a long chain. But perhaps the most impressive and certainly the most influential work on the theme is a series of woodcuts designed by Hans Holbein the Younger and first printed in 1538, showing individuals from all walks of life being dispatched one at a time by a gleeful Death. As time passed, Death started to accessorise, with a black cowl, a scythe and an hourglass: the garment gave him a more religious aspect and a little more gravitas; while the implements, derived from classical mythology, symbolised the harvesting of souls and the finite amount of time afforded each life. The Grim Reaper was now a truly terrifying apparition. (For those thinking this deep background is going too deep, be warned that Death – not death, but Death – will be paying a visit in two more songs before the end of *London Calling*.)

The powerful imagery associated with Death also turned up in the Tarot and Freemasonry, while an only slightly more jovial take on the Grim Reaper gave us the image of Old Father Time. There was some cultural slippage, too. In the African-derived – but also European Catholic-influenced, voodoo religion of Haiti and Louisiana, Bacalou is a spirit represented by a skull and crossbones, while Baron Samedi is a figure in skull-like whiteface with a funereal top hat and tails who represents death and plies his trade out by the crossroads. Confusion of voodoo with the hybrid of African traditions, European magic and Bible texts known as hoodoo is discouraged but forgivable. From its punning title onwards, the lyric of Bo Diddley's 'Who Do You Love?' is all about hoodoo, and the lyric boasts that the chimney on his house is made of a human skull.

Though the original association of the skull and crossbones with the Knights Templar had been besmirched and dishonoured by centuries of association with piratical rape and pillage, it made a return to military respectability in the eighteenth century. When Frederick the Great ascended the throne of Prussia in 1740 he formed (among other regiments) Hussar Regiment 5, under the command of Colonel von Ruesch. They wore a black uniform topped off with a hat with a prominent skull and crossbones symbol known as the *Totenkopf* ('dead man's head'). The signal was mixed, but powerful: we, the hussars, are aware of our own mortality, but are not scared of death; you, the enemy, should be very aware of your own mortality . . . because we're going to kill you. Clearly, not all traces of the buccaneering spirit had been entirely expunged. This was the start of a long Germanic tradition. Sixty-five years later, the same black uniform and *Totenkopf* headgear was sported by the Black Brunswickers in the Napoleonic Wars. At the end of the First World War, some German stormtroopers wore *Totenkopf* insignia. And so did Nazi Panzer and Luftwaffe divisions during the Second World War.

Backtracking a little: 1759 found the English fighting the French once again, this time over the rights to sizeable chunks of the New World. Colonel John Hale of the 47th Foot was sent home to England by General James Wolfe to convey news of Wolfe's victory in the Battle of Quebec. It was not a victory Wolfe himself would have time to savour: he died on the battlefield. Colonel Hale the messenger was feted for the good news rather than blamed for the bad, and was granted permission to raise his own cavalry regiment, which, by 1761, had settled on the name the 17th Light Dragoons. The helmet plate Hale chose for his men – influenced by that of the Prussian Hussars – was intended as a tribute to General Wolfe, and depicted a skull with two bones crossed (unusually) above, and OR GLORY inscribed on a banner below. In other words, give me glorious victory or give me death. Later incarnations of the regiment would simplify the image to a cap badge depicting a more traditional skull and crossbones design atop the same banner. In 1822 the 17th Light Dragoons became the 17th Lancers.

The notion of honour in death in combat was as old as civilisation itself. Although the Lancers were involved in several campaigns over subsequent years, the passage of their snappy motto into common parlance was guaranteed by their involvement in the Crimean War; specifically, the Battle of Balaklava. On 25 October 1854, a combination of the pride and incompetence of the officers in charge led to the Lancers being one of several cavalry regiments ordered to advance at speed upon distant Russian heavy artillery positions in what has gone down in history as the Charge of the Light Brigade. Inevitably, it was unsuccessful, and two thirds of the men who took part failed to make the return canter. For those impressed by such futile squandering of life, this was the very definition of the Death or Glory military spirit. The regiment's successors, the Queen's Royal Lancers (which also incorporates three other lancer regiments), are still known as the 'Death or Glory Boys'.

By 1979 'Death or Glory' was a long-established buzzphrase, and a good case could be made for Joe having simply plucked it out of the ether at random to fit the scenario he chose to write about. That said, although even the above Wiki-level information wouldn't have been so easily come by for him in those pre-Internet days, he was a determined autodidact with a particular interest in the history of warfare, and would have been familiar with at least some of the connections.

(He alludes to both the Hundred Years War and the Crimean War in 'The Card Cheat'.) And there are a couple of threads of influence that merit consideration . . .

The Clash had demonstrated a fondness for wearing military-style uniforms, insignia and motifs from their earliest days, and loved to dress up in Hollywood *Boy's Own* outfits. Pirate chic had a tradition reaching all the way back to Johnny Kidd and the Pirates via Johnny Thunders, Phil Lynott, Alex Harvey, David Bowie and Keith Richards. In 1975, when they first met Bernie Rhodes, either Mick Jones or his companion Tony James (accounts vary) was wearing a T-shirt bearing the name and logo of Malcolm McLaren's pre-Sex store. Inspired by James Dean and/or the Hell's Angels, it consisted of a skull and crossbones surrounded by the legend *Too Fast To Live, Too Young To Die*: 'Death or Glory' taken from the battlefield of honour and turned into a lifestyle slogan for drug fiends as well as the more literal sort of speedfreaks. Paul Simonon arrived in the USA for the February 1979 Pearl Harbour tour with his new and specially customised Fender Precision bass featuring a Jolly Roger sticker placed just above the controls, between the scratch plate and the strings. (This bass had just seven months to live: it's the one being destroyed on the cover of *London Calling*.) During the tour, Joe bought a peaked cap which could just about pass for the motorcycle cap Marlon Brando wears in *The Wild One* (1953), and affixed a Jolly Roger badge to the front, *Totenkopf*-style.

Paul acquired a Jolly Roger T-shirt for the Clash's 14 July Southall Defence Fund show at the Rainbow. For the same show, Joe sported a customised shirt featuring the trefoil nuclear radiation hazard warning symbol – three triangles in a circle, black on yellow – in a reference to the Three Mile Island incident. When pop artist Derek Boshier was commissioned to design the *Clash 2nd Songbook*, he was given free rein, except for one detail: Joe insisted upon having the nuclear hazard sign incorporated into the cover image. As Derek used a Pennie Smith photograph from the Rainbow show inside the book, he was familiar with both shirts and both hazard symbols on display that night: Joe's denoting radiation, Paul's denoting poison. For his cover design, Derek combined the two. He superimposed the radiation symbol on the forehead of a skull, and then placed the skull against the radiation symbol's traditional yellow background to create a doubly deadly image.

That the 'Death or Glory' symbol arrived in Clash-world just a couple of months before the song 'Death or Glory', and continued to hang around thereafter, would seem to hint that the band were aware of the connection between motto and design. If more proof is needed, it is surely supplied by 5th Column's design for the official Clash T-shirt for the September–October 1979 Take the 5th tour of the USA. It's a parody of the famous 1917 American armed forces recruitment poster, featuring a characterisation of Uncle Sam with white hair and a goatee beard and an Old Glory star on his top hat, accompanied by the slogan *I Want YOU for US Army*. In the 5th Column version, the Stars and Stripes top hat is still there, but the goatee is now an inverted red punk Mohawk, and Uncle Sam's face has been replaced by a skull and crossbones. The image has been transformed into an anti-recruitment statement, while simultaneously flying the pirate flag for the Clash's own brand of terra firma swashbuckling.

★

While Paul Simonon's take on death or glory in 'The Guns of Brixton' is as action movie-simplistic as his song's title, the same cannot be said of 'Death or Glory' itself. Joe Strummer was capable of being just as romantic as Paul, but he was also capable of recognising what First World War poet Wilfred Owen called 'the old lie' at the heart of his title's credo. That awareness is little more than a skulking presence in the background of 'Rudie Can't Fail', 'Spanish Bombs' and 'Clampdown', but in this lyric, Joe is finally ready to be more upfront with his challenge to the myth.

When *Rude Boy* filmmaker David Mingay visited the Vanilla rehearsal room in June 1979 to hear 'Rudie Can't Fail', he was also played the band's demo of 'Death or Glory', which establishes the fact that it was one of the first songs to be worked up. At the time, Joe told him that 'Death or Glory' owed a debt to Herman Hupfeld's 'As Time Goes By'. Written for the 1931 Broadway musical *Everybody's Welcome*, this song became much better known as the piano ballad played by Dooley Wilson's character Sam in the 1942 movie *Casablanca*. Sam's performance of 'As Time Goes By' for Humphrey Bogart's character Rick Blaine has the same function in *Casablanca* as Joe's performance of 'No Reason' for Ray Gange's character Ray Gange in *Rude Boy* – the filming of which scene had occurred just a couple of months before the Vanilla demo playback – so it's not unreasonable to suppose that working on 'No Reason' helped get Joe in the 'Hollywood musical convention' mindset for writing 'Death or Glory'. Johnny Green is not convinced. 'I reckon Mingay doesn't know when his leg is getting pulled,' he says. 'Or pissed on.'

David admits his memory is patchy about details. He recalls the first version he heard of 'Death or Glory' as being piano-led, and very different from the album version. 'I think it was ruined in the studio,' he says. 'It was made into a big rock song, which takes away from its origins.' There was no piano at Vanilla, and the release of *The Vanilla Tapes* reveals that the demo was particularly close to the version the Clash re-recorded at Wessex for *London Calling*. The arrangement was long established, and it was always very much a guitar song. The tune bears absolutely no relation to the sophisticated 'As Time Goes By', which was a little beyond both Joe and Mick's compositional reach. There is, however, a lyrical echo of the Hupfeld song in 'Death or Glory', and it's possible that this might be at the root of the influence that Joe implied or David inferred.

Casablanca is set at the time of its making, during the Second World War. Cynical bar owner Rick Blaine is hoping to slip out of town and avoid any involvement in the war, but ultimately makes the self-sacrificial gesture of assisting the love of his life to escape with her ex-husband instead, knowing it will be for the greater good. The song 'As Time Goes By' weighs personal feelings against momentous events, a fleeting love affair against the span of history. War is an implicit rather than explicit presence, but the combative imagery serves to rescue it from the honey pot of conventional soundtrack romance. Love will endure against the odds, and lovers feel the same way – hearts full of passion, jealousy and hate: no soft-soap there whatsoever – no matter what fate might bring: 'It's still the same old story / A fight for love or glory / A case of do or die.' Joe uses the same story / glory rhyme in the chorus of his song, and as mottos go, 'Do or Die' is a close relative of 'Death or Glory'. Equally significantly, Joe's lyric also draws upon the stories of everyday folk to paint a bigger picture.

The possibility of a cinematic origin to Joe's lyric is further supported by the opening line of the opening verse: 'cheap hood' is very much part of the vernacular of film noir. Similarly, the powerful, highly visual image of knuckles tattooed with the words LOVE and HATE comes from the 1955 Charles Laughton film *Night of the Hunter*, starring Robert Mitchum as a psychotic preacher whose hands are marked in this very manner. In the film, a struggle for the souls of innocent children ensues. In Joe's lyric it is also children who are threatened by these hands that symbolise the age-old fight between good and evil.

While some of Joe's slang and imagery is very Hollywood American, though, the rest of the scenario explored by the lyric is more redolent of British kitchen sink TV drama. In that respect, it is similar to Desmond Dekker's 'The Israelites', a regular Clash cover throughout 1978 and 1979, which was inspired by a conversation about domestic strife Dekker happened to overhear one day in a London park. Joe's cheap hood turns out to be an ageing rude boy whose dreams of the glamorous thug life eternal have been derailed by reality, which has elected to burden him instead with those usual hostages to fortune: marriage, kids and hire-purchase agreements. Like 'Clampdown', this is a song about drifting into becoming the type of person you despised when you were young. And as in that other *London Calling* song, the dead-end patriarch in 'Death or Glory' takes out his failure and frustration on the next generation, thus perpetuating a vicious cycle. While this was not Joe's life, it is possible that his living arrangements at the time – sharing the flat in Whistler Walk with his girlfriend, her mother and brothers – made it more apparent to him than ever before how easy it is to become entangled in the trappings of domesticity.

The chorus tells us that what was supposed to be a death or glory life has instead turned out to be neither one nor the other, just an unremarkable everyday existence. With the song title thus rendered ironic, Joe moves on to verse two, story two. This concerns a rock'n'roll band determined to succeed, but equally determined not to sell out their principles along the way. As his own band could state from personal experience: some chance! And though the song as a whole is not set up to be autobiographical, the phrases 'I believe in this' and 'tested by research' do invite the listener to make a connection with the Clash. Class of 1976 punk was originally all ideals, but by 1979, these had largely been obliterated by a mixture of fame, excess and contractual obligation. The Clash themselves felt hobbled by the small print in their recording contract with CBS.

Joe's deliberately provocative and grating phrase – unusually, both gratuitously coarse and lacking the saving grace of wit – 'he who fucks nuns will later join the church' testifies to how raw and painful he still found the grey area of enforced compromise.

Although verse three might also seem to be about striving rock'n'rollers, it takes the picture widescreen instead, using imagery from the striving rock'n'roller experience to tell the hard luck story of everybody who has ever woken up to discover they're middle-aged and their best days and opportunities have already passed them by. The beat of the music has become the ticking of the clock: a situation that 'must come to everyone', as Joe put it in *The Armagideon Times*. The verse's final line is ambiguous: it's hard to say whether 'we already heard your song' is meant to be reassuring or dismissive. It's almost possible to see Death standing there, scythe at the ready, fast-emptying hourglass in hand. Rictus yawn.

As with 'Clampdown', the lyrics as transcribed by Ray Lowry for the inner sleeve of *London Calling* don't tell the full story. 'Death or Glory' features two lengthy Joe Strummer ad-libs. That *The Vanilla Tapes* demo version preserves similar, if not quite identical, passages proves they weren't really ad-libs at all, but considered and polished additions intended to complement and colour the message of the main lyric.

On the album version, the first ad-lib comes during the bridge section, after the second verse (at around 1:40). It's mixed low and mumbled, and for many years proved reluctant to give up its secrets; but there are now best-guess versions on the Internet. It begins with feeling fear in the gun-sights, being advised to lie low and to not play the show, and then agrees that discretion might be the better part of valour. The Clash's relationship with Northern Ireland had been uncomfortable ever since their visit to Belfast on 20 October 1977, when they posed for some photographs at the barricades in black combat gear and leather jackets, looking like would-be freedom fighters. The following year, going through his terrorist chic phase, Joe wrote a couple of songs reflecting this interest, and took to the stage in a series of provocative home-made T-shirts. These included the *Brigate Rosse* T-shirt he wore at the Carnival Against the Nazis in Hackney on 30 April 1978, preserved for posterity in *Rude Boy*; and the *H Block* T-shirt he wore for a gig at the Roxy in Harlesden on 25

October 1978, where Keef & Co shot the video for 'Tommy Gun', ensuring a wide audience for what could all too easily be construed as a gesture of support for the IRA.

HM Prison Maze, known as the Maze or Long Kesh, was divided into H-shaped blocks, where Republican prisoners were interred. They refused to wear prison uniforms, claiming they were political prisoners, or prisoners of war, not criminals, and by 1978 their blanket protest had escalated to a dirty protest: smearing excrement on their cell walls. The protests would eventually lead to a hunger strike, which resulted in several deaths, most famously that of Bobby Sands. This was flashpoint politics. In spring 1979, when Margaret Thatcher and the Conservative Party were poised to assume power in the UK, the *NME* ran a spoof election, in which Joe's 'Riot Wing' party polled the most votes. He popped into the inky's office to deliver his manifesto, which ran in the 5 May 1979 edition. Point 11 was 'Troops and Britain out of Northern Ireland'. As he sat down at the typewriter, he said, 'I'm probably digging my own grave here.'

Shortly afterwards, Neil Spencer, then editor of the *NME*, received a letter from Northern Irish Loyalist faction the Red Hand Commando, threatening to kill Joe Strummer should the Clash set foot in Northern Ireland. Spencer forwarded it to the band, who consulted the police. Representatives of Special Branch paid a visit to Vanilla to warn Joe that this should be considered a serious threat from an active terrorist group. Matters came to a head in early July when the Undertones, attempting to arrange a major punk show at the Temple More Sports Complex in their hometown of Derry for 25 August 1979, invited the Clash to headline. Joe initially insisted on being there, providing all possible precautions were taken, but the rest of the band tried to talk him out of it.

On 11 August a news item appeared in the *NME* announcing the Clash's appearance . . . But even by then, wiser counsel had prevailed. It was made clear to Joe that an open stage in a 60,000-capacity sports hall in a small city not used to hosting major rock'n'roll gigs, and in a country divided by a long-running and murderous sectarian struggle, was not the place to prove his mettle. The show was cancelled, though the true reason was not revealed at the time, and the Undertones were offered the support slot on the Clash's Take the 5th tour by way of compensation. Thereafter, Joe kept a low profile with regard to Ireland.

When *Hot Press* sent writer John McKenna to London to interview the band at the end of 1979, it was – unusually – just Mick and Paul who spoke to him. Just a week before the hunger strike death of Bobby Sands on 5 May 1981, Joe gave a speech of support from the stage, but he did it in Madrid, and in Clash Spannish. The Clash would not play Northern Ireland again until 1984, and when they did 'Death or Glory' was not on the set list.

So this is the subject of the first ad-lib, with Joe recognising his own death-or-glory moment, and electing not to play the part of screaming target. Having been pressed into choosing discretion over valour evidently gave him pause for thought . . . quite far-ranging thought, in terms of the implications for the Clash. The last line of the ad-lib observes (approximately) 'playing the blues for pennies sure looks better now'. Having renounced Chuck Berry upon joining the Clash, Joe now found the life-affirming rebel spirit of R&B – whether belted out in a pub or busked in a subway – far more appealing a prospect than the po-faced suicide-note of political punk. In Chris Salewicz's *Redemption Song*, Kosmo Vinyl linked the subsequent downplaying of Joe's, and the Clash's, militancy directly to the death threat. The band's first major US interview, for the 17 April 1980 edition of *Rolling Stone*, led off with Paul Simonon insisting that the Clash were interested in 'politics with a small "p", like personal politics'. And that became the new party line.

The death threat was quite possibly also the real reason behind the Clash's about-face on *Rude Boy*: their determination to bury the film dated from August 1979 onwards. Had it been afforded a high-profile release, it would have fixed the Big P version of the Clash in the general public's minds for a lot longer. David Mingay was perceptive enough to recognise and even empathise with what was clearly a firm decision, rather than just an idle whim, to take that step back. 'If you confront the "ideas of today", then you find you're in a very hot seat,' he says. 'I didn't know of the death threat from Ireland. It never occurred to me at the time that Irish politics might have come home to roost. But I did think that *politics* had come home to roost. That could be something, though. Joe was flirting with death or glory. But although the rest of the band might have shared his views to some extent, they didn't want to die for them. Mick didn't want to go onstage and be afraid of a bullet. I think you can make the link, you could say that this might have led to their injunction against *Rude Boy*. The film didn't refer to Ireland, but it did refer to terrorism. I was very interested in this. One aspect of it was Joe's fascination with the Baader-Meinhof people and the *Brigate Rosse*. Squat politics. I played on the threat of that to Joe, with that *Brigate Rosse* T-shirt he wore at the Carnival in Hackney, and Ray Gange discovering it and asking him all these awkward questions about it.'

Before exploring the song's second ad-lib, some musical context is required. The composition of the tune for 'Death or Glory' doesn't appear to have made an abiding impression on anyone involved. Neither Joe nor Mick claimed the main writing credit at the time or later. This suggests that it was devised at Vanilla and worked up by the band, rather than brought in by either Mick or Joe. Evidently more memorable by far was the Wessex recording session. During the taping of the live backing track, Guy Stevens ran out onto the studio floor and started throwing chairs around. This act of vandalism doesn't appear to have done any audible damage to the take, but that may well be because this is yet another song where the live backing track has been extensively bolstered by overdubs, mostly of guitars. 'Joe's rhythm left, Mick's rhythm right, Mick's lead half-right, as standard,' says Bill Price, counting them off across the stereo picture. 'There might be a third rhythm playing accents on the "one, two" at the start of each chorus line to beef it up.' The 'one, two' is the brace of giant F major chords that announce CHORUS COMING NOW! The drums and bass lock in, and the result is at once – like 'London Calling' – martial, recalling the drums and pipes of war, and – like 'Clampdown' – urban and industrially gloomy, recalling crashing heavy machinery, piercing sirens and alarms. The former interpretation takes the song's title literally; the latter opts for irony, mimicking the relentless, grinding misery of the option that is neither death nor glory. Also relentless, towards the end of the song, are Mick's lead lines, which squirm through and choke up every available space: it's the one moment on *London Calling* that recalls *Give 'Em Enough Rope*. 'There could be more than one lead guitar occasionally,' understates Bill. 'At the end there's an extra guitar half-left.'

For much of its duration 'Death or Glory' is a classic, even main-stream, rock song. But it also has its surprises. The bridge section is almost freeform, allowing the bass and drums a brief act of skittish rebellion, threatening to slip out for another visit to the disco. The song's introduction is another wrong-footer. The drums mark – as well as keep – time, and the various guitars circle around, pretending to be aimless decoration, but really awaiting their moment. Meanwhile, the bass plays a few bars of a beautiful countermelody just long enough to establish a melancholic mood before it joins the other instruments in The Riff. It's not until the breakdown (around 2:40) that the bass restates this melodic figure. 'That could be Mick,' says Bill Price. 'It's not Paul's normal bass sound.' By now, the melancholy is almost overwhelming. Topper builds the tension by holding a steady four on the floor while rolling around the toms every two bars, Mick plays equally mournful lead lines based on ascending and descending scales, the instruments all lock into the main riff once more, and BAM, BAM, it's back into the chorus.

Joe doesn't miss the opportunity presented by this powerful emotional shift. His second ad-lib – the breakdown ad-lib – doesn't just amplify the existing lyric, it takes it up to an entirely different level, using military allusions like marching, fighting, travel, and raising hell, to evoke perseverance, endurance, unity, struggle . . . and ulti-mately victory. The main body of the song only flirts occasionally with autobiography, and the first – bridge – ad-lib is autobiographical but oblique. The second uses metaphor to maintain some distance, but, even more so than 'The Guns of Brixton', clearly reflects the Clash's own situation at the time of writing: digging in at Vanilla, feeling under pressure from CBS, besieged by negative critical opinion from the likes of Ian Penman and Garry Bushell (and even tougher reviews from the Red Hand Commando). It draws its strength from the Clash's determination not to go under without first giving it their all. As well as referring to the group, though, the frequent reiteration of 'we're gonna' is again more widely inclusive, taking the listener along for the ride.

The earlier verses offer a pessimistic or at best ambivalent outlook; by the time the breakdown ad-lib leads into the final brace of choruses, General Strummer has given the troops a pep talk and prepared them to accept nothing less than triumph over adversity. And those last choruses reclaim 'Death or Glory' as a genuinely heartfelt battle cry. If it sounds like a retrogressive step – a return to the jingoistic – then that's not the case. Having opted out of facing a bullet at Temple

More, Joe is no longer willing to advocate a kamikaze gesture in the style of the Light Brigade at Balaklava, or even Ivan in 'The Guns of Brixton', but instead extols the virtues of playing the long game, being stoical, working hard, never giving in, and refusing to be beaten.

It would be pushing it to describe 'Death or Glory' as a reggae-influenced tune, but the influence of reggae on the material the band were writing and recording at Vanilla album was clearly pervasive, and bled out onto the non-reggae songs in unusual ways. Under the chorus of *The Vanilla Tapes* version of 'Death or Glory', the backing vocals do the mouth-as-hi-hat trick – 'tsk, tsk, tsk' – beloved of original Sixties ska toasters and late Seventies ska revivalists.

On both the demo and final studio versions of the song, Joe precedes his first vocal ad-lib with another animal noise. Following on from the seagulls on 'London Calling' and the werewolf or wildebeest on 'Rudie Can't Fail' comes what can only be described as an overexcited baboon. There is unlikely to be any deep or meaningful significance to this.

'Koka Kola'

'Koka Kola' is one of the most unusual tracks on *London Calling*. It's the shortest – just one minute and 50 seconds – and it moves at a hell of a lick . . . but it doesn't sound remotely like punk rock. The buoyant bass, the near-spoken vocal and verbose lyric, sprung with puns and littered with alliteration, combine to give the impression of primitive hip hop . . . but at the time of composing the song the Clash were a year off discovering that genre, and the music here doesn't so much groove as alternate between galumphing and stuttering.

At the start of the verse, the harmony goes from G to Bm to A, when the ear would normally expect to hear Am. Once again, Mick Jones has escaped the nominal key for something more modal, this time Lydian. (Though he returns to base in the chorus.) His flanged lead guitar line takes even greater liberties with harmony and logic. By way of extreme contrast, what the bass is doing is a very old trick. Paul repeatedly goes from the root note down to the fifth and back: music-hall play-on music. Mick's lush backing vocals seductively reinforce the last word of each line of Joe's lyric. It's all very . . . odd.

The Vanilla Tapes version is much the same musically and structurally as the album version, though it is taken at a slightly more leisurely pace. Although one of the first songs the band worked up at Vanilla – like the preceding 'Death or Glory', it was probably pieced together in the room – and one of the first to which they gave a live outing, this was another track that was reworked lyrically right up until it was recorded. The Vanilla lyric is shorter, more repetitive and less polished. By the time work at Wessex had finished, the first and second verses remained much the same – save for a line change in the latter – but the chorus was tighter, there was an entirely new section of lyric for what previously had been the purely instrumental bridge, and there was an entirely new final verse.

Like 'Hateful', 'Koka Kola' was influenced directly (as opposed to indirectly via books, video, TV and the movies) by the band's experiences on their first American tour, and also like 'Hateful', it concerns – in part at least – drug abuse run amok.

The working title for the song was 'Koka Kola, Advertising and Kokaine', a phrase which, although written on the tape box when the band recorded *The Vanilla Tapes* version, does not appear in the actual lyric of that version of the song. The working title did its job by summing up the three chief elements of the subject matter. By the time it came to releasing the Wessex version, Joe had evidently decided that the elements were so interlinked, and that this interlinking was so self-evident, that 'Koka Kola' could happily stand for all three (though, just to make sure, he incorporated the original title into the revised lyric).

Coca-Cola is symbolic of America in many ways. It's a quintessentially *American* soft drink. It's the embodiment of the American Dream, in that its success is a rags-to-riches story: it was first made available in 1886 from the soda pump in a single store, Jacob's Pharmacy in Atlanta, and for months averaged sales of just nine glasses a day. That Coca-Cola went on to become arguably the most instantly recognisable brand in the world was entirely due to a distinctive and much reproduced logo, and a century-long, ever-evolving, but tirelessly aggressive advertising campaign based on a seemingly endless supply of folksy Zen-gnomic slogans. The Clash saw both Coca-Cola and Coca-Cola advertising everywhere they went on their Pearl Harbour tour of the US. By the late Seventies, the product was available in every far-flung corner of the world. So it also symbolises global imperialism.

The soda's popular diminutive, 'Coke' – which Coca-Cola the company was quick to trademark – doubles as the popular diminutive for cocaine. Which the Clash also saw everywhere they went on the Pearl Harbour tour. In the late Seventies, it seemed, not only bands, but also the entire music business – from management to promotion to distribution to journalists to DJs – were bent at the knees over mirrors and cisterns, nostrils agape and hearts pounding, as their snow-blowers set to work shifting the drifts. The other commercial arts, like the movie business, the fashion industry, magazine publishing and advertising were in there standing shoulder-to-shoulder with them, sleeves rolled up and determined to see it through. The drug was even strongly rumoured – and later proved – to have made inroads into other work-hard-play-hard champagne'n'meglomania cultures like high finance and politics. A popular T-shirt of the time borrowed the shape of Coca-Cola's world-famous white-on-red logo to proclaim the message *Enjoy Coke*. Everybody got the joke. And, hardly subtly, it's this joke that Joe is reworking when his lyric hijacks two other Coke-the-soft-drink slogans to refer to coke-the-hard-drug: 'Coke adds life' (first used in 1976) and 'the pause that refreshes' (first used in 1929).

History teaches us that it's not much of a joke, after all: it's no coincidence that Coca-Cola and cocaine have the same nickname. Invented in 1886 by Dr John Pemberton in Atlanta, Georgia, Coca-Cola was first marketed as a tonic, but just over a decade later was offering an alternative kick-in-a-bottle in the wake of recently introduced state prohibition laws forbidding the sale of alcohol. The 'cola' part of the name derived from the caffeine-rich kola nut, which provided and still provides the main lift in the pick-me-up. But the 'coca' part came from the coca leaf, which in the earliest days still included traces of cocaine. The leaf is still used in today's recipe, but even by 1905 the cocaine had been extracted first.

Joe maintains the jocular tone throughout the verses and choruses, throwing out cross-referential puns and references worthy of the advertising profession itself. 'Clinical precision' refers to cocaine's other late-nineteenth-century use as a local anaesthetic, injected directly into tissue around the area to be operated upon. 'Freeze, man, freeze' refers to both this pain-deadening affect and cocaine's resemblance, in powder form, to snow (hence another of its nicknames). The second line of the album version's chorus has the party girl beseeching 'treat me nice'. It's obvious she's asking her potential benefactor to give her some of what he's holding, and there's also the implication she's begging him not to mistreat her when he's high. But there's also a reference to 'Treat Me Nice', the B-side of Elvis Presley's 'Jailhouse Rock' (1958), a song that features more lyrical play at the lower end of the temperature gauge: if you 'come on cold', Elvis will 'freeze'; so if you don't want him to be 'cold as ice', you'd better treat him nice.

The demo version of 'Koka Kola' is a little more upfront in its sneering at coke users. A subsequently abandoned line refers to a 'silicone nose' and 'matching walls and clothes': as many rockstars and actors have since learned, long-term use of large quantities of cocaine not only rots the septum so badly that reconstructive surgery is required, it also has a deleterious impact on judgement and taste. Joe makes the latter point more amusingly in other lines that survive in the album version, painting a picture of a vacuous 'lifestyle' built around happy hours, party girls, and preposterous, pimp-style clothes fashioned from assorted exotic animal hides.

In the demo's draft version of the lyric, the context for this lifestyle remains vague. As in the album version, though, the corridors of power are gleaming and on the 51st floor. Invariably, the powerful situate themselves at the top of tall buildings to illustrate how far above the less powerful they are in other, less literal, ways: how very much closer, if not to God, then to being Gods. Mick Jones has put forward Sir C. P. Snow's *Corridors of Power* as a possible influence on the song. But this is unlikely: the novel – the ninth part of a sequence known as 'Strangers and Brothers' – which is set in Britain's political centre of Whitehall, was published in 1964, but was little-read by the late Seventies, and was therefore far away in both distance and time from any vaguely direct relevance to 'Koka Kola'. (The author's amusingly appropriate surname notwithstanding.) What the title of Snow's book did do was introduce a pithy phrase to common usage, and Joe enjoys using 'the corridors of power' here, much as he enjoyed using 'clampdown' and 'the cost of living' elsewhere.

The album version of the lyric appears to be more specific about the song's central location. A new line in the first verse, 'jumping from the windows', points towards Wall Street. Defenestration in lower Manhattan conjures up different associations in these post-9/11 days, but back in the Seventies any talk of leaping from high-rise windows immediately brought to mind the Wall Street Crash of October 1929. Reckless speculation had led to the US stock market losing 47 per cent of its value in 26 days. A sudden drop on 24 October, thereafter known as Black Thursday, was followed by panic and total collapse on 29 October, aka Black Tuesday. Rumours quickly spread that 11 unlucky speculators had thrown themselves from the high-rises in Manhattan's financial zone. This turned out to be an urban myth. There were a handful of suicides by ruined men, but none by jumping. Contemporary comedian Will Rogers worked up a bit of schtick about it, though, which helped keep the myth alive. And in truth, such an act of desperation was an appropriate symbol for the fall of the American economy: banks closed, a hundred thousand businesses went bust, hundreds of thousands more people lost their jobs and their means to feed themselves and their families.

In the album version's wholly new bridge section, Joe reveals he's already read about the cocaine exploits of the Manhattan and Berlin smart sets in the newspaper, and that word has it the white powder is now drifting through the White House. A note of exaggerated indignation is struck here. Twenty years of rock'n'roll and counter-cultural rebellion have come to nothing in terms of changing the power structure. Beatniks, rockers, hippies and punks have all, in turn, been dismissed as dirty drug fiends. And now look who's getting high and breaking the law: the very financiers and politicians who are still claiming the moral high ground and dictating how others should live their lives!

With today's multinational corporations, upgraded travel, communication and media connections, and an increasingly globally homogenised culture based largely upon the American model, the gap between the USA and UK is no longer significant enough to allow for culture shock. But in the late Seventies, too much of the British mindset was still stuck somewhere between the Second World War and the post-war Period of Austerity, while the remaining available headspace had been shaped by the decade-long economic downturn that culminated in the Winter of Discontent. National characteristics bred by the former period were diffidence, narrow-mindedness, politesse and conservatism, while the latter inspired envy, resentment, hostility and an over-developed sense of irony. (Broadly speaking, the UK punk move-ment was an extreme reaction to the earlier British traits and an extreme manifestation of the more recent ones.) In comparison, from a distance, the USA, with its materialism, success-worship and blatant hard-selling, seemed to British eyes to be brash, rude, go-getting, over-confident, transparent, and at once naïve and shameless. Once over there for the Pearl Harbour tour, though, the Clash had encountered some of the underlying ruthlessness, control and manipulation that had made America a superpower while the UK was wallowing in its multiple miseries.

Meanwhile, Coca-Cola was being marketed as the universal panacea, and adverting slogans were being passed off as 'good advice': consume Soma, listen to Big Brother. As in 'Lost in the Supermarket', the adver-tisements tell you what you ought to need in order to stop you thinking about what you really need. A signpost to this is the 'elevator going up' intro to 'Koka Kola': although ostensibly taking the listener up to the 51st floor of a Manhattan financial corporation, the 'going up' part is borrowed from the opening credits of the BBC1 department store situation comedy *Are You Being Served?* (1972–85), where the phrase precedes a list of the wares available on each floor. There's also an implied reference to the Winter of Discontent's impact upon the shop-ping experience. Inflation was also going up, and with it, of course, 'the cost of living'.

The first part of the new bridge section neatly encapsulates the Coca-Cola-advertising-cocaine theme. After naming those three elements, Joe takes a stroll down Manhattan's Broadway in the rain. The Street of Dreams, the long-established showcase for New York's – and, by extension, America's – musical and theatrical extravaganzas, Broadway has always had a schizophrenic character. Joe is referencing the Drifters' bittersweet 1963 song 'On Broadway', whose protagonist also walks along the thoroughfare in less than ideal conditions, vowing to make it as a big star while penniless and starving. At the point where Broadway cuts diagonally across Manhattan's rigid grid struc-ture at 7th Avenue, between 42nd and 47th Streets, can be found Times Square. Like London's Piccadilly Circus, this had been long established as the premier location for large-scale neon advertising signs, with the Coca-Cola sign dominating the nocturnal urban skyline. This is the sign Joe describes in 'Koka Kola'. Around the square and in the hinterland of Broadway, though, a sleazy alternative entertainment and advertising business had developed: porno cinemas, prostitution, drug dealing. Although the area has since been sanitised, by the Seventies the sleazy alternative was in danger of taking over.

This locale was one of the Clash's first impressions of New York and of America. In September 1978 Joe and Mick had finished off *Give 'Em Enough Rope* at the Record Plant, just a few blocks away at 321 West 44th Street. It's no coincidence that it is here – '42nd Street / Where hustlers hustle and pimps pimp the beat' – that Montgomery Clift reaches his lowest ebb in 'The Right Profile'. The Broadway/Times Square nexus was where high life met low life, where the American Dream bumped up against American Dirty Realism.

For the new final verse of the album version of 'Koka Kola', the viciousness of Joe's satire on contemporary mores is once again notched up to 'comic horrible' levels. As with 'Jimmy Jazz', the narrative line is more narrative ellipsis, and the sequence of events is ambiguous. Illustrating the cross-pollination of ideas among the various songs the Clash were working on at the time, like 'Jimmy Jazz' (again), 'The Guns of Brixton' and earlier Clash drugs song 'Drug Stabbing Time', 'Koka Kola' would appear to end with a raid. The other three are clearly police raids. This one could be, too: the first thing through the door is a snub-nose .44. So named because of its shortened barrel, the snub-nose revolver was originally designed for enforcers of the law, and for years was the preferred weapon of sheriffs, police detectives, federal agents and film noir PIs played by the likes of Humphrey Bogart, because it was designed to be light, easy to conceal and quick to draw and fire. The downside was that the snub nose reduced accuracy and increased both recoil and muzzle flash. Although .38 models were more common, heavier .44s were not unheard of, if slightly more unwieldy. Other parts of the circumstantial evidence available imply that this particular raid is a criminal rather than police action, though: taking coke might well be illegal, but the only people likely to burst in with guns drawn on the well-to-do while they're indulging in a little recreational hoovering are dealers or mobsters with whom they have drug- or drug-lifestyle-related debts.

The 'what you can't snort you can spatter on the floor' line is another layered coke joke. Firstly, there's the surreal toon image of the gun sucking the drug up its barrel and sneezing it back out again.

Secondly, there's a reference to the famous scene in the 1977 film *Annie Hall* where Woody Allen's (inevitably) neurotic character attends a party full of the type of Manhattan elite Joe takes a poke at in verses one and two. Offered cocaine, novice Woody works himself into such a state over correct drug-consumption etiquette that he exhales explosively instead of inhaling, causing the expensive mound to disappear along with the last vestiges of his social standing.

What really transpires in the third verse is largely irrelevant because regular or intensive coke use famously encourages paranoia. That, along with the equation 'too much coke + sudden shock = extreme panic', is what Joe is successfully striving to convey. His protagonist loses his composure in spectacular style – cue more surreal toon images of pinball eyes and a tongue like a fish (with accompanying toon sound effects) – and demonstrates the extent of his confusion by leaping out of the frying pan and into the fire or – less proverbially – escaping a gunman by flinging himself out of a 51st floor window. High he may be, but not high enough to fly. He follows the doomed trajectory of his (mythical) Wall Street Crash-era predecessors on his way down to make his own Great Depression in the sidewalk. This neat echo of the first verse's defenestration reference is also an equally neat reversal of the introduction's elevator ride: the protagonist might go up the quick way at the start, but he takes an even faster route back down at the end.

Fittingly for such a multi-storey lyric, there are morals on several levels. On an individual scale, the drug fiend executive experiences a spectacularly visualised rise and fall. Pan back, and the Big Apple is revealed to be rotten at the core. Pan back still further, and the American Dream appears to have soiled the sheets.

Why the 'k', rather than 'c', for Koka Kola and kokaine? On a prosaic level, the substitution enables Joe to take a pop at the product without using its tradename and risking legal repercussions from a powerful multinational company. But there are other reasons. Substituting a 'k' for a 'c' was a feature of self-consciously 'modern' product branding in the early part of the twentieth century. Being zany and of the moment also made it a feature in comic strips and books, notably the surreal Krazy Kat, which ran from 1913. Over time, such forced wackiness, redolent of the smarmiest excesses of the advertising profession, started to smack of the ersatz. For example,

Muzak was a company formed in the mid-Thirties to supply recorded music to retail stores and hotels – for their elevators – but the name has become synonymous with processed, cheesy background music. Ireland and Australia were among the countries that, between the Thirties and the Fifties, raised questions about having their national culture swamped by ultra-modern American products, pastimes and values. Already, they sneeringly dismissed this as 'Koka-Kola Kulture'. As the Cold War settled in during the late Forties, the Russian over-tones of substituting 'k' for 'c' fed America's Kommie paranoia, lending words thus amended a threatening edge. By the Sixties, under-ground political groups like the Yippies began to refer to the USA as Amerika: as this was the Germanic spelling of America, it intimated that the parent society was inherently Nazi. All of these associations are appropriate to the song. Joe's comments on 'Koka Kola' in *The Armagideon Times* are very much in the hokey outta-da-side-a-da-mouth tradition of a komix kaption: 'Now all the White House staff are sniffing away the giant korporation steps in and buys up all the space along Broadway – "Sure a packet is expensive, Mac! But you can use a kredits kard!"'

All of which shines some light onto the peculiar music: if the tune for 'Lost in the Supermarket' recalls both muzak and cod-disco, accom-panying a lyric describing artificial retail environments and TV commercials for disco albums, then in terms of both its brevity and awkward, forced catchiness, the tune for 'Koka Kola' could be a self-consciously zany advertising jingle. It's in the spirit – quite possibly intentionally – of the fake radio commercials the Who included between the 'proper' tracks on their 1967 album *The Who Sell Out*. (One of the ads the Who recorded but didn't use was for Coca-Cola.)

For such an apparent novelty item, the Clash remained fond of the song. Not only was it a regular feature in their repertoire for the autumn 1979 Take the 5th tour of America, but a Koka Kola poster pastiching the white-on-red Coca-Cola logo was used to advertise the 2 October show at the Agora Ballroom in Atlanta, the very city where the whole soda opera began. While other of *London Calling's* more obvious candidates for inclusion in their live set were overlooked entirely or quickly fell by the wayside, 'Koka Kola' held on to its posi-tion well into the Eighties. Possibly partly because it became ever more relevant as the Me! Me! Me! Decade progressed and the Yuppies yippeed all the way to the bank, their energies and attitudes fuelled by the stuff.

And possibly partly because the Clash themselves felt the need to keep on exorcising their own demons: Mick had fought and apparently won a year-long battle with cocaine in 1978; Joe and Paul had brief, but repeated and unresolved skirmishes with it on American tours, as Joe admitted to the *NME*'s Sean O'Hagan in 1988. Topper conducted a lengthy campaign with it, in conjunction with his steadily escalating war with heroin, until, by 1982, they had combined to prevent him advancing any further with the Clash.

The most likely reason why the band got such a kick out of the song, though, is best savoured slowly, and here at the end. 'Koka Kola' was also the latest in the long-running series of the Clash's only partially veiled digs at their record company. CBS HQ in Manhattan, home to the Epic and Columbia labels, was a 490-feet-tall, 38-storey monolith of black Canadian granite cladding and tinted glass known as Black Rock, situated just a few blocks north of Times Square at Number 51 West 52nd Street, on the corner of 6th Avenue (the Avenue of the Americas). Mmm . . . Number 51. The action in 'Koka Kola' takes place on the 51st floor . . .

The entire record industry was hit by recession in 1979 – the first decline in growth since the end of the Second World War – and CBS, the biggest player, took it hardest of all. While the industry's total sales slumped by 11 per cent on the previous year, over the same period CBS saw a drop in earnings of a devastating 46 per cent. According to Fredric Dannen's *Hit Men: Power Brokers and Fast Money Inside the Music Business*, the recession was partly due to a serious misjudgement of the size, longevity and profitability of the disco craze, partly to huge costs of hiring 'independent promoters' to ensure records got radio airplay and became hits, and partly to 'Koka Kola'-style excesses in the record companies' corridors of power.

Even while the Clash were writing and recording *London Calling*, some very bad days were being experienced at Black Rock. In Pat Gilbert's *Passion is a Fashion*, Blackhill's Andrew King described the building as an awful place where 'executives used to commit suicide by jumping down the air shaft when their ratings went down'. Again, this is urban myth. Nobody jumped for real, but more than a few were pushed during the course of the summer. On 29 June 1979 CBS

America made 53 staff redundant, and a further 120 were let go on 10 August, which – in a reference to the Crash of '29 – became known as Black Friday. Some of those who lost their jobs left the building wearing T-shirts bearing the legend *The Crash of '79*. As *Sounds* journalist Pete Silverton quipped at the time, that left the Clash just one letter away from taking all the credit. As CBS's public humiliation was occurring around the time the band were recording 'Koka Kola', and while Joe was fine-tuning the lyric, it added its not-so-secret ingredient to the song's flavour. And by performing it regularly on the Take the 5th tour, and for so long afterwards, the band took advantage of every possible opportunity to pop the top off a cold one, sit back, relax and enjoy.

'The Card Cheat'

Written while the band were recording the album in Wessex, 'The Card Cheat' was originated on Studio One's Bösendorfer Grand. Because Joe Strummer tended to monopolise the instrument during studio downtime, because pianner is very much in evidence throughout the song, and because the basic structure of the tune is uncomplicated – it's a 16-bar blues – it's tempting to attribute its genesis to him. But at the time of the *London Calling* 25th Anniversary Edition release, when asked by *Uncut*'s Adam Sweeting who was responsible for the song, Paul jerked his thumb towards Mick and said 'Beethoven here'.

What Paul was almost certainly referring to was the arranging and building of the song as recorded. Of all the members of the band, Mick was most interested in experimentation and in production techniques. Enabled by Bill Price's know-how, with 'The Card Cheat' he set out to recreate producer Phil Spector's trademark Wall of Sound. In the early to mid-Sixties Spector and his engineers achieved the original at Gold Star Recording Studios in LA by setting up a large group of session musicians – known as the Wrecking Crew – like a popular music orchestra, several of them playing the same part on the same instrument in unison. Recorded using an echo chamber, the resultant dense barrage of sound was well suited to emotional teen sagas like the Ronettes' 'Be My Baby' (1963).

The Spector sound had never really gone away. Brian Wilson picked up the idea and went doolally with it on the 'pocket symphonies' he wrote and recorded with the Beach Boys. In the early Seventies, what were – at the time – essentially retro outfits the Electric Light Orchestra and the Roy Wood-led ELO spin-off band Wizzard went for a similarly big sound, Wood using much the same techniques on Wizzard's 1972–3 run of four massive-sounding massive UK hits. Ditto early Abba and the Bruce Springsteen of *Born to Run* (1975). By this time, studio technology had advanced to the point where a large group of musicians was no longer required: the same effect could be achieved by overdubbing the same parts, double- or triple-tracking them. In the *Clash on Broadway* booklet, Mick cheerfully revealed that the 'secret' of the sound was to record everything twice. 'There's more than one piano, and the vocal has some double behind it,' says Bill Price. 'And there are many brass tracks.' Right from the beginning, the sound swells up out of the speakers and fills the room.

Stereo doesn't just come from two points: it creates a 180-degree spectrum. The further sounds are from the centre, the more the listener's perception of their volume changes. If there are two or more tracks of each instrument, they have to be balanced not only within the mix, but also against each other. On 'The Card Cheat' the horns are furthest left and right, then the pianos, then the bass, with the vocals in the centre. The even mightier-than-usual drums are spread across the whole picture. If the instruments are playing almost the same thing, but not quite – and, Topper aside, the Clash were hardly clinically precise musicians – it results in a slightly phased effect. And if there's a lot of that going on, and a good deal of it is swathed in reverb, the result is a slightly messy rumbling avalanche of sound. Surprisingly Bill says the track caused him no problems at the mixing stage, as he and Mick had been required to think about it as they went along. 'This sound would have been built up throughout the course of overdubbing,' says Bill. 'It would be practically mixed by the time recording was finished.'

When asked what motivated the Clash to take this approach to 'The Card Cheat', Bill replies, 'The opening piano riff is asking for this treatment.' But surely there was more to it than that? It's possible the band had heard that the Ramones – much admired by and a big influence on the early Clash – were currently working with Phil Spector himself on what would become the album *End of the Century*. In

January 1980 the Ramones would have a Number 8 UK hit with their version of 'Be My Baby'. Roy Wood had recently produced the Darts' remake of Gene Chandler's 1962 hit 'Duke of Earl'. It entered the UK charts on 21 July 1979 and stayed there for the entire time the Clash were recording *London Calling*, reaching a high of Number 6.

Mick's histrionic vocal could be that of a Spectoresque diva . . . until he employs a mannered dying fall on the last line of each verse and reveals the true source of his musical inspiration. That camp vocal flourish is a trademark of Mick's long-time idol Ian Hunter, employed frequently during Mott the Hoople's glam-era heyday of 1972–4. And the ghost of Mott opens the door once more to the ghost of Wizzard. Hunter was so impressed by the sound Roy Wood achieved for Wizzard's spring 1973 UK Number 1 hit 'See My Baby Jive' that he approached him to produce the *Mott* album. Unfortunately, Wood was too busy having more hits. Mott hired the engineer Roy had worked with instead, and by the time the band recorded *The Hoople* in 1974 he was helping them recreate the Wall of Sound on tracks like 'The Golden Age of Rock'n'Roll' and 'Roll Away the Stone'. That engineer was Bill Price. 'I did loads with Roy Wood, starting with "See My Baby Jive",' he says.

The impression of unstoppable momentum established by the Wall of Sound is reinforced by the song's structure. There are no choruses. Instead there's a long verse, with so little space between vocal lines that the double-tracked Micks are audibly gasping for breath. Then there's a break for Dick Hanson to rally the troops again with his lip-bustingly high – it hits top C – military trumpet solo. 'That must have been the band's idea!' says Dick; quite possibly as a nod towards the similar piccolo interlude in the Beatles' 'Penny Lane' (1967). Then there's another long verse, with the two Micks again suffering like landed fish, before a second break, a reprise of the first verse, and an outro.

Bill thinks it likely that both Joe and Mick played piano on the track, but doesn't recall who did what and where. The obvious approach would have been to have them playing in unison all the way through. For much of the song, when they're concentrating on the main riff, the pianos are well-behaved and musical. The solo around 2:20 is contained and pithy, too. But when they start to go free-form at 2.40, and again at 3.20, both pianos sound like they're getting a good

Joe-style doing: rigid chord shapes staccato up and down the keyboard, only breaking formation to play the individual notes in the shape. The pedal remains jammed down to the metal, and then Bill adds further reverb. By the time they reach the outro, the two piannerists are out of time with each other . . . and before long, they've run out of time altogether. One of them gives up, and the other picks off stray lone notes at random.

Once more, Joe avoided being tarred with the sensitive brush by handing his lyric over to Mick Jones to sing. Mick's 'Lonesome Me', demoed at Vanilla, had failed to make the shortlist for the album, but Joe's first two lines about the 'solitary man' make a good stab at summing up its sentiment. But then, Joe also touched on other symptoms of depression in 'Lost in the Supermarket', so the mood – if not the content – of the song could again have a more directly autobiographical origin.

'The Card Cheat' throws out some obvious references, but it isn't immediately clear how they are supposed to fit together. There's fear of loneliness and death; a killing over a card game; and then some contemplation of the fates of soldiers and their loved ones. The title, the barroom location, the lost girl and the gun all evoke Jimmie Rodgers's 'Gamblin' Bar Room Blues' (1932), as covered and taken into the UK singles charts in 1975 by the Sensational Alex Harvey Band. The Rodgers song itself owes much to the badman barroom gamblin', cheatin' and killin' tradition of 'Staggerlee', so there is also a carry-over influence from 'Wrong 'Em Boyo' and 'Jimmy Jazz'. Similarly, the closing section's quick-march through the history of warfare recalls the latter stages of 'Death or Glory'.

The song's working title was 'King of Hell' – as reported by Kris Needs in his mixing party sneak preview of the album for *ZigZag* magazine – and there's a Faustian flavour to proceedings. It brings to mind the legend of bluesman Robert Johnson, bartering his soul with Satan for superior guitar-picking skills out at the crossroads. Or Charlie Daniels's country-rock crossover hit, 'The Devil Went Down to Georgia' (1979), in which Lucifer – as ever, looking for a soul to steal – gets into a fiddling contest with a hot-shot young musician who brags that he'll win . . . and, contrary to the usual moral of this type of tale, does. But Joe's Gambler isn't gambling for his soul with the Devil, he's gambling for his life with Death.

Gambling was prohibited by the Church in the early fourteenth century, so during the period when the *Danse Macabre* illustrations were in regular circulation, gamblers were portrayed as being doubly unfortunate: both the Devil and Death had a vested interest in their lives. Or rather, the end of their lives. An illustration known as *The Gambler* and attributed to Hans Holbein the Younger (though possibly not by his hand) is as slyly humorous as it is grim: Death and the Devil scrap between themselves over the rights to one of three card players, Death holding the card player by his throat and the Devil holding him by his hair. Another of the card players is either pleading for his companion's life or having the temerity to attempt to intervene physically. The third appears to be taking advantage of the confusion to scoop the money off the table.

Former art-school student Joe was possibly aware of Holbein, but as a long-time film buff, he was definitely aware of Ingmar Bergman's classic 1957 film *The Seventh Seal*. The movie takes its inspiration from the *Danse Macabre* and its title from the biblical Book of Revelation's prophecy of the End of Days, when – among other manna for numerologists – the Seven Seals will be opened and the Four Horsemen, chief among them Death, will ride. The film follows a medieval knight returning from the Crusades to find his homeland stricken by the Plague. Death, in whiteface and a cowl, comes for the Knight, too. In one of the most parodied scenes in movie history – Bergman fan Woody Allen being among the perpetrators – the Knight challenges Death to a game of chess for his life. He even brags that he'll win, but is tricked into revealing his strategy, and is ultimately led away with his family and followers in an animated *Danse Macabre*. He has, however, succeeded in playing for time, and meets his end with a better understanding of himself. (He also appears to have distracted Death long enough to allow others to escape.) The moral is that nobody *beats* Death. It's about how you play the game.

In 'The Card Cheat' the Gambler is alone, contemplating his mortality. Resolving to cheat to buy more time, he hides from the reality of his situation with the help of drink and drugs. During the game, he smiles as he lays down the card he's hidden up his sleeve, and 'wins'. But after hubris, nemesis: he's identified as a cheat by the dealer, humiliated, and executed. Next there comes a seemingly random jump-cut from Gambler to Soldier – though, of course,

Bergman's Knight was both – with Joe rapidly ticking his way through the Hundred Years War, the Crimean War, the weapons of the ages, and all the Death or Glory Boys that have wielded them, before . . . well, then it all gets a bit vague.

The last couplet is confused, with the phrase 'your lover' required to function as both the last two words of the penultimate line and the first two words of the final line. Both syntax and sense fall apart. After the preceding musical and lyrical build-up, it's more of an anticlimax than a conclusion, an impression reinforced by the slow-motion crumbling of the Wall of Sound shortly afterwards. There's a death, and a thought is spared for the rose back home. Although hard to squeeze literal sense out of, the moral appears to be something like: it's not about how you die, but how you carried yourself and treated others while you were alive. So, very much like *The Seventh Seal*.

'The keeper of time' alluded to in the third line is Death's hour-glass. An almost Revelations-like lyrical milieu is established, where any phrase could have symbolic significance. The allusion to opium dens and barroom gin would seem to date the action to somewhere around the 1870s, which fits in with the Wild West gambler feel . . . but both kinds of establishment were as common in New York or even London as they were in San Francisco. Why mention opium at all, other than to again draw attention to the heroin plague via which so many of Joe's 1979 contemporaries were choosing to gamble with Death? The card that seals the Gambler's fate is the King of Spades. It has no particular association with bad luck in card games, other than being black and being a card with an unstated value of 13 in poker. It's traditionally associated with the biblical King David, who was a righteous rather than an evil king. In card-reading using a conventional deck rather than a Tarot deck – Joe dabbled with the New Age for several years before giving up such unworldly concerns for punk – it's the *Ace* of Spades that is known as the Death Card . . . (Hence Motörhead's 1980 hit 'Ace of Spades'.) Given that the working title of the Clash song was '*King* of Hell', Joe may have been intent on establishing his own personal death-card symbol. The working title also raises the possibility that the king the soldiers serve in the closing lines of the song is the King of Hell himself.

The Clash's comments about the song in *The Armagideon Times* concern its recording rather than the song itself, but that's under-standable when a band records a song about Death on a night when Death is so conspicuously busy. Joe dedicated 'The Card Cheat' to 'those in peril on the sea', and Mick elaborated on the size of the waves, 'a gigantic 25 foot the night this tune was cut'. The weather along the coast had been wild all year, and on 14 August 1979, as the Fastnet Yacht Race crossed the Irish Sea, a freak storm capsized numerous boats and killed 15 participants.

'Lover's Rock'

On 6 September 1974 the 101ers turned up to play their very first gig as support to London reggae band Matumbi at the Telegraph pub on Brixton Hill. Naïvely, Joe Strummer's band had just assumed it would be OK to borrow the headliners' equipment. Although Matumbi's van broke down, causing them to arrive two hours late, they were generous enough to agree. 'I've always supported Matumbi ever since,' Joe told *Melody Maker*'s Paolo Hewitt in 1980.

Matumbi guitarist and core member Dennis Bovell had a career worth keeping an eye on. Born in Barbados, rather than Jamaica, and raised in London, he was anything but a reggae purist, keeping his mind open to all kinds of music. Matumbi were one of the first of the British gigging reggae bands. In addition to writing and playing their own material, they acted as a pick-up outfit for visiting Jamaican singers, and quickly learned to play pretty much everything. A dub enthusiast, Dennis also ran his own London-based sound system, Jah Sufferer Hi-Fi, which allowed him to see what worked on the dance floor. As soon as he could, he seized the opportunity to sit in the producer's chair. He released largely instrumental dub albums under aliases The 4th Street Orchestra and Blackbeard, and provided the brooding backing for all Linton Kwesi Johnson's poetry'n'dub albums, beginning with 1978's *Dread Beat An' Blood* (attributed to Poet and the Roots). As a band, Matumbi could and did play roots reggae, drawing on typical Rastafarian-influenced, biblical themes, as indicated by the title of their 1978 album *Seven Seals*. But their adaptability, open-mindedness – and, happiness to earn a session fee – led to their close involvement with another, very different style of reggae.

By the mid-Seventies, the new slick, sophisticated Philadelphia and Chicago soul sounds were huge in the UK clubs, as is indicated by the fact that David Bowie borrowed heavily from the former for his *Young Americans* album (1975). While heavy dub and the deadly serious message of roots reggae didn't exactly make for a light-hearted and upbeat night out, American soul addressed the more everyday concerns of 'typical girls' in their early teens: love, lost love, the potential for love, and cheating lovers. UK-based reggae artists had a history of reflecting the current needs of the domestic market – some might claim cynically – going all the way back to the music's early days. So it was inevitable that British reggae movers and shakers would try to crash the new dance and tap a new market. In 1975 Sir Lloyd Coxsone recorded a 14-year-old talent-contest winner called Louisa Marks singing Robert Parker's cult soul number 'Caught You in a Lie' fused to a reggae riddim provided by Matumbi in their session band role. It proved popular enough to gain release in Jamaica. A new, UK-originated genre of reggae was born, though its name was only formalised a year later when Dennis Harris set up the Lover's Rock label as a subsidiary of Eve, specifically to release this type of music. (The incorrectly positioned apostrophe was soon dropped altogether . . . by everyone except Joe Strummer.)

Lovers rock singers tended to be young and female, like the genre's core audience, but it wasn't always necessarily so. Matumbi chanced their own arm in 1976 with 'After Tonight', but it was their huge reggae chart hit later that same year that really took their 'recognise no barriers' approach to its extremes. 'The Man in Me' was a laid-back lovers rock-style lope through a would-be seductive ballad, but that ballad was no sweet soul number. From Bob Dylan's 1970 album *New Morning*, it found Dylan deep into his easy-listening, keep-it-simple, back-to-the-country phase.

Lovers rock kept its eye on mainstream dance trends, and as the late Seventies progressed, the reggae-soul crossover inevitably gave way to reggae-disco. Althea and Donna's 'Up Town Top Ranking' isn't bona fide lovers – it's a Jamaican record, for a start, and its 'no pop . . . strictly roots' riddim had already been to the dance several times before in slightly different drag – but the fact that it is sung by a couple of clothes-conscious teenage girls contemplating a night out dancing and flirting at the disco indicates a lovers influence. As the UK market had been suitably lovers-prepped, it went to Number 1 in February 1978. A key part of its appeal is the girls' infectious high-pitched 'oh' vocal interjections, like a parody of a syndrum. Dennis Bovell came close to equalling its performance when he produced Janet Kay's reggae-disco lovers rock classic 'Silly Games'. It reached Number 2 in June 1979 . . . shortly before he went on to redefine punk-dub fusion with his hands-on production of *Cut*, the debut album by those less than typical girls, the Slits.

Matumbi's cover of 'The Man in Me' was released at a time that the Clash were keeping a close watch on the reggae charts. Being long-time Bob Dylan fans, Joe Strummer and Mick Jones were positively pre-disposed to the single. They made a demo of their version of Matumbi's version of the song at Vanilla, and this clearly led to some discussion about lovers rock as a genre: what the band were hearing when they went out to late-night clubs was a long way from the dub, roots reggae and late-Sixties rude-boy sounds they favoured. Just as UK punk was looking to militant reggae for a lyrical lead, UK reggae appeared to be leaving it behind. Joe had touched on the gulf between roots reggae and commercial pop reggae in '(White Man) In Hammersmith Palais', and made it clear that he had no time for the latter variety. In 1979, the new, relaxed Clash seemed willing to allow themselves and others a little more fun.

Musically, 'Lover's Rock' is a peculiar hybrid, a tale of two halves. For the first two minutes it's a simple but classic (mostly) three-chord trick of a tune: G, Am, D in the verses, with Am's near-relative C also thrown in for the choruses and the guitar intro and solo. The formal lyric is confined to this first half of the song: there are just three short verses, with the third verse the same as the first; and the choruses follow the same pattern. The reggae touch is so slight and slick it's hardly there. Mick Jones's crisp lead-guitar intro and solo seem beamed in from another time and place entirely: Mott the Hoople's 'All the Young Dudes' (1972) and Wings' 'Band on the Run' (1973) come to mind. The piano is Mick, too: confident playing that doubles the bass line at the turn-around. In principle, he sings falsetto backing vocals – a lovers trademark – but as he shadows Joe throughout, he's really singing joint lead. Topper's drums are panned across the stereo picture, with the ride cymbal to the left, the bass drum and snare central, and the toms to the right, ensuring that his fills on the latter stand out as real features.

Two minutes in, and the song takes a sharp turn into something completely different for the remaining two minutes: a busy Latino funk coda – D7, Bm, D7, G – married to a repetitive 'repeat to fade' refrain, plus markedly more entertaining Strummer ad-libs. Even before this coda starts, Topper has broken out the tambourine and the guiro, but when it hits its groove, he also throws on a shaker, cabasa, claves, a vibraslap and whistle for good measure. 'I might have gone for a curry when Topper did the percussion,' says Bill. 'We obviously had plenty of tracks.'

That the song is a pastiche is signalled very strongly by Joe: if *his* high-pitched 'po, po, po' vocal syndrum impression at 3:25 isn't enough to give it away, then his muttered aside in the outro makes sure: 'ridiculous innit? But that's what they call it'. It's very much like him throwing 'I'm the one that I want' into the outro of 'Capital Radio Two' as a jibe at Johns Olivia Newton and Travolta. 'We're in between the lands of reggae and disco, chopping up the borders. We're really chopping hard, because we've got that rock'n'roll power to chop with,' Joe told Dave McCullough of *Sounds* in July 1979, in defence of the *London Calling* material as a whole. It's a good metaphor, and it's pertinent to what the Clash are attempting with this particular song. But then Joe went on to say, 'We're really throwing reggae and disco over our shoulders. They've both had it.' What was he thinking? The impression he gave McCullough was that, if played by a rock band, a hybrid of reggae and disco no longer qualifies as either. How can it be possible for a band to rid the world of a type of music by playing it themselves?

'Lover's Rock' is only one of several songs on *London Calling* to flirt with disco, and several more of the tracks lean heavily on reggae. If the forms of disco and reggae have had it, why are the Clash playing them? And, in this case, at the same time? It makes no sense. Either Joe's understanding of what the Clash were doing with this song, and with the album as a whole, was way off-beam or – far more likely – when subjected to interrogation by a member of the press not immediately willing to embrace the band's new musical direction, he lost the courage of his convictions. To pay tribute to a genre of music requires understanding of and respect for that genre of music. The Clash had taken the trouble to demo their version of 'The Man in Me', and the attention to detail the band – or perhaps just Mick and

Topper – put into the music for 'Lover's Rock' is indicative of warm regard. Joe himself appears to be enjoying himself hugely with his vocal. There are varying degrees of homage, pastiche and borrowing involved in at least 15 of the 19 tracks on *London Calling*. If all of those songs were meant as sneeringly dismissive spoofs – piss-takes, mockeries – of the genres they reference, then that would make the Clash nothing more than a particularly sour-faced version of the Barron Knights. And, of course, that was not the case.

In the interests of balance: Matumbi could dish it out, too. A regular feature in their live shows at the time was their 'white man reggae spot', which involved playing a song with the accents placed firmly on the wrong beats.

In his formal lyric for the first section of the song, Joe takes a lateral approach to the concept of lovers rock. Instead of exploring one or more of the genre's romantic conventions, he consults a sex manual to offer some practical advice on making a little love: 'The Right Profile' is not the only lyric on *London Calling* to have been inspired by a recent good read. In *The Armagideon Times* Joe described 'Lover's Rock' as 'a book that we tried to concentrate into two verses'. Talking to *Melody Maker*'s Chris Bohn at the time of the album's release, Joe was more open about his source material. 'It's about the Chinese way of fucking. A lot of people in the Western Hemisphere have problems. No one really wants to talk about this kind of thing, but it's very common, especially with boys turning into men. You get some great bird and fuck it up, right? This song mainly tries to tell you how to do it properly . . .'

The Tao of Love & Sex: The Ancient Chinese Way to Ecstasy by Jolan Chang was first published in 1977, but draws upon 1,300-year-old texts. It sets out to correct some popular Western misconceptions about Eastern lovemaking, while also offering practical advice from oriental sages regarding occidental accidents and limitations. In the first verse of 'Lover's Rock', Joe's concern that the female partner is treated correctly reflects Chang's notes on 'The Role of Women and How to Observe Female Satisfaction' in his Chapter 2: 'Understanding the Tao of Loving'. The importance Joe places upon knowing the right place to kiss is a précis of Chang's Chapter 6: 'Erotic Kissing and the Tao'. The second verse's musings on failure to conserve seed and – whoops! – premature ejaculation, together with the outro's confession of nervousness, reflect Chang's Chapter 3: 'Ejaculation Control'. The second verse's otherwise cryptic mention of 'a thousand goes' relates to Chapter 4: 'A Thousand Loving Thrusts'. Chang is at pains to point out that his Tao is not Tantrism, but allows that Tantric teachings probably evolved from the same source material. Looks like Joe Strummer beat Sting to it . . . in a manner of speaking.

Joe also told Chris Bohn that the song was 'kind of, having a laugh'. That's the impression he gives in his coda ad-libs as he dismisses 'he-man theories', before misquoting the title of the Righteous Brothers' UK Number 1 'You've Lost that Lovin' Feeling' (1965) as 'you've lost that *grubby* feeling'. However, the 'kind of' reveals that behind such humorous touches, Joe has a serious point to make. And this is where the thinking behind the lyric starts to get as tangled as his explanation for the music.

True, the average young male was far less informed and considerate about female needs in 1979 than today, when such matters are regularly discussed in magazines, on TV and in sex-education classes; women are far more likely to instigate a forthright discussion about them; and sex is as likely to be on camera as in camera. So encouraging Clash fans to show some consideration for their partners was admirable, really. It was unusual – if not unprecedented – for a male rock'n'roll band in their mid-twenties to address the subject in such a way. That said . . . it's peculiar enough in itself to be getting sex advice from Uncle Joe, but what weird sex advice it is: somewhere between a hippy take on ancient Eastern lore and one of (the aptly named) Dr Strangelove's essence conservation rants. And that's even before Joe jumps onto a very personal hobbyhorse and strikes out for truly uncharted territory.

In the first verse, Joe introduces an unwanted, fatherless child, the result of a woman neglecting to take the Pill. In the second, we're informed that the woman won't need to take the Pill any longer once her lover has perfected the Tao techniques. *The Tao of Love & Sex* includes much talk of conserving *ching*, and of making love a hundred times without emission, but it does not directly address contraception or unplanned pregnancy . . . or, for that matter, sex in the permissive era. This element of the lyric is entirely Joe's, and has its origins in a few lines scrawled to one side of the page in an early notebook draft for 'London Calling': 'why, when it is man who is ill . . . does woman take the Pill?' Joe expounded on his theme when explaining 'Lover's Rock' to Chris Bohn. 'It's about how you can have a good time without her either having to take the Pill or have a baby. The Pill leads to dreadful depressions with some girls. Taking the Pill every day, sometimes getting fat and they don't know why, and that makes them feel worse . . . Anyway, that's why I wrote the song, even though it's a bit of a touchy subject. I don't agree with the Pill at all.'

While much of what he had to say about the Pill and depression and weight gain was true at the time, the drug came in several different varieties, and if one caused side-effects, then these could often be avoided by changing to another. For those opposed to the Pill on moral, political or long-term health grounds there were several other means of contraception available, though the 1977 song 'Protex Blue' would seem to suggest that the sheath didn't get the Clash seal of approval, either. What Joe seems to be advocating instead in 'Lover's Rock' is withdrawal. Which isn't exactly the most reliable method. And if your religion doesn't forbid contraception, or if you have no religion at all, then it's hardly forward-thinking to put your faith or lack of it in a combination of squeezing, stopping and crossing your fingers. Fine if you're a master of the Tao, perhaps; not so wise if you're still learning.

Jolan Chang was 60 when *The Tao of Love & Sex* was published. His treatise concerns itself with lovemaking in a partnership rather than on a casual basis, and as part of a disciplined and – in his own case – grimly ascetic-sounding regime. In his personal summary, Chang recounts how he typically makes love two or three times on a Sunday morning – remember, this is a thousand or so loving thrusts a go, and one emission per hundred sessions – then goes cycling for nearly the whole day, covering 20 to 30 miles, and then makes love once more before he goes to sleep. Slightly different from the weekend schedule of the average teenage or twentysomething Western male. Or, for that matter, member of the Clash. But then, Chang did live in Stockholm.

Listening to 'Lover's Rock' is not a painful experience, but the same cannot be said for contemplating the rationale behind it.

'Four Horsemen'

'Four Horsemen' was brought into Vanilla almost complete. No surprise, really, as its structure could hardly be any simpler: this is one tune that is unlikely to have kept its composer hard at work for very long. The album version has two sets of two verses with just two chords apiece, A and D; a bridge section between these sections which adds a third chord, G, to make the trick; and an outro section swinging between E and D. Four chords in total. The bridge section and outro are not complex additions, then, but the way they spin off from the verses implies that they developed from a group effort to jam what must surely have been a Joe Strummer sketch out into something less immediately predictable. This theory is supported by the demo preserved on *The Vanilla Tapes*: although the rest of the song is very much as it would appear on the album, the outro section is different, with distorted guitar and drums briefly recalling the Velvet Underground in attack mode.

Everyone taking part in the album version manages to serve the needs of the song by generating power and momentum while also finding time to showboat. Mick Jones tends to be modest about his own contributions and save his praise for others, so when he offered the opinion in *The Armagideon Times* that the piano makes this tune, it confirmed that Joe plays it. He does his usual Jerry Lee routine, again double-tracked, one in each channel, but – as Mick indicates – makes a better fist of it than elsewhere on the album, getting his fist in more or less the right place most of the time. For the most part, the pianos are simply there to drive the song, but are jacked up high in the mix just before the start of verse two, which ratchets up the excitement. The same dual role falls to Mick's guitars: rhythm re-inforcing the beat in the verse sections, with fretboard slides to get the heart racing, then a switch to restrained funky licks during the bridge, and finally an insane, squalling feedback duel between two lead guitars in the outro, criss-crossing each other as they run from side to side of the stereo picture. Topper counts in and pounds away during the verses, then slips into a holding pattern in the bridge section with some hammy crash cymbal work. By the outro, he's rolling around his kit like a drunken sailor, his 16ths on the snare reinforced by tambourine. The bass is standard Fifties rock'n'roll until the outro, when it locks into a highly melodic groove that dances around Joe's vocal line, and once again recalls the high-Sixties highpoints of Paul McCartney and Brian Wilson. And sounds like Mick Jones trying to add some last-minute class to proceedings.

All together, the tune manages to be both no frills rawk'n'rawl and very, very camp. 'This is not cheesy!' protests Bill Price. 'It's a punk song, arguably a bit over-produced. A simpler version would not have sounded out of place alongside "Janie Jones".' Bill, your taste and judgement are normally impeccable, but 'Four Horsemen' is not remotely punk. It's a four-cheese pizza with extra Parmesan. *A Quattro Cavalieri*. And highly enjoyable with it.

Unlike other songs on *London Calling*, 'Four Horsemen' has a lyric perfectly suited to the tune: a full-pelt gallop, followed by a pause for circling and whinnying, followed by a full-pelt gallop, followed by a pause for rearing, snorting, eye-rolling and mane-swinging. Joe shoves his tongue firmly into his cheek even before he swings himself into the saddle. The 'four horsemen' are, on one level, the Clash in fantasy cowboy mode. And, on another level, something nasty thundering out of the Book of Revelations. (Six years later, Clint Eastwood would play around with much the same concept in his western *Pale Rider*.) Due to a mixture of approximate translation and the frankly woolly and hallucinatory original prose stylings of John the Revelator, it's none too clear what the Four Horsemen of the Apocalypse are supposed to represent. Only the last two are named: Famine, who rides the Black Horse, and our old friend Death, who rides the Pale. The first two riders, mounted on the White and the Red Horses, were for many years traditionally described as Conquest and War. The modern mind doesn't find it either easy or satisfactory to distinguish between Conquest and War, so it has become increasingly common for the former rider to lose his place in the posse to Pestilence. Start reading what you want into the Bible, and where will it all end? As the other three riders ultimately give way to Death, anyway, it hardly seems worth losing any sleep over.

When the Clash were on tour, Joe was known to dip into the Gideon Bibles thoughtfully provided by most hotel rooms, but he hardly needed to go back to the source: other lyrics he was writing around this time show he was familiar with apocalyptic lore. Most of the Horsemen are milling around in the chorus of 'London Calling', and

Death also raises his shiny pate in 'Death or Glory' and 'The Card Cheat'. There are strong echoes of especially the first two of these songs in 'Four Horsemen'. Like 'London Calling', the song promotes self-motivation and getting involved, and like the outro to 'Death or Glory', it contemplates a long, lonely road with a lot of striving and struggle before the end. The difference in 'Four Horsemen' is that, instead of being voiced positively as encouragement, it is voiced negatively as a series of taunts.

The listener – addressed directly as 'you' – isn't open to adventure, isn't going to take the trip, and is going to be left wallowing in self-pity and looking pretty stupid by the boastful, unsympathetic (in both senses of the word) and egomaniacal Four Horsemen, who aren't waiting for anyone, aren't carrying any passengers, and aren't giving anything away. Except, that is, for the influence of Bo Diddley, this time lyrical rather than musical (though Bo wasn't much of a one for fussy chord changes either). A typical Bo Diddley lyric is composed of ribald insults and wild bragging, deriving (as would rap) from the Afro-American street-corner tradition of 'the dozens'. In 'Say Man' (1958) Bo and Jerome Green trade disses about each other's looks, clothes and girlfriends; in 'Who Do You Love?' Bo is so bad he wears a cobra snake for a necktie. Similarly, the Four Horsemen's stamina and dedication are manifest in their determination to outdrink, outspliff, outdrink, outlast and outdrink all challengers; and they're so bad that even hitchhikers won't accept a ride with them.

Writing about 'Four Horsemen' for *The Armagideon Times*, Mick Jones insisted, more in hope than expectation, that the song wasn't to be taken (auto)biographically. Clash roadies Johnny Green and Baker had celebrated their arrival in America for the February 1979 Pearl Harbour tour by buying cowboy hats, and Topper Headon had bought a set of spurs, which he promptly attached to his biker boots and wore as often as possible for the rest of the year – including the weekend break the Clash took from the recording sessions at Wessex to play the Ruisrock Festival in Turku, Finland on 4 August 1979. The band treated it like a smash-and-grab bank job, insisting – Bo Diddley-style – on being paid in cash upfront, playing drunk on Finnish vodka on Abba's equipment, getting drunker on super-strength Finnish beer back at the hotel – at which point Topper tried to pick a fight with a mountainous Finn – and then flying home hungover the following day to continue work on the album. It's highly likely that the band had recorded 'Four Horsemen' just before they flew out, because Ruisrock was the only occasion the Clash would ever play the song live. Joe's introduction was, 'OK, the Four Horsemen of the Apocalypse are quite tired and need a little drink . . .' More like the Four Beer Monsters of the Dipso Apocalypso. As soon as they were airborne again, Johnny opened his attaché case and began distributing rolls of used banknotes among the seven members of the touring party. 'Straight split, like after a bank raid,' he says. 'And we just laughed.' Having been written beforehand, the song couldn't have been 'about' this particular trip, but it might as well have been.

As a piece of self-mocking self-mythologising, it's hard to beat. The bragging continues all the way through to the coda. Sticking with the lager-lout theme, Joe paraphrases the current Heineken advertising slogan to declaim, 'We reach the parts that other combos cannot reach.' Right at the end he yells an ad-lib (very approximately) along the lines of 'We hate your rock and roll / We love your rocking soul.' What else would these particular Four Horsemen be interested in except another beer and another soul to steal?

Those are Joe's last words on the matter, but the punchline to the joke is Mick's musical one: the band set up the song for a big, corny guitars'n'drums finish, but exactly where the last beat of 'Four Horsemen' should be . . . comes the first beat of

'I'm Not Down'

The last of a trio of songs in which members of the Clash respond to their sense of being under siege at Vanilla and Wessex by taking it in turns to shout their defiance at the world. Following Paul Simonon's vocal turn on 'The Guns of Brixton' and Joe Strummer's on 'Death or Glory' comes that of Mick Jones on 'I'm Not Down'.

Interestingly, the version of the lyric preserved on *The Vanilla Tapes* does not feature the reversal of mood in the fourth verse that gives the song its edge. The original is just a litany of bad personal experiences, and as such is an example of the kind of self-pity that made Joe Strummer feel uncomfortable. Because Mick sings the song, and because it is so emotionally naked, the assumption – as with 'Lost in the Supermarket' – has long been that Mick wrote it. But the early draft is preserved in Joe's notebook in Joe's handwriting: in giving the song to his bandmate to sing, he was once again using him as a human shield.

The first verse of the Vanilla version is a general musing on the human condition. Or rather, the condition of the wealthy human: it takes its cue from the 'eye of a needle' proverb to wonder why rich men are unhappy. The second verse switches to the autobiographical first person, where it stays for the rest of the song, with the protagonist standing up to gangs of toughs wanting to do him harm, an experience all too familiar to most members of known punk bands during the late Seventies. In the first part of the extended bridge section, he's succumbing to the Black Dog of depression. In the second part of the bridge, he paraphrases the folk-nursery rhyme 'Rain rain go away / Come again another day' when he hopes the blues will 'maybe' leave for a while. By the third verse, he's accusing hard men of not knowing how tough life can really get. Even the chorus adds to the grief: he's been beaten up, thrown out, and humiliated. (This is authentic enough: Joe had lost part of a tooth in an altercation in the Speakeasy toilets in 1977; had been forcibly evicted from flats in the early Seventies; and life doesn't get much tougher than losing your only brother to suicide.) This compilation of woe gives the title – no matter how often it's repeated in the choruses and the outro – far too much work to do in order to redress the balance.

Joe clearly found his own lyric too much in this original state. As well as giving a couple of other lines minor tweaks, he completely rewrote two entire sections for the album version. His alteration to the second part of the bridge follows the lead of Mick's tune, which, after a pause for reflection, simply lifts off. Joe takes this cue to change his protagonist from passive victim to active survivor, who now insists he's sure he can turn things around for himself. And to illustrate it, Joe chooses what – for the Clash in this context – is a surprising but powerful image: the skyscraper. In 'Lost in the Supermarket' highrises are symbols of urban alienation and dehumanisation, in 'Koka Kola' they are symbols of uncaring corporate greed. In both instances, they're the Devil's fingers clawing at the heavens. But in 'I'm Not Down' they're portrayed instead as any recent first-time visitor to New York or Chicago sees the great buildings of the early twentieth century:

as symbols of man's ingenuity and potential; the soaring cathedrals of the modern, secular age; bright and shiny promises of a better tomorrow. Now we're really able to believe the protagonist's declaration that he's not giving up . . .

Joe's decision to rewrite the first verse was so last-minute that Mick had to re-record the vocal during the mixing sessions for the album that took place between 5 and 13 November 1979. By this time, Ray Lowry had completed the inner-sleeve lyric sheets, and headed back home to his native Lancashire, so Joe had to amend the lyric sheet himself. The changes are hardly dramatic and it's not obvious why he made them: the meaning of the verse stays much the same, and although the new wording makes more of the 'eye of a needle' reference by squeezing in a mention of Judgement Day, if anything the replacement verse is slightly more clumsy than the original, with its attempt to rhyme 'life' with 'lives', and its filler jumble of 'says' and 'days'. Both the original and the rewrite could be paraphrasing the Beatles' 'Can't Buy Me Love' (1964) when they muse on the old adage that being wealthy won't make you happy . . . though Joe does add a cynical twist when he wonders, if rich men can't be happy, what hope is there for the poor folk?

It may be that the language of the song as a whole is deliberately conversationally quotidian, with its repetitions, commonplaces, clichés and mangled syntax. (The worst offender being the adjective left hanging in 'A gang of jeering' . . . a gang of jeering *what?*) Save for the Skyscraper Bit, though, the result is that the lyric comes across as just a little . . . well, banal. The song is so out of character for Joe that it's hard to believe he wrote it. He's clearly well out of his comfort zone.

Luckily, the tune Mick came up with at home alone – and brought into Vanilla ready to go – is so irresistible that it gives the lyric a free pardon. Coming after the knuckle-draggingly primitive 'Four Horsemen', 'I'm Not Down' is arguably the most musical composition on the entire album. And it's packed with clues to Mick's trains of thought as composer and arranger. In 1965 John Lennon, who – like Joe Strummer after him – had not previously been one for wearing his heart on his sleeve, responded to a last-minute brief to write a title song for the Beatles' second movie, *Help!*, with a maudlin ballad about his increasingly precarious state of mind, its chorus repeatedly stating, 'I'm feeling down'. The song was perked up considerably by the in-studio arrangement, but was the first communiqué to emerge from inside the Beatlemania hurricane to indicate that all was not calm at its eye. There had always been a competitive edge to the Lennon-McCartney songwriting partnership, and a couple of months after John wrote 'Help!', the band went back into the studio to record a new song Paul McCartney had written for the single's B-side. An uptempo 12-bar rocker, it ought to be expressing abandon or fury, but instead 'I'm Down' is a knowingly ludicrous petulant whinge – a real foot-stamper in both senses of the phrase – intended as a good-natured send-up of the A-side.

Joe would have been aware that his title and subject matter were nodding to the Beatles single, and Mick was familiar enough with the reference points to take the hint. Like Paul McCartney's 'I'm Down', his tune moves too fast to be a ballad, but the plethora of minor chords and the number of changes do give the song the feel of McCartney at his most artful . . . and the bass in the intro is vaguely reminiscent of the Beatles' 'And I Love Her' (1964). The real giveaway bides its time to the dying seconds of the song though, when the staggered triplets under the high double-tracked lead vocal just scream 'BEATLES!'

Not that Mick was done there. If 'The Card Cheat' pays homage to the Wall of Sound, then 'I'm Not Down' pays homage to classic Sixties pop. Almost all of it. The repeated galloping descending bass run – following the shouted 'huh' in the intro, and then following each chorus – was a compositional hook beloved of the Kinks' Ray Davies. It worked so well in the band's June 1966 UK Number 1 hit single 'Sunny Afternoon' that he used it again in three follow-up singles, seeing the Kinks through to the end of 1967 with the Number 5 'Dead End Street', the Number 2 'Waterloo Sunset' and the Number 3 'Autumn Almanac'.

Recording the overdubs at Wessex, Mick borrowed an idea from yet another band of the era when he used a violin bow to play electric guitar. Eddie Phillips had pioneered this technique on the Creation's debut single 'Making Time' (1966). Mick was happy to admit his debt to Phillips, possibly because the rock guitarist most famous for using a bow (also inspired by Phillips) was Jimmy Page of those yet-to-be rehabilitated rock dinosaurs Led Zeppelin.

In his Clash biography, *Passion is a Fashion*, Pat Gilbert observed that the rising bass and guitar figure in the middle eight – after 'depression' – is reminiscent of the Jackson Five, and there are overtones of the polished, pop-soul-funk runs of 'I Want You Back' (1969): the uplift cannot be ignored. In *The Armagideon Times*, the ever self-deprecating Mick described his vocal in the bridge section as 'the Shirley Bassey bit in the middle', and it's possible to imagine him accompanying his delivery with Dame Shirley's trademark snaking arms and head tosses.

As ever, though, the Clash were not prepared to stay within even self-imposed boundaries, or be slaves to even one decade's worth of influence. The sparse, shimmering funky rhythm guitar running through the choruses is typical of a certain brand of tasteful, sophisticated, mid-to-late Seventies West Coast rock, the sort of thing that other members of the Clash would usually keep at bay with necklaces of garlic and bullets of silver. To stop it all sounding too polite, Mick roughs up the main rhythm guitar riff with plenty of fretboard squeaks. In *The Armagideon Times*, he likened his delivery of the second verse line 'in strange streets, o-ho' to the 'My Rio, Rio by the sea-o' line from the song 'Flying Down to Rio', performed by Fred Astaire in the 1933 movie of the same name. Picking up on this near-subliminal South American vibe, Topper's frantic contribution combines congas and tightly tuned tom-toms in order to add a hint of Salsa. Throughout the song, Mick and Joe's backing vocals reference soul and doo-wop as well as the Mop-Tops, and in the outro, the pair push the limits of their vocal range, and of pastiche, and of aural puns on the theme of up and down.

For such a Frankenstein's monster of a song, 'I'm Not Down' is hard to dislike. Either the Clash didn't share that opinion, or they found it too demanding to play live: after trying it out at their Notre Dame shows in early July 1979, they never performed it again.

'Revolution Rock'

To chart the origins of this song, it helps to establish something about reggae's development in the Seventies, the genre's attitude towards the recycling of tunes – known as riddims – and the nature of the relationship between Jamaican and UK reggae . . . or, to turn that around, the story of 'Revolution Rock' conveniently offers a potted history of all three. In 1959 Chris Blackwell set up Island Records in Jamaica, moving the label to London in 1962. Initially, he licensed master tapes of Jamaican ska to sell to the UK's immigrant West Indian market, but he quickly diversified. From 1964 he also licensed soul material from America via the Sue label – run by Guy Stevens – began to manage Birmingham R&B band the Spencer Davis Group, which he signed to Fontana, and started recording ska and R&B in the UK, one of his earliest efforts being Millie Small's 1964 multi-million-selling 'My Boy Lollipop' (another Fontana release).

When Chris relocated, one of the assets he brought with him to London was 24-year-old Wilfred Edwards, an established smooth-voiced balladeer known as the Nat King Cole of Jamaica. At first, he helped Chris sell records from his van, moving on to record, produce and write – at Blackwell's urging – under the more modern-sounding name Jackie Edwards. He continued to cover ballads, but his output responded to the requirements of the day, including duets with Millie Small, religious songs, soul songs, novelty songs, and even the belated rude-boy number 'Johnny Gunman'. By 1965 it was clear that the Spencer Davis Group weren't going to make it without a little help, so Jackie wrote them an R&B pop hit, 'Keep on Running', which reached Number 1 in the UK. He followed it up in 1966 with the equally successful 'Somebody Help Me'. In 1967, when Chris Blackwell switched the emphasis of Island to recording British rock bands, he and Lee Gopthal co-founded a subsidiary label called Trojan to take care of the reggae side of things. Jackie Edwards moved over there to produce and record, and remained at Trojan when it split from Island in 1972.

Also born in Jamaica, Danny Ray sang at Kingston talent shows in the early Sixties, modelling himself upon the recently departed Jackie Edwards. He too moved to the UK in 1965, where he joined the RAF. While stationed in Germany, he formed Danny Ray and the Vibrations and, after quitting the air force and returning to London, Danny Ray and the Falcons. The band were offered a recording contract by MCA. 'One of the first reggae acts they signed,' says Danny. 'I made my first records with them, but they didn't know how to market reggae. I used to appear down the Q Club on Praed Street, where all the reggae artists used to go. Jackie Edwards came down to see me working.

He went back to Lee Gopthal and said, "You've got to sign him." Them work out a deal with MCA, and Trojan sign me. That's how Jackie Edwards and I started working together.' Jackie produced, sang backing vocals, and supplied several of the songs for Danny's 1974 debut album *The Same One*.

A hiatus in the pair's relationship occurred when the original Trojan went into liquidation at the end of the year – the label was to undergo several resurrections – and Jackie moved back to Jamaica. In Kingston he found a musical climate very different to the one he had left 12 years earlier. Roots reggae was now established as the dominant style, with political, social and spiritual Rastafarian concerns now to the forefront of lyrical subject matter. As ever, Jackie began writing and recording songs that reflected the times.

One of these, 'Get Up' (aka 'Git Up'), carried in its title an echo of the 1973 Bob Marley and Peter Tosh Wailers classic 'Get Up, Stand Up'. The militant overtones of Jackie's song are so much window dressing, though. After insisting in the first verse that there will be a revolution if liberty is not forthcoming, he quickly switches his attention to what needs to be done in order to avoid such a calamity. When he sings 'get up' in the chorus, he's not urging the 'brothers' and 'sisters' he addresses to take up arms and fight for their rights, but to unite in resisting troublemakers looking for scapegoats, and to join hands in the cause of universal brother(-and-sister)-hood with Englishmen, Asians, Africans and Americans, as well as with fellow Jamaicans. Or as Jackie puts it in his introduction, 'We need love, people.' Musically, the song is both rhythmically strong and irrepressibly melodic. It runs just short of four minutes, with heavy guitar skanks dictating the rhythm, a jaunty walking piano line providing a strong countermelody throughout, and occasional bubbling organ runs.

Jackie had been doing some work for Bunny Lee and his house band the Aggrovators, but he had learned to keep his options open. 'Get Up' was recorded at Channel One studio for Sonia Pottinger's High Note label. The A-side was attributed to Jackie Edwards and the Revolutioners, with the flip side, 'Get Up Dub', attributed to the Revolutioners alone. The Revolutioners might sound like a band name made up expressly to fit the subject of the song in an attempt to make ageing crooner Jackie Edwards sound a bit more hardcore, but that wasn't the case. As with attribution, spelling tended to the casual on Jamaican record releases, and the Revolutioners were also sometimes listed as the Revolutioneers or the Revolutionaires, but were really the Revolutionaries, the established house band at Channel One, and the pre-eminent Jamaican session outfit of the day. The line-up was fairly fluid, but the core members usually included Radcliffe 'Duggy' Bryan on guitar, Ansell Collins on keyboards, and the first pairing of the soon-to-be superstar reggae rhythm section of bassist Robbie Shakespeare and drummer Lowell 'Sly' Dunbar. What was notable about the Revolutionaries in 1975–6 was that – thanks largely to a drumming innovation by Sly – they changed the sound of reggae. As open-minded to other musics as was Dennis Bovell in London, Sly and the other Revolutionaries also listened to disco and Philadelphia soul, and Sly adapted those drumming styles to fit within the reggae framework. The main difference was that he doubled up the drum pattern, while his fellow musicians continued to play at the original tempo: the tension made for a much tougher sound that became known as 'rockers'. (It's a paradox: influenced by the same music, albeit in different ways, UK reggae went soft, while Jamaican reggae went hard.)

Meanwhile, back in London, Danny Ray had teamed up with another ex-Trojan artist and producer named Sydney Crooks. Crooks was a member of Jamaican vocal group the Pioneers, whose 'Long Shot Kick De Bucket' had been a skinhead favourite, making Number 21 in the UK charts in 1969. In late 1976 they set up their own small independent reggae record company in Harlesden, north London, named Golden Age Music, with subsidiary labels Doctor and Pioneer, co-producing and releasing records across all three labels. 'They were all together, but we worked from two different areas,' says Danny. 'He was from the Pioneers, so his label was Pioneer. And Doctor come from my initials, DR, short for Doctor. The main label was Golden Age.'

Since the Sixties it had been common for Jamaican producers and record labels to record versions for flipsides, stripping off the vocals and playing around with the instrumental track by dropping instruments out and overdubbing others to form a dub, also known as a version. On other occasions, a completely 'new' release could result from having a DJ toast or chatter something related (or totally unrelated) in sentiment to the original track over the top. By the mid-Seventies, it was common to re-use riddims anything up to a decade old. Copyright didn't exist in Jamaica: a rival producer would get his studio band to replicate an already provenly successful riddim, then put something new over the top, thus halving the effort and expense of creation from scratch ... though not, it should be said, necessarily diminishing the amount of creativity involved: many such reworkings completely outshone the original. The larger labels, like Studio One, owned a large backlog of riddims, and could – and did – make even greater savings on costs by recycling – rather than re-recording – existing riddim tracks, simply overdubbing a few 'modern' instrumental touches onto the original master at the same time as the new vocal or toast. Smaller labels didn't have this luxury, but sometimes made up for it by trading riddims with other small labels.

When Jackie Edwards made a return visit to the UK in 1976, he brought 'Get Up' with him. 'Jackie would stay with me when he came to London. He gave me the track "Get Up",' says Danny. 'I thought it was a nice track, and I wrote "Revolution Rock", and we recorded the new vocal to the same original riddim at Morgan Studios.' Morgan was in Willesden, north London. Danny's 'Revolution Rock' became the first release on Doctor in late 1976, with a version on the B-side. The writing and production of both were co-credited to Ray and Edwards. Early the following year, Jackie's original 'Get Up' was given a UK release in its own right on the Golden Age label, but under the title 'Git Up', and as a B-side, quite possibly to divert attention from its shared roots with 'Revolution Rock'. Jackie returned the favour. He took Danny's 'Revolution Rock' and its version back to Sonia Pottinger in Jamaica, and she released them on a High Note single (as parts 1 and 2), attributed to Danny Ray and the Revolutioneers. Full circle!

Unsurprisingly, as it is the same recording, Danny's 'Revolution Rock' sounds exactly like Jackie's 'Get Up' musically, except it essays a dubby bit of echo around two minutes in, and fades out at three minutes and 10 seconds. Danny's lyric and title also take a number of leads from 'Get Up'. Like Jackie, Danny also addresses family members, though his are bona fide relatives rather than brothers and sisters in the struggle. And when he urges them to get off their seats, it isn't in order to rise up in the name of freedom or even universal love, it's simply in order to dance. The only kind of revolution he's extolling is the revolutionary – and irresistible – new rock that is the Revolutionaries' rockers riddim. He describes it as 'a heavy, heavy rock', and it's this, not marauding hordes, that will 'mash up the nation'. 'The lyrics came from going to the clubs and seeing what was happening, you know?' says Danny. 'All the dancing and getting wild. And at the time, the musical beat was changing. The Revolutionaries' drumming thing came in. It was a brand new beat, the rockers thing, so I tried to give it a new name: "Revolution Rock". So that's how it got started.' The title had enjoyed a previous life, too: as the name of a completely different 1973 release attributed to Big Youth and Prince Buster. The action in Ray's song takes place at a family-friendly blues party, where, to intentionally comic effect, Ray incites his mother, father and grandmother to join him on the dancefloor, and then worries that – in the heaving, exuberant crush – someone might step on his corns or burn his clothes with their cigarettes. Later, his Uncle Joe does get all his clothes burned off, but is so lost in the music that he dances on naked and regardless.

(All this talk of rock and rockers can be confusing. In the American-English popular music tradition, both the word 'rock' and the many different types of rock – soft, hard, heavy, prog and punk to name but a few – derive from rock'n'roll, and a rocker is either an uptempo song or a rock-music enthusiast. In the reggae tradition, a rock can be either an individual riddim or a sub-genre or style of music – like rock-steady, roots rock or lovers rock – and rockers is yet another sub-genre or style. 'Revolution Rock' and 'Clash City Rockers' have nothing to do with rock or rockers in the rock'n'roll senses of those words.)

In his sleevenotes for *Revolution Rock: A Clash Jukebox* Paul Simonon said he 'probably' bought 'Revolution Rock' from Dub Vendor on Ladbroke Grove. It then followed a typical path into the Clash repertoire for reggae covers: Paul played along with the record at home, learning the bass part as part of his practice routine, then ran through it in rehearsals, where, sooner or later, the rest of the band started to jam along. In *The Armagideon Times*, Topper claimed the Clash worked up the song in late 1978.

Chris Bohn's *Melody Maker* dismissal of the band's 5 July 1979 Notre Dame vocal version as 'appallingly trite, lyrically speaking' must have given the Clash cause for concern. Attractive though the title of the song inevitably was, it was clearly the riddim that initially appealed to the band: the *The Vanilla Tapes* version is an instrumental jam. Like the Danny Ray version, it is heavy on the guitar skanks, but is missing the piano and organ elements, neither instrument being available at Vanilla. Nor is any attempt made to replace these melodic hooks. Instead, more of a feature is made of Topper's drum work, and Baker – or, in this case, more likely Mick – plays the controls, adding variety to this four-minute version of the tune by dropping out various instruments from time to time and throwing in swathes of echo to achieve a primitive dub effect.

Even though a piano was available to the Clash in Wessex, they spurned the opportunity to introduce it to the album version, once again avoiding slavish imitation of the original (or rather, 'original') in favour of their own interpretation. This time the live backing track version has them jamming for no less than five and a half minutes, though most of the band gave up long before the end. 'I think the original track petered out into Topper jamming with himself,' says Bill Price. Much of what sounds like spontaneous communal musical improvisation was overdubbed, built up carefully track by track on top of Topper's original, free-spirited live drumming. The loud guitar skanks are still evident, but Mick also adds more shimmering, Space Echo-laden rhythm accents, and tasteful little lead guitar runs. It quickly becomes apparent that the Clash haven't entirely overlooked the Danny Ray version's piano countermelody . . . Paul Simonon has simply adapted it into a deliciously plump bass line. Mickey Gallagher adds organ, but instead of the flamboyant flourishes of the original, he contributes a pipey background wash with the Hammond's Leslie on full. Much more upfront are the Irish Horns: somewhere between punchy and punch-drunk, they bring a carnival atmosphere to proceedings. As does Topper's Latin percussion: the tom-toms treated to sound like timbales, the guiro, the vibraslap, the shaker, and some small bells all get a look in. We could be in Rio de Janeiro, Tijuana or Notting Hill.

Fittingly, the last two and a half minutes of the song is a hugely enjoyable cross between cabaret-style showcase for 'the boys in the band' and a dub out. (There are dub touches throughout the song, though they are subtler earlier on.) Following in the illustrious footsteps of Mike Oldfield on *Tubular Bells* (1973), Joe namechecks various instruments just before they get foregrounded for a few seconds: 'the organ play' cues Mickey Gallagher; 'get that cheesegrater going against the grain' prompts Topper to break out the cabasa, and Joe's last gasp boast, 'bongo jams a speciality' coincides with Topper's late flurry on that very instrument. Again, this makes it all sound live, but Joe has simply recorded his ad-lib vocal last so he can react to what's already there. The dub isn't quite so spontaneous as it sounds, either. 'All the dub effects on this song are calculated, literally: the number of milliseconds needs to be set up to get the particular effect,' says Bill Price. 'It's not true seat-of-the-pants real-time dub. Maybe it should have been. It sounded a tiny bit false to me just the now.' He's far too hard on himself. He picks out certain notes in the horn pattern, and sends them pinging from side to side in the channels. Echo is added to the guitars, and – right at the end – some heavy delay to Joe's vocal. Topper's drumming, meanwhile, is seat-of-the-pants and real-time, and he seems intent on proving that it is possible not only to jam alone, but also to do dub without any help from the desk. He has a real ball with his rolls, clatters, fills and breaks.

All of this party fun is in keeping with the spirit of Danny Ray's original lyric. Joe Strummer only uses part of that, though, preferring to rewrite the rest. The chorus remains much the same, except that the 'heavy, heavy rock' becomes a 'bad, bad rock', partly to avoid terminal terminology confusion, and partly to give what was previously a novelty comedy song a little more edge. The bridge section is also similar, except instead of getting up off their seats, everyone is now urged to smash up their seats. This is a reference to the Clash's track record for inciting such damage at live shows, most notably (but by no means unusually) at their 9 May 1977 gig at the Rainbow in Finsbury Park on the White Riot tour, when – after the venue management refused to remove them in order to allow standing and dancing – the first few rows of seats were demolished by fans and piled up on the stage. When Joe assures Ma and Pa that everything will be fine, he's not quite so convincing as Danny Ray.

The major reworking occurs in the verses. Such effete concerns as corns being stepped on, or clothes being spotted with fag burns, are not for Joe's protagonist, who's now pilled up and jittery, carrying a knife like Johnny Too Bad, and concerned about damage to his (porkpie?) hat, like Staggerlee. He's only got the one good eye, so he's clearly a rude boy or badman who's been around the block a few times. So the echoes of 'Rudie Can't Fail', 'Wrong 'Em Boyo' and 'The Guns of Brixton' are more than musical. But he's a comedy villain, really. When he tells the other dancers to be careful, he's still of one mind with Danny Ray's protagonist: he'd prefer it if things didn't turn nasty, because he's enjoying himself so much just dancing to the song. The cornball rhyming of his warnings betrays the influence of Paul Simon's '50 Ways to Leave Your Lover' (1975): 'careful how you slide, Clyde'.

The Clash version is as playful lyrically as it is musically, then. As ever, Joe goes off at something of a tangent with his outro ad-lib, but as it's in dub section, he's entitled to be as free-range as any toasting DJ. Firstly, the rude-boy train of thought leads him to present day Kingston, Jamaica, where the skirmishes of the rude boy days had escalated to political, party-backed, running gun battles and associated clampdowns. Joe addresses the coolest mobsters in Kingston, the modern-day rudies, and bids them to simmer down. Everything that crawls must die, he muses, before following this profundity with a gloriously surreal image straight out of left field: 'as cargo food goes rolling by'. It is, absolutely, food for thought. The mention of 'fixation street' in the last verse of the song proper seems to trigger an association with a different sort of fix, because the improvising Joe once again worries about young people who waste their talent shooting their days away: echoes here of 'Hateful' and 'London Calling' rather than '007 (Shanty Town)' and 'Guns Fever'.

After this, Joe switches from DJ to MC to shine the spotlight on the instrumentalists and sell the band – a bargain at $15 a day – as the play-anything-you-want-anywhere-you-want 'El Clash Combo'. This is a slice of self-deprecation that doubles as a boast: over the length of *London Calling*, the band have more than proved their versatility to themselves and their audience.

There's a few things to be said about Mick Jones's ingenious sequencing. Side four of the original LP was intended to consist of four pastiche songs-cum-comedy-cum-good time songs, the final three being segued together *Abbey Road*-style. The last of them is a reggae song, like the last songs on side one and side two of the album. 'Brand New Cadillac' and 'Revolution Rock' represent the two principal genres of cover version the Clash played in order to warm up for the writing and rehearsing sessions at Vanilla, which consequently helped establish the mood and direction of the whole project. It's fitting, then, that the former should follow the fanfare title track to set the direction for the album, and that the latter should soundtrack the wrap-up party at the end. (Of course, things don't quite work out that way, thanks to a last-minute dancecrasher . . .)

When David Mingay visited Vanilla in June 1979 to listen to 'Rudie Can't Fail' he also asked for some incidental music for *Rude Boy*. The Clash played him the instrumental demo version of 'Revolution Rock' and offered him that. When David came to Wessex in November to pick up the finished version of his end title song, Bill Price also ran him off an instrumental version of the re-recorded 'Revolution Rock'. 'It was very late on in production,' says David. 'We were waiting to mix the film, finally. I put "Revolution Rock" onto an opening scene of Ray [Gange]'s, like more conventional film music. It beefed up what was happening in certain places, gave a musical element to scenes that were otherwise a bit bare.' (As it lacks a lyric – which was Danny Ray's contribution – the instrumental should theoretically have been entitled 'Get Up', and credited to Jackie Edwards alone. As should the instrumental version on *The Vanilla Tapes* . . .)

The times came back around to find Jackie Edwards and Danny Ray where those two incorrigible old smoothies lived. Their preferred style had always been a prototypical lovers rock, and they seized the opportunity to record and produce in that style during the late Seventies and early Eighties. When Gregory Isaacs switched from roots to loverman material at the turn of the decade, Jackie even began to bill himself as the Original Cool Ruler. He died of a heart attack on 15 August 1992. Danny felt the loss of his friend and mentor keenly. 'We were very close friends, you know,' he says. He became house producer for the London-based Jet Star label from 2000 to the end of 2007, at which point he moved back to Jamaica. He remains pleased that the Clash gave his and Jackie's song exposure beyond the reggae market. 'When I first heard it, I thought, "Wow! What have they *done*?" you know,' he laughs. 'But after a while it grows on you.'

'Train in Vain'

Over the years, a considerable mystique has grown around the last song on *London Calling*. It wasn't listed on the original LP cover, inner sleeve or label, which encouraged many people to refer to it as a hidden extra track. This was interpreted as a typically generous gesture from the Clash, always keen to give the listener value for money. And in a way, it was. But it wasn't pre-planned. It has its origins in something else that was even more typical of the band: a chaotic, skin-of-the-teeth rush to pull a project together at the last minute.

In the 1991 *Clash On Broadway* booklet, Kosmo Vinyl told what subsequently became the accepted version of how 'Train in Vain' came to be, and came to be on the album. When the band returned to London after the Take the 5th tour, in his role as Clash PR, he entered into discussion with the *NME* – two of whose contributors were in the process of designing the album cover – about organising a promotional freebie. When *The Clash* was released in 1977, consecutive issues of the *NME* included coupons which could be cut out and sent off for a limited-edition EP including the (at the time) otherwise unavailable 'Capital Radio', the instrumental 'Listen', and excerpts from Tony Parsons's recent *NME* interview with the band. This time around, the idea floated was to attach a flexi-disc featuring a previously unreleased Clash song to the cover of the inky itself. In Kosmo's account, right at the end of the band's second stint in Wessex in early November 1979 – when they were overseeing overdubs and remixes for the album and recording 'Armagideon Time' for the official single – he started badgering the band to give him something for the flexi in time to meet the *NME*'s deadline. Which allowed the Clash just a day to deliver. Obligingly, Mick Jones wrote not just the tune but also the accompanying lyric overnight, and the rest of the band did everything required of them at Wessex the following day to ensure Kosmo had the complete track on time.

Kosmo's tale adds a double sucker-punch line to this heroic endeavour. Firstly, if he'd known the Clash had unreleased songs already in the can, like their cover of Booker T. and the MGs' 'Time is Tight', he would have just offered the *NME* one of those. Secondly, it turned out that the *NME* couldn't go ahead with the flexi-disc, anyway: their parent company IPC rejected the idea out of hand.

Having gone to all that trouble to give their fans a freebie, rather than put the song in the vault for another rainy day, the Clash decided to add it to the end of *London Calling*.

Johnny Green confirms that Mick came in wanting to start work on the song just as he and Baker were preparing to clear the Clash's equipment from Wessex Studio One: that is, after 'Armagideon Time' had been recorded, and the other tracks had been overdubbed. But it appears Kosmo may have compressed the timescale slightly for dramatic effect. Kris Needs was present for Mick's recording of the vocal for 'Train in Vain' on the evening of Sunday 11 November, and he returned the next day for the late-night – so late it was really Tuesday morning – playback of the now 19-track album. In his *ZigZag* preview of *London Calling*, he reported what he had been told by the band: that Mick first brought the song in on Saturday 10 November.

These accounts focus on the end game – which was what Kosmo, Johnny and Kris all witnessed – but apparently miss out an earlier part of the tale and the underlying machinations. According to Bill Price, 'Train in Vain' was not a wholly new composition. 'When we did "Train in Vain" for the *NME*, I seem to remember that we had done the backing track earlier, maybe under another name,' says Bill Price. 'I'm sure it was started, but not finished, before the American tour. At the time, I guess the band thought "Train in Vain" to be a pop song too far, and it was not originally scheduled to be on the album. But they were looking for something to do with it to keep Mick happy.' This was what was behind the approach to the *NME*. If Bill's memory is correct, then, in November the song was being completed, rather than started from scratch. 'It's Topper and Mick, not really the Clash,' says Bill. There was no time to teach Paul the bass part, and Joe had no interest in the song, because, as he told Chris Bohn just a month later, 'jealousy and heterosexual complaining songs' bored him.

Mick remained convinced that 'Train in Vain' was something special. Talking to Adam Sweeting in 2004 he implied the decision not to proceed with the flexi was made by the Clash themselves. 'I remember we thought, "This is a bit too good to give away on the *NME*, so we didn't." For 'we', read 'I'. Mick pushed hard for the song to be included on *London Calling*. He knew the album as it stood was a showcase for his talents as a tunesmith, versatile musician, studio arranger, and even producer – albeit not credited – but it was still dominated by

Joe Strummer to an unprecedented degree. Previously, the musical content had been shaped almost entirely by Mick, but as well as having to cede some control as a result of more democratic band approach to arrangements in Vanilla, Mick had also been required to give ground within the Strummer-Jones songwriting partnership: Joe had contributed more than usual on *London Calling*.

'London Calling' itself – the lead song, the project-defining song – was chiefly Joe's creation. When Mick advised Joe to rewrite the lyrics for that song, it was all about making it stronger. When Joe was dismissive of Mick's pop tunes and personal lyrics, a similar generosity of spirit was not evident. In rejecting 'Lonesome Me' and having next to nothing to do with 'Train in Vain', he was hardly being considerate of Mick's feelings. A case could also be made for double standards: while decrying Mick's tendency to bare his soul, Joe had cried into his pillow on 'Lost in the Supermarket' and 'I'm Not Down', and contemplated a lost love in 'Spanish Bombs'. Even if the wider public believed that Mick had written the lyrics for the first two of these, Mick knew that was not the case. He had been the main author or instigator of several lyrics on the Clash's first album, and at least one on the second. As of 10 November 1979, though, he had contributed none to their third. And even neophyte songwriter Paul Simonon had a lyric on there! More so than ever before, Mick's vocals were all over *London Calling*, but there was still none of his true *voice* on the record. 'Train in Vain' was his last chance to redress the balance.

'I watched the dynamic change. It was very fluid within the band, who called the shots,' says Johnny Green. 'I think, during *London Calling* Joe's power rose hugely. He'd been at a really low ebb with hepatitis when they were coming out of being a punk group, and Mick had taken control. And then with Bernie Rhodes going, Joe had taken a bit more of a dive. But I think *London Calling* allowed Joe – because of his creative input, and because of his energy and dynamism – to reassert himself over the band.' Nobody could have faulted Mick's commitment or work rate during the writing and recording of the album, but – as the lyric of 'Train in Vain' itself testifies – he had been unhappy and unproductive for some time before that. 'Even when his star was not in the ascendant, though, Mick would never give up,' says Johnny. 'He was not going to say, "Well, OK, Joe, you take it over for a while." In that way, Mick was tough.'

Even though tacking it on as the last track on the album pulled the rug from under the big finish offered by the closing suite of songs on side four, and even though the Clash had already pushed their record company's patience up to – and past – its limit by insisting on including 18 tracks on the album, never mind 19 . . . 'Train in Vain' was added to *London Calling*. 'In the end, Mick got his way,' says Bill Price. Mick had the last word, in more ways than one.

*

Like 'I'm Not Down' and 'Lonesome Me', 'Train in Vain' is a song that makes multiple references to the classics of an earlier era, both lyrically and musically. Former Drifters lead singer Ben E. King recorded 'Stand By Me' in summer 1961, taking it to Number 4 in the USA and Number 27 in the UK, but its roots went much deeper than that. In 1905 Charles Tindley, the self-educated son of slaves and a pastor who has been called the 'Father of Gospel', wrote a Christian hymn entitled 'Stand By Me'. Based on Psalm 23, verse 4 – 'Yea, though I walk through the valley of the shadow of death, I will fear no evil: for *thou art with me*' – it is a plea to the Lord for support and guidance in times of doubt and suffering. Registered by Tindley in 1916, it became an enduringly popular gospel song, recorded by Sister Rosetta Tharpe in 1941, and the Staples Singers in 1955, among others. In the late Fifties Sam Cooke, then the lead vocalist of gospel group the Soul Stirrers, amped up the drama in the verses by throwing in extra biblical references, and, with the group's manager, J. W. Alexander, claimed co-authorship of the resulting 'Stand By Me, Father'. The Soul Stirrers recorded it in 1960, by which time Sam Cooke had already left to go solo as a singer noted for secularising gospel songs, in the process helping to invent what became known as soul music. Ben E. King has admitted that his song was based on Cooke's. He followed Sam's example in three further ways: by addressing his new lyric to a woman rather than to God or his only begotten son; by going solo when the Drifters passed on his request to record the song; and by replacing the previous composer credits with his own name and those of his co-authors, the established rock-'n'roll songwriting team of Jerry Leiber and Mike Stoller.

In an early Sixties popular music scene dominated by Milquetoasts idealising teen romance, his amended lyric sounded remarkably adult. The inspiration of Psalm 23 is still evident: sung with gospel passion, the song considers love as mutual support and succour through bad times as well as good. If it gets dark and scary, even if the world crumbles, the protagonist can make it through so long as his partner is still with him. And vice versa. Something else that gives the song gravitas is its political subtext. There's an acknowledgement that, even by the early Sixties, the long walk from slavery to freedom was by no means over, and that a good deal more unity and resolve would be required along the way.

By 1968 it was a long time since country and R&B had had their baby and named it rock'n'roll, and they had pretty much D-I-V-O-R-C-E-D and gone their separate ways. But Tammy Wynette had grown up picking cotton and singing gospel, and mainstream country kept its commercial hat on and at least one eye open. The provenly popular sentiment of Ben E. King's hit had at least a subliminal influence on 'Stand By Your Man', the song Wynette co-wrote that year with her producer Billy Sherrill, especially where the song evokes 'cold and lonely' nights. While the support King advocates is anything from two-way to universal, though, Wynette's would appear to be all one-way. No matter how much your man lets you down or betrays you, she advises, forgive him, stick by him, comfort, love and support him, because, 'after all, he's just a man'. Released as a single in the USA, it reached Number 1 in the country charts and then crossed over into the mainstream chart. The album of the same name went Platinum and Tammy Wynette became a country superstar.

In the wider world, though, response was mixed. 1967 had been the year of free love, dropping out and turning on, and 1968 itself was the year of fighting in the streets and Valerie Solanas's Society for Cutting Up Men (SCUM). The values expressed in Wynette's song might have been comforting to those who had been brought up in a world where it was traditional for women to suffer and make sacrifices, but to anyone at the cutting edge of popular culture – and the particularly edgy section where the cutting up of men was done – they were either hilariously or annoyingly reactionary. Such people overlooked the implied gentle humour of Wynette's line 'after all, he's just a man': look after him because, after all, he's just a big baby. Solanas might have been an extreme example – the Anti-Tammy – but feminists would continue to dismiss Wynette as the worst kind of role model for the rest of her life. Not least because of the longevity of 'Stand By Your Man': her original version made it to Number 1 in the UK in 1975, some seven years after its initial release, by which time feminism was no longer the preserve of a radical fringe.

In 1979 the Slits' brand of feminism was muddy enough in its ideology to allow them to strip naked and plaster themselves in yet more mud for the cover of their debut album *Cut*, but it was clear enough to inspire the oddball but irresistable avant-punk-dub composition 'Typical Girls'. Although attributed to the band as a whole, the lyric is by guitarist Viv Albertine. The titular girls worry about clothes, spots, fat and smells, and conform to one of two stereotypes: either they're 'femme fatales', that is, unapproachable goddesses, a reference to the Velvet Underground song of that title; or they're downtrodden drudges who 'stand by their man', a reference – of course – to the Tammy Wynette song. The pay-off line is that the typical girl ends up with the typical boy. Viv and the Slits leave the listener in no doubt about their lack of interest in netting themselves one of those.

Whether or not he considered himself a typical boy, 'Typical Girls' must have made for tough listening for Mick Jones when it was released as a single in September 1979. Mick and Viv had become friendly at Viv's Davis Road squat in early 1976, when the personnel for the Clash were being assembled, and, much like Palmolive, she was inspired to learn an instrument and rehearse with other people in and around the squat, including Keith Levene and Sid Vicious. As the punk movement's identity came into sharper focus over the coming months, it revealed itself to be very much down on love and long-term or monogamous relationships. In this, it took its lead from Johnny Rotten's infamous 1976 dismissal of love as 'two minutes of squelching noises'. (Within a year, Rotten was involved with Nora Forster, the mother of Slits vocalist Ari Up, a relationship which has now survived for more than 30 years.)

The pressures of being in two different high-profile bands with rarely synchronised commitments would have made life difficult enough for Mick and Viv even if they hadn't been part of a scene with such highly charged sexual politics. She moved into 5 Simon Close with him in spring 1979, but the relationship ended over the summer. 'Mick used to cry and cry about Viv,' says Johnny Green.

'She really was quite hard on him. He rarely behaved like that with other women. He played the rock star normally, but with Viv, no. It's the only time I've ever seen him like that. She broke his heart. He was in love with her.'

Cut was the distillation of more than two years' work, and upon its release in September, it revealed Viv's songwriting speciality to be spiky lyrics inspired by the people she had been close to during that period: 'Instant Hit', about a boy who takes heroin because he's 'set to self-destruct', concerns Keith Levene; and 'So Tough' developed from a phone conversation she had with Johnny Rotten about Sid Vicious. Side two of *Cut* begins with a three-song suite of anti-love songs which ends with 'Typical Girls'. In the middle comes the sardonic 'Love und Romance', fluffy (male) sentiments wrapped around vicious threats. First, though, is Viv's 'Ping Pong Affair', a song in which the protagonist leaves her boyfriend sulking in his room, walks back down Ladbroke Grove alone, says that he can have his comics and records back, goes out to have fun without him . . . and doesn't miss him while the next six months pass. Who could this mystery man be?

Although it was not Viv's intention to be vindictive, her contributions to the *Cut* anti-love song triptych amounted to a rejection of both the romantic ideal and of the person who had hoped to share it with her. 1979 had already been trying enough for Mick Jones. His possessions were stolen from the Pembridge Villas pad he shared with Tony James in February – while Mick was on the Pearl Harbour tour of the US with the Clash, and Tony was in the *Top of the Pops* studio with Generation X – an event which, together with the ongoing financial problems following on from the sacking of Bernie Rhodes, resulted in Mick's temporarily moving back into the tiny second bedroom in his Nan's high-rise council flat. In April, Caroline Coon found him Simon Close, but evidently his month back at square one had been hard on him. The other members of the Clash took their partners along for the Take the 5th tour of the US in September 1979, but Mick went on his own. 'The Clash is everything to me. I have nothing else,' he told the *NME*'s Paul Morley at the time. 'I'm under the impression that I have given up everything else for it. I'm under the impression that I have lost everything: home, personal life, everything. So my dilemma in a way is that I resent the Clash.' This rare interview lapse into Suffering Artist Syndrome came less than two months before he completed 'Train in Vain'.

The song begins with the line, 'You say you stand by your man . . .' – a misreading of 'Typical Girls', which says the exact opposite – and its oft-repeated chorus is, 'You didn't stand by me.' Lyrically, then, Mick follows the chain of references back to Tammy Wynette and Ben E. King's songs, and offers a negative echo of both: the walls crumble, and he can't be happy or keep 'the wolves at bay' without the woman's love and support. In the third verse he goes on to detail his other tribulations – a job that doesn't pay, no home to call his own – but these pale in comparison to being dumped. Throughout, the spurned lover fixates on details from the break-up conversation(s), questions the truth of declarations of love made in happier times, feels sorry for himself, resigns himself to rejection, then comes back with more accusations, wheedles, and demands: 'you *must* explain!' In short, he sulks in his room.

The lyrics are unpolished to the extent that three consecutive lines in the third verse start with 'but', and the heavily recycled chorus piles up the negatives, tying itself up in nos and didn'ts as well as nots. Wounded, raw, repetitive and pouting, it's an all too painfully accurate encapsulation of a post break-up 'air-clearing conversation': the kind of post mortem that the dumpee needs to have, but the dumper would do anything to avoid. As would the dumpee's best friends, let alone members of the general public. As the self-mocking Mick wrote in *The Armagideon Times*, 'Oh the misery of it all!'

'Train in Vain' isn't the first song about lost love on *London Calling* – or, for that matter, even the first song about losing one of the Slits on *London Calling* – but it is the most naked and direct. The Clash had already chosen to ignore many of the Commandments of Punk in making the album, but defying the edict Thou Shalt Not Sing Blatant Broken-Hearted Love Songs was the boldest and most defiant move yet, and proof, if any more were needed, that Mick Jones was no longer prepared to be shamed out of displaying his emotions – or dictated to in any way – whether it be by Johnny Rotten, Bernie Rhodes or Joe Strummer.

Had Mick presented the song as a haunting and fey acoustic ballad, he would likely have found himself sitting outside Wessex's front door wearing his guitar for a hat. Luckily, the tune to which he attached his lyric saves the day: in this case, a cocky, uptempo strut which prevents the song coming over as too self-indulgent. The most distinctive feature is the clean, crisp, almost percussive guitar riff: 'spring reverb on the Roland Space Echo' according to Bill Price. Some of the other instrumentation choices might have been dictated by the limited time available: the Irish Horns weren't around for the November sessions, and Mickey Gallagher had packed up and gone home by this stage, too. In the absence of a brass section, Mick chugs along under his guitar line with a shimmering secondary harmonica riff. Topper further fattens out the sound with a shaker, and gets a handclap sound out of his drums. Mick adds an occasional piano figure for emphasis. All these elements, plus the bass, are mixed so well that each can be heard clearly and distinctly, and yet they blend perfectly into an irresistible groove.

Overall, the style is familiar, but has proven difficult to pin down. This is partly because, as music theorist Patrick Clark explains, Mick has written the song in the key of A, but hasn't established that fact by using E, the dominant chord. Again, this makes the tune modal, this time Ionic mode. In his *London Calling* album review for *Sounds*, Garry Bushell thought it sounded 'like the Stones bash through an early Tamla number', and that's not a million miles away: in 1965 the Rolling Stones' transitional second album caught them applying their twin-guitar-plus-harmonica R&B style to a selection of recent soul hits by Solomon Burke, Irma Thomas, Otis Redding and the Drifters. Circa 2008 an anonymous contributor to Wikipedia claimed the guitar riff owed much to that of American soul belter J. J. Jackson's 1966 US Number 22 hit 'But It's Alright': it is similar, but not a straight lift. The combination of scorned lover lyric and uptempo pop also vaguely recalls Fleetwood Mac's 'Second Hand News' (1977). Then, in the closing few seconds of the song, a series of elongated harmonica trills brings to mind Pete Townshend's synthesiser work in 'Baba O'Riley' (1971). And the way Mick sings 'explai-ai-ain' and 'lie-ie-ie' is, yet again, very early Beatles . . . in the latter case – more precisely – very 'Tell Me Why' (1964). Not for the first time, Mick's tune and arrangement run the gamut of styles and throw their arms around the entire Canon.

Given the chorus, the obvious title for the song would have been 'Stand By Me', but that would have been too tellingly unoriginal. In the end, Mick let the rhythm provide the name – the illustration with which he accompanies his notes on the song in *The Armagideon Times* shows a harmonica with wheels and a smoke-stack attached running down a train track – and ended up with a (presumably intentional) reference to yet another inspirational source: for their 1969 album, *Let It Bleed*, the Rolling Stones covered the 1937 Robert Johnson blues 'Love in Vain', in which the protagonist carries the suitcase of his former lover to the station, and stands there distraught, watching as the train takes her out of his life for ever.

In his *Rolling Stone* review, Tom Carson recognised the connection *London Calling* as a whole made between personal feelings and events in the wider world, and thought this made 'Train in Vain' an appropriate finale. (Looking back today, though, Tom says that theory might have had something to do with the fact that his girlfriend had just broken up with him.) Although its inclusion ruined the original planned finale for the album, it does set up another neat balance: following the introductory title track, the first song is a car song, in which a strong woman drives out of a man's life; and the last song is a train song in which another strong woman blows town and leaves her former partner licking his wounds.

Epic, the Clash's American label, were glad the song was included on the album. The title track was not really designed to appeal to the American market. Lost love is a universal theme, however, and the multiple references to the familiar music of yore on Mick's late addition made it the perfect choice for the American single. The only problem was that potentially confusing title. So it was released in the USA as 'Train in Vain (Stand By Me)'.

Joe would continue to make it clear that 'Train in Vain' was not his cup of tea. Even on the live performance video of the song shot by Don Letts, he announces that the Soul Train is about to leave from Platform 1, and 'if you don't want to come, there's always the toilets'. Again, Mick laughed last: the single made the Top 30, and helped break the Clash in America.

ound in the supermarket: the Clash check it out.

oing the right thing: the Clash headline the Southall Defence Fund
how at the Rainbow, Finsbury Park, July 14, 1979.

Working against the Clampdown: note hazard warning signs.

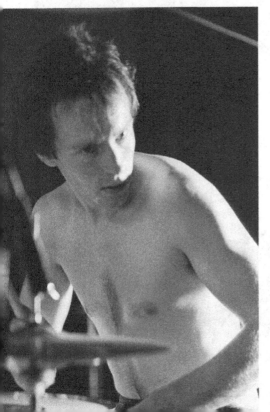

Death or Glory: The 17th Lancers cap badge and 5th Column's Take the 5th Tour T-shirt, 1979.

Four Horsemen: Topper Headon with the spurs to prove it.

Mick Jones with Clash PR Kosmo Vinyl and, in the background, cartoonist Ray Lowry, September 1979.

Tuning up, watched by Mickey Gallagher, second left, on the American leg of the 16 Tons tour, March 1980.

his bass has minutes to live.
he Palladium, New York, September 21, 1979.

The Rock And Roll
Hall Of Fame, 2006

Full circle: *Elvis Presley*, 1956;
"Have You Heard the News?"

HAVE YOU HEARD THE NEWS?
THERE'S GOOD ROCKING TONIGHT!!

Atlanta, Georgia
I forgot to mention Philadelphias' mutants – more disturbing looking people than even Liverpool or Warrington can boast. People with noses in their ears and hands growing out of the sides of their legs. Faces like a handful of stones set in dripping. Heads like hairy jellies and flaming complexions like sunset over the parrafin beds. Walking potatoes like pillows stuffed down the disappeared and gorgonzola hole where their heads there's a metal statue of a smeared all over them. These people ostentatiously giant clothes peg that all that was left behind and the Clash bus clogged on to Montreal and Toronto, visible enthusiasm displayed and 26th September. The the first serious gobbing aspired to the level of a after a touching request of this tour, although distance throat-clearing in England and this meant the audience invaded the from Joe, the long – the set and at the O'Keefe ended. On both nights about twenty or thirty stage at the end of seats died. That's New Pop. Centre in Toronto.
THIS IS AN AMAZING TOUR – Rope' as the first official The Americans had 'Give em Enough album release. (Although The Clash is said to have sold in vast quantities

Ray Lowry's *NME* dispatch
from the Take the 5th tour,
October 1, 1979.

An early Lowry sketch for the
London Calling sleeve; Elvis Presley
presents the Clash, December 1979.

High tide, hard rain, bitter cold: shooting the *London Calling* video, Royal Festival Pier, Battersea Park, December 1979.

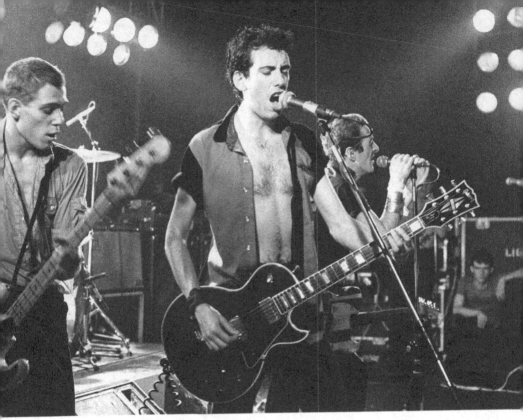

A spiritual homecoming and (almost) the end of the 16 Tons tour and the London Calling campaign: the Clash at the Hammersmith Palais, June 17, 1980.

'Armagideon Time'

'Justice Tonight' / 'Kick It Over'

'Train in Vain' is considered part of *London Calling*, despite being finished over two months after the rest of the album was recorded. 'Armagideon Time' was not included on the album, but was performed throughout the Take the 5th tour, and recorded during the same sessions as 'Train in Vain' – and completed the week before – with the express purpose of being twinned with 'London Calling' on the UK single release.

The Clash liked to warm up by playing cover versions, and they liked to add a completely new song – often a cover – to their set for each tour. When they left London on 4 September 1979 they were travelling with some recently acquired sounds, one of them being the single 'Armagideon Time' by Wilbert 'Willi' Williams (although usually credited on record covers and sleeves as Willie, he prefers Willi). On 8 September, the day they were due to play the Tribal Stomp festival, they put the record on the Cannery Row rehearsal-room deck and started playing along. When the record stopped, they kept going.

The Clash included the song in their set that same afternoon, and continued to play it every night for the rest of the tour. It quickly became the band's live reggae number of choice, habitually played as the first encore, where it asserted itself as one of the set's showcase numbers. By the end of the tour, the song was well and truly played in, and the band were keen to put their version on record while it was still 'current'.

As the Clash were aware, though, the tune was at least 11 years old, making it roughly the same vintage as the Rulers' 'Wrong Emboyo'. It was first recorded as an instrumental in the same studio as the Rulers' early material, the Jamaica Recording Studio at 13 Brentford Road, Kingston, more commonly known as Studio One, with production credited to the studio's owner Clement 'Coxsone' Dodd. Typically, no two accounts about this instrumental's origins are the same. Some call it 'Real Rock', some 'Reel Rock'. Some name the band responsible the Soul Vendors, some Sound Dimension. Some say it was first released in 1967, some in 1968.

The original single was released on Dodd's Coxsone label, and according to Al Campbell (whose song 'Don't Run Away' was on the flipside) the year was 1967. On that original single the band was credited as the Soul Vendors, and the tune listed as 'Reel Rock'. It was only on a later release of this same original tune, this time on Dodd's Studio One label, that the band was listed as Sound Demension [*sic*] and the track listed as 'Real Rock'. Though either one of the two title options could have been a spelling mistake . . .

To a degree, the confusion over the performer credit is moot. These were not different groups, just different names Coxsone Dodd used for the same house band at different times. But that doesn't make the band members on the day any easier to identify: the Soul Vendors / Sound Dimension drew upon the same core players, one or two of whom changed during this period; and on any given day, if a core player were absent, he would be substituted by whoever else happened to be hanging around. As Studio One was *the* studio at the time, a lot of hopeful musicians hung around. Two band members are certain, though. One is keyboard player Donat Roy 'Jackie' Mittoo. A musical prodigy, Jackie had formerly been involved with the Skatellites. Still only 20 years old in 1967, he was the proud owner of one of the first Hammond B-3 organs in Jamaica, and was the musical director for the Studio One sessions. Jackie not only arranged the songs, he often originated the tunes, too. And in the absence of Coxsone, he acted as de facto producer from the studio floor. The other musician who was definitely present was Vin Gordon, the even younger trombonist.

What they recorded was a simple but catchy tune with several instantly recognisable key elements, aside from the drums and skanking guitar: a stop-start bubbling bass line, an almost scattershot piano figure, an occasional three-note rising organ flourish, all of which serve the strident trombone riff: the trombone is the featured instrument, and the only one to solo (though the piano and organ take it in turns to get a little pushier towards the end).

Vin Gordon casts his memory back 40 years to give his version of events. 'It was Soul Vendors and "Real Rock": R-E-A-L, not R-E-E-L,' he says. 'I would say it was recorded late 1967. You have Patrick McDonald on guitar. A guy called Wallis on bass: I don't know his second name. Phil Callender on drums. A guy called Denzil Laing play percussion. Jackie Mittoo play organ and piano at the same time, left hand and right hand. I play trombone, and that is the second solo

I ever did.' Reports have it that the track was a jam, recorded quickly at the end of an afternoon session to make up the day's quota of material. 'It was recorded in the morning, early in the morning, starting off the day,' says Vin. 'And it was something written. I wrote out them little notes, them simple little notes, and Jackie put the chords to it. It was my melody. I wrote it out. He arrange the bass line and put the chords to it. It was a simple song, just B flat to A flat. We didn't dub it, it was live, recorded to 2-track. We took maybe two takes.' Vin has previously said that Jackie came up with the main trombone part, and he just devised his own solo. Determining and achieving due credit and payment for songwriting contributions is not always easy in America and the UK. In Jamaica, it is nigh on impossible. True author- ship was ignored or flouted for many years, and in the case of many popular songs or riddims is now hotly disputed by all who were involved and are still alive. 'Real Rock' is reputed to be the most recy- cled riddim in the history of Jamaican music.

That many of the key players are now dead is just the first of the problems. Another is that Coxsone paid Jackie Mittoo a salary to run recording sessions and to originate three new riddims per week. Because he'd paid a flat fee for these, Coxsone felt that entitled him to claim co-authorship with Jackie for the original Studio One single of 'Real Rock'. Thereafter, Coxsone owned and controlled the use of the master, and was consequently able to attribute authorship of later releases on the Coxsone label to C. Dodd and Sound Dimension. 'Coxsone wasn't even there!' laughs Vin Gordon. 'He was never in the studio when all these songs written. It was recorded by a guy called [Sylvan] Morris. He was the engineer.' And because Coxsone was not there, he neither knew (nor cared) who did contribute to the writing. 'I don't make nothing from it,' says Vin. 'I was too young.' Asked if he thinks Jackie Mittoo deserves credit, he replies, 'Of course! Jackie deserves a lot of credit for what he did. And because he made me play that, he made me do my thing.' The fine detail could be argued about for evermore, but . . . it's a Jackie Mittoo tune.

The recycling of old riddims – known in Jamaica as 'licking over' – only really got going in the early Seventies. Augustus Pablo was among the first producers to work with 'Real Rock', and one of his several versions, 'Corner Crew Dub', is included on the best-known dub album of all time, *King Tubby's Meets Rockers Uptown* (1976). Among the many artists and producers involved in licking it over between 1973 and 1979 are Hugh Mundell, Dillinger, Lee 'Scratch' Perry, Tapper Zukie, Joe Gibbs, Horace Andy, Dennis Brown, Trinity and Junior Murvin.

1979 was the year of the predominantly DJ-led 'rub-a-dub style'. Coxsone Dodd had relocated to New York by this time, but still made return trips to Jamaica, and kept both Studio One and his labels Studio One and Coxsone going, the latter now boasting a New York address. Anxious not to get left behind by the rampant exploitation of his assets, he gave DJ duo Michigan & Smiley a bunch of Studio One riddims to work with. Inevitably, 'Real Rock' was the foundation for one of their biggest tracks, 'Nice Up the Dance', included on their genre-defining album *Rub-A-Dub Style*. 'Real Rock' was now so far to the forefront on the reggae-buying public's consciousness that it begat strings of answer-records and other cash-ins, including at least another 10 more Jamaican hits during 1979 alone.

Willi Williams had voiced his first songs for Studio One in 1968, after being introduced to Coxsone Dodd by Bob Andy, but had then gone on to produce for himself in a low-key way. In 1975 he emigrated to Toronto, Canada, where he soon became friendly with fellow émigré Jackie Mittoo, who had been resident there since the end of the Sixties, running a record outlet for Studio One. Willi joined Jackie's band to play funk and soul on the local hotel circuit. 'We helped Coxsone launch his business in New York, Jackie Mittoo and myself,' says Willi. 'We used to go with him to the different stores, take him around, help do things.' A by-product of this was that Dodd arranged for Willi to record some reggae tracks at Studio One next time he was in Jamaica, with a view to releasing an album.

Over several visits and several months from late 1978 to mid-1979, Williams cut between 20 and 25 songs at Studio One. Dodd was still anxious to get more mileage out of the studio's old riddims, and made them available for Willi to version. 'I had the option of doing whatever I wanted to do,' he says. 'Some of the riddims were made on the spot, but we also used some of those that were already there. To be frank and to be honest, "Armagideon Time" was the last song I did for the album.' He used the 'Real Rock' riddim. 'You had Junior Murvin with "Cool Out Son",' says Willi. 'Joe Gibbs had done it over the riddim. This is the reason I personally wanted to do the song, because

I thought we could do something that was – not necessarily better – but equally good in competition. You had two songs on the riddim at the time, and "Armagideon Time" was the more popular one.'

It wasn't just a case of adding a new vocal. Recording standards and sound-system expectations had moved on a long way from the 2-track live-in-the-studio days of 'Real Rock'. Very much in the manner of the Clash re-recording the live tracks in the studio for *Rude Boy*, the 2-track was transferred to the modern multi-track, and additional instruments overdubbed in a more contemporary style. 'We added some other little stuff, you know,' says Willi. 'There were new instruments, because we had musicians there. There was Horsemouth Wallace on drums, Bagga Walker on bass . . . these were people who were working there at the time, because you know Studio One always have an entourage of musicians. Horsemouth use the syndrum. Me and Jackie introduce Coxsone to the syndrum in New York, because it was a new thing in the music business at the time, and Horsemouth was very thrilled.'

Reggae artists of the Rastafarian faith who recorded roots or conscious music in the mid-to-late Seventies had a tendency to portentous sermonising, and saw Jamaica's trouble and strife as a result of the corrupt and materialistic society that they dismissingly referred to as Babylon. While other Judeo-Christian religions, with varying degrees of literal-mindedness, see the apocalyptic events detailed in the Book of Revelations as future happenings, the Rastafarian faithful believed the Last Battle between God and the Devil had already been engaged. In scriptural writings, this battle is known as Armageddon, after Megiddo, the mountain in the Holy Land where it is supposed to take place; probably because it was the scene of an earlier major world-changing conflict, the Egyptian victory over the Canaanites circa 1457 BC. The Rasta belief that Armageddon was present tense became ever more powerful around the end of 1974, when Emperor Haile Selassie of Ethiopia, the Rastafarian living God, was overthrown in a coup, to die in suspicious circumstances the following year.

Rastafarianism has had a profound influence on Jamaican patois, with Rastas consciously revising the language in order to throw off the shackles of British colonialism. Although the intent is serious, their deconstruction of the language shows a good deal of wit and playfulness. Words and syllables considered unsatisfactorily negative are often substituted by more positive ones, and I-words are deemed to have special significance. I-ration, for example, means Creation. Punning is widespread. Even when written as Armageddon, Armageddon is pronounced Armagideon, which conflates Armageddon the battle with the biblical character of Gideon, a man of faith who fought and won another major war in the name of God, but whose name also means 'Destroyer'. And it didn't pass unnoticed that he had also given that name to Gideons International, the distributors of free bibles.

Just as riddims are recycled in reggae, so too are lyrical phrases, and again, usually without credit. Writers of roots material in the Seventies, in particular, drew heavily upon biblical texts, psalms and proverbs. But reggae artists were engaged in cut-throat competition, and also monitored and plagiarised each other's work. If a title or refrain had a particular resonance with the public, it was guaranteed to reappear in several other guises. Willi Williams must have been aware of former Wailers founder member Bunny Wailer's debut solo album *Blackheart Man*. Released on Mango in 1976, it features the song 'Armageddon' (aka 'Armagideon'), with the refrain, 'Woe de woe de woe / It's the Armagideon, taking place ina I-ration.' Two years later Winston McAnuff released the Crystal single 'Armageddon Time', with the refrain 'Them see ahead: Armagideon time, Revelation time'. 'I recorded that song for Derrick Harriott in 1978, but it was written three years before the actual recording,' claims Winston. 'You would have to ask Willi about the time he wrote his song.' Also in 1978 – the year before he worked on Willi's 'Armagideon Time' – Horsemouth Wallace released the album *Original Armageddon Dub*.

Willi didn't start with a completely blank page, then. Which is not to say that his lyric is second-hand or second-rate, just that he wasn't first with either the title or the subject matter. Bunny Wailer's lyric is weighty and wise, but tends to the dense and prolix. By comparison, Willi's is spare and repetitive, but gains considerably in power from its directness. The first two lines of each verse start with the phrase 'A lot of people', followed by examples of the deprivation, suffering and fear that will be visited upon the world's oppressed by the end of the day: they'll have no supper, they'll have to suffer, there will be no justice. At the end of the first verse, Willi shuffles Bunny's chorus line to make his own: 'The battle is getting hotter / In this I-ration, it's Armagideon'. The way he drawls the final word, sounding every one of its five syllables in sonorous, preaching Rasta style, freights it with maximum dread.

In the second verse, denied justice, the people will have to make a stand and fight for it. If they put their faith in Jah, he will guide them along the correct path. By the third verse, the tables have turned, and the 'lot of people' who will be running and hiding tonight are no longer the oppressed, but the routed former oppressors. Conclusion: downtrodden people must act to get their 'fraction': or, in the words of 'Get Up, Stand Up' – by those other two founding Wailers, Bob Marley and Peter Tosh – they need to stand up for their rights, and look for what's theirs on Earth.

'I look on the music as a very religious thing,' Willi told Ray Hurford and Colin Moore of *Small Axe* in 1983. 'To all the nations, internationally. To the conscious people worldwide. I'm very spiritual, in that I believe in a Creator who created us all. I check for the happenings, and match it with what I read biblically. I was in Jamaica when they had all the political violence going on. And I remember checking back in the scriptures and finding these things were just normal things. "Armagideon Time" was just like a song of consolation . . . Looking at the TV, you can see children, people from all walks of life, all nationalities, couldn't get anything. People are losing their hope in everything. So it was consoling them.'

'Armagideon Time' was rush-released as a single in Jamaica over the summer of 1979. It came out on the Coxsone label, backed with an 'Armagideon Version' attributed to Willie and the Sound Dimension. An extended, five-minute version of the A-side was released as a Studio One 12-inch, backed with 'Armagideon Version 1' and 'Armagideon Version 2'. At least one other version was released. 'The original cut of it was extended, it was on a Disco 45 12-inch, and it was the original mix from what we did in Studio One,' says Willi. 'But eventually they went and did other mixes according to the requests of the people who were dealing with the music. Different mixes. The newest mix is the clearer one, because the first mix was kind of waffle.' Authorship of all these versions was credited to Williams and Dodd.

Reggae releases seldom arrived in the UK in the same order they were issued in Jamaica. During 1979, though, 'Real Rock' appeared in the charts in several guises. Junior Murvin's 'Cool Out Son' showed in April, Trinity's 'Hog and Goat' in July, and Michigan and Smiley's

'Nice Up the Dance' in August. By September, Jah Thomas's 'Dance on the Corner' was making the lists, along with Willi Williams's 'Armagideon Time'. Strangely, just as reggae was about to undergo one of its periodic shifts of emphasis, away from roots and conscious music and towards lovers rock and dancehall via the rub-a-dub craze, roots was making something of a last stand, and what song could have been more appropriate to wave the flag than 'Armagideon Time'?

*

Back in February 1977, when recording their first album, the Clash had made the decision to depart from the prevailing punk orthodoxy and record a cover of Junior Murvin's 'Police & Thieves'. While their own 'White Riot' had been inspired by the 30 August 1976 riot at the Notting Hill Carnival, 'Police & Thieves' had been the bona fide sound-track to the riot: it was in heavy rotation on the Ladbroke Grove sound systems before and immediately following the outbreak of violence in response to heavy-handed policing. Paired together on *The Clash*, the punk and reggae songs were clearly two sides of the same coin. In 1979 there was no more fitting a reggae counterpart or echo to 'London Calling' than 'Armagideon Time'.

The Clash knew about the Jamaican riddim version tradition, and were quite taken with the idea. Their original plan was to travel down to Jamaica immediately following the Take the 5th tour and use the original Studio One 'Real Rock' riddim as the basis for their own take of 'Armagideon Time'. Unfortunately, permission was refused. Instead, the band decided to record their own version from scratch at Wessex.

The lyric was never going to be a straight reading. The band didn't purport to follow the Rastafarian faith. For Joe to have reproduced Willi's lyric entire would not only have gone against the grain creatively, but would also have left him open to charges of insincerity and, inevitably, cultural imperialism. While he could easily identify with Willi's portrait of the suffering multitudes, and his desire for them to stand up against the forces of oppression, Joe didn't believe in a for-real Armageddon, or in putting faith in God. In 'London Calling' he had insisted that people had to be self-reliant. So he modified and secularised the lyric to suit.

In so doing, he sacrificed Willi's delicately handled mid-song twist that turns victims into victors. Joe jumbles the 'a lot of people' lines up willy-nilly, so that the oppressed who have to do without supper or justice are the same folk who have to run and hide. Another arguably unfortunate touch is his decision to bring the title into the song, and add the word 'time' to the word 'Armagideon' at the end of each chorus. It makes it more accessible to the rock audience, but inevitably involves a change in phrasing, which in turn shifts the emphasis and diminishes the dread. Joe makes a more considered alteration when he urges his listeners not to 'praise Jahovah' but instead to 'kick it over'. And where Willi promises that Jah will offer guidance, Joe the Revelator insists that no one will: his downtrodden will not only have to stand and fight for themselves, they'll have to look within themselves for the motivation to do so. When he throws in the ad-lib, 'It's not Christmas time anymore', he's not just reminding folk that the season of goodwill to all men is over, he's questioning the efficacy of religious faith in this now very earthly battle.

'I wasn't too thrilled about the changing the lyrics, because as a creative person, I'd like to see my creation whole and not messed with,' says Willi Williams. 'It's understandable in that he isn't a Rasta. But at first, I was kind of pissed. I wanted to put a block on the thing, but then I decided for the creativity of music I would let it ride. I like the song except for the changes. Because what I was singing about, it was something that was very serious. And I didn't want it to be changed, because I want people to understand the whole fullness of the thing.'

There are three other ad-libs in Joe's version. As all three take their cue from what was happening musically, they are best discussed in that context. The Clash version of 'Armagideon Time' has much the same bass line and three-note organ figure as the Williams version and 'Real Rock'. Otherwise, it's very different. While the various elements sound separate and distinct in the original, the Clash go for something a little more integrated. Key to this is Mickey Gallagher, who – in addition to replicating Jackie Mittoo's periodic organ flourish – also produces a heavy, almost woozy, wash throughout. The two elements dropped – originally out of necessity when playing it live – are the piano and trombone riff and solo. Live, Mick had improvised substitutions on guitar when not playing the skank. Back in Wessex, Mick decided the song needed a lead riff, and that the only instrument for the job was an electric sitar. Typically, no forethought had gone into this decision, and Johnny Green spent much of Monday 5 November 1979 running around London trying to find one.

Over the course of *London Calling* Mick had been able to indulge himself by having a go at just about every other innovation of the classic pop groups of the Sixties. Why not this one, too? Influenced by Ravi Shankar, George Harrison had added sitar to the Beatles' 'Norwegian Wood' (1965), and Brian Jones followed suit on the Rolling Stones' 'Paint It Black' (1966). As acoustic sitar was a little too complicated to learn overnight, electric guitar companies like Danelectro saw an opportunity to produce an electric version of the instrument that was really a guitar capable of replicating the sitar's drone. It became one of the favourite left-field pop sounds of the year for 1967.

While it fills the gap originally occupied by Vin Gordon's trombone riff, what Mick plays on sitar doesn't mimic that riff. It doesn't sound remotely Indian, either, but it does sound Eastern: it comes across more like the kind of music used to soundtrack Chinese locations in hokey. This was not lost on the Clash. In the instrumental bridge section after the second verse, Topper reinforces the chopsticks feel with what sounds like a small triangle – high-pitched metal percussion, anyway – and Joe follows the rhythm vocally, offering the ad-lib, 'Ivan and Fu Man Chu / They both are coming through, yeah.'

Joe's next ad-lib comes over Mickey's introductory organ vamp to the song, and – in keeping with the East Meets West On Uncertain Territory And Terms theme – appears to combine a muezzin wail with a ramblin' cowboy ditty. 'I've stayed around and played around this old town too long / Seems like I've got to travel on . . .' could be something straight out of an outlaw ballad . . . and that's pretty close. It isn't an ad-lib at all, but a substantial quote, being the chorus lifted from a Paul 'Pablo' Clayton song called 'Gotta Move On'. At Vanilla, the Clash had covered 'The Man in Me', a song first recorded by Bob Dylan in 1970, and Joe's associative thought processes evidently took him to another song Dylan recorded that same year, this time to be found on the album *Self Portrait*.

The remaining ad-lib has its origins in a conversation Kosmo Vinyl had with the Clash about the ideal length for a single being two minutes 58 seconds. So Joe told him to stop the live tracking session for 'Armagideon Time' at that point in the song. When Kosmo's voice comes over the studio intercom to say, 'All right, time's up. Let's have you lot out of there,' the band ignore Kosmo and keep playing, and Joe replies, perfectly in time with the music, 'OK, OK, don't push us while we're *hot!*' And the song lasts for 3 minutes and 50 seconds, which proves to be the ideal length for this particular single. Kosmo was worried that he'd be chastised for spoiling the perfect take, but no one said anything . . . because it was pre-planned, and worked perfectly. Or did after it had been overdubbed and mixed.

The Clash's determination to offer something special as part of the single meant that they had always intended to pair this powerful, commercially proven – in the reggae market, at least – song with 'London Calling'. It's not quite correct to refer to it as the B-side of the 7-inch single: London Calling was the A-side, and 'Armagideon Time' the AA-side. The band spent much of the night of 5 November mixing extended dubs of the track to release on what would be their first 12-inch single. Two versions were produced, as with Coxsone Dodd's extended Studio One mix of Willi Williams's original. 'Mick and I worked the board, and I then edited together the best bits,' says Bill Price. The Clash gave these versions the alternative titles 'Justice Tonight' and 'Kick It Over', the first running to four minutes 13 seconds and the second to four minutes 37 seconds . . . or rather, they would have done had not the decision been made to segue them together into one track running for a Kosmo Vinyl-taunting eight minutes 50 seconds. 'Justice Tonight' is a fairly conservative dub, with lots of bass and reverb. 'Kick It Over', featuring Augustus Pablo-style melodica, is more experimental. It ends with the sound of firework explosions, which Joe and Johnny Green recorded prowling around outside Wessex with microphones on long leads while the local residents celebrated Bonfire Night.

Willi Williams was disparaging about the Clash's version of the song for several years after its release. Annoyed about the lyric changes, he accused the band of riding on his song with 'London Calling'. When they tried to arrange a meeting with him, he refused. Nowadays, his attitude is mellower. 'I think it was phenomenal. I think they did a good version of it,' he says. 'They did what they did, and it went across to the world and it was well accepted. And I think I was introduced to a different set of music lovers.'

The Clash initially gave him full composer credit for 'Armagideon Time' and its versions, depriving Coxsone Dodd of the 50 per cent (at least) he took from the Coxsone and Studio One label originals. The ownership of the publishing to the song was undetermined at the time the singles were released, so Willi's authorship was initially listed as Copyright Control. But all he had to do in order to collect was inform his publishers and make a claim. Jackie Mittoo also stepped forward at this time to claim his fraction. 'After the song became such a success with "Armagideon Time", he had to go fight for his rights again,' says Willi. 'So it was kind of bittersweet stuff, you know.' The composer credit for the song and its versions were amended to Williams and Mittoo on subsequent Clash compilations, beginning with 1988's *The Story of the Clash: Volume 1*. The writers continued to work together until Jackie Mittoo died of cancer on 16 December 1990 at the age of 42. On 5 May 2004 Clement 'Coxsone' Dodd died of a heart attack at 72. Willi Williams continues to live in Canada. 'Armagideon Time' remains his biggest hit, and he is still known as the Armagideon Man.

5 Packing Up and Shipping Out

Presentation, Promotion and Press

It was Bernie Rhodes who instilled in the Clash the value of working with true believers rather than jobsworths, or even people aspiring to be detached and objective. From the earliest days, the Clash delegated tasks to whoever happened to be around and showing keen, with the result that all of the Clash's key personnel were committed to the cause. Their original soundman, Micky Foote, became their first producer. Early volunteer roadie Sebastian Conran's design knowledge was pressed into service on posters and a couple of early single sleeves, even some clothing. Johnny Green became the band's roadie and personal manager because he turned up at a gig and volunteered to help. He had no experience, but was prepared to muck in and was willing to step into the breach when the Clash's previous chief roadie, Roadent, quit mid-tour. Even the first music journalists given access to the band were vetted by Bernie to make sure they were predisposed to write favourable copy, and several subsequently went to great lengths to further the band's career, Caroline Coon among them.

As long-time *NME* readers, Mick Jones and Joe Strummer knew who Pennie Smith was (rather than the other way around) when she first turned up to photograph them on 5 November 1976 at the RCA in London. And it was the Clash who invited her to come back and take more photos thereafter: they liked the way her richly textured black-and-white shots made them look, both onstage and in portraits.

They quickly became accustomed to her being around. 'I think I took the sort of pictures they'd have taken if they took photos,' says Pennie. 'We were just compatible, so I think the photos worked in the same way the music worked. We were on the same wavelength. I was the art department and they were the music department, and we just left each other to do what we do.'

Once himself a would-be cartoonist, Joe Strummer enjoyed Ray Lowry's work for the *NME*: his surreal visual riffs on roots music, popular culture and politics, and his fondness bordering on obsession for placing old bluesmen and Elvis Presley in ever-more unlikely situations. Ray first saw the Clash supporting the Sex Pistols on 9 December 1976 at the Electric Circus in Manchester, one of the few Anarchy tour gigs not to be cancelled. He began a correspondence with Joe, from which developed a friendship with Johnny Green. It was Johnny who proposed that Ray should come along on the September-October 1979 Take the 5th tour of America. Previous Clash tours had been well documented in all the usual ways, especially by the *NME*, and having Ray send back regular sketches from the road would be something different, not unlike taking a war artist to the front line: a pitch that was guaranteed to appeal to Joe Strummer's romantic side.

There was a precedent to the Smith and Lowry combination: when Chris Salewicz covered the Clash's summer 1978 Out on Parole tour of the UK for the *NME*, Pennie had contributed the photographs, and Ray a near-full-page collage of sketches and hand-scrawled notes. Both illustrators were genuine Clash enthusiasts. 'I couldn't make a racket, but if I'd been able to, I'd have made a racket like they made,' says Pennie. 'I'm the fool who was naïve enough to mail a copy of their first album to *Rolling Stone* magazine and demand that they take notice of it,' says Ray. (Ray died while this book was being written. It didn't seem right to change his contributions to the past tense.)

Over the previous three years, the Clash had built up a valuable positive relationship with the (at that time) enormously influential *NME*, and CBS were hopeful that paying for Pennie and writer Paul Morley – along with representatives from rival inkys *Sounds* and *Melody Maker* – to cover the tour in exotic America would result in upbeat reports that would overshadow some of the negative press the Clash had received of late. When neither CBS nor the *NME* proved willing to put up the money for Ray to go too, he paid his own way. Doubtless part of the reason he was chosen as the designer for *London Calling*'s album cover, and Pennie Smith was chosen to supply the photographs, was they had proved their loyalty, the Clash liked their work, and they were contributors to the pre-eminent UK music publication of the day. But the main reason was that they happened to be on hand when the band first got to hear Bill Price's initial mixes of the album in New York on 21 September 1979, and started to think about how best to present the material. Time was already getting tight to make the deadline for a pre-Christmas release in the UK, and if work on the cover did not begin until the Clash returned to London in late October, there would be no chance of making it at all.

The weekly *NME* reports Ray filed from Take the 5th, a sort of illustrated tour diary, again combined handwritten notes from the road with cartoon doodles and the odd collage element. His headings and captions included 'Brothel Creepers Over America' and 'The Soiled Pillows Tour'. In the report he sent home on 1 October 1979 (published on 13 October), he noted 'the Clash are looking more than ever like the bastard offspring of Eddie Cochran out of Gene Vincent and a Harley Davidson'. Illustrating this assertion was a reproduction of the cover of Elvis Presley's eponymous debut album, with the chunky lettering that had originally spelled ELVIS down the left hand side and PRESLEY along the bottom amended to read THE and CLASH, respectively. Unwittingly, this was step one in the evolution of his design for the front cover of *London Calling*. 'The Elvis tone of things was set by the band's own mutation into greasers, and a copy of the first Elvis album that I picked up for six dollars in Wax Trax in Chicago,' he says. More accurately, it reflected his own proclivities, and his own reading of the Clash as carriers of the flame of the original rock'n'roll artists. (His July 1978 *NME* collage illustration for the Out on Parole tour had also incorporated a vintage Elvis Presley photograph.)

Originally released in March 1956 on the RCA Victor label, the cover of *Elvis Presley* features a photograph taken on 31 July 1955 during a live performance at Fort Homer Hesterly Armory in Tampa, Florida. The dynamic black-and-white shot catches Elvis mid-song, head thrown back, eyes closed, mouth open and right hand about to strike the strings of his raised acoustic guitar. One of the first rock'n'roll action images to reach a mass audience, it helped define the genre's visual identity. The back cover credits all photos to 'PoPsie', which has caused some confusion over the years. New York paparazzo photographer William 'PoPsie' Randolph was only responsible for the four images on the back cover. Further research by Greg Williams of the Elvis Fan Club in Australia – subsequently confirmed by Presley biographer and authority Peter Guralnick – has determined that Elvis's manager Colonel Tom Parker hired a Tampa firm of commercial photographers named Robertson & Fresh to document the Fort Homer show, and it is almost certain that William 'Red' Robertson himself fulfilled the commission, and took the famous shot. Having paid for it once, the Colonel obviously didn't feel obliged to give any more credit. The member of RCA Victor's in-house design team responsible for the equally memorable lettering was also uncredited, and remains anonymous to this day.

The Clash didn't see themselves as referencing primarily white rock'n'roll, but then, nor did Presley, who owed much of his initial impact to covering songs by both black and white artists and mixing black and white genres. When *NME* writer Paul Morley joined the Take the 5th tour in late September, the Clash were already explaining the overall design concept for the new album in terms that drew attention to their black rock'n'roll, R&B, blues, jazz, soul, funk, disco, ska, rock-steady, reggae, roots and lovers influences: 'Black music, black vinyl, black-and-white cover.'

While the band were discussing sleeve design with Ray Lowry, they were also discussing possible titles for the album. A popular early contender was *The Last Testament*. It tied in with the Clash's quasi-spiritual mission to remind America and the wider world of its original rock'n'roll heritage. The first Elvis album had been reissued later in 1956 with the same cover but a slightly different tracklisting and the title *Rock'n'Roll No 1*, an attempt to establish it as the first dispatch from the new genre. Rather than envisioning the Clash album as a mere continuation of an earlier tradition, *The Last Testament* envisions it as the death-knell for that tradition: not so much the Latest Word as the Last Word. Ray Lowry's sign-off to his final report from the Take the 5th tour was 'I'd rather be back on the bus with the last rock'n'roll band,' which implies such thinking was prevalent in the Clash camp at the time. (Whether intentionally or not, the title was also a nod to the album producer's undimmed belief in music made with passion in order to communicate passion: in 1968 he had compiled an album for Island entitled *Guy Stevens' Testament of Rock and Roll*. And, as it turned out, the Clash album would be his last testament.)

The Last Testament draws attention to the songs on the album that allude to apocalypse and death, and ties in with the idea of the opening song being a final SOS from a doomed outpost. But the album hardly represented a nail in the coffin for roots rock music; rather, it was a rehabilitation of that music after the near-decade's worth of neglect it had suffered at the hands of first 'flared rock' and – for the last couple of years – punk rock. Furthermore, the Clash themselves had every intention of carrying on with their good works after its release. The title would have painted the band into another corner, and so was dropped. (But the Clash like to recycle: *The Last Testament* would reappear as the title of the Don Letts documentary about the making of *London Calling* included on the 2004 25th Anniversary Edition.)

The Clash had never previously – and would never subsequently – name an album after one of its tracks, but in this case, to paraphrase Mick Jones, 'London Calling' is the umbrella song for the album as a whole. Like the 'testament' title idea, it indicates missionary zeal, insists that America pay attention to this London group intent on reminding them what used to be good about American music (and what was still great about the roots music of the wider world), and promises to deliver a message worth hearing. It also carries the requisite apocalyptic overtones.

Ray Lowry's belief that the Clash summed up their generation like Elvis had summed up his encouraged him to persevere with what he refers to as his 'plagiarinspiration' for the cover design. Elvis had passed away just two years earlier: the King was dead, but the throne was still vacant, and there for the claiming. The work-in-progress illustrations Ray Lowry included in his 2007 memoir *The Clash: Up Close and Personal* reveal that he stuck with having the chunky pink and green lettering down the left side and along the bottom reading THE CLASH up until the band committed to calling the album *London Calling*, whereupon he realised the title – with more letters divided more equally between the two words – would be a better fit. The Pennie Smith photograph in contention for the front cover at the time he made this switch was the tightly composed yet rather conventional live group shot later used for the 1988 compilation album *The Story of the Clash: Volume 1.*

The cover was always going to feature a live shot, because the cover of the Presley original was a live shot, and because that was the way Ray was experiencing the Clash's music at the time. The last piece of the jigsaw only fell into place near the end of the tour – Ray thinks it was in Seattle on 15 October 1979 – when Pennie turned up with a whole bunch of contact sheets of photos taken earlier on the tour. Ray says they first looked through the contacts in the hotel; Pennie says on the tour bus, with further discussion later at the hotel. Pennie maintains it was Joe Strummer who selected the photograph of Paul Simonon in the act of smashing his bass on to the New York Palladium stage, which slightly disgruntles Ray, who is adamant that he was the first to spot its potential. He does allow that Joe was very quick to back him up. Initially, the most vocal opposition came from Pennie herself.

Like most professional visual artists, Pennie was proud of her vision and skill and protective of her reputation . . . and at times a little too conscious of the conventions of her chosen discipline. What she was being asked to OK was a reflex snapshot involving very little artistry on her part. Furthermore, because it was clicked off a split-second before she ducked out of the way of the rapidly advancing Simonon and his even more rapidly descending bass – she was no more than a yard away from him, but using a wide-angle lens, so 'he was closer than it looks' – it was slightly out of focus. Ray was oblivious to this when he was glancing through the contacts, because he didn't have his glasses with him, and was also – by his own admission – 'probably half-pissed at the time'. Joe was aware, but argued that it didn't matter, because the image did what all the best documentary photography does: captured a defining moment. It was Joe's spirited and necessarily lengthy defence of Ray's selection – Pennie stood her ground until well into the early hours – that clearly stuck in Pennie's mind and convinced her that Joe had selected the shot. Even after she gave in, it took her a long time to come around. 'I was completely wrong!' she laughs.

Part of the case for the defence relied on established precedent: the cover for Bob Dylan's double album *Blonde on Blonde* (1966) was also out of focus. To which the counter argument was that at least the subject of that photograph was still recognisably Bob Dylan. What the Clash and their art department were discussing was supposed to be a cover shot for a band album, and yet the image under consideration featured just one member of the Clash, and not even the frontman. Paul might have been the most glamorous member of the band, but this was hardly the most flattering representation: his face is obscured, his greased-back hair has exploded outwards in all directions, his back is hunched, his sleeveless shirt is unfastened and billowing out around him like a medieval jerkin, his skinny legs are splayed out awkwardly at 90 degrees, and the way the light shines on his right leg (left of shot) and the bare arm overlying his left leg (right of shot) combine to trick the eye into thinking . . . well, as a much later spoof of the cover would at least partly indicate, Paul looks like Quasimodo running amok with no pants on.

None of that matters, though, because it is such a dynamic image that it instantly conveys the passion, excitement and unpredictability of a Clash performance. And with not too much of a stretch of the imagination, it illustrates at least something of the spirit of the music on the album: the pounding, staccato attack of the title track and 'Four Horsemen'; the unchecked temper alluded to in 'Rudie Can't Fail' and 'Death or Glory'; the cover star's own avowed readiness to take on all comers in 'The Guns of Brixton'; Joe singing of smashing up seats in 'Revolution Rock' and threatening the chop chop in 'Jimmy Jazz'; and most of all, 'Clampdown', a song which carries the echo of its inspiration: the men on the chain gang repeatedly hoisting their hammers and smashing them down again and again against the limitations of their miserable lot in life. Somehow, the cover image communicates all of this, and instantly. (And once the *Wessex Studios Footage* had been rediscovered and included on the 25th Anniversary Edition of *London Calling*, thus preserving for posterity Guy Stevens's habit of smashing plastic chairs against the studio floor, it echoed that, too.)

The photograph was taken on 21 September 1979, during the second of the Clash's two New York showcase gigs at the Palladium. The first night had attracted a number of smart-set celebrity guests from circles the Clash would not normally have moved in, including Bianca Jagger, who danced at the side of the stage. The Palladium was a seated venue, so the paying crowd weren't as free to express themselves as the band would have liked. So Paul losing it so publicly could be interpreted as a suitably punk display of fuck-you attitude. It was tempting for the Clash to sell the bass-smashing incident that way.

Hardly surprisingly, Paul has been asked about it many times over the years. He had hurt his hip and ricked his back throwing his bass around at the Aragon Ballroom show in Chicago, and had been performing in some pain for an entire week before the Palladium show, but has never claimed this as a motive. Pushed, he has variously conceded that poor sound and a seated and unresponsive audience might have been triggers, but on other occasions, he has denied they were. He has also acknowledged that playing New York was a pressured experience, not dissimilar to playing London. The explanation he offers without prodding is no explanation at all: he just 'felt a bit funny', and in those days, when he felt a bit funny he broke things. The perfect psycho-punk statement. Like the photo itself, it says, 'Don't kid yourself that we've been tamed.'

In *The Last Testament* documentary, Kosmo Vinyl offered his theory that Elvis Presley introduced rock'n'roll on *Elvis Presley* by lifting his guitar up, while Paul Simonon symbolically killed it off on *London Calling* by bringing his bass down. It's a neat conceit, but it doesn't tell the full story. As with the working title for the album the Clash had only recently discarded, the image chosen for their new album cover does make an iconoclastic gesture, yes, but it simultaneously asserts the band's right to be considered part of a long-established tradition.

Right from the get-go, the more exciting and excitable rock'n'rollers had pushed themselves to the limits physically, and meted out harsh punishment to their instruments in the process. This had almost immediately become part of the accepted theatrics of the genre. In the mid-Fifties, Jerry Lee Lewis and Little Richard kicked away their piano stools and mashed the keys with their fists and heels, Richard jumping up on top of his grand, Lewis ripping the lid off his and throwing it clear across the stage. Even Bill Haley's double bassist clambered all over his instrument (though he did have to stop for a quiet lie down when he got to the other side). By the mid-Sixties, Pete Townshend had taken all this to extremes by smashing up his guitars onstage, and had given such wanton destruction spurious justification by claiming it as an art statement. Keith Moon joined in, and trashed his drum kits for the sheer fun of it. John's Children and the Move were among the artists who followed in the Who's debris-littered wake.

Up until Jimi Hendrix found himself following the Who onstage on the last night of the Monterey Pop Festival in 1967 – the highest-profile American performance yet for both acts – he had contented himself with such trademark showmanship as playing his guitar with his teeth, behind his head and between his legs (though not all at the same time). At the end of their Monterey slot, the Who smashed their gear. At the end of his, Hendrix set fire to his guitar, and *then* smashed it. That this was the point at which America sat up and took notice of both the Who and Hendrix was hardly a coincidence. In the punk era, the Damned made a sustained bid to assume the Who's mantle as the band most likely to trash their gear, which they celebrated in one of the songs they were finishing off in Wessex while the Clash were recording *London Calling* next door: 'Smash It Up'.

Could Paul's destructive act have been more premeditated than has been admitted? Pennie Smith is adamant that she was not party to any set-up. Having already photographed several gigs, she had intended to go out for dinner with friends on 21 September, and had only changed her mind and decided to attend the show at the last minute. Even so, she'd been shooting in a fairly desultory manner. Familiar enough with the band members to read their body language, though, she had realised that Paul was looking cross towards the end of the final encore of – fittingly enough – 'White Riot', and had just managed to get the camera to her eye when he exploded. The contact sheet reproduced in the *London Calling* 25th Anniversary Edition booklet tells part of the story, frame by frame. There's a picture in which Joe Strummer can be seen bent over to the left of the shot, but Paul is totally obscured by two roadies as, presumably, they rush to his aid. Then a shot where Paul himself is still largely obscured by a roadie, and Joe is in turn largely obscured by Paul, but the bass is clearly visible, Paul having hoisted it above his head, his hands gripped tightly around its neck. Then comes the album cover picture, with Joe – wisely – nowhere to be seen.

Pennie says she had to step around the roadies (and nearly under the bass) in order to get the key shot. She also says it was the last picture in the sequence, either because the film had run out or because

Paul left the stage at that point. The cover of the never-released *Clash 3rd Songbook* features another shot, though, this time taken from behind, with Paul facing the crowd and once again bent double smashing the bass into the ground. From a professional point of view, other than the one selected for the cover – which Pennie also found sub-standard, initially – none of these shots are of good enough quality to do anything but provide context. 'I don't mind them being used in an artsy-fartsy manner as rough notes, like the contact sheet in the reissue booklet, but not pulled out and used as photographs in their own right,' says Pennie. 'They're just part of the build-up to the *London Calling* photo.' In short, she clearly had not posed her subject, been forewarned about what he was planning to do, or even had time to think about framing her photos, or else she would have had a clearer sight-line, more time to shoot, and there would have been more images to choose from.

As evidence of his own lack of forethought, Paul Simonon has pointed out that he wasn't just throwing shapes when he brought his bass down on the Palladium stage: he gave it his all. It was his best bass too, the vintage Fender Precision that he had paid £160 for just nine months before, had lovingly customised – with Jackson Pollock-style splashes on the scratch plate, the 'Death or Glory' skull and crossbones below the strings, another sticker reading PRESSURE above, and Jamaican/Rasta red, yellow and green stripes running diagonally across the nose of the headstock – and had played during the recording sessions for *London Calling*. As well as not being cheap, it was both weighty and robust – his spare was a more recent and lighter model – yet Paul's assault split the neck diagonally through the metal frets. He also broke his watch, which stopped dead, conveniently giving the time of death for the bass as 9.50 p.m. 'I don't wear a watch normally, but I do on the road because photographers can be left off tour buses,' says Pennie. 'A few days after the Palladium show, my watch strap broke, so Paul gave me the watch he was wearing when he bashed the bass. It wasn't meant to be a memento of the photograph – although it became one, in retrospect, because the image became so famous – it was more, "Your watch strap's broken, my watch is broken, take the strap off mine and use it for yours," sort of thing. Strangely, I didn't put his strap on my watch. I just kept the whole thing. I've still got it.'

This, then, was determined ultraviolence on Paul's part. Two other points to consider: the bass was still plugged in, so his own safety wasn't a consideration; and the show was being recorded for broadcast by WNEW, so how all this went over to the wider audience of listeners wasn't, either. Surely, then, as he claims, Paul must have lost all reason for a few moments? He has admitted that his temper is 'like a light switch, off and on'. But he'd had plenty of practice destroying property for casual kicks as a teenager, and didn't need to be genuinely furious to break things.

Johnny Green has always suspected that Paul was simply making show. When Paul first raised his bass, Johnny says he ran to ask him what the matter was, and Paul almost calmly told him to fuck off, he was all right. Backstage after the incident, Paul showed no signs of being upset or angry. Instead, he joked about having to use the spare bass for the rest of the tour. It's also worth bearing in mind that he didn't crack up mid-set or even mid-song, but right at the end of the last song of the encore: convenient timing. Johnny Green's theory – offered in *A Riot of Our Own* – is that Paul was trying to impress his New York girlfriend, Debbie Kronick, in her home town. If it were premeditated, it's unlikely he had such a small and local audience in mind. The bass destruction couldn't be seen on the radio – and on the recording manifests itself more as a confusion of sound than an explosion – but Paul knew there were other ways of getting across to the masses.

When first approached by Mick Jones in spring 1976 to join the band that would become the Clash, Paul was at first considered as a second guitarist. That didn't work out, because he showed no natural aptitude for the instrument, much to his initial disappointment. 'I had these grand dreams of being Pete Townshend,' he told Scott Rowley of *Bassist* magazine in 1999. 'I wanted to do [the windmilling arm] and smash guitars and all that stuff. So once I was handed the bass, I thought, "I'll just pretend I'm playing guitar." Which is pretty much what I did from day one. I took one instrument and treated it like it was another one, not musically, but physically.' And this wasn't an ambition arrived at retrospectively. As early as 1978 Paul had told the *NME*'s Chris Salewicz, 'I want to be able to stick the bass behind my neck and play it like Jimi Hendrix played the guitar.' He'd seen Dee Dee Ramone wear his bass slung low, and really punishing it; he'd seen Richard Hell leaping around with his. And he'd seen his friend Sid Vicious – who picked up the instrument after he did – take much the same reference points and go on to use the bass more as a posing prop-cum-occasional weapon than as a musical instrument. In his leather drainpipes and biker boots, Paul as captured by Pennie's lens in September 1979 closely resembles his friend Sid Vicious on the Sex Pistols January 1978 American tour, when Sid was getting punched in the mouth, slashing his chest and hitting members of the crowd with *his* white Fender Precision bass.

Not that Paul had to look outside his own band for showman- ship pointers. All three of the Clash frontmen liked to run across stage and launch themselves into the air. Mick Jones, in particular, was partial to Townshend-like scissor kicks, star-jumps and jack- knives. The tour posters, flyers and ads for the October-December 1978 Sort It Out tour feature a photograph of him caught in mid- scissor kick. But when it came to maltreating equipment, Joe Strummer had been leading the field and incrementally upping the ante for some time. At the Clash's Southall Defence Fund concert at the Rainbow, Finsbury Park, on 14 July 1979 Joe had lost his temper, removed his main guitar, the white Fender Esquire, and sent it looping high over the drum riser (with its lead still attached). Pennie Smith was present, and her shot catching the guitar mid-arc was given half of the *NME*'s back page, more space than Paul Morley's inevitably less memorable review of the gig itself. Throughout the Take the 5th tour, Joe would take off his guitar mid-song and centre- stage, then casually fling it into the wings, where Johnny Green would be expected to dive and catch it. Pennie Smith also snapped this routine one night, in a photograph that would later be used on the cover of the 1980 Dutch single picture sleeve for 'Rudie Can't Fail'; and, 11 years after that, the front cover of the Clash compila- tion album *The Singles*. So there was no lack of precedent for Paul's outburst. He knew what a band member needed to do if he wanted to be the centre of pictorial attention.

Pennie hadn't been the only one to notice what was happening. The Clash's lighting man Warren Steadman must take some credit for both picking up on and picking out what Paul was doing. Pennie's photograph shows that a Super Trooper is aimed right at Paul, turning his figure (and bass) into an exercise in chiaroscuro. By comparison, everything in the background is muted, seen through the haze of light, which means it tends to be overlooked. But the drama is not confined to the foreground. Immediately behind Paul, both his and Joe's microphone stands are lying flat on the stage, poleaxed by earlier Simonon swings. Over Paul's left shoulder, a figure far too burly-looking to be a band member, his right elbow raised at an awkward angle, is hurrying towards another figure mostly obscured by the upraised body of the bass. When Pennie subsequently included the picture in her photobook *The Clash: Before and After* (1980) Mick Jones supplied a caption offering an explanation . . . Mick was the obscured figure. A girl named Colleen had just climbed onstage and run towards him, and was being chased by the burly man, 'a New York-style bouncer'. In his version, Mick grabbed Colleen and pulled her safely off-stage, before Keith Moon fan and disciple Topper Headon took his cue from Paul and 'the kit exploded into the orchestra pit'. In Mick's fanciful description, it was like a 'scene from a movie'. Which, again, makes it a highly appropriate cover for an album imbued with silver-screen imagery.

Blow Up (1966) – a film which features its own famous example of instrument destruction, this time a guitar courtesy of the Yardbirds' Jeff Beck – revolved around the titular photograph which, upon close inspection, turns out to have captured unexpected evidence. In the case of Pennie's picture, that evidence is that the Palladium audience was the opposite of unresponsive. Which Eleanor Flicker, who was present at the show and is now a moderator at the *Strummernews* website, can confirm. 'I do remember thinking that the sound was a bit murky and not that great,' she says. 'It didn't take away from the performance, though, which was brilliant. I remember the tremendous energy and anticipation of the crowd and the band. The audience was totally into it.' The onstage chaos at the end was 'kind of trippy, but not totally surprising, because the whole show was wild and they kind of built up to it', but Eleanor was in row 30, too far back to see everything that happened at the end.

Of the reviewers present at the time, Robert Palmer of *The New York Times* wasn't impressed by either the band or the sound, dismissing the Clash as a 'garage band with pretensions', but Ira Robbins of *Trouser Press* described it as a 'sloppy mess of a wonderful show', and both 'fun and exciting'. Lester Bangs thought the performance was not as together as had been the February Pearl Harbour tour show at the same venue, but believed the band's energy overcame sound and equipment problems. In the report he filed for the *NME*, Van Gosse wasn't aware of any problems: he maintained the band's musicality had *improved* since their February visit, and added that they put everything into getting the music across. His report cuts out after 'What's My Name', though, which hints that he did, too. Which means he missed 'White Riot', and the bass-smashing episode. Strangely, in spite of the spotlight, it seems to have passed unnoticed or at least unremarked by all the other writers, too, and no photographers other than Pennie Smith appear to have recorded it visually. Rather than documenting an Event, then, Pennie's photograph – or 'our bastard child', as she and Paul now refer to the unplanned arrival – ultimately served to create an Event after the event.

Spontaneous outburst or considered stunt? We'll never know for sure. Following the show the broken bass was retrieved and packed away. But Paul never had it repaired. As soon as the photograph was chosen for the album cover, he knew it was an Iconic Object. He also knew that what he was wearing when Pennie clicked the shutter had instantly become an Iconic Image. The look the photograph immortalised – biker boots, leather trousers, slicked-back hair, short-sleeved black shirt – was to remain his stage outfit of choice for at least the next two years.

*

Disagreements between the director and cinematographer continued in the editing suite . . . or rather, the art department at CBS's offices in London's Soho Square, where Ray Lowry found a space in late October 1979 to realise his vision. Ray asked Pennie to crop the original rectangular, portrait-shaped photograph square and blow it up to 12-inch LP size. Pennie resisted at first. This was partly on general principles, because she didn't like her images to be cropped other than how she might choose to crop them herself. In this particular instance, though, she also felt strongly that the upper part of the image was a vital part of the shot, capturing the darkness of the offstage area and providing necessary contrast with the spotlit stage area. (Captioning another photograph taken in the same venue for *The Clash: Before and After*, she noted that she had only ever seen that particular quality of light at the Palladium.) She had a point. Sacrificing the top third leaves the light unexplained, and the remainder of the background a blurry grey wash.

The alternative option, reproducing the full portrait image on a square LP cover, would have necessitated leaving a wide border on either side. Not only would this not have worked with the Presley lettering, it would also have required Paul Simonon's figure to be much smaller in relation to the surface area of the cover as a whole, diluting its impact. To Ray, the stage lights and lighting contrasts in the upper part of the picture were 'inessentials': unnecessary distractions from the action. He got his way with regard to the album cover, but to this day, when Pennie sanctions reproduction of the photograph for any other purpose, it is of the full image. (Incidentally, the photograph on the cover of *Elvis Presley* was also cropped, losing Elvis's untamed pelvis and guitarist Scotty Moore.)

Communication difficulties between Ray and Pennie continued. 'I asked her to put one of those rough, photographic black borders around it,' says Ray. 'You do it with the enlarger. She didn't quite get that and, at first, sent me a copy with a black border just drawn around it. No good. And second time around it wasn't quite right either, because most of the border got bled off in the printing process.' He thought it would be straining their relationship to ask again. 'It should have a rough black border around it. Serendipity, perhaps, that it doesn't.' The top, bottom and right edges of the original LP release reveals traces of the otherwise 'bled off' border, but by the time *London Calling* made it to CD this had been 'cleaned up': that is, completely removed.

Ray positioned the band's name as unobtrusively as possible top left in simple white italics, then added the Presley-style lettering by hand, leaving the letters blank for the printers to drop in the pink and green. He was so determined to ensure that they got it right that, according to Johnny Green, he was on press while the sleeve was being printed. 'It was no easy task getting that cover as I knew God wanted it to be,' says Ray. And there was one last compromise to be made. As he had done with Derek Boshier and the *Clash 2nd Songbook*, Joe allowed Ray free rein . . . except for one detail.

Either these touches were genuinely important to him, or a subtle Strummer way of exercising control, of putting his marker on a project. Ray had envisaged a Fifties-type sleeve, with a laminated front and a matt back, but was overruled. 'Joe's only input was to insist that the cover not be laminated,' he says. 'He wanted it to be totally matt, no gloss.'

The back cover was exactly as Ray wanted it, layout, typography and images. On LPs from the Fifties and early Sixties, the front would traditionally carry the attention-grabbing image, and the back would be a comparatively drab and functional affair, providing information about the recording and the artist, accompanied by one or two more unexceptional promotional shots. *Elvis Presley* was true to type. Ray paid tribute to this convention while subtly updating it. His back cover is very much *designed*. Above the band's name appears the first use on a Clash record cover of the five-pointed star, initially adapted as an item of clothing insignia by Paul Simonon from memorabilia brought back from his January 1978 holiday in Russia, and already well on its way to becoming a Clash-associated symbol. Neat blocks of text provide the song titles and main credits. The titles, text blocks and the CBS logo are all positioned neatly around Pennie Smith's back-cover photos. These are also cropped, not square this time, but into unusually stretched landscape and portrait shapes. And they are far from being perfunctory promo space-fillers. As Paul had been given the front sleeve, Ray – persisting with the theme of musicians doing something unusual with the tools of their trade – selected shots that allowed the other three band members to come over as exciting performers, too.

Pennie took the left-hand landscape picture at Armadillo World Headquarters in Austin on 4 October 1979. Looking like a snarling Vince Taylor or Gene Vincent, Joe Strummer stands in front of the drum riser and holds his microphone stand out at full extension into the kit, as though trying to feed the mike to a flailing Topper Headon. It captures the moment in the set, during the breakdown section of 'Clampdown', when Joe would habitually inform the audience that he was going 'to take them into the engine room' to visit the stoker in chief. It was a routine, but an honest routine, because any band is only as good as its drummer. It's another light-blasted picture, this time from underneath: white figures and instruments against a dark background.

The portrait shot of Mick Jones, taken by Pennie at the Agora Ballroom in Atlanta, Georgia, on 2 October, is unusual in that it doesn't go for the obvious – Mick in mid-leap – but catches him looking not unlike a young Montgomery Clift, mid-stage and apparently mid-twist, balancing the base of his Gibson Les Paul on the palm of his right hand as though preparing to hoist it into the wings, Joe Strummer-style. A second glance reveals this not to be the case: the strap is still securely fastened around his shoulder. (And Mick loved his guitars so much that he cried if one got damaged.) The tangle of leads around his feet indicates that he might just be trying to spin himself out of a knot. Pennie is stage right again, and up on high, shooting down, giving her an unusual perspective. Like Paul on the front cover, Mick is spotlit, his body slightly to the right of centre of the sunburst oval shape made by the Super Trooper, the hand balancing the guitar at dead centre. The light is so powerful it shows up the grain of the wood on the stage, which seems to radiate outwards. This effect, together with Mick's contorted shape and the centrifugal force evidently in play on the guitar, creates the impression of pure energy exploding outwards in all directions.

What surprised Ray most about his time in the CBS art room is that no one from CBS attempted to interfere in any way. He recalls they all seemed engrossed in the cover for a new Shakin' Stevens record. He had expected to have to fight about everything, from the unconventional cover image to the 'borrowed' lettering. While it was all too easy to interpret this as evidence that CBS didn't care about the Clash's presentation, or even that they were too scared of a rebuke to show interest, it was simply a matter of it being well established and well understood that the band always took care of their own record-cover designs.

Partly to keep costs down for the Clash's BOGOF offer, and partly so Ray could stay true to his source of inspiration, the decision had been made to house both discs in a single outer jacket. In order to compensate for the otherwise minimalist packaging, Joe's lyrics, more photos and some additional credits were to be included on the two inner sleeves. Although Joe's earlier lyrics had been included in the first two Clash-authorised songbooks, this was the first time he had been willing to include them with the album itself. As well as being indicative of a relaxation of punk's rules of presentation – part minimalist aesthetic, part aversion to anything smacking of self-indulgence – it demonstrates how much more confident Joe was about the standard of his recent work. In January 1980, while the Clash were in Scotland on the 16 Tons tour, Joe told *Sounds'* Robbi Millar that people used to come up to him and complain that the lyrics weren't included with the first two albums. 'Well, of course, this time we did, and one guy in Edinburgh comes up and says to me, "Why do you *always* put the lyrics on the album?" I creased up laughing. I could see that one coming.'

Joe handed Ray a sheaf of his lyrics, and Ray wrote them out by hand – in much the same way and style as he had filed his *NME* reports from Take the 5th – in the correct order over the four sides of the inner sleeves. Having no need of or affection for CBS's professional facilities, Ray did this part of the job in more casual surroundings: the place where some of the lyrics had first been drafted. 'It was all done at Gaby's place in Chelsea where Joe was staying,' he recalls. The style reflected the relaxed location. Ray wrote out the lyrics in rough block capitals and in rough blocks of text on the diagonal, a side's worth of songs for each side of the album . . . except for side two, the lyrics for which splurge out in more casual shapes, with three of the five songs – arbitrarily – reproduced in lower case. Side three also includes the additional credits.

More of Pennie's photos are featured. On the first three sides, they are also placed on the diagonal, dropped in and around the blocks of text on sides one and three, but necessarily squeezed down the right-hand side on the more chaotic side two. On side four they are placed at higgledy-piggledy angles in the bottom-right corner. There's no rhyme or reason to any of this, and the ratio of photos per side is dictated by available space, naturally greater on the sides with less text. Thus, there are 10 photos on side one, 12 on two, 13 on three and 16 on four. That's 51 in total: an embarrassment of riches. Unlike the outer cover photographs, these are not exclusively live perform-ance shots – except for those illustrating side two – and include photos of the band in dressing rooms, at soundchecks, in transit, posing in front of cars and pinball machines and Niagara Falls. There are photos of venues, musical guests (Mickey Gallagher with Mick, bottom right, side two; Joe Ely with Stetson, top right, side three), girlfriends (Gaby with Joe and Paul, bottom right, side one; Debbie with Paul, bottom right, side four) and the on-the-road support team (Baker with Topper, extreme left, side three; Johnny Green standing and holding court, bottom right, side three; Kosmo Vinyl with a fridge, bottom centre, side four).

As they were all taken on the Take the 5th tour, which took place between the main recording and the final recording and mixing sessions for the album, these images could not be more chronologically appropriate. They give the album packaging a photo-diary or travelogue feel, amplify the mood of the album, and communicate the experience that shaped some of the songs. They were all taken in America though, and capture the Clash dressed in their retro-rocker gear, which arguably over-emphasises *London Calling*'s American influences and themes at the expense of the British and Jamaican and universal influences and themes. The shots are reproduced with black borders, as preferred by Ray, and as full standard portrait or landscape prints, as preferred by Pennie. The generous quantity of images and scrapbook presentation Ray chose guarantees a slow release of ambience: there's always something new to see. The downside is that the photographs are reproduced so small on the original LP – each of them little more than postage-stamp size – and there are so many of them crammed into the available space that it doesn't do the individual images many favours. (By the time the album appeared on CD, they were down to thumbnail size.) Pennie says she had no problem with this. 'I'm an artist in my brain, not a photographer,' she says. 'I very rarely gave the Clash, or anyone, a picture I didn't like. As long as they weren't throwing them away, it was quite cute that they looked like postage stamps. You're allowed to do that, it's art.'

The serious credits appear on the outer back cover: generously, Guy Stevens gets sole production credit; slightly less generously, given that he was responsible for the mix, and co-produced some material with Mick Jones, Bill Price is only listed as chief engineer. His assistant, Jerry Green, is acknowledged, as is Wessex studio, photographer Pennie Smith and designer Ray Lowry. The inner sleeve (side three) 'creditz' – jotted down by Joe Strummer for Ray to copy out by hand – mostly acknowledge the other people who assisted the Clash in the studio during recording and on the Take the 5th tour. Organist Mickey Gallagher is the only other musician named.

The ever-competitive Joe Strummer apparently could not bring himself to list the horn section under their chosen professional name, the Rumour Brass, which derived from their time supporting Graham Parker and the Rumour. As Joe hadn't made a note of the names of the individual musicians – saxophonists John 'Irish' Earle and Ray Beavis and trumpet player Dick Hanson – he collectively renamed them the Irish Horns, after the nickname of their leader. 'It wasn't our idea, and we were quite annoyed to discover the name had been invented,' says Ray Beavis. 'We never used it again.'

Baker Glare is drum roadie Barry August, poached from Bernie Rhodes's second band, the Subway Sect, during the course of the spring 1977 White Riot tour. He was rechristened by Paul Simonon, because he thought he looked like a baker. 'Glare' only lasted for the duration of 1979, and was evidently inspired by Baker's sunny disposition. The 'pre-production' credit refers to his taking charge of the portastudio for the Vanilla demos, while 'whistling' acknowledges his contribution to 'Jimmy Jazz'. Johnny Green is John Broad, who also changed identity during his first tour with the Clash, the autumn 1977 Out of Control tour. He was initially nicknamed Johnny Greenglasses, after the lime-green frames on the spectacles he favoured at that time, but acquired the shortened version after taking advantage of an unclaimed motel bed provisionally booked for a Dagenham Plastics representative named John Green. A cross between chief roadie and ungentleman's ungentleman, Johnny was too wild a spirit and new to the way things were done in the USA to be the Clash's road manager for Take the 5th. The credit 'roadholding' neatly sidesteps the issue of his official job title. As his own rip-roaring account of the tour in *A Riot of Our Own* testifies, the degree to which Johnny held himself together on the tour, let along anything else, is debatable.

As his biblical credit implies, Warren Steadman was in charge of lighting for Take the 5th. Kosmo Vinyl was the band's newly acquired publicist and unofficial stylist, a role he would fulfil until the band split. His given name is Mark Dunk. 'The Quest' was the title Kosmo gave the Clash's campaign to reintroduce America to the music they invented, rock'n'roll (which, of course, ties in with the album cover design and its rejected working titles). 'Have you heard the news?' was one of Take the 5th's catchphrases. The answer is, 'There's good rockin' tonight.' It's a reference to Elvis Presley's 1954 Sun Records single – his second ever – 'Good Rockin' Tonight', a song written and first recorded by Roy Brown. Ray Lowry used it as the headline for the 1 October 1979 *NME* report that first featured his appropriation of Elvis's debut album cover. Kosmo came as part of a package with Peter Jenner and Andrew King of Blackhill Enterprises, but the band's new management team are not credited. Joe had been ambivalent about the still temporary arrangement, and Blackhill had evidently not yet done enough to win him over.

The 'hello' to James Stevens is on behalf of his father, Guy, who was separated from his wife and child. Poignantly for a man whose overriding passion in life was music, Guy's son was born deaf. Alex and Kris are Alex Michon and Krystyna Kolowska. Alex was taken on by Bernie Rhodes in spring 1977 to help design and then make the Clash's earliest custom-made outfits, which *NME* journalist Nick Kent at the time described as 'Pop Star Army Fatigues'. She in turn recruited her friend Krys. They produced all the Clash's gear up until the band split with Bernie and started wearing suits instead. But after the band returned from America in late October, Alex and Krys were asked to make some shirts for the upcoming Christmas gigs and 16 Tons tour scheduled for January 1980. The 'clobber' credit acknowledges the duo's latest commission, but also thanks them for their previously uncredited contribution to the Clash's look over the past three years.

The Clash encountered 'Howard McNee' on their 4 August 1979 jaunt to play the Ruisrock Festival in Turku, Finland. Howard was based there, working as an English teacher. When he heard the band were making a new album, he cheekily asked Joe to give him a credit, and three months later Joe remembered . . . almost. Howard's real surname is, apparently, McGee. There's another mistake in the credit immediately below. Joe was under the impression that the Clash's contract with CBS in the UK and Epic in the USA was for five albums over five years. Annoyed that the record company instead on counting the double *London Calling* as a single album (despite the band's own subterfuge on that matter), Joe added the tally marks as a taunt: three down, only two to go. Shortly afterwards, though, Blackhill examined the CBS contract and reported back to the Clash that they had some possibly good news and some very likely bad news. The possibly good news was that CBS had not specified in print that double albums should count as single album releases.

(Though, as the Clash themselves had insisted *London Calling* was a single, this point was still debatable.) The likely bad news was that there were option clauses allowing CBS to extend the contract by a further five albums if they so wished . . . and then by a further three. So the tally marks should read, three or four down, anything up to 10 to go. At the end of the year, asked if the Clash regretted signing to CBS by *Hot Press*'s John McKenna, Mick replied, 'This group has no regrets. But that might be one of the ones it has.'

Joe clearly nearly forgot to mention 'Britain's no 1' DJ, Barry Myers, who had helped keep the rockin' mood of both Pearl Harbour and Take the 5th going with his pre- and post-Clash performance song selections, and was usually credited on the tour flyers as 'England's No 1 DJ': a promotion, then. He is deliberately misnamed 'Birry' as a joke – according to Pat Gilbert's *Passion is a Fashion* (2004) – at the expense of his fondness for biryani.

As the earlier credit to Alex and Krys hints, Joe was keen to make good for the band's failure to include acknowledgements on earlier albums. *London Calling* is dedicated to Henry Bowles and Peter Evans. From mid-1977 to early 1978, Joe had a room in sometime Clash helper and designer Sebastian Conran's house at 31 Albany Street, Camden Town. So did several other people involved with the Clash. Another housemate was Henry Bowles, who had such a street-credible London accent he was asked to record a couple of early Clash radio ads. On 23 October 1977 Henry accompanied some of the others to a Subway Sect gig at the Bell pub in Pentonville Road. Someone threw a firework in the bar. Krys Kolowska was talking to him at the time, and is adamant that it wasn't Henry. But because he happened to be laughing, the bouncers presumed he was responsible. Several of them dragged him outside and hit him so hard he fell on the pavement and fractured his skull. He died in hospital on 4 November 1977, just 24 years old. Thereafter, Joe involved himself in a campaign to ensure all music venue bouncers were properly registered. (Henry's fellow dedicatee, Peter Evans, remains a mystery figure.)

When Ray Lowry finished work on the inner sleeves, he returned home to Lancashire. The Clash were still tinkering with *London Calling* in Wessex at the time, and while mixing the album, Joe rewrote the first verse of 'I'm Not Down'. With printing deadlines looming, and Ray unavailable, Joe made the changes to the lyric sheet himself.

'It is Joe's fair hand, yes,' says Ray. 'He was most apologetic about sullying the thing with his writing.' Joe also dropped in two last-minute credits: M Jones – piano and J Strummer – pianner. The spelling says everything about the difference in their styles and proficiency. He also added the peculiar and misleading note: 'Recorded Winter '79'. *London Calling* was recorded August, mixed September, and completed in early November 1979.

An anonymous CBS typist added a few more significant credits: publishing credits. Carlin Music for Vince Taylor's 'Brand New Cadillac', Island Music for Jackie Edwards and Danny Ray's 'Revolution Rock', and 'Copyright Control' for the – at the time – unrepresented C. Alphanso's 'Wrong 'Em Boyo'. By the time of the 1999 CD issue, Edwards's estate was represented by Fairwood Music, Ray by Panache Music, and Alphanso's estate by MCPS.

London Calling was also the first time that the Clash's own songs had been attributed to both Nineden Ltd (their self-owned publishing company) and Riva Music Ltd (who administered it) on the inner sleeve, as opposed to just the label copy. Riva had previously only collected for Strummer-Jones songs in the UK, Eire, Europe and Australasia, but before the album was even recorded, Dennis Collopy did another couple of deals with the Clash. One was to collect for Paul Simonon and Topper Headon songs as well, which initially required the Clash to establish another limited company, Dorisimo Ltd, in June 1979. (When the Clash moved on from Riva the following year, their new deal was for the rights to songs by all four Clash members to be collected via Nineden, and the Clash subsequently used Dorisimo for other purposes.) The second, more significant, deal was for Riva to pick up the rights to collect in America for Nineden as well.

The Clash were not quite in a strong enough position to demand their own vanity label at CBS, but they did get part of the way there. In the UK, the band's previous two albums had been given standard CBS matrix numbers, but the initial LP edition of *London Calling* was issued as CLASH 3. Standard CBS labels of the period were orange at the top fading to yellow at the bottom, and featured the CBS 'walking eye' logo and 'CBS' in fat white lettering. In keeping with Ray Lowry and the Clash's vision for the album being – save for the Elvis lettering – entirely black and white from outer cover to the vinyl within, *London*

Calling was issued with plain white labels, with the lettering in black . . . And although the record company's 'walking eye' logo appeared above the band's name and the album title, 'CBS' itself was reduced to small print. This at least gave the appearance that the Clash had slipped free of corporate control, with the white labels (together with the packaging as a whole) also evoking both a valuable promo artefact and a bootleg.

The last detail of the original, detailed package was on the vinyl itself: on side four, scratched into the run-off between the last track and the label is the legend TRACK 5 IS 'TRAIN IN VAIN'. As the song was added to the album too late even for Joe Strummer to scrawl its title to the inner sleeve, this inscription was the last opportunity to identify it. It was added on 13 November 1979 at CBS studios in Whitfield Street, London, by mastering engineer Tim Young. 'That's my handwriting, but it came from Mick Jones,' says Tim. 'He turned up in the afternoon and told me to do that.' (As was customary, Tim also signed his own name, as 'TY' on the fourth side, and as 'Tim Tom' – his middle name is Thomas – on the run-off of the other three sides.)

As well-informed music fans, Joe Strummer and Mick Jones were conscious that releasing a double album featuring such a variety of material would inevitably invite comparisons with the very short list of acknowledged great double albums from the past. Which is not to say that double albums were in short supply; just that the reputation of the double had been tarnished by meandering prog epics, unfocussed rock operas and self-indulgent live sets. Hard as it was to deliver a great single album, it was more than doubly difficult to sustain brilliance over four sides. Given their own musical tastes, the kind of music they had drawn upon, and the flavour of Joe's lyrics, the Clash doubtless anticipated *London Calling* being compared – whether positively or negatively – with Bob Dylan's *Blonde on Blonde* (1966), the Beatles' *White Album* (officially known as *The Beatles*) (1968), and the Rolling Stones' *Exile on Main St.* (1972) in particular: each of them an acknowledged double-barrelled contribution to the rock Canon. While it showed considerable chutzpah for them to record a double in the face of prevailing punk opinion, it showed even more for them to, once again, serve notice of their desire to go up against such big guns.

While almost every previous commentator on *London Calling* has made this observation with relation to the contents of *London Calling*, however, it does not seem to have been discussed with relation to the packaging. On his design for the 'London Calling' single, Ray Lowry makes overt references to the Beatles, the Stones and Dylan in addition to Elvis Presley (see below), but because his most obvious point of reference with the album sleeve was Elvis, it appears to have passed largely unnoticed the degree to which his design for the album also consciously (if slightly more subtly) references the other three artists.

When Ray Lowry and Joe Strummer first argued with Pennie Smith about the cover of *London Calling*, their main line of defence of the out-of-focus photograph of Paul Simonon was the precedent set by the Jerry Schatzberg shot of Bob Dylan used on the outer gatefold cover of *Blonde on Blonde*. Dylan had plenty of in-focus Schatzberg shots to choose from, but opted for a picture taken outside New York's old Chelsea meat market. As much attention had already been paid to his earlier album sleeves, Dylan knew it would be subjected to intensive analysis, so there was an element of wind-up, of perversity, in the choice. And in failing to fix its subject with pin-sharp clarity, the photograph allows him to remain elusive and enigmatic. As with Pennie Smith's Palladium shot, though, this was more by accident than design. 'It was very cold – hence the scarf around his neck – and we were shivering,' Schatzberg explained to *The Sunday Herald*'s Alan Taylor in 2008. But as discussions had brought *Blonde on Blonde* to mind, it's likely that another element of its cover design influenced Ray Lowry: the inside of the gatefold of the original issue features nine black-and-white photographs stretched into unusually long and thin portrait or landscape shapes, just like the two shots on the back cover of *London Calling*.

The following year, the Beatles hired pop artist Peter Blake to realise their concept for *Sgt. Pepper's Lonely Hearts Club* band. Although a single album, it boasts a gatefold sleeve, a photo collage on the front and – for the first time on a popular music album – the lyrics reproduced on the back. When it came to package their 1968 double album, the Beatles hired another British pop artist, Richard Hamilton. He decided to buck the trend, and came up with the ultimate minimalist idea: an eponymous album with a plain white sleeve bearing no title

or band name. It was subsequently decided to add a serial number to
the front, referencing both bootlegs (at that time a fairly recent development, usually housed in plain white sleeves, hence the title of the
famous Bob Dylan bootleg *The Great White Wonder*) and limited edition
art prints. A last-minute failure of nerve led to *The Beatles* being
embossed on the front. But the outer sleeve was memorable enough
for public opinion to re-title the record *The White Album*. Hamilton's
contribution wasn't all conceptual, though: he asked the Beatles to
give him personal photographs, and used them to create a collage to
appear on one side of a fold-out poster insert, while the other side
again reproduced the lyrics.

A tradition had been established that the Greatest Rock'n'Roll
Band In The World – a title the Stones felt justified in claiming once
the Beatles split – should have its record covers by one of the world's
foremost visual artists. The cover of the Stones' 1971 album *Sticky
Fingers* was designed by Andy Warhol. The following year they
recorded a double album of loose, muddy rock'n'roll, R&B, blues,
soul and country tracks, which they titled *Exile on Main St.* in wry
acknowledgement of their recently acquired tax-exile status.
Although recorded by a British band resident in France, this was
American roots music. The visual artist chosen to illustrate the cover
was photographer Robert Frank, best known for his 1958 black-and-
white photo-documentary book *The Americans*, photographs taken
during the course of a road trip around the USA. With a foreword
by Jack Kerouac, it is the visual equivalent of the latter's Beat
Generation bible *On the Road*, which had been published the
preceding year. The overall design of *Exile On Main St.* is by underground culture designer – and surf artist – John Van Hamersveld,
using Frank's photos. He went for something self-consciously Beat.
Although the outer sleeve houses both discs in the same pocket, it
has an envelope-style gatefold as well as two inner sleeves. The front
cover is a black-and-white collage from *The Americans*, the back cover
a black-and-white collage of more recent shots of the Rolling Stones
in the studio and hanging around on Main Street, Los Angeles. The
gatefold envelope interiors mix elements of the two. So do the inner
sleeves. For the front cover, Hamersveld used a deliberately slap-
dash handwritten scrawl for the band name and album, and for the
inner sleeves he also wrote out the song titles and credits (though

not lyrics). As he himself later claimed, this was the punk aesthetic four years before punk.

The similarities with *London Calling* are too many to be entirely coincidental: a wide range of predominately black-influenced roots musics on an 18-track double album in a single, matt black-and-white sleeve with a retro-theme, featuring American road-trip photography and hand-scrawled titles and notes. (Had the plan to promote *London Calling* with a flexi-disc freebie in the *NME* come off, the connections would have reached eerie proportions: the Rolling Stones had done exactly the same thing with *Exile on Main St.*)

The packaging for *London Calling* is *Elvis Presley* crossed with *Exile on Main St.*, with a hint or two of *Blonde on Blonde* and *The White Album*.

★

Ray Lowry's commission didn't end with the design for the album. He was also asked to come up with something for the planned UK single releases, in both 7-inch and 12-inch formats; the 7-inch backing 'London Calling' with 'Armagideon Time', the 12-inch placing both those tracks on one side and the latter's dub version(s) 'Justice Tonight'/'Kick It Over' on the reverse. Ray opted to continue with the Elvis 'plagiarinspiration' theme. In the late Fifties Elvis's UK singles were released on the HMV label, and the standard HMV 78 rpm and 45 rpm company singles bags of the era featured the 'dancing Fifties teens' illustration that Ray appropriated for the back sleeve of the Clash single. The original design was intended to fit around a central label hole, so Ray modified it slightly to make the composition work better for a sleeve without a hole: he moved a distant background couple from the centre to the left side, and brought the foreground dancers closer together in the centre. Other than that, it's a straight steal. The hand-lettered italic typography Ray uses for the titles on both sides of the single is also remarkably close in style to the lettering used for the strapline 'For The Tops in Pops' on the original HMV bag.

The image on the front of Ray's sleeve is of a Fifties teenage couple sitting on the floor next to a Dansette-type record player, listening to a record and with other records and their sleeves strewn all around them. Ray admitted this was 'another rip-off', but this time it's of a general style rather than a particular image. Among others, its nods to a late Fifties company sleeve used by Columbia records (the C of CBS), but Ray relies more on his own talents as an illustrator. The kids are in the process of digging the debut albums by Elvis Presley, the Beatles, the Rolling Stones and – even more anachronistically – the Sex Pistols and the Clash themselves. The odd one out, shown face down, is Bob Dylan's *Highway 61 Revisited* (and even that, arguably, is Dylan's debut full electric album). These were all touchstone records for Ray, and again made the connection between the best punk bands and the greats of yesteryear. They were also, he claimed, the records the Clash were listening to at the time. In 2004 he admitted to Simon Harper of *The Clash* magazine that he was consciously referencing the '1977' lyric 'No Elvis, Beatles or the Rolling Stones / In 1977' in a way that turned that rejection on its head: the Clash had worked their way through their 'kill your fathers' period, and were now embracing their creative forebears. The tribute to the artists depicted is not intended in any way sarcastically, but is instead wholly genuine.

The reggae side of things had been overlooked by the design department so far, but Ray makes amends by using three different background colours on three different versions of the standard 7-inch single: red, yellow or green, the traditional Rasta and reggae colours, derived from the Ethiopian flag. In this subtle way he brings together the rock and reggae elements of the songs, the single and the Clash's influences. It's a touch that only reveals itself when all three sleeve variations are displayed side by side, which, naturally, also made for added collectability when the single was released on 7 December 1979. (The contradiction between pegging album prices to save fans money and using gimmicks like different singles sleeves and formats to part them from more of it was something the Clash never really got to grips with.) Mercifully, the 12-inch single was identical in design, and only came in yellow. This was the Clash's first 12-inch, and unlike many earlier punk 12-inch singles the use of format is justified by the nature of the content: the extended dub versions need all the space they can get. Like the album, both the 7-inch and 12-inch single formats have plain white record labels rather than the standard CBS orange.

Even when Ray submitted all of his finished designs for the album and single, no one at CBS in the UK, or Epic in the USA, voiced any concern about possible legal repercussions from a rival major record company. 'We didn't bother about clearing the various borrowings,' says Ray. 'I'm afraid I was on a mission, and really couldn't have given a fuck at the time. Punk rock and all that, old boy. As far as I know, nobody got any grief from anywhere. Nobody even knows who put the Elvis album cover together, so we were on pretty solid ground, there. No legals.'

Asked if he was well reimbursed for his efforts, he replied: 'For doing the *London Calling* album cover, plus those little single sleeves, I was paid – wait for it – nine hundred pounds in toto. Finito. Absurdo.' As £900 in 1979 would have been roughly the equivalent of £4,000 in 2007, it's not that absurdo . . . but, then again, he had spent approximately that amount of his own money going along on the Take the 5th tour. Ray did not depart from the Clash's employ with any bad feeling. He chose not to hang around and put himself forward for future Clash commissions because – an entirely honourable and slightly self-conscious man – he didn't want to be seen as a freeloader. As he admits, he was also a little jaded. He went back to the cartooning day job.

The single of 'London Calling' backed with 'Armagideon Time' was released in the UK on 7 December 1979. Both Andy Gill at the *NME* and Ian Birch in *Melody Maker* commented on its apocalyptic lyrics and new musical maturity. Gill admired their 'terse restraint' and credited Guy Stevens for the 'powerful cleanliness of the production'. Birch enjoyed the song's 'irresistibly rolling gait' and believed Joe's lyrics benefited from 'the natural assurance and clarity' of their delivery. As a taster for the album, the single had done its job: both reviewers said they were keen to hear *London Calling*.

Don Letts, another long-time associate of the band, was invited to make a video for 'London Calling'. Don had taught himself how to use a Super-8 to make *The Punk Rock Movie* and *Rankin' Movie*, and had recently shot a video for PiL. The concept for the 'London Calling' promo was to film the band playing not just 'by the river' but so close to it they were on it. The location chosen was the Royal Festival Pier in Battersea Park, at the midpoint between Albert Bridge and Chelsea Bridge, which was, again, on the route of the Number 19 bus. According to Mick Jones, who evidently did his homework, the pier was built in 1951 specifically for royalty arriving at the park for the opening of the Festival of Britain. The idea was to set the band's equipment up on the pier, and film them performing 'London Calling' from a boat in the river. Don Letts tells a well-polished anecdote about how – being a Rasta – he didn't do water, and therefore didn't understand that the Thames was tidal, which meant that when he wanted to start filming the boat was a good 10 feet lower down than he had anticipated. The band and crew had to wait for the water level to rise and other adjustments to be made. It was early December, windy and very cold. And then it started to rain. Pennie Smith tried to keep people occupied by taking photographs, and Johnny Green sent out for a warming bottle of brandy, most of which he consumed himself.

Finally, as twilight turned to night, Don was able to get enough material in the can to put together a video. Having been introduced to a couple of good tailors by Kosmo Vinyl, the band had modified their collective look a little to throw the Forties Brighton spiv style in on top of American mobster, cowboy, and rocker. They had overcoats, and hats, and bandannas. The overall effect was somewhere between *The Wild Bunch* (1969), the early years De Niro sequences from *The Godfather Part II* (1974), and *Brighton Rock*. Although shot in colour, the combination of retro clothing styles and dusk and gave it all a film noir aspect: everything black and white except for pinkish faces and flashes of blue suede brothel creepers, a red tie, pocket handkerchief and hatband. The lashing rain and the menacing black river add an appropriately biblical element to proceedings. All this, as Don has cheerfully admitted, was achieved almost entirely by accident. 'Like everything with punk rock, we made our problems our assets,' he told *Uncut* in 2003. When the shoot was finished, a soaking, freezing and drunk Johnny Green expressed his misery at the prospect of being left behind for another couple of hours to dismantle the equipment by heaving one of the – hired – monitors into the river. The band's own gear was so waterlogged that the following day's rehearsals for the upcoming Christmas gigs and January tour had to be cancelled.

The single rose quickly up the charts. Joe was invited on to BBC Radio 1's *Round Table* to be a member of a panel discussing other record releases, and while on air expressed his doubts that 'London

Calling' would make the Top 10 without the band promoting it on *Top Of The Pops*, which they still refused to do. With a nod to the second track of the album, DJ Annie Nightingale bet him a Cadillac that it would. In the event, it stalled at Number 11 – the Clash's highest chart appearance so far, and all the more impressive at a time of year when by far the most singles are sold – leaving Annie in something of a pickle. Luckily for her, a regular listener offered her a Cadillac with which to pay her debt. Unable to drive, and – at that time still a good deal more concerned than he would be in later life about the message that owning such an ostentatiously American rock'n'roll motor car would send – Joe decided to donate it to a raffle, the proceeds from which would go to benefit the recession-hit English steel town of Corby. The slightly disgruntled winner discovered that the Cadillac was anything but brand new . . . instead, it was so old and decrepit it didn't even go.

A week after the single, the album was released. In the UK it was cheekily promoted with a full-page music press ad showing rock'n'roll-era Elvis Presley in a gold lamé suit holding a copy of *London Calling*: a lovely visual pun. 'Young Mr Strummer himself came up with the press ad idea,' says Ray Lowry. 'At the time, I thought we might get some trouble with that one, but – as far as I know – nothing ensued. Shows you how much the boy went along with the rock'n'roll thing, which at the time I thought might be pushing it a bit.'

It was time for the inky reviews, and with the consensus opinion from the earlier part of 1979 being less than complimentary about the Clash's new material, the band's confidence must have wavered slightly during the few days prior to release. At the *NME* Charles Shaar Murray was uncomfortable with the macho bluster of 'The Guns of Brixton', what he took to be the self-glorification of 'Four Horsemen', and the questionable sexual politics of 'Lover's Rock'. But he began by saying this was the first of the Clash's albums 'to be equal to their legend', and the first to sound right. The band were 'writing, singing and playing for their lives', but also 'purely for fun'. After that, he became effusive: 'The Clash have been criticised for being a "straight-ahead rock-and-roll band", which is specious in the extreme. The Clash love rock and roll, which is why they play it, but they want it to live up to its promises, which is why they play it the way they do.' He commended them for putting their money where their mouths were on pricing. The Clash should be very proud, he concluded. 'This is the one.'

At *Melody Maker* James Truman also believed the Clash had come back from the low-point of *Give 'Em Enough Rope* with their best album so far. 'The Clash have discovered America, and by the same process, themselves.' At *Sounds*, though, Garry Bushell had not changed his opinion markedly in the last six months: in a review headlined 'Give 'Em Enough Dope' – by no means the last time the ganja-loving Clash would hear *that* one – he poured scorn on the whole endeavour: 'Unable to go forward, they've clutched at straws, ending up retro-gressing via Strummer's R&B past and Jones's Keith Richards fixation to the outlaw imagery of the Stones and tired old rock clichés.' He gave it just two out of five stars. BBC London DJ and critic Charlie Gillett commented that some songs sounded like 'second-rate Bob Dylan with horns'.

As if to validate the predictions of the album's title song and its video, strange tidal forces came into play following the release of *London Calling*. The swirls, eddies, ebbs, flows and rips evident in the response of some sectors of the music press had been created and stirred up by a three-year storm of punk propaganda. Over the next month or two, other critics' opinions started to come through as asides in other features and reviews. Writers who expected the mode of the music to have been forever changed by punk found the retro flavour of *London Calling* somewhere between inappropriate for the times and hugely disappointing. To put it in context, and perhaps paradoxically, the same qualities that make *London Calling* sound like a timeless classic today could make it sound dated in post-punk, city-shaken 1979.

At the time, a more radical future seemed to be offered by the needling funk of Gang of Four and Talking Heads, the industrial gloom of Joy Division, the icy, cerebral prog of Magazine and the wailing kraut-rock dub of PiL. While *London Calling* was a new direc-tion for a punk band like the Clash, it also sounded – as claimed by Garry Bushell, and contested by Charles Shaar Murray – like a back-wards step from punk to trad rock. The Elvis and Stones references in the packaging didn't help, and nor did the American tour photo-graphs, and the American roots musics and America-referencing lyrics within. The Jam managed to remain critically popular despite being even more obviously traditional than the Clash by simply remaining determinedly English in outlook and reference. Over two years later, Joe would affect bemusement at accusations of 'going American'. 'I never thought about beefburgers once, or Mickey Mouse, or the Statue of Liberty,' he blustered to the *NME*'s Roz Reines. Maybe not, but he clearly did think about Coca-Cola, Cadillacs and 42nd Street.

Given that it was released in the final month of the year, 'London Calling' did well to be voted the third Best Single of 1979 in the *NME*'s year end critics' poll, following behind the Jam's 'Eton Rifles' at Number 1, and the Specials' Bernie Rhodes-quoting 'Gangsters'. The Clash beat Gloria Gaynor's 'I Will Survive' at 4, and a plethora of hits that remain radio regulars even to this day by artists as diverse as Chic, Michael Jackson and his brothers, Earth, Wind & Fire, Eddie Grant, M, the Police, Elvis Costello, XTC, Talking Heads, Blondie and the Pretenders.

A strong single has an instant impact. Given that the album was only available for a couple of weeks before the *NME* critics were polled, and had 19 songs for listeners to digest, it's perhaps not so surprising that *London Calling* was only voted eighth Best Album. Listing its rivals should give a better sense of the musical climate of the time: *Fear of Music* by Talking Heads came top, then *Metal Box* by PiL, *Unknown Pleasures* by Joy Division, *Setting Sons* by the Jam, *Entertainment!* by Gang of Four, *Armed Forces* by Elvis Costello, and – almost unbelievably, seeing it was considered to be such a let down after *New Boots and Panties* – *Do It Yourself* by Mickey Gallagher's other band, Ian Dury and the Blockheads. Among those trailing behind the Clash were the now Rumour Brass-free Graham Parker with *Squeezing Out Sparks*, *The Specials*, *The Undertones*, *Cut* by the Slits, *Regatta de Blanc* by the Police, and *Rust Never Sleeps* by Neil Young. It was a great year for music.

There was no singles poll at the *Melody Maker*, and the album showed less well, coming in at number 10 in the critics' Top 20 of the year, behind Talking Heads, the Gang of Four, *Forces of Victory* by Linton Kwesi Johnson, the Slits, the Jam, Graham Parker, *Off the Wall* by Michael Jackson, *I Am* by Earth, Wind & Fire and PiL. *London Calling* failed to show at all in the *Sounds* critics' Top 10 albums of the year, which led with the Specials, Talking Heads, the Slits, the Jam and Graham Parker.

With regard to the British artists appearing on the above lists, the key themes to pull out as 'signs of the times' are the legacy of the Winter of Discontent's economic squeeze and concern about the implications of the move to the Right signalled by Margaret Thatcher's election victory. Some are dark, depressive, brooding and insular; some are concerned with spiritual, cultural and moral bankruptcy; and some demonstrate anxiety about political extremism, aggressive policing, and the threat of war and conscription. *London Calling* ticks most of these boxes.

The critical reaction to the band over 1979 as a whole undoubtedly influenced the inky readership's initial response to the album – the view of the Everypunk on the Number 19 Omnibus, so to speak – to the extent that the Clash ceded their premier position in the *NME* readers' polls to the Jam in several categories. Although the Clash themselves didn't realise it at the time, though, the wider marketplace was catching up to punk, and preparing to open its arms in a tentative way to the more approachable side of New Wave music: as in, new wave music with tunes that bore some relation to the music of the past. As well as retaining their loyal core following, the Clash had just made an album that would prove accessible to people who liked the Stones and Dylan and Springsteen, and – for that matter – the Police, the Specials, the Jam and the Boomtown Rats. The album did better than the single, climbing to Number 9 and remaining on the charts for 20 weeks. It went Gold by the end of December 1979. That is, immediately.

The Clash spent December back in the rehearsal room. Not Vanilla, but another by-the-hour concern in south London, this time in Disraeli Road, Putney. Almost as if consciously bookending the *London Calling* recording experience, they had arranged another brace of self-promoted, low-key London gigs followed by a higher-profile benefit show. The first two shows were to be held on Christmas Day and Boxing Day at the 250-capacity Acklam Hall community centre under the Westway. The benefit, on 27 December at the Hammersmith Odeon, was one of four Concerts for the People of Kampuchea (the former and future Cambodia), recently freed from the grasp of their evil *presidenté*. The Clash played as special 'surprise' guests of Ian Dury and the Blockheads, with Matumbi of 'The Man in Me' fame also on the bill.

Like the Notre Dame shows almost six months earlier, the first two shows were real DIY efforts. Unusually for the Clash, the PA was the cheapest they could find. Pennie Smith took photos of the band posing round at Mick's Nan's flat in their transatlantic noir gangster threads to be used on a free Christmas card. She also donated a Take the 5th tour photo of Mick dancing in a straw boater and a red clown's nose to be used on a poster advertising the event. Kosmo paid for the posters to be printed out of his own pocket, and spent Christmas Eve putting them up around Notting Hill. On Christmas Day, Johnny Green and Baker struggled in to set up despite the lack of public transport, and Kosmo entered into the spirit of the event by turning up to MC in a gold lamé Elvis suit.

The Clash had a new sartorial element of their own to add to their ever-growing wardrobe: Alex Michon and Krys Kolowska had been asked to make some two-colour, Fifties-style bowling shirts – black back and sleeves, white, red, blue or yellow chest panels – which would remain a staple part of the band's onstage costume for the following year.

Pennie couldn't make it, but the Clash's favourite American photographer, Bob Gruen, was present to document the show. Montgomery Clift had featured on the flyer for the July Notre Dame shows playing his bugle as Robert E. Lee Prewitt. For the Acklam Hall gigs, Paul Simonon had acquired a real bugle, and tried to persuade Baker to play the band onstage. It proved too much for the drum roadie, but it turned out that Bob Gruen knew how to squeeze a sound out of the instrument. He did the honours for both shows, and again before the encore at the Concert for Kampuchea.

Although the price of admission to the Acklam Hall gigs was just 50p, the first show was quiet – people simply didn't believe the band would be playing at that venue on Christmas Day – but word had got around by the following day, to the extent that a bunch of skinheads mounted a stage invasion during 'White Riot'. The 101ers had played the Acklam Hall, too, and as 'Keys to Your Heart' had just been re-released on Big Beat, the Clash included it in their set.

The Kampuchea show was uncomfortable for the Clash. It was a favour for the Office, but they were conscious of playing second fiddle to Blackhill's other band, the Blockheads, and it was definitely not their crowd. Reviewing the show Paul Rambali became the latest *NME* journalist to find the Clash's approach to the stage raised a lot of questions. Mickey Gallagher again appeared with the Clash – as he would for the upcoming tour – and Mick Jones took the opportunity to return the favour, dressed in black and playing Joe's butterscotch Telecaster on the Blockheads' 'Sweet Gene Vincent'. This annoyed Joe, almost as much as Joe's insistence on the Clash encoring with the chaos-inciting 'White Riot' annoyed Mick. It wasn't quite the celebratory end to the year the Clash might have hoped for. With the band members tired, and having just committed themselves to the best part of another six months on the road, the always-present tensions in the Clash camp were destined to boil over on more than one occasion in the near future.

5 January 1980 saw the opening night of the two-month-long UK leg of the 16 Tons tour. It was named after the song '16 Tons', recorded in 1946 by Merle Travis, but taken to Number 1 in the USA by Tennessee Ernie Ford in 1955. Another vintage bit of Americana, it fitted right in with the Clash's retro vibe, but it was chosen because of its pertinent chorus: the coal miner protagonist works all day, shifts 16 tons of coal, and gets nothing but one day older and deeper in debt. If Saint Peter calls him, he won't be able to go, because he owes his soul to the company store. Once again, the Clash had to borrow from CBS in order to go back on the road.

The main support was supposed to be Toots and the Maytals (of 'Pressure Drop' fame), but they pulled out at the last moment. Ian Dury and the Blockheads repaid a debt by supporting on the first night in Aylesbury, but after that Mikey Dread was drafted in as a replacement. Don Letts had made tapes of Mikey's Jamaican radio show *Dread at the Controls* for Paul Simonon, and his inventiveness not only as a DJ, but also as a toaster impressed the band immensely. He was in London at the time, and was invited to be a solo support, aided only with a combination of tapes and live sound effects, like squeaky toys and matchboxes. Gradually, one or two at a time, the crew and the band started slipping onstage behind him to skank along with bandannas pulled down low over their faces. Mikey also guested during the Clash's encore, adding a toast to 'Armagideon Time'.

The *London Calling* songs played regularly on the tour were 'London Calling', now with its proper lyric, 'Brand New Cadillac', 'Jimmy Jazz', 'Clampdown', 'The Guns of Brixton', 'Koka Kola', 'Wrong 'Em Boyo', and a newly worked-up 'Train in Vain'. Plus 'Armagideon Time'. More occasionally, the band played 'Death or Glory', 'Rudie Can't Fail', 'Revolution Rock' and 'Spanish Bombs'. The other song for Palmolive, 'Keys to Your Heart', also continued to make an occasional appearance. Mikey Dread – who quickly saw where the Clash were coming from – tried to persuade them to cover Alton Ellis's rude-boy classic 'Dance Crasher', but it never got past soundchecks. The band had more fun messing around with Percy Mayfield's tribute to Jack Kerouac's *On the Road*, 'Hit the Road, Jack' as recorded in 1961 by Ray Charles and brought back into the Clash's ken by Big Youth's 1976 DJ reggae cover: the band would usually segue it into their version of 'Police & Thieves'.

The Clash's UK fans adapted quickly to their new material, even 'Jimmy Jazz'. 'I *never* thought I'd see the Apollo full of Scotsmen pogoing to it! Never, never, never!' Joe told Robbi Millar of *Sounds* in Glasgow in late January. Not that it would be all plain sailing when the tour hit Europe that May. 'I remember a skinhead getting me in Berlin and saying, "Vot is that!? My grandmother likes 'Wrong 'Em Boyo!'" He was on the edge. He couldn't believe it,' Joe told *Musician*'s Bill Flanagan in 1988. It can't really have come as much of a surprise to the Clash that their new music was more accessible to a wider demographic (one line from 'Death or Glory', perhaps, excepted). It was less aggressive, less musically brutal, less lyrically barbed: no longer aimed solely at expressing anger and frustration to teenagers and twentysomethings. That the Clash were now perceived as an established (if not quite Establishment) rock band, rather than just a bunch of offensive upstarts, was testified to by BBC1's mainstream tea-time news magazine show *Nationwide*'s decision to send a film crew to Scotland to file a report on the UK tour.

Whether or not the Clash discussed this among themselves, they did acknowledge it in more subtle ways. They now felt it was OK for their families to see what they were doing. Joe's father, Ron Mellor, had come along on 5 July 1979 to the first Notre Dame show; Mick's mother Renee had attended the first night of the Take the 5th tour on 12 August in Minneapolis, and even Stella, Mick's 80-year-old Nan, had come along to the Christmas Day show at the Acklam Hall (and had liked it too, with the caveat that it was 'a bit loud'). At the 6 January 1980 16 Tons tour show at the Odeon in Canterbury, a box was set aside for Paul's father and step-mother and Topper's parents, and Johnny Green attended to their every need.

While Mick was happy with a less frenetic atmosphere, Joe was conflicted. Mick finally refused to play 'White Riot' at the Top Rank in Sheffield on 27 January, whereupon Joe physically attacked him, requiring Mick to go on for the encore with a bandanna over his bloodied face. In Hamburg on 20 May, taunting from the aggressively radical punk audience – who believed *London Calling* represented a sell-out – provoked Joe to lash out from the stage with his guitar. He was arrested and cautioned. More importantly, at the root of this was a fundamental disagreement about what the Clash should be. Mick wanted to move on, develop, experiment. Joe was interested in this too, up to a point, but it was more important for him that the Clash should embody a spirit and an ideal, something that was partly to do with Class of 1976 punk and also partly to do with Class of 1955 rock'n'roll. Anything too safe or too pop, anything too self-indulgent or elaborate, and his hackles started to rise.

After a month on the road in the UK, the Clash took advantage of a day off on 2 February 1980 to book into Pluto studios in Manchester to record 'Bankrobber' as the band's next UK single. Mikey Dread produced, and supplied the DJ toast B-side 'Rockers Galore . . . UK Tour'. Joe expressed the intention of releasing it in late February, the first instalment of a planned yearlong Singles Bonanza, with the band recording and releasing one single after another throughout 1980. The plan hit an immediate snag: the Clash's great friend and champion, Maurice Oberstein, Head of CBS UK, apparently refused point-blank to release 'Bankrobber'. The quote attributed to him by Joe Strummer – redolent more of Joe Strummer's turn of phrase than Obie's – was that 'it sounds like all of David Bowie's records played backwards'. 'We loved the single!' objects Muff Winwood. 'If Maurice Oberstein said that, then it was all the art of the game.' Far more likely, the Clash just issued that statement because they refused to accept the real reason, which was purely business-related and consequently both slightly embarrassing for them and far less newsworthy for the indies.

Yet again the Clash were trying to pressure CBS into releasing a brand-new, non-album UK single too soon after the release of an album that had not yet had chance to fulfil its potential. And this time, the issue was further complicated by the fact that the same album had been available for less than a month in the USA, and the first American single from that album was still current. 'The Clash weren't dealing with their own increasing success by then,' says Muff. 'If you put out a record in the UK, and it becomes a hit, it becomes a hit in other countries in the world about two months later, including America. If you then go and put another record out within two months, all the other territories around the world go completely berserk. They say, "Hang on a minute. Our press people are just talking about record A, and all of a sudden they're getting information from their contacts in London about record B!" And the radio station stops playing record A because – guess what? – there's a hot new one just come over from England in the post and they're gonna play that instead, because it's cooler to play the new one. So you end up with neither of them being hits, because they're not coordinated in their release.' All a Singles Bonanza would achieve was to compound the confusion. It made more sense to release a second single from *London Calling*. The Clash dug their heels in, refused to release anything at all in the UK until CBS did their bidding, and went to the press. Stalemate.

On the 16 Tons tour for the first time the Clash were persuaded by Blackhill to take a professionally run merchandising stall on the road with them. Although manned from day to day by *Rude Boy* actor Terry McQuade, it was overseen by Terry Razor, who was in charge of merchandising at Stiff. The Clash also agreed to a tour programme. Wary of the standard expensive, glossy rip-offs offered by established rock bands at the time, they jiggled the concept a bit and came up with a rough'n'ready fanzine-style, black-and-white, A4-sized magazine retailing for 40p called *The Armagideon Times*. Rather than selling one programme for the entire duration of the tour, the plan was to produce a new issue to coincide with each substantial new development in Clashworld – each new leg of the tour, and/or each new instalment in the planned Singles Bonanza – and make it an ongoing publication, like a cross between *Sniffin' Glue* and *The Beatles Monthly*.

In addition to a history of the Clash to date written by Joe and Mick, the first 24-page edition includes a five-page guide to the songs on the *London Calling* album, with handwritten notes and sketches by all four members of the band. Co-designed by long-time Clash associate Robin 'Banks' Crocker, it features photographs by Pennie

Smith from the 'London Calling' video shoot and the 1979 Christmas card shoot at Mick's Nan's flat. The cover is a blow-up of the Paul Simonon image from the album cover. These familiar touches aside, though, if any illustration were required of how the Blackhill-Blockheads-Stiff connection was encroaching on the Clash's previously fiercely protected individualism, it was provided by the magazine: as well as the other co-designer being Terry Razor, art is by the Stiff Records design team of 'Jules and Eddie', and of four and a half pages of ads, a full page is devoted to Blackhill, and a half page to the Blockheads.

The Clash were not happy with this. *The Armagideon Times No. 2*, again 24 pages, was published in mid-February to cover the latter part of the UK leg of the tour. The co-editors are now Robin Banks and Kris Needs. Photographs – much more professionally reproduced – are again by Pennie Smith, this time from the 16 Tons tour, and the recording session for the 'Bankrobber' single. The band and crew, and DJ Barry Myers, contribute in slightly sardonic 'fave colour'-type questionnaires, and there is a page devoted to support act Mikey Dread. There's not an ad or a sniff of a Stiff in the entire publication: Mickey Gallagher doesn't get to do a questionnaire, and although the address given for Clash correspondence is that of the Blackhill office, the management team are not mentioned by name.

It was perhaps a little graceless of the Clash to distance themselves quite so pointedly, given the significant role that the Blackhill-Blockheads-Stiff axis had played in *London Calling* and the 1979 and 1980 tours, and was destined to play in the making of *Sandinista!*. Jules Balme – of Jules and Eddie – for example, would go on to design the sleeve for that album and for future Clash albums. In the end, though, it was CBS's refusal to release 'Bankrobber' in February 1980, and the resulting collapse of the Clash Singles Bonanza, that prevented there being any more editions of *The Armagideon Times* proper.

Although Epic had finally come around to the album being a double, they had not rolled over entirely. For the reasons Muff Winwood outlines in Part 3, they maintained it was not possible for them to offer 'two for the price of one', but they compromised with a 'special price' of $10, still well below the standard amount asked for a double at that time. Some of the fine detail of the packaging

was also sacrificed for the Epic release in the USA (and other territories: they also had the rights to release Clash material in Canada,
Brazil, Japan, Australia, and New Zealand). The album was given a
standard Epic matrix number. Only the demo copies were given
white labels: the main release has standard Epic labels, white italic
logo on a black-fading-to-blue background. Releasing the album later
than CBS UK, they were able to take advantage of that few weeks'
grace to add a sticker to the cover announcing '19 new songs including
the Hidden Cut "Train in Vain (Stand By Me)" (last song on side
4) . . . This album contains lyric content which may be offensive to
some members of the public.' Surprises of any sort were clearly out
of the question.

To promote the album Epic came up with an impressive, almost
Andy Warholesque, poster using treated multiple reproductions of the
album cover. Four images of *London Calling* are reproduced in a column
down the right-hand side, with four rows – alternately back-washed
with pink or green – of multiple negative images of Paul Simonon's
hunched figure running into them from the left.

Early American reviews were thin on the ground, but John Rockwell
at *The New York Times* was in print by 4 January. He praised songs full
of 'ingenious touches' and arrangements, and while he observed that
love and sex were more provenly successful themes than politics in
America, he believed that Epic wouldn't have any problems selling the
band to a mass audience: '*London Calling* may just be that increasingly
rare phenomenon, an album prized for its seriousness, even as it
reaches out to the millions.' *The New York Rocker*'s review saw the
Clash continuing 'to mature and progress at a stunning rate', and
concluded that their music now 'embraces all that is vital in rock-
'n'roll and black music of the last 20 years': 'There's just no limit to
where they can go.'

Filing for the *Village Voice* in early February, John Piccarella believed
that double albums were 'an expansive gamble on greatness', but that
'*London Calling* is a great one' . . . though he had his doubts about
'Lost in the Supermarket', 'whose bored, homebody lyrics sound as
though they were written by Jones's mother'. Reluctantly, recognising
the predictability of the comparison, he likened the album to the
Rolling Stones' *Exile on Main St.*, 'both albums achieve a far-reaching
redefinition of rock-and-roll history within the consistency of one

band's style', but asserted that the Clash's 'rude-boy maverick rebel-lion' carried a 'moral commitment' the Stones would not have aspired to. He was impressed by the Clash's honourable intentions in selling their double cheap, but felt compelled to point out that by releasing the album in the UK before Christmas the band had 'unwittingly' ensured that 25,000 American fans bought it on import 'at inflated prices', which in turn robbed the Epic version of sales and the band of a higher chart placing.

The album made Number 27 in the US charts anyway, but Epic were in no hurry to release a single. They did send a couple of promo singles/EPs out, though: a 10-inch white label of 'Clampdown' backed with 'Brand New Cadillac' and 'Spanish Bombs', and a 12-inch white label featuring 'Clampdown' and 'Lost in the Supermarket' on the A-side, and 'The Card Cheat' and 'London Calling' on the flip. It's plain that 'London Calling' was not considered a priority, and 'Clampdown' being the lead track on both promos signifies that it was the early frontrunner for release as a single. In the event, on 12 February, a little closer to the Clash's planned visit for the American leg of the 16 Tons tour, Mick's mainstream-friendly – but hardly typical – 'hidden extra track' was chosen as the A-side of the official release, its title length-ened to 'Train in Vain (Stand By Me)'; 'London Calling' was relegated to the B-side: two tracks culled from an album that had already been available for several weeks, with nothing extra to tempt those who had already bought that album. The UK single sleeve was not adapt-able, so Epic issued it in a standard 1979 Epic company bag, which – as picture sleeves were by that time very much standard for punk or new-wave releases – only served to further diminish its desirability as an artefact. It still climbed to Number 27 in the charts, and in the process helped make the Clash more palatable for American audi-ences: a bunch of rebel rockers with soft centres, rather than a bunch of angry politicos with big boots and foul mouths.

To promote the single, Don Letts filmed the Clash performing 'Train in Vain' during their 16 Tons show at Lewisham Odeon on 18 February 1979. Mickey Gallagher's organ is almost inaudible, but it's a rousing version. The Clash are immaculate in black again, and – perhaps with America in mind – once again more Fifties rock'n'roll than Brighton spiv: Paul looks exactly like he does on the cover of *London Calling*, and the rest of the band exactly like they do in the

'I Fought the Law' sequence from *Rude Boy*. Don also filmed 'Clampdown' at the same show, which indicates that song was still a contender for a single release in various territories. In Australia, Epic had also circulated a 12-inch white label, this time featuring 'Stand By Me (Train in Vain)' (*sic*) and 'Clampdown', backed with 'London Calling' and 'Lost in the Supermarket'. In the event, Australia was the only territory that gave 'Clampdown' an official single release, as a 7-inch backed with 'The Guns of Brixton'. It has a picture sleeve, very obviously something knocked up by the local Epic in-house team, featuring a poor live photograph of the Clash accompanied by clunky yellow typography.

The American leg of 16 Tons was just 9 dates in 10 days, from 1–10 March 1980. In part this was to keep costs down and avoid the funding problems of the last two visits. The travelling contingent was noticeably smaller than last time, but Johnny Green, Baker, Kosmo, Mickey Gallagher and Barry Myers were included. Also along for the jaunt were Mikey Dread and, filling the now traditional role of original R&B star, Lee Dorsey, whose performance of his 1966 American Number 8 hit 'Working in the Coalmine' fitted in perfectly with the Clash's nightly play-on music of '16 Tons'. Because the band were concentrating on key markets spread out across the States, they had to fly between shows, which took some of the sting out of the experience. The last night was Detroit, where the Clash played a benefit show for Jackie Wilson and visited the original Motown studio.

The key American reviews for *London Calling* belatedly emerged in April. *Rolling Stone*'s Tom Carson pointed out that expectations were high, that the Clash were contenders for the title of the Greatest Rock'n'Roll Band in the World, a role which – and here he unknowingly echoed the Clash's own *Last Testament*-type thinking – was 'about synonymous with being the music's last hope'. He celebrated *London Calling* as 'merry and tough, passionate and large-spirited', and noted how it is not merely an exercise in romantic rock'n'roll rebellion, but an album that explores the whole of rock's history for its sounds, and its library of myths and legends for its themes. Over at the not quite so widely influential but more street-conscious *Creem*, Billy Altman had positive things to say about the production, the guitar playing and many of the individual songs, but seemed more interested in exploring his theory that the title track's dire warnings are so powerful that they overwhelm the rest of the album. The humour in such humorous songs as 'Koka Kola', 'Four Horsemen' and 'Revolution Rock' failed to translate for him. He found the lyrical vision relentlessly dark and worthy: 'The four sides of *London Calling* have me feeling like I've been levelled by the weight of the world.'

An even more positive boost than the *Rolling Stone* review came two weeks later, on 17 April 1980, when the magazine ran a four-page Clash cover interview-cum-history. In America, as the 1973 Dr Hook song claims, getting the cover of *Rolling Stone* was a big promotional deal. While James Henke's piece was important in giving the band that all-important third dimension for their American audience, Annie Leibovitz's photograph of Joe Strummer and Mick Jones – Joe all in black with rolled sleeves, red bandanna and red comb in his back pocket, Mick wearing an Alex Michon bowling shirt and smoking a cigarette – did everything necessary to sell the band as effortlessly cool Champions of the Quest.

Just a week later, on 25 April, the Clash made their debut American TV appearance on ABC's late-night comedy show *Fridays* to perform four songs, and give the viewing public a cleverly conceived introduction to both *London Calling* and the Clash live experience (and, slightly more unfortunately, Mick Jones's purple Kid Creole suit). First Joe took centre stage to sing 'London Calling', then Mick to sing the American A-side, 'Train in Vain'. After a break for some comedy and a costume change, Paul swapped instruments with Joe to sing 'The Guns of Brixton'. And to complete this stunning display of range and versatility, Joe climbed up on Mickey Gallagher's organ for the introduction of a powerhouse 'Clampdown'. It's hard to believe anyone under 40 who saw *Fridays* was able to resist paying a visit to their friendly neighbourhood record store on Saturday.

After a fortnight off in London – during which period the *Rude Boy* film was officially released, with legal action threatened but ultimately not taken by the Clash – the 16 Tons tour recommenced in Europe, committing the exhausted band to another six weeks on the road. Every effort was being made to promote *London Calling* as thoroughly and extensively as possible, and that extended to record releases. Both *London Calling* the album and 'London Calling' the single had been released in mainland Europe in the UK sleeves. The album did well in Scandinavia, reaching Number 2 in Sweden and Number 4 in Norway.

Half a year later, though, a new release was required to give the European leg of the tour some currency.

Talking to Robbi Millar of *Sounds* a few days before the 'Bankrobber' recording session, Joe had mentioned the possibility of releasing a three-track combination of old and new for the Clash's next UK single. Had discussions gone more smoothly, and the Singles Bonanza not been an obstacle, a compromise might well have been reached grouping 'Bankrobber' with a couple of tracks from *London Calling*. That very compromise was agreed with CBS Europe in June 1980, at which time a three-track Dutch pressing of a 7-inch 33 rpm maxi-single with 'Train in Vain' on the A-side and 'Bankrobber' and 'Rockers Galore . . . UK Tour' on the flip was released. The CBS pressing plant in Haarlem in the Netherlands was used for discs intended to supply most of Continental Europe, so a Dutch pressing does not mean that the single was available only in the Netherlands. The version with sleeve details in English was also made available in Germany and France and very likely elsewhere (and, via Epic, pressings would also be issued in Brazil, Australia and New Zealand).

'Fucking hell! The fucking Dutch single of fucking "Train in Frigging Vain"?' responds Ray Lowry when asked if he was involved in its design. 'Never seen it, thank God.' Nothing to do with him, then. Which did not prevent the anonymous CBS in-house designer responsible from appropriating elements of Ray's rough drafts for the *London Calling* album, where – as with this single – the Presley typography was used to spell THE down the left side and CLASH along the bottom. The song titles are hand-scrawled at the top, also in an approximation of Ray's italic title for the 'London Calling' single. The front cover features a live action photograph of the A-side's composer and vocalist, Mick Jones, caught mid-skank and mid-exhale during the Clash's Christmas Day 1979 gig at the Acklam Hall. On the back cover is a photo of the Clash plus organist Mickey Gallagher at Niagara Falls, wearing hats and goofing around like the early Beatles during the Take the 5th tour. This is the only time that Mickey appears in a Clash group shot on a record sleeve . . . even though he was not involved in the European leg of 16 Tons. Proof that the release was Clash-sanctioned is provided by the photographer credit for both shots: Paul's girlfriend Debra Kronick. This is a – temporary – break with the new tradition of Pennie Smith being responsible for all photos of the band used on official releases; but it does continue the trend of the Clash involving supporters and friends whenever possible. In Spain, the same single with much the same typography was released with a Pennie Smith Take the 5th tour action photo on the front cover, this time of Topper Headon hoisting his towel aloft while leaving his drum kit at the end of a set. The back cover features a portrait of Mikey Dread, and the sleeve notes are in Spanish (not Clash Spannish).

A second three-track single pressed in the Netherlands slightly later features 'Rudie Can't Fail' on the A-side, and – strangely – the same additional tracks as 'Train in Vain' on the flip. The typography and design are also the same, but the front cover now features Pennie's shot of Joe Strummer throwing his Esquire into the wings on the Take the 5th tour. So there was another conceptual link between the parent album and the three Continental European singles lifted from the album: each release features a 1979 live action shot of a different member of the band.

The first of the above three singles is the most significant in terms of wider influence on the Clash story, because it was also imported into the UK, with the band's connivance. It sold well on the strength of including the otherwise unavailable, but – thanks to the row with CBS UK – much publicised 'Bankrobber'. The Clash just wanted the song to be heard, but the inevitable result was that common financial sense won out. CBS finally caved in and agreed to release 'Bankrobber' as a UK single in its own right in August 1980. Whereupon, despite the number of import copies already sold, it climbed to Number 12, the band's second-best performance so far. The Clash proclaimed this a victory. If it was, it was a pyrrhic one. Had the band agreed to 'Train in Vain' being released in the UK in February, CBS would probably have been happy for 'Bankrobber' to follow in April or May. By August, CBS had killed the concept of the Singles Bonanza stone dead. Meanwhile, the band had stockpiled so much material during the period of stalemate that they were starting to get unhealthy CBS-baiting notions of following up the unwelcome double album London Calling with the triple album Sandinista!.

The 16 Tons tour wound down messily, with some postponed UK gigs interspersed with a handful of European festival appearances, but its spiritual Big Finish was a two-night stand at the Hammersmith

Palais on 16 and 17 June 1980, with Mickey Gallagher back on keyboards and Mikey Dread back as support and guest toaster.

By early 1980 it was time to think about putting together a *Clash 3rd Songbook* to cover the *London Calling* material. In keeping with the 'friends of the band' ethos, Johnny Green's girlfriend – and soon to be wife – Lindy Poltock was put in charge of design. The songbook went through the production process to the point of the printing of proof copies, but was ultimately abandoned.

Bernie Rhodes's music publishing administration deal with Riva was for just three years, and was due to terminate in October 1980. With the Clash now an established and proven group, Blackhill were in a position to cut a new administration deal with a sizeable advance attached, and generate some instant income for the songwriting band members . . . which by this time, meant all four members of the Clash. Riva tried to extend their deal, but were outbid by Warner Brothers Music. 'Had we published another songbook in the last months of our deal with the Clash, we wouldn't have been able to get our money back,' says Dennis Collopy. 'Also, as soon as they printed the lyrics on *London Calling*, there was no real business rationale for the songbook. I have to say, had we stayed in the game, we would have probably still done it. But if you talk to a corporate publisher like Warner Brothers Publications – at the time one of the most successful print music companies in the world – to them it would be, what's the point of putting out a songbook if the lyrics are already on the album sleeve?'

The cover of the songbook again recycles Ray Lowry's original idea for the Presley lettering, as used on the European singles sleeves. The book is illustrated throughout with Pennie Smith's photographs of the period, which – like the lyrics – were in danger of over-exposure thanks to their use on the album sleeve, to accompany *NME* features, in the first two issues of *The Armagideon Times*, and in Pennie's own forthcoming Clash photobook. The two shots used on the songbook cover are worthy of note, though, as both of them come from the bass-smashing sequence that also provided the cover for *London Calling*. The first was not to be seen again for many years, until Pennie's original contact sheet was reproduced in the booklet accompanying the 2004 25th Anniversary Edition of *London Calling*. The second has never been published in any other context at all. The other notable thing about the book is its rarity: the copy given to Lindy would appear to be the only one still in existence. Sadly, Lindy herself died in 1983 after a sudden illness. 'I've stuck Lindy's songbook in the vaults for my many children's future well-being,' says Johnny Green.

Not long after *London Calling*'s release, Pennie Smith was approached by Peter Hogan of Pete Townshend's publishing company, Eel Pie, at Townshend's behest, about doing a photobook on the Clash. 'I went away and printed the pictures I thought would work, laid them out over the floor, then took a draft rough to the Clash who were in Germany at the time,' says Pennie. 'The night Joe nearly got arrested [20 May 1980], I was whizzing up to the gig to say, "This is going to be it, roughly," and Joe was driving away in a taxi. He grabbed me, and we were in Norway before I knew it. I didn't get home for another three weeks: that was the way the Clash worked, which was great!' During that period, the band members – except for Topper, who was having too much fun elsewhere – provided amusing captions, which added considerably to the book's appeal. Although it covers the period from 1978–1980 in the UK, Europe and the USA, the book gives the impression of focussing on the Clash in America, so it, too, is like a travelogue. Writing for *Mojo* in 1994, Will Birch memorably described it as a record of the Clash's 'great trash and vaudeville, cost-to-coast fancy dress party'. It makes for a strong visual companion piece to the *London Calling* album. 'The band had no artistic say in it,' Pennie is quick to point out. Joe confirmed as much when the *Melody Maker*'s Paolo Hewitt tackled him about this latest boost to Clash mythology in late 1980. 'There's not a lot we had to do with it,' he said. 'She's an artist herself, and that's one of her testaments.' First published in October 1980, it is still in print today.

Such was the level of interest for all things Clash in America that by autumn 1980 Epic were actively looking for more material to meet demand. The solution was a 10-inch album (no gimmick knowingly left unexplored) entitled *Black Market Clash* and released in October 1980. One side cobbles together tracks left off the American version of *The Clash* to make way for non-album singles with some early single B-sides and rarities. The other side includes 'Armagideon Time' and its versions, and 'Bankrobber' and its (Mikey Dread-free) version, and therefore can be seen as an addendum to *London Calling*. CBS UK's attempts to get the Clash to sanction its release at home failed, but the inclusion of the original 'Capital Radio' and the band's otherwise unavailable cover of Booker T. and the MGs' 'Time is Tight' ensured that the album did good business in the UK on import.

By the time Americans got to cast their votes in the 1980 year-end music polls, they were in the exact opposite position of their UK counterparts the previous year: they'd had a full year to accustom themselves to the album. Of course, familiarity can breed contempt, or at least lead to boredom, allowing more recent releases to replace earlier ones in the critics' affections. Fortunately, that wasn't the case with *London Calling*. *Rolling Stone* critics made it Album of the Year over runners-up *The River* by Bruce Springsteen and *Remain in Light* by Talking Heads. Shortly afterwards, the magazine's readers' poll gave the top accolade to Springsteen, but placed *London Calling* in the runners-up list alongside *The Wall* by Pink Floyd, *Back in Black* by AC/DC and *Emotional Rescue* by the Rolling Stones. *Creem* typically followed a more hard-edged rock'n'roll agenda, but in 1980, though, its readers were close to being as one mind with those of *Rolling Stone*, placing *London Calling* at Number 4 behind Springsteen, AC/DC and the Stones. The album cover was voted best of the year, and 'Train in Vain' the sixth Best Single.

The acknowledged king of the annual critics' polls was the 'Pazz and Jop' survey derived from Top 10 lists supplied by 300 music critics from across the nation and compiled by music critic Robert Christgau for New York's venerable alternative arts paper *Village Voice*. In 1980, *London Calling* was Best Album, above Springsteen, Talking Heads, *The Pretenders* and PiL's *Second Edition* (aka *Metal Box*). In the single of the year list, 'Train in Vain (Stand By Me)'/'London Calling' (both sides were listed) was voted joint fourth with the Pretenders' 'Brass in Pocket', behind Kurtis Blow's 'The Breaks', Joy Division's 'Love Will Tear Us Apart' and Blondie's 'Call Me'. *London Calling* was again Number 1 – with an A+ rating – in Robert Christgau's personal album of the year list, ahead of Prince's *Dirty Mind*, *Remain in Light*, and Chic's *Real People*.

With a *Rolling Stone* front cover under their belts, and sitting on top of both that magazine's and the *Village Voice* polls, the Clash had clearly won the hearts and minds of the USA's tastemakers with *London Calling*. They still had a way to go to translate that into mass acceptance and mass sales in America, but the position they found themselves in at the end of 1980 was enviable.

Things were looking up financially, too. Their records were selling, and the CBS debt was slowly being whittled away. There was the advance from Warner Brothers Music. And extending the Riva music publishing deal to cover the USA back in June 1979 also proved to be highly beneficial for the Clash's songwriters. (A 'collection period' agreement meant Riva continued to collect money generated by their efforts even after Warner Brothers took over.) Outside America, mechanical songwriting royalties amounted to a fixed percentage of the overall price of the album, in the Clash's case 8.5 per cent. 'Whether you've got five songs on it or 500, it's never going to be more than that amount of money,' says Dennis Collopy. The American system, however, was based upon a fixed royalty rate per song. In order to avoid paying hefty royalties, CBS America and other majors habitually required their artists to sign what is today known as a 'controlled composition clause'. It doesn't apply to cover versions, just artist-composed songs, but it's a convention that assumes that there are no more than 10 songs per album. 'It's considered to be the maximum amount that American labels are going to pay for,' says Dennis. 'And though the band delivered a double album, because of their insistence that it be priced as a single album, CBS in America [Epic] did not want to pay more than they would have been obliged to pay for a single album. And I said, "I don't care. I'm the band's publisher, and I say it's a double album." I hit them with a full mechanical publishing royalty claim for the Clash songs, which caused a massive ruckus, but we prevailed, because Riva wasn't a signatory to the recording agreement. And the record company just said, "Well, we'll have to take our losses off the band's [artist] royalties, then."' The choice the Clash were faced with in America was: either Riva collected songwriting royalties from Epic for all 16 of the band's album compositions, and passed them on directly to the band, and the Clash's debt to CBS increased slightly; or Riva collected on just 10 band compositions, and the Clash's debt to CBS decreased slightly. Or to put it another way: more money now or less money now. The Clash opted for more money now. 'And we got paid in full!' says Dennis. 'It was a magnificent thing. I was very proud of that.'

As this last late tussle didn't affect them directly, CBS UK were also able to look back on the previous year's *London Calling* campaign with considerable satisfaction. 'I think everything just worked right,' says Muff Winwood. 'The timing of the release was right, the music was right, the sleeve was right. The video for the single was fantastic. Sometimes that just happens. And not always because of the genius of the people involved, but sometimes by sheer luck. Everything came together just right. Nobody can claim responsibility for that.'

6 . . . to the World's End

Returns

Both chronologically and stylistically, Joe Strummer's first post-*London Calling* composition, 'Bankrobber', sits midway between that album and its follow up, *Sandinista!*, and would have been at home on either. Like the previous year's *The Cost of Living* EP, it represents a period of transition. Originally a ska-meets-R&B hybrid called 'Bank Robbing Song' in the vein of 'Rudie Can't Fail' or 'Wrong 'Em Boyo', with bottleneck blues guitar by Mick Jones, it was reworked with a heavy dub sound in the studio at Mikey Dread's suggestion and with his production assistance. It pushed the Clash further down the contemporary reggae route the band had already returned to with 'Revolution Rock' and 'Armagideon Time', despite Joe having disowned that style of music a year earlier.

The lyrical inspiration for 'Bankrobber' came in part from 'I Fought the Law', in part from visiting the site of John Dillinger's death on the Take the 5th tour, in part from fooling around with Bob Dylan's 'Billy' in Wessex, in part from Paul Clayton's 'Gotta Move On', as hijacked for 'Armagideon Time'. Joe's reference to the Hole in the Wall towards the end conjures up another bunch of cowboys: the Hole in the Wall Gang, also known as the Wild Bunch. They inspired two very different westerns in 1969, but it's clear that Joe was thinking more of the good-natured, non-violent heroes of *Butch Cassidy and the Sundance Kid* and its spin-off ABC TV series *Alias Smith and Jones* (1971–3). The latter fictional outlaws might have carried guns, but 'in all the trains and

banks they robbed, they never shot anyone', and Joe's Daddy never hurt nobody, neither.

'Bankrobber' sold well, and Radio One DJ John Peel enthused about it, but it did not endear itself to the inky critics, who showed a tendency to take the lyric at face value. The *Sounds* reviewer pointed out that Joe's Daddy was not a bankrobber but a Foreign Office diplomat. Woody Guthrie and Bob Dylan had never been called to account for singing about bankrobbers, and in May 1979 the Clash themselves had released a song about 'robbing people with a six gun' without anyone turning a hair. Why was 'Bankrobber' being interpreted so literally, and deemed so unacceptable? After all, beneath the outlaw ballad trappings, it's just another song exhorting listeners to enjoy life and not be slaves to the machine, in the tradition of 'Clampdown' et al. In some respects it was the Clash's own fault: they had banged the authenticity drums so hard for the first couple of years of their existence that commentators found it difficult not to keep on judging them by those standards. 'Bankrobber' is a Strummer original (as opposed to a cover), and although it starts off as a third-person narrative, it quickly slips into the inclusive first-person plural, before winding up in the first-person singular, with Joe as the leader of the gang. Back in 1974, when he was still calling himself Woody, the very first song Joe Strummer wrote and committed to tape, 'Crummy Bum Blues', expressed a desire to be 'an intelligent bankrobber'. Neither song was meant to be seriously autobiographical, but both smack of fantasy role-playing, movie-fed romanticism. Further blurring the lines was the UK picture sleeve for the single, featuring a photograph of notorious real-life, modern-day bankrobber John McVicar, a former UK Public Enemy Number 1, only recently released from prison. The inky critics were evidently starting to wonder if the band themselves knew where fact stopped and fiction started. It was a good question, the answer to which remained elusive for the rest of the Clash's career, and beyond. From 1980 to 1985, although the Clash would still get the odd good review in the UK music press, the voices expressing disapproval and outright mockery would grow louder.

In mid-March 1980, following the American leg of the 16 Tons tour, the Clash tried to make up for their disappointment at not getting to record 'Armagideon Time' at Kingston's Studio One – where the Willi Williams version, and the original 'Real Rock' riddim had both been recorded – by booking into the rival Channel One, where Jackie Edwards had recorded 'Get Up', the original riddim for 'Revolution Rock'. Again with Mikey Dread's assistance, they gave a reggae makeover to an old 101ers cover, 'Junco Partner'. First copyrighted under that title by Bob Shad and Robert Ellen, and first recorded by James Wayne in 1952, it was a bona fide badman ballad deriving from Willi 'Drive 'Em Down' Hall's Thirties barrelhouse piano composition 'Junker's Blues', the tune of which had also been appropriated for Fats Domino's 'The Fat Man' (1949) and Lloyd Price's 'Lawdy Miss Clawdy (1952). Although the song is unapologetic about the need to get high (on heroin, cocaine and cannabis, and whatever else might be going) the details about jail time, pawning possessions and pimping girlfriends paint an anything-but-glamorous picture of the junkie lifestyle. In that respect, then, it continues in the anti-heroin tradition of 'Hateful' and 'London Calling'. As ever, Joe can't resist personalising a cover: the possessions he tries to pawn are those rude-boy essentials a ratchet and pistol, and the girl he also tries to raise money on is his 'sweet Gabriella'.

The wall Joe had built between his previous and current life and band was coming down. During 1980 he would participate with Richard Dudanski and other former members of the 101ers in compiling and releasing *Elgin Avenue Breakdown*, an album of the band's studio and live recordings on the Andalusia! label, named in honour of the Romero sisters, Palmolive and Esperanza, and including the 101ers' version of 'Junco Partner'.

The Clash's hopes of recording more material in Jamaica were dashed by demands for money with menaces by local rude boys, prompting a rapid departure. Paul Simonon went to Vancouver to work on *Ladies and Gentlemen, the Fabulous Stains* for the next six weeks, Topper Headon to London. Expecting to help out with the recording of a new Joe Ely album, Mick and Joe headed for New York. When that project fell through, they booked a week in the Power Station to work on some ideas towards a new Clash album. As with *London Calling*, there was no new material at first, so – with help from visiting guests – they played and recorded retro covers like 'Louie Louie', Prince Buster's ska classic 'Madness' (1963) – indicating that the Clash were still monitoring the ska revival – and 'Police on My Back' (1967) by Eddie Grant's multiracial London pop-R&B band the Equals.

Deciding they wanted to keep going, they begged money from CBS UK and booked the first three weeks of April at Electric Lady. Bill Price agreed to come over. A few days into the sessions, Mickey Gallagher received another short-notice phone call, and was asked to bring his fellow Blockhead Norman Watt-Roy with him to deputise for Paul. The conscripts flew out with Topper.

Mickey had already been given an indication that the Clash wanted to persevere with and develop the keyboard-augmented sound of *London Calling*. Just a couple of weeks earlier, when he was due to return to London to start work on the next Ian Dury album at the end of the American leg of the 16 Tons tour, he had been waiting in the hotel lobby for a lift to the airport when Mick and Joe took him into a side room. 'They asked, "Well, do you want to join the band?"' says Mickey. 'They made me an offer, but of course it was at the last minute. People had just got off the plane and come to the hotel for me, and then I was put on the spot. Blackhill said, "Make a decision," so I did. I couldn't really get close to the Clash, the way I was with the Blockheads, and there was always trouble over your money.'

By the end of the Electric Lady sessions, the Clash had around 20 songs and dub versions in various stages of completion. As with *London Calling*, the making of the album was interrupted by a tour, in this case the European leg of 16 Tons. Then, in mid-August 1980, the band reconvened at Wessex Studios to complete the album, with Bill Price and Jerry Green engineering. (Jerry oversaw a lot of the overdubs, and took over entirely when Bill went on a pre-booked holiday for a couple of weeks.) The idea was originally to complete the existing material, but the band continued writing, and the finishing line got pushed further and further back until the end of September. CBS had been making nervous noises about the possibility of the album being another double. By the time the tracks in the can got up around the 30 mark, Mick decided that it was going to be a triple. In the last couple of weeks, the band worked frenziedly to push the track total up to 36. Bill Price was again charged with overseeing the mix.

This time the demand made of CBS was *three* for the price of one. 'We all just shoved our heads in our hands and said, "Oh no, not again!"' says Muff Winwood, whimpering at the memory. '"This is happening every time! It never stops!" Every time we thought we'd made them understand what they needed to do to control their career on a worldwide basis, every time we thought we'd finally got through, there'd be another crazy situation. Again, we could deal with it in the UK, we had flexibility, we had the UK media and marketplace behind the group, so we knew we could do it. But in other countries . . . they went *crazy* from one side of the word to the other. And we were getting all the flak! "How can you do this to us? We've helped you so much to make the Clash big here in Germany, and now you do this to us!"' CBS had said no to the Singles Bonanza: surely they could have said enough is enough here as well? 'We did tell them that enough was enough, and laid out all the sensible reasons why, but they just said, "No effing way! We're *doing* this." We couldn't go to the studio and take the tapes off them . . .'

Mick has claimed that the Clash held the master tapes to ransom until they got their own way, and they had Bill Price take copies home for added security. Some stiff bargaining was involved: the UK 'Special Price' would be the same as for a deluxe single album, that is £5.99; it would again only count as a single album with regard to the band's obligation to the record company; and the Clash would receive no artist royalties – not to be confused with songwriting royalties – on the first 200,000 copies sold in the UK. (To put this in context: at that time only 180,000 copies of *London Calling* had sold at home; so they were effectively forgoing their UK royalties.) Epic refused to have their arm twisted to the same degree, but the triple album retailed for a Special Price of $14.98 in the USA, a dollar less than the list price for Bruce Springsteen's current double album, *The River*.

Generous though the Clash were, *Sandinista!* was judged by almost everyone – CBS, Blackhill, the music press, the fans – to be an act of utter folly. If *London Calling* is a short double, then *Sandinista!* is a long triple. It has 36 tracks to *London Calling*'s 19, and runs two hours 25 minutes to its predecessor's one hour five minutes. The Clash had recorded 32 originals in the three years prior to recording *London Calling*, and 16 for that album. Even with all the covers and versions stripped out, *Sandinista!* still contains 25 new Clash songs. With this one release, then, they increased the size of their original song catalogue by 50 per cent. That has to pose questions about quality control. The standard joke at the time of release was that, as triples go, *Sandinista!* would have made a good single album. There is a lot of filler, and some instances of glaring self-indulgence, but it's closer to the truth to say there's a strong double album waiting to be discovered in *Sandinista!*: by no means the equal of its predecessor, but close enough in subject and style to justify the price of admission for anyone who appreciates *London Calling*.

When the Clash began work on *London Calling*, playing cover versions was the spark for a lengthy and productive writing and rehearsal process. With *Sandinista!*, the available band members recorded some covers. And then recorded some new songs. There was no rehearsal, and no preparatory writing process: the Vanilla stage was omitted completely. So was the Guy Stevens stage. It was impossible to create a band vibe while recording live backing tracks, because the full band wasn't there. The new songs were built up from fragments improvised in the studio. The discipline and polish of rehearsal is what *Sandinista!* misses most: while it is possible to add much fine detail at the overdub stage – and Mick, Topper and the numerous guest musicians did – it is not so easy to change the structure or substantially rearrange a song once it has been tracked. Writing and arranging at Vanilla had been organic, with people throwing in ideas, those ideas being tested, and only the best kept and worked on further. On the new sessions, there was a culture of experimentation for experimentation's sake. The evidence in the grooves indicates that the Clash had taken the inkies' criticism that *London Calling* was safe, traditional and retrogressive to heart, and had gone out of their way to be as outlandish as possible.

The Clash's songwriting process became both more and less varied. To try and make some sense of that apparently contradictory statement: less varied, in that the music now almost always came first, with Joe working on lyrics to fit the growing library of tunes in his studio spliffbunker throughout the lengthy recording process; more varied, in that the initial musical spur could come from anyone. The Clash had toyed with the idea of a group credit for compositions at Vanilla, but now that group credit became a reality: on *Sandinista!* songs were no longer attributed to Strummer-Jones, but to the Clash. That decision was fudged and hedged almost immediately afterwards. Revenue would not be divided equally among the band members: for music-publishing purposes, each song was credited to whatever permutation of band members had worked on the song.

As Topper Headon later pointed out, this meant the general public never knew the extent of his songwriting contribution to the Clash. Thirteen of the 25 new originals are still Strummer-Jones songs, but no less than eight more are by Strummer-Jones-Headon, and – from a Clash-centric viewpoint – it should probably be nine: the four-way credit to 'Lightning Strikes' is probably an error, as Paul Simonon was not present at the time. Most of the songs involving Topper's input were either developed from his musical ideas – notably the funk tune that became 'Ivan Meets GI Joe' – or from Topper jamming with fellow multi-instrumentalist Mick Jones, the two of them sharing bass and piano duties as well as their more traditional roles.

Determining true authorship is further complicated by Mickey Gallagher and Norman Watt-Roy's presence. They would later complain that they didn't receive due credit or pay for their compositional input. It's now accepted that Mick Jones's tendency to come to the studio late meant that a few of the rough jams from which songs were developed – most obviously 'The Magnificent Seven' and 'Lightning Strikes' – were originated by the Blockheads duo with Topper. The duo have also claimed they were involved in the early stages of 'Hitsville UK', 'Charlie Don't Surf' and 'Something About England', all three of which are listed as Strummer-Jones songs.

By the time the recording sessions resumed at Wessex in August 1980, Topper was more interested in drugs than writing, whereas Paul Simonon was keen to make sure he didn't miss out on publishing income entirely. He is co-credited with Mick and Joe on 'Broadway', while both 'Rebel Waltz' and 'The Crooked Beat', the latter of which he sings, are Strummer-Simonon songs, and betray a distinct lack of melodic invention.

During the sessions, the Clash recorded some material with collaborators that was originally intended for the use of those collaborators. When the band started scrabbling around to find the 36 tracks they felt they needed to make up the triple – and turn the album into a documentary of its own making – they decided to include material by Tymon Dogg and Mikey Dread, too. While on the previous album guest musicians had been limited to organ and horns, the extent of their contributions limited and determined in advance, *Sandinista!* was an open house, with everyone from Void-Oids guitarist Ivan Julien, to Topper's Dover buddies the Barnacles, to Den Hegarty, to a steel band, to Mick's new girlfriend Ellen Foley, joining three Blockheads and the Clash on the album. It's perhaps not surprising that it lost focus.

On *London Calling* reggae stakes out a large claim, but never threatens to overwhelm the album as a whole. On *Sandinista!* reggae and dub dominate. While funk and disco make their presence felt on *London Calling*, they lead off on *Sandinista!*, and because they are by this time associated with the new New York street phenomenon of hip hop, the Clash are less concerned with using irony to distance themselves from the dance. (Even Joe.) Latino and Caribbean touches also appear in a couple of Soca-influenced songs, 'Corner Soul' and 'Let's Go Crazy'. 'There are elements of *Sandinista!* that were years ahead of their time, and advanced the world of record-making,' insists Bill Price. There's no doubt that the album paved the way for the rave-influenced groove rock of the late Eighties, but even the diplomatic Bill allows that 'perhaps' not everything on the album was worthy of inclusion. Although still evident in some songs, the principle victim was Mick Jones's commercial Sixties pop-writing touch. In addition to all the left-field experiments in sound, though, there is still some room for the traditional. The jazzy blues of 'Jimmy Jazz' finds a kindred spirit in the more uptempo jazzy R&B of Mose Allison's 'Look Here'.

The freewheeling structures allow Joe to be even more Beat-like in his lyrical meanderings on tracks like 'If Music Could Talk', and more playful with genre expectations, as with 'The Magnificent Seven'. Overall, the lyrical flavour is similar to that of *London Calling*, but with the world-political slant touched on in 'Clampdown' coming through more strongly. After stepping away from that subject matter for much of *London Calling*, it is as though Joe now felt it was safe to return to it with a more considered perspective than was evident on *Give 'Em Enough Rope*. To go with the world music, he provides a world news-paper. (Something the design for the lyric sheet makes clear.) He would later claim that he was no longer interested in being a Little Englander: the Clash were an international band now, and had the right – if not quite an obligation – to reflect that status and experience lyrically as well as musically. David Mingay recognises a return to political comment, but sees the shift in emphasis as another stage in the Clash's strategic retreat from direct accountability. 'Bernie had said to Joe that they mustn't do love songs, which is why they did songs like "Hate & War",' he says. 'He also said that they mustn't sing about other countries, because it was cowardly not to talk about your own politics. But with *Sandinista!* they did just that: they talked about other people's politics.'

Despite significant differences, *Sandinista!* can still be seen as a natural progression from *London Calling*. Like 'Rudie Can't Fail', 'Somebody Got Murdered' was commissioned for a film, William Freidkin's *Cruising* (1980) (but not used). Like 'Lost in the Supermarket', the song was directly inspired by life on the World's End Estate. Or, rather, loss of life: the attendant at the subterranean car park was killed during a robbery that netted his assailants just £5. Upon his return to London, Joe would move out of Whistler Walk, first into a squat, and then into a rented flat on Ladbroke Grove with Gaby. Mick's 'Up in Heaven (Not Only Here)' was – at last – his own 'Lost in the Supermarket'-style take on high-rise life, this time very much informed by his Wilmcote House experience. 'Train in Vain' has a soulmate in the Motown sound of 'Hitsville UK'. Mick's referencing of blues mythology train imagery in the final *London Calling* track also brought out the competitive side of Joe, who comes back with the hobo train fantasy 'Version City'. Reflecting on the underbelly of New York – as previously seen in 'Koka-Kola' and 'The Right Profile' – from the point of view of a down-and-out inspired 'Broadway'. 'Spanish Bombs'-style folk history lessons and 'Death and Glory' and 'The Card Cheat'-style musings on the conflicts of yore are to be found in 'Rebel Waltz' and 'Something About England'. Live, the Clash had taken to counting 'Clampdown' off with a military 'hup, two, three, four'. That, and talk of conscription being reintroduced in the USA, and the Cold War heating up, fed into new song 'The Call Up'. Also like 'Clampdown' (and an ever-growing list), it explores the theme of 'why should we work?', and, like 'The Card Cheat', it sheds a tear for the 'rose' the soldier leaves behind. Further *Apocalypse Now!* allusions can be found in 'Charlie Don't Surf'. The Cold War meets 'the giant hits discotheque album' on 'Ivan Meets GI Joe', where – *London Calling* having set a precedent by opening the door of the vocal booth to Paul Simonon – Topper Headon gets to sing lead. The whiff of evil *presidentés* permeates the album, but is especially pungent on 'Washington Bullets'.

Like 'Junco Partner', 'The Junkie Slip' nods back to 'Hateful' in detailing and bemoaning the inevitable fate of the addict. All eyes on

Topper . . . except, apparently, Topper's, even though this is one of the tracks he co-wrote. 'The Leader' is a 'Brand New Cadillac'-type Fifties rocker with lyrics influenced – like 'The Right Profile' – by a 'warts and all' book, this time the 1963 *Denning Report* on the Profumo scandal. 'Police On My Back' is another Sixties rude-boy-cum-badman cover that the Clash make their own. In the spirit of the band's up-to-the-minute reggae covers 'Revolution Rock' and 'Armagideon Time' comes the self-penned 'One More Time', a more realistic take – with the exception, perhaps, of the kung fu-kicking crone – on ghetto misery than 'The Guns of Brixton'. The violent stance of the latter is also rebuked in the a cappella snatch of the original sung by Maria Gallagher (Mickey's four-year-old daughter), and by the plaintive 'Kingston Advice', about the all-too-real violence the Clash witnessed in Jamaica. Paul Simonon does get to revisit his 'south London reggae' theme on 'The Crooked Beat', with the non-violent lyric this time by Joe Strummer. Sadly, the song lacks a killer bass line, a tune, or a bearable vocal. In his *Rolling Stone* review of *London Calling*, Tom Carson described the jocular self-mythologising of 'Four Horseman' as 'the movie soundtrack to a rock & roll version of *The Seven Samurai*' (1954), a movie remade for Hollywood as *The Magnificent Seven* (1960). Joe read the review shortly before recording 'The Magnificent Seven', which also reprises the call-and-response chain-gang chant of 'Clampdown', and the Clash's perennial 'why work?' theme. As does 'The Equaliser', another song betraying the influence of Karl Marx.

Although Jules Balme oversaw the design of *Sandinista!*, the packaging has many similar elements to that for *London Calling*. Partly for budgetary reasons, the three original LPs are again housed in a single sleeve, also with a matt finish. The colour palette is even simpler: instead of black and white and pink and green, it's black and white and red (like the 'Bankrobber' single sleeve). The Elvis Presley typography has gone, but the lettering – this time placed more conventionally at the top and bottom of the picture – remains bold and chunky, and the Clash star is still part of the group logo. Ray Lowry had wanted a black border around the front cover image on the last album; Jules Balme uses a white border on this one. The front cover photograph is again by Pennie Smith, though this time it's a purpose-posed group shot taken behind Kings Cross train station. It's reproduced in full portrait format, uncropped, necessitating a secondary wide black border down both sides, and making the individual figures of the Clash members appear distant and small. A bad move, according to Ray Lowry. 'Does it work?' he asked in *The Clash: Up Close and Personal*. 'Does it heck!'

The inner sleeves are plain, but the lyrics are included on a foldout insert entitled *Armagideon Times No 3*, to follow on from and tie in with the earlier Clash publications promoting *London Calling* and the 16 Tons tour. The lyrics are once more written out by hand, and again by a popular cartoonist, this time Steve Bell, political cartoonist for the *Guardian*, and creator of the long-running strip *If . . ..* The Clash get custom-designed record labels; CBS is again reduced to small print. The band's new music publishers – as of October 1980 – Warner Brothers Music aren't mentioned at all. The band were allowed their own matrix number, but instead of going for the vanity option this time they decided that – as with their choice of album title – they would use it for political ends: to draw attention to the political struggle in Nicaragua following the 19 July 1979 overthrow of 'evil *presidenté*' General Anastasio Somoza Debayle by the *Frente Sandinista de Liberación Nacional*. Hence FSLN1.

On the new album's inset credits, the Blackhill management team are charmlessly listed as 'the Two Ogres', and *Sandinista!* represented the beginning of the end for their handshake arrangement with the Clash. With Mick visiting Ellen Foley in New York, Joe handled most of the press interviews in late 1980, and had to face most of the disbelief and scorn. By the end of the year, Joe had mixed feelings about the album himself. His creative relationship with Mick had been severely strained during the making of *Sandinista!*. Their personal relationship was about to get a lot worse when, early in February 1981, Joe demanded that Bernie Rhodes be reinstated as Clash manager, and Paul Simonon agreed that life in the Clash was becoming a little too much like life in any other rock'n'roll band. Kosmo Vinyl accepted the invitation to stay on. Peter Jenner and Andrew King were let go with next to no payment for their trouble, which they blamed for the ultimate demise of Blackhill in 1982.

Epic's response to *Sandinista!*, and to Bernie's return, was to once again refuse to help out with funding for a proposed two-month tour of America. Bernie instead booked a month-long tour of Europe from late April 1981 – named the Impossible Mission tour after the band's candid assessment of their chances of learning all the new songs – and then came up with an inspired alternative live strategy to tie in with the release of 'The Magnificent Seven' single: a series of magnificent seven-night residencies. Less slog for more media coverage.

Early in April 1981 the Clash booked back in to Vanilla Rehearsal Studios on Causton Street to begin rehearsals for the live shows, and work up even more new material for a new single. Mickey Gallagher was persuaded to play keyboards, and Baker was deputised to invite Johnny Green – now back in London – to return to the fold. It was like something out of a movie, in theory. 'I wanted to reunite the old firm, like in *The Wild Bunch*,' Joe told Gavin Martin for *Uncut* in 1999. 'Get the old gang together and ride again.'

Mickey is quick to dispel the notion that Vanilla held any inherent promises of magic. 'It was a dingy little studio,' he says. 'It was just a space. It wasn't that wonderful. You didn't think, "Oh I've just *got* to come back here again!"' The keyboard set-up they had for me to rehearse on was ridiculous. They had a Wurlitzer piano, and taped over the top was a little Casio synth player thing, you know, where the notes are really small. I thought, "You're taking the fucking piss here, you know!"' While Joe and Topper wanted Mickey along to play as he had done for *London Calling* and *Sandinista!*, and Paul preferred the band as a four-piece, Mick was determined to continue pushing the Clash's music into the future. Synths were part of this vision, along with ever-more heavily treated guitars, electronic percussion and dance beats. For now, the others were walking on eggshells around him because of the Bernie situation.

Mickey just shrugged and got on with it. At teatime on his first day, he was introduced to another Vanilla institution: a game of football in the playground over the road with various friends of the band. Mickey remembers everyone else putting on trainers, while he had 'these silly piano player's leather-soled shoes on, and a biker jacket', but thought he should show willing. 'It was this mad game of football,' he says. 'So rough!' While he was trying to kick a ball at shoulder height, his standing shoe slipped, and he fell heavily on his elbow and back. His sympathetic teammates put him in goal for the rest of the game. 'I had these people whacking balls at me, hitting me in the face and all sorts.' He completed the day's rehearsal feeling a bit stiff, but it wasn't until he got home and took off his jacket that he realised he'd broken his elbow. 'So I was seriously out of the game,' he laughs. 'I phoned them up to tell them, and they just went, "Oh, all right. See ya!"' Two weeks later, he discovered he'd also dislocated his back. That was it for Mickey and playing with the Clash . . . and for playing with anyone else for a good few months, either.

Johnny Green lasted just 24 hours longer. 'I went down to Vanilla, and I noticed the atmosphere there,' he says. 'I did the second day, and I said to Joe, "Can I talk to you?" We went round to the White Swan, and I said, "Look, this is crap, Joe. The music's shit, and you don't look like a band anymore. What's going on?" And he had tears in his eyes, and he just said, "I don't know, Johnny." And I said, "I don't want any part of it."'

So much for the Wild Bunch riding again.

The new music produced by the sessions included what became 'Sean Flynn' and 'Car Jamming', but the only song to be fully realised at this point was 'This is Radio Clash', an uneasy meeting of a Rhodes-Vinyl concept, a collectively written funk groove, and a Strummer lyric. All compromise and accommodation and no passion, it failed to set pulses racing or the charts on fire when released later in the year. It does continue the radio-as-essential-means-of-communication theme of 'London Calling' and 'Capital Radio', echoing the original BBC radio call sign 'This is London calling . . .' in its title, claiming that it's being broadcast on 'pirate satellite', and interrupting all programmes to again send out an SOS: 'please save us, not the whale'.

Following on from the Impossible Mission tour was the Clash's residency at Bond's Casino on Times Square – the key location in 'Koka Kola', 'The Right Profile' and now 'Broadway' – which, thanks to fire regulations and all kinds of club-war shenanigans, had to be expanded from the planned seven shows to 17, running from 28 May to 13 June 1981 (including two matinees). This sent media coverage through the roof, and did more than the band's previous tours to break them in the States. Bob Gruen reprised his Monty Clift bugle introductions.

Back in London, the Clash were stunned by the news of Guy Stevens's death on 29 August 1981: just two years after he had finished work on *London Calling*. The Clash attended the funeral. They were due to commence a UK tour in early October, but were also due to deliver another album to CBS by the end of the year. Joe was determined not to repeat the *Sandinista!* experience, but with just over a month before the tour, it didn't leave the Clash a lot of options for writing and rehearsing material. Returning to Vanilla hadn't worked out, but, invoking the spirit of Guy, Joe pushed for a solution to recording that was a cross between *The Vanilla Tapes* and *London Calling*; and was exactly how the Rolling Stones recorded *Exile on Main St*. In 1979, it might have been naïve of Joe to think that an album could be recorded in a rehearsal room by a drum roadie on a TEAC 4-track, but in 1981 there was no reason why it couldn't be recorded in a rehearsal room by a trained and proven engineer using a top-of-the-range mobile studio. Ear Studios in the People's Hall, Freston Road, in Notting Hill was booked as the rehearsal room. The Rolling Stones' 24-track mobile (which had recorded the Lyceum show for *Rude Boy* nearly three years before) was parked outside, and Bill Price's number two, Jerry Green was hired to man the controls.

'The Right Profile' might have been – in Johnny Green's opinion – a disguised tribute to Guy Stevens, but one of the first songs recorded at Ear was 'Midnight to Stevens', Joe and Mick's direct and heartfelt ballad tribute to the producer, eventually released on the *Clash On Broadway* box set in 1991. Joe's lyric recounts his pub crawl in search of Guy prior to hiring him for *London Calling*, makes the point that sales justify the means, praises Guy's work at the Scene Club in Ham Yard, and reminds the world that he championed Chuck Berry, helped make the London R&B scene happen, and played a major role in the success of 'A Whiter Shade of Pale'. Romantically – inevitably – it concludes that the wild side of life is the right side to choose.

Early the following year, Joe would tell *NME* stringer Roz Reines that the Clash had set out to bring their world bag of musical influences together and combine them into a unified sound. Superficially, rehearsals went well, with various permutations of the Clash members writing and recording half a dozen new songs, and the band also getting four of them ready for a live road test in October 1981. But there was still a strained atmosphere between the experimentation-favouring musos (Mick and Topper) and the retro-enthusiast entertainers (Joe and Paul), with the management team of Bernie and Kosmo now transparently siding with the latter pair. Rehearsals were uncomfortable and co-operation limited. Any remaining hint of goodwill was dashed when Mick insisted that – after the upcoming tour – recording must recommence in a proper studio,

Electric Lady in New York. And in December that's what did happen. It meant that in 1981 the Clash would fail for the first time to meet their obligation to deliver an album a year to CBS. It also meant that they would have to record without a familiar face behind the console: Bill Price was otherwise engaged, and Jerry Green had just become a father, and was not prepared to travel.

So, yet again, album sessions were interrupted by a tour, and yet again, the Clash ended up writing and recording the material while running up bills in an expensive studio, with Mick producing and genuine team spirit nowhere to be found. More so even than on *Sandinista!*, the Clash members were rarely present all at the same time. Paul lost patience very quickly. Finding himself alone in the studio one day, Topper applied himself and recorded the master track for 'Rock the Casbah' on his own, drums, piano and bass. Recording continued throughout December – a new song, 'Straight to Hell', was finished on New Year's Eve – and into January 1982. On 5 January Joe phoned Jerry Green and begged him to come out for three days to help record vocal overdubs. Jerry ended up staying three weeks. Towards the end, the Clash had two studios going simultaneously, with Joe recording vocals and Mick recording guitars. (The other two Clash members had gone home.) There were relatively few guest musicians, but as Paul Simonon later remarked, Mick's obsession with effects was such that he was able and determined to make his guitar sound like anything except a guitar. By the day Mick and Joe had to fly to Japan to meet the others for a month-long Australasian tour, the album was another double – the band's third proposed multi-disc release in a row – going by the working title *Rat Patrol from Fort Bragg*. It featured 17 or 18 tracks, at least seven of which ran for more than five minutes.

Joe rejected Mick's mix, causing him great offence. The rest of the band tried to produce a compromise mix in Australia, but failed. Upon the Clash's return to the UK, Glyn Johns – famed for salvaging the single Who album *Who's Next* (1971) from its original unwieldy double incarnation as *Lifehouse* – was brought in to edit and remix the tapes to produce the 12-track single album *Combat Rock*, eventually released in May 1982. This is the fate that could have easily befallen *London Calling*, and in some respects it was harsh treatment of both the material and of Mick Jones. After the excesses and disappointments of

Sandinista!, though, it wasn't just a sensible move, but a necessary one. 'It wasn't us,' says Muff of the decision to cut the album down. 'I think the band had finally twigged. They'd been to America a few times, they'd seen how it worked there for themselves. And lots of other people would have told them they were crazy: people in other bands, producers, people they liked. Experience. You keep on putting out doubles and triples, you've got no career and nobody loves you any more. Being loved by people is a big drug.' It was Joe and Bernie who overruled Mick, but the moment of awakening did come in America. An engineer working on the new record told Joe he had been unable to buy a copy of *Sandinista!* – the Clash's current album – in New York. As Muff had predicted, the distributors simply weren't working the non-cost effictive triple.

As if to prove a point, they did work *Combat Rock*, and it went on to sell twice as many copies as *London Calling* in the USA. 'It's getting that balance of a band that's breaking the rules, and a monumental organisation that has to put the records out to the people,' says Muff. 'It was like a speedboat and a battleship. They both have to start out at the same time and get to the end of the line at the same time . . . against some big waves.' The end of the line wasn't too far away.

Mick's guitar effects give the album the opposite of an organic feel, and the attempt to create a coherent and unified Clash sound – the type of 'funky multinational anthem' Joe sings about on 'Car Jamming' – takes it further away from the compendium of roots musics that is *London Calling*. That said, there are still echoes of that album to be found. Most obviously in the way Joe's lead track 'Know Your Rights' recalls 'London Calling' with its staccato beat and public address theme . . . though, sadly, not in its quality. Similarly, Mick repeats his 'Train in Vain' trick with 'Should I Stay or Should I Go': a percussive Sixties-sounding riff, this time owing much to Mitch Ryder and the Detroit Wheels' 1966 US Number 17 hit 'Little Latin Lupe Lu'; and a lyric about problems in his romantic life, this time with current girl-friend Ellen Foley. Predictably, Joe wasn't impressed, going so far as to write a (genuinely funny) Mick-mocking version of the lyric, found among his papers after his death. To make the actual lyric more palat-able (to Joe), he and Joe Ely shouted the backing vocals in Clash Spannish. Again, Mick laughed last: at the time of their original release as singles, Joe's song reached Number 43 in the UK, while Mick's made

Number 17, and would one day give the Clash their only UK Number 1. Back in 1982, Topper's song was the biggest hit of all, reaching Number 8 in the USA . . . but the drummer had little cause to rejoice by then.

'Car Jamming' is a Bo Diddley-goes-Motown groove, with a lyric touching on advertising, in the manner of 'Koka Kola', and soulless selling, like 'Lost in the Supermarket'. It star-spots Lauren Bacall, much as 'The Right Profile' did Montgomery Clift. When the Clash included a sample of a real TV commercial promoting the lavatory-cleaning products of the Flushco company, they weren't as clever as they had been with Coca-Cola. Flushco took legal action, requiring Epic to halt a repressing of the album in July 1982 until the sample could be removed. 'Overpowered by Funk' finds Joe once again mocking a musical style even as the Clash play it – as on 'Lover's Rock', 'Lost in the Supermarket', and 'Capital Radio Two' – it's 'asinine, stupefying', apparently. 'Red Angel Dragnet' is Paul Simonon's Ringo track: plodding reggae again missing Mick Jones's tuneful touch, with a lyric by Joe tackling Manhattan vigilantes rather than south London desperados. It does provide one of the album's very few references to London, though when it quotes the 'bobbies bicycling two by two' line from Roger Miller's 'England Swings'.

If 'London Calling' can be seen as a lyrical take on David Bowie's 'Panic in Detroit' meets 'Diamond Dogs', then 'Atom Tan' is reminiscent of Bowie's 'Five Years' (1972): a countdown to oblivion. 'Ghetto Defendant' is the latest in Joe's anti-heroin broadsides, returning to the conspiracy theory that it was made freely available in urban flashpoint areas during the late Sixties to pacify and demoralise black militants. Like 'Atom Tan', and like 'London Calling', it comes packed with apocalyptic imagery. 'Straight to Hell' also touches on 'Hateful'-style drug addiction, and uses Coca-Cola as a signifier of America in a negative context. Together with several other songs on the album, it brings the historical war stories of 'Spanish Bombs', 'Death or Glory' and 'The Card Cheat' a little more up to date. In the tradition established by 'The Right Profile', the inspiration for 'Sean Flynn' came from a book passed around the Clash camp: Michael Herr's Vietnam memoir, *Dispatches* (1977). The main character from 'Death or Glory', 'The Card Cheat' and 'Four Horsemen' gets top billing again in 'Death is a Star': as Joe later explained, when people go to cowboy, gangster and war films, Death is who they are really paying to see.

London Calling was – unfairly – accused of being primarily American in focus, but that is undeniably true of *Combat Rock*. It is even more of a cinematic album, too, with tracks referring to films and film stars, quoting films, using filmic imagery, or even – as in the case of 'Sean Flynn' – sounding more like incidental soundtrack music than songs. The Vietnam War meets contemporary crime and drug-plagued New York, and the feel is pitched somewhere between *Apocalypse Now!* and *Taxi Driver*, as quoted from – at length – by Kosmo Vinyl in 'Red Angel Dragnet'. The Clash had been hanging out with Robert De Niro and talking to Martin Scorsese about appearing in a movie he was developing called *The Gangs of New York*. (Development took some time: it was eventually made in 2002.) Since 'Koka Kola' and 'The Right Profile', the Times Square sleaze pits that are also the prowling ground of *Taxi Driver*'s Travis Bickle – you can see the Bond's Casino sign reflected in the rear-view mirror of his cab in the film's opening sequence – had become almost as central to Clash mythology as the Westway in Notting Hill, and both the film and the Bickle character help lock Joe into the 'urban Vietnam' imagery he explores throughout *Combat Rock*.

The album cover continues some of the traditions established by *London Calling*, while shifting the goalposts slightly. Jules Balme designs. The typography is again bright and bold, and incorporates the Clash star. The front-cover photo is by Pennie Smith, taken during the band's late February 1982 visit to Thailand to capture the Vietnam vibe. In a real departure, it's in colour. Pennie had no time for colour photography, and as band portraits go, it's a bit of a half-hearted snapshot. The border is aerosol grey. This time around, the inner sleeve features lyrics written in hand by a slightly different sort of visual artist: New York graffiti artist Futura 2000 (who also raps on 'Overpowered by Funk'). Originally, the lyrics were incorporated into a piece of graffiti art. While Ray Lowry had to cope with a verse being replaced, Futura had to cope with his entire work being cut and pasted to incorporate changes. In songs where only the odd line was altered, though, the discrepancies were allowed to stand. The lyric sheet also features the credit – reproduced faintly, as though it knows it doesn't really belong there any longer – 'Inspiration Guy Stevens'.

'CBS' is again in small print on the record label, with the title and 'The Clash' writ large in red. The matrix number follows in the tradition of *Sandinista!*, this time supporting the rebel forces in Nicaragua's neighbours El Salvador, *Frente Farabundo Martí para la Liberacion Nacional*: hence FMLN2. This is tokenism. With the arguable exception of 'Inoculated City', this new Clash album isn't looking at contemporary conflicts, though the way its release coincided with the UK-Argentina Falklands War helped disguise this at the time.

The Garden of Eden of the *London Calling* experience – all the band working together supportively and exploring each other's interests in a generous and open-minded manner throughout the three Rs of riting, rehearsing and recording – was a place the Strummer-Jones-Simonon-Headon line-up of the Clash would never get to revisit. Topper was sacked for his drug use and unreliability on 21 May 1982. When the band lost him, they lost their ability to jam, improvise and work collectively. Songwriting options were back to Strummer-Jones. Joe and Mick no longer had any time for each other's music, or each other as people, and both had egos too large to allow them to find some workable common ground. Joe later characterised this period of the Clash – perhaps a little fancifully – as failed collaboration by post: he would stick lyrics through the letterbox of Mick's flat, and sometimes Mick would put them to beatbox funk grooves that Joe hated. Mick, conversely, remembers Bernie insisting the band write music in a 'New Orleans style', a directive he pointedly ignored.

Early in 1983 Joe directed a 50-minute black-and-white silent movie called *Hell W10* starring the Clash and their various friends. Notting Hill locations and a cops-and-robbers plot allowed the entire band to live out some long-time fantasies. Joe got to make his own film noir. Paul got to play 'Earl', a Notting Hill (or Brixton) Ivan or Pinkie, complete with a gun and a poor-boy cap. There were roles for Pennie Smith and Tony James, among others, but it failed to turn the Clash and their extended circle back into one big happy family.

Later that year, Clash money was invested in Lucky Eight, a rehearsal room with built-in demo studio facility in the band's old haunt at the British Rail Yards in Camden Town. Their upgraded, self-owned version of Vanilla-plus-TEAC, it could have been Joe's ideal rehearsal-cum-writing space, but all it saw was a lot of sulking and silences. The Clash had become unworkable. The *NME* news pages of 10 September 1983 carried the statement that Mick Jones had been fired. Within a matter of days he had started recruiting members for the band that would become Big Audio Dynamite (BAD).

Having shed its two musical members, the odds were not good that the rump of the Clash would be able to make another great record without some outside musical help. Drummer Pete Howard had already been hired, and was soon joined by guitarists Nick Sheppard and Greg White. Paul decided that Greg was not a rock-'n'roll name, so Greg was rechristened Vince, after the author of 'Brand New Cadillac'.

Rehearsals started promisingly enough, with new Strummer songs in a wide variety of styles being rehearsed by the full band. But then the new direction hardened into back-to-basics punk. Joe once again found himself writing to Bernie Rhodes's direction, and it soon became clear to the new members that they would always be hired hands rather than genuine collaborators. Before long, Joe was again 'posting' his contribution: leaving the others tapes of lyrics and rough chords for them to 'arrange' during rehearsals at which he was rarely present. (In fairness, Joe had other priorities: during this period his father died, his mother was diagnosed as terminally ill, and he and Gaby had their first daughter.) Then even that responsibility was taken away from the new boys. Bernie Rhodes hijacked the recording process and hired outside musicians to programme and record most of what was eventually released in late 1985 as the bizarre punk-hip hop album *Cut the Crap*. Songwriting was credited to Strummer-Rhodes. Universally agreed to be the absolute nadir of the Clash catalogue, it's hard to believe it was made by the same band that made *London Calling*. Or even *The Clash*. And, of course, it wasn't.

Even this version of the Clash – the Clash Mark 2 – continued to play material from *London Calling* live. The title track opened every show from January to September 1984, and powerful rockers 'Clampdown' and 'Brand New Cadillac' were set regulars. So was Paul Simonon's vocal feature 'The Guns of Brixton'. They also occasionally played 'Spanish Bombs', 'Koka Kola', 'Death or Glory' and 'Armagideon Time'. When the Clash Mark 2 went out on their northern UK busking tour in May 1985, 'The Guns of Brixton' and 'Brand New Cadillac' were both aired, along with covers of several other rock'n'roll classics. It was to be the Clash's last hurrah: the band split a few months afterwards.

*

In late 1984, towards the end of the Clash Mark 2, a troubled Joe Strummer disappeared off to Granada in Andalusia, Spain. During this period he met and befriended members and associates of a local band called 091. The following June he returned with Gaby and his baby daughter, and spent the summer in a house belonging to Palmolive's brother. Towards the end of the year he was in Madrid, hiding from the nightmare of the Clash's final days and trying to produce an album by 091, *Mas De Cien Lobos*, in the spontaneous Guy Stevens style. Like Guy, he found the record company didn't speak his language, and like Guy, he had to accept the indignity of the mix being completed in his absence. Taking a break from what had become another tense situation, he finally made the pilgrimage to the area near Viznar where Federico García Lorca's body is buried in a mass unmarked grave, and smoked a spliff in his honour. That December, he visited Lorca's birthplace, where more spliffs were smoked, and Joe also marked the occasion by singing 'Spanish Bombs' a capella.

In early 1986 Joe came up with a couple of songs for the sound-track of Alex Cox's film *Sid and Nancy* – as he had previously done for *Grutzi Elvis* and *Rude Boy* – and in spring Alex took him to the desert near Almeria, also in Andalusia, to shoot the video for the single 'Love Kills'. It had been a popular location for spaghetti westerns, and the video inevitably involved Joe wielding a gun. Shortly afterwards, he and Alex hatched a plot to shoot a modern-day spoof spaghetti western in Almeria called *Straight To Hell*, starring Joe, Elvis Costello and members of the Pogues. Joe got to play a hired killer, and method acted the role Monty Clift-style: to the extent of never washing and sleeping in his increasingly grubby black suit.

Thus was the personal and Lorcan connection with Spain as explored in 'Spanish Bombs', and the spaghetti western soundtrack connection as explored in 'The Guns of Brixton', and the general *London Calling* western-gangster-noir mythos all wrapped up neatly in one bundle of experience for Joe. Andalusia was destined to remain an important part of his life for the rest of his life. He would holiday in the coastal town of San José every August, when he was not obliged by other commitments to be elsewhere, often bringing friends along, Paul Simonon among them.

Over the summer of 1984 Topper Headon celebrated cleaning up by recording a big band version of Gene Krupa's 'Drumming Man' at Wessex with the help of Mickey Gallagher, and co-produced by long-time Clash engineer Jerry Green. Knowing Topper could write, Jerry persuaded him to form his own band. They recorded a couple of jazzy type R&B instrumentals, and secured a recording contract with Mercury. In July and August 1985 Topper was back in Wessex Studio One with Jerry to record an album of entirely self-composed material. Although it would be marketed as a solo album, Topper was accompanied by Mickey, a couple of former Van Morrison band members, vocalist Jimmy Helms, and a four-piece horn section. He wasn't quite able to recapture the *London Calling* vibe 'on his own' – he's no lyricist, for a start – but 'When You're Down' revisits the theme of 'I'm Not Down', and 'Just Another Hit' and 'Monkey on My Back' work the same seam as 'Hateful'. Released the following January, *Waking Up* got positive reviews, but Topper was soon using again.

Before long, there were no more songs about kicking heroin, just days running into years spent living the life of 'Hateful', 'Junco Partner' and 'Junkie Slip' . . . losing friends, running out of money, pawning possessions and spending time in jail. In February 1987 Topper was charged with supplying heroin to someone who overdosed and died. The court case hung over his head for the rest of the year, and he was sentenced to 15 months that November, of which he served 10. Numerous clean-up attempts and lapses followed.

Although Topper and Paul Simonon had been let go by CBS, Joe and Mick were still held to contract. BAD's late 1985 album title, *This is Big Audio Dynamite*, continues the 'call sign' tradition of 'London Calling' and 'This is Radio Clash'. Musically, BAD moved on – as Mick had been determined to do ever since *Sandinista!* – from the retro-rock-meets-classic reggae blueprint of *London Calling*, but with lyrics mostly by Clash-sympatico band member Don Letts, the album doesn't quite leave the imagery of those years behind. A fascination with movie history is evident, and there are samples from spaghetti westerns and London gangster flicks. The packaging brings both elements together to illustrate Mick's concept of the Wild West End . . . not far

different from The Guns of Notting Hill: on the front cover, a bestub-
bled Mick wears a cowboy hat pulled low over his eyes, while holding
a fistful of dynamite. Inside, BAD commence what was to become a
tradition of incorporating an image of high-rise Ladbroke Grove landmark Trellick Tower in the packaging: echoes of 'Lost in the
Supermarket' and 'I'm Not Down', as well as 'London's Burning' and
'Up in Heaven (Not Only Here)'.

The two having made peace in late 1985, Mick played guitar on
Joe's 'Love Kills', and both Joe and Paul Simonon appeared as cops in
the Wild West End video for the BAD single 'Medicine Show'. In June
1986 Joe dropped into the central London studio where BAD were
recording their second album, and didn't leave. He ended up co-
producing, naming the album *No 10 Upping Street*, and co-writing five
of the nine tracks. Two of these have (different) elements of 'London
Calling' about them. Although 'V13' is the tag of a Venice, Los Angeles,
street gang, the incorporation of the *EastEnders* TV soap theme tune,
and its references to fallout from the explosion at the Chernobyl
nuclear reactor on 26 April 1986 – Three Mile Island turned nasty –
give it a futurist-apocalyptic feel. 'Sightsee MC!', meanwhile, is similar
in tone to one of Joe's earlier drafts for 'London Calling', with its
alternative tourist guide to the capital: the 'midnight shutdown' in the
first verse; the high-rise slums (and a reference to a 'Koka Kola'-style
window-jumper) in the second; and, in the third, a reference to the
Broadwater Farm riot of 6 October 1985, which followed on closely
from the latest Brixton riot a week earlier, jumping a train of Clash
references careering all the way back through 'The Guns of Brixton'
to 'White Riot'.

Mick was still pursuing his infatuation with hip hop, but the
album's lead track 'C'mon Every Beatbox' (which didn't involve Joe)
is an update of Eddie Cochran's 'C'mon Everybody' (1958), indicating a revived interest in early rock'n'roll. After Mick had re-
explored the works of Elvis Presley and Hank Williams, the next
BAD album promised a rootsier approach. Entitled *Tighten Up Vol 88*
after the Trojan reggae compilation album series, and with a cover
painting of a blues party by Paul Simonon, it uses a sample of
'Duelling Banjos' (aka 'Feudin' Banjos') (1955), and includes
'Esquerita', about the early rock'n'rolling pianist who taught Little
Richard everything he knows. Unfortunately, the album itself was a

limp affair. Far better was follow-up *Megatop Phoenix*, released the following year, after Mick had recovered from a life-threatening illness. Recorded at Kinks mainman Ray Davies's Konk studios, it was co-produced by Bill Price.

For Joe Strummer, *Straight to Hell* would be the start of an alternative acting and composing career. In January 1987 he travelled to Nicaragua as part of Alex's repertory company to film *Walker*, for which he also wrote and recorded a well-received, largely instrumental country-meets-Latino soundtrack score. That summer he was invited to guest with the Pogues on Ireland's RTE TV programme *The Session*, where they did a Pogued-up version of 'London Calling'. When the band's guitarist Phil Chevron was taken ill in November, Joe was asked to deputise for him on a month-long tour. Each night he was given own feature spot in the encores, performing 'I Fought the Law' and 'London Calling'.

Towards the end of the Clash, while Joe Strummer was hiding out in Spain, Bernie Rhodes had tried to persuade Paul Simonon to continue with a Mark 3 incarnation of the Clash. Even after the band split, they did persevere with a variation on that idea. At Bernie's suggestion, in 1987 Paul and his friend Nigel Dixon – former vocalist for rockabilly revival band Whirlwind – took an *Easy Rider*-style motorcycle trip across the south-western USA to soak up some inspiration. (Where once the four members of the Clash had written songs about Hollywood movie archetypes, now, it seemed, they were separately living out those roles.) Bernie expected Paul and Nigel to come back to London and work with him. Instead, they based themselves in LA, rode with a celebrity biker gang and began to put together the band Havana 3am. Bernie took the hint, and instead involved himself with a Clash-alike band called Twenty Flight Rockers for a couple of years.

March 1988 saw the release of the first Clash compilation album. Sony had taken over CBS that year, but Sony continued using old CBS labels for Clash and other releases: Columbia in the UK and Epic in the USA. The working title for this 'best of' was *Revolution Rock*, after the *London Calling* track, but it was ultimately issued as *The Story of the Clash: Volume 1*. Initially available as both a double LP and a double CD, it is oriented largely towards the band's singles releases, but the 28 tracks still include a proportionately high six from *London Calling*, plus 'Armagideon Time'. The sleeve, again designed by Jules Balme, features a live Pennie Smith photograph: coincidentally, the one Ray Lowry had initially mocked up for *London Calling* before replacing it with the bass-smashing picture. Less coincidentally, the two tracks released from the album as singles in the UK were the ones Joe had recently performed with the Pogues. The first, 'I Fought the Law', reached Number 29 in the charts. The second, 'London Calling', included two other tracks from *London Calling* not found on the new hits album, 'Brand New Cadillac' and 'Rudie Can't Fail'. The 7-inch single was also available in a box-set package with a T-shirt and two badges, and the other options were a 12-inch single and a CD single, both of which had an additional, non-*London Calling* track. Despite this multi-format hard sell, the single stalled at Number 46.

The following year, Sony released all the Clash albums on mid-priced CD. *London Calling* now fitted comfortably onto a single disc, and had 'Train in Vain' listed on the sleeve: two of its former key characteristics jettisoned forever without a second thought.

The Alex Cox connection continued to create opportunities for Joe. In April 1988 he was asked to compose the soundtrack to Marisa Silver's film *Permanent Record*. He wrote an album's worth of songs, the flavour of which can be gauged from the name he gave the band he put together to record them: the Latino Rockabilly War. The material has a loose, busked quality – more *The Vanilla Tapes* than *London Calling* – and shows that Joe's personal tastes had not changed much in the last decade. Summer 1988 found him touring the UK with the Latino Rockabilly War. He played 'London Calling', but to bulk up his own new material he mostly favoured Clash-associated covers like 'I Fought the Law', 'Brand New Cadillac' and 'Armagideon Time' rather than Clash originals. In August, he was acting again, this time in Jim Jarmusch's *Mystery Train*, a film made and set in Memphis, as an English rocker called Johnny but nicknamed Elvis. Given that Johnny was Joe's real name, an element of typecasting was involved: the part was written with him in mind.

Straight afterwards, Joe went to LA to record *Earthquake Weather*, his bona fide debut post-Clash album proper, using the Latino Rockabilly War as his backing band. Most of the songs were written shortly beforehand, with lyrics composed on drives around the city. As he had done with the Clash Mark 2, Joe gave tapes of rough sketches of songs to the other band members, and told them to arrange their own parts. Although three months of sessions were booked between November 1988 and February 1989, the album was mostly recorded live in the studio and (three or four songs excepted) rather than raw and direct it sounds muddy and uninspired. There are elements of rock and R&B and jazz and even reggae, but the album has neither the tunes nor the textural depth of the Clash at their peak. Most surprisingly, it lacks a convincing lyrical voice. If 'Jimmy Jazz' was a slice of Tom Waits-style pseudo-jazz-meets-film-noir busking, then this album is far too much more of the same. And 'Leopardskin Limousines' is as blatant a lost-love-song – albeit couched in self-conscious hipster jargon – as anything that Mick Jones had provoked Joe's gag reflex with in 1979. The strong first track and lead single 'Gangsterville' is a 'London Calling'-style City as Microcosm of a World in Decline song, this time inspired by the (fantasy) mobsters of LA rather than the mobs of Soho. Other than the inclusion of a rock-steady-era cover version of the Tennors' 'Ride Your Donkey' (1968) and Tim Young doing the mastering, there are precious few other parallels that can be drawn with *London Calling*. It must have been a conscious decision, as Joe's recent soundtrack work was far more true to the spirit of that era. The album flopped miserably, the accompanying tour lost money, and Joe lost much of his self-belief.

As he was spending a lot of time in California, in summer 1987 he had bought himself a light blue 1955 Cadillac Fleetwood: already four years old when Vince Taylor's song was written, it was the perfect period for a fantasy rock'n'roll vehicle. Joe parked it outside the studio where he was recording *Earthquake Weather*. One night a drug dealer's stray bullet went through the door, a detail of which Joe was inordinately proud. The Caddy features on the sleeve of the 'Gangsterville' single, and also in the video, with Joe driving it, posing with it, and – far more true to life – popping up its hood to fix it. It wasn't in much better shape than the Caddy Annie Nightingale had given him in 1979, but Joe stuck with it. In 'Who Would Love This Car But Me?', a song he co-wrote for Brian Setzer's 2001 automotive-themed rock album *Ignition!*, its many faults and failings are lovingly described . . . right down to the bullet hole in the door.

In early summer 1990 Joe was asked to produce the Pogues' next album, *Hell's Ditch*. He method-acted this role, too. Wearing a Nicaraguan cowboy hat for the duration, he cast himself in the role of Guy Stevens to psych the Pogues up: there was a lot of shouting and a fair bit of damage to equipment. His moods were so volatile that the band nicknamed him Strumboli. One of Shane MacGowan's songs, 'Lorca's Novena', touched on subject matter close to Joe's heart. After recording was completed, Shane quit the band, and Joe was asked to deputise for him on a world tour lasting until the following March. Again, this incorporated a Clash mini-set including 'London Calling'.

Havana 3am had relocated to London in 1988, but took a while to get going. Watching them at the Borderline in London in January 1990, the NME's Stephen Dalton described the band's new jointly composed songs as variations on a London Calling theme, rockabilly-meets-reggae-meets-funk-meets-spaghetti-western-soundtracks. Only, as made clear by the reviews of that show, and of the band's self-titled debut album, theirs was not the most inspired mining of that seam. While Joe Strummer at least had some choice in selecting 'London Calling' as his post-Clash signature tune, Paul didn't have the same luxury, and 'The Guns of Brixton' remained his live vocal feature throughout his time with Havana 3am. The song was given an unexpected second wind in February 1990. Norman Cook, the future Fat Boy Slim, then trading as Beats International, married the lyric and vocal melody of the SOS Band's 'Just Be Good to Me' to the bass riff of 'The Guns of Brixton' in a proto-mash-up released as 'Dub Be Good to Me'. When the song went to Number 1 in February 1990 and stayed there for four weeks, going Gold on 1 March with sales of more than 400,000 copies, Paul felt justified in asking for a share of the publishing. Soon afterwards, he commissioned DJ Jeremy Healey to do some dance and dub remixes of the original – involving re-recording the drum track and adding harmonica, among other touches – which were released under the Clash name in July 1990 as 'Return to Brixton'. It peaked at Number 57. Even the best bass line can wear out its welcome.

By early 1991 Paul had lost interest in Havana 3am, and was talking of stopping and devoting himself to painting. But Nigel Dixon had been diagnosed with cancer, and so Paul persevered to keep his terminally ill friend occupied and positive for another year. After that, he retired from music, though he did continue to play along to reggae and spaghetti western records on either bass or guitar for his own amusement . . .

and he did contribute to a track called 'Boom or Bust' recorded by Joe Strummer for a Japanese compilation album in 1995.

After the defection of the other members of the original BAD to form Screaming Target in 1989, Mick formed BAD II and recorded *Kool Aid* in 1990. Reviewing it for *Q*, Ian MacMillan heard echoes of the Clash, and specifically *London Calling*, in its sound. With a couple of changes, the album was reissued in July 1991 as *The Globe*.

That year another unexpected windfall came the Clash's way when they were approached to sanction the use of 'Should I Stay or Should I Go' for the latest in a provenly popular series of UK television advertisements for Levi's jeans. As a consequence, the re-released single climbed to Number 1 in the UK charts in February. Sony responded by re-releasing *The Story of the Clash: Volume 1*, and then re-releasing 'Rock the Casbah'. A re-re-release of 'London Calling', this time in a miniature of the original album sleeve with different typography, and backed with 'Brand New Cadillac' and 'Return to Brixton', made Number 64 in June 1991.

To capitalise further, Sony rush-released a second UK Clash compilation album, *The Singles*, in November. Again, a visual echo of the Clash's most famous album was employed to sell it: the cover features the Pennie Smith Take the 5th tour photograph of Joe Strummer launching his guitar into the air, as previously used on the sleeve of the 1980 European release of 'Rudie Can't Fail', only with new, far busier typography. It peaked at Number 68 on the charts. The album's release was preceded in October by a single of yet another *London Calling* track, 'Train in Vain' (its first official UK outing). It has the same typography as the album, but in a reference to the 1980 European release of 'Train in Vain' (and, again, to the 'action picture' *London Calling*-era European singles generally), it features a sleeve photograph of Mick Jones mid-scissor kick. It failed to chart.

Far more impressive a compilation was the 1991 career overview triple CD *Clash On Broadway*, originally released in America only by Sony as part of the Epic Legacy series. Offering 64 tracks and running to more than three hours 30 minutes, it makes even *Sandinista!* look petite, but has the quality to justify its length. In addition to including 11 of the 19 tracks from *London Calling*, plus 'Armagideon Time' – the only Clash album proportionately better represented is *The Clash* – it also features two of the 1976 Guy Stevens Polydor demos, plus the tribute song 'Midnight to Stevens'. It has a Pennie Smith group photograph on the front cover (supported by one of Bob Gruen's) and there is much use of the Clash star emblem. As a nod to *London Calling*, the set also includes a 'hidden extra' track tucked away on the end of the last disc, in this case 'The Street Parade'. Back on friendly terms with the former Clash members, Kosmo Vinyl helped oversee the project, and interviewed all the Wild Bunch – the band plus the likes of Johnny Green, the Baker and Mickey Gallagher – for the accompanying booklet. For a few years afterwards, Kosmo was Joe's semi-official manager. When the box set was released in the UK in 1994, he was involved in negotiations for a possible Strummer-Jones-Simonon-Headon Clash reunion, but on this occasion – as on previous and subsequent occasions – it was not to be.

In 1996 Joe Strummer appeared in French director François-Jacques Ossang's movie *Docteur Chance*, set in northern Chile, playing a character named Vince Taylor. If that sounds like an uncanny coincidence, it wasn't: the film had been several years in development, and the part was originally written with the real (since deceased) Vince Taylor in mind. That same year, BAD II covered a song by another early British rock'n'roller for *The Flintstones* movie: the highly appropriate 'Rock with the Caveman', written by Lionel Bart and recorded by Tommy Steele in 1956 for his first UK hit, reaching Number 13. *F-Punk*, which turned out to be the last BAD (II) album to be officially released on disc, came the following year. In parts, it is far more overtly a return to the sound of the Clash than *Kool-Aid*, but unfortunately the Clash album it most resembles is *Cut the Crap*. The sleeve's pastiche of the *London Calling* sleeve, complete with pink and green Presley lettering, and the inclusion of a 'hidden extra' track – a cover of David Bowie's 'Suffragette City' – couldn't help but seem a little hopeful.

In August 1998 Joe was invited to present a series of four weekly radio shows entitled *London Calling* for the BBC's World Service (formerly the Overseas Service). Not only did this bring the title of the Clash album full circle, it represented a long-held ambition for Joe: he might not have ended up founding his own radio station, but he did get his own programme, reaching millions of listeners worldwide. It proved to be a success, and he would repeat the exercise in 2000 with two more series of six and four shows, respectively. He always insisted on playing vinyl discs rather than CDs, and the 19 January 2000 show could have been broadcast straight from Vanilla 19 years earlier: it included Sonny Okosun's 'Fire in Soweto', Bo Diddley's 'Nursery Rhyme' (1963) and Elvis Presley's 'Crawfish'.

★

It's probably no coincidence that the next wave of Clash activity coincided with the 20th anniversary of *London Calling*: conventional wisdom has it that 20 years is how long it takes to achieve true classic status.

In October 1999 the Clash authorised the release of a compilation album of 17 live performances covering the period 1978 to 1982. The process of sourcing, shortlisting and producing the material had taken more than a year. Mick Jones produced without taking full credit (given, as was traditional, to the Clash), Bill Price mixed, and Tim Young mastered. Having used live performance shots on the covers of both *The Story of the Clash: Volume 1* and *The Singles*, the band rang the changes by featuring a photograph of the Westway on the cover, but the package did still include some Pennie Smith live photographs. The band had never played 'The Right Profile' in concert, but naming the album *From Here to Eternity* reinforced the Clash's personal mythology by referencing a track from their most feted album, while simultaneously staking their own claim on immortality. The live album was released in tandem with the official Don Letts band documentary *Westway to the World*, so there were opportunities for cross-reference and cross-promotion between projects and titles.

The album includes three of *London Calling*'s four set regular big production numbers: 'London Calling', 'Train in Vain' and 'The Guns of Brixton', and while there is no room for 'Clampdown', 'Armagideon Time' is also included. Only the last of these songs – recorded during the 16 Tons tour on 18 February 1980 at the Lewisham Odeon – features the *London Calling*-period line-up, with Mickey Gallagher on organ and Mikey Dread providing the toast. Selecting versions of the other *London Calling* tracks from later shows – Bond's Casino on 13 June 1981 and, in the case of 'London Calling' itself, the Orpheum in Boston on 7 September 1982 – could be justified as offering snapshots of the songs at later stages in their live evolution. That argument fails to convince, though. Topper was not at his best by summer 1981, and had been sacked by spring 1982. Overall, a disproportionately high eight of the live album's tracks are from the autumn 1982 Combat Rock tour of the USA, with Terry Chimes standing in on drums. This was not a conscious decision to devalue Topper's contribution to the Clash. Bill Price explains that, while 'dozens of shows were very well-recorded on 24-track [during the Combat Rock tour] only a handful of shows with Topper on drums were ever recorded, some of them none too well'. Given the choice available, as much material as possible featuring Topper was included. Even at the time of *From Here to Eternity's* release, Joe – who had little to do with the album – said he didn't believe the Clash had played more than one good gig after Topper left. It was an overstatement, but a strong indication that he for one did not believe the album was truly representative.

Bill Price was kept busy during 1999. The Clash's entire back catalogue, including *London Calling*, was reissued on CD that October in 'restored and re-mastered' versions, a process which Bill oversaw. 'The object of the Clash remastering was to improve upon the original [1989] CD releases,' he says. 'Some of which, to be honest, had just been transferred onto CD rather than mastered, sometimes from production copies of the original master tape using now obsolete technology.' 'You hear a lot of stuff about original pressings, the implication being that nothing ever matches the first cut of an album,' says Tim Young. 'Complete rubbish. Quite often, reissues sound much, much better. People move heaven and earth and pay real money for originals. "I've got to get the one that's got TRACK 5 IS 'TRAIN IN VAIN' written on the fourth side! It must sound better than anything else!" and it doesn't.' Tim maintains the best way to hear *London Calling* is on the 1999 CD version, remastered by Ray Staff and Bob Whitney under Bill's supervision. 'That's the best sounding version to get, which was absolutely nothing to do with me,' he says. 'I've got to be honest about it. It was done from the original master tapes.'

'Firstly, we obtained the actual masters, as opposed to copies that had been filed for mass production and export, then we baked them to restore the tape to its original conditions,' says Bill. 'We got the finest ¼-inch transport with the latest electronics to play them on.' This is where his version departs from Tim's modest account: apparently, efforts were made to preserve the integrity of the 1979 mastering. 'We got pristine copies of the original vinyl, and played them on Ray Staff's Neumann lathe using the finest Shure pickup, a £200,000 record player,' continues Bill. 'Very few people would ever hear the vinyl at that quality. The later Clash albums were very well mastered, so when it came to *London Calling* we referred to Tim Young's original notes on levels and EQs and attempted to match the vinyl. It was totally subjective, albeit we knew the direction in which to go. Having got the sounds, we mastered it to the highest level that Ray would allow me to use. The CD also benefited from a lack of pre-echo and snap, crackle and pop, relative to the vinyl.'

Four different Clash tribute albums were released in 1999, too: hardly a coincidence. In fairness, the only authorised one had been conceived more than two years earlier. In 1996 Jason Rothberg persuaded Joe Strummer to contribute a new track to a human rights album called *Generations 1* he was overseeing in LA for the Miles Copeland-backed label Ark 21, and from that grew the idea of the Clash tribute album *Burning London*. Jason commissioned 21 tracks from leading left-field artists of the day – there was a distinct Californian bias – and Joe approved the final listing for the 12-track album. Originally intended to be a September 1997 release on Ark 21, it was co-opted by Sony and released on Epic in March 1999 to tie in with the other Clash activity. Part of the proceeds still went to benefit the Children's Hospital Los Angeles High Risk Youth Program. Five of the covers – almost half – were of songs originally to be found on *London Calling*: 'Hateful' by No Doubt, fronted by Gwen Stefani, and with Billy Idol guesting on backing vocals; 'Train in Vain' by Third Eye Blind; 'Clampdown' by the Indigo Girls; 'Rudie Can't Fail' by the Mighty Mighty Bosstones; and 'Lost in the Supermarket' by the Afghan Whigs, with Topper Headon playing drums and lead singer Greg Dulli throwing in snippets of 'Train in Vain' and Ben E. King's 'Stand By Me' at the close.

By the end of 1999 the definition of 'tribute album' was starting to get a little strained, with the phrase 'cash-in' springing more readily to mind. The other three projects feature Clash songs performed by significantly lesser-known bands. *City Rockers* has 18 tracks in total, eight of which hail from *London Calling*, the only familiar name being the Dropkick Murphys, who cover 'The Guns of Brixton'. *Backclash* has 16 tracks, of which five are from *London Calling* (one song is covered twice). *Police State* has just two out of 12.

After a relatively low-key decade, Joe Strummer also timed his move back into the musical spotlight with new band the Mescaleros and new album *Rock Art and the X-Ray Style* to coincide with the issue of *From Here to Eternity* and the Clash CD remasters. Opening track 'Tony Adams' is another 'London Calling'-type broadcast – 'Late news breaking, this just in' – only this time with the 'city of madness' being New York: with solar flares (the sun zooming in), snowflakes (the Ice Age coming), and other end-of-the-world indicators like power cuts (engines stopping running) and neon advertising signs blowing on Broadway. While that song offers a touch of reggae, Joe's interest in retro-rock is catered for by 'The Road to Rock'n'Roll', which he wrote with Johnny Cash in mind. The closing ballad 'Willesden to Cricklewood' is a gentler, more positive take on 'Sightsee MC!', and therefore bears a similar relation to the early drafts of 'London Calling'. Mostly, though, it's a world-dance-groove-oriented collection, with tracks built up slowly by men with machines, and sessioners over-dubbing, rather then a genuine band rehearsing or tracking live. The much-acclaimed album found Joe working with Ant Genn, his first equal co-writing partner since Mick Jones departed the Clash. Bill Price was invited to mix the result, though his mix was ultimately not used.

Ant Genn proved effective as Joe's writing foil, but he had a heroin habit that made Topper look like a dilettante, and was not around for the Mescaleros' follow-up, *Global a Go-Go*. Released in 2001, that album was worked up from improvisations by the live band, plus a guesting Tymon Dogg, and if it resembles any Clash release at all, it's *Sandinista!* The title track, though, was inspired by Joe's stints as a BBC World Service DJ, and once again opens with late news breaking as Joe enjoys the prospect of more radio-induced, cross-cultural pollination.

In May 2001 Joe Strummer, Mick Jones, Paul Simonon and Topper Headon took the stage together for the first time in 20 years and – as it turned out – the last time ever to collect the Clash's Ivor Novello award for lifetime achievement. Joe dedicated it to Guy Stevens. According to Chris Salewicz's Strummer biography, Joe and Mick wrote half-a-dozen new songs together around this time, ostensibly as security for Joe should the Mescaleros fail to come up with enough material for *Global a Go-Go*. When Mick asked him why the Strummer-Jones songs had not been used, Joe told him he was saving them for the 'next Clash album'. They remain unreleased.

In September that year, Bob Gruen published *The Clash*, a book of his Clash photographs, which fills in the gaps around Pennie Smith's *Before and After*. It covers the autumn 1978 New York mixing sessions for *Give 'Em Enough Rope*, the February 1979 Pearl Harbour tour, the Christmas 1979 Acklam Hall gigs and the Concert for Kampuchea, and the March 1980 US leg of the 16 Tons tour, as well as some earlier and later material.

In 2002 the snappily titled unofficial tribute album *A Punk Tribute to the Clash* was released. Although it includes some recognisable names – including Chelsea frontman Gene October and UK Subs frontman Charlie Harper – this only serves to make it seem more cynical or desperate. Of 12 tracks, three are from *London Calling*: 'Train in Vain' by Knox (of the Vibrators), 'London Calling' by Mike Peters (of the Alarm), and 'The Guns of Brixton' by RTZ Global.

When the Mescaleros played live, Joe still flung his guitar into the wings for his guitar roadie to catch, Take The 5th-style, and the band played a significant number of songs associated with the Clash. In 1999, there would typically be around four Clash originals, including Joe's signature tune, 'London Calling', 'Rudie Can't Fail' and two or three of the covers the band had recorded, including 'Brand New Cadillac'. Both 'London Calling' and 'Brand New Cadillac' had faded away by the end of 2000, but 'Armagideon Time' came in during 2002. The only *London Calling* song to be featured regularly for the entire duration of the Mescaleros' career was 'Rudie Can't Fail'. Joe played it during his last ever show, and also a week earlier, on 15 November 2002 at Acton Town Hall, where the Mescaleros were performing at a benefit show for striking firemen. That night, Joe dedicated the song to Mick Jones's newly arrived baby daughter. This might have been what prompted Mick to join the band onstage for the three-song Clash encore, playing live with Joe for the first time since 1983. David Mingay was also present, purely by chance: he didn't even know the Mescaleros were appearing. Afterwards he chatted with Joe about 'Rudie Can't Fail', and Joe happily told the *Rude Boy* co-director that it was still one of the most popular Clash songs. 'So it did chime with the fans, and people did understand the message,' says David.

As was customary, Joe had spent his 50th birthday – 21 Aug 2002 – in Spain, drinking with former 101ers member Richard Dudanski. That year, he talked about playing a tribute to Lorca nearby to tie in with his next birthday. That birthday never came, but Richard, Tymon Dogg,

Mick Jones and some other old friends travelled to Granada in Andalusia to do the honours, playing a mixture of Clash songs and 101ers songs. Afterwards, Joe's daughters travelled down to San José with his ashes, and sprinkled them into the sea.

The third, posthumously released, Joe Strummer and the Mescaleros album *Streetcore* (2003) sends tremors all the way back along the line of his career. Opening track 'Coma Girl' was recorded live in one take, Guy Stevens-style, and the sleeve notes Joe wrote during his last studio sessions give every indication that he would have pursued this approach had he not died before recording was completed. There's more late news breaking and another London City Guide in 'Burnin' Streets'. 'Midnight Jam' is a collage of announcements from Joe's *London Calling* World Service radio broadcasts. 'Ramshackle Day Parade' is an acknowledgement that Joe's head had always been full of American movies: gangsters and cowboys and soldiers. 'Silver and Gold' is a cover of a 1960 Fats Domino and Bobby Charles song more commonly known as 'Before I Grow Too Old': a nod back to New Orleans when the music beloved of Joe Strummer was young and was recorded quickly and cheaply on basic equipment.

Rude Boy had been released at least twice before on video, but in 2003 it was afforded a Special Edition DVD release with extras and interviews. It still features 'Rudie Can't Fail' and the instrumental 'Revolution Rock', as well as the only available Joe Strummer versions of 'No Reason' and 'Let the Good Times Roll'.

Uncut magazine marked its December 2003 publication of a poll feature on the Clash's greatest songs with two different freebie CDs of Clash covers, featuring 15 tracks apiece (with a couple of other related songs thrown in), most of them by contemporary artists in a traditional rock or acoustic vein. Shortly afterwards came a trio of more conceptual 'tribute' projects. The title of *This is Rockabilly Clash* (2003) tells no lies. Of 14 tracks reworked rockabilly style, four are from *London Calling* (one of them twice). The following year came *Charlie Does Surf*, another title that reveals the agenda. Of 18 surf instrumental takes on Clash tunes by bands from all over the world (but mostly North America), seven are of songs from *London Calling*, including 'Train in Vain' by Susan and the SurfTones and 'Clampdown' by the Urban Surf Kings.

Arguably the most entertaining – and certainly the most imaginative – of all the Clash tributes was an international download project conceived to anticipate the 25th anniversary of *London Calling*. In February 2004 the Prank Monkey, aka Culture Deluxe, threw down an open challenge to anyone interested in subjecting any of the album's tracks to the remix and mash-up treatment. As early as April 2004 a free download version of *London Booted* was made available, featuring 19 tracks reworking the entire album in its original sequence (plus a few spares), with all downloaders asked to donate to charities, including the Joe Strummer Future Forests project on the Isle of Skye. In September 2005 the core 19 tracks were issued as a double LP, with all profits again going to charity. The wit and invention keeps on coming on tracks including: Dunproofin's 'Bubba's Got a Brand New Cadillac' (Clash vs Bubba Sparx); Eve Massacre's 'The Power of Rebelution Can't Fail' (vs Madonna and Jurassic 5); Instamatic's 'Spanish Bombs (Over Baghdad)' (vs Outkast); McSleazy's 'Lost Souls in the Supermarket'; DJ Riko's 'Build 'Em Up, Clamp 'Em Down' (vs Fatboy Slim); Miss Frenchie's 'Fuck 'Em Boyo' (vs Peaches); Jimmi Jammes' 'This Girl Wants a Cheat' (vs Christine Aguilera); and '10,000 Spoons' 'Four Hoarse Men' (vs Prodigy). Well worth the price of a tree.

From 4–18 September 2004 the London Print Studios on the Harrow Road, at the northern end of Ladbroke Grove, hosted the *Joe Strummer Past, Present & Future* exhibition. As well as memorabilia collected by Joe on his travels, photographs, tickets and set lists, it included a number of 101ers lyric sheets plus the notebook drafts of many of his lyrics for *London Calling*.

In October that year (rather than leaving it until the literal mid-December last minute) Sony celebrated the 25th anniversary of *London Calling* by releasing a double CD-plus-DVD box-set special edition. The first CD features the 1999 remaster of the original double album, and the second CD features *The Vanilla Tapes*, that is, 21 of the 37 Vanilla demos Mick Jones had recently discovered in his lock-up. They aren't recordings anyone but a fan would want to listen to repeatedly, but Greil Marcus's assessment of them as unlistenable crap is too hard. The DVD includes *The Last Testament*, Don Letts's 30-minute documentary about the making of the album, incorporating new interviews by Mick Jones and Paul Simonon, and older ones (with footage taken from *Westway to the World*) by Joe Strummer and Topper Headon, plus excerpts from the BBC1 TV *Nationwide* feature about the 16 Tons tour, first broadcast on 18 February 1980. There is also the *Wessex Studios Footage*, early August 1979 black-and-white home video of Guy Stevens creating havoc while the Clash record. Last comes Don Letts's original promotional video for 'London Calling', and live promotional films for 'Train in Vain' and 'Clampdown', shot at the Clash's Lewisham Odeon show on 18 February 1980.

Jules Balme's clever design for the CD-sized box folds out into four panels, and comes in an open-sided plastic slipcover. It incorporates the original album cover art, details from the 'Armagideon Time' side of Ray Lowry's original HMV 'dancing teens' UK single sleeve design, and stills taken by Pennie Smith during the filming of the 'London Calling' video. The discs themselves are grey, pink and green: the colour palette of the original album release. The right-hand outer panel houses a two-sided foldout adaptation of Ray Lowry's original inner-sleeve lyric sheets. The left-hand outer panel houses a 36-page booklet featuring detailed information about the contents of the discs, plus the Clash's handwritten and hand-drawn notes on the songs, as originally included in the first issue of *The Armagideon Times*. It also features details from Pennie Smith's contact sheets for the 21 September 1979 Palladium show that provided the cover shot, the making of the 'London Calling' video, the December 1979 Christmas card shoot, and a few gigs from the Take the 5th tour, together with Ray Lowry's illustration for the 'London Calling' side of the original UK single, and his rough sketch for the album cover. New material includes a psychogeographical exploration of the Clash's London by Tom Vague, and Pat Gilbert's account of the story behind *The Vanilla Tapes*.

Given the embarrassment of riches included in all media, it seems churlish to find fault. Room could perhaps have been found for 'Armagideon Time' and its versions. Someone could have investigated whether any warm-up covers or outtakes recorded during the Wessex sessions still survived (and if not, said so). *The Last Testament* documentary is a little perfunctory, with neither Mick nor Paul being forthcoming with details about the writing or recording of individual songs. And the *Wessex Studios Footage* is problematic: as a fly-on-the-wall document it's a godsend, and once it was rediscovered by Kosmo it absolutely had to be included . . . but it's hard to enjoy watching Guy Stevens in the throes of his compulsive, addictive behaviour, knowing – as all viewers now know – that the death it is leading to is just around the corner. These are minor caveats, though: the box set has been assembled with taste and care, and is a worthy monument to the original album.

Official merchandising was something of which the Clash had previously been wary. In 1977 Bernie Rhodes had attempted to get a venture called Upstarts underway with early Clash helper and designer Sebastian Conran, which fizzled out as Sebastian drifted away from the band later that year. In 1979 T-shirt designers and printers 5th Column were brought in to produce T-shirts for the Pearl Harbour and Take the 5th tours, which were then made more widely available. From 1980 onwards, the Clash took their own stalls on the road with them to sell badges, posters and T-shirts. But all of this was low-key, and hardly qualified as a comprehensive and concerted merchandising strategy. Even at the time, the opportunities for pirates and bootleggers did not past unnoticed or unexploited, and by the time the Clash were considered hip again – post-split – the opportunities offered by Internet marketing and sales meant that for many years people other than the Clash were in a position to make a lot of money from bootleg merchandise. By far the most popular image was the iconic *London Calling* sleeve, adorning everything from knock-off T-shirts to mouse mats to Zippo-style lighters.

While they were still a going concern, the Clash had rejected exploitation, limiting their potential income to money for record sales from the record company, for live shows from promoters, and for songwriting from music publishers. Now the Clash had disbanded, there was no live revenue at all, and although money was still coming through from record reissues and publishing, by the mid-Noughties, the band – like other artists new and old – were coming to the realisation that these sources could not be relied upon indefinitely as major income streams. Music was increasingly being downloaded for nothing or next to it, with these acquisitions passing largely unrecorded, let alone levied. This affected both record company royalties and music publishing royalties. For those artists still active, live revenue became more important, and for all artists, soundtracks, advertisements and merchandising could no longer be ignored or scorned.

For the Clash, their principled stands on these issues had toppled one by one from the early Nineties onwards. Permission to use songs on soundtracks for edgy and simpatico London-based indie films had given way by the Noughties to permission to use 'London Calling' in any flick involving a trip to London. After refusing to let Clash songs be used to advertise British Telecom, pop or beer, the Clash had been involved in promoting Levi's, Technics and Jaguar. In 2004 merchandising was the last domino to fall. The timing was significant: the Clash were inducted into the Rock and Roll Hall Of Fame in March 2003, which raised their profile considerably; and the *London Calling* 25th Anniversary Edition focussed new attention on what was already considered to be the band's crowning glory. Five years earlier, the Clash had revived their limited company Dorisimo – originally established 20 years before for Paul Simonon and Topper Headon's songwriting – to handle the band's co-production of *Westway to the World*. In 2001 it was used to set up the Clash's official website. And now it was used to market a range of official merchandise.

As it rolled out from 2004 onwards, official Clash merchandise has remained true to a Clash-associated colour palette and a number of strong, Clash-associated designs. Chief among them is the *London Calling* cover image, which has adorned posters, T-shirts, badges, stickers, sew-on patches, fridge magnets, mugs, coasters, key rings and 'stash' tins. Another recurring image known as 'Skull', features Japanese kanji over a 'Death or Glory' skull and crossbones, and appears on T-shirts, badges, coasters, shot-glasses, and playing cards. Overall, Dorisimo's merchandising has been on a Beatles-type scale. It hasn't relied upon *London Calling* exclusively, but it has leaned on it heavily, recognising and demonstrating that the album is the major selling point when it comes to Clash iconography.

Back in 2002 Mick Jones was asked to produce *Up the Bracket*, the first album by the Libertines. Deciding to honour their punky take on things, he took a leaf out of the Guy Stevens book, recorded it live in the studio, and worried about the detail later. He did the same for the 2004 follow up, *The Libertines*, and – after the band split – in 2005 with *Down in Albion*, the first album by Pete Doherty's new band, Babyshambles. Bill Price was brought in to mix the last two projects, and Tim Young mastered *The Libertines*.

Seemingly retired from making music, Paul Simonon proved to be a good enough painter to be taken seriously. Although his first post-Clash works explored urban musical and sub-cultural themes, he moved away from that subject matter during the Nineties, while persevering with his easily identifiable figurative style. He painted everything from portraits to beach landscapes, but the work that made the most impact was a series exhibited in October 2002 at the private Hazlitt, Gooden & Fox gallery in Piccadilly under the title *From Hammersmith to Greenwich*, in the tradition of Thomas Shotter Boys's 1842 series *London As It Is*. Large canvases of views along the River Thames, most of them painted from an elevated vantage point, they are 'London Calling' in oils. The foreword for the exhibition catalogue was written by Peter Ackroyd, author of *London: The Biography*. Appropriately enough, then, one of Paul's works, *The Thames from Millbank* – painted from Jeffrey Archer's penthouse apartment, located close to Vauxhall Bridge, a brick's throw from the site of the former Vanilla Rehearsal Studios – was subsequently chosen to illustrate another psychogeographical guide to the capital, Ed Glinert's *London Compendium: A Street-by-Street Exploration of the Hidden Metropolis*, published by Penguin in 2003.

Although on civil terms – and in regular contact thanks to their co-directorship of Nineden and Dorisimo, and involvement in other Clash business affairs – Mick and Paul had not had much to do with each other socially since the band split up. They did, however, move in the same London creative, media and fashion circles, and were both invited to supermodel Kate Moss's Rock'n'Roll Circus-themed 31st birthday party, held at her home in the Chilterns on 16 January 2005. Both accepted when Kate asked them to provide the entertainment as part of a one-off garage supergroup also including Primal Scream's Bobby Gillespie, Spiritualised's Jason Pierce and Supergrass's Danny Goffey. Paul had not played publicly since the last days of Havana 3am, and had been the only member of the Clash still expressing his reluctance to perform at the Clash's Rock and Roll Hall of Fame induction when Joe Strummer's death put an end to further discussion. At the time, Paul had been concerned about cheapening the Clash's legacy, but now Clash reunions and reformations were no longer on the agenda, he felt relaxed enough to jam a bunch of oldies for fun at a private (if hardly low-key) shindig. The party would be remembered for a more tabloid-newsworthy event – it saw the beginning of Kate's ill-starred relationship with Pete Doherty – but it was also the first time Paul and Mick had played together since the latter's sacking from the Clash in September 1983.

There were two significant spin-offs. One was that Kate visited the studio while Mick was producing the first Babyshambles album. On 15 September 2005 the *Daily Mirror* ran a front cover exposé constructed around mobile-phone footage of Miss Moss allegedly snorting cocaine, with Mick Jones implicated by association: that 'Koka Kola' world revisited, 26 years on.

More interestingly, it was news of Paul Simonon's emergence from retirement that prompted Damon Albarn to invite him to play on what evolved into the 'supergroup' album project *The Good, the Bad and the Queen*. Of the Britpop-era bands, Blur's work had been closest to the London-centric songwriting tradition of the Sixties. Conversations Damon had with Paul about the current state of the capital, the nation and the world helped the new project take shape throughout 2005 and 2006. Paul plays reggae-inflected bass throughout, which, in combination with former Verve guitarist Simon Tong and ex-Fela Kuti drummer Tony Allen and producer Danger Mouse, helped create a multicultural musical stew. The title obviously owes something to the spaghetti western of nearly the same name, but also to Lee Perry's spaghetti western-influenced dub, evoking both 'The Guns of Brixton' and Paul's childhood. Although more melancholy and sedate than *London Calling*, *The Good, the Bad and the Queen* is an inheritor of its ability to capture and reflect not only the city but also the national and international mood. Upon its release early in 2007 it too was hailed as an instant classic and was named Album of the Year by the *Observer Music Magazine*.

The front cover (and the disc itself) features an illustration of London burning attributed to Paul's recent inspiration, Thomas Shotter Boys, and Paul himself provides cartoons to illustrate the lyrics, just as he did for the first issue of *The Armagideon Times*. Pennie Smith took the band photo positioned behind the disc tray. It carries an unintentional echo of the damage being inflicted on the cover of *London Calling*. Instead of dishing it out, this time Paul has clearly been on the receiving end: he's sporting two black eyes and a plaster across the bridge of his nose. For the publicity photos, promo films and accompanying live tour, the group wore suits and hats and rolled jeans, sartorial nods to Blur's *Modern Life is Rubbish* (1993) period and the Clash's *London Calling* period. Thus it was arguably the least likely member of the Clash who was involved in making something comparable to *London Calling* in terms of content, popularity and the spirit of its making. At the end of the first gig to promote the album, on 27 January 2007 in Bristol, Paul even succumbed to what he later described as a moment of madness and sang 'The Guns of Brixton'. After that, the band decided to let the new project stand on its own merits.

In 2007 Mick Jones involved Bill Price in mixing *The Last Post*, the first physical album – as opposed to download – release by Carbon/Silicon, the band he formed in 2002 with old friend Tony James. There are occasional lyrical echoes of the Clash to be found in Tony's lyrics. 'Caesar's Palace' revisits the consumer angst of 'Lost in the Supermarket', 'War on Culture' touches on Mick's experience of being damned by association in a tabloid newspaper cocaine scandal, while the album title references the provisional title for *London Calling*, *The Last Testament*. 'It's about the band being the last stand for culture,' joked Mick to *Uncut*. The following January, Carbon/Silicon began a series of weekly concerts at the Inn on the Green in Ladbroke Grove. On the first night, 11 January 2008, Topper Headon – now clean – sat in for the encores, performing Mick's signature Clash songs 'Should I Stay or Should I Go' and 'Train in Vain'. It was the first time they had played together for 25 years, making Mick the only member of the Clash to have played live with all three other members of the *London Calling*-era Clash since they disbanded.

Three years after the Clash's induction into the Rock and Roll Hall of Fame, the Hall's Museum in Cleveland put together an exhibition entitled *Revolution Rock: The Story of the Clash* (a combination of the title rejected for the band's original compilation album and the title that replaced it). Among the exhibits were some of Joe's handwritten draft lyrics, including those for 'London Calling' and 'Clampdown', as previously seen at the *Joe Strummer: Past, Present & Future* exhibition in London. Also on display were Mick and Joe's most recognisable Clash-era guitars, but the centrepiece – or, at least, the item that received the most media attention – was the wreckage of the bass Paul is seen smashing on the cover of *London Calling*. Opening on 21 October 2006 *Revolution Rock* was originally intended to run until the following spring, but proved so popular it remained open until 7 October 2007. On 24 November 2008 the Cleveland Clash exhibition was resurrected as one of the opening attractions at the Hall of Fame's new Annex in New York, where, in a reference to *London Calling*, the three-dimensional exhibits were housed in replica vintage red 'London' telephone boxes.

On 2 October 2006, a couple of weeks before the original Cleveland exhibition, the Trojan label, which had been part of the Sanctuary group since 2001, released a compilation album of songs covered by the Clash called *Revolution Rock: A Clash Jukebox*. It features 21 tracks selected by Paul Simonon, who, with the aid of Chris Salewicz, also supplies the sleeve notes. In addition to other songs the Clash played around the period they made *London Calling*, it includes the original versions of the covers featured on the album, 'Brand New Cadillac' by Vince Taylor, 'Revolution Rock' by Danny Ray, 'Wrong Emboyo' by the Rulers (plus, for good measure, 'Stagger Lee' by Lloyd Price) as well as 'Armagideon Time' by Willi Williams. Unfortunately, the album fell down a crack when Universal took over Sanctuary in June 2007.

That year, *London Calling* was inducted into the Grammy Hall of Fame, and 2008 saw a rash of official releases. The first artefact to emerge in April in the USA (October in the UK) was a Don Letts-overseen live compilation-cum-documentary DVD confusingly also named *Revolution Rock*. Of its 22 tracks, five are performances of *London Calling* tracks, all with Topper on drums: 'Train in Vain' and 'Clampdown' are the same Lewisham Odeon promos that appear on the 25th Anniversary Edition of *London Calling*; and 'London Calling' is the Bonds Casino version that appears in audio form on *From Here to Eternity*. 'The Guns of Brixton' is from the Clash's April 1980 appearance on the ABC TV show *Fridays*; and 'Brand New Cadillac' is from a January 1982 performance at the Sun Plaza in Tokyo.

In October 2008 came the Clash audio release *Live at the Shea Stadium*, the band's first single-concert live album, recorded by Glyn Johns when the band played support to the Who there on 13 October 1982. The original intention was to release it as a stopgap live album in 1983, but this was abandoned when Mick Jones was sacked that year. Later, many of the individual tracks had been in the running for inclusion on *From Here to Eternity*, until 'better' versions were uncovered from an earlier 1982 show at the Orpheum Theater in Boston. Although generally well received, *Live at the Shea Stadium* catches the Clash with a hard rockin' sound geared to American stadia. Some fans expressed surprise that Sony BMG (as they were by now) couldn't have found a Clash headlining show from 1979 or 1980 that caught the band in their *London Calling* period, with their *London Calling* line-up. Bill Price has already partly answered that one, but the other part of the answer is surely that the Shea show was ready to go and therefore the easiest and cheapest option. 'It's not really the Clash,' Topper Headon told Sean Egan for *Billboard* at the time of release. What it does demonstrate is that, nearly three years after its release, *London Calling* still provided the dramatic heart of the Clash live experience. All four of the songs the band had chosen to introduce themselves to America with on the *Fridays* TV show are still part of the stripped-down, support-act-length, 14-song set, and they are accompanied by the perennial 'Armagideon Time' and less regular 'Spanish Bombs'. A limited edition 7-inch vinyl picture-disc single of 'London Calling' was issued to promote the album.

As sales of physical copies of the disc were unlikely to be high, Dorisimo drummed up some more merchandising business: at least three official T-shirts adapting the Shea Stadium album cover artwork were produced, one of them bearing the legend *Revolution Rock* just to cover all the bases.

Published at the same time, again with the involvement of Dorisimo, was the coffee-table book *The Clash* – another overused title – billed as the story of the band, by the band. It recycled and extended the interview material from 1999's *Westway to the World*, and features a lot of photographs and memorabilia, including reproductions of pages from the *Clash 2nd Songbook* and excerpts from both issues of *The Armagideon Times*. Less impressively, none of the *London Calling* draft lyric and other notebook material on show at the 2004 and 2006 exhibitions was included. Like the other two releases, it involved little new input from the surviving Clash members, or from Joe Strummer's estate, and had a perfunctory feel. 'Joe would be turning in his grave if he'd seen what the band have become today,' Topper Headon told Sean Egan at the time. 'You know what the Clash originally stood for, and we don't stand for that anymore. The Clash were 30 years ago. None of us are really that bothered any more, so people are moving in and making money out of it.'

★

The first serious critics' Greatest Album of All Time polls were conducted in the mid-Seventies, celebrating (approximately) the tenth anniversary of the album as the principal form of delivery for popular music. (Before 1965, pop was all about singles.) Another decade passed before such polls really started to catch on. By the mid-Eighties popular music was no longer considered disposable: its contribution to the wider culture was acknowledged, and its history valued. It wasn't just bold adventurers – like the teenage Joe Strummer of 20 years earlier – who investigated roots: younger buyers generally were no longer content to live exclusively in the moment. Thanks to the CD format, older buyers found themselves making much the same trip from the opposite direction: revisiting the music of their youth, and then – their interest revitalised – investigating the new. The walls between the youth market and the nostalgia market crumbled, and the precedent was set for enthusiasts remaining enthusiastic for life. Polls and the information accompanying them provided useful buying guides for those looking to assemble core collections, and at the same time knowingly exploited the anoraky psyche of the committed collector: lists, lovely lists. A poll issue of a music publication was a guaranteed bestseller.

Whatever publications or organisations happened to commission and publish the critics' Greatest Albums polls, they threw up surprisingly few surprises. *Rolling Stone*, *Mojo*, broadsheet newspapers, Guinness and Virgin might have been expected to pay homage to the long-recognised pillars of rock culture, but most of the same pillars also recur in *NME* polls and those of other even more left-field publications. A 1985 *Sounds* poll put *The Clash* at Number 1, and a *Spin* poll from 1989 was similarly self-consciously alternative, but otherwise – on both sides of the Atlantic, and elsewhere, too – all critics' polls have tended to reshuffle much the same Top 30 pack. And the critics' choices have also been reflected in the music publications' readers' polls. (Either the critics have been right, the readers have been easily led, or – and this became more pertinent from the early Nineties onwards – the magazines have been hitting their target markets with unerring accuracy.) Mass polls of record buyers conducted by mainstream publications and radio and TV channels (or alliances of such bodies) have tended to make room for a few flavour-of-the-moment mega-sellers, and have crammed even more Beatles albums into the

Top 10 than other polls, but otherwise even they have not departed too much from the script.

This, then, is the Canon According to 25 Years of Greatest Album polls (roughly chronologically): the Beatles' *Revolver* (1966), *Sgt. Pepper's Lonely Hearts Club Band* (1967), *The White Album* (1968) and *Abbey Road* (1969). Bob Dylan's *Bringing It All Back Home* (1965), *Highway 61 Revisited* (1965), *Blonde on Blonde* (1966) and *Blood on the Tracks* (1974). The Rolling Stones' *Let It Bleed* (1969) and *Exile on Main St.* (1972). James Brown's *Live at the Apollo*, the Beach Boys' *Pet Sounds* (1966), Otis Redding's *Otis Blue* (1966), *The Velvet Underground & Nico* (1967), the Jimi Hendrix Experience's *Are You Experienced* (1967), *The Doors* (1967), Love's *Forever Changes* (1968), Van Morrison's *Astral Weeks* (1968), *The Band* (1969), Marvin Gaye's *What's Going On* (1971), the Who's *Who's Next* (1971), David Bowie's *Hunky Dory* (1971) and *The Rise and Fall of Ziggy Stardust and the Spiders from Mars* (1972), Pink Floyd's *The Dark Side of the Moon* (1973), Elvis Presley's *Sun Collection* (1975) and Bruce Springsteen's *Born to Run* (1975).

The first two punk albums to show were *The Clash* and the Sex Pistols' *Never Mind the Bollocks* (both 1977). They were later joined by their American counterparts, Patti Smith's *Horses* (1975) and Television's *Marquee Moon* (1977) and post-punk's sole representative, Joy Division's *Closer* (1980). The late Michael Jackson's *Thriller* (1982) proved to be an undeniable force. As the Nineties and Noughties wore on, alternative rock shifted shape to add the following to the list: the Smiths' *The Queen Is Dead* (1986), U2's *The Joshua Tree* (1987), *The Stone Roses* (1989), Nirvana's *Nevermind* (1991), R.E.M.'s *Automatic for the People* (1992), Oasis's *Definitely Maybe* (1994) and Radiohead's *The Bends* (1994) and *OK Computer* (1997). Hip hop's regular representative is Public Enemy's *It Takes a Nation of Millions to Hold Us Back* (1988). Other albums have appeared and disappeared, including works by Stevie Wonder, Alanis Morissette and Eminem, but the above are the upper-reach regulars. The Greatest Albums of All Time, it seems, are mostly by white male rock artists. Only a few females make the grade, soul and funk get a token nod, hip hop and heavy metal are almost wholly overlooked, and there is no such thing as reggae.

It was the early Nineties before *London Calling* truly supplanted *The Clash* as the Clash's best. Critics' Greatest Album showings for the band's third album have run as follows: 1985: *Sounds* Number 54; 1987:

Paul Gambaccini's poll Number 40; *Spin* Number 1; 1993: the *NME* Number 13 and *The Times* Number 45; 1994: Guinness Number 54; 1995: *Mojo* Number 23; 1997: the *Guardian* Number 17; 2000: *Melody Maker* Number 28; 2003: *NME* Number 12 and *Rolling Stone* Number 8. In 2006 America's *Time* magazine dispensed with the competitive element, and listed albums without placings, *London Calling* included.

Readers' Greatest Albums showings for *London Calling* have been: 1988: *NME* Number 28; 1996: *Mojo* Number 22; 1998: *Q* Number 32; 2002: *Rolling Stone* Number 14; 2003: *Q* Number 14; 2006: *Q* Number 20. Mass vox pops have placed the album in the following positions: 1997: the *Guardian*-Channel 4 TV-HMV Music of the Millennium (36,000 UK record buyers) Number 36, and Virgin Record Buyers Number 96; 1998: *The Virgin All-Time Top 1000 Albums*, edited by Colin Larkin (reportedly of 200,000 music enthusiasts from the UK, the USA and wider world) Number 37; 2005: Channel 4 (500,000 viewers, voting via the Channel 4 website) Number 44; 2006: the *NME.com-Guinness Book of Hit Singles and Albums* (40,000 voters) Number 12.

The poll formula has been tweaked from time to time to offer some variety. In 1987 *Rolling Stone* celebrated its 20th anniversary with a critics' listing of the Top 100 Albums of the Last 20 Years, and *London Calling* came in at Number 14. Flushed with its success, *Rolling Stone* ran another poll in 1989 to determine the Best Albums of the Eighties, and this time *London Calling* placed at Number 1, despite only qualifying for inclusion by the skin of its teeth. In 1993 the *NME* critics' Best of the Seventies list put it at Number 6 (behind *The Clash* at Number 3: by this stage something of a freak result). In 1998 *Q*'s Best of the Seventies poll put *London Calling* at Number 1. (Bestowing upon the Clash the unique honour of achieving Best Album of the Decade in two consecutive decades with the same album.) In 2004 *Pitchfork*'s critics' best of the Seventies made it Number 2. In 2000 French publication *Les Inrockuptibles* ran a readers' poll of the Top 25 Albums of the Last 25 years, placing *London Calling* at Number 10.

In addition to polls with qualification limited by period of release, there have also been polls with qualification limited by nationality of the artist. In 2004 the *Music Monthly* magazine supplement of the *Observer* – the *Guardian*'s sister Sunday paper – consulted critics, music industry figures and pop stars in a bid to determine the best British Albums Ever Made. *London Calling* was Number 3. Also that year, observing the same criterion, *Q*'s critics made it Number 5. In 2006 the *NME* critics made it Number 8. In 2006 *Classic Rock*'s rock with a capital R critics, photographers, DJs and singers made it Number 46. The year before, though, heavy metal magazine *Kerrang!* conducted a readers' poll of British albums and *London Calling* showed at Number 7 in among the Black Sabbaths, Iron Maidens and Led Zeppelins. Qualification by format: a 1991 *NME* poll of the Best Double Albums Ever put *London Calling* at Number 4 after *Blonde on Blonde*, *The White Album* and Captain Beefheart's *Trout Mask Replica* (1969).

Predictability of results wasn't the only reason straightforward Greatest Album of All Time Polls started to dry up in the Noughties: changes in the way music was being consumed meant that the album was starting to feel like old currency. There were ways around this. In 2002 *Spin* critics polled on the Greatest Bands of All Time placed the Clash at Number 7, identifying their Classic Album as *London Calling*, while the same type of poll at the *NME* made the band Number 12. In 2007 – the same year *London Calling* was inducted into the Grammy Hall of Fame as a 'recording of lasting qualitative or historical significance' at least 25 years old – the *NME* invented its own Hall of Fame honouring albums at least 10 years old that had influenced subsequent generations of musicians and still sounded as fresh today as at the time of their release. *London Calling* again made the grade. It proved catching. That same year, *Mojo* ran a poll entitled Big Bangs: 100 Records that Changed the World, for which only records that 'made us see the world differently' and were among 'the most influential and inspirational' qualified for inclusion. Moving away from the album-centric viewpoint, these could be either albums or singles: *London Calling* came in at Number 24 behind a Top 5 of 'Tutti Frutti' by Little Richard, 'I Want to Hold Your Hand' by the Beatles, 'Heartbreak Hotel' by Elvis Presley, *The Freewheelin' Bob Dylan* and *Autobahn* by Kraftwerk.

Swedish statistician Henrik Franzon is responsible for the website *Acclaimed Music*, and maintains he has developed a programme that makes appropriate adjustments for the date of polls, qualification limitations and regional bias to combine all the critics' (not readers') polls he has been able to locate to determine the most highly acclaimed albums of all time. His overall listing currently has *London Calling* at Number 10. (Regional variations: critics from the USA and Canada make it Number 9, from the UK and Ireland Number 7, and from the Rest of the World Number 10.) This seems a little generous. Running an eye over the album's major poll placings listed above gives the impression that it averages somewhere closer to the mid-20s. After pausing for a moment to consider the quality – in some cases, the near-Holy Relic status – of the 25 (or so) albums that tend to appear higher, and then pausing for several more moments to consider all the ground-breaking, heart-warming, foot-stomping, mind-expanding albums that rarely make the lists at all (let alone their upper reaches), a reasonable person would have to concede that it is still a remarkable achievement. *London Calling* is sitting impressively close to the top of the pile, showing no sign of slipping, and throwing a long and intimidating shadow back down the slope.

Enough polls, already. The other way the general public votes (or, rather, used to vote until comparatively recently) is with its wallet. According to the British Phonographic Industry (BPI), *London Calling* went Gold in the UK almost immediately with sales of 100,000, and both *Trouser Press* and *Rolling Stone* reported it had sold around 180,000 copies in the UK by the end of 1980. Thirty years after its release, though, it has officially yet to go Platinum with sales of 300,000. According to the Recording Industry Association of America (RIAA), the album went Gold in the USA with sales of 500,000 in December 1991, and Platinum with sales of 1 million in February 1996. Because other countries started recording the information and offering awards at different times (and some still don't), there are no wholly dependable records for worldwide sales. Comparing a Wikipedia listing of the biggest-selling albums of all time – its information taken from a variety of credited and mostly credible sources – to the official RIAA awards suggests a very rough rule-of-thumb ratio: worldwide sales tend to be approximately 2.5 to 3 times American sales. (This doesn't take into account that some artists do well in the UK and/or Europe and elsewhere without ever breaking America, and vice versa.) Applying this rule, total international sales of *London Calling* are likely to be somewhere around 3 million. Of course, first home taping and then CD burning, illegal downloading and file-sharing, and the longstanding tradition of blatant piracy in some countries, have allowed many more people than that to acquire or at least hear the album over the years.

To put this in perspective, the current RIAA USA award status (with worldwide sales following in brackets) of some of *London Calling's* poll rivals is as follows: *Thriller* 28 million (over 100 million, allegedly), *Dark Side of the Moon* 15 million (40 million), *Sgt. Pepper* 11 million (32 million), *Nevermind* 10 million (26 million), and *The Joshua Tree* 10 million (25 million). Anyone so inclined can do their own calculations using the following official RIAA USA award figures: *The White Album* 19 million, *Born to Run* 6 million, *Revolver* 5 million and *Are You Experienced* 4 million. *London Calling* isn't the only case where sales aren't the true full measure of perceived import: according to the RIAA, like the Clash's *Combat Rock*, *Blonde on Blonde*, *Let It Bleed* and *OK Computer* are currently on 2 million American sales apiece; and like *London Calling* itself, *Highway 61 Revisited*, *Exile on Main St.*, *Pet Sounds*, *Never Mind the Bollocks* and *The Bends* are on 1 million. Only halfway there at Gold status are *Astral Weeks*, *What's Going On*, *Ziggy Stardust* and *The Queen Is Dead*.

An artist's best album is not always their best-selling album. Quite often, it's the one released after the masterpiece that benefits from both word of mouth and the big publicity push. There has been a tendency to assume – because they insisted they were poor for so long – that the former members of the band never made any money from the Clash. That is far from the case. Caroline Coon was right to take the long-term view. The Clash's back catalogue has done very well by them over the years, and *London Calling* and its songs – re-issued, re-packaged, licensed and merchandised – have played a sizeable part in that provision.

That conceded, Joe Strummer wasn't misrepresenting the Clash's situation in 1988 – nor would he have been 20 years later – when he told *Musician*'s Bill Flanagan: 'If you look at our record sales, nothing sold until *Combat Rock* and "Rock the Casbah". I'd say we sold a *speck* overall to what U2 sell now. We made it, but in another way. We made it in the culture.'

While it's not easy to determine which artists have been influenced by *London Calling* in particular rather than by the Clash in general, *London Calling* played a significant part in making the Clash more than just a cult band, and many would be happy to acknowledge a debt. U2, for example. In 1988 they released *Rattle and Hum*, a 17-track double album recorded both live and in the studio during the course of their 1987 Joshua Tree tour of the USA. Incorporating rootsier styles than the band had been previously been associated with – including touches of blues, country and folk – it appropriates the Bo Diddley beat for 'Desire', and offers a guest spot to the equally venerable blues artist B. B. King. The front cover combines blocky title lettering with a dramatic black-and-white live photograph of Bono picking out the hunched figure of the Edge with a spotlight. The design of the inner sleeves is also like a tidier version of that for *London Calling*. The album was accompanied by a film of the same title, like a moving version of Pennie Smith's stills documentary of the Clash's Take the 5th tour. On 10 March 2003 the Edge made a heartfelt speech inducting the Clash into the Rock and Roll Hall of Fame as 'without doubt, next to the Stones, the greatest rock'n'roll band of all time'.

It was *London Calling* that raised Ian Hunter's opinion of Mick Jones enough to inspire him to write a song, 'Theatre of the Absurd', based on a conversation the two had about the Clash's reggae-rock crossover explorations. In December 1980 Mick was invited to help Ian and his producer – and another hero – Mick Ronson work on the song in the studio. He ended up staying to co-produce the album *Short Back and Sides*.

Bruce Springsteen also took note. Joe Strummer might have nicked a bit of his stagecraft from Springsteen back in 1975, but he later contended that it was *London Calling* that inspired the Clash's fellow CBS artiste to release *The River* as a 20-track double LP in a single sleeve, featuring a more mixed bag of direct rock'n'roll songs than he had recorded before. One of these new numbers concerns a Cadillac that comes to take Bruce's baby away, while a symbolic river runs through the doomladen title track. Bruce also started exploring a more socially conscious lyrical direction with *Born in the USA* (1984). In an effort to help the Clash pay tribute to Joe Strummer, Springsteen offered to perform with the surviving members of the band at their Rock and Roll Hall of Fame induction. They politely declined, but Bruce paid his own tribute anyway at the 45th Annual Grammy Awards on 23 February 2003, when he and a supergroup comprising Miami Steven Van Zandt of the E-Street Band, Elvis Costello and Pete Thomas of the Attractions, Dave Grohl of the Foo Fighters and Tony Kanal of No Doubt performed 'London Calling'. 'This one's for Joe,' announced Bruce, before everyone involved attacked the song as though their own lives depended upon it.

Bob Dylan first saw the Clash on the Take the 5th tour, and was intrigued. (His son Jakob became a loyal Clash fan.) It might well have been *London Calling* that prompted Bob's return from exploring born-again spirituality to more worldly concerns and his decision to use Sly and Robbie's reggae rhythm section on *Infidels* (1983). Bob invited Paul Simonon to play on 'Sally Sue Brown' for the *Down in the Groove* (1988) album, and the following year sent Joe Strummer a song for *Earthquake Weather* (though Joe didn't use it). It would be good to think Dylan's decision to host the very wonderful *Theme Time Radio Hour* from 2006 onwards was in part inspired by Strummer's adventures on the wheels of steel for the World Service. Bob performed 'London Calling' twice during his November 2005 shows at the Brixton Academy.

Although what is meant by 'the culture' these days gives a lot of room to popular music, its catchment area is much wider than that. *London Calling* and its songs have made their presence felt in areas both predictable and remarkable. It's not possible to list every example here, but the following should provide a flavour . . .

In the USA Jimmy Khezrie named his first hip hop and sportswear store after 'Jimmy Jazz' in 1989, and the business has since grown into a 65-store chain. In 2000 Polish punk Zdzislaw Jodko, nicknamed Dzidek, called his record label-cum-publishing venture after the song.

'Rudie Can't Fail' was used as the play-on music when Rudy Giuliani appeared at the MTV Awards in August 2002, at a time when New York and the wider world were still reeling from 9/11 and full of warmth towards the former mayor of the city. On a superficial level, then, it must have seemed like the perfect theme song for Rudy's short-lived run for the Republican nomination as presidential candidate in 2008 . . . until someone listened to the lyric. In September 2002 Green Day bassist Mike Dirnt paid more credible homage when he named his Emeryville, California, diner Rudy's Can't Fail Café.

'Lost in the Supermarket' was covered by Ben Folds especially for the closing credits of the 2006 animated comedy film *Over the Hedge* . . . the hedge in question being a large one in the suburbs a mixed bunch of woodland critters can't see over. Joe Strummer's use of the expression 'lost in the supermarket' as a metaphor for alienation in modern society has acquired an almost philosophical status, and the song and its title have been much referenced in text-books on consumerism, business, economics, design, health and spirituality. Plus it's also given its name to a 2008 indie-rock cookbook. So on the money did the lyric prove in summing up contemporary malaise that it has even been put forward as a possible influence on Don Delillo's classic post-modern novel of urban alienation, *White Noise* (1985).

Although the Clash are not the Strokes' most obvious punk forbears, the latter band covered 'Clampdown' during their July 2004 UK gigs as a comment on the previous year's invasion of Iraq. The Manic Street Preachers are more clearly built on a Clash template, and singer-guitarist James Dean Bradfield performed 'Clampdown' on his October 2006 solo tour. Again, the song's title and chorus are quoted in textbooks, this time typically on political and legal themes.

Decried by some as an example of irresponsible fantasy at the time of its release, 'The Guns of Brixton' has proved to be remarkably true-to-life. By 1981 high unemployment and a growing local crime rate had made for a powder keg situation in Brixton. Police responded in early April with Operation Swamp '81, an aggressive application of the already unpopular and contentious Sus law. On 10 April 1981 a crowd tried to intervene in the arrest of a young black man on Railton Road. Back-up was called, and police presence in the area increased into the following day, at which point a full-scale riot kicked off, with the crowd even resorting to petrol bombs, a first for England. The Brixton riot preceded major riots throughout UK over the summer, when predominately black areas of most of the major cities erupted, including Handsworth in Birmingham, Toxteth in Liverpool, Southall in London, and Moss Side in Manchester. Along with the Specials' 'Ghost Town', 'The Guns of Brixton' became an unofficial anthem for this unrest: not a soundtrack to a film, but a soundtrack to reality. And long-running reality, at that. There were other serious riots in Brixton in 1985 and 1995.

That it has been covered so extensively over the years cannot be solely attributed to adolescent fascination with its rebellious stance. For such a genre-specific song, it has invited a wide variety of styles: punk and rock and reggae-tinged versions, yes, but also acoustic, Tex-Mex, hip hop and bossa nova. For such a location-specific song, it has been covered by British, French, German, Polish, Italian, American, Canadian, Argentinean, Peruvian and Australian artists. And for a song so steeped in personal mythology, it still leaves enough space for reinterpretation. Time has proved the ultimate test: 'The Guns of Brixton' has been accepted as not just a great bass line, but also a great song. The bass line proved hard to resist, though. After being co-opted by Beats International in 1990, it was sampled again in 2004 for Californian hip hop group Cypress Hill's single 'What's Your Number?'. Clash fan Tim Armstrong of Rancid played guitar, and also appears in the video.

Joe Strummer's prescience was proven once more when the drug-fuelled selfish, materialist, hedonist lifestyle he described in 'Koka Kola' – further encouraged by Reaganomics – became the Dream for the Bright Young Things of the arts, fashion and finance worlds during the Eighties. Jay McInerney's *Bright Lights, Big City* (1984) explored Manhattan's fashion and media Kokaine Kulture, initiated a literary sub-genre, and was filmed in 1988. That was the same year his novel *Story of My Life* repeated the trick for the worlds of acting and finance, and the year after Hollywood had investigated the 51st floor in *Wall Street*. In 1991 Bret Easton Ellis's novel *American Psycho* let a serial killer loose into this amoral world of sex and drugs and money and designer labels . . . and nobody noticed or cared.

Annie Lennox recorded a soulful version of 'Train in Vain' for her 1995 covers album *Medusa*. Dwight Yoakam explored the country contribution to the song's bloodline on his 1997 covers album *Under the Covers*. The song has also been attempted by the Black Crowes, the Manic Street Preachers and Rancid, among others. Garbage came up with 'Stupid Girl' by jamming along to its sampled and looped drum rhythm. Released as a single in 1996 it became Garbage's biggest hit, reaching Number 25 in the US mainstream charts, and Number 4 in the UK, also winning a BMI award for Best Pop Song. Honourably, the band acknowledged their debt by crediting its composition to Garbage-Strummer-Jones . . . which was a little hard on Mick Jones, who wrote the original song entirely on his own, and even harder on Topper Headon, who came up with the drum part.

'London Calling' has also had its moments in the polls. In 1999 a *Q* readers' poll of the Top 100 Singles of All Time placed it at Number 42. In 2002 it was Number 9 in the *NME* critics' 100 Greatest Singles of All Time list. In 2004 *Rolling Stone* placed it at Number 15 in its list of the 500 Greatest Songs of All Time.

'London Calling' is a classic example of a song that has become so familiar that its underlying meaning is overlooked in favour of making more superficial connections. It's a powerful, instantly recognisable, highly memorable song about London by a (retrospectively) much-loved classic rock band from London, and, to cap it all, it has a fanfare for an introduction . . . so it's the perfect song to signify, evoke, celebrate or promote the capital. Forget the flood warnings and the zombies of death, and think Big Ben, red buses, black taxis and red telephone boxes. 'London Calling' can be (and has been) made to stand for London is trying to get in touch with you, or London is inviting you, beseeching you, drawing you in . . . especially on TV or in the movies.

As the BBC local station serving the capital, Radio London has more right than most to call a regular programme feature *London Calling*, and it would be no surprise if they'd arrived at the name by following the direct route back to the call sign for the BBC's original 1922 London-wide radio broadcasts. But the segment, which showcases up-and-coming music artists, is presented by former punk fanzine writer Gary Crowley and is named after the Clash song. Among his featured guests in 2007 were up-and-coming new band Carbon/Silicon.

In 2002 the Ford Motor Company's North American unit decided that the best way to sell their new Jaguar X-Type compact saloon car in the USA was to emphasise the Jag's quintessential Britishness. The ad wrote itself: scenes of an X-Type breezing serenely and expensively through a London cityscape of red buses, red telephone booths and Big Ben. Joe Strummer was initially a little reluctant to come forward and justify his decision to permit 'London Calling' to be used to promote what was, if not quite top-of-the-range, still an expensive motor vehicle aimed at the executive market. 'It just seemed churlish for a writer to refuse to have their music used on an advert, and so I figured, only advertise the things you think are cool,' he finally admitted on the official *Strummersite*. 'If you're in a group and you all make it together, then everybody deserves something, especially 20-odd years after the fact.'

In the early Noughties 'London Calling' became one of the regular tunes played at Loftus Road, the home ground of Queens Park Rangers, which pleased regular supporter Mick Jones no end. Another QPR fan was former Head of CBS UK Maurice Oberstein. He was so taken with the club that he asked to have half his ashes sprinkled over the centre circle following his death from leukaemia on 13 August 2001 . . . so no escaping 'London Calling' for Obie, either.

On 5 April 2006 it was widely reported that a taxi driver had become suspicious of the antics of Harraj Mann, a young Hartlepool man he had picked up and taken to Durham Tees Valley Airport. The cabbie called the police to inform them that Mann had plugged his MP3 player into the taxi's system, and passionately sung along to songs with suspiciously inflammatory lyrics. The flight departure was halted, and Mann was removed from the plane and questioned. The songs in question proved to be Led Zeppelin's 'The Immigrant Song' and the Clash's 'London Calling': the Hammer of the Gods meets the Zombies of Death.

From the song to the album of the same title: in or around London, it has given its name to an annual music business conference, a short film festival, an arts leaflet distributor, and a building contractor, among other ventures. Further afield, London Calling is the name of a regular rock festival held at the Paradiso in Amsterdam, and of dance clubs in Johannesburg, Tokyo, Helsinki and St Louis, Missouri, as well as a pub restaurant in Bogotá, Columbia, a mod-style clothes shop in Rome and an eBay shop selling flip-flops in Portugal. The album has also recently given its name to a pair of designer surfer shorts, a designer kids' shirt, a designer handbag and a pair of designer sunglasses. Should you so desire, you could have a night out at London Calling on just about every continent, dressed from head to toe in London Calling. (Just don't expect to pull.)

Over the years, the cover of *London Calling* has been celebrated in ways both fair and foul. *Q* has been particularly attentive: in addition to putting Pennie Smith's photograph on the cover of a 25 Classic Rock Photographs supplement in 1992, the magazine voted the album cover the ninth best of all time in 2001. The following year, the leading music photographers and writers who contributed to the magazine's 100 Greatest Rock'n'Roll Photographs of All Time poll put it in first place. 'Any music fan would love the sheer excitement it conveys,' said editor of the *Q* special edition Paul du Noyer. 'Aesthetically, it's just a beautiful thing to look at. Most of all, it's a classic picture because it captures the ultimate rock'n'roll moment: total loss of control.' That same year, the *NME* gave Pennie a Godlike Genius award for her services to the paper.

In October 2000 a magazine advertisement for Technics DVD Audio equipment projected a hologram of the Paul Simonon figure from the *London Calling* cover into an upmarket designer-minimalist lounge. 'The main thought behind the ad was that DVD Audio creates a 3-D sound so real that you can feel the performance taking place in your living room,' says David Bonney, the Advertising Manager at Panasonic UK Ltd. 'There were also sound demographic reasons: our target market of mid-thirties to mid-forties males would instantly recognise and relate to the picture.' Similar thinking inspired the cover for *The Guardian Book of Rock & Roll* (2008), edited by Michael Hann, which manages the neat trick of referencing four generations of rock with one image. The photo on the cover is a live shot of Radiohead's Thom Yorke with a guitar round his neck, but the pose is an echo of the cover of Bruce Springsteen's *Born to Run*. Meanwhile, the combination of the black-and-white photograph, the prominently displayed guitar, and the pink-and-green lettering nod to both Elvis's debut and to *London Calling*.

Record-sleeve parodies of the Clash cover combining the Presley-style lettering with a live action shot are common. Probably the first was the 1984 album *Sexo Chungo* by Spanish punk band Siniestro Total, the cover of which shows a set of bagpipes being smashed. Joe Strummer was so amused by it that he bought a copy to display on his wall at home. Pursuing the theme, New York speed-metal ukulele funsters Uke Til You Puke's *Pure Speed, Pure Ukulele* (1992) shows a uke being trashed. Polish Pogues-type band Emerald's Jimmy Jazz label release *Folk No More* (2006) gives the treatment to an accordion. Cowpunk band Pronghorn's *Londis Calling* (2007) offs a banjo. Belgian techno DJ Marco Bailey's eponymous 2004 album sets about a turntable with a baseball bat, and Berlin-based synth outfit Egotronic's eponymous 2008 album trashes an electronic keyboard. Clash tribute album *London Booted* (2005) dispatches a PC.

The enraged Simonon image has also proved popular for parody posters, flyers and ads by and aimed at groups of bike couriers, surfers and skateboarders smashing bikes, surfboards and skateboards: it's a strong, rebellious, instantly recognisable image and an easy one to tweak for comic effect. In the Clash's most imaginative merchandising venture to date – one that acknowledged and exploited the apparent affinity between their most famous album and the skateboarding fraternity – Dorisimo Ltd approached skatewear manufacturers Globe International Ltd in 2007 and invited them to collaborate on a Clash skate shoe. The result, named .45 Clash, uses the standard Clash merchandising colour palette of black, red and white, reproduces excerpts from Ray Lowry's handwritten inner-sleeve lyric of 'London Calling' on the collar and a 'Death or Glory' skull and crossbones on the tongue. Promotion made the most of the punk-skate interface: a short film shows a bunch of moody skaters smashing their boards down onto the road, soundtracked by 'London Calling', before finally freeze-framing on a young skate-punk in a near perfect replica of the Simonon pose.

Other parodies have included a businessman smashing his briefcase and a nude glamour model smashing a vacuum cleaner. Possibly the most surreal appropriation of all, though, has to be the 2007 collaboration between Roen – a Japanese fashion design company with a dark, vaguely street sensibility – the Walt Disney Company, and the Medicom Toy Company. The result was a 15-cm-high figurine known as Guitar Mickey: Mickey Mouse standing with legs splayed, hunched over, one eye closed tight in concentration, as the silver guitar he has clutched by its neck comes arcing over his shoulder. Some artists make it in the culture; others *really* make it in the culture . . .

By the late Noughties both Ray Lowry and Pennie Smith had decided to do something about the exploitation of the image they had created. Ray's response was typically self-effacing and low-key. Having illustrated Johnny Green's Clash memoir *A Riot of Our Own* a decade earlier, in 2007 he produced his own illustrated account of the Take the 5th tour and the process of designing the album cover for *The Clash: Up Close and Personal*. Ray was a highly successful cartoonist by profession and an artist by inclination, rarely a designer, and even more rarely a design plagiarist. He would doubtless have been resignedly amused to know that, following his death on 14 October 2008, a large reproduction of the *London Calling* cover would dominate the page carrying his obituary in the *Guardian*.

Pennie had always been able to make an income from selling the right to produce what Ray described in his book as her 'forever photograph' to media outlets, but as she notes it was used far more often without her receiving due payment. Around the same time as Ray's book came out, Pennie came to an arrangement with Proud Galleries to sell a limited-edition run of signed, 16-inch by 20-inch silver gelatin prints of the image per year, at £4,700 each. (Small world: Proud are popular culture photography specialists whose Camden Town gallery occupies the very premises that once housed the Clash's original rehearsal room, Rehearsals Rehearsals.) Despite the hundreds of other memorable photographs she has taken of the Clash, and thousands of other major artists, Pennie has no illusions about what image will appear next to her own death notice (hopefully many years in the future). 'It's become a trademark,' she acknowledges.

Perhaps inevitably, when Joe Strummer died on 22 December 2002, only one cover of one record – out of all the records Joe Strummer made both with and without the Clash – was used to illustrate the many news accounts and the obituaries published in the UK press. To sum up what he gave the world in one picture, newspapers as diverse in target market as the *Guardian*, the *Daily Telegraph*, the *Daily Express* and the *Sun* all chose the cover of *London Calling*.

Of the albums he made with the band, Mick Jones prefers *The Clash*, but he, too, is doubtless reconciled to having the cover of *London Calling* as his media tombstone. Topper Headon, whose professional and personal life fell away so dramatically soon after completing the album, is as surprised as anyone that it hasn't already been used for his. Having cleaned up in the early Noughties, he acknowledges the album as his personal best as a musician, believes it to represent the peak of both the Clash's creative endeavours and relationship as a band, and is delighted to see it featuring so highly in the polls of the Greatest Albums of All Time. 'It's a nice feeling to know that, even if I was to die tomorrow, I've contributed something to music,' he told *Uncut* in 2004. Given that he is the cover star, it will almost certainly be *London Calling*, rather than any of his own acclaimed artworks, that will illustrate Paul Simonon's official farewells.

'When I think of the Clash, I think of Paul Simonon slamming the bass,' Joe Strummer told Charles Shaar Murray three years before his own death. 'When all's said and done about the songs and the lyrics, I always think of Paul Simonon smashing that thing around. And that says it all: I'd like to think the Clash were revolutionaries, but we loved a bit of posing as well.'

In addition to Joe, Ray, Guy and Obie, saxophonist John 'Irish' Earle and inspiration Bo Diddley have also passed on since *London Calling* was first released. Human beings we expect to go (though not always so soon), but we tend to think of buildings and institutions as being more permanent. As Paul Simonon's friend Peter Ackroyd has demonstrated, though, a city is a constantly evolving thing. It might not die completely, but parts of it do, all the time. And piece-by-piece, the London of *London Calling* is slipping away.

Mick's Nan's flat at 111 Wilmcote House is still there, though the block has had a facelift in recent years and looks far snazzier than of yore. Mick moved out for good in 1979, and Stella left to go into sheltered accommodation nearby in the early Eighties. (She died in 1989.) The Salters' old flat at 31 Whistler Walk is also still there, in this case considerably more worn-looking from the outside than it was in 1979, when it was just a couple of years old. Joe moved out with Gaby in mid-1980, and Frances and the rest of the family had also left by 1982. The supermarket of 'Lost in the Supermarket' is still there, under different ownership. Paul moved out of 42b Oxford Gardens in 1983, initially to a small house over the road at Number 53 Oxford Gardens. Over the years since, the original basement flat that inspired him to write 'The Guns of Brixton' has been modernised and extensively remodelled, the corridor walls removed to increase the sense of space and allow more light into the property. In October 2008 the flat was put on the market at an asking price of £400,000. Future doorstep confrontations with the police seem unlikely.

Vanilla Rehearsal Studios no longer exist, and nor does the rest of 36 Causton Street as the Clash knew it. In 1993, the entire site was demolished (along with the neighbouring site) to be redeveloped by the London Diocesan Fund, formerly based at Number 30. It is now divided between the London Diocesan House, fronting Causton Street, a small paved garden area behind, and an old people's home. On the other side of the road, though, the children's playground formerly used by the Clash FC is still there for anyone contemplating a commemorative kick-around.

The shell of Wessex Studios remains more or less intact, but the insides have been ripped out to make way for eight apartments and one townhouse of between 600 and 1,100 square feet each. The residential complex, protected by new electronic security gates, is now known as the Recording Studio, and boasts (appropriately enough) high-quality soundproofing. The strapline used by the Neptune Group to market the residences was, 'The Recording Studio may not make you a rock star – but at least you can live like one.' It's a long way from *Never Mind the Bollocks* . . . or is it?

The Royal Festival Pier was judged unsafe in the Nineties, and demolished. Plans to build a replacement in 2000 as part of a general restoration programme for Battersea Park were abandoned. All that remains of the location for the Clash's 'London Calling' video is a coffee-table-sized block of algae-slick concrete against the river wall, from which protrude a couple of submerged concrete rails and a rusty tangle of reinforcing wire. It would seem the River Thames is still capable of swallowing the Works of Man.

The Number 19 bus follows the same route as it did in 1979, from Battersea to Highbury, but it's no longer the same type of bus that Joe Strummer jumped back then (whenever he couldn't afford a taxi). The AEC Routemaster double-decker was introduced in 1954, its most recognisable feature being its open rear platform. Although produced in both red and green, it was to be the red version that caught the eye and imprinted itself upon the public consciousness. The Routemaster was embraced as a design classic, and became a tourist icon for the Swinging Sixties and beyond, like red telephone boxes, red post boxes, black taxis and Big Ben: to the Rest of the World, it was not just a symbol of London, but by extension a symbol of England, Great Britain and the UK (however much the rest of the UK might resent that). Although hard-wearing and adaptable, by 2005 the vehicle was 40 or 50 years behind the times. The open platform was considered a health-and-safety risk, and (perhaps more significantly) the rear entrance required the increasingly hard-to-justify expense of a two-person crew, the driver plus a conductor to collect fares. On the route of the 19 bus, the Routemaster was withdrawn from service on 1 April 2005.

Much of the Clash's London of 1979 might have disappeared, but their valedictory radio message is still being broadcast: London is still calling. In the UK 'Should I Stay or Should I Go' was (eventually) the Clash's biggest hit, and 'Bankrobber' did nearly as well as 'London Calling'. In 2003, when *Uncut* magazine invited its 63-strong 'All-Star' panel of musicians and band associates to vote on the best Clash track ever, it was '(White Man) In Hammersmith Palais' and 'Complete Control' that came first and second, leaving 'London Calling' in third place. Although it might not be the absolute forerunner commercially or critically, though when it comes to radio or TV programmes, if a Clash-related anniversary is to be marked, or a reference to the band is to be illustrated in song, 'London Calling' is almost always the track selected. (To the point that the predictability is slightly depressing.) What used to be Joe Strummer's signature tune is now the Clash's. It is asked to represent not just the band's landmark album, but also their entire career. There's an even wider application, too. From time to time the song has been pressed into service by TV, radio and other media to symbolise the punk movement in general, and – on occasion – the entire history of British rock.

As Greatest Albums of All Time go, *London Calling* offers more to get your teeth into than most. Built upon rootsy musical foundations without being mired in the past or overly reverent to tradition, its lyrics tackle life's major demands and questions, and do so perceptively enough to earn nods of recognition, while remaining oblique enough to intrigue. People and buildings go, but the world doesn't change that much. Police continue to wield batons, workers continue to be exploited, immigrants continue to be victimised. Heroin and cocaine consumption and levels of related crime increase. Evil *presidentés* (both abroad and closer to home) pay their dues or get away with it. Greed and want drive the cycle of boom and bust. Rivers still flood, and the globe continues to warm up (and may yet freeze). And there will always be personal heartbreak. But *London Calling* doesn't continue to speak to people because it wallows in doom and despair. The main reasons for its longevity are its defiant spirit, its power to uplift, and its determination to lead by example: it looks anger, fear, impotence and self-doubt in the eye, then pulls on its boots and goes out to face the day. That's a good feeling to get from a record, or from any piece of art or entertainment. When it was first released, it was two for the price of one. Now it's priceless.

TERMINUS

Photographs and Illustrations

Tom Casey: *Section One* p. 2 (b)
Caroline Coon / Camera Press: *Section One* p. 7 (b)
Bob Gruen: *Section One* pp. 1 (t), 6 (b); *Section Two* pp. 1 (t), 4 (b)
London Diocesan Fund (courtesy of, additonal detail provided by Tom Casey) *Section One* p. 2 (m)
Ray Lowry / See Gallery: *Section Two* p. 6 (m & bl)
David Mingay (courtesy of): *Section One* p. 7 (tr)
Bill Price (courtesy of): *Section One* p. 6 (t)
Pennie Smith: *Section One* pp. 3, 4 (b); *Section Two* pp. 4 (t), 5 (main), 7
Virginia Turbett: *Section One* pp. 1 (b), 7 (tl), 8 (t); *Section Two* pp. 1 (b), 2 (tl, tr, bl & br), 3 (b), 8 (t & b)
Nick Wesolowski: *Section One* p. 5 (t)
Don Whistance: *Section One* p. 4 (t)
Nox Archives provided all other images. *Section Two* p. 5 (insert) photographer at present unknown (contact the author via marcusgray.co.uk)

Creditz

I began work on the prototype of *Route 19 Revisited* in late 2003, put it aside the following year for 'family reasons' (as the politicians like to put it), returned to it in 2007, and completed it in 2009. Interviews took

place throughout this period. Thanks for their time and insight to, alphabetically: Chiswick (and Ace) label boss and producer Roger Armstrong;
Ray Beavis of the Rumour Brass (aka the Irish Horns); Gary Brooker
of Procol Harum; Rod Byers (aka Roddy Radiation) of the Specials;
Derek Boshier, designer of the *Clash 2nd Songbook*; Michael Campbell,
son of reggae artist and 'Wrong Emboyo' songwriter Clive Alphanso
Campbell; Dennis Collopy, previously of Riva Music; former Clash
manager Caroline Coon; former Deviants frontman and London underground scenemaker Mick Farren; Clash concertgoer Eleanor Flicker;
Mickey Gallagher of the Blockheads; *Rude Boy* actor Ray Gange; reggae
engineer and record-label founder Graeme Goodall; Vin Gordon of the
Soul Vendors; Dick Hanson of the Rumour Brass; reggae artist Winston
McAnuff; *Rude Boy* filmmaker David Mingay; *London Calling* engineer
and mixer Bill Price; reggae artist, producer and 'Revolution Rock' co-
writer Danny Ray; *London Calling* cover photographer Pennie Smith;
London Calling mastering engineer Tim Young; reggae artist and
'Armagideon Time' co-writer Willi Williams; and former CBS A&R
man Muff Winwood. As he was without a phone at the time, cartoonist,
artist and *London Calling* cover designer Ray Lowry (RIP) answered my
questions mostly by letter and postcard, though we did also manage a
payphone conversation. Although neither of us would describe it as an
interview, I conducted an on/off e-mail correspondence with original
(and final) Clash manager Bernie Rhodes for 18 months, during which
we discussed his upbringing and contribution to shaping the Clash.

    London Calling second engineer Jerry Green seems to have dropped
off the radar in recent years, but luckily I had already talked to him in
some detail in 1993 for my Clash biography *Last Gang in Town*. I also
interviewed Clash roadie-cum-personal manager Johnny Green for eight
hours in 1993. I did contact him again, and he answered a couple of
specific factual questions, but – reasonably enough – he declined to
submit himself to another full grilling, as he thought he wouldn't have
anything more to add that we hadn't already covered. I was unable to
use much of that interview material in *Last Gang in Town*, but I have
drawn upon it extensively here. I've also used a quote apiece from interviews of that period with former Polydor A&R man Chris Parry, ex-
Sex Pistol Glen Matlock, and two-times Clash drummer Terry Chimes.

    When my investigation into the fate of the Rulers' producer Carl
'Sir JJ' Johnson looked to be in danger of hitting a brick wall, respected

reggae writer David Katz was good enough to let me see (and use excerpts from) the archive of interviews he had amassed for *Solid Foundation: An Oral History of Reggae* (2003), specifically with Sir JJ artists Leonard Dillon of the Ethiopians and Roy Shirley, and Sir JJ's friend and fellow producer Alvin 'GG' Ranglin. David also discussed the subject anew on my behalf with reggae artist and producer Niney the Observer.

Joe Strummer is no longer with us, of course, and no new interview material with the surviving members of the Clash is included in this book, either: the period of writing coincided with official band projects *The Last Testament* (2004) and *The Clash* (2008). I would have welcomed the opportunity to talk to them, but I don't believe that their non-appearance has left a gaping void. To date, nobody else has persuaded Mick Jones to detail his compositional or recording methods for individual songs: he has claimed poor memory on more than one occasion, and I suspect he also likes to preserve a little mystique. Although both Paul Simonon and Topper Headon were more involved with the arranging and recording of *London Calling* than with previous recordings, neither was as close to the heart of the creative process as Joe and Mick. And Paul and Topper were certainly less concerned with planning and politicking. I don't mean to suggest that the three surviving members of the Clash have never said anything of note about the making of the album . . . just that I doubt there is much they are able or willing to say that they haven't said already.

I found the most concentrated sources of the Clash's own thoughts on the album's songs and their recording to be: the band's track-by-track guide in the first edition of *The Armagideon Times* (1980), which was also included in the booklet for the 25th Anniversary Edition of *London Calling*; Joe Strummer and Paul Simonon's introductions to the band's greatest hits, as recorded by an anonymous interviewer for *Melody Maker* (1988); Kosmo Vinyl's interviews for the *Clash On Broadway* box-set booklet (1991); and the interview with Paul and Mick Jones conducted by Adam Sweeting for *Uncut* (2004) to coincide with the release of the 25th Anniversary Edition of *London Calling*. Two interviews with Joe Strummer that are roughly contemporary with the making of the album, by Charles Shaar Murray of the *NME* and Chris Bohn of *Melody Maker*, were also particularly useful. My thanks to Adam,

Charlie and Chris for their generosity in allowing me to quote so freely from their work.

Other writers whose interviews have provided Clash quotes and key information are, alphabetically: Jon Bennett, *Mojo* (2002); Ian Burrell, the *Independent* (2004); Garry Bushell, *Sounds* (1978) and, with Dave McCullough, *Sounds* (1979); Matthew Caws, *Guitar World* (1995); Caroline Coon, *Melody Maker* (1976 and 1977); Sean Egan, *Billboard* (2008); Bill Flanagan, *Musician* (1988); David Fricke, *Rolling Stone* (1981); Vic Garbarini, *Musician* (1981); Pat Gilbert and the *Q Classic* Clash special team (2005); Simon Goddard, *Uncut* (2003); James Henke, *Rolling Stone* (1980); Paolo Hewitt, *Melody Maker* (1980); Danny Kelly, *The Word* (2005); Judy McGuire, *Punk* (2003); John McKenna, *Hot Press* (1979); Gavin Martin, *Uncut* (1999); Robbi Millar, *Sounds* (1980); Mikko Montonen, *Soundi* (1979); Paul Morley, *NME* (1979); Kris Needs, *ZigZag* (1977); Sean O'Hagan, *NME* (1988); Tony Parsons, *NME* (1977); Clint Roswell, *Musician* (1981); Scott Rowley, *Bassist* (1999); Chris Salewicz, *NME* (1978) and *The Face* (1981); Jane Simon, *Sounds* (1985); Pete Silverton, *Sounds* (1978); Steve Walsh and Mark Perry, *Sniffin' Glue* (1976); and the Unknown Interviewer for *Negative Reaction* (1978).

As a means of providing essential context, I have also included excerpts from contemporary reviews of *London Calling*, other Clash releases between 1978 and 1980, and various live performances of the era. Special mentions are due to Garry Bushell and Dave McCullough's unimpressed and concerned *Sounds* review of the Clash's Notre Dame shows (1979), and Ian Penman's scathing yet perceptive *NME* reviews of a late 1978 Clash show and of *The Cost of Living* EP (1979), not least because these provocations gave the band something to kick against. Garry's *Sounds* review of the completed album (1979) was damning, too, and again raised some pertinent issues for debate; as did Billy Altman's ambivalent response for *Creem* (1980). More empathetic were Charles Shaar Murray's *NME* review (1979), and Tom Carson's almost scarily on-the-money review for *Rolling Stone* (1980). Other reviews drawn upon: Ian Birch, *Melody Maker* (1979); Chris Bohn, *Melody Maker* (1979); Andy Gill, *NME* (1979); Charlie Gillet, Radio London (1979); Van Gosse, *NME* (1979); Nick Kent, *NME* (1978); Greil Marcus, *Rolling Stone* (1978); Paul Morley, *NME* (1979); Kris Needs, *ZigZag* (1979); Robert Palmer, *The New York Times* (1979); John Piccarella, *Village Voice* (1980); Paul Rambali (1980); Ira Robins, *Trouser Press* (1979); John Rockwell,

The New York Times (1980); Jon Savage, *Melody Maker* (1978); James Truman, *Melody Maker* (1979); and the Unknown Reviewer for *The New York Rocker* (1980).

In those instances where I have lifted more than a few words from interviews or reviews, I have attempted to get in touch with the writer in order to seek permission to quote. All those I contacted granted it freely. In cases where I was unable to get through, I have quoted as sparingly as possible, and given what I hope the writers will agree is due credit. All concerned have my sincere gratitude.

Although Bill Price patiently answered more than 120 questions on aspects of his work with the Clash, I didn't quiz him too much on technical details pertaining to the Wessex Studio set up for *London Calling*. This was because I had already secured permission from *Mix* magazine's Editorial Director Tom Kenny to consult and quote substantially from an interview covering those topics conducted by *Mix*'s then-Technical Editor Chris Michie in 2000. An engineer himself, Chris had previously worked with Bill at AIR studios, and was therefore able to pose questions from an insider's perspective that simply wouldn't have occurred to me, and – furthermore – elicit information that would have confused me without his expert interpretation. I'd like to thank Chris effusively, and also Tom and *Mix* for their cooperation. The original, full-length interviews covering Bill's career and the recording of the track 'London Calling' – first published in October and November 2000, respectively – can be read at mixonline.com, while the latter is also included in the *Mix* book *Classic Tracks*.

London Calling producer Guy Stevens died in 1981. Surprisingly, for one so influential, his life has not been extensively documented. This makes the ubiquitous Charles Shaar Murray's 1979 *NME* interview-cum-career-overview all the more important. The full text can be found in his 'greatest hits' book *Shots from the Hip*. Roy Carr's *London Calling*-contemporary *NME* interview, although much shorter, was also useful. I'm grateful to both for their permission to quote. Campbell Devine's excellent Mott the Hoople biography *All the Young Dudes* (1998) is highly informative about Guy's role in that band's story, and also proved invaluable.

Thanks for interviews with – or features about – other characters involved in the story to: Oliver Hall (and editor Jason Gross) for Greil

Marcus, *Perfect Sound Forever* (furious.com/perfect) (2005); Simon Harper for Ray Lowry and Pennie Smith, *The Clash* magazine (2004); Ray Hurford and Colin Moore for Willi Williams, *Small Axe Annex* (myweb.tiscali.co.uk/smallaxe) (1983); Chris May for Lee 'Scratch' Perry, *Black Music* (1977); Joe Moretti for his recollections of working with Vince Taylor, *Joe Moretti International* (joemoretti.org) (2002); Pierre Perrone for Maurice Oberstein (obituary), the *Independent* (2001); Adam Sweeting for Maurice Oberstein, the *Guardian* (1993); Kieron Tyler for Vince Taylor, *Mojo* (2000). Also Paul du Noyer for the *Q* Album Covers special edition (2002); Michael Oldstein for John Van Hamersveld and *Exile on Main St.* for *Goldmine* (goldminemag.com) (2008); Alan Taylor for Jerry Schatzberg and *Blonde on Blonde* for the *Sunday Herald* (2008). General background: *The Gleaner* (Jamaica) (1964–75), the *Guardian*, the *Observer*, *Mojo*, *NME*, *Q*, *Rolling Stone*, *Uncut*.

Official Clash source material, chronologically: Mick Jones, Paul Simonon, Caroline Coon, Barry Miles et al., *Clash Songbook* (1978); Derek Boshier, Dennis Collopy et al., *Clash 2nd Songbook* (1979); Don Letts (interviews by Mal Peachey), *Westway to the World* (1999); *The Clash: The Complete Chord Songbook* (2004); *London Calling* 25th Anniversary Edition (2004), including *The Vanilla Tapes* and Pat Gilbert liner notes; Don Letts, *The Last Testament*, plus the *Wessex Studios Footage*; the *Joe Strummer Past, Present & Future* exhibition at the London Print Studios (4–18 September 2004); Julien Temple, *The Future is Unwritten* (2006).

Unofficial Clash source material, chronologically: Jack Hazan and David Mingay, *Rude Boy* (1980), plus DVD extras interviews with Jack, David and Ray Gange (2003); Pennie Smith, *The Clash: Before and After* (1980); Marcus Gray, *Last Gang in Town: The Story and Myth of the Clash* (1995); Johnny Green with Garry Barker, *A Riot of Our Own* (1997); Bob Gruen with Chris Salewicz, *The Clash* (2001); Chris Knowles, *Clash City Showdown* (2003); Pat Gilbert, *Passion is a Fashion: The Real Story of the Clash* (2004); Anthony Davie, *Joe Strummer and the Mescaleros: Vision of a Homeland* (2004); Kris Needs, *Joe Strummer and the Legend of the Clash* (2005); Chris Salewicz, *Redemption Song: The Definitive Biography of Joe Strummer* (2006); Vince White, *Out of Control: The Last Days of the Clash* (2007); Ray Lowry, *Up Close and Personal* (2007).

Deeper background. Spikes: Lester Bangs, *Psychotic Reactions and Carburetor Dung* (1988); Jon Savage, *England's Dreaming: The Sex Pistols and Punk Rock* (1991); John Robb, *Punk Rock: An Oral History* (2006). Suits: Frederic Dannen, *Hit Men: Power Brokers and Fast Money Inside the Music Business* (1990). Threads: Paul Gorman, *The Look: Adventures in Pop & Rock Fashion* (2001). Dreads: Steve Barrow and Peter Dalton, *The Rough Guide to Reggae* (2001); Lloyd Bradley, *Bass Culture: When Reggae Was King* (2000); David Katz, *Solid Foundation: An Oral History of Reggae* (2003). Faces: Craig Bromberg, *The Wicked Ways of Malcolm McLaren* (1989); David Katz, *People Funny Boy: The Genius of Lee 'Scratch' Perry* (2000); Don Letts with David Nobakht, *Culture Clash: Dread Meets Punk Rockers* (2007); Horace Panter, *Ska'd for Life: A Personal Journey with the Specials* (2007). Checks: MC Strong, *The Great Rock Discography*; *A–Z London*; *King James Bible*; *Concise Oxford Dictionary*.

Individual *London Calling* tracks: Richard Matheson, *I Am Legend* (1954); Boris Sagal, *Omega Man* (1971); David Bowie, *Diamond Dogs* (1974); *Rude Boy* Trojan box set (2002); George Orwell, *Homage to Catalonia* (1938); the poems of Federico García Lorca; Patricia Boswell, *Montgomery Clift* (1978); Perry Henzell, *The Harder They Come* (1972); Graham Greene, *Brighton Rock* (1938); Boulting Brothers, *Brighton Rock* (1947); Poet and the Roots, *Dread Beat An' Blood* (1978); Michael Curtiz, *Casablanca* (1942); John and Alan Lomax, *American Ballads & Folk Songs* (1934); Greil Marcus, *Mystery Train* (1975); Cecil Brown, *Stagolee Shot Billy* (2003); Hans Holbein the Younger, *Dance of Death* (c. 1523–6); Ingmar Bergman, *The Seventh Seal* (1957); Jolan Chang, *The Tao of Love & Sex: The Ancient Chinese Way to Ecstasy* (1977).

Internet research. General: *Friends Reunited*, MySpace, YouTube, Google, Yahoo, and the much-maligned Wikipedia (it might not be the last word, but it's often a good place to start). Business: Companies House (companieshouse.gov.uk). Movies: the *Internet Movie Database* (imdb.com). Music: Henrik Franzon at *Acclaimed Music* (acclaimed-music.net); *everyHit.com*; *Rocklist* (rocklistmusic.co.uk), *Second Hand Songs* (secondhandsongs.com); *Timepieces* (timepieces.nl); British Recorded Music Industry (bpi.co.uk); International Federation of the Phonographic Industry (ifpi.org); Recording Industry Association of America (riaa.com). The Clash: *Black Market Clash* (homepage.mac.com/blackmarketclash) was useful for information about and reviews of live shows; Don J. Whistance's *The Clash Website* (theclash.org) is a repository for all things Clash, especially good for armchair trips around the Clash's London. *London Calling* parody album covers: Elvis Presley album cover galleries at Chucky G's *Am I Right* (amiright.com) and *Rate Your Music* (rateyourmusic.com). Reggae: *Dance Crasher* (dancecrasher.co.uk) for label information and Black Music's UK Seventies singles charts, *Reggae Fever* (shop.reggaefever.ch), *Reggae Vibes* (reggae-vibes.com), for interviews; *Riddimbase* (riddimbase.org) for 'Real Rock' riddim information; *Roots Archives* (roots-archives.com); *Strictly Vibes Reggae Database* (strictly-vibes.com); *Tapir's Reggae Discographies* (xs4all.nl) for UK label information and Seventies singles charts.

Internet interactive. *The Clash: If Music Could Talk* (clashcity.com) when it was Satch's and still the home of Deep Clash Theory. Big thanks to Teddy B., John S., Chris K. and Inder, and everyone else who joined in an informed, heated or just plain abusive 'discussion'. Sorry not to name more names: partly the fault of the Great Crash of Wheneveritwas; partly my failure to write thank you notes as I was going along. Also *Strummer News* (strummernews.com) and *Strummersite*. Reggae: *Chatty Mouth* (djgreedyg.proboards.com), occasionally edgy, but always informative 'reasoning'. General thanks to Steve Rice and Lancou 2. For the Rulers and Sir JJ: Herbert, Hotmilk, Lollabella, Oldbroom, Penny Reel, Reggae Postman, Skanick, Taffy. For 'Real Rock' and 'Armagideon Time': Edward George, Finbar, Inyaki, Mrs Trellis, Tim P., Mr Swing Easy, Wellcharge, Zapatoo, Zonard. And anyone at Jamaicans.com who volunteered a definition of 'Wrong Emboyo'.

Foot slogging. Thanks to the British Library, the Guildhall Library, London Metropolitan Archive, and Westminster Central Reference Library.

Thanks to anyone who ever held a poll (see Part 6).

Other useful information was provided by: Mike Bates at Battersea Park (batterseapark.org); David Bonney, Advertising Manager at Panasonic UK Ltd; Dave Callaghan and Niall McLean at MCPS; Tom Casey, Janet Eaves and Mary Nada at the London Diocesan Fund, 36 Causton Street; Jules Montero of the World's End Estate Residents' Association. Zoë Street Howe knows about the Slits. Thanks to Peter

Guralnick and Greg Williams of the Elvis Presley Fan Club in Australia. Thanks to Nick Bowman for the Rulers compilation, and Neil Scaplehorn at Ace for Vince Taylor's *Jet Black Leather Machine*. Kudos to Ade Marks for interpreting the intro to 'Clampdown'.

For information used briefly or as background in Part 6 – and more extensively in the additional material on the afterlife of *London Calling* to be found at marcusgray.co.uk – alphabetically: Doug Curtis of Clockwork Productions and the London Calling club, St Louis, Missouri (londoncalling.us); Stephen Jules Ehrhardt of London Calling, Tokyo (london-calling.jp); Neil Hepburn at Beau Bo d'Or (bbdo.co.uk) and Tim Gillespie aka Doghouse (stablesound.co.uk) and Claire at Eclectech (eclectech.co.uk); Michael Jaworski of the Cops and the Sunset Tavern, Seattle (sunsettavern.com); Zdzislaw 'Dzidek' Jodko of Jimmy Jazz Records, Poland (jimmyjazz.pl); Christine Johnston of Wonderboy (and Martin Duffy) (wonderboyclothing.com); Jimmy Khezrie of Jimmy Jazz Clothing & Shoes (jimmyjazz.com); Miss L. at London Calling club, Helsinki (myspace.com/londoncallingclub); Paul Ladley at Clampdown Records, Ashton-under-Lyne (clampdown-records.com); Keiron 'Seamouse' Lewis of Pinniped Studios (pinniped-studios.com); Matthew McNear of C&D Wireless; Josh 'Chet' Minyard of Spanish Bombs; Andrew Moir of London Calling Arts Ltd, London (londoncalling.com); Jason Rothberg; Rory Taylor (rorytaylor.com); Xander at the House of Pistard (houseofpistard.com).

My grasp of music theory is tenuous at best. Rather than wing it, I consulted experts. Among the many hats worn by my good friend Jason Hazeley are those of songwriter, live and studio musician, arranger and musical director. In the early days of my research, I asked him to lend me a fresh pair of ears – the Clash not being his bag, exactly – and he spoke of *London Calling*'s modes and metres, identified many of Mick Jones's songwriterly influences and tics, gave me a stupid person's guide to Topper Headon's percussive box of tricks, and took me on a guided tour of Bill Price's stereo picture. When the book was at the draft stage, I came across a fascinating booklet entitled *Clash Theory*, downloadable from theorypunk.com, the website of Seattle-based composer and music theorist Patrick Clark. After a brief email correspondence, he agreed to look through the music sections of *Route 19 Revisited*, discussed modes and metres in even more depth, and came up with a number of corrections and suggestions that would never have occurred to me (or, possibly, anyone else). With regard to the musical discussion in this book: anything that advances the sum of human understanding can probably be attributed to Jason and/or Patrick; anything that is embarrassingly wrong can almost certainly be blamed on me not understanding what they were talking about.

Contacts. Special thanks to Tim Young for providing the introductions to Bill Price and Muff Winwood. Also: Dave Callaghan for Michael Campbell; Rich Deakin for Mick Farren; Daniel Hearsaya Garcia for Mickey Gallagher; the Musicians' Union for Ray Beavis; Ray Beavis for Dick Hanson; Alex Ogg for Roger Armstrong and James Sleigh; Simon Morgan for Alex Ogg; Jussi Huhtala of Pop Media and Timo Kanerva of *Soundi* for Mikko Montonen.

Song quotation advice provided by James Sleigh. Contractual advice from Kate Pool at the Society of Authors. Writerly advice and moral support from NBT. Thanks for timely and doubly useful commissions to Michael Hann at the *Guardian's Film & Music* section, and Scott Rowley at *Classic Rock*. Thanks to Sean Body (RIP). Apologies and appreciation to Julian Alexander of LAW. Thanks to David Dunton of Harvey Klinger for being an agent of good fortune in America, Adrian Loudermilk for swimming with sharks, and Gilles Yepremian for French connections.

At Random House: my gratitude to Dan Franklin for a decade's worth of patience and the Get Out Of Jail Free card; Ian Pindar for copy-editing; Matthew Broughton for designing the cover; Neil Bradford for designing the photo section; Tom Avery for more editing, and comms; Ben Murphy for the index; Stephen Hull for the website.

Photographs: thanks to Tom Casey, Caroline Coon (and Elizabeth Kerr at Camera Press), Bob Gruen (and Bill May), Pennie Smith (and Tony Vesely), Virginia Turbett, Nick Wesolowski, Don Whistance and all at Nox Archives. And Les Savine for offer Number 19. Special mentions to Pennie and Virginia for their flexibility. Illustrations: London Diocesan Fund (Janet Eaves, Mary Nada and Tom Casey), Ray Lowry (Julian Williams at See Gallery), David Mingay and Bill Price. Sam Lowry – Hello!

Thanks to Jeff Doherty, Jules Gray, Chris Knowles, Simon Morgan and Alex Ogg for feedback and uplift.

Hello to the Kerlins. Fond farewells to Maureen and Darnley Gray and to Vivienne Nurse.

Thanks and much love for patience and understanding (at least some of the time) to Caroline and Joe.

'Hidden extra' material at www.marcusgray.co.uk

INDEX

Printed in the United States
by Baker & Taylor Publisher Services